D0843609

THE BEATLES AS MUSICIANS

THE BEATLES AS MUSICIANS

Revolver through the *Anthology*

WALTER EVERETT

New York   Oxford

Oxford University Press

1999

DISCARD
LCCC LIBRARY

Oxford University Press

Oxford   New York
Athens   Auckland   Bangkok   Bogotá   Buenos Aires   Calcutta
Cape Town   Chennai   Dar es Salaam   Delhi   Florence   Hong Kong   Istanbul
Karachi   Kuala Lumpur   Madrid   Melbourne   Mexico City   Mumbai
Nairobi   Paris   São Paulo   Singapore   Taipei   Tokyo   Toronto   Warsaw

and associated companies in
Berlin   Ibadan

Copyright © 1999 by Oxford University Press, Inc.

Published by Oxford University Press, Inc.
198 Madison Avenue, New York, New York 10016

Oxford is a registered trademark of Oxford University Press

All rights reserved. No part of this publication may be reproduced,
stored in a retrieval system, or transmitted, in any form or by any means,
electronic, mechanical, photocopying, recording, or otherwise,
without the prior permission of Oxford University Press.

Library of Congress Cataloging-in-Publication Data
Everett, Walter, 1954–
The Beatles as musicians : Revolver through
the Anthology / Walter Everett.
p.   cm.
Includes bibliographical references and index.
ISBN 0-19-509553-7; 0-19-512941-5 (pbk.)
1. Beatles.   2. Rock music—1961–1970—Analysis, appreciation.
I. Title.
MT146.E94   1999
782.42166'092'2— dc21   98-23704

9 8 7 6 5 4 3

Printed in the United States of America
on acid-free paper

For Barbara, John, and Tim

11-13-00   24.95

PREFACE

Poetry and Music

The Beatles' lyrics have been discussed for better than thirty years. We know that it need not be a stream-of-consciousness lexicon from Lennon or a detailed character study from McCartney to be a Beatles composition rich in singular words and meanings; each of more than 750 different word roots is heard in only a single Beatles song. For example, the knowledgeable Beatles listener will know in which particular song each of these words appears: "sympathize," "cows," "scarlet," "butterflies," "opaque," "lemonade," "darning," "poppies," "fuse," "turnstile," "handkerchief," "hogshead," "illusion," "bootlace," "snow-peaked," "velvet," "glimmering," "disease," "limousine," and "bellyfull."[1] Similarly, we know that the rich vocabulary expresses a wide variety of themes in a multitude of poetic styles and systems.

The Beatles' accompanying music has not enjoyed the same amount of attention, even though it is as rich as their lyrics. Their melodic shapes, contrapuntal relationships, harmonic functions, rhythmic articulations, formal designs, colors, and textures draw from many different tonal languages and appear in countless recombinations to bring individual tonal meanings to their poetry. For instance, the progression ♭III–IV–V appears in many Beatles songs, with differing meanings determined by varied contexts. In "Please Please Me," this progression, G–A–B, convenient because of the parallel chord fingerings on the guitar, adds a bluesy pentatonic demand to an otherwise politely diatonic song in a major key. In "Lucy in the Sky with Diamonds," the same progression is expanded for a deep excursion into another world when ♭III (B♭) becomes a key unto itself, an intermediate chord is added between IV and V, and V is sustained for a full measure. In the bizarre "I Am the Walrus," the same progression, there C–D–E, is momentarily given a nearly atonal syntax, taking from its context a whole-tone quality. It is the uncanny ear of the Beatles that allows these three chords, ♭III–IV–V, to assume such a variety of individual meanings across their career.

Goals and Critical Stance

The purpose of this book is to examine and celebrate the musical practices and structures in the Beatles' performance and composition from the music's earliest incarnations through finished product, during the second half of their career as a group, charting the musical techniques and patterns that emerge at various points and adapt to changing needs as the Beatles' styles and goals continuously evolve. We shall pick up and put aside various methodological tools as the material demands, and this material consists not only of the "canon"—the Beatles' LPs, singles, and CDs recorded in London and officially released by EMI—but of every available document of a Beatle's musical activity during the period covered. This book results from the study of many thousands of audio, video, print, and multimedia sources, including the close consultation of uncounted audio recordings of the Beatles' compositional process, traced through tapes that are heard and treated as the equivalents of compositional sketches and drafts. The reader will find particularly useful both the thoroughness with which every known recording is contextualized both historically and musically, and the fact that aspects of the Beatles' instruments, vocal production techniques, recording equipment, and studio procedures—the essence of their performance practice—are exposed here as in no other source. "Bootleg" drafts are discussed and documented in all thoroughness considered necessary, so as to portray the compositional genesis of a song and its arrangement and to permit the reader to seek copies of specific sources.

It may seem incongruous, or at least unusual, to approach a body of popular music that was composed and performed by young men who did not read musical notation (and was intently followed by millions with no musical indoctrination whatsoever) with analytical methods that only a musician with some degree of training could appreciate. Two years' study of college-level music theory would be essential to following much of this book's theoretical discussion, and some of the points raised are more advanced still. An appended table of chord functions (describing the most characteristic functions of all chords mentioned in this book) and the glossary (with its succinct definitions to some fifty-five terms used in this book) should help the less initiated stay on course.[2] Of the thousands of books and articles related to the Beatles, only a small proportion deals seriously with their music, and only a few rare writers have done so from a perspective molded by formal musical study; seldom has an analysis of a Beatles song appeared that can be called in any way thorough. Yet this book suggests that there are many musical reasons worthy of considered speculation that place the Beatles' work among the most listened-to music of all time. The fact is that even though these recording artists and their millions of listeners are rarely if ever consciously aware of the structural reasons behind the dynamic energy in "I Saw Her Standing There," the poignant nostalgia in "Yesterday," the organized confusion of "A Day in the Life," or the exuberant joy in "Here Comes the Sun," it is the musical structures themselves, more so than the visual cues in performance or the loudness of the given amplification system, that call forth most of the audience's intellectual, emotional, and physical responses.[3]

This book traverses the complete history of the Beatles' composition, performance, and recording practices in the second half of their career. As it would be virtually impossible to do justice to the Beatles' work within a single book, the author intends to present this chronology in two volumes, divided between the end of 1965 and the beginning of 1966. The point of division pays homage to the stylistic innovations of *Revolver* (1966) and thus groups together here the Beatles' most experimental and final works, and it also happens to fall exactly at the midpoint of the telling of the story. Each chapter is devoted to the projects of one year and is presented in sections that alternate a chronological summary of the musical events over a given period, with a detailed track-by-track discussion of every song composed by a Beatle through the group's duration. The musical detail, aspects of which are frequently related to similar patterns in other songs by the Beatles or by their peers, and which is occasionally summarized for a global perspective on the group's musical interests, remains the book's central concern, while the accompanying historical information should be viewed as a contextual backdrop. The approach to each song covers its compositional inspiration, heavily documented from the most unimpeachable sources; its recording history, including the identification of every part, its performer and instrument; and its most salient musical features, presented in an analysis of the text that often features comparisons of the dominant musical and poetic goals. Innovations are carefully noted as they appear, and some important compositions require several pages for full appreciation. Some later songs that introduce nothing new of note, on the other hand, are given short shrift.

The book's various analytical approaches are suggested by the musical materials themselves, and they cover as wide a range as do the Beatles' eclectic interests. The early Beatles' least challenging harmonies, forms, colors, and structures — twelve-bar blues forms, four-square phrases, simple guitar arrangements, diatonic and pentatonic components, live recording — were replaced in the later phases of their career by more interesting and complex features — innovative forms and colors, irregular phrase rhythms, chromatic ornaments and key shifts, multilayered and electronically altered studio productions. At some times, harmony and voice leading are the main focus; at others the interplay of rhythm and meter is center stage; and at still others the recording process itself is primary. But from the simplest to the most advanced discussion, techniques are always based on the piece-specific characteristics of the works themselves.

Not only do analytical methods depend on the works studied; so do decisions of format. For instance, the contents of *Revolver* are addressed in chronological order by date of recording, but the validity of this approach is overridden by other factors in subsequent albums. The most unified works, *Sgt. Pepper's Lonely Hearts Club Band* and *Abbey Road*, are discussed in order of presentation; the songs written by independent group members for the "White album" and *Let It Be* are grouped by composer; and the scant offerings for the *Magical Mystery Tour* project are subjectively ordered by their value as compositions. The book's coherence is hopefully not found in predictable, absolutist approaches to every issue but in the contextualization of every detail, the interpretation of the meaning of every analytical finding, the relating of one Beatles technique to another, even—as in the thumbnail summary introducing chapter 2—the placement of the Beatles' work into the surrounding history of rock.

While this book is historically oriented and aims to be comprehensive in its way, it must remain light in its extramusical references, all of which have been extensively covered elsewhere. Except for the most important matters, facts of biography appear only to set the musical context. For instance, the "Christ" controversy of 1966 is mentioned only as a factor in the Beatles' decision to end their performance tours. A portrait of Allen Klein is necessary only for its place in forming an understanding of the Beatles' music-business problems of 1969. Notes on the handful of artists most important to the late-period Beatles that cannot find their way into the main body of text are presented in Appendix B. The interested reader will learn much more about the Beatles' lives and careers in such document studies as those by Mark Lewisohn (particularly 1988) and Allen J. Wiener (especially regarding activities of the ex-Beatles). Many useful interviews and biographical studies, several by those very close to the principals, and hundreds of valuable audio and video sources will help the interested reader fill these gaps.

There are those who say that the Beatles' music is numinous, that an appreciation of it is not enhanced by any intellectual understanding. Others say that any example of popular music is to be evaluated not in relation to its internal musical issues but solely in terms of its social reception, or that popular music cannot be analyzed to useful ends with tools "created" for the appreciation of classical music, even when exactly the same, or interestingly related, compositional techniques are employed in both arenas. Any discussion of musical issues, these folks might say, should be restricted to the ideas of which the composers, performers, arrangers, and consumers are conscious as they interact with it, even if these people have no vocabulary for, or cognitive understanding of, most musical characteristics. While those with such beliefs are certainly free to limit their own investigations in any desired way, I would hope that the present study, which delves as deeply into the realm of the musical imagination as it does into the technical, would suggest to them that their own endeavors might be enhanced by an objective hearing of the music that they endow with such spiritual and cultural significance. Some critics would have it that sustained reflection on nontraditional sources such as popular music of any sort must represent a "hidden-agenda" promotion for the canonization of such documents by the academic community—that, for instance, the uncovering of a complex yet satisfyingly coherent voice leading is necessarily an argument toward high valuation as an expressive work of art.[4] To them, I can only say that this study tells the story of why this listener enjoys the Beatles' music with an ear turned toward compositional method, performance practice, and recording procedure. Whether such matters find acceptance in the curriculum is of less import than is having a reader, or a group of readers—yes, perhaps in a seminar setting—find one or more of my observations or interpretations rewarding or even "cool." And, along these lines, it should be noted that for every single example noted in these pages for its "classically" molded harmonic and voice-leading patterns, two others pursuing very different means toward coherent expression, perhaps even lacking a tonal center entirely, are presented without a thought of apology. Neither let it be said that this book's use of the musical text itself as the primary source is a means to devalue work by others in cultural, social and media studies, critical theory, and reception history; rather, I view all of these approaches, as well as other less scholarly approaches, as complementary and informative to the well-read, well-balanced listener.

This book contains a wealth of fully documented factual information weighed from thousands of materials and identifies in every possible instance the earliest or most authoritative sources, which the reader may wish to pursue for more detailed coverage of a particular topic. These two volumes, when both available, will thus constitute the first referenced guide to all important litera ture about the Beatles, as well as the only complete study of their musical history from the group's inception to its end. But the book also presents both many original interpretations and new means for deriving interpretations. In many cases, my own explanation as to the "meaning" of a given passage or song—often based on combined elements of the musical and poetic texts, along with knowledge of the composers' biography and intent—is offered, but all listeners must solve the Beatles' many mysteries for themselves. My conjecture and fantasies are intended not as edicts but in the hope that the presented facts and proposed methods should aid reader-listeners in delving through the many ambiguities and selecting factors that create their own unified hearings that are in isomorphic harmony with the subject.

A great amount of detail is provided on the Beatles' instruments, which are identified here—by ear as well as by reliable documents—in far greater detail than in any other source. Much of this information, gathered in twenty-three entries in Appendix A, would be useful in evaluating the varied qualities of tone production, but many of the visual descriptions would also be helpful in dating photographs that often appear elsewhere with incorrect dates. Much other detail —on the Beatles' listening tastes, circumstances of composition, singing and playing techniques, studio method, facts relating to British and American record releases and success—is included in the hope of making this volume a thorough reference tool, yet I have striven to present the information in a readable fashion. It is recommended in the strongest way that the reader listen with care to the recordings discussed in the text—for example, you would be able thus to determine who is playing each of the four guitars in some given texture.

Savor, if you will, the information on recording procedure and musical structure as a guide to thoughtful listening; the speed-reader will be sorely disappointed!

Some will wish to learn more about their favorite Beatles songs, others to learn of songs they never knew existed. The voracious reader, especially one with a theoretical bent, may read from cover to cover, but the book is organized and labeled so that many passages of historical and historiographical study are separate from the more analytical prose, allowing readers to navigate their preferred channels. It is hoped that in the end the reader will not only learn the pillars in the evolution of the composers' harmonic vocabulary (which are clearly marked in these pages), the artists' means of studio experimentation (which are all documented here), or my own particular hearing of any given work, but will also learn something about how an appropriate interpretive approach may be devised for deriving the manifold meanings of all such factors in a song by the Beatles or, for that matter, by others.

Terminology and Mechanics

Some notes on terminology may be useful at this point. The text refers to chords in two ways; if function within a key is not immediately relevant, chords will be identified by root, quality, and figured-bass symbol. An uppercase root name signifies a major quality; lowercase, minor or diminished. Triad and seventh qualities are then designated by upper- or lowercase m. Thus, the label $A\flat Mm_5^6$ refers to the chord built with major triad and minor seventh above the root $A\flat$, presented with C in the bass. If a chord's tonal function is a point of discussion, the key will be established, and the chord's function and position will be designated by roman numeral, always uppercase, and any necessary figured-bass. Any figured-bass and roman designations may be altered by accidentals if deviations from the diatonic scale occur. Normal usages are listed in the Table of Chord Functions. On rare occasions, nontriadic chords or other note groupings are referred to by their numeric pitch-class description, which accounts for the intervals among the members of the grouping reduced to an octave-equivalent prime form. Thus, the [025] designation refers to a three-note group, a "trichord," whose members may be arrayed within a single octave in such a way that they form two unordered intervals from reference point "zero," at distances of two and five half-steps, respectively — for example, A–C–D, B♭–C–E♭, C–D–F, C–E♭–F, G–A–C, or G–B♭–C, to name all [025] collections including C.

An important distinction must be drawn here between this book's usage and that found elsewhere involving terminology for formal sections. Rock musicians use the terms "verse," "chorus," "refrain," and "bridge" differently than those working with the traditional pre-1950s popular song. The rock usages are adhered to, and they are defined in the text as they are introduced and again in the glossary. Phrase groups and periods are designated as in basic form texts by Wallace Berry and Douglass Green.

The expression of musical ideas in this book would have been very difficult were it not for the appearance of *The Beatles: Complete Scores* (London: Wise Publications, 1989; distributed in the United States by Hal Leonard Publishing Corporation, 1993), an 1,100-page compendium of practically full scores of every song appearing on an EMI single or LP during the years 1962–70. The scores are not without faults, but they will certainly not be replaced in the near future.[5] The reader will wish to consult the Wise edition in reading the analytical commentary in this volume. This book refers to Wise rehearsal letters in a consistent font and method: **A** refers to the entire section appearing between rehearsal letters **A** and **B**; **B**+5–8 refers to the fifth through eighth measures following the double bar at **B**; **C**–2 refers to the second measure before the double bar at **C**. But timings programmed into compact discs are also given whenever they are considered relevant, and these cues would be of particular value to those without recourse to the scores.[6] All chart information for singles and LPs is drawn from *Billboard* (for the United States) and *Melody Maker* (for the United Kingdom) unless stated otherwise; these and other contemporaneous periodicals are also worth seeking out.

The musical examples in this book are chiefly of two kinds: (1) transcriptions of sound recordings, intended as supplements to the Wise scores—their exclusion there necessitates their appearance here to clarify points of discussion; and (2) voice-leading graphs and other analytical constructions that present my arguments in musical notation. I have striven to ensure that all quotations of text and music, for which permission has not been secured, conform to all criteria of "fair use" law by their insubstantial length, their scholarly purpose, their never before having been printed, and their unperformable nature. Hopefully their appearance here along with the discussion will encourage readers to seek out the Wise scores for full versions of the songs quoted here.

In this book's musical quotations, all of which I have transcribed myself except for the orchestral passage from "A Day in the Life," which was prepared by Glenn Palmer, all instruments are notated as they sound. Specific pitch designation will conform to the following system: c^1 refers to Middle C, g^1 is a fifth above, and c^2 is an octave above; f lies a fifth below Middle C, c an octave below, and C two octaves below. Singers' pitches notated with the transposing treble clef are referred to as notated, as representations of their functional registers, rather than as sounding. Careted arabic numerals refer to scale degrees.

ACKNOWLEDGMENTS

I would like to thank the many who have contributed to and supported this work. Oxford editors Maribeth Anderson Payne, Jonathan Wiener, Jessica Ryan, and Soo Mee Kwon and their perceptive and helpful staff, anonymous readers, and consultants have provided expert assistance whenever and wherever needed. Grants from the Horace H. Rackham School of Graduate Studies, the Office of the Vice President for Research, and the School of Music, all at the University of Michigan, have made possible the travel, purchase of materials, use of equipment, and compensation for clerical help necessary to complete this project. Devoted administrators Ralph Lewis and Andy Mead were generous in providing assistance from Joe Braun, Ben Broening, Glenn Palmer, Nancy Rao, Eric Santos, and Laura Sherman. Calvin Elliker and Charles Reynolds made Music Library resources available; networking and software help came from Mike Gould, Robert Newcomb, John Schaffer, and Charles Rand; and additional administrative assistance was provided by Paul Boylan, Morris Risenhoover, Diana Cubberly, Diane Schlemmer, and Julie Smigielski at the University of Michigan School of Music, Warren George at the College-Conservatory of Music of the University of Cincinnati, Peter Silvestri and Lynnae Crawford at MPL Communications, Jeff Rosen and Libby Rohman at Special Rider Music, and Rosemarie Gawelko at Warner Bros. Publications. The author is grateful for assistance provided by Roger Luther (EJE Research), Dick Boak (C. F. Martin & Co.), Hans Schöller (Karl Höfner), Mike Armstrong (Hammond Suzuki), and Charles Heuck (Ludwig and Musser). Thanks to James Kendrick of Thacher Proffitt &

Wood for legal advice. Rick Everett supplied the beautiful guitars that were essential for this study.

I am grateful for the ideas and support from many theorists, composers, and musicologists over many years, some not credited in the body of the text: Jim Borders, Matthew Brown, Lori Burns, John Covach, David Damschroder, Jim Dapogny, Dai Griffiths, Henry Gwiazda, Dave Headlam, Rick Hermann, Arthur Komar, Tim Koozin, Jonathan Kramer, Steve Larson, Betsy Marvin, bruce mcclung, Allan Moore, Bill Rothstein, Lewis Rowell, Frank Samarotto, Deborah Stein, and Marty Sweidel.

Thanks also to Morris, Pam, and Meredith Everett; to Mark Lapidos, Dave Stein, Judy Liao, Jody Forsberg, Karin Laine, Belinda Ficher, and Konchna Ramchandran; and to John Golden, Bill Keane, Myron Allen, Kevin Addis, Ronnie Mann, Joe Petrillo, Howard Maymon, Mark Bogosian, Bob Thompson, William Marx, Don Whittaker, Robin Mountenay, Jeff Wood, Bob Murphy, Michael Piret, Tom Caldwell, Monica Roberts, Natalie Matovinovic, and Roger Vogel.

Ann Arbor and Interlochen   *W. E.*
September 1997

Contents

THE BEATLES AS MUSICIANS

THE BEATLES IN LONDON

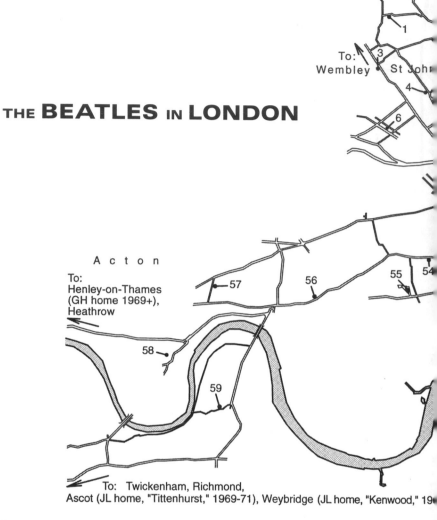

A c t o n

To:
Henley-on-Thames
(GH home 1969+),
Heathrow

To: Wembley St John

To: Twickenham, Richmond,
Ascot (JL home, "Tittenhurst," 1969-71), Weybridge (JL home, "Kenwood," 19

1. Decca Studios, 165 Broadhurst Gardens
2. The Roundhouse, 100 Chalk Farm Road
3. Gaumont State Cinema, 195–99 Kilburn High Road
4. EMI Studios, 3 Abbey Road
5. 7 Cavendish Avenue (Paul McCartney's home, 1966–)
6. BBC Maida Vale Studios, Delaware Road
7. Paddington Station, Praed Street
8. Lisson Gallery, 66–68 Bell Street
9. Marylebone Magistrate, 181 Marylebone Road
10. Montagu Square (Starr's flat, 1964–69)
11. Apple boutique, 94 Baker Street
12. 57 Wimpole Street (Asher home)
13. EMI House, 20 Manchester Square
14. Apple offices (1968–69), 95 Wigmore Street
15. BBC Broadcasting House, Portland Place
16. Associated Independent Recording, Oxford Circus

17. Scala Theatre, Charlotte Street
18. Regent Sound, 164–66 Tottenham Court Road
19. Royal Academy of Dramatic Art, Gower Street (Brian Epstein's school, 1956–57)
20. British Library and Museum, Great Russell Street
21. Indica Books/International Times, Southampton Row
22. Sadler's Wells Theatre, Rosebery Street
23. Guildhall School of Music (George Martin's school, 1947–50)
24. Kingsway/DeLane Lea Recording Studios, 129 Kingsway
25. Lyceum Ballroom, Wellington Street
26. NEMS office (1963–66), 13 Monmouth Street
27. Old Vic Theatre, 103 The Cut
28. Saville Theatre, 135–49 Shaftesbury Avenue
29. Northern Songs/Dick James Music (1963–64), Charing Cross Road

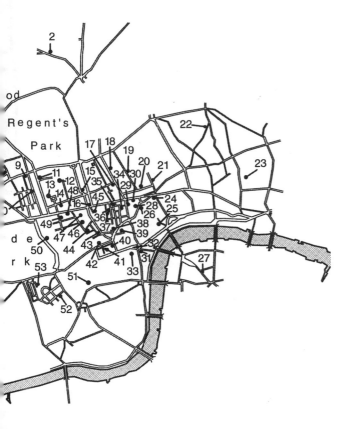

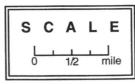

S home, "Sunny Heights," 1965-8), Esher (GH home, "Kinfauns," 1964-9)

30. Northern Songs/Dick James Music (1964–69), 71–75 New Oxford Road
31. Playhouse Theatre, Northumberland Avenue
32. Trafalgar Square
33. Institute of Contemporary Arts, 12 Carlton House Terrace
34. MPL Communications, 1 Soho Square
35. Radha Krishna Temple, Soho Street
36. Trident Studios, 17 St. Anne's Court
37. Blue Gardenia Club, St. Anne's Court
38. Piccadilly Theatre, Denman Street
39. Prince of Wales Theatre, 31 Coventry Street
40. BBC Paris Studio, Regent Street
41. Indica Gallery, 6 Mason's Yard
42. Pigalle Club, Piccadilly
43. Apple offices and studios (1968–95), 3 Saville Row
44. London Arts Gallery, 22 New Bond Street
45. London Palladium, 8 Argyll Street

46. BBC Aeolian Hall, 135–37 New Bond Street
47. Chappell Recording Studios, 52 Maddox Street
48. HMV Record Store, 363 Oxford Street
49. Fraser Gallery, 69 Duke Street
50. Grosvenor House Hotel, Park Lane
51. Buckingham Palace
52. 13 Chapel Street (Brian Epstein's home, 1964–67)
53. William Mews (George Harrison's and Ringo Starr's homes, 1963–64)
54. Royal Albert Hall, Kensington Gore
55. 13 Emperor's Gate (John Lennon's home, 1963–64)
56. Hammersmith Odeon Cinema
57. Queen Charlotte's Maternity Hospital, Goldhawk Road
58. Chiswick House conservatory, Burlington Lane
59. Olympic Studios, Church Road, Barnes

ONE-WAY TICKET, YEAH

The Beatles' career from 1956 through 1965 represents a one-way trip from powerful teenage identifications with Elvis Presley and Buddy Holly, through a dominion achieved with their own well-crafted, adolescent-inspiring refrain of "yeah, yeah, yeah," to an increasingly serious focus on the artistic expression of their experience and hopes. Whereas the Beatles could do little wrong with critics or fans in this ascendancy, their image would occasionally be tarnished and their future would often be stamped as uncertain in their remarkable final years together, 1966–70. It was during the earlier period that the group mastered what was given them; from 1966 onward, their confident and constant drive for originality in the production of studio masterworks would push the rest of the rock-music world to reset its goals from the ground up. The Beatles would no longer be seen by their peers as producers of a style that begged to be imitated before the fad had passed but as visionaries who were able to convince the establishment that each new rock album might have a fundamentally different set of rules and that these rules would be dictated by the artists. And from 1966 to the present day, the Beatles' highly personalized music would be understood by their audience in as many different ways as there are listeners.

While the Beatles' activity in the years following 1965 is the subject of this volume, the highly creative work of this period can be appreciated only in the context of what had come before. So we begin with a brief précis of the group's development through the release of *Rubber Soul* in December 1965. This introductory sketch will highlight the earliest musical influences on the band, its general approaches to composition, instrumental and vocal performance techniques, lyric writing, rhythmic, formal, harmonic and melodic practices and innovations, and early recording procedures. It will then present more extended discussions of one composition each by John Lennon and Paul McCartney. Table 1.1 provides a time line summarizing the major events of the first "half" of the Beatles' career.

Early Influences on the Beatles

A teenage John Lennon picked up the guitar because of its simplicity of expression, as demonstrated by skiffle artist Lonnie Donegan, and because of the magnetism of Elvis Presley's recordings from 1954 to 1956. Paul McCartney, who inherited his sense of harmony from his vaudeville-playing father, Jim,

Table 1.1 Time Line of Major Events for the Beatles, 1940–1965

1940
July 7:	Ringo Starr born as Richard Starkey, Liverpool
Oct. 9:	John Lennon born, Liverpool

1942
June 18:	Paul McCartney born, Liverpool

1943
Feb. 25:	George Harrison born, Liverpool

1956
Mar.?	John Lennon, guitarist, forms skiffle band, the Quarry Men

1957
July 6:	Paul McCartney meets John Lennon
Oct. 18:	Paul McCartney first performs with Quarry Men, as guitarist

1958
Feb. or Mar.:	George Harrison joins Quarry Men as guitarist
Summer:	John's mother killed; Quarry Men regroup only sporadically over following year for private engagements

1960
Summer:	Quarry Men renamed the Beatles
Aug. 17:	Beatles begin professional training with long sets in Hamburg clubs, over several visits through Dec. 31, 1962

1961
Feb. 9:	Beatles begin long series of lunchtime concerts in The Cavern, Liverpool, the last on Aug. 3, 1963
Apr.:	Paul McCartney becomes the Beatles' bassist
June 22:	Beatles' first commercial recordings, backing Tony Sheridan, made in Hamburg
July, Sept.:	"My Bonnie" and other tracks released in Germany
Summer:	"Merseybeat," personified in the music of the Beatles, recognized as a dominant style in Liverpool
Dec. 10:	Beatles accept Brian Epstein's management offer

1962
Jan. 1:	Beatles audition unsuccessfully for Decca Records
Mar. 7:	First BBC radio broadcast recorded; further radio and television appearances follow the group's recording career, promoting discs but also documenting the group's cover arrangements as performed in 1961–62
June 6:	First EMI recording session with George Martin, who signs the group to Parlophone (his label with EMI), in London
Aug. 18:	Ringo Starr joins the Beatles as drummer, crystallizing the quartet
Aug. 22:	First television filming, Cavern Club; not aired until 1963
Sept. 4, 11:	Recordings for first single at EMI Studios, Abbey Road, London
Oct. 5:	"Love Me Do"/"P.S. I Love You" released as first Parlophone single in United Kingdom
Nov. 26:	Recordings for single at EMI, London

1963
Jan. 11:	"Please Please Me"/"Ask Me Why" released in United Kingdom
Feb. 11:	Recordings for first LP at EMI, London
Feb. 23–Mar. 3:	Beatles' first British theater tour, supporting Helen Shapiro
Late Feb.:	"Please Please Me" becomes the Beatles' first national #1 single
Mar. 5:	Recordings for single at EMI, London
Mar. 22:	*Please Please Me* released as the Beatles' first LP in the United Kingdom; will remain at #1 for thirty weeks into November
Apr. 11:	"From Me to You"/"Thank You Girl" released in United Kingdom

Table 1.1 (*continued*)

May 18–June 9:	British tour, headlining alongside Roy Orbison
July 1:	Recordings for single at EMI, London
July 18–Oct. 23:	Recordings for LP at EMI, London
Aug. 23:	"She Loves You"/"I'll Get You" released in United Kingdom
Oct. 13:	Televised concert at London Palladium; "Beatlemania" is journalists' term for mass hysteria surrounding the theater
Oct. 17:	Recordings for single at EMI, London
Oct. 24–30:	Tour of Sweden
Nov.:	Capitol Records signs the Beatles for release of recordings in United States
Nov. 4:	Royal Variety Show, Prince of Wales Theatre; John shows cheek with Queen Mother's audience
Nov. 22:	*With the Beatles* released in United Kingdom
Nov. 29:	"I Want to Hold Your Hand"/"This Boy" released in United Kingdom
Dec. 24:	London Christmas concerts begin; they continue through Jan. 11, 1964
Dec. 26:	"I Want to Hold Your Hand"/"I Saw Her Standing There" released in United States to top the singles charts for seven weeks; onset of the "British Invasion" in America

1964

Jan. 29, Feb. 25:	Recordings for German market and for new single, EMI studios in Paris and London
Feb. 7–16:	Minitour of United States, including first appearances on "The Ed Sullivan Show"
Feb. 25–Apr. 16:	Recordings for soundtrack of first film, EMI, London
Mar. 2–Apr. 24:	Shooting of first film, London and southern England locations
Mar. 20:	"Can't Buy Me Love"/"You Can't Do That" released in United Kingdom
Mar. 23:	Publication of John Lennon's first book, *In His Own Write*
June 1–3:	Recordings to fill soundtrack LP, EMI, London
June 4–30:	Concert tours of northern Europe, Oceania
June 19:	*Long Tall Sally* released as EP single in United Kingdom
July 6:	World premiere of film *A Hard Day's Night*, London
July 10:	Single "A Hard Day's Night"/"Things We Said Today" and LP *A Hard Day's Night* released in United Kingdom
July 12–Aug. 16:	Concerts in England and Sweden
Aug. 11–Oct. 26:	Recordings for LP and single at EMI, London
Aug. 19–Sept. 20:	Concert tour of the United States
Oct. 9–Nov. 10:	British concert tour
Nov. 27:	"I Feel Fine"/"She's a Woman" released in United Kingdom
Dec. 4:	*Beatles for Sale* released in United Kingdom
Dec. 24:	London Christmas concerts begin; they continue through Jan. 16, 1965

1965

Feb. 15–Apr. 13:	Recordings for soundtrack of second film, EMI, London
Feb. 23–May 11:	Shooting of second film in the Bahamas, Austria, and the United Kingdom
Apr. 9:	"Ticket to Ride"/"Yes It Is" released in United Kingdom
May 10–June 17:	Recordings for U.S. market and to fill soundtrack LP and single, EMI, London
June 14:	*Beatles VI* released in United States with "Bad Boy," not made available to British market until Dec. 10, 1966

(*continued*)

Table 1.1 (*continued*)

June 20–July 3:	Concerts in France, Italy, and Spain
July 23:	"Help!"/"I'm Down" released in United Kingdom
Aug. 6:	*Help!* released in United Kingdom
Aug. 14–31:	U.S. tour
Oct. 12–Nov. 11:	Recordings for LP and single at EMI, London
Dec. 3:	Single "We Can Work It Out"/"Day Tripper" and LP *Rubber Soul* released in United Kingdom
Dec. 3–12:	Final U.K. tour

shared these passions with Lennon. Both of these future Beatles joined George Harrison in a mutual admiration for both the raw energy of Jerry Lee Lewis and the rockabilly vocal and guitar ornaments of Carl Perkins. This brew of musical interests in these young players grew from a simmer to a boil, ever stronger through 1960, with their imitation of the compositional style of Buddy Holly and their adoption of rhythm-and-blues techniques as practiced by the witty guitarist Chuck Berry, the energetic Little Richard, and the humorous and skillful Coasters. The Beatles' music was to integrate the extremes of rock and roll: the crude and the clever, the raw and the finished. As rarefied as their music would quickly become, the group was never to disown their rock and roll. The early LPs are full of original rockers, such as "Hold Me Tight" and "I Wanna Be Your Man"; they are still a rock-and-roll cover band in *Beatles for Sale*; and they would close concerts only with their loudest numbers: the Isley Brothers' "Twist and Shout" through 1963, Little Richard's "Long Tall Sally" in 1964, and McCartney's own "I'm Down" in 1965. In later years, McCartney was often to be labeled the balladeer, as against the more rock-rooted Lennon, and this overgeneralization has led the former to whine loudly as to his basic rock-and-roll credentials (viz. "Helter Skelter" and "She Came In through the Bathroom Window").

Lennon and McCartney, the Young Composers

This is not the place to list or discuss all of the original compositions that predate the Beatles' recording career, but it should be noted that we know of forty-seven complete songs or fragments possibly begun before 1963. By early 1963 Lennon and McCartney found that their muse was within easy calling distance, and their craftsmanship and imagination increased with their productivity as the Beatles wrote and released eighteen original compositions in 1963, twenty-four in 1964, and thirty in 1965. In 1963, most new songs were composed and arranged in miraculously productive stolen moments in hotel rooms between concert dates. Lennon and McCartney wrote "From Me to You," "She Loves You," and "I Want to Hold Your Hand" as full collaborations, "nose to nose," just days before their respective recordings, and a few simple "arranging" decisions might be finalized when the group gathered at EMI. Progressively more time would be

reserved for leisurely composition in the following years, when Lennon and Mc-
Cartney would revert to their pre-1963 practice of writing separately, or would
collaborate by contributing contrasting sections to each others' partially worked-
out songs. But by 1965 a growing portion of the writing of both lyrics and musical structure was accomplished during precious studio time.

Before we proceed with a general overview of the band's performance and
composition techniques through 1965, we might benefit from a look at the
basic performance-related personality traits and the aesthetic goals of the
charismatic figures of Lennon and McCartney. For although George Harrison
became more confident of his own composing abilities in 1965, with four offerings on the LPs produced that year, Lennon and McCartney are by far the
dominant composers of the early Beatles.

Impossible to discipline as a teen, John as a young Beatle could publicly defy
convention only through his cruel juvenile humor, which was a staple of the
group's stage act. When Paul yukked it up on stage by announcing one song
or another as having been recorded by "our favorite American group, Sophie
Tucker," one would not think that insult was the intent. John, on the other hand,
made it abundantly clear that he was ridiculing the afflicted—particularly
with his exaggerated imitations of those with spastic paralysis and harelips.
More acceptable was his frequent stage reference to Peggy Lee in his introduction to "Till There Was You," which she had recorded, as "Peggy Leg." To the
world at large, John was cheeky but sophisticated when he was heard to have
announced "Twist and Shout" to the queen mother and the entire audience at
the Royal Variety performance (1963) thus: "For our last number I'd like to ask
your help. For the people in the cheaper seats, clap your hands, and the rest of
you, if you'd just rattle your jewelry." Only a handful knew that for manager
Brian Epstein, this was a private and very cruel joke, for Lennon had informed
Brian prior to the performance that he was considering hurling an obscene insult at the royal family at this point in the show; Brian could not have been sure
what to expect.

McCartney may be said to have constantly developed—as a means to
entertain—a focused musical talent with an ear for counterpoint and other aspects of craft in the demonstration of a universally agreed-upon common language that he did much to enrich. Conversely, Lennon's mature music is best
appreciated as the daring product of a largely unconscious, searching but
undisciplined artistic sensibility, a less-than-perfect vehicle for expressing
deeply held personal truths. Lennon had little regard for the mastery of the
niceties of received compositional dictates or for the dull expectations of the
bulk of his audience. Not that McCartney's music is without import, but his pro-
nouncements of hopes for the world—such as his wish for a more humble re-
spect for the natural environment and the animal kingdom—often come
across as overstated public-relations billboards, all too rarely having the subtle but vital poetic impact of "Blackbird" (1968), his simply elegant apotheosis
for the civil rights struggle. Not that Lennon always resisted being heavy-
handed, but even the blunt nature of his dire agitprop work (see *Some Time in
New York City*) was an artistic stance promoting the direct expression of utili-

tarian ideals. And not that Lennon's frequent disregard for technical precision, in realms of craft that lay beyond his interest and patience, hampered his ability to reach others. On the contrary, his sometimes strange music would commonly set in motion deep and strong sympathetic vibrations among the many millions of his devoted listeners.

These sorts of differences between Lennon and McCartney are sometimes explained as a manifestation of class distinction between the two. Lennon is seen as the intellectually inquisitive middle-class boy with the leisure to read all of his auntie's books on struggling artists and while away his childhood in wordplay, daydreaming, and picture drawing; at about seven, he illustrated a cartoon book he called *Sport and Speed Illustrated*; at age eleven, he painted the pictures used on the cover of *Walls and Bridges*.[1] This is the boy whose most difficult-to-express artistic outpourings were first to find a limited audience in his hilarious and cruel books of vignettes, poetry, and cartoons, *In His Own Write* (containing many materials written as a teen and published as a book in 1964) and its sequel, *A Spaniard in the Works* (1965). Upon his collaboration with Yoko Ono, beginning in 1968, such off-the-wall musings were to burst forth suddenly — to a stunned reception — in the aforementioned media plus nontonal music, film, lithography, and improvisational "happenings," and they found perhaps their most productive voice in the cathartic album *John Lennon/ Plastic Ono Band*. Conversely, McCartney is seen as the sentimental, nonintellectual working-class craftsman who counts his pay in smiles and then moves on to the next project, toiling to get every note just right.

There is some truth in these caricatures, but it must be remembered that Lennon was genuine in his lifelong adulation for the most simplistic and visceral rock and roll — even the basic Bo Diddley could move him strongly — and that relatively complex tonal relationships came to be second nature for McCartney early on, requiring less toil and allowing for more imagination by 1966. Also important is the understanding that it was McCartney (a hip London bachelor in 1966) who introduced Lennon (then a suburban family man) to the proprietors of the Indica Gallery, where John met Yoko, and that it was McCartney who introduced the Beatles to the worlds of Stockhausen and Bach, leading to a revolution in the expressive capacity of mainstream rock music. The horrible shock of Lennon's death in 1980 pushed McCartney to create one of his most inspired, personal, and (nearly) unaffected works, "Here Today" (recorded in 1981 for *Tug of War*), a haunting tribute to the partnership as it began in the fields behind St. Peter's Woolton Parish Church, Liverpool.

Differences in the working methods of Lennon and McCartney can be summarized briefly. It is common for McCartney to compose his tunes long before lyrics are decided on. At times, Paul would write his tune with nonsense lyrics that would be replaced later: "Yesterday" began as "Scrambled Eggs," "I've Just Seen a Face" as "Auntie Gin's Theme," and "It's Only Love" as "That's a Nice Hat." John would usually prod Paul to improve the worst of his wordings, but occasionally he would prevent his partner from disturbing an odd unconsciously produced line that he liked. Thus the provisional line in "Hey Jude," "The movement you need is on your shoulder," remains despite the fact that

McCartney had hoped to find something more directly meaningful. Much of McCartney's solo work has suffered for the lack of such trusted editing of his lyrics, which are rife with commonplace images, poorly chosen words, and grammatical errors.

Beatles producer George Martin often said that McCartney usually began with music, Lennon with lyrics. "Now, Paul would help John musically, because I think that he had a greater understanding of the theory of music, and harmony and so on, and he would be able to make a thing more well-rounded; John tended to drive the car without a clutch rather, he'd just go from one gear to another. On the other hand again, John would have perhaps more of a mastery of imagery and words and would make Paul work harder at his lyrics."[2] Other McCartney songs were conceived as instrumental numbers, such as "Michelle," the tune of which the composer was to carry for at least two years before adding lyrics. The circumstances of "When I'm Sixty-Four" remind us of Jim McCartney's dilemma with "Walking in the Park with Eloise": Paul's dad, looking for help with an instrumental number, asked his family, "Can anyone think of any words to this?" In the case of "When I'm Sixty-Four," a vaudeville song Paul closely associated with his father, the lyrics arrived about eight years after the tune.[3] This apparent difficulty with lyrics, coupled with an occasional lack of sensitivity, would at times get under Lennon's skin. In 1980 John related this story about "Eleanor Rigby" (1966): "Paul had the theme, the whole bit about Eleanor Rigby in the church where a wedding had been. He knew he had this song and he needed help, but rather than ask me to do the lyrics, he said, 'Hey, you guys, finish up the lyrics.' . . . I sat there with Mal Evans, a road manager who was a telephone installer, and Neil Aspinall, a student accountant who became a road manager, and it was the three of us he was talking to. . . . Actually, he meant for me to do it, but he wouldn't ask. How *dare* he throw it out in the air like that?"[4]

Performance Techniques of the Early Beatles

The following review of the Beatles' performing techniques through 1965 is directed from the sonic foundation upward: we'll look in turn at aspects of Ringo Starr's drumming, Paul McCartney's bass playing, John Lennon's rhythm guitar work, George Harrison's lead guitar playing, and the group's vocal techniques. This lineup was rather fixed through 1965, but come *Revolver* in the spring of 1966, such conventional assignments significantly diminished in importance, an approach that would make stage performances of these songs, by the performers on the record, impossible. Our coverage here of the basic aspects of performance-related, finger-driven, melodic and harmonic devices will then allow us to turn to a more global perspective on poetic and tonal construction in the Beatles' music.

Ringo backed the Beatles with the perfect percussive foundation for their hard-driving yet imaginative music. Featuring his Ludwig Super-Classic set from June 1963 onward, his basic pattern consisted of an articulation of strong beats on the bass drum (often emphasized with a dotted rhythm) and backbeats on the snare; all eighths would often be marked on the closed hi-hat or the rivet-sizzling ride cymbal. If it were time to excite the crowd with a "raver," as in "Boys" or "Money," the crash cymbal would be used extensively, but this noise was more often reserved for the articulation of a song's structural points—note how often the various formal sections of the Beatles' early songs are differentiated with contrasting cymbal shadings. Ringo's use of the two toms was both idiosyncratic and effective, particularly in his off-balance, propulsive fills that would increase the tension at divisions between phrases and sections.

Paul McCartney's Höfner violin bass provided a distinctive visual image, even if its naturally dull sound was further masked by primitive recording techniques in the first few albums. Although he'd played the instrument for only two months prior to the June 1961 Sheridan recordings, his arpeggiation-based ostinati and alternations of roots and fifths in dotted rhythm are among the qualities of those early tapes that point most clearly in the direction of the Beatles' own emerging sound. In 1963, McCartney often bolstered his sound with hollow vertical open fifths, marking song divisions in "It Won't Be Long" (at 0:47–0:52), "All I've Got to Do" (0:03–0:14), and "I Want to Hold Your Hand" (0:58–1:01), and leaned toward the melodic as he began to play walking major scales in "All My Loving." McCartney continually expanded his techniques, particularly as he developed his ear for functional and contrapuntal relationships between lowest and highest registers. After all, he possessed the highest voice among his group members and played the lowest-sounding instrument, so considering his melodic gifts, it was only natural that he gain, with practice, an eloquent authority over the structure-governing outer voices of the Beatles' music.

Although he rarely put the bass aside on stage, he did so increasingly in the studio. McCartney purchased an Epiphone Casino electric lead guitar in late 1964 and dubbed lead tracks onto three cuts for *Help!* His use of the Epiphone Texan acoustic guitar on "Yesterday" and elsewhere augmented the multi-acoustic guitar texture that Lennon and Harrison cultivated many times on *Help!* and *Rubber Soul*. After acquiring a Rickenbacker bass, McCartney provided an entirely new and limpid tonal foundation for *Rubber Soul* and later efforts. Here the instrument achieved remarkable melodic independence, largely because McCartney would often play piano or acoustic guitar for the basic tracks and then overdub the bass onto its own tape track. Thus relieved of the function of underpinning the live ensemble, McCartney brought his melodic sense to bear with ornamental bass melodies in many of the album's compositions.

Lennon's vital instrumental function in the early Beatles was to fill the texture with chords on rhythm guitar. His two main instruments were the three-quarter-length Rickenbacker Capri (purchased in 1960) and the amplified-acoustic Gibson Jumbo (heard in many early EMI recordings), but he expanded his arsenal in 1965 with the folk-inspired Fender Villager acoustic twelve-string and the hard-rocking Stratocaster. His favorite guitar in the later Beatles years was the Epiphone Casino that he purchased at the end of 1964. Lennon's rhythm style changed little during this early period—he already commanded a full range of barre chords, often embellished with "boogie" neighbors, by 1961.[5] Lennon took great pride in his occasional lead lines, as in "You Can't Do That" and "I Feel Fine," but the Rickenbacker provided only a dull timbre and was not suitable for soloing.

George Harrison pursued increasingly bright colors from the guitars he chose, culminating in the Stratocaster solo for "Nowhere Man." His early lead playing is chiefly done with three Gretsch instruments, particularly the Country Gentleman model used from June 1963 through the end of 1965, but the early LPs also feature his rhythm work and broken chords on the Gibson Jumbo. His playing is marked by the Carl Perkins–inspired rockabilly style (as in the "All My Loving" solo), Buddy Holly diatonicism, and bluesy Chuck Berry–derived pentatonic-minor licks that punctuate phrases (as in "She Loves You"). A mannered tremolo strumming and frequent dependence on tremolo-arm bending disappear in the early going as Harrison begins to create his own style. This is marked by the constant use of nonresolving tones frozen into chords (as in the frequent endings on added-sixth or added-ninth chords, very idiomatic to the instrument, or the $\flat$VII^9 chord that opens "A Hard Day's Night"), and the doubling of lead lines in octaves (as in "Please Please Me"). The latter technique achieves a bright texture that prepares Harrison for the capabilities of the Rickenbacker electric twelve-string, four of its courses tuned in brilliant octaves. This guitar, acquired in February 1964, was especially effective for the "chiming" effect that Harrison had tried to achieve on the Country Gent in songs' middle sections, such as in "Thank You Girl," but which rang out much more clearly on the twelve-string in such tracks as "I Should Have Known Better." Harrison showcased his attention to timbral detail on a Ramirez classical nylon-string guitar in the lead lines of "And I Love Her," where the vibrato is sensitive, position shifts and glissandi are tasteful, and tonal qualities are contrasted by varying the distances of plucking from the bridge. In 1965, Harrison used a volume/tone control extensively, allowing for a ghostly articulation technique, particularly when applied to natural harmonics, as in "Yes It Is." The vibrant Fender Stratocaster introduced in early 1965 became a staple of the Beatles' sound two years thence and can also be seen as a precursor to the exceedingly brilliant waveforms of the sitar that Harrison introduced in *Rubber Soul* and used as his main instrument in 1966–68.

This basic instrumentation served the Beatles well through 1965. Early augmentation involved simple percussion (maracas, claves, cowbell, tambourine, overdubbed handclaps) and Lennon's harmonica. Occasionally, producer George Martin added keyboard whenever the texture could benefit from some thickening, or for coloristic effect. McCartney took to the piano for "Little Child," and Lennon added electric piano to three *Help!* tracks. The latter returned the keyboard to the Beatles' stage act with the Vox Continental electronic organ and gave the harmonium its first of several Beatles assignments in late 1965, a time when various Beatles and assistants also played the studio's Hammond B-3 organ. Outside performers were contracted for the first time in 1965 for "You've Got to Hide Your Love Away" and "Yesterday"; the latter featured a string quartet that essentially doubled McCartney's guitarwork to fantastic effect.

To conserve their voices during the long Hamburg sets, for the most part the Beatles' earliest repertoire comprised solo vocal numbers. The singers developed their own approaches to vocal ornamentation: Lennon's was particularly expressive, with soulful graces, melismas, Preslian roulades, sprezzatura, and timbre shadings. McCartney broke into falsetto to overdrive his Little Richard–style shouts, but Lennon's falsetto was more refined and melodious, usually restricted to retransitional "woos" in emulation of Roy Orbison. Lennon's hard-rock style was typified by vocal notes repeated in a Chuck Berry–like stream. Harrison's and Starr's vocal styles were colorful but otherwise undistinguished, capable of a much narrower range, flexibility, and accuracy than those of the two leaders.

As their recording career developed, Lennon and McCartney devised various vocal duet techniques, largely derived from Carl and Jay Perkins, the Everly Brothers, and Buddy Holly's dual-track vocals. Typically, Lennon would sing the structural line, and McCartney the descant above. They would occasionally sing in octaves for an unusual expressive effect, as when Lennon brought profundity to McCartney's otherwise prettily innocuous "Tell Me What You See," but much more often they worked in parallel thirds or sixths with touches of oblique and contrary motion, all balanced particularly well in "If I Fell." A hallmark of the 1963–64 hits was to have the two begin in unison and break into parts to emphasize the latter part of each verse.

Ensemble models for three-part and solo/chorus vocal arrangements came from the Jordanaires (Elvis Presley's backing group), the Crickets (Buddy Holly's), the Coasters, and various Motown and other "girl groups." Beginning with the chorus to "Ask Me Why," McCartney, Harrison, and Lennon experimented with nonresolving tones added to chords, obviously an extension of Harrison's guitar technique in the three-part added-sixth chord sung at the end of "She Loves You." This approach was taken to the extreme in the pandiatonic clusters that create great tension even with a slow tempo in "This Boy."

Early Lyrics

To what use were these voices put? The Beatles' early lyrics were direct, innocent, joyful celebrations of adolescent love, almost thoughtlessly perpetuating pop conventions. Lennon's lifelong sense of wordplay, emblematized in the group's name, showed in titles such as "Please Please Me" and "A Hard Day's Night," and McCartney answered well with "Eight Days a Week" and "Rubber Soul." Lennon began to explore his own insecurities in more expressive ways in "Misery," "If I Fell," and "I'm a Loser," this last a watershed in artistically portrayed negative self-views leading to "Help!" and "Nowhere Man." Lennon credits the deeper penetration of self in his lyrics to his listening to Bob Dylan. But the new directions taken with topics in *Rubber Soul*, from the clandestine affair of "Norwegian Wood" to the moralistic sermon of "The Word," are somewhat offset by the cruel, selfish warning in the closing track, "Run for Your Life." Beginning in 1966, such incongruous juxtapositions would have much more the aura of intentional irony, as the Beatles' attention to such matters was quickly to come into sharp focus.

Early Rhythmic Techniques

Supported by varied approaches to drumming in every single song, the early Beatles' rhythmic surface is broken up imaginatively with lively syncopations in accompanimental, instrumental solo and vocal parts, and spiced up with "shuffle" triplet eighths. More dramatic rhythmic effects include the ensemble stop time, as in the "You Can't Do That" refrain (at 0:23–0:24), and the quarter-note triplets that bring "I Want to Hold Your Hand" to a rein-tightening halt. The Beatles would catch their listeners off guard with time-suspending disso-nant opening chords sustained as if by fermata in "All I've Got to Do" and "A Hard Day's Night," and with the ametrical, eccentric bass/guitar counterpoint that opens "Drive My Car." The Beatles' sense of rhythm was so supreme that McCartney could sing the same structural voice leading over the same chords in both the main and contrasting sections of "Yesterday" and yet produce two very different melodies, largely by virtue of unexpected rhythmic displace-ments that expressively reflect the singer's considered probing of his own un-certainty. At a structural level, the Beatles' command of rhythmic effects is cel-ebrated in nearly every song, right from "Love Me Do," with elided phrases as in "Not a Second Time" and—audible everywhere—contrasting phrase lengths produced by the addition or deletion of measures or beats from proto-typically symmetrical units. The Beatles do not explore mixed meter, as heard in the later "All You Need Is Love," in their early music.

Early Formal Designs

Aside from occasional large-scale variations in phrase rhythm and a few sur-prises in tonal direction, there are few deviations from normal formal designs in the Beatles' early music. Terms for structural sections to be employed in this book are "verse," "refrain," "chorus," "bridge," "solo," "introduction," and "coda." They are used here as the musicians themselves used them, and their natures and functions will be described in turn in the following paragraphs.

The verse is to be understood as a unit that usually prolongs the tonic (it need not begin with a I chord), although it may sometimes lead into the chorus with a transitional dominant, as in "Hold Me Tight" (at 1:10–1:11). The musi-cal structure of the verse nearly always recurs at least once with a different set of lyrics, but further stanzas appear in neither "Love Me Do" nor "Not a Second Time." Often, as in "I Feel Fine," a verse section begins with one or more inter-changeable lines of text, and this is followed, before harmonic and grouping closure, by a recurring line or two of lyrics. This constant, recurring brief po-etic text will carry the song's main theme, sometimes in ironic or otherwise hu-morous juxtaposition to instances enumerated in the verses. In this event, we speak of a verse-refrain construction; the refrain consists of the repeated text. If a refrain is present, that is the usual source of the song's title. Sometimes, as in "What You're Doing," the first verse begins with the same line that concludes it; in succeeding verses, the first line will change, while the conclusory refrain will be constant.

The Beatles' verses are often to be heard in an *aaba* or *aabc* pattern that constitutes the *S*tatement of a melodic idea, a *R*estatement at the same or contrasting pitch level, a *D*eparture that introduces contrasting motivic material, and a *C*onclusion that may or may not recapitulate the opening phrase. This, the "SRDC" structure of phrase functions, is the basis of most of the Beatles' verses throughout their career, so in the pages that follow we will often refer to the "D-gesture" or the "C-phrase"; recollection of the "SRDC" device will allow the reader to contextualize these formal labels as they appear later.

The chorus, which gets its name from a usual thickening of texture from the addition of backing vocals, is always a discrete section that nearly always prolongs the tonic and carries an unvaried poetic text. Rarely, as in "It's Only Love" (at 0:49 – 0:50), the chorus will end on V— an applied V, if need be — acting as retransition to the beginning of the following verse. When closing the song or when followed by a bridge, the chorus invariably ends on the tonic. If there is no refrain, the song's main poetic theme and title are always present in the chorus. Either the refrain or chorus may be omitted; the Beatles wrote dozens of songs, including "Yesterday," with a refrain but no chorus, and dozens of others, such as "It Won't Be Long," with a chorus but no refrain. In such unusual cases as "She Loves You" and "All My Loving," both chorus and refrain may be present. Occasionally, as in "There's a Place," neither a refrain nor a chorus is heard.

In common academic parlance, the term "bridge" usually refers to a transition, but this is not strictly its connotation in the parsing of pop music. In this domain the name is applied much more often to a section that contrasts with the verse, a middle section that the Beatles call a "bridge" or — regardless of its length — a "middle eight." The bridge usually ends on the dominant, but not in "There's a Place" and a few other experimental 1963 structures. The bridge, then, often culminates in a strong retransitional V, often with an improvisatory vocal exclamation that leads into the return of a verse, a practice stemming primarily from urban rhythm and blues, via early Presley, as exemplified by "This Boy" (1:21–1:27). The bass $\hat{5}$ at this point is often approached by an intensifying half-step, either from below with an applied chord, or from above with the upper neighbor ♭VI. The retransitional V itself is often ornamented by added sixth or ninth. Harmonic contrast with other sections is usually strong; if a verse and chorus are harmonically bland and diatonic, the bridge may be far-ranging and chromatic, as in "It Won't Be Long."

The improvisatory instrumental solo usually follows a chorus and may either repeat the harmonic structure of the verse, as in "Don't Bother Me," or may be newly minted but related closely to the verse, as in "All My Loving." A few solos, as in "Little Child" and "I Saw Her Standing There," follow a twelve-bar blues format that does not appear elsewhere in those songs. If a song has a verse-refrain combination, a verse-based instrumental solo will often be inter-rupted before harmonic closure by a vocal rearticulation of the refrain, as hap-pens in "From Me to You" (1:10–1:16).

So as to stir anticipation, the introduction—though it must be motivically tied to the piece as a whole—is likely to be the song's most colorfully varied and harmonically unstable event, in the extreme in "If I Fell." Codas are not neces-sary, but until 1966, when they appear they always prolong the tonic. They may be brief, and if so they are often based on the song's introduction. Con-versely, they may consist of long repetitions and, as in "I'm Down," may raise the rock-and-roll spirit to a higher level of excitement than does the song proper, as if in preparation for the ultimate coda of "Hey Jude." Codas often con-sist of a repeated passage that either fades out or comes to a full close, often on a tonic embellished by added sixth, seventh, or ninth or a combination of these. By early 1963, the Beatles recognize the dynamic attraction of a strong coda, and they provide surprising yet conclusive reharmonizations of insistently re-peated motives to close such songs as "From Me to You," "She Loves You," "I Want to Hold Your Hand," and "Yes It Is." With "Ticket to Ride," the Beatles ex-periment with codas of new but related material, a device that was to become a hallmark of later work.

Tonal Materials in the Early Music of the Beatles

Following Buddy Holly and some of the simplest rock music of the 1950s, most of the earliest Lennon-McCartney compositions were restricted to three major-chord roots: I, V, and the dominant preparatory IV. Minor sevenths were added to any of these scale degrees, but otherwise most early songs were fully dia-tonic. By 1963, the harmonic palette was abundantly colorful. Lennon heard the expressive alternation of I–VI–I–VI in Arthur Alexander's songs and used it himself in "It Won't Be Long" and "Not a Second Time." The often weak III triad, which comes off as a colorful substitute for I^6 when following I over an ascending bass arpeggiation, was given an unusual assignment by Lennon and McCartney. In "She Loves You" and "I Want to Hold Your Hand," the mediant was featured in support of the melodic $\hat{7}$, which thus lost its typical role as goal-directed leading-tone to $\hat{8}$ and instead evoked a unique aura of sensitivity and sympathy. Lennon again used III to portray his sensitive side in "I'll Cry Instead."

The Beatles' earliest compositions were nearly all diatonic, in the major mode, after Buddy Holly. But as a testament to their budding interests in the bluer manifestations of rockabilly, such as the recordings of Elvis Presley and Carl Perkins, and in rhythm and blues, the Beatles began to incorporate more and more blues-based scale degrees in their vocal and instrumental perfor-mance and composition. As in the tradition of blues vocalists and guitarists, the underlying harmony drawn from the diatonic world of the major mode would often serve as a backdrop for highlighted solo blue notes. These blue notes usu-ally describe the content of the pentatonic minor scale, all of its "steps" created

Example 1.1 Trichords in the pentatonic minor scale.

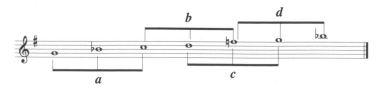

by major seconds and minor thirds, as illustrated in example 1.1. Note that "$\hat{2}$"
and "$\hat{6}$" of the pentatonic minor scale are nonexistent, but for convenience,
they will be counted as placeholders. These scale degrees are certainly featured
often as passing tones within the system. Note also that the scale allows for
both roots and corresponding minor sevenths of I♭7, IV♭7, and V7, all highly
characteristic sonorities in the pentatonic minor world.

The brackets labeled *a*, *b*, *c*, and *d* in example 1.1 mark the four ubiquitous
[025] trichords that distinguish the scale's often realized potential for motivic
construction. For instance, a blues tune might take the [025] motive of trichord
d as heard over the tonic and transpose it to trichord *b* over the dominant.
Among examples performed by the Quarry Men, the bare [025] trichord is the
basis for melodies in "Be-Bop-a-Lula," where the verse features the *c*-trichord;
the chorus transposes an *a* motive over IV to *c* over I. Similarly, the verse of "I'm
Talking about You" (*d*), the chorus of "Dream Baby" (*c* over I transposed to *a*
over IV), and both the verse (*c*) and refrain (*d*) of "Heartbreak Hotel" are all
based on melodic treatments of the [025] trichord.[6] We will occasionally speak,
in the chapters that follow, of the *c*- or *d*-trichord, and these designations refer
to the positions of these motivic devices within their respective tonal contexts,
as described within the scale in example 1.1.

The Beatles entered the chromatic world with simple applied dominants, as
heard in both Carl Perkins bridges and McCartney's vaudeville background.
These appear in late 1961 with "Like Dreamers Do" and in 1963 with the coda
of "Little Child"; by that year, applied chords would be used for shock value, as
in the use of V7/VI, which paints jealousy a bright green in "You Can't Do
That" (at 0:52–0:53). Augmented-sixth chords appear occasionally, as in the
deflationist retransition in "I Call Your Name" (0:51–0:53). Lennon became
fond of descending chromatic lines, which govern altered chord colors in the
bridge of "It Won't Be Long," the coda of "Tell Me Why," Harrison's guitar part
in an episode from "I'll Be Back" (1:03–1:07), and many passages in *Rubber
Soul*. Lennon composed a brief but stunning chromatic effect, involving a tonicization of III♯/V worthy of Liszt, in the tentatively groping introduction to "If
I Fell."

Free and expressive mixtures of parallel major and minor modes, and the
importation of scale degrees from the pentatonic minor and other scale forms,
gave the Beatles' early music one of its defining characteristics. Opposite-mode
scale degrees such as ♭$\hat{6}$ in major, heard in "Love of the Loved" in 1961, and ♯$\hat{3}$
in minor, heard in "I'll Be Back" in 1964, were often expressively tied to the text.

The pentatonic minor scale (e.g., G–B♭–C–D–F–G) was basic to "Love Me Do," and by the time of "Please Please Me" and "I Saw Her Standing There," the Beatles were freely mixing elements of parallel major, minor, and pentatonic minor scales, all for very specific and powerful effects. The Beatles established and continued to update their lexicon of the meanings of chords thus derived from mixed modes. The ♭VII chord, for example, was first borrowed into major in "P.S. I Love You," where it served as a passing chord from the similarly modal ♭VI on its way to I, later to become a basic function in *Sgt. Pepper's Lonely Hearts Club Band*. In "All My Loving" (0:10–0:11), ♭VII was used to contrapuntally prepare the seventh of V⁷ in the verse cadence. ♭VII attains its two most powerful and often mimicked meanings in (1) the Mixolydian/pentatonic neighbor system, where I in the major key is ornamented by its lower–neighboring ♭VII (as in "A Hard Day's Night," "I'm a Loser," "Every Little Thing," and many others), and (2) the so-called double-plagal cadence, ♭VII–IV–I, where ♭VII acts as a pentatonic IV of IV (as in "The Night Before" and countless followers, perhaps best represented by the coda of "Hey Jude"). Freely altered chords (such as the original openers to "All I've Got to Do" and "A Hard Day's Night"), occasional jazz chords (such as the V♯⁹ that powers "You Can't Do That" at 0:22–0:23), an occasionally pandiatonic approach to vocal dissonance (as in "This Boy" and "Tell Me Why") and the emphasis on the dissonant 4–3 suspension throughout *Rubber Soul* show that the Beatles often consider the major triad a simple platform for involved and ear-catching statements.

These innovations are responsible not only for a large aspect of the Beatles' late sound but also for qualities that brought "rock" away from "rock and roll" in the 1960s. But the Beatles went much further than their peers with such borrowings. The Beatles borrowed from the Phrygian mode to create the ♭II⁷ that substitutes for V⁷ in the retransitions of "Things We Said Today" (at 1:13–1:14) and "You're Going to Lose That Girl" (1:07–1:08). They create a Lydian effect when they use ♯$\hat{4}$ not as an applied leading-tone to $\hat{5}$ but within a descending chromatic scale from $\hat{5}$ to $\hat{3}$, as in many songs, from "She Loves You" and "I Call Your Name" through "Eight Days a Week" and "Yesterday" to "You Won't See Me" and "In My Life." And the haunting Dorian mode becomes a favorite collection for George Harrison in "Don't Bother Me." Harrison's "Think for Yourself" is a tour de force of altered scale degrees leading to such an ambiguity of scale membership that its tonal quality forms the perfect conspirator with the text's and the rhythm's hesitations and unexpected turns. Before long, both Lennon and Harrison will employ such techniques to portray their questioning of their own identities, and the Beatles' remarkable command over such a wide body of tonal resources will soon allow them to venture into the strange worlds of "Only a Northern Song," "Strawberry Fields Forever," and "I Am the Walrus."

Most of the Beatles' tonicizations involved not the dominant (as would be expected in common-practice repertoires) but various dominant-preparations. As in "From Me to You," IV would often be tonicized at the beginning of the bridge. This was a 1950s convention, probably because the spotlight on the home key's relaxed flat side at the beginning of the bridge made all the more effective the emphasis on the key's sharp side at the end of the bridge with a fleeting tonicization of V or with V⁺ for the retransition into the ensuing verse. Sometimes the flat side would be intensified further, as with the tonicization of ♭VI in the "Michelle" bridge or with that of ♭III in the bridges of "You're Going to Lose That Girl" and "That Means a Lot." The diatonic VI is tonicized in many songs; in "Day Tripper," this occurs in a most complex yet sure-handed and expressive way, requiring a nearly incredible German sixth applied to VI (at 0:39–0:40). These rather remote tonicizations are testament to the Beatles' command of the structural values of a wide variety of altered scale degrees, and they make it clear that the celebrated later lyrics and unearthly tone colors are not the only primary domains in which the group's curiosity and discipline led to major achievements.

Whereas nearly all of the Beatles' early music—no matter how deeply it may be chromatically embellished—follows a clear tonal plan with goal-directed structural voice leading and harmonic motion, a few songs venture outside these bounds. Both "And I Love Her" and "Girl" derive some of their expressive power from a double-tonic complex resulting in a conflict of priority between tonal areas suggestive of relative major and minor.[7] Any question as to just which area, "I" or "VI," should be understood as tonic, results only in ambiguity, as neither song settles the issue with finality. Such uncertainty of tonal centers colors a few later Beatles compositions as well, always for expressive effect.

Not only does most early Beatles music present a clear tonal plan, but it usually does so with a great deal of structural tonal tension that is not heard as regularly in later work. As if a direct reflection of the Beatles' turn from libidinous excitement to spiritual and psychotropic contemplation, such energetic harmonies as the retransitional augmented dominant chord in "From Me to You," "The One after 909," and the later, softer "It's Only Love" disappear in the face of the more tonally relaxed experimentations of "Norwegian Wood (This Bird Has Flown)" and "Tomorrow Never Knows." Of course, registral contrasts, vocal ornamentation, rhythmic emphasis, and masterful pacing play just as great a part as tonal statement in the concerted tension brought about in such marvels as "She Loves You," "I Want to Hold Your Hand," and "This Boy," and many of these aspects play lesser roles in later Beatles music.

Early Recording Studio Practice

By the end of 1965, the Beatles had not yet glimpsed the incredible colors still to be discovered in the tape manipulations and studio effects that were to become de rigueur for them and most other rock musicians in the coming years, and eight-track recording was still nearly three years away. Nevertheless, the group's basic recording method had come far from the fall of 1962, and many of their innovations to come were to affect details more than the general procedures adopted for *Rubber Soul*.

George Martin, the head of EMI's Parlophone label, signed the Beatles as artists in the spring of 1962. He produced every piece of their work through the middle of 1967 in EMI's studios on Abbey Road, in suburban St. John's Wood near Regent's Park.[8] Early on, the Beatles worked exclusively in the midsize Studio Two, but in later years they would have recourse to both the cavernous orchestra hall, Studio One, and the intimate solo setting, Studio Three. Well into 1963, the group would complete most of their composing and arranging before they entered the studio, at which time the producer and his staff might make adjustments, such as having McCartney rather than Lennon sing the chorus of "Love Me Do," raising the tempo of "Please Please Me," or rearranging the song's form so as to begin with an ear-catching chorus, as done with "She Loves You."

Martin made a specialty of introductions and endings, which for many listeners were perhaps the most crucial moments of a two- to three-minute song. In the Beatles' first albums, little editing was required, but a disproportionate amount of that done was intended to perfect the first and last seconds of a recording. This attention is quite evident in the rudely spliced final chord to "Roll Over Beethoven," but most of Martin's cutting was much more artful. It may be true that the Beatles' later innovations in these functions, from the startling opening chord of "A Hard Day's Night" to the mysterious coda of "Strawberry Fields Forever," were direct results of Martin's strong encouragement to get these moments perfect in the very first products. The same concern manifested itself on a larger level, as Martin would also be sure that the song order devised for each LP would permit both sides to begin and end with the album's strongest material.

Martin's work on the floor was not always done when the song's arrangement was complete. He often played along on the Beatles' recordings while an assistant in the control room (Norman Smith was the Beatles' balance engineer through 1965; Geoff Emerick took over after that) would monitor sound levels and direct the tape operator. Martin's simple but effective work on the studio's Steinway grand ranged from the sensitive in "Not a Second Time" to the raucous in "Long Tall Sally," as he added piano, celesta, Hammond B-3, or harmonium to fifteen songs through the recording of *Rubber Soul*. His tremolo playing in "What You're Doing" set the stage for McCartney's later forays into barrelhouse playing, and the licks he traded with Harrison in "You Like Me Too Much" anticipated by two years the Beatles' fascination with imitative counterpoint. For "Misery," he devised what he has called the "wind-up piano," recording a piano part at half-speed an octave low so it would sound rhythmically precise but with an altered sound envelope when replayed at correct speed. This was the production technique that graced his solo clavichord-like part in "In My Life." And Martin was certainly not above picking up a tambourine when the texture required density and smack and the Beatles' hands were full. But without question, his greatest contribution to the arrangement of a Beatles record through 1965 was the introduction of a string quartet in "Yesterday." He justly receives great recognition for this innovation, even though he derived the voice leading for the string parts almost entirely from McCartney's guitar playing and from that composer's verbal suggestions.

The Beatles taped their first four singles and two albums in a twin-track monophonic format, requiring all-but-live performances, with vocals generally placed on one track and instrumental parts simultaneously recorded on the other, separated thus to allow a later crude coloring and balancing of the two in a mono mix. Overdubs, which at this time required "bouncing down" all of the previously recorded material into a single "second-generation" track, were to be avoided because of the degradation of the signal/noise ratio and were restricted to a rare double-tracked lead vocal, the handclaps that could beef up the basic rhythm, a part from Lennon's harmonica, or an afterthought from George Martin's keyboard.

Once the arrangement had been worked out and the basic tracks and overdubs recorded, the Beatles' work was done. Martin and his engineer would complete the editing and then the mixing of the tracks. During the mixing process, more bite could be added through the compression of the amplitude range, filters could redistribute amplitudes among various frequency bands, and sparing echo could be applied. Any of these processes was available for either or both tracks, and a fade-out might be added for an ending, as in "Boys" and "Chains." The mix would be fed directly to the mono or stereo master tape, and, in the case of an LP, nonmagnetic leader would be spliced between tracks for the silent rills. As a final step in the recording process, amplitude peaks in the finished master tape would be limited to industry standards in cutting the "mother" used to press the vinyl, in order to keep the consumer's stylus from jumping the groove. Because of their lack of studio experience and their heavy concert schedule, the Beatles rarely attended mixing sessions, let alone disc cutting, for their early work.

In October 1963, the Beatles and EMI graduated to four-track recording, which divided the first "rhythm" performance over three tracks (one for bass, drums, and rhythm guitar; a second for lead guitar; and a third for vocals), thus reserving a fourth track for overdubbed vocals and/or solo instrumental lines. Given this new flexibility, the Beatles began to re-record their vocals after a basic track had been perfected, and by the recording of "Help!," Harrison was able to perform more complex guitar licks and more than a single part because he had the luxury of taping his lines separately from the rest of the ensemble. McCartney might compose a lyrical bass line for a song weeks after all else had been committed to tape, a practice that was to have a strong impact on *Revolver* and *Sgt. Pepper*. With such procedures in place, the group might first arrive at the studio with scant lyrics and little idea of a song's final arrangement, yet promptly begin a recording of its final product; from here it was only a small step to converting the resources of the recording studio into basic tools of composition. This direction was also manifest in the growth of the Beatles' home studios, beginning with Harrison's and then Lennon's purchases of equipment in 1964, allowing for the recording and adaptation of multitrack drafts through all phases of composition.

By 1965, the Beatles would routinely fill their basic tracks and then bounce these down to one or two reduced second-generation tracks for further superimposition. This allowed for more flexibility in the composition and recording process (five different guitars plus bass can be heard in "It's Only Love"), more control in the balancing and coloring of each individual instrument, and, with *Help!*, a more satisfying stereo mix. And while their first recording sessions observed EMI's strict schedule, their own heavy obligations and fantastic success allowed them carte blanche to record at their convenience, moving more consistently to late-night sessions. For *Rubber Soul*, the Beatles recorded in Studio Two for 113 hours over thirteen days, and as the deadline for delivery of the master tape approached, they completed their taping and mixing sessions at successive times of 1 A.M., 3 A.M., 4 A.M., and finally 7 A.M.

Only the most rudimentary electronic effects were employed during these years: various echo devices (to an extreme in "Everybody's Trying to Be My Baby"), compression of Lennon's guitar signal (as in "Don't Bother Me"), the pan-pot fade-in that opens "Eight Days a Week," and McCartney's fuzz-box distortion for the line that doubles his bass in "Think for Yourself" the most important among them. But as Martin's engineers had to struggle with capturing such complex sounds as those emanating from George Harrison's sitar, and as the group began to turn from merely exotic colors to those produced entirely in their own imaginations, the moptops came to govern the control room as well as the studio floor, and in December 1965 they stood at the brink of recording history.

Now that the Beatles' early compositional, performance, and production techniques have been surveyed in a general way, perhaps we can gain a fuller understanding of the platform upon which they built their more complex later work by looking in a more detailed way at a pair of representative early pieces. This will also permit an early demonstration of some of the analytical techniques, structural voice-leading analysis in particular, to appear in the coming chapters. We'll look first at McCartney's juvenile "You'll Be Mine," a comical skeleton of a simple song that suggests the sort of entertainment the Beatles would have provided their 1960 audiences. Then we'll consider a mature early work, Lennon's "If I Fell," from the 1964 soundtrack to *A Hard Day's Night*.

"You'll Be Mine"

We know "You'll Be Mine," a ballad in shuffle rhythm, only from a homemade low-fidelity tape probably made in the spring of 1960. The recording seems to feature its composer, Paul McCartney, on lead vocal as he strums his Zenith guitar, with a contact microphone attached to the top of the acoustic instrument's bass f-hole and plugged into a primitive blue El Pico amplifier. John Lennon supplies backing vocals and rhythm on his Höfner Model 126B electric guitar, with the Truvoice amplifier he appropriated from the Liverpool College of Art, and Harrison plays his Futurama Resonet, sharing McCartney's amplifier. No bassist or drummer are present.

Example 1.2a provides a reduction of the first two verses (**A** and **B**) and the bridge (**C**) of "You'll Be Mine," as heard on *The Beatles Anthology, Volume 1*, indicating only McCartney's and Lennon's vocal parts above a roman numeral la-

Example 1.2a "You'll Be Mine" (Lennon–McCartney). © 1995 MPL Communications, Inc. Used by permission of MPL Communications, Inc.

(continued)

beling of the guitar chording. McCartney delivers his melody in a corny, overly supported pseudo-dramatic style also practiced in "Besame Mucho," even though his half-written lyrics are neither dramatic nor even convincing. Lennon's vocal melody enters at **B** (0:27), mocking his partner with a wordless falsetto "descant" that doubles the structure of Paul's tune an octave higher. The tune, like many of McCartney's melodies (compare "Love of the Loved" or "Hello Goodbye"), is based on a descending sequence (c$\sharp$2–g$\sharp$1, b1–f$\sharp$1, a1–e1, at mm. 2–4). The low comedy peaks in the spoken bridge (0:47–1:08), with John in a ridiculous basso profundo range. This passage could be an imitation of the Ink Spots, a reference made stronger by Paul's expert control of dynamics and melodic instincts in his wordless "harmony" vocal that ends in quite an emotive baroque arpeggiation of an applied V of V, or perhaps of Elvis Presley's spoken bridge in "That's When Your Heartaches Begin," a song the Beatles perform elsewhere on the 1960 source tape. The put-on lyrics in this bridge are typical of Lennon's prose and poetry but would have been unthinkable to

Example 1.2a (*continued*)

record as a Beatles song until "You Know My Name (Look Up the Number)" was taped in 1967.

As an introduction to McCartney's writing, the melodic and harmonic structures of the verse to "You'll Be Mine" are worthy of further consideration. In example 1.2b, the structure of the vocal melody is given in the treble staff; the bass staff indicates the load-bearing chord members. As customary in such sketches, note values indicate not rhythmic lengths but rather weightings of structural value (notes with open noteheads are ornamented by those with closed noteheads), flags indicate neighboring function, and dotted slurs connect repeated tones or anticipations.[9] The graph thus demonstrates the hierarchy of structural value among the pitches of McCartney's tune, typically rich with such relationships.

The sketch represents the voice leading in the verse and may be compared

Example 1.2b Analysis of "You'll Be Mine."

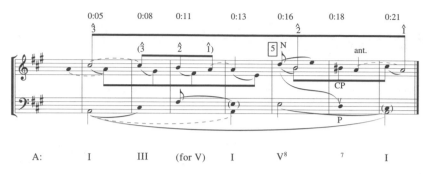

with the melody and roman numerals shown in example 1.2a. Previewing many Beatles tunes, this is a polyphonic melody with two "voices," both performed by one singer who alternates between the pitches of one line and those of the other. The two voices are differentiated in the treble staff of example 1.2b, where the "upper voice" is presented stems-up, the "lower" stems-down. The first four bars prolong an arpeggiation of I: note the bass slur tying A to A and the stepwise upper-voice descent from the third of the tonic triad to its root ($\hat{3}$–$\hat{2}$–$\hat{1}$), both outer parts exemplifying the control exerted here by the tonic harmony. The colorful chord progression within this expansion of tonic predicts those heard in the Beatles' early hits: III (C#m) supports $\hat{7}$ in measure 2 with a solid perfect fifth below so that it need not lead back up to $\hat{8}$, and an F#m triad (VI) substitutes for the V that would have been a more common and functional support for $\hat{2}$. Instead of enjoying support as the solid fifth of V, $\hat{2}$ is actually harmonized as an accented dissonant passing tone against the sounding VI, creating a strong desire for continued motion. The dominant is expanded in measures 5–6, and tonic returns in measure 7. The seventh of V[7], D, is heard first in the voice in measure 5 but is transferred to the bass a bar later (note the arrow's indication of such a transfer in the sketch), there heard as the root of a IV[7] chord. The progression V–IV–I, very common in rock music, is usually considered a backward motion, as IV more normally prepares V, which then wishes very strongly to resolve to I. As commonly happens in the ninth and tenth bars of a twelve-bar blues, especially in blues-derived rock, the "IV" merely doubles and intensifies the implied passing seventh of the V[7] for which it stands. So what might have served as an upper neighbor to the vocal c#[2] (note the flag on d[2] in the graph) becomes instead, in a blues convention, a passing tone down to C# in the bass. All to clarify a commonly misunderstood harmonic function heard in countless thousands of blues tunes!

Had example 1.2b continued through the bridge, it would have emphasized McCartney's soaring register, in which he highlights the structural upper voice in his highest tones, c#[3] (m. 20, 0:57) passing to b[2] (m. 23, 1:05), whose descent to a final a[2]—which would thus complete the $\hat{3}$–$\hat{2}$–$\hat{1}$ line in a closing perfect authentic cadence—is interrupted by the retransitional dominant. This is the typical manner in which the early music of the Beatles creates great tension in the bridge, demanding the return of the verse section as all four Beatles wildly shake their long-haired heads! In addition to covering a bit of ground in reading a voice-leading graph, we have been able to learn from a rather silly song something of McCartney's preferences for melodic construction, his sense of the interaction between melody and harmonic color, dissonance treatment, and his borrowing from a blues voice-leading type into a different rock idiom.

"If I Fell"

Lennon's ballad for *A Hard Day's Night*, "If I Fell," was probably written during the American "Sullivan" tour of early February 1964. When recorded in one session at EMI on February 27, the eventual arrangement comprised Paul's Höfner bass, Ringo's Ludwigs, predominantly soft damped rim shots, and John's Gibson Jumbo guitar all on one track, vocals from both Lennon and McCartney on another, Harrison's Rickenbacker twelve-string chiming the introduction's downbeats and arpeggiating in eighths through the song proper on a third track, and overdubs of Lennon's vocal introduction and of Harrison's guitar, heard only in the first ending (0:38–0:40) and on the very final chord, on the fourth. The mixture-enhanced IVb–V^7 cadence of this first ending and the motivically related coda are not yet present on one early solo Lennon draft tape, suggesting that Harrison may have decided himself to add this minor subdominant chord, most likely in reference to its important role in the bridge (1:05–1:08).[10]

Example 1.3 demonstrates the structural voice leading of "If I Fell." In the chromatically complex introduction, the singer enters a love relationship tentatively, looking for assurances that he will not be treated as he has been in the past. The tentative nature of the enterprise is reflected in the introduction's remarkable tonal relationships. The structure of the singer's melody here represents a straightforward interrupted $\hat{3}$-line in D major; note that the structural upper voice, indicated stems-up with open noteheads, descends from $\hat{3}$ to $\hat{2}$ but does not continue to the goal, $\hat{1}$, as the harmonic progression does not reach beyond V; the vertical parallel lines mark the interruption at the end of the second system. Although the melodic structure is straightforward—compare the goal-identifying interruption here with that noted above in the bridge of "You'll Be Mine"—the harmony is quite confused. The piece opens with a tonicization of C♯ major, emphasized at 0:05–0:06 by the utterly consonant octave leap on what is soon (at 0:18) to be treated as $\hat{7}$ in D major. Ultimately, C♯ major is to be understood as III of V, as clarified by the roman numerals beneath the bass staff. This opening prolongation of V is made even more complex by the dual roles of D triads: the D-major chord heard within the tonicization of C♯ (at 0:03–0:04) seems to serve as a substitute for the local V, a chord suggested in the graph by the implied G♯ in parentheses and by the "T6" indication that G♯ is transposed by six half-steps to D. The D-major triad at 0:12–0:13 is heard retrospectively both as the emerging tonic, befitting the discovery mentioned in the poetic text, and as a passing chord between III/V and II. A dissonant neigh-

Example 1.3 Analysis of "If I Fell."

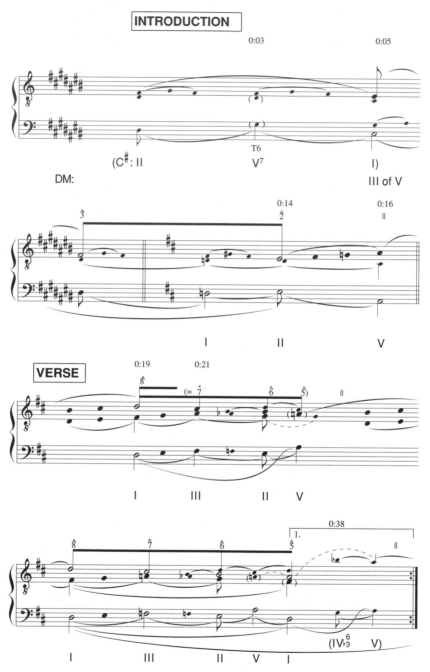

(*continued*)

Example 1.3 (*continued*)

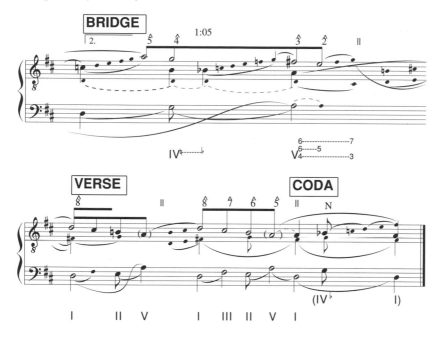

boring vocal g♯¹ at 0:12 prevents the D from taking hold as tonic right away and of course recalls the "T6" tritone, D-G♯. The introduction searches for, and finally finds, the motive that will enable the beginning of the verse: the initial rise of d♯¹–e♯¹–f♯¹, the song's first three notes, the first two of which are reduced out of the graph to indicate their status as superficial ornaments, twice becomes "normalized" to d¹–e¹–f♯¹, once at each D triad. Once on firmer ground, the second normalized motive leads to a rise all the way to a¹ (d¹–e¹–f♯¹–g¹–a¹, 0:14–0:16), which is the basis of Lennon's harmony vocal part in the verse (0:18–0:21).[11]

As if having gained new confidence from finally finding its way via the strong I–II⁷–V⁷ progression at the end of the introduction, harmony is strongly functional through the song proper (verse and bridge) and is supported with a commonplace bass line. The song's repeated I–II–V–(I) harmonic structure—see the third and fourth systems of example 1.3—is rescued from the threat of tedium by the colorful Beatlesque III triad (0:21), a passing diminished chord (0:22), and the minor-mode mixture of Harrison's guitar tag (0:38). The altered scale degrees predict an inner-voice chromatic descent of d²–c♯²–c♮²–b¹–b♭¹–a¹ in the bridge—note the pitches shown with stems down—describing past "pain" with the age-old ♭6̂–5̂ motif, recaptured as the song's germ in the coda.

But if the harmony is solid, the fundamental line, the structural upper voice, is not. First, the introduction's interrupted promise of a complete 3̂-line is never fulfilled; F♯ remains prominent in the verse, but only in an inner voice that takes the F♯ to its upper neighbor G, normalizing the upper-neighbor G♯ of the introduction, and back. Much more of a determining factor for the voice leading is an upper line that descends from $\hat{8}$ to $\hat{5}$, passing from McCartney's vocal part into Lennon's. The line stops at $\hat{5}$ in the verse but continues its descent above a tonicization of IV in the bridge, which is built on a melodic sequence; note the rise to a^2 presented a step lower, rising next time to g^2. The continuation is allowed by a register transfer signaled by the bright mixture-enhanced Rickenbacker figure in the first ending, as Harrison's guitar predicts the upper range of McCartney's bridge vocal. The structural upper line continues all the way down to a retransitory $\hat{2}$, where it is interrupted by the fear that the new relationship is "in vain." The verse returns, and, with it, the beginning of a new $\hat{8}$-line. The descent, however, never again progresses below $\hat{5}$, where the line ends. Once the song's continually interrupted structural voice leading is understood, the expressive aim seems obvious — the whole point of this song is that the singer cannot decide whether or not he should "fall." Thus, closure on $\hat{1}$ is never achieved. "If I Fell" is a marvelous example of chromaticism and unfulfilled voice leading in the service of artistic purpose, the portrayal of a trepidation born of remembered pain.

The Beatles' great confidence led them to repeat their most successful approaches. Musically, this self-borrowing was nearly always hidden to outsiders by the great wealth of ideas flowing at any one time, constantly providing new contexts and meanings for familiar materials. But staleness was felt within the inner circle. A glance at the time line above suggests that because they had reached the top of their field by early 1964, their manager could not think beyond the schedule of that year to compile one any different for the next. But the details suggest something different. The group had found their composing and recording activity much more personally rewarding than television appearances, which had been totally replaced by filmed promotional shorts, or radio performances, which had ended in 1965, or the grueling personal appearances that were to continue on a much briefer schedule to an end in the summer of 1966. Beginning with *Revolver*, for many critics the Beatles' most important work, the group would no longer submit product on a fixed schedule but would work — late into the morning when the iron was hot — to the dictates of their compositions. *Rubber Soul* is of course an important album, with its rich multipart vocals brimming with expressive dissonance treatment, a deep exploration of different guitars and the capos that produced different colors from familiar finger patterns, surprising new timbres and electronic effects, a more soulful pentatonic approach to vocal and instrumental melody tinged by frequent twelve-bar jams that accompanied the more serious recording, and a fairly consistent search for meaningful ideas in lyrics. But in 1966, the Beatles' drive for exploration was soon to affect every aspect of their craft from first draft through final mix.

ONE

ANOTHER KIND OF MIND THERE

The Meaning of Within (1966)

The time line (Table 1.2) shows an obvious curtailment of activity compared with preceding years. Largely because more time was devoted to recording *Revolver* than any previous LP, this album and a prior single were the only new Beatles product released in 1966. But the recordings were stunning. Reflective of their reading of Timothy Leary, their own experiences with LSD, and an exploration of Hindustani music and philosophy, *Revolver* was fundamentally unlike any rock album that had preceded it. The recording of its new and colorized sounds was inaugurated by a few bizarre homemade tape loops brought to EMI by McCartney, pushed beyond normal limits by expressive uses of audio filters, and introduced on the final product by a time-defying "one, two, three, four" countdown clearly worlds removed from that which opened *Please Please Me*. *Revolver* was an innovative example of electronic music as much as it advanced the leading edge of the rock world.

The Beatles' passion for studio creativity kept the band focused and intact through a difficult year of press-bashing, tours from hell, and extensive year-end solo projects conducted amid anxious rumors of the band's demise. With the end of the final concert tour, the Beatles virtually abandoned ensemble playing; rarely — prior to last-ditch efforts in 1969 — would they again perform a song in its entirety in a live format, even within the friendly confines of the studio. Indeed, the group had begun to break up in 1966 as its members discovered that they had individual lives with interests that were not always fully harmonious with those of their mates, a divergence that naturally would grow

Table 1.2 Time Line of Major Events for the Beatles, 1966

Apr. 6–June 22:	Recordings and postproduction for LP and single at EMI, London
June 10:	"Paperback Writer"/"Rain" released in United Kingdom
June 16:	Last "live" television appearance, miming single
June 24–July 4:	Concerts in West Germany, Tokyo, and Manila
Aug. 5:	*Revolver* released in United Kingdom
Aug. 12–29:	U.S. tour; final live performances for ticketed audience
Sept. 6–Nov. 6:	John Lennon shooting *How I Won the War*, West Germany and Spain; composes "Strawberry Fields Forever"
Sept. 14–Oct. 22:	George Harrison in India, studying sitar under Ravi Shankar
Nov.–Dec.:	Paul McCartney writes material for *The Family Way* soundtrack
Nov. 24:	Beatles return to EMI, London, to begin work ostensibly for next LP

ever larger in the group's final years together. But the beginning of 1966 was a heady and most promising time . . .

Early 1966: McCartney and the Avant-garde

Little has been documented about the Beatles' first three months of 1966; presumably, the period had been reserved for a film project that never materialized. No performances were scheduled before May, so a January dubbing session for a television film was the only group project prior to April recording sessions.[1]

Whereas the other Beatles resided in the suburbs west of London, McCartney bought a home on Cavendish Avenue in St. John's Wood, a very short walk from EMI Studios, in April 1965.[2] McCartney, the swinging London bachelor, had fallen in with the underground pop culturati—writers such as William Burroughs and Allen Ginsberg, filmmakers such as Michael Antonioni, and art critics such as John Dunbar—whom he had met as early as 1963 through singers Peter Asher and Marianne Faithfull. In January 1966, McCartney helped Asher, Dunbar, and Barry Miles open the youth-oriented Indica Bookshop on Southampton Row; the following October, he aided Miles in founding the underground paper *International Times*. McCartney attended avant-garde concerts of music by Karlheinz Stockhausen and Luciano Berio, began collecting the surrealistic paintings of René Magritte, and made his own avant-garde films; Andy Warhol once sat through a home screening on Cavendish Avenue.[3] Two such films, *The Defeat of the Dog* and *The Next Spring Then*, were described by one guest in *Punch* magazine: "They were not like ordinary people's home movies. There were over-exposures, double-exposures, blinding orange lights, quick cuts from professional wrestling to a crowded car park to a close-up of a television weather map. There were long still shots of a grey cloudy sky and a wet, grey pavement, jumping Chinese ivory carvings and affectionate slow-motion studies of his sheepdog Martha and his cat. The accompanying music, on a record player and faultlessly synchronised, was by the Modern Jazz Quartet and Bach." All of these activities represented a drive to discover the new aesthetic experience and would reverberate with the new sound images the Beatles would discover, especially with the promotional films made for "Strawberry Fields Forever" and "A Day in the Life" in 1967.[4]

McCartney's dabbling was more serious in his home recording studio, which was based on a coupled pair of Brennell tape machines. "He's become an expert at recording and double-tracking—he'll start with a basic sound on one tape, re-record something over it and then repeat the process umpteen times using two tape decks. He specializes in curious space noises and electronic music."[5] McCartney once threatened to release a solo LP called *Paul McCartney Goes Too Far*, but Lennon called his bluff, and the notion came to nothing. Lennon, on the other hand, would complete such exercises in 1968 and 1969. McCartney's home recordings, whether demos for the Beatles or something more experimental, became a regular practice and culminated in the more conservative homemade solo LPs, *McCartney* (1969–70) and *McCartney II* (1979–80).[6] "In interviews with Miles, Paul talked about the yearnings he felt for grasping what was unheard in music and unseen in film: 'To see the potential in it all. To take a note and wreck it and see in that note what else there is in it, that a simple act like distorting it has caused. . . . I'd like a lot more things to happen like they did when you were kids, when you didn't know how the conjuror did it, and were happy just to see it there and say, "Well, it's magic."' "[7] This desire for the distortion of sound and the yearning for the mystical is reflected in the timbres and structures of the Beatles' only LP of 1966, for which *Abracadabra* and *Magic Circles* were considered as titles.

A New Beginning: *Revolver*

American projects dominated the early plans for the Beatles' spring 1966 recordings, perhaps in accord with the fact that the film considered for shooting in early 1966 was to be a western. Motown Records in Detroit announced that the Beatles had commissioned two songs from their writers Holland-Dozier-Holland, and the group was also reported to have scheduled recording sessions in Memphis.[8] Instead, the Beatles cut sixteen of their own compositions at the usual EMI Studios, although the intimate Studio Three would often be used as well as the more familiar Studio Two.[9] In the end, the characteristics of American C&W and R&B so unadulterated in *Rubber Soul* would not appear nearly to such an extent in the new songs.

Revolver, as the LP was to be called, is an often mystifying blend of more new sounds from guitar and unusual instruments, sound effects, and non-Western materials, all engineered with creative wizardry. These sounds accompany newly demanding poetic texts that explore levels of consciousness other than simple wakeful awareness.[10] The sixteen songs for the LP and single were recorded, mixed, and edited on thirty-seven days between April 6 and June 22.[11] Building on the *Rubber Soul* process, much composition and arranging was done in the studio; the group devoted an average of eighteen hours of studio time to each song, ranging from just under ten for "She Said She Said" to some thirty-three for "Got to Get You into My Life." " 'We're quite big with EMI at the moment,' understated Ringo. 'They don't argue if we take the time we want.' "[12]

The Beatles' sound was altered with both acoustic and electronic effects. Geoff Emerick was assigned as engineer to the *Revolver* sessions when Norman Smith—who had worked the controls for every Beatles session through 1965— became head of Parlophone upon George Martin's resignation. Emerick provides an example of the new sound-distortion techniques: "I moved the bass drum microphone much closer to the drum than had been done before. There's an early picture of the Beatles wearing a woollen jumper with four necks. I stuffed that inside the drum to deaden the sound. Then we put the sound through Fairchild 600 valve limiters and compressors. It became [Ringo's drum] sound of *Revolver* and *Pepper* really."[13] Through 1966 and 1967, the Beatles pushed against all boundaries: at turns, Lennon would ask to sound like the Dalai Lama chanting from a mountaintop, would wish a passage to sound "orange," or would say a listener should be able to taste sawdust; it was up to the imagination of George Martin's team to find a way. Additionally, *Revolver* introduced a technical alternative to the tedious double-tracking of vocals. Artificial Double-Tracking (ADT), invented by Ken Townshend during a Cilla Black session, allowed an existing lead vocal track to be duplicated out of phase, but with steady pitch, by a variable 24–30 milliseconds on a second tape machine during mixing.[14]

The Beatles apparently sensed early on that the LP was to indicate a new beginning; before the pioneering first recording for the album was to receive its eventual title, "Tomorrow Never Knows," it was referred to as "Mark I." The album begins with Harrison's artificial, off-tempo, secretive-sounding count-off, "one, two, three, four, one, two," added to the top of the otherwise completed "Taxman." This beginning contrasts strongly with the opening sounds of the Beatles' first LP, McCartney's energizing count-off to "I Saw Her Standing There"; the contrast is especially one between a live performance in the early work and a studio creation in the later.[15] Serious artistic ambitions signaled by *Rubber Soul* were fulfilled with a newly mature confidence and strong creative individuality in *Revolver*. We shall document the compositional and recording histories, and interpret the final results, for each of the sixteen new songs in turn, taken in order of the date of each one's preliminary recording session.

One Song Each from Lennon, McCartney, and Harrison

"Tomorrow Never Knows"   The LP sessions began with the Beatles' first recording that was to reflect the LSD experience.[16] The lyrics of "Tomorrow Never Knows" are the group's first to not rely on any rhyme scheme. This results from the fact that they are taken directly from a prose source: a set of instructions for a drug-enhanced search for spiritual bliss given in *The Psy-*

chedelic Experience, an interpretation of the Tibetan Book of the Dead—the Buddhist guide to nirvana—written by Timothy Leary and Richard Alpert.[17] LSD leads to realms of consciousness analogous to the illumination achieved by Tibetan-taught meditation on the nature of death and rebirth. Leary and his colleagues believed that psychedelic drugs cause and permit the ego to become lost among the nervous system's encoded memories of all human history. Therefore, Leary and Alpert thought it valuable to provide a yoga-based manual for the control of awareness beyond this drug-induced death of the ego.[18] The instructions therein that would allow a surrender of the ego, such as "turn off your mind, relax, float downstream," a quotation only slightly altered in the song, guided Lennon's early conception of "Tomorrow Never Knows": "I'd imagined in my head that in the background you would hear thousands of monks chanting. That was impractical of course and we did something different."[19]

The song's title was Ringo's twist of the phrase "tomorrow never comes" and, like "A Hard Day's Night," was once considered as the title for the Beatles' 1965 film until "*Help!*" was supplied.[20] Lennon remembered the phrase and, two months after the backing tracks were recorded as "Mark I," applied the Ringoism to the song during mixing for the LP, "to sort of take the edge off the heavy philosophical lyrics."[21] Beginning with this song and continuing through his final recordings, Lennon was to lead the Beatles and his listeners through a fantasy world of dreams, Lewis Carroll, and the circus; the hypnotic meditative state of relaxation of the mind and body, in which ideas and wishes are observed but not followed, and in which initiative is an alien force, is heard here and reverberates in such later pieces as "Across the Universe."

Beatles assistant Neil Aspinall recalls the five-hour April 6 session for the basic track of "Tomorrow Never Knows": "The boys had been storing up all sorts of thoughts for the album and a lot of them came pouring out at that first session! The words were written before the tune and there was no getting away from the fact that the words were very powerful. So all four boys were anxious to build a tune and a backing which would be as strong as the actual lyrics. The basic tune was written during the first hours of the recording session."[22] The track, guided by such a "powerful" text, was eventually deemed strong enough to conclude the album.

Take 1 of "Mark I" (not part of the original release but made available on Beatles 1996a) features a basic track consisting of a heavily slowed-down, reverberating percussive tape loop with slowed-down guitar repeating the ostinato of example 1.4a. Overdubs (which begin at the ostinato's tempo but gradually go out of phase) consisted only of Ringo's heavily compressed drums, which provided a Motown-like straight backbeat without the eventual syncopation, and Lennon's vocal, which was amplified through a Leslie speaker.[23] Before further overdubs were made, this entire version was scrapped for a new set of basic tracks that were to include the characteristic bass, tamboura, organ, and tape effects. The tamboura is a long-necked Indian gourd instrument with four to six strings tuned to $\hat{1}$ and $\hat{5}$, always plucked open to furnish a simple, open drone. The use of non-Western instruments thus begins on the album's first day of

Example 1.4a "Tomorrow Never Knows," compositional draft, Take 1 (Lennon-McCartney). © 1966 Northern Songs.

work. The vocal melody's arpeggiation is a heavily slowed-down version of Bo Diddley's 1955 eponymous R&B hit; the connection is strengthened by the harmonic restriction to I and its modal lower neighbor, ♭VII. (This connection is interestingly similar to that drawn between McCartney's "Got to Get You into My Life" and Stevie Wonder's "Uptight (Everybody's Alright)," in n. 44 below.)

Some tape reduction (i.e., "bouncing" a full tape down to one or two tracks of a second generation) may have been required, but the following summary of the contents of the final stereo mix, which was based on Take 3, could have been produced with only four tracks. The first recordings other than outtakes from April 6 are heard on two tracks, one placed in the center of the stereo image and one on the right. The center is devoted to an ostinato more completely repetitive than that of "If You've Got Trouble" (a 1965 outtake heard on Beatles 1996a). The ostinato is heard continuously in Ringo's damped, limited, and compressed drums, with an odd accent on the second half of every third beat and a constant cymbal sheen, and McCartney's bass and Harrison's tamboura, both simply droning on the tonic, C.[24] The right channel has a second track with Lennon's tambourine, an organ, and Martin's honky-tonk piano. Perhaps Mal Evans plays the simple Hammond organ part, as he did on "You Won't See Me"; it is heard only as ♭VII resolves to I at **A+5−8** (0:19−0:22) and in the coda (2:20 through the fade). Martin's piano enters the coda with a flourish at 2:43, with a coloring duplicated later in the year for the "Strawberry Fields Forever" coda. This second track is interrupted abruptly between 0:52 and 1:49, and laid in this place is Harrison's guitar solo overdubbed on the same day. This solo (**B+7−16**, 1:08−1:24) marks an important event in the Beatles' history—it was recorded backward, as well as being treated with a fuzz box and run through the Leslie cabinet. What was recorded as a typical blues solo in C pentatonic minor takes on a vaguely Eastern sound, due to the "otherworldly" articulation and complex rhythms, when reversed. Only part of this original guitar recording survives in the finished mix, as the solo is surrounded by forty seconds of blank tape on its own track.

Lennon added his lead vocal on a third track, heard center, the same day. The first verses were recorded straight, but the vocal following the solo (beginning at 1:26) is also run through the Leslie speaker. Martin recalled, "He wanted to sound like a Dalai Lama singing on a hilltop. . . . So I put his voice through a loudspeaker and rotated it. It actually did come out as that strangled sort of cry from the hillside."[25]

McCartney applied his magic on the fourth track, added in a five-hour session on April 7. This track is wild, panning between left and center (and occasionally right), yet another Beatles innovation. It contains five tape loops made

Example 1.4b–f "Tomorrow Never Knows," tape loops, Take 3 (Lennon-McCartney). © 1966 Northern Songs.

by McCartney at home.[26] The loops are said to contain McCartney's laughter and distorted and/or sped-up guitars, but the origins remain mystifyingly obscure even when the song is played backward and/or at half- or quarter-speed.[27] Particularly in comparison with the end of "Strawberry Fields Forever," some of the loops sound less like a guitar and more like a Mellotron, a keyboard instrument on which each key activates a length of tape chosen by a stop tab—flute, string, or brass—and which then emulates the basic timbre but not the articulation of a symphonic player; Lennon owned a Mellotron by the end of 1965. In a historic EMI session portentous for the Beatles and other rock musicians, the five loops were added to the empty track, one from each of five tape machines, the short loops spooled on pencils; new engineer Emerick "played the faders like a modern day synthesizer," synchronizing the appearances of the various loops with the preexisting recordings.[28]

Examples 1.4b–f attempt to represent the contents of the loops in traditional notation. Example 1.4b sounds like a seagull—a far cry from the same sound in the Shangri-Las' "(Remember) Walkin' in the Sand," particularly when it swoops from left to center at 0:07–0:11 and left to right at 1:57–2:04; it appears a total of five times. Example 1.4c, featured eight times, never for more than four seconds, is a sustained chord that usually accompanies the organ's ♭VII (as at 0:18–0:22, 0:34–0:37, and 0:48–0:52) and suggests its function when the organ is tacet (1:12–1:15 and 1:20–1:23). Example 1.4d, heard seven times, is a giddy, highly ornamented Mellotron-like string sound that is normally heard very fast (as at 0:22–0:26), but its tape machine is slowed down for a solo (0:56–1:03) and elsewhere. It is twice heard changing from fast to slow, as at 2:08–2:27.[29] Example 1.4e, given eight appearances, is another string sound, featured panning left to center (0:53–0:56) before the tape solo and back to left (1:04–1:07) afterward. Example 1.4f is the pitch g^2 sounding on a rubbed wineglass rim, heard only once, at 1:28 on the right. Remarkably, the loops harmonize with the organ and the vocal, which continuously alternates between a C-major arpeggiation and a cadential [025] trichord c, to conform to the C Mixolydian scale, and the tamboura, ostinati, mystical timbres, and poetic text have led some commentators to conjure up Hindustani modes.[30] Perhaps Lennon and McCartney were sampling Harrison's Indian recordings during the early months of 1966. The loops seem to exemplify Timothy Leary's description of the "pure sensations of cellular and sub-cellular processes [that] are subjectively described as internal sounds: clicking, thudding, clashing, [coughing], ringing, tapping, moaning, shrill whistles . . . raw, molecular, dancing units of energy" perceived during the psychedelic experience.[31]

Having to reduce the four working tracks to a two-track mix proved very challenging for Martin's staff. They attempted twelve mono and six stereo mixes of "Tomorrow Never Knows" between April 27 and June 22 before best versions were so marked. During this process, the tamboura opening was given a fade-in and the first, non-Leslied, portion of Lennon's lead vocal was doubled with Ken Townshend's Artificial Double-Tracking, with the nearly duplicate signal added to the right channel in stereo.[32]

Harrison steeped himself in Indian music and in readings on Indian culture and religion. In India, "social structure, eating habits, in fact every action is related to a religious philosophy, be it Hindu, Muslim, or another. So it is with Indian music. Before a musician of the classical tradition begins to practice or to perform he offers prayers."[33] Regardless of the level of the Beatles' spiritual and Indian consciousness, the circular wheels in the poetry of the track, especially in the karma set forth in the conclusion, "Play the game Existence to the end of the beginning," are perfectly suggested by cyclic tape loops, backward tapes, and unending drones. "There's only the continuous downstream unfolding of the same melody going nowhere, like time, or consciousness, until it circles around to a conclusion that is also a rebirth."[34] Perhaps this song and the similarly circular "I'm Only Sleeping," in accord with the Beatles' rudimentary knowledge of the Indian concept of time as a wheel, inspired the LP's title, *Magic Circles*, which was to become *Revolver*.[35]

"Got to Get You into My Life"   Lennon says that McCartney's "Got to Get You into My Life" describes the composer's "experience taking acid," but the composer's relationship with actress Jane Asher may also figure into the nonspecific lyrics.[36] This was the first track begun after "Tomorrow Never Knows," and there are unexpected similarities in tonal structure as well as the possible LSD connection, but the recording evolved over the course of more than two months to something quite different from Lennon's song. "Got to Get You into My Life" was in fact chosen as the LP's foil to "Tomorrow Never Knows," appearing just before that album closer.

Basic tracks were attempted on April 7, but the group started from scratch on the following day. The aborted Take 5 from April 7 (heard on Beatles 1996a) has a basic track of harmonium, compressed drums, bass, and acoustic guitar, all in the vein of "Tomorrow Never Knows." McCartney superimposed a lead vocal to that basic track, and backing vocals and tambourine were added by McCartney, Lennon, and Harrison. These backing vocals, ranging from the second verse's Indian *gamak*-like dissonant ornaments shown in example 1.5 to the *Rubber Soul*–like retransitional "I need your love" (2:08+), were scrapped in favor of a solo McCartney vocal.[37] But none of this was to be released.

From Take 8 of April 8, the new basic track chosen for further work, we hear McCartney's bass (as in "Tomorrow Never Knows," maintaining a $\hat{1}$ pedal through the neighboring $\flat$VII of $\mathbf{A}+3-4$), Starr's heavily limited drums (note

Example 1.5 "Got to Get You into My Life," compositional draft (Lennon-McCartney). © 1966 Northern Songs.

the dull sound of the closed hi-hat in the introduction), and a rhythm guitar (Lennon's?) that is often edited out, all on the left channel.[38] A second track from the initial rhythm recording, heard center, has a tambourine (Harrison's?), often doubling the hi-hat and—in the coda only, entering at **D+3**—Martin's rearticulated tonic chord on the organ.

On May 18, three trumpets and two tenor saxes, with mikes right in the bells and the signal heavily limited for a very compact sound, were added to a third track (heard right). The trumpets double their parts in an additional take for the ending, in a tape reduction that also allows McCartney to add a lead vocal, superimposed on the organ/tambourine track.[39] As in "Tomorrow Never Knows," the vocal line moves from the jagged arpeggiation of a major tonic chord (verse, **A+1–2**) to pentatonic materials (chorus, **B+1–2**). Unlike in Lennon's song, McCartney provides a contrasting passage with a prolonged III (**A+9–12**), providing consonant support for $\hat{7}$, $\sharp\hat{2}$, as did so many 1963 songs in the same key, G major. The mediant then moves up through IV (**A+13**) to an authentic cadence (**A+14–15**).[40] The fourth track, heard center, features McCartney's double-tracked vocal, a quiet fuzz guitar that is mostly edited out, and—added on June 17, necessitating a further tape reduction—Harrison's loudly ringing Leslie-treated guitar solo for the coda, entering at 1:44.[41]

Lennon and McCartney wished to have a soul arrangement for the horns.[42] Nothing had been notated, but McCartney and the players worked out their voicings at a piano and dubbed their parts while monitoring the basic track through headphones.[43] The brass sonority, suggestive of both *Sgt. Pepper* and the "White album" to come, rings of a Muscle Shoals production, but the lines, particularly in the chromatically descending D-gesture at **A+9–12** (0:21–0:28), lean more toward Motown slickness. Additionally, McCartney's articulation of four strong quarters in the bass invokes the Supremes of 1964.[44]

"Got to Get You into My Life" has always been one of the LP's most popular tracks; it rose to the Top Ten in July–August 1976, when Capitol released it as a single in support of a compilation LP. McCartney coproduced a version for Cliff Bennett and the Rebel Rousers, a band close to the Beatles since Hamburg days, which peaked at #6 in the United Kingdom on September 17, 1966, and Earth, Wind and Fire took the song back into the Top Ten in September 1978. The composer performed his song on stage for the first time with Wings in 1979.

"Love You To"   "Love You To" is the first of Harrison's Hindustani (North Indian) compositions, followed by "Within You Without You" (1967), "The Inner Light," the *Wonderwall* soundtrack (both 1968), and other projects with the Radha Krishna Temple and Ravi Shankar. The song is perhaps most important for the Beatles because its change of meter, a normal event for Indian listeners, would have an effect on Lennon's fully English compositions within weeks. George's later Indian texts run to the philosophical and the selfless, but the lyrics of "Love You To"—while they preach against Western greed—express the same bitterness that characterizes "Don't Bother Me" and "Think for Yourself."[45]

Following his Byrds-inspired use of the sitar, Harrison heard Ravi Shankar's ensemble in concert in London in late 1965, and in June 1966 he began a tutelage with that master (b. 1920, Benares) that was to intensify later in the year.[46] After the release of "Norwegian Wood (This Bird Has Flown)" on *Rubber Soul*, rock musicians' interest in Indian sounds multiplied rapidly; the sitar was played by Brian Jones of the Rolling Stones ("Paint It Black," May 1966), by Donovan ("Sunshine Superman," July 1966), and by future Yardbird Jimmy Page and was imitated by Yardbird guitarist Jeff Beck ("Shapes of Things," March 1966). The London firm Jennings made a guitar effects box in 1966 that would add the sitar's play of harmonics to a guitar signal.[47] By April 1966, the Byrds and the Kinks claimed to play "raga-rock," and by the summer, the Hollies ("Bus Stop," June 1966) joined in.[48] But Harrison had led the way.

"Love You To" was taped on April 11 and 13. From the first day's session, we hear an Indian group, largely recruited from London's Asian Music Circle, on the center channel, open fifths on Harrison's electric rhythm guitar on the right, and a dub in the center that sounds like a volume-pedal-controlled fuzz guitar on the $\flat$VII chords at **B**, reminiscent of one loop, example 1.4c, from "Tomorrow Never Knows."[49] The Indian instrumentation includes a *svaramandal*, a Punjabi table harp with between ten and thirty brass and steel strings, all of which are played in two rapidly descending arpeggiations in the opening bar. We also hear the tabla, a pair of hand-played drums played by Anil Bhagwat; sitar, which is probably played by Harrison; and drones on a tamboura.[50] This tape was reduced on April 13, when vocals by Harrison and McCartney, mostly in unison except for cadences where Paul sustains his upper $\hat{1}$, replaced previous efforts, and Starr added a tambourine (all this is heard right). The tapes were mixed into mono on the same day, and into stereo on June 21. In mixing, ADT was applied to both vocals, the second signal fed to the left channel.[51] All this time, the composer—habitually shy in this domain—had offered only "Granny Smith" as a working title. The odd locution of the final title, a twist on the lyrics' "Love to you" and misspelled for years in American releases as "Love You Too," was apparently supplied only after all of the album's master tapes had been fully compiled.

A bit of detail on the instrumentation, formal procedure, pitch, and rhythmic organization of North Indian music as practiced in this song is in order, due to the important role that Harrison allows it in several of his compositions for the Beatles. Hindustani vocal music traditionally has the singer accompanied by a single melodic instrument (sitar, *dilruba, sarod, shenai*, or *sarangi*), a drone (tamboura or harmonium), and drums (tabla); such is the case with "Love You To."[52] Even in this short—under three minutes—pop tune, elements of Indian structures are followed. The unmeasured thirty-five-second introduction corresponds to the Indian *alap*, which ends with an establishment of the tempo before the beginning of the song proper, the Indian *dhrupad*, as it is called in vocal music. As in India, the motives in the *dhrupad* are developed by improvisatory sections.

"In alap . . . a musician re-creates as imaginatively as possible the personality and mood of the rag chosen. . . . The intent in alap is to build a climax on the psychological effect of constantly rising pitch register"; this is normally accomplished in a rise of three octaves, but is abbreviated here.[53] After the svaramandal opening, the tonic (*sa* = $\hat{1}$) is introduced traditionally by the tamboura, droning with an open fifth (*pa* = $\hat{5}$) above. The song's scale is slowly introduced by the sitar in an unmeasured, improvised melody—the barlines of the Wise edition distract but are convenient for reference—that at first descends from *pa* to *sa*, and this pitch is confirmed with a string bend from b♭¹ in measure 6. The sitar then climbs with faster tempo and increasing rhythmic drive, corresponding to the Indian *jor*, and concludes with the characteristic motive, bringing the tension to a peak at **A**–3 before the tabla introduces the pulse in the *jhala*, which traditionally has the sitar repeat *sa* on a drone string (as in **A**–1–?)

Outside the ornamental f♯2 of measure 3, Harrison plays in a mode equivalent to his apparently favorite scale, the Dorian mode (here on C). The scale is a major component of the Hindustani pitch system, which classifies hundreds of rags by scale content (ascending and descending), characteristic motives (*pakads*), typical ornaments (*gamaks*), and associations with time of day, season, and mood. "Love You To" follows the pitches of the *Kafi thata*, equivalent to the Dorian mode, and follows typical Hindustani adherence to the upper tetrachord, but no real rags are present.

At **A** (beginning at 0:35), Harrison and instrumentalists initiate the *dhrupad*, constrained by the metric system, the *tala*. Bhagwat, the tabla player, recalls, "George . . . suggested I play something in the Ravi Shankar style, 16-beats, though he agreed that I should improvise."[54] Sixteen beats is the greatest possible length for a *tala*, hundreds of which are classified by their own accent patterns. Phrase patterns normally end on the first count (*sam*), representing the Indian cyclic image of time, but this is not evident here. More traditional is the idea of improvisation, as Harrison's sitar playing answers his singing differently in each verse; note how the sitar motives shown at **A** were predicted by the *alap*.

The sitar's *jor* motive of **A**–3 is taken up by the singer at **B** (0:54), where the meter changes for the first time in a Beatles composition. As in the first two *Revolver* recordings, ♭VII is expressed as a neighbor to I; following "Tomorrow Never Knows," this is the song's only chord change, as its Indian nature precludes any suggestion of harmonic movement. The sitar solo (**C**, 1:35–1:54) climbs an octave, concluding with the b♭2–c³ bend (**C**+5) previously heard in the lower octave in the *alap*, and continues with many rhythmic accents against the regular *tala*. Following the last verse, the instrumental ensemble improvises again, with the tabla player speeding up (at 2:35) as traditional. Highly unorthodox is the fade-out, as traditional practice would call for a long improvisation at this point which may, perhaps, still exist on the working tape.

One might wonder how George Martin reacted so well to such unusual material as he'd been given this week; he probably recalled his sound effects work with Peter Sellers and the Goons. He had even recorded sitar and tabla in a 1959 Sellers spoof of "Wouldn't It Be Loverly."

The 1966 Single

The three composing Beatles had devoted a week of sessions to the near-completion of three LP tracks and now deliberately approached their choices for what was to become the year's only Beatles single not also on an album, "Paperback Writer"/"Rain." Both were recorded and mixed for mono on April 13–16.[55]

"Paperback Writer"   It was on a drive to Lennon's home that McCartney came up with the idea for "Paperback Writer," perhaps in reaction to his involvement with the Indica Bookshop or in regard to Lennon's own success as an author.[56] McCartney's manuscript contains all of the song's lyrics—except for one variant conjunction in the last line—in four paragraphs, written in the form of a letter signed "Yours sincerely, Ian Iachimoe." This bizarre name is McCartney's transcription of his own, as heard on reversed tape.[57] As if to please his Auntie Lil, who had asked, "Why do you always write songs about love?," McCartney composed the first of his many character studies. Placement of the introduction and various riffs are indicated, of course without musical notation, on the manuscript.[58] Like "Tomorrow Never Knows" and "Love You To," "Paperback Writer" features only one chord other than tonic; in this case, IV serves as its neighbor. The loud guitar riff moving $\hat{8}$–$\flat\hat{7}$ reminds John Lennon of "Day Tripper" in one interview, but the extended opening tonic seems closer to "Ticket to Ride," especially with vocal ascents to $\flat\hat{7}$ appearing over tonic in both "Ticket to Ride" (**A**+5) and "Paperback Writer" (**A**+3).[59]

As in "Ticket to Ride," likewise the first A-side in its year of production, McCartney plays lead on his Casino, now distorted and played through a Leslie speaker. Taped on April 13, the backing track consists of Starr's Ludwigs (again, the cymbals crash at crucial points in the refrain, at **B**–2, 0:28, followed by a tom fill), Lennon's tambourine, Harrison's lightly ringing Leslied Gibson SG (which chimes on second beats through the verse, **A**+1–8, 0:13–0:24), and McCartney's lead ("Guitar I," having both the I$\flat$7 ostinato riff, mm. 5–6, 0:06–0:12, and the boogie pattern in the verse that looks ahead to "Revolution"). All of this is heard on the left channel.[60]

The following day saw McCartney's lead vocal, featuring Chuck Berry–like repeated notes for a narrative effect, recorded alone on one track heard in the center, and many attempted instrumental overdubs.[61] The last three seconds of

Example 1.6a "Paperback Writer" (Lennon-McCartney). © 1966 Northern Songs.

one such take, featuring a Leslied jangle box and Martin's Vox Continental organ part, can be heard at the end of a pre-mix tape of Take 2 (Beatles 1990d). The final instrumental additions include Harrison's lead guitar for the two fills at **C**–1–2 (1:35–1:36) and McCartney's Rickenbacker on its own track, taped along with unison falsetto vocals from Lennon and Harrison, which are shown on the lowest staff of examples 1.6a and 1.6b.[62] All of these additions are reduced to one track, heard right. Reductions cleared a fourth track for more backing vocals from Lennon and Harrison, including a celebrated rendition of "Frère Jacques" as a countermelody—McCartney's idea—that begins at 1:02. This track is wild, heard at center for choruses (**C**) and right elsewhere. The vocal arrangement for the chorus, which introduces the song, is given as example 1.6a. This texture exhibits a Hindemithian growth of dissonant intervals (cf. the aborted "Got to Get You into My Life" vocals of ex. 1.5) that finally contains three harmonic seconds, almost as many as in the electronic loop of example 1.4c.[63] The vocal parts become more complex in the mono mix done the same day, as McCartney's lead is subjected to ADT (fed to center), which is slowed down for a heavy tape echo in each refrain (**C**–1–2), where $\flat\hat{7}$ rises to $\hat{8}$ to complete an [025] trichord. With little melodic or harmonic interest, the song persuades by electronic gimmickry and through the circular notion that the attractively ingenuous would-be paperback writer sings of his main character, who himself wishes to be a paperback writer.

Example 1.6b "Paperback Writer" (Lennon-McCartney). © 1966 Northern Songs.

"Rain"   Lennon's "Rain" is well known for its coda, which employs reversed tapes of the Beatles' singing. John Lennon claims that this was his design and innovation, but George Martin counters that *he* demonstrated to the Beatles how it could be done, and they jumped to accept it.[64] Actually, Harrison had already recorded his guitar backward on April 6, so all published recollections of these events seem a bit inexact. The vocal parts were apparently lifted from the beginning of the track and fitted, in reverse, against the Beatles' instrumental coda. Advancing upon the ending of "Ticket to Ride," "Rain" then possesses a coda related to the body of the tune, but detached in significant ways. This was to be a technique developed to a greater extent in "Strawberry Fields Forever" and "I Am the Walrus," as well as in many non-Beatles records.[65]

Basic tracks were recorded on April 14 in a five-hour session. From that day's work we have drums and Lennon's distorted Gretsch Nashville guitar, both recorded much *faster* than heard, introducing a subtle but rich tone of queasy hesitation that could be likened to the nausea of an acid trip, in the center; the composer's overdubbed lead vocal, recorded about a major second *lower* than heard, resulting in the brilliant iridescence of an acid-streaked sunshine, is heard on the left.[66] McCartney likely recorded a bass line at the same time, but this would have been replaced by a new high-ranging take (heard just right of center) on April 16. The bass was perhaps re-recorded to better harmonize with Lennon's guitar in the chorus, maintaining static tonic harmony as did "Got to Get You into My Life," while the vocals suggest IV at **B**+3−4 (0:53−0:57). Such a retake might have been effective in better matching the drumming, as with the bassist's hammer-ons that synchronize with the drummer's flams at **E**−2 (2:27−2:29). This bass "solo," like that in the same range at the end of "Paperback Writer" and like passages in "I'll Cry Instead," *Rubber Soul*, and "I'm Only Sleeping" to come, provides a rare pre-1967 showcase for McCartney's instrument reminiscent of London soul playing, as in the Zombies' "She's Not There" (1964). Ringo has come to regard his drumming in "Rain" as his best. It is certainly complex, while, along with his next drumming for the Beatles, on "Doctor Robert," it contains (in the chorus) some of his longest rests ever.[67] Lennon's guitar riff—especially if the tuning shown in the score is accurate, allowing a celebration of the hollow body's open strings in the chorus—is related to, but much simpler than, that in "I Feel Fine."

Also on April 16, the Beatles cut a fourth track with Ringo's tambourine and backing vocals from the others, including a descant part from John for the chorus (**B**) and responsorial parts from Paul and George (heard right). The reversed vocals were sent to Lennon's lead vocal track on the left.[68] Lennon's mordents in the two-part chorus (**B**+2, 0:52) sound less like his 1963 ornamentation and more like the Hindustani *gamak*; this intriguing sonority was taken over by several rock groups. Such mordents especially mark examples by the Moody Blues ("The Sun Set," 1967), the Hollies ("King Midas in Reverse," October 1967), and Crosby, Stills and Nash ("Guinnevere," June 1969). If the melody in "Paperback Writer" draws from Chuck Berry, then the tune of the verse in "Rain" might be said to come from Bob Dylan; compare the verse of "Rain" to Dylan's "She Belongs to Me" (April 1965), a twelve-bar blues that omits the dominant, preferring a Beatlesque final line of II^7_4–IV–I. "Rain" was mixed for mono the same day it was overdubbed, with Lennon's vocal altered by ADT on the same channel. Because release was projected only for the monophonic single, no stereo mix of "Rain" was produced until December 2, 1969.[69]

Rain or shine? Alive or dead? I or IV? Forward or backward? For Lennon, it makes no difference; for the Eastern spiritualist and the LSD-experienced, the material world is an illusion. The composer particularly wished to convey "the feeling that the physical world was insubstantial compared to the world of the mind."[70]

Remaining LP Tracks

"Doctor Robert"   Robert Freymann is said to have been a New York medicine man who administered mixtures of vitamins and mind-altering substances, including then-legal hallucinogens or amphetamines, to his well-to-do clientele.[71] Lennon thought the practice a suitable topic for a song, perhaps as a vignette-sketch answer to "Paperback Writer," with musical and poetic overtones of "Drive My Car." So he wrote "Doctor Robert," perhaps with McCartney's help in the bridge.[72] The result contained the most overt drug references of any published Beatles song, and the Beatles found musical ways to portray the doctor as a saint.

All instruments were recorded on April 17. We hear the basic track of Rickenbacker bass, drums, Harrison's maracas, and Lennon's distorted guitar in the center. Overdubs include Lennon's harmonium on the right, and Harrison's hot overdubbed Leslied lead on a third track that is basically channeled to the right but has its signal split by ADT to the left (bridge, **B**+1–8, 0:55–1:14) with the $\hat{2}$ pedal or to the center (after 1:10). Lennon's guitar ("Guitar I" in the score) is either the Nashville or the Casino; the timbre and the $\hat{3}$–$\hat{4}$–$\hat{3}$ figuration are straight out of "Rain." Harrison's lead ("Guitar II") enters in the second ending (at 0:55). Lennon's lead and McCartney's descant vocals were added to the fourth track on April 19; these are heard, by ADT, both left and right throughout. Mono mixes were performed on April 19, May 12, and June 21, stereo mixes on May 20. Not only was ADT added, but a fade-out was given to the full ending, probably to mask an extended jam of forty-three seconds that completed the original recording.[73]

The tune, in A, begins as simply as did that of "Paperback Writer" and emphasizes a long-held $I\flat^7$ in a similar way but then must rise from a^1 to $a\sharp^1$ (**A**+9, at 0:17) as the harmony shifts from I^7 to VI^7_4, reminiscent of the move in "Day Tripper" (**B**+1) to $F\sharp^7$—there II^7_4. $F\sharp^7$ resolves to a tonicized B^7 for the extraterrestrial bridge (**B**), where the drums and [025] bass ostinato are exchanged for a sanctified harmonium, $\hat{1}$ pedals on bass and lead guitar, and evangelical moving vocal parts. A retransition moves normally through E back to the tonic for the succeeding verse, but the song cadences on B. Unlike the tonal ambiguity of "And I Love Her" and "Girl," which contrasted two areas that worked like relative major and minor of each other, "Doctor Robert" prescribes two contrasting tonal areas without organic connections between them and thus uses structural pitch relations to contrast the normal, worka-day world portrayed by dull motives in A major with a supercharged, blissful state in B. Such irregular tonal contrasts will be exercised more often in the psychedelic songs of 1967.

"And Your Bird Can Sing"   Lennon claims "And Your Bird Can Sing" as his own, and he sings the lead part; before the last verse, McCartney adds only four bars of descant, and nothing in the bridge, **B**. But for some reason, McCartney alone has signed the manuscript, which had been written before recording began, under the title "You Don't Get Me."[74] The lyrics must be Lennon's, although the idea of a broken bird, second bridge, resurfaces in his partner's "Blackbird" as well as in his own "Revolution 9" (both 1968). They reflect a song that had been performed by both the Quarry Men and Bob Dylan, Blind Lemon Jefferson's "Corrine Corrina": "I got a bird that whistles, I got a bird that sings, but I ain't got Corrina — life don't mean a thing." The $\hat{3}$–$\hat{4}$–$\hat{3}$ vocal figure in "And Your Bird Can Sing," also current in Lennon's finger-friendly guitar parts for "Rain" and "Doctor Robert," rhythmically matches that in Dylan's 1963 version of "Corrine Corrine."[75]

A great deal of work took place on April 20, with an attempted basic track of drums, Rickenbacker twelve-string, and guide vocals from Lennon and Mc-Cartney, and dubs of two more Lennon vocals and others by McCartney and Harrison, plus bass, tambourine, and a Casino duet in thirds by Harrison and McCartney; Take 2 is heard on Beatles 1996a. But all of this was aborted and the recording was remade, start to finish, on the 26th.[76] Judging by Take 2, the guitarists likely performed the song with capos that raised D-major fingerings a whole step. The eventual basic track, which required thirteen takes to perfect, is heard center: drums, Lennon's rhythm guitar (which has quarter-note chords throughout, as shown at **A**+1–7), and an unusually intricate Casino duet by Harrison ("Guitar I," melodic parts) and McCartney ("Guitar II"). The latter said, "We wrote [the duet] at the session and learned it on the spot — but it was thought out. George learned it, then I learned the harmony to it, then we sat and played it."[77] McCartney dubbed a busy, octave-rich Rick-enbacker bass part, heard right-center. A third track with rich three-part vo-cals and, in the bridge, 1963-style handclaps is heavily compressed and sent to both far right and far left via ADT. A fourth track has tambourine and Ringo's added cymbals augmenting the previous trap parts, a procedure that looks to-ward "Strawberry Fields Forever." The added cymbals include the crash at the start and just before and after the bridge (0:33 and 0:51), and the hi-hat "ka-chit" on the second half of fourth beats within the bridge. A splice at 1:54 al-lows the nontonic ending — with McCartney's bass reminder of "Paperback Writer"/"Rain" — to be chosen from an earlier take; the aborted Take 2 had vamped forever on tonic for a mix-down fade.

Because "And Your Bird Can Sing" represents Lennon's closest current ap-proximation to a traditional voice-leading structure, with the upper line de-scending to $\hat{1}$, but differs from it in expressive ways, the song is sketched here as example 1.7. A glance at the graph shows an upper line descending $\hat{3}$–$\hat{2}$–$\hat{1}$,

Example 1.7 Analysis of "And Your Bird Can Sing."

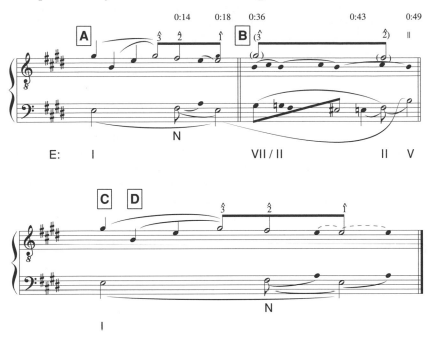

shown in open noteheads, through the verse (**A**), and then normally interrupted at $\hat{2}$ (at 0:45) in the bridge; only at this retransitional point (heard
0:49–0:50) does any dominant make itself known. Thus, the descent in the
verse is given merely a fleeting contrapuntal, rather than firm harmonic, support; note the example's flag on the neighboring F♯ in the bass at 0:14. The lack
of firmly supported directed movement in the verse portrays the problem about
which Lennon sings—the woman to whom he is speaking is too wrapped up in
material possessions to hear his message. In the final verse, when he moans
that she can't hear him, he tries to break through with a three-part vocal setting. The emphasis on attempted communication gives the guitar duet the air
of a wake-up call; their energetic tonic arpeggiation at **B**+5 (0:43), and
tellingly at "You may be awoken" (1:12), certainly recalls the "calling" quality
of classical horn fifths.

The upper line in the bridge is taken by Harrison's guitar countermelody,
which moves essentially in parallel octaves above the downbeats in the bass,
while Lennon sings a noncommittal b¹–c♯²–b¹ neighbor figure. The chromatic descent in the bridge, g♯–g♮–f♯–e♯, which transposes the same chromatic scale degrees of the D-gesture of the recent "Got to Get You into My
Life" down a minor third, unfolds a dissonant sonority, an applied diminished
VII/II triad. The prolonged strong-yet-uncertain dissonance effectively portrays the painful and aimless "broken" bird in the second bridge, and then resolves to the II triad at **B**+6 (0:45). Lennon's lyrics indicate that this resolu-

tion to a diatonic function acts as a signpost ("Look in my direction") that awakens the listener to more meaningful concerns. The interruption on the strongly motivated V (0:49–0:50) supports his promise, "I'll be 'round," with both harmonic and melodic tendencies. The expressiveness of Lennon's vocal is noted by John Robertson: "He had by now mastered the art of sounding devastatingly indifferent, overwhelmingly powerful, and slightly vulnerable, all at the same time, and seldom was his voice as gripping as it was throughout this album."[78]

"Taxman"   As a group, the Beatles released few songs with overt political messages. Outraged at their tax rate of 95 percent, Harrison composed the sarcastic "Taxman," who here proclaims, "Should 5 percent appear too small, be thankful I don't take it all." Harrison's defiance was expressed musically in the great volume of the percussion and distorted electric guitars, the constantly displaced vocal accents—reminding the listener of those in Harrison's "I Need You" and "If I Needed Someone," both from 1965, the modal substitution of $\flat\hat{7}$ for $\natural\hat{7}$, and the jarringly frozen $\text{I}^{\sharp 9}_{7}$ sonority.[79] But this song does not urge tax revolt; it has more the sound of a helpless taxpayer in misery. Lennon remembers helping Harrison with the lyrics; he probably suggested scrapping several lines that appear only in manuscript: "You may work hard trying to get some bread—you won't get it before [you're] dead," and "Now what I let you keep for free—won't take long to get back to me."[80] Lennon is known to have added the line, "Now my advice for those who die: declare the pennies on your eyes."

After work from April 20 was left unused, ten new takes of the basic track were made on the 21st. The four tracks were filled that day with drums and bass, Harrison's distorted rhythm guitar ("Guitar II") and overdubs of his vocal, and Lennon-McCartney backing vocals (in the chorus, **B**, and the bridge, **C**). The following day, these four tracks were reduced to two, with the vocals mixed together (Harrison's lead vocal was heavily compressed and treated with ADT) and the signal from the drums/bass track split between the guitar and vocal tracks. In the final mix, these first recordings are heard with guitar left, bass and drums left-center, and vocals center. Immediately following the reduction, a third track was given a tambourine (entering in the second verse, **A**, at 0:32) and McCartney's distorted Casino with heavy use of the Bigsby and feedback through the Vox amplifier ("Guitar I," entering at **D** and continuing, 1:12 to the end), heard right. Then the fourth track was filled with cowbell (added in the second chorus, from 0:46), heard right. With the tracks again filled, Lennon and McCartney wished to add more backing vocals, and punched out part of the Casino/tambourine track to sing "Ha, ha, Mr. Wilson; Ha, ha, Mr. Heath" (even in the second verse, from which it was apparently deleted in the mix). Example 1.8, from the revised Take 11 on Beatles 1996a, indicates the backing vocals that had adorned the third verse at 1:38 before Wilson and Heath were invoked. Despite having finished previous mixes, the "count-off" introduction was copied left, right, and center on May 16; remixes of this new version were abandoned when a new ending was created on June 21, made by splicing an alternate mix of the **D** section (here with a cowbell) onto what had been a cold ending but is faded out in the final mixes.[81]

Example 1.8 "Taxman," compositional draft (Harrison). © 1966 Northern Songs.

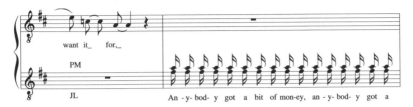

McCartney imitates Motown bassist James Jamerson with the active lines and glissandi at **C** (0:55–1:08). In the third verse (1:32–1:44), his distorted guitar recalls *Rubber Soul* textures, as in "Think for Yourself," by doubling his own pentatonic bass line (again outlining the static yet jarring I♭7 chord) in octaves, and in the fourth verse (1:54–2:12) it ornaments the line further by taking the ostinato up to f♮² each time. The transition to the coda (**F**–1–2, 2:20–2:23), which employs scale-defying pitches f♮² and c♮², includes the song's only chord other than the constant I♭7 and the chorus's double-plagal cadence—the year's first example of this favorite 1965 technique. Harrison recalls McCartney's guitar offering: "In those days, for me to be allowed to do my one song on the album, it was like, 'Great. I don't care who plays what. This is my big chance.' So in Paul's way of saying, 'I'll help you out, I'll play this bit,' I wasn't going to argue with that. . . . I was pleased to have him play that bit on 'Taxman.' If you notice, he did like a little Indian bit on it for me."[82] The Indian-styled ornaments (particularly in **D**+5, 1:18–1:19) are a strong feature of the solo, which traverses two octaves in the same Dorian-like mode adapted by Harrison in "Love You To." In "Taxman," McCartney's music protests just as loudly as does that of the composer.

"I'm Only Sleeping"   When the Beatles finished at the studios before midnight, they would often spend a few hours together afterward; as a result, they usually slept until two or three in the afternoon. As will be done again in "Watching the Wheels" (1980), Lennon defends his dreamy retreat from the world in "I'm Only Sleeping," the first of many dream-related songs. Two manuscripts are documented; a signed, complete set of lyrics is seen in Campbell and Murphy 1980 (vi). More interesting is an early draft seen in Shotton and Schaffner 1983 (123), written on the back of a letter dated April 25, two days before sessions began on the recording. No bridge (**C**) is yet present, but the buoyant first verse (**A**) takes shape:

> Got to get to sleep
> ~~When I'm woken early in the morning.~~
> ~~Lift my head stay in bed.~~
> When I wake up early in the morning,
> ~~Lift my head stay in bed~~
> ~~Got to get to sleep while I'm still yawning.~~
> Lift my head I'm still yawning.
> I'm sleeping.
> When I wake up early in the morning
> Lift my head I'm still yawning
> When I'm in the middle of a dream
> Stay in bed float ~~down~~ up stream. . . .

The Beatles create unusual timbres for "I'm Only Sleeping" with the vari-speed technique; as with "Rain," instrumental parts were recorded higher, and the lead vocal lower, than heard in the eventual recording. Although the song sounds a semitone lower, it was taped in E minor on April 27 and certainly not with the E♭ tuning shown in the score. On this day, the Beatles recorded eleven takes of Rickenbacker bass, drums, and Lennon's Gibson Jumbo ("Guitar II"). All of these were later reduced to a single track, heard left-center.[83] Lennon sang his lead vocal two days later, taped at 45 cps for replay at 50 cps, creating a dreamy timbre that floats particularly well on the high sustained tones.[84] This track was sent, with ADT, to both left and right channels. On May 5, Harrison taped two slithering reversed guitar parts that manifest the unreal condition: "Guitar I" and, with distortion, "Guitar II" at **D** and **F**. These tracks later became one and are heard center. The eventual fourth track, with McCartney's descant vocal at **C** and **E** and weightless backing vocals by McCartney and Harrison throughout, was recorded on May 6 and is heard both left and right via ADT. Mixes were attempted on May 6, 12, and 20 and completed on June 6.

Several alternate mixes contain different reversed guitar parts; the British stereo mix (that heard on the CD) is given in the score; the British mono mix omits the first five notes of **A**+7; the mono and stereo mixes used on American LPs contain one passage (given here as ex. 1.9) not shown in the score and omit the line within **A**. The mono mix for a French EP, also on a bootleg titled *Casualties*, is said to contain still other lines; I have not reviewed this version.[85] As if in homage to this recording, two-part backward guitars are heard in Crosby, Stills and Nash's "Pre-Road Downs" (June 1969).

Just as the lyrics show disdain for those in a hurry to get somewhere, the tonal structure would like to hover without direction. It almost can't—the verse's S-gesture (**A**+1–4, 0:00–0:09) moves strongly from I through III to V⁷ as the composer lifts his head—but he changes his mind, stays in bed, and drifts. Drifting characterizes the D-gesture (**B**+1–3, 0:21–0:28) much more than it does the earlier lines, as the tune, the backing vocals, and the underlying chords reverse themselves in circles, just as Harrison's guitars do. Structurally, the melody descends as if into a pillow, from $\hat{8}$ into the inner voice $\hat{5}$: e♭² (supported by I, **A**+1)–d♭² (supported by III, **B**+1)–c♭² (supported by a neighboring IV, **B**+4)–b♭¹ (supported by the returning I, **B**+5–6). "I'm Only Sleep-

Example 1.9 "I'm Only Sleeping" (Lennon-McCartney). © 1966 Northern Songs.

ing" has no structural melody that descends forcefully to the tonic, but only to the noncommittal fifth scale degree, as did the structural upper voice in "If I Fell."[86] While the coda is not strictly a separate section, the song trails off without conclusion in dreaming reversed guitars in a manner later heard in "Flying" and "Long, Long, Long." From the melodic and harmonic devices to the unreal colors, Lennon and his supporting cast have created sounds in "I'm Only Sleeping" that make for particularly expressive text painting.

"Eleanor Rigby"   Playing with the rhythm of a name he'd invented at the piano, Miss Daisy Hawkins, McCartney noticed a Bristol shop named Rigby's in January 1966, while visiting actress girlfriend Jane Asher (who was performing there). McCartney thought of actress friend Eleanor Bron, and Eleanor Rigby was born.[87] Once he'd established that Rigby was a church cleaning woman, he brought the idea and tune to Lennon in Weybridge, and the two created a lonely Father Mackenzie and considered the possibility of a verse about a dustbin browser.[88] Lennon contends that he wrote most of the Rigby lyrics; McCartney answers, "Yeah. About half a line." Old Woolton friend and one-time Quarry Man Pete Shotton, who claims to have been present at the Weybridge gathering, says that Ringo had the priest darning his socks, that Shotton himself suggested that Mackenzie bury Rigby in the end, and that Lennon's entire contribution, witnessed by him, was to oppose Shotton's burial suggestion, which became, of course, the basis of the last verse. Lennon recalls approving the chorus lyric (see ex. 1.10) in the studio, as it was created by McCartney and Harrison, likely after the instruments had already been taped. The last verse, about which Shotton writes, is not present in McCartney's manuscript and so probably was created in the studio.[89] No matter who composed the lyrics, and it likely was a group effort, McCartney has overseen another character study whose lines are etched in very clear focus.

Perhaps trying to re-create "Yesterday" or perhaps because Jane Asher had him listening to Vivaldi, McCartney suggested strings to George Martin when he demonstrated the new song on piano; the string octet — a double quartet, particularly in its articulations, was much more Martin's arrangement than was "Yesterday." The producer says, "I was very much inspired by Bernard Herrmann, in particular a score he did for the Truffaut film [*Fahrenheit 451*]. That really impressed me, especially the strident string writing."[90] The eight players were recorded, mikes right on the strings, on April 28, two per track, requiring a reduction to one track, heard center.[91] The instruments have a dry, gritty timbre, particularly effective when the cellos double the melody as the priest wipes

Example 1.10 "Eleanor Rigby" (Lennon-McCartney). © 1966 Northern Songs.

dirt from his hands in **B**+7–9. As in "Yesterday," the cellos have several poignant lines, including tonic arpeggios in the chorus and full C-major scales in the second verse, and the first violins play a sustained inverted pedal in the last verse.

Two vocal tracks were taped on April 29, with McCartney's lead vocal on the right and backing parts from Lennon and Harrison in the choruses on the left. ADT sends the lead vocal signal to the left for refrains (**C**) but to the right in the last refrain, where the out-of-phase signals are combined on the same channel.

The fourth track was used on June 6, nullifying an already suitable mono mix, when the composer added a vocal countermelody to the last refrain, sung through the Leslie speaker and augmented on the same channel, the left, with ADT. All released mixes were made on June 22.

"Eleanor Rigby" is another *Revolver* song with minimal harmonic implications; the tonic Em and a neighboring C are its only chords. Again, the Dorian scale appears, with C$\sharp$ functioning at two levels—in the surface vocal sequence of **B**+2–3 (0:15–0:19), and within the violas' chromatic descent in **C** (0:31–0:45), which is reminiscent of, but very different from, Harrison's backing vocal descent in the bridge of "It Won't Be Long." The scale, like the story's inhabitants, doesn't quite seem to fit, and a battle for priority ensues between C and C$\sharp$; the former wins, perhaps because in each refrain and chorus it enlists the help of the pitiable tritone-completing B$\flat$.

"Eleanor Rigby" was chosen as the LP's second song, following "Taxman." Beatles author Tim Riley says that "the corruption of 'Taxman' and the utter finality of Eleanor's fate makes the world of *Revolver* more ominous than any other pair of opening songs could."[92] Rigby and Mackenzie are sad in their loneliness and in the obvious futility of their lives, the poetry carries a "Nowhere Man"–like extension of their condition to all of humanity, and McCartney's images are vivid and yet common enough to elicit enormous compassion for these lost souls. Conversely, only those in the highest earning brackets would be likely to feel an overwhelming compassion for the ultrarich victims of Harrison's Taxman.

Although the Beatles play no instruments on this recording, McCartney accompanies himself on a Martin D-28 for "Eleanor Rigby" with the Gabrieli String Quartet, adding new effects, in his 1984 film, *Give My Regards to Broad Street*. The film features a seven-minute dream scene scored by Martin and McCartney in which the song is developed in the following sequence of minor keys: e–e$\flat$–e–d–e–c–e, briefly citing Herrmann's score for *Psycho* along the way. A popular number with soul artists who were expanding their repertoires, "Eleanor Rigby" was taken into the Top Forty by both Ray Charles (July 1968) and Aretha Franklin (November 1969).

"For No One"   Paul wrote "For No One" while on a March 1966 Swiss vacation.[93] The manuscript (seen in Campbell and Murphy 1980, xli) is titled "WHY DID IT DIE?"; the first two verses are written as released, but the first chorus, third verse, second chorus, and fourth verse, all to be substantially altered, are given there as:

> *Chorus*
> Why did it die?_____you'd like to know.
> Cry—and blame her.
>
> But you wait
> You're too late
> As you're deciding why the wrong one wins,
>   the end begins and you will lose her

(Why let it die_____
I'd like to know
Try — to save it.)

~~She wants you~~
~~you need~~
You want her
You need (love) her
So make her see that you believe it may
                    work out one day, you need each other.

The dissemination of monitor tapes made during two recording sessions makes possible the close study of the recording process.[94] The basic tracks were laid in C major, in ten takes on May 9, with McCartney on the Steinway and Starr on drums, each on a separate track but with some acoustic leakage. The piano is given added reverberation from the control room, beginning with Take 9. The first two verses (**A** and **B**) and first bridge (**C**) of the piano part from Take 10, that used in the final mix, are excerpted, for two measures each, in examples 1.11 a–c (as a correction to the Wise scores). Note the thickening of the texture with left-hand octaves for the second verse. The verse's repeated drum pattern is given as example 1.11 d. The third track, also taped in C on May 9, successively adds McCartney's clavichord, heard throughout (see ex. 1.11 e for an instance of how this part differs from that of the piano); Ringo's hi-hat, played on beats two and four (entering in the second verse); maracas, shaken on all eighths (entering in the bridges); and a tambourine doubling the maracas (entering in the second bridge). On May 16, McCartney dubbed his solo vocal, sung in B and compressed as well as sped up, onto the fourth track, and the tape was transferred, reducing all to one vocal and one instrumental track. The new third track was filled with bass and a second tambourine, both of which enter in the first bridge; the bass, played in B major — the slower tempo must have appealed to the composer — essentially doubles the keyboard line but extends the ascent to a tonicized $\hat{2}$ in the bridge (at 0:29–0:31).

On May 19, Alan Civil was brought in to add a horn solo to four bars in the middle (**D**) and to the final chord as well. One wonders what led Martin to think of this instrument — was it the arpeggiating nature of McCartney's melody, or his nostalgic text?[95] In any case, Martin had known Civil — a frequent EMI artist, usually recording solo or orchestral jobs in Studio One while Martin worked in Two — since about 1950, and he thought the hornist could do the job. Civil says the four bars requiring the solo were played to him several times and he was asked to "busk" along. Although Martin recalls that the composer suggested the melody, Civil says, "McCartney sang nothing. Nobody seemed to know what they wanted at all, even George Martin. And you think they'd have written something down, but, no, they didn't." Responding to such suggestions from McCartney as "Try something a bit higher," the final result was Civil's own melody: "I was entirely responsible for inventing the motive; I never thought of anything as *high* as that, though, actually, because that's not a distinctive horn sound, as such." Civil recorded in B: "The engineer pulled the pitch down to B♭ but the effect sounded odd — we then raised it to B♮ and I played the horn

Example 1.11a–c "For No One" (Lennon-McCartney). © 1966 Northern Songs.

Example 1.11d "For No One" (Lennon-McCartney). © 1966 Northern Songs.

Example 1.11e "For No One" (Lennon-McCartney). © 1966 Northern Songs.

counter in that key on a B♭ horn."[96] Both mono and stereo mixes were made on June 21. The latter has McCartney's vocal center; the right channel has one track with piano, drums, clavichord, hi-hat, maracas, and first tambourine; the left channel carries the two remaining working tracks—that of the bass and second tambourine and that of the horn.

An unusually large-scale structural motion from $d\sharp^2$ (supported by tonic, **A**) through $c\sharp^2$ (supported by II, **C**) to a half cadence with $4-3$ suspension on an implied $c\sharp^2$ over the dominant (**C**+5) gives the song a large sweep that also characterizes the individual melodic arches shaped in the verse and the more agitated bridge. Pianist Joel Hastings notes similarities between the opening phrases of "For No One" and "Yesterday," although the songs are in contrasting modes: both have stepwise descents in the bass passing from I through VI to IV while the singer optimistically arpeggiates up a sixth, and both move to a nostalgic, backward-looking $\hat{3}/I$.[97] The subtle, fleeting $G\natural$s sung over $\flat$VII evoke the bitterness of the realization of loss.

Like "And Your Bird Can Sing," "For No One" does not conclude on tonic because it uncharacteristically and mysteriously ends with the bridge (**C**) rather than with the verse (**A**). Like "We Can Work It Out," the passage ends with V^{4-3}; the earlier song, though, as would have happened in any pre-*Revolver* song, adds a codetta to confirm the tonic. The lack of resolution shows the ambiguity in the relationship of which the singer speaks, the final note from the horn suggests one last retreat to fond memories, and the $4-3$ suspension is "the musical equivalent of a sigh, the sorrow and self-obsession of a lover left behind," all in a distant galant style.[98]

"Yellow Submarine"   With the exception of "For No One," the eight sessions over the first three weeks of May were devoted to superimpositions for, and editing and mixing of, previous recordings. Needing five more tracks for the LP, the Beatles started fresh on May 26. All six hours on this day and all twelve hours of the next session, June 1, were devoted to the recording of "Yellow Submarine." McCartney, inspired by a Greek confection called "submarine" that is dropped into water, wrote the song for children to chant. McCartney: "It's got to be very easy—there isn't a single big word. Kids will understand it easier than adults."[99] He then realized it was a perfect number for Ringo, who had yet to contribute vocally to the album. Lennon added some lyrics, and Scottish singer Donovan Leitch contributed a line of his own, "Sky of blue, sea of green."[100] Manuscripts exist on two scraps of paper (given in Campbell and Murphy 1980, 368, 382); one has the verse at **D** completely scratched out with Lennon's marginal note, "Disgusting!! See me." As Nicholas Schaffner said, "John and Paul coupled some incredibly disarming and idiotic lyrics about their improbable conveyance with an equally simple and ridiculous melody, and it proved to be the perfect vehicle for Ringo's goofy, toneless voice."[101]

The basic track contains Lennon's Jumbo, Harrison's tambourine, Ringo's drums (entering at **A**+5), and McCartney's bass (entering at **B**); this is all heard left. Also taped on May 26 were Ringo's lead vocal and all four Beatles singing the chorus (**C**); all are heard right.[102] As in "Rain" and "I'm Only Sleeping," instruments were recorded a half-step higher and vocals a half-step lower than now heard (in G♭). Tape reductions made room for the "Goon"-type sound effects performed in the second session. A raid of the Studio Two trap room availed the EMI staff, the Beatles, and their guests of enough noisemakers to convey the deep-sea party atmosphere of both the sub and the overindulging on two additional separately taped tracks (sometimes combined dead center, as for the brass band at **D**+7–8, at other times split left-center and right-center). Heard are Harrison swirling water in a metal bathtub (beginning at 0:18); Rolling Stone Brian Jones clinking glasses, supplying party chatter, and playing the ocarina at **D**; Lennon blowing bubbles in a bucket through a straw and shouting off-mike in the echo chamber, studio staff rattling chains in a metal tub, and ships' bells at **E**; and a manic Lennon mocking Ringo's every measure the second time through **B** (entering at **B**+2 in the mono mix and **B**+3 in stereo), into a hand-held mike plugged into his Vox guitar amp.[103] All who were not working the controls, including the Beatles; Martin; Emerick; assistants Evans, Aspinall, and Alf Bicknell; and friends Jones, Pattie Harrison, and Marianne Faithfull join in the final chorus in the center, along with the original chorus on the right. Mono mixes were made on June 2 and 3, stereo on June 22. Incredibly, this fun piece of nonsense required twice as much studio time as did the Beatles' entire first LP.

"*I Want to Tell You*"   Apparently, Lennon did not yet have another song ready — he had not introduced anything for five weeks, as Harrison was given an unprecedented and thereafter unequaled three songs on a single Beatles LP. This third composition, "I Want to Tell You," deals with the difficulty of communication. His manuscript shows several lines that were abandoned as extraneous, such as "If you should see me, and need my love to pass the time . . ."[104] Referred to as "Laxton's Superb"— like the Granny Smith, an apple variety — during the session, the song's basic track and most of its overdubs were made on June 2. First taped were Harrison's Leslied guitar (the fade-in would be supplied during mixing), Starr's drums, McCartney's compressed piano, and Lennon's tambourine; these go to the center, along with overdubbed maracas, all reduced to one track. A second track, with Harrison's earnest lead vocal and handclaps (entering the second time through **B**), was compressed, sped up, divided by ADT, and sent to both left and right channels. A third track, with backing vocals by Lennon and McCartney, is heard right-center. All three singers re-create the parallel planing triads of Harrison's "If I Needed Someone," and as in "Taxman," McCartney adds *gamak*-like ornaments to his part in the coda. Repeating the process used in "For No One," McCartney overdubs a bass line, recorded onto the fourth track on June 3. Mixes were done on June 3, 6, and 21.

The tied triplets of the guitar's introduction, which is related to the dotted-rhythm I♭7 bass riff in "Rain," should be taken as a warning of metric effects to follow. Two extra beats (**A**+4, beats one and two) have the first phrase stutter to five full bars, and, by virtue of lumbering rests, the second phrase goes to six bars. The lumbering effect is heightened by the clumsy finger-tapping impatience in McCartney's ♭$\hat{6}$–$\hat{5}$ figure in the piano (**A**+6–9, 0:25–0:32), but Harrison seems to counter this restlessness later when he sings, "I don't mind. . . . I could wait forever, I've got time." Given the lyrics that seem to describe an eternity in reaching an understanding, these effects convey stammering and searching for ideas.[105] As in the opening of "Eight Days a Week," which also fades in, and all other Beatles examples of the Lydian $II_{\sharp}^{7}$, the singer seems surprised that the delayed B^{7} chord ($\mathbf{A}$+4, 0:22–0:24) resolves normally (at 0:25) as an applied V, rather than moving to IV. Either way, though, an inner voice descends chromatically, e–d$\sharp$–d$\natural$–c$\sharp$, through $\mathbf{A}$+4–11. Because the singer must repeat himself and try harder to articulate his point most clearly, he repeats this chromatic descent in the bridge ($\mathbf{C}$), there beginning as high as f$\sharp$ (at 0:57) and descending by half-steps all the way to c$\sharp$ ($\mathbf{C}$+7; follow the right hand of the piano part through 1:08), through the changes of mode on II (the B^{o7} chord at $\mathbf{C}$+6 substitutes for V^{7}). Harrison hopes that understanding will eventually be consummated ("maybe you'd understand") as he completes a $\hat{3}$ ($\mathbf{A}$–$\mathbf{B}$)–$\hat{2}$ ($\mathbf{C}$+1)–$\hat{1}$ ($\mathbf{C}$+7) descent to close the bridge with a perfect authentic cadence, a natural emblem for any coming together. Harrison has melded his lifelong intrigue with altered chord colors with the descending chromatic line that Lennon seems to have taught McCartney to appreciate, here quite fitting in a portrayal of the search for understanding. Until 1968, Harrison would be pursuing such an idea in most of his work, but in Indian music rather than the rock idiom exemplified here.

"Good Day Sunshine"   McCartney, influenced by the Lovin' Spoonful's "Daydream," wrote "Good Day Sunshine" on a sunny day at Lennon's home piano in suburban Weybridge.[106] The manuscript (Campbell and Murphy 1980, xiii) has indications that the instruments, originally to feature a guitar solo, were recorded in the unusual key of B major, as heard. As in "For No One," McCartney played piano ("Piano II") and Starr played drums for the basic track, taped on June 8. The composer's lead vocal for verses ($\mathbf{B}$) went on a second track, Lennon's and McCartney's vocals in the chorus ($\mathbf{A}$) onto a third, and the bass was added on the fourth. These tracks were reduced to two, so that in the eventual stereo mix, the piano sounds left, all vocals sound center, and bass and drums are left-center. The next day, Starr added more crash cymbals, bass drum, and snare to choruses (entering in the second beat before $\mathbf{A}$) and toms (at $\mathbf{C}$) or rim tapping elsewhere. At the same time, McCartney added a shuffling lead piano part ("Piano I"), and those available clapped hands for the last verse and chorus. This track and the fourth—on which Martin recorded the tremolo-rich honky-tonk piano solo, $\mathbf{C}$, at some slower speed, and McCartney, Lennon, and Harrison added vocals for the coda (these last are given as ex. 1.12 so the complex of voices may be heard for its individual parts)—are heard right, but the vocals are given tape echo that repeats the signal right ($\mathbf{E}$+3) and then left ($\mathbf{E}$+4).[107] Mixes were made on June 9 and 22.

The chorus is metrically relaxed, in a carefree manner enjoyed three years later in Harrison's "Here Comes the Sun." The vocals are loose and syncopated, with all chords sung in dotted quarters, as are the instruments at a larger level, with chord changes dividing the $\frac{4}{4}$ time with alternating bars of $\frac{3}{4}$ and $\frac{5}{4}$. The

Example 1.12 "Good Day Sunshine" (Lennon-McCartney). © 1966 Northern Songs.

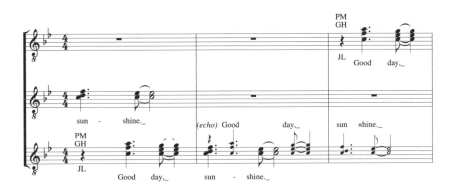

tonal center is likewise emancipated as if by the sunshine, as the B-major introduction reveals itself as V of V of A, thereby repeating the two keys of "Doctor Robert," but not until **B+1**, where B major is again immediately tonicized in a string of vaudevillian applied V⁷s. McCartney slides artfully to D major for Martin's piano solo, and a fourth, nonresolving tonal center is heard when the final chorus ascends a half-step from B major, trailing off to the clouds, as did "And Your Bird Can Sing." The reverberating polyphony of this chorus is reminiscent of the Beach Boys' "Fun, Fun, Fun" (February 1964), "Help Me, Rhonda" (April 1965), and "God Only Knows" (May 1966), not to mention Lennon/McCartney's barbershop $^{b7}_{5} - ^{6}_{b3} - ^{b6}_{4} - ^{5}_{3}$ "Moonlight Bay" cadence sung on the "Morecambe and Wise" television show in 1963.[108] Martin's playing gives the track more of a barrelhouse atmosphere than the Spoonful's jugband quality, the use of three keyboards paves the road from "For No One" (with its two keyboards) to "Penny Lane" (where they're beyond number), and the venture into vaudeville will give McCartney the necessary brazenness to resurrect the decade-old "When I'm Sixty-Four" at the end of the year.

"Here, There and Everywhere"   The Beatles were set to fly to Germany on June 23, and by the 14th they had not finished their work for the LP; McCartney told

a reporter, "I'm just writing one more number, then it's finished," and Lennon said, "I've got something going; about three lines so far" (McCartney: "Have you? That's good"); both last-minute compositions would make the album.[109]

One of McCartney's gems, "Here, There and Everywhere," is supposed to have grown from his hearing of the Beach Boys' "God Only Knows" (brand new in May 1966) at the side of the Weybridge pool, but as the composer says, "you wouldn't have known."[110] After several takes were attempted on June 14, a re-make was begun on the 16th, when most of the recording was done.[111] First — as in "For No One" and "Good Day Sunshine"—McCartney played a duet with Starr for the basic track, this time a rhythm part on Casino with drums, ac-companied at **C**+3−4 and in the final two bars ("Guitar I") by Harrison's elec-tric twelve-string. The Rickenbacker's so-called Rick-O Sound stereo capability is taken advantage of at **C**, the signal sent to two amps, miked separately to the Casino/drum track and to a second track; the tone pedal colors the song's final five notes. Then bass was added to a third track of Take 13; the fourth was filled with backing vocals from McCartney, Lennon, and Harrison and (beginning at **C**+8 but more audible a bar later) finger snaps. The bass and basic track were reduced to one track, along with a sped-up overdubbed lead vocal from Mc-Cartney, sustaining the upper line at **C**+9−10, all parts now heard right. This and the backing-vocal track (left-center, with reverb) and Ricky-12 "pre-echo" (left) joined a doubled lead vocal (left, descending at **C**+9−10) added on the 17th. The track was mixed on June 17 and 21. Although the recording process itself was complicated by the composer's slow-to-coalesce vision of the final arrangement, what with only a few Beatles working at a time, and despite its full backing harmonies, "Here, There and Everywhere" presents the sparest and most relaxed texture of the LP.

In order to indicate a few of the motivic and harmonic ideas expressed in "Here, There and Everywhere," its structure is sketched as example 1.13. In the tonally mysterious and tempo-free introduction (**A**), note how the passing mo-tion in the bass, B–B♭–A (0:02−0:06), imitates a similar descent in the alto register as sung by McCartney (in lead and backing lines), g^1–($f\sharp^1$)–$f\natural^1$ (0:01−0:06), representing a great development from the G–G♯–A–B♭ opening of "You Like Me Too Much." This song is also a masterpiece of registral relation-ships. One dotted slur in the graph indicates how the introductory pitches in the alto line continue to descend following a registral shift (at 0:05) that reaches over the upper voice to $f\natural^2$; this gesture will be repeated diatonically in the verse when a second alto descent, from b^1 through a^1 and g^1 (0:25−0:27), dramatically shifts up to $f\sharp^2$ at **B**+7 (0:28).[112] McCartney recaptures this regis-tral dialog by concluding his song with an ascending arpeggiation (**D**+3−4) to allow $f\sharp^2$ to finally resolve in the song's final note to g^2. The B♭ chord of measure 2 is the opening sonority of the bridge (**C**+1, 0:56), which borrows from the parallel minor for four bars. Both the boundary-embracing registral interplay and the unexpected move to B♭ help portray the composer's "everywhere." Nowhere else does a Beatles introduction so well prepare a listener for the most striking and expressive tonal events that lie ahead.

The function of the first two verses (twice through **B**) is to begin with an un-

Example 1.13 Analysis of "Here, There and Everywhere."

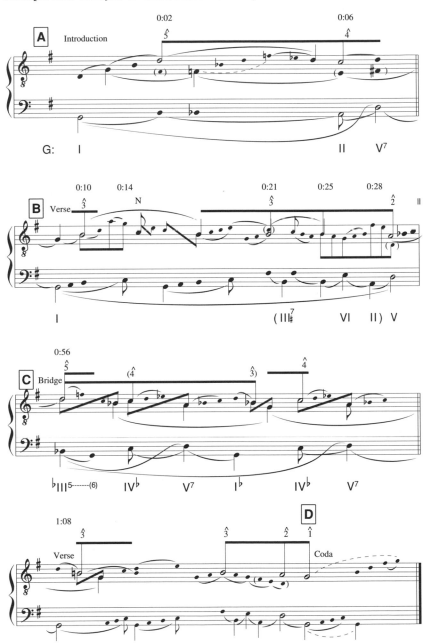

Example 1.14a "She Said She Said," compositional draft (Lennon-McCartney). ©
1966 Northern Songs.

equivocally strong metric placement of "Here" and "There" on the situation-
defining tonic but to end with some question (What is there? [Some special
quality that she possesses]. . . . Who is speaking? [Some unnoticed outsider]) in
a back-relating half cadence at **B**+8, as the phrases were structured in the
"Michelle" verses. In fact, the arrival on tonic for "There" at the top of the second verse helps answer the question posed at the end of the first, by virtue of
the repeated word, "there"; the unnameable "something"—also a key word in
"I Want to Hold Your Hand"—exists in his relationship with her, as described
in the second verse. Everything changes from certainty to question at **B**+5
(0:21), where "a wave of her hand" lifts the singer into unknown chromatic territory, but he finds his way back to the V⁷ through conventional fifth motions,
III♯–VI–II–V.

The unexpected turn to mixture from G minor represents both the globe-
encompassing nature of "Everywhere"—places not seen even in the circle of
fifths ending the verse—and the anxious "care" from which the singer is ex-
empted; the sketch emphasizes how unfolded thirds descend sequentially at **C**,
suggesting closeness as she is beside him.[113] The opening of the bridge not only
recaptures the B♭ chord and the beginning of the fundamental line ($\hat{5}$–$\hat{4}$) from
the introduction, but its beginning on d² (**C**+1) satisfies the need of the verse's
e², left hanging at **B**+4 and **B**+7, to descend in register.[114] This beautiful piece
accomplished, McCartney rested his muse for five months.

"She Said She Said"   During a party in Benedict Canyon on August 24, 1965,
with Lennon trying to relax on LSD, Peter Fonda brought up a childhood op-
eration in which he'd technically died on the table. He said, "I know what it's
like to be dead." Lennon, who wanted no part of a ghost story while his mind
was in such a tenuous state, replied, "Who put all that shit in your head?"
Along with memories of childhood provoked by a sad mood and a change of
pronoun from "he" to a more mainstream boy/girl "she," Lennon had the materials for "She Said She Said," which came to represent the afternoon's altered
mental state as well as the words of the conversation.[115]

Example 1.14b "She Said She Said," compositional draft (Lennon-McCartney). © 1966 Northern Songs.

Example 1.14c "She Said She Said," compositional draft (Lennon-McCartney). © 1966 Northern Songs.

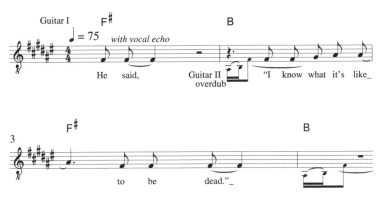

Example 1.14 shows drafts transcribed from Lennon's working tapes (heard on Beatles 1993b) that are supposed to have been taped in March 1966.[116] Examples 1.14a and 1.14b resemble Dylan's prosody, the latter with a "Doctor Robert"–like tonicized II$^\sharp$ (mm. 8–9). Examples 1.14c and 1.14d were made with electric guitar overdubs; the melodic structure approaches the eventual tune; note also the out-of-phase overdub, possibly suggesting the extensive guitar imitation in the final recording. In 1.14e, the transposition up a third im-

Example 1.14d "She Said She Said," compositional draft (Lennon-McCartney). ©
1966 Northern Songs.

(*continued*)

proves the vocal range and gives rise to the muster-passing double-plagal chord
structure, and the first two verses are basically intact, but the bridge (**B**) has
lyrics that seem to experiment with a "Baby's in Black" plot, and its metric problem has yet to be solved. These tapes show that it is quite possible that Lennon
had no more than three lines or so when the song was due in the studio; the
Beatles were confident nonetheless.[117] A nine-hour session beginning at 7 P.M.

Example 1.14d (*continued*)

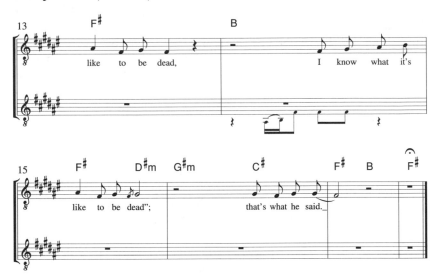

Example 1.14e "She Said She Said," compositional draft (Lennon-McCartney). ©
1966 Northern Songs.

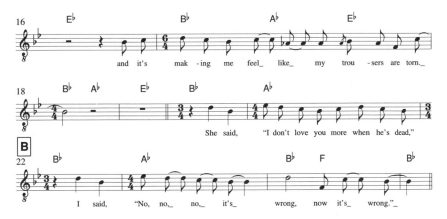

on June 21, the day before the LP's master tape was to be compiled, allowed
many rehearsals and a relatively simple recording. We hear drums with
"Rain"–like accents on the left; bass, Lennon's sped-up lead vocal, and backing
vocals from Lennon and Harrison center; and Lennon's rhythm guitar ("Guitar
II"), Harrison's distorted lead guitar ("Guitar I"), and Lennon's harmonium
right. McCartney recalls that an argument led to Harrison's playing bass on this
track (Miles 1979, 288). George had been photographed with a Burns bass during these sessions; this recording would then mark his first bass playing on a
Beatles track since his chromatic overdub onto "I Want to Hold Your Hand."

Lennon, who is uncomfortable with his feeling that he's "never been born"—Dylan sings "He not busy being born is busy dying" in "It's Alright, Ma (I'm Only Bleeding)" (May 1965)—reassures himself with memories of an untroubled early childhood that announce themselves with a change to $\frac{3}{4}$ in the bridge.[118] The move to another "time"—meter, childhood—ambiguous at first, may suggest the mystical, dreamlike changes in perceptions of environment and time experienced among the subjective effects of LSD. After "Love You To," "She Said She Said" is only the second example of contrasting meter in a Beatles song; the following LP, *Sgt. Pepper*, includes five songs with middle sections in contrasting meters—four by Lennon and one by Harrison.[119]

As LSD distorts the perception of time, it intensifies the vividness of colors and the glow of light. In "She Said She Said," this glow can be heard in the frequent use of the crash cymbal, with its white noise of partials, the distortion of the lead guitar, which in measure 1 sounds a♭ twice, on the second and seventh eighths—not through the striking of a string, but through harmonics in feedback, and in the high pedal in the harmonium (b♭4—an octave higher than shown in the score) that fades in and out of the first two verses. Subsequent î pedals, in succeedingly lower registers—b♭ in the rhythm guitar for the last verse, and B♭ in the bass for the coda—trace a registral descent from the harmonium's b♭4. At least two voice-leading effects have peculiar qualities that may relate to "other realities" encountered by an LSD user: streams of parallel fifths and sevenths between the vocals and bass (as at **A+2**) and vocal parallel fourths with crossed voices (as at **A+5**), both somewhat atypical of the Beatles' singing, sound otherworldly.

The LSD user's visual reverberations, or "trails," images similar to strobe photographs of moving objects, are heard in this music's various kinds of imitation. In the verse, Harrison's distorted lead guitar follows several of Lennon's vocal lines at a measure's distance at the unison, repeating a technique used on the sitar in "Norwegian Wood." There is also some foreshadowing of vocals by the lead guitar: the first measure of the guitar's introduction is sung by Lennon in **A+4–5** and **B+4**, and the pitches of the guitar's descent in **B+5–6** are sung two bars later by Harrison. Imitation is most obvious in the vocal parts of the coda, thrown into double time by Starr's pattern change, where Harrison sings Lennon's vocal part a measure later at the unison. This passage, reminiscent of the polyphonic coda to "Good Day Sunshine," is apparently the source of the song's imitative title—"She Said, She Said," which appears nowhere else in the text. Harmonic stasis is a result of both the repetitious double-plagal succession, heard elsewhere in *Revolver* only in "Taxman," and the lack of a true dominant. The song is in the Mixolydian mode; nowhere does a leading tone appear.[120] In addition to the reverberating imitation, the droning, cyclical I–♭VII–IV–I harmonic pattern is a further type of repetition that may be related to the timeless quality of both an LSD trip and the mantra-based meditation in Indian practice. Various effects of the drug LSD, then, are musically depicted so that "She Said She Said" may accurately reflect the tone of Lennon's reaction to Fonda's revelation.

After Martin and the Beatles finished mixing the LP, they began a brief Eurasian tour. The title they finally decided on, *Revolver*, was cabled to EMI from Japan on July 2.[121] The front cover was an ironically monochromatic illustration by Klaus Voorman, with superimposed photographs of individual Beatle heads cut from magazines and newspapers by Lennon, McCartney, and Pete Shotton.[122] The back cover shows the Beatles with their new "granny glasses," the shade lenses in basic geometrical shapes, as worn first by the Byrds and the Lovin' Spoonful. The track order, continuing Martin's general practice of placing the album's strongest tracks at the beginning and end of each side, is as follows:

Side 1	*Side 2*
"Taxman"	"Good Day Sunshine"
"Eleanor Rigby"	"And Your Bird Can Sing"
"I'm Only Sleeping"	"For No One"
"Love You To"	"Doctor Robert"
"Here, There and Everywhere"	"I Want to Tell You"
"Yellow Submarine"	"Got to Get You into My Life"
"She Said She Said"	"Tomorrow Never Knows"

For its radical experimentation in composition—strongly embracing Eastern thought, qualities of the mind, and many new topics expressed in new, often simple tonal structures that occasionally receive unexpected twists—and such recording practices as reversed tapes, artificial phase shifting, electronically altered timbres, sound effects, and new stereo imaging, *Revolver* is frequently cited as the Beatles' most profound work, or at least right up there with *Sgt. Pepper's Lonely Hearts Club Band* and *Abbey Road*. EMI announced orders of over 300,000 copies in advance of the August release (and by the end of September, covers of ten *Revolver* songs had been reviewed in *Melody Maker*), but by 1970, *Revolver* stood only tenth in American Beatles album sales, at 1.5 million copies, behind *Meet the Beatles, A Hard Day's Night, Rubber Soul*, and all subsequent group efforts other than *Yellow Submarine*.[123] The album's influences on progressive British rock have often been noted in the pages above, but nowhere is *Revolver* concentrated more heavily than in the Moody Blues' *In Search of the Lost Chord* (August 1968), with "Legend of a Mind" based on "Tomorrow Never Knows" and "She Said She Said," "Ride My See Saw" taking McCartney's guitar work from "Taxman," the I–$\flat$VII–I function from "Tomorrow Never Knows," and vocal nonharmonic tones from "Good Day Sunshine," plus the general wash of tabla, sitar, autoharp—as svaramandal, Mellotron, and ADT. But perhaps the greatest influence that *Revolver* was to have on the Beatles' followers was its general emancipation from the Western pop norms of melody, harmony, instrumentation, formal structure, rhythm, and engineering. This was the artistic freedom that was to allow the Beatles to turn to imaginary alter egos to produce their 1967 masterpiece, *Sgt. Pepper's Lonely Hearts Club Band*, emancipating the composers even from themselves.

"I'm Not a Beatle Anymore"

The Final Concerts

Records released in the United Kingdom and United States from the spring sessions include the following:

"Paperback Writer"/"Rain," Capitol 5651, May 23 (peak position on chart: #1 for two weeks/B-side peaked at #23); Parlophone R 5452, June 10 (#1 for four weeks)

"Yesterday" . . . and Today, LP (U.S.), Capitol (S)T 2553, June 15 (#1 for five weeks)

Revolver, LP (U.K.), Parlophone PMC/PCS 7009, August 5 (#1 for nine weeks); (U.S.) Capitol (S)T 2576, August 8 (#1 for six weeks; eventually 3 million copies sold)

"Yellow Submarine"/"Eleanor Rigby," promoted in the United Kingdom as a double-A-sided single, Parlophone R 5493, August 5 (#1 for three weeks); Capitol 5715, August 8 (#2 for one week/#23)

Nine different mimed promotional films for "Paperback Writer" and "Rain" were filmed by "Ready, Steady, Go!" director Michael Lindsay-Hogg at EMI Studio One and an exterior London location on May 19 and 20; they premiered on June 3.[124] The Beatles also had one live television appearance, miming both songs on "Top of the Pops" on June 16. No films or appearances were planned for the release of "Yellow Submarine," the first British Beatles single to be culled from an LP, apparently a move to head off sales of cover versions of its B-side, "Eleanor Rigby."[125]

The Beatles played concerts in five cities; in Germany, they shared the bill with Cliff Bennett and the Rebel Rousers and with Peter and Gordon. The itinerary:

June 24: Munich (two shows)
June 25: Essen (two shows)
June 26: Hamburg (two shows in the group's first visit since 1962)
June 30–July 2: Tokyo (five shows, three booked in April and two added in May)
July 4: Manila (two shows)

The set list comprised the following:

"Rock and Roll Music" (abbreviated)	"Yesterday"
"She's a Woman"	"I Wanna Be Your Man"
"If I Needed Someone"	"Nowhere Man"
"Day Tripper"	"Paperback Writer"
"Baby's in Black"	"I'm Down"
"I Feel Fine"	

Instrumentation included McCartney's Höfner bass and Starr's Ludwigs; Harrison and Lennon now relied on the Casinos, but Harrison played one of the 1965 Rickenbacker twelve-strings on "If I Needed Someone." For "I'm Down," Lennon played the Casino rather than the organ, which sat onstage unused.

The Beatles played all instruments through new 150-watt Vox amps. On this tour, "Yesterday" was given the same electric backing as the other songs, without retuning down from G major, thereby straining McCartney's range (this is seen in volume 5 of Beatles 1996c). The other notable changes in arrangements are the lack of the rising-scale guitar part in the instrumental passage in "Day Tripper"—Harrison plays the lead and Lennon the chords—and the Indian-style ornamentation McCartney added to a descant part in "If I Needed Someone," just as he did at the end of "I Want to Tell You," on July 1.

But there are countless differences between the recorded versions and those played on these dates. Due to the ridiculous crowd noise and the group's blatant carelessness, the underrehearsed performances in many cases trivialize the music. Before "I'm Down" in the Munich evening show, Paul huddles with George, appealing to him for the opening words, which he can't recall. Lennon can't resist the opportunity to throw his partner off and suggests to him, off-mike but in rhythm, "You feel down though you're laughing at me." McCartney then erroneously begins with the second verse, and his cohorts laugh when he can't recover the second time through **A**. On July 1 alone, Lennon plays II$\sharp$ instead of IV in "Day Tripper," McCartney can't find the lyrics to the "Baby's in Black" bridge, and Lennon confuses pronouns in "I Feel Fine." The experience had become a joke—the Beatles were now at home in the studio but not at all in live performance. Lennon said their concerts had "nothing to do with music any more. They're just bloody tribal rites."[126]

Due to a miscommunication between Epstein, promoters, and the presidential family in the Philippines, the Beatles failed to show at a palace reception hosted by Imelda Marcos. Mrs. Marcos interpreted this as a public snub, withdrew all security protection, and harassed the roughed-up Beatles entourage with bureaucratic delays at the airport upon departure.[127] The group had three days to recover with a stopover in New Delhi, where all purchased more Indian instruments.

The American tour went no better. No longer the darlings of the press, the Beatles took far-reaching criticism in advance of their August visit. The first wave of anti-Beatles protest, and a cool reaction to the new single among some record retailers, appeared at the end of May when a Pittsburgh disc jockey broadcast an interview in which the Beatles—whom Epstein had never allowed to comment on the Vietnam War—dismissed Barry Sadler's jingoistic "Ballad of the Green Berets."[128] Discontent within the industry was the reaction to the Beatles' notorious so-called Butcher cover for *"Yesterday" . . . and Today*. This album grew out of Capitol Records' impatience in waiting for Beatles product from London—they wanted a new record in the racks for the tour, so they gathered tracks from 1965 yet to appear on an American album ("Yesterday" and "We Can Work It Out" and their B-sides, and four songs from *Rubber Soul*), and were able to secure three *Revolver* tracks ("I'm Only Sleeping," "Doctor Robert," and "And Your Bird Can Sing") in advance, to complete an eleven-song LP. Originally, the cover appeared as photographed on March 25 with the group in butchers' aprons, holding decapitated dolls and slabs of meat, as a sly commentary on the American practice of matching year-old leftovers with new experimental artwork, thereby mutilating the product. Harsh reaction to promotional copies from radio and retail people led to a June 14 decision in Hollywood to recast the cover with a bland pose, requiring the destruction or pasting-over of close to a million jackets, and creating one of the earliest globally sought Beatles collectibles. But it cost Capitol Records some $200,000 to try to preserve the Beatles' spotless image.[129]

The Beatles forgot these problems when vocal puritanical Americans read comments made by Lennon that had been published to no reaction in England on March 4. Lennon had told his friend Maureen Cleave of the London *Evening Standard* of his recent readings in theology, adding, "Christianity will go. It will vanish and shrink. I needn't argue with that; I'm right and I will be proved right. We're more popular than Jesus now." Upon a July 29 reprinting of this interview in the American magazine *Datebook*, a furor swept through the United States, particularly in the southern Bible Belt. Within a week, a national radio boycott was called for by disc jockeys in Birmingham, Alabama, and Longview, Texas, and some thirty stations in eleven states complied. Bonfires of Beatles paraphernalia were organized throughout the South, and the Ku Klux Klan picketed in Washington and were televised threatening the Beatles and their management. Epstein inadvertently kept the story in the papers with an advance trip to New York, offering to cancel any dates at a promoter's discretion. Worried about the possibility of attempted assassination in Memphis, Brian convinced John to recant his inflammatory statements in the first press conference of the tour, in Chicago, when the Beatle expressed his profound unhappiness that his misinterpreted words "had created another little place of hate in the world."[130]

The American tour went ahead with the same repertoire heard on the Eurasian dates, with not a single song rehearsed from *Revolver*, now available in stores. The Beatles were supported by the Remains, Bobby Hebb, the Cyrkle, and the Ronettes, as follows:

August 12: Chicago (two shows)	August 19: Memphis (two shows)
August 13: Detroit (two shows)	August 21: Cincinnati (replacing
August 14: Cleveland (replacing	the previous day's rain-out)
a Louisville show canceled in April)	August 21: St. Louis
August 15: Washington, D.C.	August 23: New York
August 16: Philadelphia	August 25: Seattle (two shows)
August 17: Toronto (two shows)	August 28: Los Angeles
August 18: East Boston	August 29: San Francisco

The tour had some high points; Dylan's new album, *Blonde on Blonde*, was heard for the first time in Cleveland; Harrison was able to find new Indian albums for his collection; and the Beatles met with old friends Derek Taylor, David Crosby, and Brian and Carl Wilson of the Beach Boys while resting in Beverly Hills.[131] But tension was high. Now that the Beatles' innocence was lost, Lennon had a new freedom to denounce American racism and the Vietnam War, applauding draft dodgers in the Toronto press conference, thus effectively beginning a peace campaign that was to dominate his relationship with the press from 1969.[132] Ticket sales in the country's biggest stadiums were disappointing; many seats went unsold, even for New York's single appearance. The group had privately decided that these were to be their last concerts, and when the final show was over, Harrison said, "Well, I guess that's it, I'm not a Beatle anymore."[133]

Solo Projects

Other than hack pop writers, what performers before the Beatles had ever abandoned live appearances while continuing a musical career? The move could easily have been the end of the group, and the Beatles drifted apart—amid rumors that they were planning to leave Epstein—in the fall of 1966. Starr's activities between August 29 and November 24 have remained private, but the individual projects of the others are known and relevant to the group's musical history.

In between increasingly infrequent Beatles recordings, Harrison's guitar was to take back seat to the sitar, which he maintains he practiced for hours every day. He and his wife spent September 14 through October 22 in India (Bombay, Kashmir, and Rishikesh); George studied sitar under Ravi Shankar and his assistant, Shambu Das, and Pattie played dilruba.[134] In a 1968 documentary film called *The Road*, Shankar says, "It is strange to see pop musicians with sitars. When George Harrison came to me, I didn't know what to think, but I found he really wanted to learn." In tandem with the music study, the two pursued spiritual development as well, practicing yoga and meditation under the direction of yogis.[135] Harrison returned to London with his sitar exercises and chants of "Hare krishna," along with a new moustache that was to be copied by McCartney (while on an autumn safari in Kenya) and then (by the time of a December 20 television interview) by the others.

How I Won the War   Lennon went to Celle, West Germany, on September 5 to begin his role of Musketeer Gripweed in Dick Lester's film *How I Won the War*. Shooting moved to Carboneras, Spain, for September 18 through November 6.[136] It was a great release for Lennon, who said later, "I was always waiting for a reason to get out of the Beatles from the day I made *How I Won the War* in 1966."[137] "I was thinking, well, this is like the end really. You know, there's no more touring. . . . I really started considering what can one do? Considering the life without the Beatles—what would it be? And I spent that six weeks thinking about that."[138] Lennon returned to London with a severe army haircut and austere prescription granny glasses, but also with most of the song that he, George Martin, and many others consider his most original and personal statement, "Strawberry Fields Forever."

The Family Way   It was reported in August that the Beatles' long-delayed third film, to be produced by Shenson and written by television scripter Owen Holder, was to include not only the usual six or seven new songs, to be recorded in September, but also their own incidental music, and shooting was to begin in January 1967.[139] Plans were delayed in a November meeting, and subsequently put off indefinitely.[140] But McCartney was keen on writing film music, so he had NEMS find such a job.[141] They found what was to be called *The Family Way*, a Hayley Mills film set in northern England. McCartney wrote the title theme and a love theme, "Love in the Open Air," and made some suggestions as to instrumentation, and Martin scored many settings, each to fit various moods, and recorded the soundtrack in November–December.[142]

The themes were recorded by Martin's orchestra on December 10, released on the soundtrack LP and as a single (released December 23, 1966, in the United Kingdom, and April 24, 1967, in the United States; the film first played in London, December 18, 1966), and the opening of the title theme appears here as example 1.15. Shown are the introductory brass ritornello (**A**; martial drum and off-the-string viola parts are omitted) and the beginning of the first solo organ episode (**B**). The ritornello's tonal conceit, a motion from E major through G major (**A**+2, repeated **A**+6) to E minor (**A**+3, repeated **A**+7), is a transposition down a minor third of the harmonies surrounding the beginning of the bridge of "Here, There and Everywhere." The first organ episode develops the area of G, and—continuing beyond the excerpt—the second episode is much more unstable, touching on E minor, B minor, F♯ minor, and E major, leading to a ritornello in A major (**D**). Later, a brass episode in A is followed by a ritornello in D major, closing in D minor. Although some incomplete ideas for piano in the manner of an early-Baroque suite would grace McCartney's opening of the Beatles' 1970 film, *Let It Be*, the sort of work done here does not reappear in finished McCartney products before the breakup of the Beatles.

McCartney returned from his Kenya holiday in November, at which time he was photographed in his Cavendish Avenue music room with his new-fashioned pop-art multicolored piano and an odd instrument called a Tubon, a cylindrical lap-held two-and-a-half-octave keyboard with various stops and effects.[143] On returning from India, Harrison improved his own music room by stocking his jukebox with singles by the Beach Boys, the Mamas and the Papas, the Lovin' Spoonful, and the Stones.[144]

Of course, the Beatles did not break up in the fall of 1966, but the seed of their eventual dissolution was planted at this time, not only by their newfound independence but also by John's meeting an avant-garde artist who in two years' time would fully divert his attention from his boyhood mates. John met Yoko Ono (b. 1933 in Tokyo; she moved to Scarsdale in 1952 for schooling at Sarah Lawrence) on November 9 when invited to a preview of her show "Unfinished Paintings and Objects" at the Indica Gallery, known to John through Paul.[145] Lennon recalls: "It was 200 quid to watch the apple decompose . . . and she came up and handed me a card which said 'Breathe' on it, one of her instructions, so I just went (pant). This was our meeting."[146] Ono had little reputation in London but had given concerts as a performance artist (before the term was in use) at the Carnegie Recital Hall in 1961 and 1965, had toured Japan with John Cage in 1962, and had frequent New York appearances, especially with a group known as Fluxus. "Drawing on the legacy of Surrealist and Dadaist soirées of the early decades of the century, Fluxus artists often reduced

Example 1.15 "Theme from *The Family Way*" (McCartney). © 1967 Northern Songs.

their Events . . . to unitary gestures enacted in unadorned settings by performers wearing ordinary street clothes. . . . Because of the focus on single-gesture actions, this type of Fluxus Event was easily expressed as written performance instructions."[147] Ono's Zen-disciplined yet twisted instructionals created artwork not in visual space but in the perceiver's mind; the thoughtful reaction to the concept *was* the work of art, a post-Platonic notion that was to impassion Lennon. Among her conceptual artworks ("the concept [was] more important than the object," as Lennon recalled on the day of his death [Lennon 1980]) were "custom-made underwear in vicuna to 'accent your special defects.' There was a crying machine 'which drops tears and cries for you when coin is deposited . . . $3,000'; and, for half that price, a Sky Machine which 'produces nothing when coin is deposited.' . . . In 1964, Yoko published a book of her 'works' called *Grapefruit*. . . . Opening the book at random I read 'Map piece: Draw a map to get lost.'"[148] Lennon knew nothing of her conceptual art, and she claimed not to have known of his work either. Over the next few months John saw Yoko only on rare occasions, as at an opening for Claes Oldenberg a few weeks after the Indica meeting, but she was to seek his support professionally and win his heart in mid-1967.[149]

By the end of 1966, EMI was growing impatient with the lack of new Beatles recordings, so British Christmas gift-givers had to be satisfied with a compilation LP, *A Collection of Beatles Oldies*, a gathering of non-LP singles, several requiring new stereo mixes (Parlophone PMC/PCS 7016, released December 9). Fan club members received the usual Beatles Christmas message, called "Pantomime" (recorded on November 25), featuring Paul playing piano through original numbers such as the music hall–flavored "Everywhere It's Christmas"—as silly as the future "You Know My Name (Look Up the Number)"—and "Please Don't Bring Your Banjo Back," and several brief Monty Python–type skits with more elaborate off-the-cuff music than heard before in these fan club offerings.[150] Aside from this, McCartney produced a recording of Smokey Robinson's song "From Head to Toe" by the Escorts (released on November 18), and the Beatles finally returned to EMI on November 24 for the first of twelve year-end days of work toward their follow-up LP to *Revolver*. They began with Lennon's new song written in Spain.

I KNOW WHEN IT'S A DREAM

"Strawberry Fields Forever"

Late-1966 sessions began with "Strawberry Fields Forever." Whereas Lennon had referred to his youth in "Help!" and "She Said She Said," he makes a personal statement about his nature as shaped by unresolved childhood problems in "Strawberry Fields," the name of an orphanage a few hundred yards from Mendips that he and his friends would often visit — a place of happy memories.[1] When released as a single backed with McCartney's companion piece about his own childhood memories, "Penny Lane," the record was packaged in a sleeve featuring snapshots of the Beatles as babies, although the musical references to Liverpool would remain obscure to the Beatles' listeners for years. Writing in Almería, Spain, perhaps Lennon needed both a break from the Beatles and an uncertain future in order to grapple musically with such deeply private thoughts; such certainly seems the case with *Plastic Ono Band*, his first LP produced after the final breakup of the Beatles.

Composition

Lennon "wanted the lyrics to be like conversation."[2] One verse (the first time through **B**) has one end rhyme ("you see"/"to me"), and the chorus (**A**) has one internal rhyme ("Fields"/"real"). Otherwise the text flows freely, giving rise to a highly irregular rhythm and meter as the singer disagrees with himself while performing, clarifying his message as he goes along, voicing colloquial "you know"'s to his confidant. Lennon says that the images in the poetry express his awakening as a youth to the fact that his plane of awareness seemed higher than that of those around him; for "No one I think is in my tree" (originally the song's first line), read, "Nobody seems to be as hip as me, therefore I must be crazy or a genius."[3] The higher plane did not provide the composer with an air of superiority but, on the contrary, made him feel like an outsider; in "Strawberry Fields Forever," Lennon's identity problems — "It's getting hard to be someone" — are traced in the first verse to others' (disdainful?) misapprehensions of him: "Living is easy with eyes closed, misunderstanding all you see." Lennon places these childhood and adolescent memories in the context of a dream: "But you know I know when it's a dream." Because "nothing is real," the singer can be ambivalent about his anxiety and express resignation at not being understood, shrugging off his vexation: "You can't, you know, tune in but it's all right; that is, I think it's not too bad"; he has learned to live with his problem. Ambivalence is well expressed by the dominant at **B**+7 (0:51–0:52), which, amplifying the text, seems unsure of where to turn and stumbles backward through IV to I (0:52–0:55).

We are privileged to have available (on Beatles 1997) many working tapes of "Strawberry Fields Forever" at various stages of composition, arranging, and studio recording. About eight minutes of tape, recorded in Almería prior to Lennon's return to London on November 7, document the song's origins, as John sings along with a nylon-stringed classical guitar. The evolution of "Strawberry Fields" continues through about seventeen minutes of tapes made at Lennon's Kenwood studio, where he overdubbed vocals, Casino fingerpicking, and/or Mellotron figures onto previously recorded rhythm tracks made with the Casino alone. Finally, working four-track tapes by the Beatles of Takes 1–7, an acetate of one mono remix of Take 7, Takes 25 and 26, and the commercially released mono and two different stereo mixes of the final product (totalling some forty-two minutes of studio work) come to us from EMI sessions held over the final five weeks of 1966. These tapes present the song in various keys between A and C, with some of the variation attributable to vari-speed recording (whereby any of the basic tracks or overdubs could have been taped at speeds other than that used for playback), unreliable guitar tunings, the conceivable use of a capo, and incorrectly mastered bootlegs. Lennon's voice sounds "natural" on the earliest A-major tapes, but McCartney demonstrates his Mellotron introduction in C major in Beatles 1995b; the discrepancy remains difficult to rectify without crediting the group with transposition abilities not often demonstrated elsewhere. Most likely, Lennon used a capo to maintain A-major left-hand work, and McCartney was able to adjust fairly naturally at the keyboard from A to C.

Example 1.16a represents the entirety of Lennon's first recorded runthrough, which was to become the skeleton for the eventual second verse. No lyrics exist yet above the inner-part chromatic descent (E–D$\sharp$–D$\natural$) in the two bars following the initial repeat mark, but they are filled in gradually—first with a sustained "no one . . ." and then, in the third pass, as shown in example 1.16b. Nothe the melodic simplification here, as a single common-tone B is sung above the changing chords, in the manner once devised by Lennon for the "She Loves You" coda and the chorus of "Help!" In this third pass, Lennon strums for the first time the chords of the "Strawberry Fields" chorus, but no words are yet present there. The fourth run-through adds some lyrics to the chorus, significantly, "nothing is real, nothing to get mad about," but there is no reference to the Liverpool orphanage until the following rehearsal (recorded in a different acoustic environment, perhaps on a later date), which also introduces the first line of the third verse.

The home sessions at Kenwood see the completion of the conversational third verse and experimentation with instrumental textures. Lennon is heard woodshedding on a variety of right-hand fingerpicking techniques on the Casino; early C-major introductions are represented in examples 1.16c and d, showing a simply figurated tonic. An intricate folk effect is introduced in 1.16d, highly reminiscent of Dylan's "Boots of Spanish Leather" (February 1964), perhaps a

Example 1.16a "Strawberry Fields Forever" compositional draft (Lennon-McCartney). © 1967 Northern Songs.

song recalled in Spain while the composer was practicing his fingerpicking, a technique he was not to master until 1968. Having little luck with his finger-work, Lennon simplifies the style once again and we hear the song open as in example 1.16e. Note that Lennon still begins with what was to be the second verse, and he proceeds directly to the third before singing the chorus—at first "let me take you back," but forever after, "let me take you down"—which had not yet existed in examples 1.16a and b. Otherwise, except for the later-supplied introduction, first verse and coda, the structures of the Kenwood run-throughs are as recorded, although the Beatles (at **B+**1) add the transposed equivalent to a bass G, which takes on the quality of a root, to Lennon's D-minor chord at **B+**2 (ex. 1.16e). The last Kenwood tape also includes Mellotron overdubs, al-ternating a bell-like wine glass rubbing effect for verses against a pipe organ

Example 1.16b "Strawberry Fields Forever" compositional draft (Lennon-McCartney). © 1967 Northern Songs.

Example 1.16c "Strawberry Fields Forever" compositional draft (Lennon-McCartney). © 1967 Northern Songs.

Example 1.16d "Strawberry Fields Forever" compositional draft (Lennon-McCartney). © 1967 Northern Songs.

with heavy tremulant for choruses. Right from the first EMI recordings, this function would be borne by McCartney's Mellotron part.

The Recording

The very complex procedure by which this song was recorded had a strong effect on its resulting tramontane sound quality. Two full versions were done. After listening to an acetate of the early Beatles version, Take 7, sounding in A, Lennon decided it sounded "too heavy" and wanted it rescored and performed

Example 1.16e "Strawberry Fields Forever" compositional draft (Lennon-McCartney). © 1967 Northern Songs.

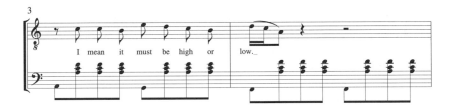

faster.[4] A second version was recorded with four trumpets and three cellos, taped at a fast clip in C to sound (on replay) in B. Lennon liked the beginning of the first version and the ending of the second and asked George Martin to splice them together. " 'Well, there are only two things against it," said Martin. "One is that they're in different keys. The other is that they're in different tempos." Replied Lennon, "Yeah, but you can do something about it, I know. You can fix it, George."[5] When the speeds of both tapes were adjusted to match the pitch— actually, Part I sounds midway between A and B♭, and Part II is much closer to B♭, the tempos of both were roughly the same, c. ♩ = 96. The procedure gives Lennon's vocals an unreal, dreamlike timbre common through much of *Revolver* and *Sgt. Pepper*, especially in the second, slowed-down portion of the song.

On November 24 at EMI, Lennon played the song on acoustic guitar, and the group rehearsed and recorded Take 1 in A, with Lennon's Casino and McCartney's Mellotron (heard in the first verse only), Starr's drums, and Harrison's bass line played on electric guitar. Overdubs atop Take 1 included the composer's lead vocal (double-tracked for the refrain only), Harrison's two-part slide on Stratocaster (introduced in the first chorus), and dreamlike backing vocals from McCartney and Harrison in the third verse, appearing only in this outtake and for some reason not included when mixed for *The Beatles Anthology*. Examples 1.16f–h represent excerpts of this version; although the tape sounds in B major, instruments were certainly recorded in A, and the vocals around B♭.[6] Note that by the unreleased Take 1 (see ex. 1.16f), Lennon has written the reproachful first verse, and McCartney has composed the eventual Mellotron introduction, although it still serves only an accompanimental role. The backing vocals for the third verse (ex. 1.16g) were derived from the Mellotron part. Example 1.16h shows the original coda—note the transposition of the verse down a fifth, ending on its V[7], and Lennon's fingerpicking of the final six bars; the like of such odd chords would only be released in "Glass Onion."[7] Despite the elaborate overdubs, Take 1 was perhaps considered from the start to be a practice demo for study purposes; the Casino is nonchalantly out of tune. Whatever the original intent, the Beatles rejected this approach, deciding within a few days that McCartney would overdub bass, and began all over again on November 28 and 29, recording basic tracks and adding overdubs to Take 4 and then again to Take 6.

Takes 5–7, taped on November 29, result in Part I of the finished master, continuing through the second beat of **B**+2 (0:59), second time through. From the basic tracks, we hear Mellotron, on which McCartney plays the introduction from Take 2 onward, featuring the pitch-bend knob at **A**+2–3 (as demonstrated visually in volume 6 of Beatles 1996c), drums, and maracas (which Harrison picks up in Take 2) on Track 1, and Lennon's elaborately picked Casino on Track 2. Harrison played slide on his Stratocaster, and McCartney added a bass line on Track 3. Lennon added his lead vocal (probably recorded slightly above A major) on Track 4, and this was treated to ADT (in choruses only) in a reduction of everything to two tracks, with both vocal signals mixed with the Casino, now heard center, as the new guitars were added to the Mellotron/percussion track (left).[8] A further dub contains what sounds like an electric piano; this is heard right. Part I is edited (at some time after acetates were cut on November 29) at the start of **D**, as the basic tracks still moved directly from first to second verses; the edit provided an additional chorus.

Part II is a multigeneration, heavily overdubbed edit of two takes made of a rhythm track on December 8 (probably joined just before **C**), with Starr's drums, McCartney's bongos, Harrison's timpani, Lennon's maracas, and Mal Evans's tambourine. It was at the end of this take that Lennon added off-mike nonsense such as "cranberry sauce" and "calm down, Ringo, calm down." This was reduced to one track and interrupted during each verse by Starr's backward cymbals, drums, maracas, and bongos; this is heard left. Harrison's reverb-enshrouded svaramandal was recorded on December 9; on the 1971 stereo mix heard on the compact disc, this track is "wild" (moving from right to left and back).[9] The third track, which is heard right on the CD, but was wild in the original American stereo mix, contains the December 15 overdub of Martin's score for fully divided trumpets and celli (based on the temporarily scrapped Mellotron and Casino parts and recorded in C to allow for a normal tuning of the cellos' open C strings), the guitar's repeated $b\flat^1$ in the coda, and the Moorish "Tomorrow Never Knows"–like Mellotron loop at the end. Completing the mix are Lennon's two vocal parts (taped December 15 and 21), more percussion, and the honky-tonk piano that enters at **C**–1; this is all heard center. It may have been McCartney's idea to retain the song's long fade-out/fade-in, free-form coda; not only was he the true avant-gardist at this point, but the passage resembles the released mixes of his "Helter Skelter" (1968). If true, this theory would help explain Lennon's memory of a casual, experimental air that McCartney brought to this recording, an air which the composer felt prompted

Example 1.16f "Strawberry Fields Forever" compositional draft (Lennon-McCartney). © 1967 Northern Songs.

Example 1.16g "Strawberry Fields Forever" compositional draft (Lennon-McCartney). © 1967 Northern Songs.

Example 1.16h "Strawberry Fields Forever" compositional draft (Lennon-McCart-ney). © 1967 Northern Songs.

attempts to "sabotage" his songs.[10] Mono and stereo speed-adjusted mixes and edits of the two parts of "Strawberry Fields Forever" were made on December 22 and 29. The odd colors and glissandi of the Mellotron, Stratocaster, and svaramandal somehow fit the otherworldly effect created by the vari-speed recording technique, and the coda's bizarre percussion tracks and mumbling were stranger still.

Musical Expression

One portion of the verse (**B**+5–6, 0:44–0:49) moves through the progression IV–V–I–VI, nearly as the bridges began in "I Want to Hold Your Hand" and "Yes It Is"; otherwise, this bizarre song has appropriately few references to previously used harmonic structures. The introduction composes-out the tonic, with the bass descending F–D–B♭. Ambiguity is at work in this passage: upon the arrival of d^1 in the bass (m. 3, 0:06), one might regard G as $\hat{1}$. But the tonic sonority of B♭ is actually incipient once d^1 appears in the bass, and B♭ is the functioning bass pitch throughout this extra-full, six-beat unfolding. Things are not quite what they seem: the °7 chord (A–C–E♭–G♭, m. 2) is VII of B♭, not of G, and pitch-class G at measure 3 is just a temporary substitute for pitch-class F, to which it resolves very soon after its appearance. When this equivocal point, g^1 over d^1 in the introduction, returns in the first verse (**B**+3, 0:39), it accompanies the word "misunderstanding," the cause of Lennon's anxiety; the singer seems to be challenging the listener to follow and make sense of the ambiguous surface harmonies. The verse is especially open to misunderstanding, in light of the ambivalent IV–V–IV–I oscillation (**B**+7–8, 0:50–0:55) mentioned above.

Text and music operate as a unit at the beginning of the chorus (**A**), where the slow stop-time line "Let me take you down" is as removed from the flow of time, as if by a composed-out fermata, as is the extended anacrusis of the similarly anticipatory opening of "There's a Place." This line follows the opening up of the lowest register ("take you down") with the low, hollow bass fifth (**A**+1), and the vocal descends d^2–$b♭^1$–f^1 (**A**+1–2), from the high end of the singer's range. Stability is threatened when $\hat{1}$ undergoes an identity crisis at **A**+2–10, wavering between B♭ and B♮. The A♭ in the bass leads to G at **A**+5 (0:20), supporting the heavily altered progression V♭–VI♮, as the text bears the singer's maya-invoking motto "Nothing is real." Reality is certainly in question when $\hat{7}$ is flatted (in a minor dominant) and $\hat{1}$ raised (in a major submediant) without having been necessitated by strong reasons of voice leading; A and B♭ would have "worked" quite as well but would have had nothing to say about "unreality."

Percussion is heard in retrograde, through reversed tapes, in the second and third verses, which describe the past anxieties of Lennon's youth. It is only during the choruses' brief reminders of the fact that "nothing is real" that we are not in a backward world of the past.[11] The odd coda, a long but largely unornamented tonic, fades out with a sort of "Reveille" figure on the piano. Is someone attempting to awaken the singer from his dream?

Lennon is apparently trying to communicate a jaded indifference (in the V–IV shrug of the shoulders) to the unreality (through the references to dreaming and the b♭–b♮ oscillation) of his misunderstood past (ambiguity in the introduction, reversed tapes). Regardless of the seeming indifference, he would like some company as he revisits Strawberry Fields.[12]

"Penny Lane"

Composition and Recording

In its first draft, John Lennon's "In My Life" (*Rubber Soul*) originally referred to Penny Lane, the Liverpool district in which he had first lived. Less than two weeks after the Beatles recorded the basic tracks for that song, McCartney told an interviewer that he'd been considering writing a song about that same place.[13] Lennon's writing "Strawberry Fields Forever" finally prodded McCartney into action.[14] "Penny Lane" brought fame to the workplaces of its barber, banker, and fireman, all surrounding the bus roundabout in the Penny Lane circus of suburban Liverpool.

At least three tape reductions were made during the recording of "Penny Lane," which began with a solo McCartney piano part; the Beatles would have profited by sixteen-track equipment two full years before EMI allowed them eight-track machines. All of the work from sessions on December 29 and 30 and January 4, 5, and 6 is reduced to the center channel; this includes sped-up vocals (McCartney's lead and—at **C**+5–6 [0:43–0:48]—Lennon's falsetto descant; the word is "there," not "wet," at **C**+5), sped-up bass and drums (the latter tacet through **A**), Lennon's limited and slowed-down congas (**E**), tambourine (**D** and second time through **B**), harmonium (sustaining b^3 at **E**+6–7 [1:18–1:23] and **F**+9 [2:05–2:11], with the subtle single-note effect used in "You Won't See Me" and "She Said She Said"), and four piano tracks. The four piano performances alternate McCartney's quarter-note chords on the basic track with a superimposed second piano at **A**+4–8 (0:07–0:17) and all analogous passages; a third piano is added at **C** (0:35–0:51) and on the final chord, run through a Vox guitar amp with a ringing full reverb for stylized "foggy" whole-note chords in the retrospective choruses; a fourth piano effect, with shorter articulation, is heard in the first three bars of **E** (1:08–1:14).

Still four more overdub sessions were required. Martin added a score for four flutes, one doubling piccolo, and two trumpets, one doubling flügelhorn, on January 9; this is heard right.[15] The flutes have Percy Faith–like repeated staccato chords in verses **A** and **B**, and the second time through **D**; the piccolo waves "hello" above the repeated $^{6-5}_{4-3}$ motion at **A**+8 (0:15–0:17). Brass is heard in choruses, **C**, and in the (unnotated) solo before **E** (1:05–1:08). Word-painting effects, including the firebell (heard left at the references to the fireman, first time through **D**+7–8 and second time through **B**+6) and the roaring bus (center, third beat in bar before **F**, 2:32), were taped on January 10.[16] Two more trumpets (**C** and second time through **D**+7–8) and string bass

Example 1.17a "Penny Lane" (Lennon-McCartney). © 1967 Northern Songs.

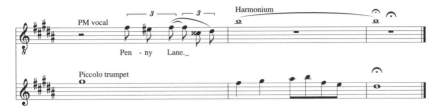

Example 1.17b "Penny Lane" compositional draft (Lennon-McCartney). © 1967 Northern Songs.

(simulating the barber's "trim" at **B**+2−5, 2:03−2:07) were added on the 12th; they are heard left with the effects. The record's final touch is perhaps the song's most distinctive: David Mason's regally British baroque four-valve B♭ piccolo trumpet added on January 17, six days after McCartney heard Mason's solo performance on the instrument in Bach's second *Brandenburg Concerto* on the BBC. The solo was taken from Martin's jottings of McCartney's humming, mixed to the right for the solo at **E**, its pitch structure inverting the verse's descent, and to the left for the coda (where a♮s, not the score's a♭s, are played).[17] Many additional parts, including Harrison's lead guitar, Lennon's rhythm guitar, handclaps, a pair of oboes doubling on English horns, and several more pianos, were erased before the master was completed, and Mason's final trumpet flourish (ex. 1.17a) is heard only in the mono American promotional single (and its accompanying film), the version played on American radio in 1967. Example 1.17b (from Beatles 1996a, which also restores the final trumpet flourish and extra piano parts and splices some studio chatter onto the end) shows the instrumental break as it existed before Mason's solo was taped: a pair of English horns answered by trumpet.

Structure and Affect

The song's verse features a schizoid comparison of jaunty triplet eighths in B major ($\mathbf{A}+1-3$), with the gloomy conclusion of this opening phrase suddenly shifting to B minor for the half cadence, $I\natural–V^{4-3}$ ($\mathbf{A}+5-8$), the suspension a reminder of the refrain in "We Can Work It Out." The altered minor tonic is colored by an overdubbed chromatic descent, $\natural\hat{7}–\sharp\hat{6}–\natural\hat{6}–\hat{5}$, the pensive quality of which is most appropriate for the ontological twist—suggested by Lennon's metaphysical $\flat\hat{1}$ self-perception in "Strawberry Fields" as well as by a taste of Pirandello?—in the final verse, where the nurse "feels as if she's in a play," unaware that she actually *is* in a play. In tandem with the post–"Yellow Submarine" tone painting with the bell, bus, string bass, and reverberating piano, all of which make specific references, the baroque trumpet may promote a general association with recollections of the past, as do the Bach-like keyboard solo in "In My Life" and the string quartet in "Yesterday."

An unusual tonal contrast exists between this B-major verse and the A-major chorus ($\mathbf{C}$), reversing the direction of the good-time tonal emancipations of the similarly piano-rich "Good Day Sunshine" and "Doctor Robert."[18] In "Penny Lane," the modulation is effected simply by moving from V of B to V of A, perhaps effecting the downshifting audible at the bus roundabout. This motion sounds, upon first hearing, like the V–IV articulation of the final phrase of a rock blues, or perhaps a reference to that idea from "Strawberry Fields," but is confirmed at the arrival of the chorus as a "very strange" ($\mathbf{C}-1$) approach to a new tonal center. At $\mathbf{F}-1$, the bus takes the listener to a chorus in B for the song's conclusion, effecting an overall transcendence from $b^1–c\sharp^2–d\sharp^2$ (at $\mathbf{A}-1$) through $c\sharp^2–d^2–e^2$ ($\mathbf{C}-1$) to $d\sharp^2–e^2–f\sharp^2$ ($\mathbf{F}-1$). The chorus also shifts perspective from the pure narration of local events to the author's subjective ("foggy") memories.[19] The slower harmonic rhythm of the chorus begins with $I^{8-6}–IV$, with its repeated quarters in the bass taken from the D-gesture of "I Saw Her Standing There," before returning to B major ("meanwhile back") through a direct motion to its dominant. Wilfrid Mellers captures the song's essence: "For both musical and verbal reasons the song comes out as childishly merry yet dreamily wild at the same time. The hallucinatory feeling concerns problems of identity rather than drugs specifically, asking what, among our childhood memories, is reality and what is illusion."[20] McCartney recalls his intentions for Lennon's new song and then for bringing both personal sides of the single into universal awareness: Strawberry Fields was "a magical childhood place for [John] and we transformed it into the sort of psychedelic dream; it was like everybody's magic place instead of ours—we took them from being little localized things to make them more global."[21]

Single Release

As the Beatles declined offers from concert promoters—without publicly acknowledging their firm decision to stop touring—and the industry grew impatient over the lack of an announcement of a third film, reports of both a group breakup and a decision to replace Epstein were widespread by November 1966.[22] These rumors were not fully refuted until the arrival of the new record. Martin remembers "Strawberry Fields Forever" and "Penny Lane" as the first two songs recorded for the intended follow-up LP to *Revolver* but taken instead for a double-A-sided single when EMI and Brian Epstein pressured him for a record release.[23] But contemporaneous reports have a different story. In early November, before Martin had heard either song, he stated: "The Beatles will probably have a new single out in time for Christmas. EMI are hoping to get the group into the studios at the end of this month to record material for a new single which will be rush-released in December in time for the Christmas sales boom."[24]

However divined, the record was released in the United States (as Capitol 5810) on February 13 ("Penny Lane" achieved #1 for one week, and "Strawberry Fields Forever" peaked at #8—a weak showing, considering sales of 1.1 million in three days), and in the United Kingdom (Parlophone R5570) on February 17 (topping the chart for three weeks). The accompanying promotional film, directed by Peter Goldmann (recommended by Klaus Voorman), features backward shots, multiple superimages, and—for the coda of "Strawberry Fields Forever"—black-and-white negatives.[25] Many Beatles experts agree with George Martin, who says, "In my estimation it was the best record we ever made."[26] As bizarre as the record and film were, the Beatles' public were still unprepared for the shock that greeted the group's subsequent release, *Sgt. Pepper's Lonely Hearts Club Band*. This single and LP capture the Beatles at their peak of creativity, and the introspective psychedelia in the words and sounds of these records would revolutionize popular music even more thoroughly than the Beatles did in 1964.

TWO

YELLOW MATTER CUSTARD, GREEN SLOP PIE (1967)

Several important projects for the Beatles appear in the time line (table 2.1), but in the domain of popular music, 1967 is simply the year of *Sgt. Pepper*. Rock music — barely more than a decade old — had been rapidly maturing but achieved with this album a pinnacle of artistic vision, good times, and far-reaching impact far beyond its peers, such as could never again appear in any one product. The rock world has known albums of serious artistry by Yes and Pink Floyd, of recreational value by Michael Jackson and the B-52s, and of influence by the Sex Pistols and Nirvana, but no object in its entire history can match the immediacy and power with which a collection of songs exemplifies all of these aspects so intensely above and beyond its fellows as *Sgt. Pepper's Lonely Hearts Club Band*.

Even a summary listing of the highly expressive LP's most important attributes goes on and on: its individual songs, spanning styles from soft chamber music to arena rockers, are interconnected by album-spanning devices of theme, meter, and imagery; following the lead taken in the early-1967 single, all manner of outside musicians are recruited, electronic effects are taken advantage of, and the Beatles' own performances are highly polished, so as to produce the seemingly perfect blend of colorful surface effects; subjects of lyrics run the gamut from detailed fantasy worlds to many areas of social and spiritual significance, as never before in the genre; two songs clock in at over five minutes, then an unprecedented feature of a mainstream pop LP but a pacesetting feature for all that followed; tonal systems call on modal mixture that refers to 1962 compositions, range deeply into both the sharp and the flat sides

Table 2.1   Time Line of Major Events for the Beatles, 1967

Dec. 6, 1966–Apr. 21, 1967:	Recordings for *Sgt. Pepper*, EMI and Regent Studios, London
Jan. 5:	Recordings for the "Carnival of Light," EMI, London
Jan. 30–31, Feb. 7:	Shooting of "Strawberry Fields Forever" and "Penny Lane" promotional films, Kent
Feb. 13–June 2:	Recordings for *Yellow Submarine* soundtrack, EMI and De Lane Lea Studios, London
Feb. 17:	"Penny Lane"/"Strawberry Fields Forever" released in United Kingdom
Apr. 25–Nov. 17:	Recordings and mixing for "Magical Mystery Tour" soundtrack, EMI and Chappell Studios, London
May 11:	Recording of "Baby You're a Rich Man," Olympic Studios, London
May 17–June 9:	Recordings and mixing for "You Know My Name (Look Up the Number)," EMI, London
June 1:	*Sgt. Pepper's Lonely Hearts Club Band* released in United Kingdom
June 14–26:	Recording and mixing of "All You Need Is Love," Olympic and EMI Studios, London
July 7:	"All You Need Is Love"/"Baby You're a Rich Man" released in United Kingdom
Aug. 27:	Death of Brian Epstein, London
Sept. 11–Oct. 31:	Filming of "Magical Mystery Tour," southern England and France
Oct. 2–Nov. 2:	Recording of "Hello Goodbye," EMI, London
Nov. 22–Jan. 30, 1967:	Harrison recording *Wonderwall* soundtrack, London and Bombay EMI studios
Nov. 24:	"Hello Goodbye"/"I Am the Walrus" released in United Kingdom
Dec. 7:	Opening of Apple boutique, London
Dec. 8:	*Magical Mystery Tour* EP set released in United Kingdom
Dec. 26:	BBC telecast of "Magical Mystery Tour"

for profound scale-degree contrast, and continue an experimentation with progressive tonality begun in *Revolver* and "Penny Lane." All of this seems possible because of the serendipitous peakings of McCartney's leadership, Lennon's imagination, Harrison's confidence, and Starr's competence. And the album ranks as George Martin's favorite among the group's LPs; it certainly marks his most effective work as a producer.

During the year, the Beatles also produced "All You Need Is Love" for a historic live worldwide telecast and wrote songs with lasting appeal—led by Lennon's obscure "I Am the Walrus" and McCartney's haunting "The Fool on the Hill"—for their year-end project, the made-for-television film "Magical Mystery Tour." Most of this chapter will document the composition, recording, and analysis of the year's individual new songs, but it will begin with a look at the music of the Beatles' peers through their last years as a group, will feature an examination of the *Sgt. Pepper* LP as a totality, and will conclude with a summary of the Beatles' midperiod characteristics.

Popular Music, 1967–1969

Many aspects of popular music changed radically during the Beatles' last years, and our musicians took the lead in many ways. The following pages will trace the central trends introduced by some of the most important rock artists of this period, so as to suggest the Beatles' influence on their peers and also to provide a broader context for their own later innovations.

The most fundamental conversion in the late 1960s is seen in the phenomenal growth of the LP market and its effect on musical content. In terms of success in the American album charts, the Beatles were the most popular artists of the 1960s: they topped a full third of the weekly charts throughout their six-year domination. It may be surprising that Frank Sinatra was a close second for the same decade.[1] This fact reflects the orientation of record albums toward adults, particularly in connection with the universal demand for the more costly stereo equipment generally used in their play, a demand increasing very early in the 1960s in the United States, with the United Kingdom about six years behind. The soundtrack album for *The Sound of Music*, for instance, hardly the typical teenager's party music, remained on the U.S. LP charts from March 1965 through October 1969, longer than any other record of the decade; its run was even stronger in the United Kingdom. Overall LP sales rose steadily from 1959, grew alongside the advent of prerecorded cassettes in 1966, pulled ahead of singles sales by 1967, and peaked in the late 1970s and early 1980s. This growth was represented increasingly by the youth market, largely created by the Beatles. The only albums released prior to 1970 that sold 7 million or more copies in the United States through 1992 are the Beatles' *Abbey Road* (9 million), *Sgt. Pepper's Lonely Hearts Club Band* (8), and *The Beatles* (7).[2] In comparison, only one of Presley's ninety-six LPs from 1956 through 1992 sold as many as 2 million; in 1958, Van Cliburn sold far more LPs than Presley. Conversely, popular artists account for the vast majority of album sales by the late 1970s; highest multiplatinum sales are for Michael Jackson's *Thriller* (1982, 21 million copies), Fleetwood Mac's *Rumours* (1977, 13 million), and Pink Floyd's *Dark Side of the Moon* (1973, 12 million). The LP format allowed for much freer musical expression, as well as greater potential commercial reward, than the singles market; it also fostered more emphasis on original composition by group members, with cover versions—once common LP fillers, even for the Beatles—fast becoming curiosities.

Singles dominated radio playlists through the end of the 1960s, and their sales were still strong through the mid-1970s. Table 2.2 lists all artists, British in boldface, that achieved a total of four or more weeks at #1 in the British and American singles charts for the years 1967–69. Note that despite a much relaxed release schedule, the Beatles totaled more weeks at #1 than their top three competitors combined.

Market concerns aside, rock music of the late 1960s reveled in mind-expanding drugs, free love, long hair, reincarnation and nirvana, the brotherhood of man, and world peace. All of these topics, for instance, are neatly dis-

Table 2.2 British and American Singles-Chart Success for Top Artists, 1967–1969

Artist	U.K. Chart Entries			U.S. Chart Entries		
	Wks #1	Wks Top 5	Wks Top 10	Wks #1	Wks Top 5	Wks Top 10
Beatles	24	51	62	20	44	67
Monkees	5	18	26	10	26	35
Rolling Stones	8	17	24	5	18	24
Engelbert Humperdinck	10	38	60	0	4	5
Marvin Gaye / Tammi Terrell	3	9	15	7	11	20
Archies	6	10	10	4	10	12
Rascals	0	0	4	9	21	31
Fifth Dimension	0	0	0	9	18	30
Zager and Evans	3	6	7	6	7	9
Tommy James & the Shondells	5	6	7	2	18	35
Bobbie Gentry	3	6	9	4	8	9
Nancy / Frank Sinatra	2	11	18	4	9	15
Tommy Roe	2	5	7	4	7	9
Diana Ross & and the Supremes	0	9	18	5	28	46
Doors	0	0	0	5	18	26
Mary Hopkin	5	12	17	0	6	7
Bobby Goldsboro	0	6	8	5	9	11
Lulu	0	4	15	5	8	9
Herb Alpert	1	5	9	4	7	8
Procol Harum	5	8	13	0	2	6
Louis Armstrong	5	10	12	0	0	0
Paul Mauriat (French)	0	0	0	5	8	10
Tom Jones	4	24	46	0	0	4
Gary Puckett & the Union Gap	4	9	15	0	15	27
Box Tops	0	0	5	4	13	14
Association	0	0	0	4	13	19
Sly & the Family Stone	0	0	0	4	11	18
Otis Redding	0	3	6	4	8	11
Scaffold	4	10	16	0	0	0
Sandie Shaw	4	9	16	0	0	0
Peter Sarstedt	4	7	8	0	0	0
Esther & Abi Ofarim	4	6	7	0	0	0

posed of in the "tribal" musical *Hair* (New York's original cast LP was released in July 1968). Live performances reached a new level of excitement with the new proliferation of light shows and far heavier amplification than before possible, particularly with stacks of 200-watt Marshall amps, all developed in San Francisco in 1965, catching on in New York and London by early 1967 and—before long—considered essential to a world concert tour, which might require thirty tons of equipment. In San Francisco, the Grateful Dead were the house band at communal "acid-tests," psychedelic happenings where music was among a number of sensory stimuli programmed to accompany the LSD experience. These gatherings and the popularity of local rock shows at the Avalon Ballroom and Bill Graham's Fillmore Auditorium led to the "Human Be-In" of

January 1967 (featuring Jefferson Airplane and Janis Joplin), which in turn inspired the addition of rock acts to the Monterey International Pop Festival of June that year (with Jimi Hendrix, the Dead, Janis Joplin, and the Who). Monterey itself was the blueprint for free concerts in London's Hyde Park in the summers of 1968 and 1969 and for festivals at Woodstock (Hendrix; Crosby, Stills and Nash; the Who) and the Isle of Wight (Bob Dylan, the Who, the Moody Blues, King Crimson) in August 1969 that came to be strong social statements, airing the youth movement's antiwar and antiestablishment concerns as well as constituting musical celebrations.

The London scene was dominated by small clubs such as the UFO and the Speakeasy, which flourished in 1967–68 as regular venues for "underground" groups such as the Who, Jimi Hendrix, Cream, Tomorrow, the Small Faces, and John Mayall. Among many highlights, Paul McCartney attended Pink Floyd's debut with light show at the Roundhouse in January 1967, and Jimmy Page awed Led Zeppelin fans with the tremolo he achieved on his guitar with a violin bow at the Marquee Club in December 1968. Aside from the rare booking of the Albert Hall for a pop concert, central London was without a large stage for rock shows until Brian Epstein leased the Saville Theatre, where beginning in January 1967 he booked and promoted Sunday shows by Cream, Fairport Convention, the Incredible String Band, Pink Floyd, Tomorrow, The Who, the Nice, and Ten Years After, as well as Little Richard, Chuck Berry, and Fats Domino. It was at the Saville that McCartney thrilled to hear Hendrix play the title track of *Sgt. Pepper* only three days after the LP's official release date.[3]

Trends in Rock Recordings: The United States

Following the Beatles' lead, a few pop acts that had thrived on hit singles matured and concentrated on albums in the late 1960s. Representative are the Beach Boys, driven by Brian Wilson's fertile yet fragile imagination, and the Rascals, led into new territory by Felix Cavaliere, who was to tour with Ringo in 1995. Both groups embraced Indian teachings and promoted peace and enlightened brotherhood. The Beach Boys entered a particularly experimental phase, noted by the radical fragmentation of their pieces, such as the multiply spliced "Heroes and Villains" and much of the LPs *Smiley Smile* (September 1967) and *Friends* (July 1968); the latter included several partial songs. In these and most similar cases, such changes of direction merely confused audiences and led to commercial failure; *Friends* did not make the Top 100. Among other established American acts, Bob Dylan was sidelined for two years by a motorcycle accident until he surprised the world with his simple country-styled LP *John Wesley Harding* (January 1968), scored for single voice, acoustic guitar (or, in two songs, piano), bass, and drums; two songs are graced by an additional pedal steel guitar, which points to the next LP, *Nashville Skyline* (May 1969). It has often been suggested that the simplicity of *Harding* inspired the Beatles to leave the complex colors of psychedelia behind in 1968. This shift toward simplicity occurred at the same time that Motown acts such as the Temptations and Marvin Gaye, under the production of Norman Whitfield, were given more complex "psychedelic" arrangements.

Opposing these established acts were such "underground" rock groups as the Fugs (of New York) and the Mothers of Invention (of Los Angeles). The latter, formed by Frank Zappa in 1965, celebrated its lack of commercial potential the way hippies paraded their shoulder-length-and-longer hair as a "freak flag"; only four of eleven Mothers LPs released before 1971 reached the Top 100, and only one—probably because it was a takeoff on *Sgt. Pepper*—reached #30. Zappa's main message for the left-behinds of the Great Society, usually expressed in a contemptuously satirical tone, was that they must shun the dominant culture and learn to think for themselves. Zappa's musical vehicle relies on noise (from his raucous guitar, electronic effects, backward tapes, tape-speed manipulation, idiosyncratic orchestrations, and Varèse-based atonal harmonies), a lack of harmonic function (many songs, as in *Freak Out!*, simply alternate between tonic and its neighboring ♭VII), and poststructural pastiches full of references to Ives, Stravinsky, and Holst alongside those of the Supremes, the Beach Boys, Berry, and the Kingsmen.

The hypnotically repeating I–♭VII–I neighbor motion became the basis for entire songs and seemingly interminable pentatonic improvisations by West Coast groups such as the Jefferson Airplane ("It's No Secret" on *Takes Off*, September 1966, and "She Has Funny Cars" on *Surrealistic Pillow*, February 1967), Quicksilver Messenger Service ("Who Do You Love," for twenty-five minutes of *Happy Trails*, March 1967), Big Brother and the Holding Company ("Down on Me," August 1967), and Country Joe and the Fish, who would also alternate, in a Dorian setting, the tonic with its *upper* neighbor II. The Dead could build a whole song on this recurring neighbor motion but (as in the twenty-three-minute performance of "Dark Star" preserved on *Live/Dead*, December 1969) would usually provide contrasting "space" filled in a variety of ways ranging from jugband licks to several minutes of artfully varied feedback from two guitars and bass. The Airplane also specialized in unusual mode mixture and asymmetrical phrase rhythm, while the Dead produced a highly inventive mix of electronic effects (their bassist Phil Lesh studied some with Berio, and Jerry Garcia was fond of "phasing" the harmonics on his vocal tracks), imaginative percussion (the two drummers exploit a wide array of instruments), multitudinous textures (exhibited at one extreme in the 8'30" a cappella vocal solo by Garcia in "What's Become of the Baby," *Aoxomoxoa*, June 1969), and irregular phrase lengths and meters ("The Eleven," *Live/Dead*, which continuously alternates fast bars of $\frac{6}{8}$ and $\frac{5}{8}$). Big Brother's spotlight was always on blues singer Janis Joplin, whose sandpaper voice expressed a great range of emotions through controlled, subtle, and highly effective variations of register, dynamics, clarity of diction, diaphragm support, locus of tone production, multiphonics, vibrato, ornamentation, intonation, articulation, and rhythmic placement, all with an ear carefully attuned to a song's formal structure.

Three other Los Angeles bands—the Doors; Crosby, Stills and Nash; and Spirit—are worth brief mentions. The first is highly celebrated for Jim Morrison's brooding poetry but little for its usually monotonous music, and the second is revered for its post-Byrds/post-Hollies three-part vocal harmonies, most characteristically in parallel motion, as if based on the Beatles' "If I Needed

Someone," and post–Buffalo Springfield guitar work. The last, Spirit, is not nearly as popular, although it is the most colorful of the three. Spirit marries improbable aspects of the Beatles, as with the *Rubber Soul*–like backing vocals of "Uncle Jack" or the backward guitar of "Topango Windows," and the Mothers, as with the 3+3+2 meter of "Fresh Garbage," reminiscent of the Mothers' less earnest *Absolutely Free*, in their LPs *Spirit* (April 1968), *The Family That Plays Together* (January 1969), and *Clear Spirit* (August 1969).

New British Rock

The Beatles' experimental timbres, rhythms, tonal structures, and poetic texts in *Rubber Soul* and *Revolver* encouraged a legion of young bands that were to create progressive rock in the early 1970s. But a few older groups kept pace. The Rolling Stones came of age in the late 1960s; *Aftermath* (July 1966) was their first LP to contain only Jagger/Richard originals, but their next efforts, *Between the Buttons* and *Their Satanic Majesties Request* (both from 1967), were heavily dependent on the Beatles. The revolution-inciting *Beggar's Banquet* (December 1968) and *Let It Bleed* (December 1969) were fully self-assured, and the Stones' 1969 American tour broke all previous box-office records. The Who, a successful singles band, proved with the nine-minute, five-section self-styled "mini-opera" "A Quick One, While He's Away" (*A Quick One*, December 1966) that Pete Townshend had expansive and dramatic ideas well suited to the LP. This propensity led to the "rock opera" (really a cantata) *Tommy* (June 1969, two LPs), two years in the making, during which time Townshend composed and recorded home demos in McCartney-like auto-multitracking. Taking a page from Indian philosophy, *Tommy* is an allegory for the illusory nature of our waking lives and the infinite reality that can be perceived only by denying the material world; the composer says, "I decided that the hero had to be deaf, dumb, and blind, so that, seen from our already limited point of view, his limitations would be symbolic of our own."[4]

Light shows and hallucinogenic trances were nearly necessary for the appreciation of the early Pink Floyd, led by Syd Barrett until his nervous collapse. Their first LP, *Piper at the Gates of Dawn* (August 1967), is a pentatonic-based ("Pow R. Toch") or fully atonal ("Interstellar Overdrive") minimalist freak-out featuring Barrett's Fender Telecaster and Rick Wright's Farfisa organ, with no emphasis on periodic phrase lengths or recognizable cadences. The great self-negation of Barrett's "Jug Band Blues" (*A Saucerful of Secrets*, July 1968) depends on Lennon's "Strawberry Fields Forever." One-time Beatles engineer Norman Smith produced these LPs at EMI.

Just as far-out as the Floyd but guided by a tonal center was the Jimi Hendrix Experience (November 1966–February 1969), a trio with Hendrix (guitar, usually a Stratocaster), Noel Redding (bass), and Mitch Mitchell (drums).[5] The group was down-to-earth enough to score four British Top Ten hits but wild enough to introduce a wide range of pyrotechnics—often aided by lighter fluid—on the guitar, including heavy distortion for a fluid sustain, all manner of feedback, wide vibrato, nonstandard tunings, switching of pickups during notes and chords, two-handed hammer-ons and string tapping for novel articulations, backward tape, and the wah-wah pedal (permitting controlled sweeps of harmonics) as early as June 1967. Additionally, Hendrix's velvet vocals were often filtered, phased (sweeping through their harmonics, as with the wah), and manipulated by varied tape speeds. A middle ground between Hendrix and Floyd was straddled by Soft Machine, who also pioneered in distortion and feedback as they wove freely improvisatory paths in and out of tonal realms, flaunting complex wind-ensemble passages in asymmetrical yet repeating meters and phrase lengths, which might or might not relate to Western scales.

Much more pop-oriented in their melodies, harmonies, and forms, but just as spacey in their pseudo-"deep" incantations and lyrics, were the Moody Blues, as that group's membership was reconstituted in September 1966. Aided by Holst-like orchestrations, *Days of Future Passed* (December 1967) was a true concept album, tracing the moods of one day from dawn through peak hour into the night. Incongruous but well-meaning were their next offerings, Mellotron-drenched warnings against an overly mechanized society, but the sounds and the stereophonic panning fit well their pot-headed eternal voyages through the vastness of space. When Denny Laine left the Moodies, he toured with his Electric String Band, comprising two violins, two cellos, and a rhythm section, thus simultaneously getting McCartney's ear (leading to collaborations in the 1970s) and breaking ground for the Beatlesque Electric Light Orchestra. The loud, pre-heavy-metal King Crimson (1969–74) were just as dependent on a Mellotron wash for spacey effects as the Moodies but were also in possession of a far more virtuosic guitarist, Robert Fripp on a heavily distorted Les Paul, and bassist Greg Lake.

The ambitious group Tomorrow was led by backward-tape aficionado Keith West, who composed *The Teenage Opera*, staged in London in 1967; their eponymous LP (February 1968) included a cover of "Strawberry Fields Forever." But Tomorrow is best known as the hothouse for guitarist Steve Howe, member of Yes from 1971. In its first incarnation in July 1968, Yes included singer Jon Anderson, bassist Chris Squire, drummer Bill Bruford, guitarist Peter Banks (who applied a wah and a tone-pedal control to his Rickenbacker twelve-string), and keyboardist Tony Kaye, all honing their vocal harmonies with covers of the Beatles, the Byrds, and the Fifth Dimension.

Schooled within the Yardbirds and John Mayall's Blues Breakers, the premier British guitarists—Eric Clapton, Jeff Beck, Peter Green, Jimmy Page, Alvin Lee, and Mick Taylor—were masters of many hues of the blues. Clapton left the 'birds in 1965 when their sound became too "pop" for his taste and formed the original power trio Cream in June 1966, with Jack Bruce on bass and Ginger Baker on drums.[6] Maintaining his stand against commercial exploitation, Clapton refused in late 1967 to record any further singles, but by the end of 1968, after their announced breakup, Cream's management began to pull singles from their LPs. Clapton's playing, on the Strat, Les Paul, or SG, is marked by a fluid level of distortion (occasionally, as in "White Room" [*Wheels of Fire*, August 1968], allowing some light feedback from open strings), various degrees of finger and wrist vibrato, string bending and slides (a wide range of phrasing, articulation, and ornamentation is displayed in "Sitting on Top of the World" [*Wheels*]), and wah-wah pedal (hear the inventive blend of wah, bass, and cymbals in "Tales of Brave Ulysses" [*Disraeli Gears*, November 1967]). Clapton usually plays two or three guitar parts in the studio LPs: distorted lead, rhythm chording, and fuzz ostinato (even using two electric twelve-strings in "Dance the Night Away" [*Gears*]). The registrally alive solo in "Sleepy Time Time" (*Fresh Cream*, October 1966) shows a sensitive range of dynamics and unexpected choices of melodic intervals and scale degrees, especially in creating a Dorian sound in a pentatonic context. Bruce and Baker were also virtuosos (the drum solo in "Toad" [*Wheels*] often has the hi-hat, ride cymbal, bass drum, and toms offering complementary rhythms at once), so the initial LP, *Fresh Cream*, is uneven, as the performers don't always support each other. Ensemble is much tighter in *Gears*, and by *Wheels* it is hard to find a better balance of three such great and sympathetic talents than in "Crossroads" or "Spoonful," wherein Clapton often responds to Bruce's fuzz-bass lead in imaginative ways, and toms, cymbals, and snare imitate guitar parts; in the latter, the textural counterpoint maintains interest for seventeen minutes on a single chord. *Wheels* also introduces songs and passages in asymmetrical ("White Room," "Passing the Time") and mixed ("Those Were the Days") meters and alters vocals with a Leslie cabinet ("As You Said").

The Yardbirds split in September 1968, leaving four who renamed themselves Led Zeppelin and produced their first LPs in January (eponymous) and October (*II*) 1969. Jimmy Page played Telecaster, Les Paul, and other guitars as fast as Eddie Van Halen would in the 1980s; Robert Plant sang lead (sometimes with Leslie, as on "What Is and What Should Never Be" [*Led Zeppelin II*]); John Paul Jones added bass and keyboards; and John Bonham played loud yet complex and subtle drums, all instruments and vocals evidencing a great range of filtering. These first two LPs specialize in a powerful doubling of bass and guitar for pentatonic (post–"Day Tripper") ostinati, as in "Good Times Bad Times" (*Led Zeppelin*) and "Heartbreaker" and "Living, Loving Maid" (both *Led Zeppelin II*); three lead guitars and bass are doubled in four different registers for the chromatic ostinato in "Dazed and Confused" (*Led Zeppelin*), and "Bring It On Home" (*Led Zeppelin II*) adds a third guitar, in thirds, above two others doubling the bass at the unison.

To whom were the Beatles listening? Lennon remained a Dylan fan and took a liking to Hendrix, Harrison turned off Western pop in preference for North Indian classical music, and McCartney became a devotee of the clubs. His favorite act was the Incredible String Band, whose LP *The 5000 Spirits* he called the best album of 1967. As in the nine-and-a-half-minute "Maya" (*The Big Huge*, November 1968), this Scottish quartet would routinely alternate metrically free passages of winsome acoustic folk chants, graced by pretty and striking vocal slides and other ornaments, with up-tempo ragalike sections in regular rhythm. McCartney no doubt admired the folk melodies as well as the odd colors produced by contrasts of sitar, tin whistle, Irish harp, and all manner of keyboards and guitars.

The Beatles in Early 1967

Brian Epstein's interest in the Saville Theatre has been noted; by late 1966, no longer occupied on a daily basis by his nontouring Beatles, he continued to add an occasional act to his management roster, such as the Paramounts, who became Procol Harum. Then in January 1967, NEMS merged with Robert Stigwood (manager of the Who and Cream), to whom Epstein relinquished managerial duties. Brian continued to negotiate for the Beatles, anticipating the October expiration of his management contract with the group, and in fact secured for them new nine-year contracts with EMI and Capitol in January that multiplied the group's recording royalties from 7 cents per LP and 1 cent per single in the United Kingdom (and half that in the United States) to a percentage of wholesale prices, on a sliding scale of 10–15 percent in the United Kingdom (and 10–17.5 percent in the United States). In April 1967 the Beatles renewed their legal partnership as Beatles & Co., binding until 1977.

While Lennon continued postproduction dubbing for *How I Won the War* in February through March, McCartney went underground. In October 1966, he had helped Barry Miles establish the underground paper *International Times*, a London counterpart to the *Berkeley Barb*. The opening celebration had been held at a club called the Roundhouse, which then asked McCartney to contribute a sound tape for a happening called the "Carnival of Light" scheduled for January 28 and February 4. On January 5, the Beatles constructed for this purpose a fourteen-minute tape of drum, organ, and guitar, overshadowed by sound effects and what Mark Lewisohn has described as "John and Paul screaming dementedly and bawling aloud random phrases like 'Are you alright?' and 'Barcelona!' "[7] McCartney would never have considered such a tape for release as a Beatles product, but Lewisohn's report makes this recording sound like a study for Lennon's "Revolution 9."

Harrison immersed himself in all things Indian, turning from Leary to Yogananda to the *Bhagavadgita*. This last is a book concerning the moral battle fought in this life and the exploration of the inner soul in order to attain an illumined and divine consciousness, joy within, and spiritual freedom in the afterlife. One editor elaborates:

> Man, on the threshold of higher life, feels disappointed with the glamour of the world and yet illusions cling to him and he cherishes them. He forgets his divine ancestry and becomes attached to his personality and is agitated by the conflicting forces of the world. Before he wakes up to the world of spirit and accepts the obligations imposed by it, he has to fight the enemies of selfishness and stupidity, and overcome the dark ignorance of his self-centered ego. Man cut off from spiritual nature has to be restored to it. It is the evolution of the human soul that is portrayed here. There are no limits of time and space to it. The fight takes place every moment in the soul of man.[8]

The recollection of one's ancestral past as a basis for redemption, and the seeing of "the Self abiding in all beings and all beings in the Self," becomes a central tenet in Harrison's lifework, perhaps most obviously in the soon-to-be-recorded "Within You Without You."[9]

Sgt. Pepper's Lonely Hearts Club Band

The Lennon-led idea of recording songs connected with childhood, which inspired the three Beatles recordings of November–December 1966, did not govern the Beatles' next LP, although its references to Lewis Carroll and the circus probably reflect boyhood interests. Instead, a different theme was instead invented by McCartney. Bored, he says, with writing unconnected individual songs, "it was now to do more like writing your novel."[10] Liberated by the end of touring, McCartney's thoughts were expansive; he hit upon an alter ego for the Beatles, a band that the Beatles could pretend to be: "Everything about the album will be imagined from the perspective of these people, so it doesn't have to be us, it doesn't have to be the kind of song *you* want to write, it could be the song *they* might want to write."[11] "We were getting a little bit fed up of being the Beatles, because everything we did had to be the Beatles, and I felt we were getting trapped in this whole idea of 'what kind of songs does John do? What does George do? Paul does the ballads.' It was all getting so bloody predictable."[12] The facade became Sgt. Pepper's Lonely Hearts Club Band; its full name, says Lennon, was inspired by the lengthy names of the San Francisco groups and coined by Mal Evans.[13] The band was designed as an Edwardian military outfit; antiquarian turns of phrase age many songs, and the record sleeve's opulent, brightly colored satin military uniforms (chartreuse, fuchsia, sky blue, and tomato!) seem just one psychedelic step beyond the fawn-colored Nehru soldier's jackets with sheriff's badges worn at Shea in 1965.[14] The alter egos also magnify the Beatles' always present sense of their musical history. On *Revolver*, the group had announced "Mark I" by rewriting the count-off for the LP; with *Sgt. Pepper*, the jacket puts drab waxwork figures of the 1964-era group itself to one side to bring to center stage the new, improved rainbow-embracing band. The "Pepper" idea, which allowed the Beatles to remove themselves from the public by an extra layer—they were now giving a performance of a performance, to be distributed on vinyl, all a far cry from what had become the horror of a live show—was very much characteristic of play-actor McCartney. Lennon always said he preferred the White album (1968): "The music was better for me on the double album, because I'm being myself on it."[15] Anyway, both Lennon and Starr feel that the "Pepper" concept embraces only the LP's first two songs and the reprise.[16] Other unities will, however, become apparent and will be discussed during and following the analysis of the individual tracks, which will be taken up in the order on which they appear on the LP.

Sgt. Pepper marks the beginning of McCartney's domination of the group's creative direction; he was to provide the impetus and direction for most of the Beatles' remaining projects, singles as well as LPs, and increasingly asserted his will in all details while recording his own compositions. Half of *Sgt. Pepper's* songs are McCartney's, but the LP's most significant individual contributions— "A Day in the Life" and "Lucy in the Sky with Diamonds"—are predominantly Lennon's. Other methods evolved as well: Lennon now wrote predominantly at keyboards, and McCartney was becoming more of a guitarist, playing both his Casino and a new Esquire Custom on the LP, although the Rickenbacker bass remained his lead instrument. Not only was the bass increasingly to the fore in terms of compositional interest and balance among the other forces, but its "natural" ambience was removed as a result of being directly injected into the recording console rather than having the amplifier's speaker miked, allowing a potentially purer and richer capture of the instrument's own harmonics.[17] Ringo replaced his toms' plastic heads with loose calfskins, allowing a deeper timbre.[18] Harrison has been accused of participating in few *Sgt. Pepper* sessions, but he has denied this. The sitarist does seem to play maracas almost as much as lead guitar in 1967, but his contribution to the album is strong in several ways.

Some of the LP was recorded in a party atmosphere; Mick Jagger, Donovan, and David Crosby were among the many guests to celebrate the proceedings. Ringo, however, was largely bored by the five-month project; he was always on call, awaiting orders. After taping the basic track, he might have to wait weeks to superimpose a single hi-hat to beef up the original percussion, which would often have gotten buried under several succeeding mixdowns. "The biggest memory I have of *Sgt. Pepper*," he recalled, "is I learned to play chess on it."[19] Given the complexity of the album's arrangements, it is amazing to note that Martin's engineers were still limited to four tracks.[20] In many songs, the basic tracks are made easily distinguishable by the mixdown process; lumped together, they lack the vibrancy of the many overdubs. Between Lewisohn (1988) and Martin (1994), most of the album's track-by-track recording details have been fairly well documented. Overdub and mixing sessions for some songs overlapped heavily with the recording of the basic tracks of others, but a general sense of the album's recording history can be gleaned from a schedule of the initial recording for each piece:

December 6, 1966:	"When I'm Sixty-Four"
January 19, 1967:	"A Day in the Life"
February 1:	"Sgt. Pepper's Lonely Hearts Club Band"
February 8:	"Good Morning Good Morning"
February 9:	"Fixing a Hole"
(February 13:	"Only a Northern Song")
February 17:	"Being for the Benefit of Mr. Kite"
February 23:	"Lovely Rita"
February 28:	"Lucy in the Sky with Diamonds"
March 9:	"Getting Better"
March 15:	"Within You Without You"
March 17:	"She's Leaving Home"
March 29:	"With a Little Help from My Friends"
April 1:	"Sgt. Pepper's Lonely Hearts Club Band (Reprise)"
April 21:	run-out groove

Principal recording was completed on April 3, as McCartney wished to be in the United States to join Jane Asher on her birthday on the 5th. The master tape was compiled on April 21, the disc mother cut on April 28, and the LP released on June 1.[21] Now for the track-by-track analysis of the final product.

"Sgt. Pepper's Lonely Hearts Club Band"

The LP opens with pit violins warming up and an audience in anticipation of a concert. This effect has some precedent in the Byrds' "So You Want to Be a Rock and Roll Star" (January 1967), which had included a screaming audience. Martin recalls of the Beatles' opening track, "Always there's the audience punctuating the whole [song]. Together with the audience and the horns, it's an exciting thing saying come enjoy our show, listen to us, we're a great band."[22] The basic track and vocals for the title song were taped on February 1 and 2, comprising Ringo's drums, engineer Emerick getting "the snap of the hammer hitting the skin" of the bass drum, and Harrison's rhythm guitar ("Guitar II") on Track 1.[23] At the same time, McCartney's bass was direct-injected to Track 2, its rhythm at **A** and **C** just as insistent as his Little Richard-styled lead vocal (Track 4), which is supported by McCartney/Lennon/Harrison backing vocals on Track 3. Instruments were reduced to a new Track 1 (heard center), vocals to Track 4 (wild, but always right for the lead vocal), and then a month later (on March 3), Track 3 was given four horns at **B**, **D–1**, **E**, and the "**Coda**," its parts sung individually by McCartney to the players.[24] In between these horn passages (always heard left), Harrison filled Track 3 by "dropping in" his heavily distorted lead guitar ("Guitar I"), but McCartney overdubbed a solo (not notated in the score) on his Esquire for the repeat of **A**; both new guitars are heard right. Finally, on March 6, Track 2 and small gaps of Track 3 received ambient live-performance effects: crowd murmuring (the sound effect taken from the EMI tape archives), violins (from the orchestral session tapes for "A Day in the Life"), the audience's pleased reaction (taped by Martin in 1961) to McCartney's disingenuously proclaimed desire to invite the audience home, and (at 2:01, left and right) audience screams (from a Hollywood Bowl performance by the Beatles).[25]

The title track introduces two new formal devices. The two-part horn episode at **B** (0:43–0:54), which like "From Me to You" tonicizes IV and then emphasizes V[7] for the retransition, is given lyrics to become the bridge at **E** (1:25–1:37). Additionally, the *aa'b* chorus, **C–D**, contains twelve bars but is unrelated to the blues pattern. (Moore 1997, 27–30, notes the song's 12 + 5 + 12 + 5 + 12-bar architecture.) But the song's strength lies in the [025] basis of chord patterns, truly the dominating pitch function that brings rock out of rock and roll. In the introduction and verse, McCartney's Lydian II♯ progression is built of parallel major-minor seventh chords whose roots define one [025] collection, G–A–C. We have here none of the voice leading of "Yesterday," which cadences with the same progression, although the repeated vocal î draws a connection to "She Loves You." But the Lydian progression becomes pentatonic for the chorus, where an [025] set is formed by the roots of I–♭III–IV–I, G–B♭–C.[26] Here, the blues-rock progression is amplified by heavily distorted "power chords" ("Guitar I," **C**, 0:55–1:13, right), guitar doublings of the roots in parallel fifths in the style of the Who. Sgt. Pepper's band may tune up their violins and amuse with their horns and quaint flattery of the audience, but it is hard-rocking Paul and the Beatles that make Hendrix want to play the number.

"With a Little Help from My Friends"

By the end of March, Ringo still had no lead vocal. So for the last-written song for the album, Lennon met McCartney at Cavendish Avenue, where they wrote "With a Little Help from My Friends," based on a germ Paul called "Bad Finger Boogie," the host at piano and his guest on guitar.[27] They began with the chorus and a simple melody, and it was Lennon's idea to begin each verse with a question. Lennon defended the song's line "I get high with a little help from my friends" against charges that it was drug-related: "It's really about a little help from my friends, it's a sincere message." But another of Lennon's verses, " 'What do you see when you turn off the light?' I can't tell you but I know it's mine," is more poetic and less directly sincere.[28] Another lyric gave Ringo pause: "The original line was 'what would you do if I sang out of tune? Would you throw tomatoes at me,' and I would not sing that line [recalling the jelly beans thrown at the group on stage in 1963] so they changed it."[29]

"With a Little Help from My Friends" was taped in two days (March 29 and 30), mixed for mono on the next, and then mixed for stereo on April 7; all mixes required crossfading with the Hollywood Bowl cheers that welcome Ringo. The basic track consisted of McCartney's piano on Track 1, Harrison's treble-y Strat rhythm guitar (including the flourish at 0:04) on Track 2, Martin's Hammond triplets for the introduction on Track 4, and Ringo's drums (featuring the two-bar fill just before **C**) and Lennon's cowbell (audible at 0:42) on Track 3. All were reduced to a new Track 1, which is heard center. Overdubs were limited to three more instruments: McCartney's high-register, direct-injected Rickenbacker bass replete with neighbors and passing tones, Ringo's tambourine, and one very distorted Harrison guitar lead-in at 0:37 (**C**–1–3) on Track 2 (heard right). Tracks 3–4 were filled with vocals (Ringo's lead, always heard center; Lennon and McCartney backing, heard at times left, right, and center).[30]

The LP opener had promised the singer Billy Shears, so the recording of "With a Little Help from My Friends" brings in both the singer and a new key center with a four-bar fanfare, ♭VI–♭VII–I, long ago the cadence from "P.S. I Love You," in E major (see sketch in ex. 2.1). This segue amounts to the first link between two consecutive songs on a Beatles album, instantly creating the expectation that this record will have an overall coherence. Such an expectation would be frustrated in some ways by the songs that follow, but a strong connection might be noted between the final piano-heavy E-major chord that ends this song (at 2:39) and the very similar sonority that concludes the album's closer, "A Day in the Life."

As for the introduction of the name Billy Shears, McCartney "thought that's a great little name, it's an Eleanor-Rigby-type name [and] it was purely and simply a device to get the next song in."[31] The ♭VI–♭VII–I fanfare progression itself ties the song together, as it reappears in the coda, there with a vocal octave jump even more strongly reminiscent of the same device in the refrain of "P.S. I Love You," while backing vocals provide there an oblique descent, as heard in "Please Please Me." Are we supposed to hear Billy Shears as the one-time star of the 1962–63 Beatles?

Example 2.1   Analysis of "With a Little Help from My Friends."

Like the title song, "With a Little Help from My Friends" features the ♭VII–IV–I double-plagal cadence. In the major-key context provided by the Beatles, often with continuous repetitions (as in the "Hey Jude" coda), this progression was to become ubiquitous following the release of *Sgt. Pepper*. The most prominent early appearances of its countless examples to come are heard in the Moodies' "Tuesday Afternoon" and "Peak Hour" (December 1967), Donovan's "Hurdy Gurdy Man" (June 1968), Traffic's "You Can All Join In" (October 1968), the Stones' "Sympathy for the Devil" (December 1968), the Who's "See Me, Feel Me" (June 1969), and the Airplane's "Volunteers" (November 1969).

Ringo's vocal quality, produced without diaphragm support, is both earnest and vulnerable. Example 2.1 indicates that, as in "Nowhere Man" (also in E major), McCartneian filled-in thirds ornament a simple $\hat{5}$-line, indicated in the open noteheads, that is strongly directional despite the singer's stated lack of confidence. The descent in the questioning verse (**A**) is tentative, lost among the ornamental notes and distracted by a minor II chord, while the chorus (**B**) offers enough support from friends to make the final descent sure and straight above the neighborly reassurance of the thrice-performed double-plagal cadence. The introduction's stepwise rise from e^2 to $g\sharp^2$ is reversed in the bridge (**E+1–2**, 1:13–1:16) and then by a reply with the same motive an octave lower (**E+3–4**, 1:17–1:20). In a very clever arrangement, the bridge informs the final verse (**F**) by reversing the Q/A relationship between Ringo and his supporters, finally having the backing singers ask the leading questions and Ringo respond with certainty. In the end, the insecure Ringo really does get "high" with a little help from his friends: "It took a lot of coaxing from Paul to get me to sing that last note—I just felt it was very high."[32]

"Lucy in the Sky with Diamonds"

One day in February 1967, a nearly four-year-old Julian Lennon returned home from nursery school with his painting of a classmate. McCartney has described this artwork as a representation of a girl floating among the stars in the sky, in a child's typically Chagall-like fashion.[33] Lennon asked his son what he called the picture, and Julian replied, "Lucy, in the sky, with diamonds." The title reminded the composer of the dreamy final poem of one of his own favorite books as a child, Lewis Carroll's *Through the Looking Glass*, "A boat beneath a sunny sky":

> Still she haunts me, phantomwise,
> Alice moving under skies
> Never seen by waking eyes.[34]

Lennon began writing fantasy lyrics based on images drawn from both *Through the Looking Glass* and *Alice's Adventures in Wonderland* and chanted them on an unchanging note above his trademark chromatically descending bass line. The composer has maintained that he was never consciously aware that the title, "Lucy in the Sky with Diamonds," forms an acrostic of the initials LSD, but given the Beatles' involvement with psychotropic drugs, it is not at all inappropriate to hear the poem's references to a "girl with kaleidoscope eyes," "cellophane flowers of yellow and green towering over your head," and "plasticine porters with looking-glass ties"—as well as the intended Carroll-based dream fantasy—as psychedelic images, especially as illuminated by the highly colorful effects provided by the Beatles.[35] Whether dream-based, drug-based, or both, the song's amphibolous phantasms entice the listener away from all concerns with reality.[36]

The song's colorful surface effects depend on novel instrumentation and engineering. The basic tracks, recorded on March 1 following a full eight-hour rehearsal, consist of Lennon's piano and Harrison's acoustic guitar (with a "wow" phasing effect—very noticeable at 1:43—added in the reduction mixdown) on Track 1, heard mostly in the chorus, McCartney's Lowrey organ (with the bell stop on verses, featuring a slower decay than would be available from the Hammond) on Track 2, Ringo's drums on Track 3, and Lennon's guide vocal on Track 4.[37] This last was wiped by Harrison's tamboura, which enters at 0:18 and is a particularly effective blender in the retransition from the Leslie guitar of the chorus, **C**, to the bell stop and cymbals in the verse, **A**. All basic tracks were mixed down to a new Track 1 at 49 cps, heard left. The next day, the new Track 4 was given McCartney's overdubbed bass and Harrison's Strat slide with Leslie (doubling the vocal at **B** and bass at **C**, and sounding particularly like an organ at 3:16), heard right. Completing the recording, Tracks 2 and 3 were each filled with lead vocals by Lennon and, in the chorus, a descant part by McCartney, both heard center. One pair of these vocals was recorded at 45 cps and the other, with heavier echo, at 48.5 cps, so the verse (**A**) begins (at 0:06) with a slightly fast vocal, then blends both speeds (**A**+14, 0:24), and then the transition (**B**, at 0:32) has only the helium-light higher-speed vocal; both tracks are heard in the chorus. In comparison to the stereo mix (done April 1), the mono mix (March 3) has more ADT and compression and is heard a halfstep lower, all adding to the "phasing effect."

"Lucy"'s tonal structure strays from norms, just as her lyrics and colors do. The song modulates from A (**A**) through B♭ (**B**) to G (**C**), but the graph in ex-

Example 2.2 Analysis of "Lucy in the Sky with Diamonds."

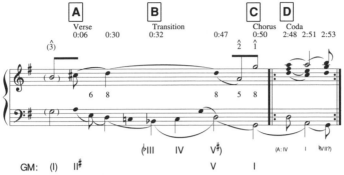

ample 2.2 suggests how rehearsal letters **A**, **B**, and **C** can be heard overall as an incomplete progression, II♯–V–I in G. In this verse-transition-chorus combination, structural counterpoint, particularly with the solid octaves established at V and I, unifies the tonal scheme. The bass B♭ might seem to weaken the sense of G major, but the B♭ leads to the prolongation of a mixture-based progression, ♭III–IV–V, thus an expanded version of a cadence from "Please Please Me." So through the verse, transition, and chorus, counterpoint and harmony seem to cooperate at deep levels to unify the superficially unrelated keys of A, B♭, and G. We then can hear the retransition to the second verse in the last three bars of **C** (1:00–1:08) from G major, through key centers D to A, in the context of G major, even though the singers and organ articulate a sustained choral plagal cadence settling on A.

In the repeated coda, however, we understand that we must have slipped down the rabbit's hole and entered the progressive-tonality world of "Doctor Robert" and "Penny Lane." Here, the retransition's plagal cadence takes on greater significance, and A major sounds more like tonic than it does II♯ by virtue of the double-plagal cadence that has G resolving to D, which in turn resolves to A. So while the voice leading continues to make sense, the coda's chordal roots are intertwined as on a Möbius strip, with resolution on neither G nor A possible. The tonal distinction between the G-major chorus and its A-major environs is amplified in a subtle yet powerful way by the metric modulation that allows the verse's triple meter to melt into the chorus's quadruple without disruption, and vice versa.[38]

Despite the novel musical effects in "Lucy in the Sky with Diamonds," it was the otherworldly lyrics that seem to have most caught the imagination of other pop musicians, as suggested by the derivative texts of "Judy in Disguise (with Glasses)" (John Fred and His Playboy Band, November 1967), "Jelly Jungle (of Orange Marmalade)" (the Lemon Pipers, May 1968), "Let There Be More Light" (Pink Floyd, July 1968), and "Jelly Covered Cloud" (the Scaffold, 1969).

"Getting Better"

In the first week of March, the weather's improvement reminded McCartney of one source of amusement the Beatles had found in the summer of 1964. During a tour that year, a drummer named Jimmy Nicol replaced Ringo during a brief illness. Asked by the press every day as to his progress, Nicol always replied, "It's getting better." Lennon and McCartney began their song "Getting Better" in Cavendish Avenue and on March 9 took it to the studios, where composing continued.[39] We have a few notes on the composers' thoughts on the lyrics: McCartney has described Lennon's throwaway line "It can't get no worse" as "very good. Against the spirit of that song, which was all super-optimistic — then there's that lovely little sardonic line. Typical John."[40] Lennon discloses an ugly past in the second bridge (**F**), wherein he confesses cruelties to women, having since changed his ways.[41]

Judging by the final product (Lewisohn 1988 and Martin 1994 do not quite agree on the song's recording history), recording began on March 9, perhaps with Lennon's Capri ("Guitar II," which boogies in the verse, **A**) and Ringo's drums (heavy with hi-hat) on Track 1 and George Martin's pianette ("E. Piano") on Track 2. The pianette was an amplified piano, described by Martin as "a cross between a harpsichord and a Fender Rhodes," that had been left in the studio from an earlier session.[42] The next day, Ringo dubbed more drums on Track 3 and McCartney played bass on Track 4. Tracks 1 and 2 were mixed to a new Track 1, and Tracks 3 and 4 to a new Track 2. Martin played the strings of the pianette with mallets (mislabeled "Guitar I" and, at **C**, "E. Piano") for Track 3, and Harrison added a tamboura (mislabeled "Sitar") to Track 4 for the second bridge (**F**). A third generation of tape was created on March 21, with the most recent Tracks 1 and 4 mixed to a new Track 1 (heard left), Track 3 remaining independent (heard right except for 0:11–0:24, when it is heard left), and Track 2 simultaneously dubbed with McCartney's lead vocal (heard center). On March 23, a new Track 4 was given a doubled McCartney lead vocal and backing vocals by Lennon and Harrison (center).[43] A further mixdown made room for Ringo's bongos (heard right). Mono mixes were made on March 23, and a single stereo mix on April 17.

"Getting Better" is the LP's first track with no harmonic innovations; *Revolver* is recalled as the chorus, **B**, transposes I–II–III–IV from "Here, There and Everywhere," while the overlapping vocals recall "Good Day Sunshine." The bass, however, is unusually adventurous in accenting nonroots on downbeats, and nonchord tones are emphasized by both the IV^9 chord in the introduction, in Martin's octaves against Lennon's guitar, and the tag to the chorus (vocals at **E+4**). The tempo and shuffle rhythm, if not the guitar part at **A**, might be heard as a precursor to the single version of "Revolution" (1968).

"Fixing a Hole"

Inspired by repairs he'd had to make to his Scottish farmhouse (says Beatles aide Alistair Taylor) and perhaps by the line "a hole in the roof where the rain leaks in" that he had sung in Presley's "We're Gonna Move," McCartney wrote "Fixing a Hole," the bridge of which (**B**) also refers to fans outside his St. John's Wood door.[44] The lyric is vague, but Wilfrid Mellers hears some universal meaning; he finds it a "subtly mysterious little song about the nature of identity. He's fixing the holes, papering over the cracks, in the shell that protects him in order that his mind may 'wander where it will go': so what looks like imprisonment is really freedom."[45] In Miles 1997 (314–5), McCartney attributes his inspiration for the song to a wish to letting his mind wander freely.

This song has one of the simplest arrangements on the LP. The basic track, cut on February 9 at Regent Sound Studios (as EMI was booked up), has Ringo's drums, McCartney's bass, and Martin's harpsichord (the voice leading of which comes untransposed from the intro to "Michelle") on Track 1 (heard left), and Harrison's sometimes double-stopped distorted Strat guitar (gain, treble, and bass controls all turned up very high, according to George Martin) on Track 2 (right).[46] These were then augmented by McCartney's lead vocal with echo on Track 3 (center) and backing vocals by McCartney, Lennon, and Harrison on Track 4 (right). On February 21, this tape was reduced to allow McCartney to double-track his lead vocal for the bridges and refrain ("where it will go," "there I will go," once — at 0:34 — masking a previous raw edge; center). The song was mixed for mono the same day and for stereo on April 7; as with the end of "Got to Get You into My Life," the mono mix retains a few seconds of vocal scatting faded out of the stereo.

The song's melody in the verse-refrain (**A**) is based in the F-pentatonic-minor scale, supported in the bass by simple arpeggiations of F minor, in support of primary tone $\flat\hat{3}$. Passing Dorian touches of G, however, prefigure the emphasis that this pitch class will attain as the stubbornly unchanging structural upper-voice $\hat{2}$ in the major-mode bridge's retransition (**B**+5–8, 0:50–0:58). The same [025] collection emphasized in the bridge of "Michelle," $f^2-e\flat^2-c^2$, is featured here in the pentatonic verse. Tim Riley reads the singer's changing attitude in the changes of mode: "The indecisive major-minor intro to 'Fixing a Hole' maps out its harmonic symbolism: the first part of each verse begins in major and slips quickly into minor, as Paul sings of how repairing leaks sets his thoughts spinning. In the second part of each verse, on the words 'And it really doesn't matter if I'm wrong [I'm] right,' the harmony shifts back to major, and a new outlook shines through: satisfaction, self-assurance, and positivism."[47] The coda fulfills the simple $\flat\hat{3}-\hat{2}-\hat{1}$ descent in a Dorian context.

"She's Leaving Home"

The Beatles' identification with youth was at a peak in 1967.[48] This was evident not only in their new growth of facial hair and donning of psychedelic clothes and flowers — all outward appearances of the hippie counterculture — but also in their criticism of the lack of understanding between disagreeing peoples, including those on the opposite sides of the "generation gap." Nowhere is this concern more apparent than in McCartney's "She's Leaving Home."

McCartney has written an unusually descriptive narration for "She's Leaving Home," which was inspired by a *Daily Mail* story on teenage runaways.[49] In less than three and a half minutes, the song provides vivid characterizations of a lonely girl who runs away from her selfish yet well-meaning parents in order to meet, and possibly elope with, a man. The first verse (**A-B**) portrays the protagonist, who seems lonelier in her namelessness, as a quiet ("silently," "quietly") though troubled girl. Her inability to express her inner tensions is apparent both in the incomplete note "that she hoped would say more," which she leaves her parents, and in the way she stifles her crying. Her crying can be inferred from "clutching her handkerchief"; or possibly she is both crying and sneezing, as suggested by the rhythmic play of assonant onomatopoeia in "*Kitch*en *Clutch*ing her hand*k*er*ch*ief." In the second verse (**D-E**), the girl's quiet is contrasted with her parents' self-indulgent noisiness ("snores," "breaks down and cries"). The girl ends up having her first uninhibited "fun" in the third and final verse (**G**) as she keeps a tryst with a man, a car salesman who is probably as freely active and noisy as she would like to be.

The three choruses (**C**, **F**, and **H**) are set antiphonally, separating the narration from the parents' questioning of the daughter's motivation for leaving. The narration is heard in McCartney's double-tracked unison falsetto lead vocals, and the parents are portrayed in Lennon's double-tracked unison full-voice backing vocals. The puns in the choruses on the homonyms "buy" and "by" with the answering "bye, bye" reflect the stimulus-response relationship of the parents' selfishness and the daughter's leaving. For example, the parents wail in the first chorus, "We gave her everything money could buy," which they must follow with "Bye, bye"; in the second chorus, the parents plead, "We struggled hard all our lives to get by" . . . "Bye, bye." Further characterization exists in the repetitions of the choruses' first phrases, which mimic a stereotypical parents' harping: "We gave her most of our lives; sacrificed most of our lives," and "We never thought of ourselves; never a thought for ourselves."[50] The song's ultimate sadness is presented in the third chorus, in the parents' overdue understanding of the fact that they cannot buy their daughter's happiness.

As in previous songs of loneliness, "Eleanor Rigby" and "For No One," "She's Leaving Home" includes instrumental parts played by non-Beatles. The accompaniment is scored for harp and string nonet (four violins, two violas, two celli, and string bass). The original score was prepared by Decca's producer/arranger Mike Leander, whom Paul had met when Marianne Faithfull recorded "Yesterday," and it was recorded on March 20 by Martin, who adjusted some of Leander's rhythms slightly.[51] Other technical oddities are the edits in the string parts at **D** and **G** and the fact that the sped-up British mono release is the only one to include the piece in F; all other releases are in E major.

The string arrangement is closely related to the meaning of the text. Descent in the line "she goes downstairs" is pictured by the introduction of the string bass (0:28) and by the descending scale in the violins at **B**+6−8 (0:35−0:39, added to the cello's statement first heard in **A**+6−8). The mother's distress ("Daddy, our baby's gone") is signaled by the upper strings' Morse code−like rhythmic pattern on a single pitch at **E**+5−7 (1:46−1:51). The relatively high register of this passage depicts the tone of the mother's cry, as well as the fact that she is standing "at the top of the stairs." The daughter's "thoughtless" behavior, referred to by the mother, is suggested by the carefree waltzlike accent pattern in the bass (**F**–1–4, 1:58–2:03). The string trills at **G**+9–11 (2:42–2:46) reveal the girl's tension as she is "waiting" for her appointment, and the perfectly regular articulation of repeated pitches in the strings (**G**+13–16, 2:48–2:53) portrays the "motor trade." The parents recognize their misguided approach at the culmination of an arpeggio (**H**+1–12, resolving to the vocal c♯2 in **H**+13) ascending to the first violins' highest pitches (3:07–3:10). In this passage the Mixolydian d♮2 (**H**+5–6, emphasized by the violins' glissando), which functions as an unorthodox ♭7̂, seems to signify what was "wrong," the cliché that "fun is the one thing that money can't buy"; the listener may recall the strong D♮ in the bass at **C**+11–12 (1:05–1:07, not shown in the Wise score) at the first mention of the parents' "wrong," materialistic values. The "wrong" passing D♮, when transferred from the bass region to the violins in **H**+5 (2:59–3:01) as the parents, at the first realization of their error, claim "We didn't know it was wrong," suggests that the error of their ways can enter the parents' higher levels of consciousness only when the ungrammatical pitch-class D♮ has risen to the strings' higher register.

Distance between the daughter and her home and parents is the central theme, both in the distance caused by their inabilities to communicate (the "generation gap") and in the physical distance caused by the girl's leaving home. This distance is heard, most abstractly yet most significantly, in the distance between the song's basic tonal structures and its surface of knotty intricacies. The girl's increasing distance from home, for example, is symbolized in the methodical addition of pandiatonic voices against a three-bar phrase first appearing in the cello as the girl gets farther from home. The original phrase (**A**+6–8, 0:12–0:16) is heard as the girl is still in her bedroom; when she goes downstairs (**B**+6–8, 0:35–0:39), the cello line is blurred somewhat by its odd contrapuntal relation—particularly the parallel ninths in **B**+8—with the added line in the violins. As if to assure the listener of the correlation between the ideas of distance and the treatment of the cello passage, the parents' still being in their bedroom is represented by the return of the single cello line in the second verse (**D**+6–8, 1:25–1:29); however, the last appearance of the passage, when the girl "is far away" (**G**+6–8, 2:38–2:42), is completely disguised by the addition of two inner voices to the counterpoint heard after **B**; the result is a pandiatonic stream of nonfunctional triads, seventh, and ninth sonorities, all prolonging the bass C♯. Irony abounds as McCartney, Lennon, Leander, and Martin do their best to portray a tearful distance between generations, while bringing together a chamber-music setting for a turn-of-the-century Edwardian domestic drama on an LP that was to become a primary symbol of the world's youth movement.

"Being for the Benefit of Mr. Kite"

Lennon's lyrics for "Tomorrow Never Knows" were based on a few phrases from Timothy Leary, but nearly the entire lyrics for "Being for the Benefit for Mr.

Kite," including the quaint Victorian-era title, were, as Lennon says, "a straight lift" from a poster advertising a circus in Rochdale in 1843 that the composer found in an antique shop while shooting the "Strawberry Fields Forever"/ "Penny Lane" promotional clips in Kent.[52] This lazy-cum-objet-trouvé approach to composition was to further infect the work of the Beatles, particularly Lennon's. The Victorian circus tune ends the LP's first side with a strong connection to the Edwardian imagery of the opening track.

In beginning the arrangement, Lennon had told Martin that he wanted "to smell the sawdust."[53] The incredibly involved recording procedure certainly brought the text's circus atmosphere to life. The song's basic track was laid down on February 17, with McCartney's bass on Track 1, Lennon's guide vocal on Track 2, Ringo's drums (with damped hi-hat for a marching cymbal effect in the verses and a snare roll for the first ending's retransition) on Track 3, and Martin's harmonium on Track 4.[54] A reduction brought bass and harmonium to a new Track 1 (left) and drums to Track 2 (center). Lennon recorded two lead vocals — mostly in unison, but in harmony for the dramatic conclusion to each verse — at 49 cps on Tracks 3 and 4, compressed and given some echo for verse conclusions during mixing (both heard right).[55] On February 28, the introduction and retransition were fortified by different-sized harmonicas played by Harrison, Starr, Neil Aspinall, and Mal Evans (the last on bass harmonica) while Lennon doubled the tune on Hammond and Martin banged away on the retransitional dominant on a piano. This was dropped into Track 4 (heard right).[56] The composer decided that he wanted the waltz (**B**) to "swirl up and around."[57] So the next day, drop-ins were inserted into Tracks 3 and 4. Track 3 is heard on the right; to this, Martin added chromatic runs on the Hammond while Lennon "tooted" some chords on the Lowrey and McCartney played an electronically modified acoustic guitar solo for the waltz. This was all taped at half-speed, allowing for super-fast mechanical runs, the articulation of which is sharply clipped. Track 4 is heard on the left during the waltz and is wild in the coda; to this was added an effects tape of some nineteen snippets of steam organ march excerpts compiled by Martin and assembled by Geoff Emerick on February 20, providing an unrecognizable wash of circus calliopes.[58] Finally, on March 31, bits of an organ and shaker bells were dropped into Ringo's drum track for the waltz; mixes were completed on this day (mono) and on April 7 (stereo).

But the track's superficial effects do not account for all of the musical fantasy; larger-scale swirling is created by novel harmonic relationships. Tonalities of C minor, D minor, and E minor, indicated in example 2.3, are each supported by traditional tonal means but do not relate to each other in a coherent way. D minor abandons its role as tonicized II of C, as it did briefly in the introduction, to declare itself a new full-fledged tonal center (as at **A**+7, 0:22), and the process is repeated a step higher in the waltz (**B**) and coda, moving from D minor to E minor each time. Retransitional fanfares on the dominant (as at 0:36) twice bring the piece back to C minor, but the coda trails off in E minor. Neither C, D, nor E can claim traditional authority as a single tonal center, especially with the same melodic/harmonic material appearing in each key.

Example 2.3 Analysis of "Being for the Benefit of Mr. Kite."

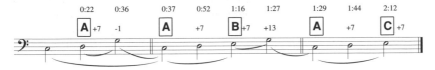

Rather, the three centers can be heard as the rings of a circus, with action taking place in all arenas and no particular object of attention the "correct" one. Martin takes and deserves much credit for the song's effect, but this barrel-of-monkeys structural innovation is certainly Lennon's own and is one closely related to a similar effect achieved in the following year in his tonally slithery "Sexy Sadie."

"Within You Without You"

Harrison had written, and the Beatles had recorded, "Only a Northern Song" for *Sgt. Pepper*. Martin recalled: "I groaned inside when I heard it. We did make a recording of it on 14 February, but I knew it was never going to make it.... I suggested he come up with something a bit better."[59] Harrison returned with "Within You Without You," which Lennon calls "one of George's best songs."[60] This is the first product of Harrison's studies of sitar, meditation, and Hindu beliefs, and the tune was written on a harmonium at friend Klaus Voorman's house in Hampstead, with words based on dinner conversation that evening.[61] "Harrison's lyrics draw heavily on traditional Hindu concepts. There is the suggestion of a deeper reality behind the illusion (*maya*) of ordinary tangible existence ('We were talking about the space between us all, And the people—who hide themselves behind a wall of illusion, never glimpse the truth . . .'). There is an affirmation of (divine?) love, *bhakti*: ('. . . with our love—we could save the world;') and of the existence of the infinite reality (God, *atma, brahman*) within the individual ('Try to realize it's all within yourself; . . . life flows on within you and without you')."[62]

The relatively simple recording began on March 15, with members of the Eastern Music Circle of Finchley, London.[63] Track 1 consisted of three tambouras, two played by Harrison and Neil Aspinall, Track 2 of tabla and svaramandal, and Track 4 of a bowed dilruba playing the melody at 52.5 cps. On March 22, another dilruba doubled the first (after **A**) on Track 3, and a tape reduction took the dilrubas to a new Track 2 (heard right) and the other instruments to Track 1 (left). Recording was completed on April 3: Martin's score for eight violins and three celli, attempting to imitate the slides and bends of the dilrubas, at Martin's direction, was played on Track 3 (center, entering for the last two bars of the first ending), and Harrison's lead vocal, also replete with slides, sitar, and (at 3:31) svaramandal, was added to Track 4 (center).[64] Mono and stereo mixing, adding ADT to the vocal, but in mono not until after the first verse, was done on April 4, and both masters required editing (surrounding **C**, at 2:23 and 3:41) from a length of 6'25". Harrison asked to have some laughter added to the end of the track as a deflatory foil; this was found in the sound effects archives and added to the right channel but does little other than create incongruity, and it is certainly unnecessary, as the following witty yet empty song would have accomplished the desired purpose. The composer is the only Beatle heard on the track.[65]

While pitch material adheres to the *Khamaj thata*, equivalent to the Mixolydian mode, and certain *pakad*-like motives—particularly the opening tritone-defining E–F–G–B♭—acquire prominence, no specific raga is followed.[66] Harrison says, "I was continually playing Indian [exercises] called Sargams, which are the bases of the different Ragas. That's why around this time I couldn't help writing tunes like this which were based upon unusual scales."[67] Still, the upper tetrachord is altered (introducing e♭2 at **B**–6–8) to reflect motivic unity, transposing the [025] collection, E-B♭-C, to C-E♭-F, in accord with Hindustani practice.[68]

As in "Love You To," "Within You Without You" has a Hindustani-like form, proceeding from an unmeasured *alap*-like introduction on tambouras (0:00–0:04), a statement of motivic material within the bounds of an octave on a solo melody instrument (dilruba, beginning at 0:04), and the announcement of the pentatonic portion of the scale on svaramandal (0:19–0:23). The tabla set the tempo (the *jhala*, at 0:23) before the verse (*gat*) begins (**A**) with a contextualization of the introductory motive. The first chorus (**B**, signaled by the tabla's characteristically flurried cadence at 1:57–1:58) is followed by an improvisatory passage (**C**) in $\frac{5}{8}$ (♩♩ ♫♩ ♩♩ ♫♩, the *jhaptal tala*).[69] This metrically alive section has the sitar alternately imitating or doubling the solo dilruba, punctuated by Martin's pizzicato score, that comes to rest with the *tihai*, a thrice-heard cadential pattern (ending on the fermata, **C**+27–28, beginning at 3:24).[70] Another free *alap* then brings in the final hearing of the *gat* above the composer's earnest counting. The seriousness of musical purpose gives this track much more weight than the gospel-sermon "The Word."[71]

"When I'm Sixty-Four"

Beginning life c. 1957–58 as an instrumental number, McCartney's "When I'm Sixty-Four" returned to its composer's consciousness around the time of his dad's sixty-fourth birthday, in July 1966, and took final form by that September, perhaps coincidentally the month that the music-hall style was revived by the New Vaudeville Band's "Winchester Cathedral."[72] It was likely in the studio that Lennon made his contribution, naming the grandchildren Vera, Chuck, and Dave.[73]

"When I'm Sixty-Four" is the earliest recording to make the LP. In the atmosphere of childhood-oriented "Strawberry Fields Forever" and "Penny Lane," the basic track was recorded on December 6, 1966, with McCartney's tubalike oom-pah bass and Ringo's brushed snare, bass drum, and cymbal on Track 1. That day's overdubs included McCartney's spare piano on Track 2, more brushwork on Track 3 (wiping the guide vocal), and (for the last verse, **C**)

Lennon's distorted Casino on Track 4. Two days later, these were all mixed to a new Track 1 (heard center), and McCartney taped his lead vocal on Track 4 (left). The Beatles made their final contributions on December 20, with Track 3 filled by McCartney/Lennon/Harrison backing vocals (right) and Ringo's tubular bells. The bells suggest an angelic approval of the singer's petition when heard at left at 0:57, and at 1:53—where their syncopation follows McCartney's homey brogue—they suggest the young ones bouncing on Grandma's knee. Track 2 (right) was reserved for the December 21 taping of Martin's score of two clarinets, the first providing a nifty alto countermelody for the third verse, and bass clarinet, doubling the bass guitar for the retransitional arpeggiation of V⁷ at **C**–1–2. The mono mix was perfected on December 30, the stereo on April 16, 1967; all mixes were sped up from C to D♭, as the composer wished to carry a youthful air.[74]

Rightly recognized by Tim Riley as "the McCartney side of Elvis's corny hokum," this penchant for the audience-charming vaudeville sketch led to McCartney's preferences that Lennon detested the most.[75] The style, reflected by Fred Astaire's prominent picture on the cover, calls for the album's most extensive use of applied dominants, which appear in the refrain (**B**–2–3) and in a tonicization of VI in the bridge (**B**), and the wide array of jaunty chromatic neighbors and passing tones comparable to those in McCartney's dad's "Walking in the Park with Eloise." While the senior-citizen age of the protagonist of "When I'm Sixty-Four" has been connected to the album's "Lonely Hearts Club" banner, this song—the first to be recorded for the LP—has little in common with the album's remainder.

"Lovely Rita"

"Lovely Rita" was another McCartney composition that his partner later said he disliked because the subject revealed no personal experience but instead was an invented story about a "third party."[76] This party was one Meta Davis, a traffic warden who'd issued McCartney a parking ticket and whom the composer remade into a lovable yet military woman (perhaps a Sergeant?) while he was "bopping about on the piano at Liverpool."[77]

Recording of "Lovely Rita" began with a now rare live instrumental performance by all four on February 23, with Harrison's and Lennon's acoustic guitars—the Jumbos now have their pickups below the soundhole for more of a treble sound—on Tracks 1 and 2 respectively, Ringo's drums on Track 3, and McCartney's echo-laden piano on Track 4. These tracks were bounced down to a new Track 1 (heard left), and McCartney dubbed a bass part onto a second track (center).[78] The next day, a third track was given McCartney's lead vocal (taped about a semitone low to sound sped-up, center), and Track 4, taped March 7, features three-part backing vocals aided at times by metal-comb-and-tissue-paper and effects such as the pop of the wine bottle "over dinner" at 1:27 (right).[79] On March 21, the day Lennon was unable to record vocals for "Getting Better," Martin used the booked studio time to drop a barrelhouse piano solo (**E**) into Track 4, recorded a whole step slow and re-

Example 2.4 Kellogg's jingle.

The seven recording/mixing sessions for "Good Morning" were nearly all
ceiving a high-frequency sheen of organlike wow from a sticky piece of editing tape on the capstan of the tape echo machine.[80] Mixing was completed on
March 21 (for mono) and April 17 (stereo); an extensive piano introduction
disappeared during mixing, but the long aimless coda remains. (Lennon's "un-
dermining" of McCartney's song in the coda is a topic of interesting remarks
in Moore 1997, 49.)

"Lovely Rita" repeats the double-plagal cadence from "With a Little Help
from My Friends" in the verse (**B**+1, 0:23–0:25) and in the introduction
(where the cadential vocal d[2] is missing from the score) and chorus (**A**, tonicizing the dominant), and the track also maintains harmonic interest in its deep
descent by sequential fifths into the flat side, I–IV–♭VII–♭III (**C**+1–2,
0:33–0:38) before finding the dominant a bar later. As for formal relations, the
verse's *abba* phrase relationship (**B–D**) is not seen elsewhere in the Beatles'
work. Perhaps the song's most attractive feature is the soaring phrase of arch-
shaped backing vocals at 0:55–1:09.

"Good Morning Good Morning"

Resignation in the face of frustrating misunderstanding had been a central
theme of "Strawberry Fields Forever" and "I Want to Tell You," but the acqui-
escence of "Good Morning Good Morning" reflects only the composer's televi-
sion-accompanied ennui. While writing at the piano, Lennon's ear was caught
by a Kellogg's Corn Flakes jingle (excerpted here in ex. 2.4) blaring from a television in the background.[81] This was adapted for the song's refrain. Example
2.5 presents part of an early draft of the resulting song, probably dating from
late January or the first week of February. By the time of this recording, the
lyrics and melody of the first two verses (**B–C**) and bridge (**D**) are as finished,
but—in addition to a transposition up a major third—there were still major
metric adjustments and minor harmonic changes to follow.

The seven recording/mixing sessions for "Good Morning" were nearly all
more than a week apart from each other. The basic track was taped on February 8; Ringo's drums, with coda fills like those in "Strawberry Fields Forever,"
and Harrison's Casino rhythm part were on separate tracks. The other two
tracks were not filled until February 16, when McCartney recorded his bass and
Lennon his lead vocal.[82] A reduction to two tracks separated the instruments
from the vocal. Martin scored parts suggested by Lennon (on guitar) for members of Sounds Inc., including two tenor saxes, baritone sax, two trombones,
and French horn; these, largely a single line in unison or octaves, often func-

Example 2.5 "Good Morning Good Morning" compositional draft (Lennon-McCartney). © 1967 Northern Songs.

tioning as the bass line, were taped with mikes down the bells on their own track on March 13.[83] On February 28, Lennon added to Track 4 a vocal harmony part for the second bridge (**F**) and last verse (**G**), containing some harsh harmonic intervals against the first vocal that point the way to "Cold Turkey." A second reduction put the Beatles' instruments on Track 1 (left), Sounds Inc. on Track 2 (right, with ADT—"anything to make it sound unlike brass playing," recalls one tape operator), and the signals from both of Lennon's vocal tracks sent equally to both (now heard center), with all signals heavily compressed.[84] The new Track 3 was filled the same day with Lennon/McCartney backing vocals and handclaps and McCartney's searing Indian-ornamented distorted Esquire with vibrato $\hat{1}$ in the introduction (heard right) and solo, **E–G** (center, with ADT). Track 4 was given a series of animal effects (center for the Kellogg's cock in the opening, then wild—especially for the foxhunt—during the coda) on March 28 and 29. Based on an idea of Lennon's, the animals (cock, birds, cat, dogs, horses, sheep, tigers, elephant, foxhunt, and chickens, all sounds borrowed from the EMI archives; a sea lion was also considered but rejected) were taped in an order that attempted to have each successive animal capable of frightening or devouring its predecessor.[85] The complex mixes, requiring crossfading through the effects track into the following song, were made on April 6 and 19. Serendipitously, a chicken was unintentionally imitated by Harrison's clucking descending fourth on raucous lead guitar.[86]

Several writers have praised the song's shifting meters (well notated in the score—in the verse, 0:11–0:33—as three bars of $\frac{5}{4}$ followed by single bars of $\frac{3}{4}, \frac{4}{4}, \frac{5}{4}$, two of $\frac{3}{4}$ and two of $\frac{4}{4}$) as "unforced" expression of "natural speech rhythms."[87] They may sound unforced, but comparison of the tape draft excerpted in example 2.5 with the finished recording shows that Lennon's final choices of irregularly related accents were probably the result of a good bit of industry. Another writer says, "The verse is metrically flexible to a degree never before encountered in the Beatles' music, [having] an unusually disruptive effect on the momentum which is compounded by the extraordinary harmonic rhythm. The opening two measures of $\frac{5}{4}$ meter, for example, exhibit an alternation of I and ♭VII chords in the following pattern: I (three beats) – ♭VII (five) – I (two; the last of which is replaced by cymbal and bass drum)."[88] It is this disruption of the norm — borrowing the Mixolydian progression from the opening complaint of "A Hard Day's Night" — that perfectly expresses Lennon's grievance against complacency.[89]

"Sgt. Pepper's Lonely Hearts Club Band (Reprise)"

It was Neil Aspinall's idea to close the LP with a reprise of the title song, but McCartney is truly himself playing the audience with his stage patter, expressed elsewhere as "and we all hope that you've enjoyed the show — have you enjoyed the show?," and with the energy-intensifying truck-driver's modulation from F major to G (at 0:40 – 0:44).[90] The Beatles met in the great Studio One on April 1, just before McCartney left the country, to record the song as follows: Harrison's Casino, Lennon's Hammond, McCartney's bass (Track 1), and Starr's drums (Track 4) all performed live (center). Vocals were overdubbed with McCartney, Starr, and tambourine on Track 2 (left) and Lennon and Harrison on Track 3 (right).[91] The mono mix was completed the same day, while the stereo was delayed until April 20; both mixes incorporate audience reactions from the EMI tape library. The truck-driver's modulation, unknown in other Beatles tracks although related to the progressive tonal scheme of "Mr. Kite," allows the Reprise to introduce the G-major tonality of the LP's following, final composition.

"A Day in the Life"

As is the case with both *Revolver* and the White album, the most monumental piece on *Sgt. Pepper's Lonely Hearts Club Band* was Lennon's and was the first to be recorded. Its weight is measured by its length (at 5'03", a balance to "Within You Without You"); its profound use of orchestra, piano, and drums; its thought-provoking contrast of sections; Lennon's precise yet echo-laden enunciation of his lyrics; but most of all by its mysterious and poetic approach to serious topics that come together in a larger, direct message to its listeners, an embodiment of the central ideal for which the Beatles stood: that a truly meaningful life can be had only when one is aware of one's self and one's surroundings and overcomes the status quo. "A Day in the Life" represents the Beatles' wake-up call for whomever might be listening. The song is not merely a warning of an ashy apocalypse, as it has often been taken, but suggests that there is yet hope for the phoenix.

The song took shape on December 19, 1966, at Weybridge as Lennon played piano with the *Daily Mail* propped on the rack, and inspiration for a first verse (**A–B**) came from the day's lead story about the senseless death of a wealthy young friend of the Beatles who'd sped his Lotus into a parked van.[92] Lennon's reaction to the death, a laugh, provokes an air of emotional detachment that determines the song's dark affect. A second item about potholes in Blackburn, Lancashire, caught his attention on January 17 and became the basis for the enigmatic final verse (**G**).[93] Drawn to the holes, Lennon says, "There was still one word missing in that verse when we came to record. I knew the line had to go 'Now they know how many holes it takes to fill the Albert Hall.' It was a nonsense verse really, but for some reason I couldn't think of the verb. What did the holes do to the Albert Hall? It was Terry [Doran] who said 'fill' the Albert Hall."[94] The second verse (**C**) refers obliquely to John's current film project, *How I Won the War*. Three major factors render these passages aimless and thus as emotionally void as Lennon's alien echoing tone: (1) they are free-flowing without clear rhythmic goals (bars number 10+9 in the phrases of the first verse, and 22 for the other verses with transitions); (2) voice leading progresses nowhere as the vocal alternates an [025] collection (b^1–d^2–e^2) with a similar grouping a third lower; and (3) the key of G is often undermined by Mixolydian touches, and cadences are avoided as the dominant (perhaps the fleeting last ♪ before **B**?) is always slighted.

In Cavendish Avenue, John played his verses to Paul, who offered as a bridge (**D–E**) an independently written song fragment, a vaudeville number related to a Dorothy Fields song from 1930 ("Grab your coat and get your hat" is the opening line of "On the Sunny Side of the Street").[95] As in the verses, the vocal melody here seems to prolong b^1 but is not led anywhere by an authentic cadence, instead carried by strong Mixolydian moments that stretch the meter from the equivalent of two bars of $\frac{2}{4}$ to a disheveled three. McCartney's ditty — a remembrance of his catching the bus for school and climbing to the top for a ciggy, an early "Penny Lane" castoff?— grows in stature between Lennon's verses. Given the combination, one hears a commentary on the dismal "Good Morning Good Morning" sort of meaninglessness of daily life and the possibility that "a smoke" could lead to a dream, here the intangibly wordless retransition (**F**), far above the waking nightmare of mundane existence.[96] Realizing that the "smoke" might be interpreted as a reference to marijuana, the composers decided to go all out and proselytize for pot.[97] Lennon: "Paul's contribution was the beautiful little lick in the song, 'I'd love to turn you on,' that he'd had floating around in his head and couldn't use. I thought it was a damn good piece of work"; McCartney: "This was the only one in the album written as a deliberate provocation. . . . But what we want is to turn you on to the truth rather than pot."[98] Martin has a practical interpretation of the wordless "dream" at **F**: "The vocal wailings . . . definitely contributed to its reception as a 'marijuana dream.' To us, though, those vocals were no more than an inventive way of getting back to the original key!"[99] This dreamy, hopeful retransition repeats the "P.S. I Love You" cadence—♭**VI**–♭**VII**–**I**: C–D–E in five bars, **F**+1–5, repeated, 2:49–3:14—from the opening and close of "With a Little Help from My Friends," now expanded by a sequence involving the double-plagal cadence taken from the same song, but coming from two extra steps from the flat side: ♭**VI**–♭**III**–♭**VII**–**IV**–**I**: *C*–*G*–*D*–*A*–*E*. This (quadriplagal?) pro-

Example 2.6 "A Day in the Life" full-score realization (Lennon-McCartney). © 1967
Northern Songs.

(continued)

gression comes untransposed from Jimi Hendrix's first single, "Hey Joe," a favorite of McCartney's, released on December 23, 1966, and performed on "Top
of the Pops" on the night the Beatles recorded this track.[100]

At first it was unclear how to progress from Lennon's verse to McCartney's
bridge, but it was certain that a transition would be necessary, especially as the
key changes from G to E, so McCartney thought the song should be recorded
with twenty-four essentially empty bars (twelve, as measured in the score) and
put aside until a solution presented itself.[101] George Martin has credited both
composers with the concept of booking a full orchestra to fill the gap; he says
McCartney wanted a "freak-out" and Lennon a "tremendous build-up, from
nothing up to something absolutely like the end of the world."[102] We must recall

Example 2.6 (*continued*)

Each instrument is to gliss in free 8th-note pulse ad libitum
Any coordination between parts is to be avoided

(*continued*)

that McCartney was then fascinated by the avant-garde, attending concerts of
music by Berio and by Stockhausen, whose pensive portrait graces the *Sgt. Pepper* cover. Martin scored string parts to imitate Lennon's slow-trill "turn you on"
refrain and also a ten-bar retransition (**F**) for violas and celli, then wrote out a
skeletal score for Penderecki-like aleatoric counterpoint that would have each
member of the orchestra begin pianissimo on lowest available note, rise poco a
poco with a few guide notes along the way, and conclude the fingered glissando
together fortissimo on the highest attainable member of an E-major triad; see a
re-creation of what would have been played in example 2.6.[103] It was decided
that this approach would serve as the song's conclusion as well as transition. The
progression from G to E is ultimately nonfunctional, and as in "Being for the

Example 2.6 (*continued*)

Benefit of Mr. Kite," neither tonal center can claim total authority. Transcendence, the orchestra's goal, is much more to the point than structural harmonic cohesion.[104]

The Recording Process   "A Day in the Life" received work over the course of eight sessions. The basic track was laid on January 19, two days after the "holes" story appeared in the paper. Take 4 from that day consisted of Lennon's Jumbo, McCartney's piano, Harrison's maracas, and Starr's bongos on Track 1, and Lennon's expressive vocal with heavy tape echo feeding back live, with Mal Evans's counting of the twenty-four filler bars, on Track 4.[105] As a joke, Evans set off an alarm clock at the end of the twenty-four bars (at 2:18) that could not be eradicated from future reductions.[106] Although preserved inadvertently, it was the perfect prelude to McCartney's "woke up" section, as neat and rousing a spot weld as the cluck/guitar that opens the LP's reprise. Track 2 received another echoing Lennon vocal, as did Track 3, on which McCartney also augmented the introductory piano chords; the Lennon vocals were simultaneous with each other only on the refrains.

On January 20, a reduction mix to Take 6 kept Track 1 as is and combined the other three as Track 2, on which McCartney added a vocal to the bridge.[107] Another Lennon vocal—he still had not added his vocal part to the dream sequence at **F**—and rough takes of McCartney's bass (entering at **A**+7) and Starr's drums (at **B**+2) completed the day's work.[108] A demo acetate of this tape was prepared on January 30; only the piano, the rough bass, and Evans's counting is heard during the "twenty-four" transitional bars; a declicked version is heard on Beatles 1991a. None of Take 6 survives in the finished product other than the new reduction of previous work. On February 3, Lennon and McCartney punched in new vocals for the bridge and retransition on Track 2 (and a good bit of cavorting can be heard in the background here), new bass and drum parts were added to Track 3, and McCartney added a bit more piano (at **B**+4, beats 3–4, and **C**–1, beats 3–4) to Track 4. The Beatles had finally completed their own performances for the body of the song, but there was still much to do.

The orchestral passages were taped on February 10, with all players in concert dress as per the wishes of McCartney, who also saw to it that costume hats, masks, paws, and so on were available for orchestra members and party guests who wished to wear them.[109] The festivities were recorded by seven cameras as part of a projected film of the album, with plans to prepare a different sequence for each song.[110] The forty-piece orchestra (winds 1/2/2/1/1; brass 2/3/3/1; percussion, harp, and strings 12/4/4/2) taped its glissando once on Track 4 and again on all four tracks of a second tape; these two tapes were then to be synchronized during mixing (with a sudden splice on the downbeat of **D**–2).[111] At this point, the recording ended on the downbeat of the final "twenty-fourth" bar, without a conclusion having been decided upon. McCartney proposed a chorus of long-sustained choral open fifths on E and B, perhaps reminiscent of the monks Lennon had imagined for "Tomorrow Never Knows"; this was attempted but proved unsatisfactory. On February 22, another edit piece for the ending was made with E-major triads articulated simultaneously on three pianos—dampers depressed—by McCartney, Lennon, Starr and Evans, and on harmonium by Martin. Emerick worked the faders to allow for a forty-five-second sustain; the sustain is almost necessary, as this chord must carry the entire weight of the LP "and the whole weight of *Sergeant Pepper* is a lot of weight."[112] The piece was edited to mono mixes done on February 13 and stereo ones of February 23, both crossfaded with applause from the reprise.[113] In the stereo mix, Track 1 (the basic instrumental track) remains left, Track 3 (bass and drums) and Track 4 (orchestra and a little piano) center, and Track 2 (vocals) pans wildly all over the spectrum. Tim Riley finds emotional content in the engineering: "During the last lines of the first verse, Lennon's voice moves slowly from the far right toward the center as the song becomes more aware of itself and the music gains intensity. . . . By the end of the verse Lennon's voice has travelled all the way over to the far left channel, and the journey of awestruck disbelief is complete."[114]

Given the album's stage-performance context, "A Day in the Life" might be considered an encore, but David Pichaske suggests that the song "is parenthetical, outside the performance context, a new perspective on all that has gone before."[115] The track seems to carry a more immediate message than can be made by a stage band, so the Beatles have stepped out of their costumes in order to better connect with the audience. The producer worried that the statement was pretentious: "One part of me said, 'We're being a bit self-indulgent, we're going a little bit over the top,' and the other part of me said, 'It's bloody marvelous!'"[116] Most critics have agreed with the latter sentiment.

The Concentric "Run-Out" Groove

The LP was not over before the surprise appearance of a bit of McCartney-suggested silliness. A 15 kHz signal led to the vinyl's repeating inner groove, normally tacet but here filled with a two-second tape of vocal gibberish (sounding like Lennon saying "been so high," answered by McCartney's "never could be any other way") captured on April 21.[117] The inner groove, which repeated as long as the record turned with the stylus engaged, was intended to be a mantra for those with manual turntables.[118] The Beatles gave the album, pressed without the normal rills between tracks and including a packed inner groove, their all.

Sgt. Pepper as a Whole

Despite the project's mass—Emerick found it took 700 hours to record the LP— a number of specific musical devices relate some songs to others, and mention has already been made of most. Sgt. Pepper is not quite the "concept album" that McCartney might have wished, but the song order results in a surprising structural coherence.[119] In fact, other musicians have been tempted to describe a large-scale harmonic/contrapuntal plan for the album as a whole. Its musical unity results not from these factors, however, but from motivic relationships between key areas, particularly involving C, E, and G. The album begins in G major ("Sgt. Pepper"), then segues into E ("With a Little Help") — not a harmonic relationship, but one that is replicated within the closing song ("A Day in the Life"). Each side ends with a song that begins elsewhere but closes in E. Side 2 begins in C ("Within You"), featuring the motive E–(F)–G in its various melodies, not unlike the C–D–E–C–D–E motive formed by the tonal areas in the closing song of Side 1 ("Mr. Kite"), which also refers to the C–D–E segue from the first into the second song. The key areas of the first three songs of Side 2, C ("Within You")–D♭ ("When I'm Sixty-Four")–E♭ ("Lovely Rita"), might be heard as an altered version of the same motive, and it has already been noted that the reprise changes key from F to G to prepare the final song in a manner that reflects the preparation of "With a Little Help." So there seem to be some motivic connections among the openings and closings of the two sides. Additionally, progressive tonality, a previous issue for the Beatles only recently, beginning with *Revolver*, is heard in "Lucy in the Sky," "Mr. Kite," and the reprise, while "With a Little Help," "Lucy in the Sky," and "Mr. Kite" begin in areas other than tonic. There is a strong sense that the album is greater than the sum of its parts, and it is worth noting that except for the "run-out" groove this was both the first Beatles LP to enjoy uniform worldwide release and the first American Beatles album on Capitol that—as per normal British practice—was not ransacked for a single.

Much of the album's intrigue is no doubt a debt to its packaging; before *Sgt. Pepper*, four-color treatment had not been common on the front of LP sleeves, let alone on the reverse or the inside of a gatefold sleeve. Printed lyrics were a first, and yet all of this was to become commonplace rapidly. Rather than depend on EMI's staid art department, the Beatles took over the cover and, through McCartney's friend Robert Fraser, hired a team of pop designers and photographers to break new ground. McCartney said he wanted the cover to depict Sgt. Pepper's band, so the Beatles are holding a French horn, trumpet, English horn, and piccolo (reminiscent of the Airplane's holding a French horn, soprano saxophone, violin, and recorder on *Surrealistic Pillow*, March 1967) on a park rostrum, surrounded by a park flower bed and their audience.[120] For the first pressing, the unique paper inner sleeve was of a graduated white, pink, and red motif designed by the Dutch trio the Fool, whose illustration for the gatefold was rejected as not to scale.[121] Brian Epstein, whose task it was to oversee the securing of scores of permissions for the cover photos, had second thoughts and wanted the whole cover scrapped, asking the Beatles in vain to issue the LP in a plain brown paper jacket.[122] The Beatles ignored this request, and George Martin also had a request denied when EMI did not see the point in listing his chief engineer, Geoff Emerick, in the sleeve credits.

Reception of *Pepper*

In the United Kingdom, *Sgt. Pepper's Lonely Hearts Club Band* (Parlophone PCM/PCS 7027) was rush-released six days ahead of its official date, June 1; it entered the charts at #1, where it stayed for twenty-two weeks. The album became the biggest-selling British LP of all time until the 1969 release of *Abbey Road*, selling 250,000 copies in its first week, 521,000 by August, and 1 million by April 1973. The American version (Capitol [S]MAS 2653) was released on June 2, held the #1 spot for 15 weeks, and charted for a full 175 weeks. Advance sales were over 1 million; American sales reached 2.5 million through August and eventually topped 8 million. By 1981, six years before the release of the compact disc, the album had sold more than 10 million copies worldwide.

The LP was mentioned in one song by Johnny Rivers ("Summer Rain," November 1967) and led to copycat LPs by the Stones (*Their Satanic Majesties Request*, December 1967) and the Small Faces (*Ogden's Nut Gone Flake*, June 1968), and a parody by the Mothers (*We're Only in It for the Money*, March 1968).[123] Covering the actual songs of *Sgt. Pepper* was more challenging to the pop world, although versions of "With a Little Help from My Friends," "When I'm Sixty-Four," and "She's Leaving Home" were released in the United Kingdom by other artists before June 1967 was half over.

Critics hear the LP as "a sort of pop music master class": "Gone are the frothy pitches to teen-aged libidos. They are trying hard to say important things. At times they are succeeding."[124] With some hyperbole, Timothy Leary, who must have heard himself in "Tomorrow Never Knows," calls the Beatles "the wisest, holiest, most effective avatars the human race has ever produced."[125] Allen Ginsberg declares, "After the apocalypse of Hitler and the apocalypse of the Bomb, there was here an exclamation of joy, the rediscovery of joy and what it is to be alive. . . . They showed an awareness that we make up our own fate, and they have decided to make a cheerful fate. They have decided to be generous to Lovely Rita, or to be generous to Sgt Pepper himself, turn him from an authority figure to a figure of comic humour, a vaudeville turn."[126]

When *Rolling Stone* magazine polled seventeen diverse critics in 1987 to rank the "100 Best Albums of the Last Twenty Years," *Sgt. Pepper's Lonely Hearts Club Band* was chosen the best of the best, with the justification that the album — fresh and inventive, artistically ambitious and yet "their funniest record ever" — revolutionized rock and roll.[127] Now at their high-water mark, the Beatles would never again have such an impact.

"All You Need Is Love"/"Baby You're a Rich Man" and Some Shelf-Sitters

"All You Need Is Love"

The Beatles were invited to represent England as one of fourteen countries contributing segments to the world's first live global satellite broadcast, called "Our World." They decided to be shown in the studio working on a new song. Specifically for the event, Lennon wrote "All You Need Is Love," which was his last composition to be chosen as an A-side for the next two years. Lennon has been criticized for the simple and naive nature of this sermon, but this message came not only from his flower-power convictions but also from a desire to be intelligible to the hundreds of millions of viewers across twenty-four countries who would receive the live feed.

The verse's mixed meters, an irregular but repeated alternation of $\frac{4}{4}$ and $\frac{3}{4}$ bars, show the composer's same impatience with empty upbeats that he demonstrated in "Good Morning Good Morning." The mixed meters have received attention elsewhere, but the powerful message of its voice leading has not. The vocal melody of the verse (**B**, introduced in **A** by the universally understood backing vocals only) is a simple $\hat{3}$-line that attempts to progress $\hat{3}$–$\hat{2}$–$\hat{1}$, as it does twice on the surface in **B**+1–2 (0:27–0:29) and **B**+3–4 (0:31–0:33). But the arrival of $\hat{1}$ is undercut each time by a pessimistic minor VI that signifies what can't be done, can't be made, or isn't known. The chords here alternate G–Em–G–Em, just as in "Not a Second Time"; the likeness to that early song is disguised here by the passing bass F$\sharp$, Lennon's current fancy, as heard many times in *Sgt. Pepper*. The retransition, prolonging $\hat{2}$ over V (at **C**–2–3, 0:40–0:43), provides a newly reassuring confidence—"It's easy"—and the simple chorus (**C**) easily completes the $\hat{3}$–$\hat{2}$–$\hat{1}$ descent with the powerful but simple truth "Love is all you need." The confident chorus works *through* the previously troubling VI in vaudeville style, passing from I through an applied V_3^4 to VI (**C**+5–6, 1:11–1:13), thereby encouraging the bass to continue its stepwise descent to a predominant IV. The bass descends below a hallowed trumpet line (1:11–1:18) that finds the way, in stepwise contrary motion, to its own $\hat{1}$, making the cadence a breeze: like they've been saying, love is all you need.

Not leaving everything to chance, Martin made sure that the broadcast was not to be completely live. A basic track was taped on June 14 at Olympic Sound Studios, with Lennon on harpsichord, Ringo on drums, McCartney bowing a string bass, and Harrison getting occasional sounds out of a violin; this was reduced to a new Track 1. Five days later Track 2 received piano from Martin, heard best in the introduction and in the barrelhouse right-hand octave tremolos (**C**+2 [2:17] and two bars later), and banjo from an uncharacteristically vaudevillian Lennon, and vocals went onto Tracks 3 and 4; these additions were mixed to a new Track 1 on June 21.[128] The Beatles asked Martin for an orchestral score and gave him carte blanche for the long ending that was to have been faded out in mixing; for this he chose to arrange a mélange of incipits from Bach's F-major keyboard invention for two trumpets (one of which would be played by "Penny Lane"'s David Mason), Glenn Miller's arrangement of "In the Mood" for two tenor saxophones, and "Greensleeves" for celli and violins.[129] For good measure, he wrote out brass parts, doubling his piano octaves, for "Le Marseillaise" as an opening fanfare, presumably to reflect the global nature of the broadcast. The chamber orchestra rehearsed with the Beatles on June 23, and all rehearsed with the BBC television crew on the 24th.

June 25 saw the live broadcast from Studio One, a seven-minute segment showing the group adding backing vocals to the end of the instrumental track, after which Martin announced, "We'll get the musicians in now"; the Beatles always referred to their classically trained session players as "the musicians." These players took their seats, Richard Lush cued the backing track (Track 1 of the June 21 mix), Geoff Emerick readied the balance controls, and the song was performed with more drums by Starr, McCartney introducing his newly painted Rickenbacker bass (entering at **B**) and Harrison his gussied-up Casino (most audible for the four-bar solo and for each time through the last two bars of **B**), all placed onto Track 2. In the same televised performance, Track 3 of the tape captured the live lead vocal by Lennon (including the final scatting of "She Loves You," in its original key, onto Track 4) and the orchestra (two tenor saxes, two trumpets, two trombones, accordion, four violins, two celli), plus tambourine and a chorus of friends (Mick Jagger, Keith Richard, Eric Clapton, Graham Nash, etc.).[130] After the broadcast, a bit of "cheating" took place in preparation for the single release of the broadcast: Ringo augmented the tambourine with a snare roll in the "Marseillaise" opening, repeating his recent rudiment performance from "Being for the Benefit of Mr. Kite," and Lennon recut some of the vocal. The mono mix for the rush-released single was made the next day, but the stereo was delayed until October 29, 1968, when it was needed for the soundtrack LP for *Yellow Submarine*. The stereo mix has Track 1 left, 2 and 4 center, and 3 right.

The anthem is certainly utopian (if a bit vague), especially in contrast to the pessimism of Bob Dylan's "It's Alright Ma (I'm Only Bleeding)": "Advertising signs . . . con you into thinking you're the one that can do what's never been done, that can win what's never been won" (May 1965), but the sincerity of "All You Need Is Love" is what Harrison remembers about his lost friend in his anthem to Lennon, "All Those Years Ago" (May 1981).

"Baby You're a Rich Man"

In May, the Beatles were contracted to provide at least three new songs for a feature-length cartoon film, *Yellow Submarine*, that was to be released in mid-1968. "Baby You're a Rich Man" was originally recorded for the film but did not count among the contracted three because it appeared first as the B-side to "All You Need Is Love."[131] Combining a chorus (**B**, 1:15–1:44) of McCartney's with a verse (**A**, 0:20–0:47) of Lennon's that repeats the Q/A approach of "With a Little Help from My Friends," the song asks an unnamed Brian Epstein what it's like to be one of the "beautiful people." This appellation was used of both communal hippies and those who mingle with the most celebrated entertainers.[132]

The track was recorded in its entirety on May 11 at Olympic Studios, with a basic track consisting of Lennon on piano, Ringo on drums, plus maracas and tambourine, all heard right. This tape received simple instrumental overdubs, including Lennon's Clavioline with a double-reed setting, Harrison's guitar (left), McCartney's backward piano (fading in and out, 1:45–2:09) and bass (partially muted in the opening, recalling the octaves of "Rain"), and engineer Eddie Kramer's vibraphone (only an $a\sharp^3$ at **A**+3, 0:53, resolving to b^3, is audible, center). This was mixed down to two tracks for vocal dubs (Lennon singing lead, Lennon and McCartney backing) with some echoing handclaps, heard center. The Clavioline was a three-octave (F to f^2) monophonic keyboard with immediate response, containing guitar, strings, brass, winds, and organ effects, with knee-swell, reverb, and tremolo. The instrument was apparently found at Olympic, as it is heard on no other Beatles recordings. The mono mix was made the same day, but a stereo mix was unavailable before the 1981 release of a new British EP compilation, *The Beatles* (SGE 1). Less than two weeks following the "Our World" telecast, the "All You Need Is Love"/"Baby You're a Rich Man" single was released on July 7 in the United Kingdom (Parlophone R 5620, #1 for three weeks) and on July 17 in the United States (Capitol 5964, #1 for one week).

"Baby You're a Rich Man" seems to be in G Mixolydian for the opening, with a *Revolver*-like use of a G chord moving to F over a "tonic" pedal at **A**+4–5. But from **A**+7, it is clear that C major is the key. This song reminds the listener of "Norwegian Wood," with its non-Western melodic instrument—the Clavioline plays clearly Indian-styled *gamak*-laden lines based on McCartney's guitar leads of the past year—in an otherwise rock context.

"Only a Northern Song," "All Together Now," and
"It's All Too Much"

When the Beatles signed their *Yellow Submarine* contract with United Artists, which they erroneously thought fulfilled their three-picture obligation (even though it was to be a cartoon feature using actors' voices), they already had one track in the can. This was the *Sgt. Pepper* reject recorded in February, Harrison's "Only a Northern Song," now destined for the film. Frustrated by his royalty deal with Northern Songs, a replay of his beef with the government in "Taxman," Harrison thumbed his nose at his publisher with verses (**A**) loaded with ill-behaved tones, including the eleventh chord on II (**A**+5−6, 0:18−0:23, with the unruly eleventh in the lowest register) and the lack of resolution of $\hat{7}$ and chordal seventh in **A**+8−9 (0:26−0:31).[133] Worse, the song features a chorus (**B**) that has its dominant move back to II⁷ (**B**+1−2, 0:54−0:58, "It doesn't really matter what chords I play") and flaunts a gratuitous parenthetical tonicization of the major submediant (**B**+2−5, 0:56−1:05). The wrong-mode chords reflect Harrison's lifelong dependence on modal and chromatically altered scale degrees, but this density of their usage would have been unthinkable before "Strawberry Fields Forever."

Basic tracks, with Harrison on organ, Lennon on tambourine, McCartney on bass, and Starr on drums, were taped on February 13 and reduced the next day to make room for two tracks of Harrison's lead vocals. Additional overdubs on April 20 include trumpet from McCartney (*McCartney World Tour* 1989, 55), Lennon's piano, and assorted percussion including glockenspiel, much of it highly sped-up.[134] The track was mixed for mono the next day and remains one of only two post-1963 Beatles releases never to be mixed for stereo.[135]

For *Yellow Submarine*, McCartney produced the undistinguished, simplistic three-chord skiffle number "All Together Now." Completed and mixed for mono on May 12, the track includes McCartney's acoustic guitar, Lennon's banjo, plastic sax, and harmonica on the left; bass, handclaps, bass drum, triangle, and other percussion center; McCartney's lead vocal right; and backing vocals by Lennon and all in the studio, left, right, and center.

Harrison had some unspecified LSD experiences "which were later confirmed in meditation," and these inspired "It's All Too Much," another film track that, with its restriction to two chords and new tolerance for extended endings, creates none of the interest that *Pepper* does.[136] The basic track, taped May 25 at De Lane Lea Studios, has Harrison on organ, Lennon on lead guitar, McCartney on bass, and Starr on drums; these and woodblock, cowbell, and tambourine (superimposed on May 26) are heard center. Lennon's introductory Bigsby-bent feedback, perhaps the song's best feature, sounds more like Jimi Hendrix than like "I Feel Fine." Harrison's lead vocal, Lennon/McCartney backing vocals, handclaps, and more percussion were taped on May 26; these are heard in a *Revolver*-like ADT mix on both left and right. Four trumpets—again, David Mason joins the Beatles, and Clarke's "Prince of Denmark March" is quoted in the coda à la "All You Need Is Love"—and buzzing bass clarinet were added on June 2 (all heard right). The mono mix was made on October 12, the stereo (for the soundtrack LP) on October 16, 1968.[137] Martin was to be caught in a copyright infringement for his June borrowing of "In the Mood" for "All You Need Is Love," but apparently Harrison's breach in "It's All too Much," citing and repeating in the coda a line from the Merseys' 1966 record, "Sorrow," was acceptable, as it was allowed to pass without dispute.[138] Tapes of these three 1967 *Yellow Submarine* songs were copied in November for film production.[139] Martin need not have worried about "A Day in the Life" being pretentious; it is tracks like this that are indeed too much.

"You Know My Name (Look Up the Number)"

The cover of the 1967 London telephone directory was marked "You have their NAME? Look up their NUMBER."[140] Lennon saw this in Cavendish Avenue, and by the time he and Paul turned the corner to the studio, he'd come up with "You Know My Name (Look Up the Number)," which was conceived as a Four Tops–like number until McCartney added touches inspired by the Bonzo Dog Doo Dah Band.[141] Various instrumental versions of the song were recorded on May 17 and June 7 and 8; five sections were edited together on June 9 for a rhythm track originally 6'08" in length. No vocals were added until April 30, 1969, when the track was mixed for mono. Editing to 4'19" took place on November 26, 1969, and the song was finally released as the B-side of the Beatles' last British single in 1970.[142]

On the finished track in addition to McCartney's piano, which is heard throughout, we hear one section (through **A**, ending with a splice at 0:46) with McCartney's added bass (as in "Baby You're a Rich Man," the opening is partially muted), Ringo's drums, tambourine, and Lennon/McCartney vocals. Sections **B** and **C**, ending when spliced at 2:16, offer bongos, shaker, and other percussion, with applause sprinkled in for an authentic nightclub atmosphere, and more vocals from Lennon and McCartney. Sections **D** and **E** (2:16 to the splice at 3:03) contain drums, bongos, traps (including whistle), and vocals by the same two Beatles and by Mal Evans, who is also heard shoveling gravel with a spade, this taped along with vocals in 1969. Concluding sections **F** and **G** feature drums, McCartney's string bass (pizzicato), a strummed acoustic guitar, and Lennon/McCartney vocals. At **G** (3:51), Harrison adds a vibraphone, and Brian Jones of the Stones contributes a brief tenor sax solo to complete the lounge-act ensemble (McCartney credits Jones's sax with the impetus for the song's recording in Miles 1997, 436–7). McCartney affects a good imitation of cocktail jazz with an augmented applied dominant (V^+/VI, **A**+2), many suspended chords (especially ninths: II^9_7, **A**+4; IV^9, **F**+4; and II^9_3, **F**+8), an applied diminished chord (VII°/V7, **E**+6), and a I^{add6} (**E**+8–10 and the final chord). As "Denis O'Bell," a takeoff on the name of Beatles assistant Denis O'Dell, McCartney has adopted the Billy Shears persona.

The satire is expert, and the fun infectious, but this single, especially as its release was held back time and time again, seems more to document something of the atmosphere of the Beatles at work—as did their Christmas records for the fan club—than to join the ranks of their compositions. But Lennon fought hard to have it finally released, probably not only because he found it fun but also because it showed the Beatles with their guard down, "warts and all." The record may thus be seen as an internal effort to demythologize the Beatles, and it is significant that its spring 1970 release accompanied the formal announcement of the group's breakup, McCartney relenting to its release under the Beatles' name only as part of a bitter feud with his ex-partner. But from 1967, we hear only banter and buffoonery.

The Summer of 1967

The Beatles' involvement with psychedelic drugs was probably at a peak in 1967, and McCartney was roundly criticized for admitting his LSD experience to a *Life* magazine reporter for a June 1967 story.[143] On May 18, Lennon and McCartney had sung backing vocals on the Rolling Stones' B-side "We Love You," a song that was written as a thank-you to fans for their support during widely publicized drug trials leading to suspended prison sentences for several of the Stones. On July 24 a full-page ad appeared in the London *Times* urging the legalization of marijuana, with endorsements by the Beatles, Epstein, and fifty-nine other notables. A more productive collaboration at this time was McCartney's work as a board member for June's Monterey Pop Festival, organized by once-time Beatles publicist Derek Taylor. It was McCartney who made the historically significant suggestion that Jimi Hendrix be booked, and all four Beatles also collaborated on a drawing for the program booklet.[144]

McCartney was busy in the studio in July, producing tracks for the Scaffold with an all-star lineup that included Graham Nash, Dave Mason, and Jimi Hendrix, and producing and playing piano on his 1962 composition, then called "Catswalk" but released in 1967 as "Catcall," for the traditional jazz outfit called Chris Barber's Band.[145] At the same time, various Beatles vacationed in Greece; Lennon bought a bouzouki there, and all four considered purchasing Greek island retreats.[146] Harrison spent several weeks in Los Angeles, seeing Ravi Shankar at the Hollywood Bowl, then taking a famed August 8 excursion to Haight-Ashbury to witness hippie life firsthand and finding it surprisingly repulsive.[147]

In February 1967, Pattie Harrison had joined the Spiritual Regeneration movement, led by Maharishi Mahesh Yogi. The Maharishi taught courses at his Himalayan ashram in Rishikesh, India, and toured worldwide lecturing on his brand of transcendence, which required indoctrination in the general principles of the *Vedas*, the *Upanishads*, and the *Bhagavadgita*, followed by only an hour's meditation daily. The Maharishi increased his number of followers tenfold, to 150,000, after the Beatles expressed their interest by attending a London lecture (August 24) and a weekend conference in Bangor, Wales (beginning the next day), and planning an Indian retreat for the autumn.[148]

It was in Bangor that the Beatles learned of the death of Brian Epstein in his Belgravia home, due to a cumulative poisoning from prescribed barbiturates and antidepressants; he had attempted suicide twice in the previous year.[149] It is doubly unfortunate that his death coincided with the low standard reached with the mediocre recordings approved for the *Yellow Submarine* soundtrack; Lennon said on hearing of Epstein's death, "I knew we were in trouble then."[150] Although I have already suggested a few contributing factors that had occurred earlier, many trace the end of the Beatles to the death of Epstein.

Lennon's kindred spirit, Yoko Ono, had some success in England in 1967. She toured the northern provinces—the Liverpool *Daily Post* called her "the high priestess of the happening" in March—and had London club performances such as in the "14-Hour Technicolor Dream" at the Alexandra Palace in April, with McCartney attending, and the opening of the Electric Garden Club in May.[151] Ono became a sensation with private summer showings of her feature-length *Film No. 4 (Bottoms)*, a projection of 365 sets of hindquarters walking in place, and she also attracted attention in August with her installation "Wrapping Piece," completely covering the Trafalgar Square lions in white fabric. Yoko hooked John's support for her artwork with a copy of her book *Grapefruit*, which she sent to him the following spring; he may have likened the instructionals therein as similar to Timothy Leary's. With a £5,000 contribution, he finally sponsored her "Yoko Plus Me" show—a.k.a. "Half a Wind Show," where the entire contents of an all-white bedroom were displayed neatly cut in half—at the Lisson Gallery, October 9–November 14, 1967. Thus began a collaboration that in the coming year would change his life and have great significance for the Beatles.

Grapefruit is worth further consideration. Yoko Ono printed 500 copies of her book of one-page performance instructionals (individually dated 1953 to 1964), *Grapefruit*, in Tokyo in 1964; it was reprinted with additional material in New York in 1970. Indicating her media in an apparently arbitrary fashion, the book contains fifty-one pieces of music, forty-six paintings, sixty-two events, seventeen poems, twelve objects, five film scripts, and seven dances, nearly all of which are simple instructions to the reader. Lennon has said that the verses of "Imagine" (1971) are his own instructionals, and many connections can be found between items in this book and the Beatles' later lyrics. Samples:

> LINE PIECE: Draw a line with yourself. Go on drawing until you disappear. [music, 1964]
>
> PAINTING FOR THE SKIES: Drill a hole in the sky. Cut out a paper the same size as the hole. Burn the paper. The sky should be pure blue. [painting, 1962]
>
> SLEEPING PIECE I: Write all the things you want to do. Ask others to do them and sleep until they finish doing them. Sleep as long as you can.
>
> SLEEPING PIECE II: Write all the things you intend to do. Show that to somebody. Let him sleep for you until you finish doing them. Do for as long as you can. [paintings, 1960]
>
> WALK PIECE: Stir inside of your brains with a penis until things are mixed well. Take a walk. [painting, 1961; although whimsical, this piece seems inspired by a particularly grisly incident recounted in William Burroughs's hallucinatory novel, *Naked Lunch* (1959)]
>
> SUPPLY GOODS STORE PIECE: Open a supply goods store where you sell body supplies: Tail / Hair / Lump / Hump / Horn / Halo / The third eye / etc. [object, 1964]

Aside from scant contact with the press, the Beatles were largely out of the public eye in 1967. McCartney submitted to a radio interview in late June, and Lennon, Harrison, and the Maharishi appeared on "The [David] Frost Programme," taped September 29. In October, the Beatles refused a $1 million offer from Sid Bernstein to perform live, beginning a long series of many such ignored bids.

Magical Mystery Tour

By June, the Beatles' plans to make a TV film for world distribution based on the *Sgt. Pepper* LP were replaced by a new McCartney idea. This was to film a loosely narrated musical program based both on elements of the coach trips with secret destinations that were an attraction of the English shore and on the 1965 bus tour of Ken Kesey's fifteen or so Merry Pranksters, an LSD-enhanced round-trip from the San Francisco Bay area to the New York World's Fair; forty-five hours of film were shot during this trip.[152] We already know from *Revolver* that McCartney was fascinated by magic and from "Penny Lane" and "A Day in the Life" that a bus trip suggests to him a magical reverie. While he was in California in April, the Kesey influence took hold, and on the April 11 flight back to London, McCartney drew a clock-face storyboard, divided into eight segments that already describe many aspects of the completed film, *Magical Mystery Tour*.[153] To Lennon's irritation, McCartney took the reins, typed up a schedule and to-do list, and asked Harrison and Lennon to write songs and to concoct scripts to fit his basic plan.[154] Lennon came up with "I Am the Walrus" and the "Jessie's Dream" sequence, Harrison with "Blue Jay Way." One other thing — the film was to be produced, shot, and edited by the Beatles (after all, Paul and Ringo were handy with cameras . . .); Beatles assistant Denis O'Dell was the nominal producer. Harrison shows remarkable hubris with his justification for the homemade approach: "The moment you get involved with other people, it goes wrong."[155] The Beatles were to discover that a little reliance on professionals might have helped this project commercially. Instead, we have quite a document of their artistic shortcomings.

The bus, actors, and crew were hired, songs were recorded, and location shooting took place September 11–15 and 19–24; editing and the recording of incidental music required eleven weeks.[156] A synopsis of the finished film would mention Ringo's on-bus arguments with his Aunt Jessie; Paul cavorting on a hilltop in Nice for "Fool on the Hill"; Victor Spinetti (a friend who'd acted in *Help!*) repeating a previous comic role as a drill sergeant; a surreal marathon featuring wrestling midgets and blindfolded vicars (competing with a musical score of tape-reversed Rossini); "Flying," with color-filtered aerial shots of Iceland (supposedly outtakes from *Dr. Strangelove*); the Beatles and Evans posing as coach-guiding magicians above the clouds; an orchestral arrangement of "And I Love Her" for a tender love scene between Aunt Jessie and Buster Bloodvessel; "I Am the Walrus" played by animal-suited Beatles at a West Malling, Kent, airfield; heavy Jessie's dreams of spaghetti shoveled onto her plate by waiter John Lennon; Harrison playing a chalk-on-pavement "organ" for "Blue Jay Way"; an accordion-led bus singalong (running through "I've Got a Lovely Bunch of Coconuts," "Toot Toot Tootsie (Goo'bye)," "The Happy Wanderer," "When Irish Eyes Are Smiling," "When the Red, Red Robin Comes Bob-Bob-Bobbin' Along," "Never on Sunday," and Offenbach's "Can-Can"); a striptease show supported by the Bonzo Dog Doo Dah Band (playing "Death Cab for Cutie," a "Don't Be Cruel" derivative; another performance by Traffic did not make the cut); and a tinsel-spangled Busby Berkeley–styled dance finale with a cast of thousands for "Your Mother Should Know." The end product had some good music lost in a wandering storyline and poor production values and was unfortunately broadcast by the BBC (December 26, 1967) in black and white, dooming the project to reviews so damning that American executives canceled a broadcast scheduled for Easter weekend.[157] The record of the Beatles' music for the film, marketed in the United Kingdom as a six-song two-EP set (Parlophone SMMT 1/2, released December 8, 1967, with a lavish twenty-four-page booklet and lyrics insert), fared much better, with an advance order of over 250,000, final sales doubling that, and a #1 placement in the singles chart despite competing against much less costly single-disc records.

"Magical Mystery Tour"

McCartney set to work on the film's theme song immediately on his April return to London. He entered the studio—unusually, in the small Studio Three, where all of the work for this track took place—on April 25. He began with very few ideas, so Mal Evans was asked to find some actual posters advertising mystery tours, as such a thing had worked well for John's "Mr. Kite." Mal came up dry, so they invented their own come-ons: "Roll up, roll up," "Trip of a lifetime," "Satisfaction guaranteed."[158] In rehearsal, McCartney made known his wish for a trumpet fanfare, and Evans, taking dictation, wrote down their double-plagal chords: D, A, and E.[159] The basic track consisted of piano (McCartney), Gibson Jumbo (Lennon), Strat through the Leslie cabinet (Harrison), and drums, heavy on the snare (Starr), and was reduced to a new Track 1. Also on April 25, a tape loop was made of bus noises from the archives; this would not be added until November.[160] On April 26, Track 2 received a bass part (McCartney); Track 3, tom-tom, tambourine, maracas, finger cymbals, and cowbell (Evans, Aspinall, and unknown Beatles); and Track 4, sped-up, echoing backing vocals (McCartney, Lennon, and Harrison) at **A**, **B**, **D**, and **E** (large noteheads only). A second reduction combined Track 1 with Track 3 (left), and 2 with 4 (center). On April 27, lead vocals from Lennon and McCartney were added to Track 3 at **A**, **B**, **E**, and **F** (small noteheads only), and on May 3 the tape was filled with three sped-up trumpets added to Track 4 (right, where a celesta is also audible during the fade).[161] Recording was completed on November 7, when McCartney added a new vocal introduction (center, wiping a previous highly sped-up Lennon effort at introduction and spoken interlude that in an earlier mix—heard in Beatles 1992f—had already gone into film production).

During both mono and stereo mixing on the same day, bus effects were added live, wild, panning from channel to channel.

I agree with those who call "Magical Mystery Tour" a warmed-over "Sgt. Pepper"-type fanfare/invitation to what's to follow.[162] Additionally, it should be noted that the "Sgt. Pepper" progression, I–bIII–IV–I, is the basis of both the chorus (**A**) and the verse (**B**). Of new interest here, however, are the rare inclusion of both a chorus and a refrain (**C**), and the tonicization in that refrain of b VII, D major, employing a "Lucy in the Sky"–like $\hat{8}$–b$\hat{7}$–$\hat{6}$–b$\hat{6}$ bass descent (at 0:32–0:38). In order to effect the distant modulation, bIII–IV of E in **C**–1–2 is reinterpreted, "Penny Lane"–style, as IV–V in D. The return to E is accomplished through a *misterioso* retransitional interlude (**D**, 1:13–1:26) that neatly prolongs the dominant. Instead of returning to E, the last refrain (**F**) elects to cadence in D, reminiscent of the structure of the "Penny Lane" close, and in fact drifts into the parallel minor, repeating the idea of the "Lovely Rita" fade. The transcendent modulation is not accompanied by compelling enough lyrics or sufficient melodic interest, let alone enough of the "Penny Lane" magic, to rise to greatness.

"I Am the Walrus"

Probably in August 1967, John Lennon read a fan's letter indicating that a literature master at Lennon's old high school was directing interpretations of various Beatles lyrics.[163] As this very institution, Quarry Bank Grammar School, had once branded the future composer as "bound to fail," the Beatle howled over the absurd extremes of Liverpool's civic pride in particular and music criticism in general, and he decided to confound his scholarly and journalistic audiences by writing a song so inscrutable that it could only yield the most laughable attempt at analytical parsing.[164] Lennon is supposed to have sought from Quarry Bank schoolmate Pete Shotton the half-remembered words to their schoolboy chant:

> Yellow matter custard, green slop pie,
> All mixed together with a dead dog's eye,
> Slap it on a butty, ten foot thick,
> Then wash it all down with a cup of cold sick.[165]

This and more rhapsodic childhood fantasies were mixed together with more borrowings from Lewis Carroll to create "I Am the Walrus"; Lennon even seems to compare the Duchess's image of flying pigs (*Alice's Adventures*, "The Mock Turtle's Story") with his own "Lucy in the Sky with Diamonds."[166] Unlike the luminous, wonderful "Lucy," also derived from the *Alice* books, the mysterious, chaotic "Walrus" is a wonderfully dark, snide portrait of unstable unfortunates.

Lennon strung his poetic images together as Bob Dylan did in 1965–66. The composer says of "I Am the Walrus," "I was writing obscurely, a la Dylan, never *saying* what you mean, but giving the *impression* of something. . . . The intellectuals . . . read all this into Dylan or the Beatles. Dylan got away with murder.

I thought, well, I can write this crap, too. You know, you just stick a few images together, thread them together, and you call it poetry."[167] During these years, Dylan would often imbue his mysteriously evocative lyrics with sensitive and original views on human nature; these songs would be populated with a delirious mix of historical, literary, and carnival figures and expressed with imagery and associations often likened to those of the French symbolists whose poems Dylan knew in translation. "I Am the Walrus" resonates with the characters and situations described in Dylan's "Like a Rolling Stone," "Ballad of a Thin Man," and "Tombstone Blues," but perhaps most with "Desolation Row," the second verse of which follows:

> Einstein disguised as Robin Hood, with his memories in a trunk
> Passed this way an hour ago with his friend, a jealous monk.
> Now he looked so immaculately frightful as he bummed a cigarette,
> And he went off sniffing drainpipes and reciting the alphabet.
> You would not think to look at him, but he was famous long ago,
> Playing the electric violin on Desolation Row.[168]

> "Desolation Row" (Bob Dylan). Copyright ©1965, by
> Warner Bros. Music, Copyright renewed 1993 by
> Special Rider Music. All Rights Reserved. International
> Copyright Secured. Reprinted by permission.

While this verse is often an erratic jumble of unconnectable events, one is left with an impression of Einstein as misguided protector of the free world, reciting his equations in isolation, and as a modern-day Nero, fiddling in the wake of nuclear devastation. But it was Dylan's incoherent manner, not his message, that stimulated Lennon with the tongue-in-cheek "I Am the Walrus." This incoherent manner carried on after the "Walrus" joke in "Glass Onion," "Happiness Is a Warm Gun," "Dig a Pony," "Come Together," and others, as if Lennon were masking his true nature, taking refuge in obscure personal jokes. In his last years as a Beatle, he was often to be unconcerned with communicating with the Beatles' commercial audience, which in his eyes was to become more McCartney's than his. Trapped while a Beatle, he would emerge from this mystical corner with the very direct *Plastic Ono Band* recordings as soon as he was released from the group.

The very week that Lennon was mixing the tracks for "I Am the Walrus," he began his collaborative association with Yoko Ono, whose past work with Cage and her other background in aleatoric music may have influenced the Beatle. On September 29, 1967, Lennon turned on a radio in the studio control room and captured whatever he could pick up, capriciously mixing the broadcast directly into the final master of "Walrus."[169] The BBC added the perfect touch to Lennon's obscure and dismal composition; the coda of "I Am the Walrus" is darkened by a death scene (Act IV, scene vi, ll. 224–25 and 251–59) from the ferocious and bewildering tragedy *King Lear*, the identifiable extracts of which are given here:[170]

> GLO. Now, good sir, [what are you?]
> EDG. A most poor man, made tame to fortune's [blows]

osw. Slave, thou hast slain me. Villain, take my purse.
　　[If] ever [thou wilt thrive,] bury my body,
　　And give the letters which thou findst about me
　　To Edmund Earl of Gloucester. Seek him out
　　Upon the British party. Oh, untimely death!
　　Death!
edg. I know thee well—a serviceable villain,
　　As duteous to the vices of thy mistress
　　As badness would desire.
glo.　　　　　　　　　　　What, is he dead?
edg. Sit you down, father, rest you.

Another line, "O matter and impertinency mixed! Reason in madness!"
(IV.vi.178–79), is Edgar's characterization of Lear's speech as a mixture of
sense and nonsense; this appears only a few lines before the *Lear* text becomes
recognizable in "I Am the Walrus." Edgar's description reminds me of George
Martin's words: " 'I Am the Walrus' was organized—it was organized chaos."[171]
The nonsense peaks in the coda, the unusual musical aspects of which are to
be discussed below, where the Lear text joins the walrus's grunts and snorts
(voiced by Lennon) and a professional chorus simultaneously intoning the forever repeated and marvelously ambiguous lines "Oompah, oompah, stick it up
your jumper" (eight men) and "Everybody's got one! Everybody's got one!"
(eight women).[172]

　　As impenetrable as the images of "I Am the Walrus" are, the song can be
heard as a continuation of Lennon's exploration of his own identity, which he
had begun in earnest with "She Said She Said" and "Strawberry Fields Forever."
The opening line, "I am he as you are he as you are me and we are all together,"
recalls Alice's identity crisis in chapter 2 of her *Adventures* (1865), where she
asks, "*Was* I the same when I got up this morning? . . . I'm sure I'm not Ada.
. . . and I'm sure I can't be Mabel. . . . Besides, *she's* she, and *I'm* I. . . . Who am I,
then?" Lennon is the eggman, the nonsense riddler Humpty Dumpty; he is
Tweedledee's Walrus, a costumed conversationalist "of shoes and ships and
sealing wax, of cabbages and kings, and why the sea is boiling hot, and whether
pigs have wings." The Quarry Bank lecturers are eggheads, expert textperts,
kicking Edgar Allan Poe, that master of melancholy and terror. The composer's
drug-inspired paranoia, a by-product of his use of LSD, is reflected in the opening vocal melody, which he hoped would imply the slow trill of a police siren.[173]
His angst is likewise heard in the trilling falsetto cry in a rough mix (heard on
Beatles 1992f) of **C**+1–2, really the song's emotional germ exposed as a raw
nerve, performed in the final version by slow trills in the cellos and the women's
chorus.[174]

　　"I Am the Walrus" underwent a rather complex recording, considering the
relatively moderate instrumentation that results. Basic tracks (Lennon's electric piano, Harrison's Stratocaster, McCartney's Rickenbacker, Starr's drums)
and Lennon's Mellotron overdub were taped on September 5. These were reduced the next day to two tracks to allow for more bass and drums, Lennon's
sped-up lead vocal, and, on the fourth track, tambourine. On September 6,

Example 2.7 Analysis of "I Am the Walrus."

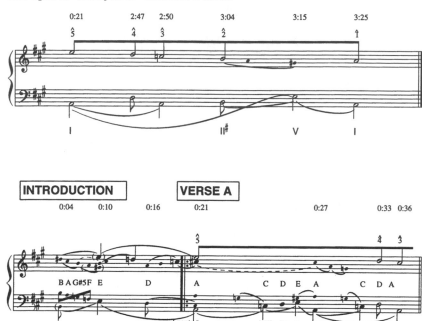

(continued)

mono mixes were made for acetates; different test mixes from this day appear on Beatles 1992c (without tambourine, and with **D**–1 silenced in the mix) and on Beatles 1991a (with tambourine and with **D**–1 spliced out of the mix).[175] On September 27, a simultaneous reduction mix/superimposition session placed the dubbed drums, bass, and Lennon's compressed ADT vocal (heard center); added a bass clarinet to the basic track, Mellotron, and tambourine (left); and taped eight violins, four celli, and three horns on a third track (right).[176] The chorus was then added to the fourth track (right). On September 28, experimental recording, mixing, and editing took place, followed by the next day's final mono mixing (with the *Lear* radio feed added simultaneously) and editing of two separate mixes. The stereo mix and edit were done on November 6.[177]

Because of the song's highly expressive deep-level tonal structures, themselves suggestive of the composer's deep levels of narration based on his tongue-in-cheek stance, we will savor here some of the musical patterns that contrast background and foreground events in order to carry Lennon's message. The voice leading in this song's background structure, as sketched in the first system of example 2.7, is deceptively "normal," but it does raise eyebrows with the depth of the minor-mode mixture ($\natural\hat{3}$), the relatively weak contrapuntal support of $\hat{4}$—the texture provides only a neighboring IV chord here— and with the assertion of such a deep chromatic II$\sharp$ chord. At the middle-

Example 2.7 (*continued*)

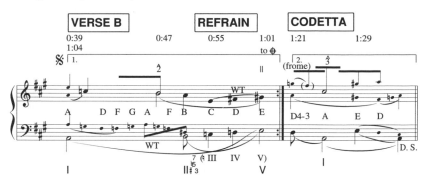

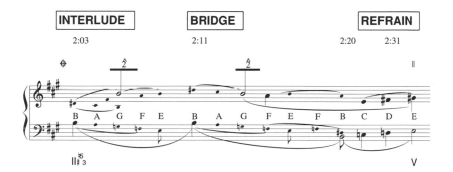

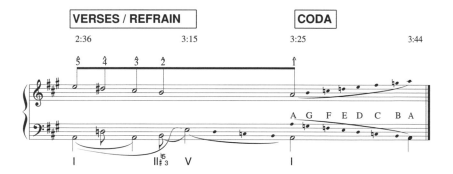

ground level, harmonic norms are violated in the bridge (2:11–2:25) and else-where by the unfolding of II♯ as a whole-tone sonority, spelled B–D♯–F♮–A, ex-pressed with G as a passing tone.

The song's foreground harmony, however, cynically challenges the under-lying tonal centricity at nearly every turn. This is illustrated in the example's second-through-fifth systems. Chord roots and colors obfuscate the scale— after the introduction, every triad is major (chord designations appear between the foreground staves in ex. 2.7), and the seven different roots are all from the

A natural-minor scale. In the repeating coda, this scale descends for three and a half functional octaves (remaining in one actual register) in the low strings and bass, completing the stepwise planing of major triads that never quite reaches an octave in the song proper. At the same time, the upper strings rise the same number of octaves through the A Dorian scale. Despite this modal mixture, the song's basic quality is perceived as major because of the qualities of the I, IV, and V triads. Chord succession in verse A and the refrain is drawn from the pentatonic minor scale (A–C–D–E–G–A). In more tonal contexts, the progression ♭III♭5–IV–V, heard recently in "Lucy in the Sky with Diamonds," sounds as if borrowed from this pentatonic minor mode; the chromatic bass a–g–f♯–f♮, **B**+1–2, also comes from "Lucy." Here, however, the chords C–D–E are lent a whole-tone quality despite their perfect fifths by the preceding (and complementary) II♯ sonority. In other words, one whole-tone scale, B–C♯–D♯–F–G–A (see outer voices at 0:04–0:09 or 0:44–0:54), is directly followed by its opposite, C–D–E–F♯–G♯–A♯ (outer voices, 0:55–1:03). Deep voice leading, particularly with the strong final upper-voice arrival on Î, is strong enough to keep "I Am the Walrus" tonal, but there is little sense of coherent chord spelling and grammar beyond the contrapuntal structure. A masterful welding of poetic and musical nonsense.

"I Am the Walrus" was released not only with the *Magical Mystery Tour* EP set but also as the B-side to "Hello Goodbye."[178] While the public hardly knew what to make of "Walrus," it was given rehearings of the Joycean "googooga-joob" refrain in Simon and Garfunkel's "Mrs. Robinson" (April 1968) and in the first line of verse in Chicago's "South California Purples" (May 1969). It may also have been the model for the otherwise rare whole-tone harmony in the coda to Eric Clapton's "Layla" (November 1970, there V$^{9}_{7\,♭5}$).

"The Fool on the Hill"

The basic track of McCartney's "The Fool on the Hill," which has been documented in demo form as early as March 1967 (Miles 1997, 366), was recorded on September 25 but largely remade the next day; after this work we hear McCartney's piano, Ringo's drums and finger cymbals, and Harrison's acoustic twelve-string guitar on the left, McCartney's lead vocal and plastic recorder solo with heavy breath-tremolo ("Flute II" at **C**, 1:24–1:36, and **E**) in the center, and Lennon's and Harrison's "backward"-articulated harmonicas (as at 0:58–1:07) on the right. Overdubs include a double-tracked lead vocal (September 27) for the refrains (**B**+7–14; center), three flutes (October 20; right, but also left for all refrains after the first), and a chattering sped-up tape effect (like the "bird" sound in "Tomorrow Never Knows") panning left to right, "spinning 'round" at 2:40. The mono mix (October 25) reduced the length of the track from 4'25" to 2'58", and the stereo (November 1) to 2'55".

"The Fool on the Hill" is the story of one whose innocent nature isolates him from an ostracizing society. The structure of each strophe is tripartite: parts **A** and **B**+1–6 comprise the D-major verse, and **B**+7–14 is the D-minor refrain. Each section has its own tonal character, befitting the changing narrative

Example 2.8a Analysis of "Fool on the Hill."

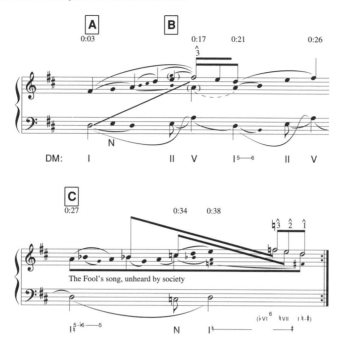

points of view regarding the fool's unsuccessful position as defined by social norms.[179] The following analysis illustrates how harmony and structural voice leading can make such a statement.

The bass is static throughout **A**; as the fool is described as "keeping perfectly still," the tonic scale degree is sustained as a pedal below neighboring II chords until **B+**1 (0:17). This lack of motion also promotes the timeless nature of the fool's existence—he is "alone" and "still" "day after day." At the same time, the ear climbs gently upward, following the stepwise ascent from $f\sharp^1$ to primary tone $f\sharp^2$ (see the first system of the sketch in ex. 2.8a), finally locating the fool in **B–**2, at the top of the hill, sitting "perfectly still" on a dissonant anticipatory e^2.

This static introductory gesture leads to **B+**1–6 (0:17–0:26), a passage marked by cadentially strong II–V–I motions in the bass that support first a descent from $\hat{3}$ to $\hat{1}$ and then another rise to $f\sharp^2$ that goes unanswered by any second descent. As opposed to the neutral narrative attitude in **A**, **B+**1–6 shows the fool to be judged by social convention and found wanting: "Nobody wants to know him, they can see that he's just a fool"; "nobody ever hears him, or the sound he appears to make." The judgment against the fool tolls unequivocally in a businesslike doubled harmonic rhythm in **B+**2–3 with the orderly $\hat{3}$–$\hat{2}$–$\hat{1}$ descent over the bass fifth motions doubled in low octaves. The lack of an answering descent in **B+**6–7 reflects the fool's lack of engagement with social convention: as remarked at this point in all of the three strophes, "he never

Example 2.8b "Fool on the Hill" compositional draft (Lennon-McCartney). © 1967 Northern Songs.

gives an answer," "he never seems to notice," and finally, "he never shows his feelings."

Instead of answering with his own conventional 3̂–2̂–1̂ descent, the fool presents *his* very different perspective in **B**+7–14 (0:27–0:40). We hear a rising motion from an inner voice a¹ to the final 1̂. This minor-mode line must be the fool's song, to which nobody pays attention, as it is buried in the inner voices until it rises to meet the upper voice on the open-notehead f♮²— the masses apparently care only about the law-giving outer parts. The fool's melody opens with a 5̂–♭6̂–5̂ neighboring motion that apparently recomposes the major-mode 5–6 exchange sung on I in **A**+6–7, 8–9, 10–11, and 12. The 5–6 exchange is also performed on the piano through the 5–6–5 motion in the neighboring chords of **A**, and frozen into the tonic sonority itself, as no D-major chord is ever heard without its accompanying panconsonant sixth. In **B**+7–14, we are back in the timeless world of static harmony, with only a lower-neighbor C-major chord pulling away from tonic. The final 3̂–2̂–1̂ cadence is distorted by the minor mode and by the unusual interwoven unfoldings—note the graph's diagonal beams, suggesting the manner by which the world's normal structure is filtered by the fool's highly individual sort of comprehension. This descent is not his called-for answer to the world's judgment but rather a re-creation of how he hears the world spinning its wheels, literally "spinning 'round," an image painted in several foreground cadential parts; note the similarity between the "spinning" chromatic piano part, **C**–1–4, and the electric guitar overdub on "Here, There and Everywhere." The spinning effect is enhanced by the calliope-like harmonicas at **C**, which recall the atmosphere of "Being for the Benefit of Mr. Kite." The fool, who has no destination, cares nothing for—and likely does not understand—the world's harmonic progressions and goal-directed lines.[180]

There are a few reasons for considering this song as an autobiographical effort, perhaps as McCartney's answer to Lennon's "Nowhere Man." The notion of self-portrait-as-fool is magnified in the song's first draft, taped by a solo McCartney on September 6, nearly three weeks before his group began work on the recording.[181] In this early version, the composer's penchant for vaudeville gives the song's 5–6 motive a foolishly corny conclusion, shown as example 2.8b; perhaps a joke, the unelected idea is ironically appropriate in portraying the distance between McCartney and his peers with a flashy finish that expresses little other than a self-mockery of the entire effort.

*"Blue Jay Way," "Your Mother Should Know," and
Incidental Film Music (Including "Flying")*

Harrison composed a tune at the Hammond organ in a rented Los Angeles house on the foggy night of August 1, 1967, while waiting for friends Derek and Joan Taylor. This situation forms the basis of the "slightly Indian" (as Harrison calls it) song "Blue Jay Way," named for the street where the house was located.[182] The song's "slightly Indian" quality is due to the unusual Lydian scale altered with an occasional ♭$\hat{3}$, setting the stage for "Glass Onion" and for Donovan's "Peregrine" (October 1968), related to ragas *Kosalam* and *Multani*, but not replicating their practice.[183] The track consists of Harrison's droning Hammond, Ringo's drums, and McCartney's bass (taped September 6) heard left. Additions to this basic track include backing vocals from the three singing Beatles (September 7), Lennon's tambourine (October 6), backward snippets of vocal harmony (probably inserted on November 7), and a "Strawberry Fields Forever"–like solo cello (October 6) center, and Harrison's double-tracked vocal (September 7) right. All vocals and organ are submitted to extensive phasing, creating a light ADT-like sweep of upper partials.[184] A demo mix was made on September 16 (before the addition of the cello, the tambourine, and the backward tapes, as heard on Beatles 1991a and 1992f) for miming during the film shooting. The released stereo and mono mixes were both made and edited on November 7; the mono mix does not feature the tape-reversed vocals that punctuate every vocal phrase in the verses of the stereo mix. The backward tapes, odd scale degrees, and colorful engineering create the most mysterious Beatles sound between "Strawberry Fields" and "Glass Onion," but the dull lyrics do not match them in import.

"Your Mother Should Know" is McCartney's kitschy film-ending song-and-dance music-hall production number. (It was begun just weeks after the recording of "Catcall," which begins with a similar syncopated ascending octave-arpeggiation of a minor triad.) The vaudeville style of applied V[7]s (**A**+3 and 7–8; the key center of A minor is a pretense) leads to a very unbalanced roll of anacrustic harmonies, so the eleven-bar phrase (**A**, 0:04–0:26) seems to be divided oddly but intriguingly as 4+1+2+3+1. This lack of balance will be recaptured in slightly different ways in Lennon's "Sexy Sadie" (1968) and "Because" (1969), and the tone of McCartney's bridge here is reheard in his "Martha My Dear" (1968). The basic track from August 22, taped at Chappell Studios, contained McCartney's echoing piano, Ringo's drums, and Harrison's tambourine; this tape was reduced for a double-tracked McCartney lead vocal plus McCartney/Lennon/Harrison backing vocals.[185] Another reduction on September 29 made room for the composer's bass and Lennon's organ, which often provides interesting sustained dissonances and countermelodies. The mono mix was made on October 2, and the stereo on November 6. We hear piano, bass, and drums center, tambourine and organ right, and vocals roving from left (for the first two verses) to right (third verse and refrain) and back to left (last verse). "When I'm Sixty-Four" is a quaint and touching number improved by its *Sgt. Pepper* surroundings, but "Your Mother Should Know" is little other than a curiosity; McCartney apparently hoped that rich pitch and rhythmic tricks would allow him an empty salute to the Astaire era.

"Flying," which long had "Aerial Tour Instrumental" as a working title, was composed for the film's sequence of monochrome above-the-clouds *Strangelove* outtakes and is the first of a few Beatles copyrights to credit all four as writers. The song, about as weak a composition as anything released since "Mr. Moonlight," is a major-mode twelve-bar blues in C with three choruses and tritone-heavy coda of Mellotron loops, featuring the harmonic interval c^1-$f\sharp^1$ and the melodic interval f^1-b^1, which tonally presages the coda to "Glass Onion." The basic track (Ringo's drums, Harrison's acoustic Leslie guitar ["Guitar II"], Mc-Cartney's bass, and Lennon's organ ["Keyboard I," entering at **B**]) was taped on one track on September 8 and is heard left. The Beatles filled the tape once with three tracks' worth of backward organs, heard on one September 8, 1967, acetate on Beatles 1992f, but these were erased the next day. Also taped on September 8 were Lennon's Mellotron ("Keyboard II," with the double-reed sound later used in "The Continuing Story of Bungalow Bill," entering at **B**) and all Beatles chanting the final chorus, in unison except for the octave-low croak on A at 1:16, until the final four descant-decorated bars (center). On September 28, Lennon taped a second Mellotron (not shown in the score, entering at **B**), Starr maracas, Harrison a second acoustic guitar, and McCartney the two-part guitar solo ("Guitar I"), heard right.[186] The second Mellotron features the "Strawberry Fields Forever" flute stop, and the second acoustic guitar has sustained chords that are heard only in the mono mix. Also on September 28, tape loops, Mellotron effects, and backward tapes by Lennon and Starr were added to Track 4, creating the coda (heard center), and the mono mix and edit from 9'36" to 2'14" were completed, eliminating a long recording of drums, banjo, pizzicato string bass, vocals, and sax lifted from the EMI library. The stereo mix and edit were done on November 7.

Incidental music intended for the film also includes three other Beatles compositions. "Jessie's Dream" was Lennon's composition for his dream scene, a minute-long pre–"Revolution 9" piano/guitar/tape piece essentially alternating E minor and D$\sharp$ minor triads as shown in example 2.9 until overcome by a vocal chant of "The Volga Boatmen," all recorded privately and heard on Beatles 1992f. Also recorded for the soundtrack were some uncopyrighted Mellotron music (a pandiatonic C-major fifty-second wash heard in the film as "the magic is beginning to work," recorded privately, heard on Beatles 1992f) and "Shirley's Wild Accordion," an unused and unheard Maclen composition notated for accordionist Shirley Evans by Mike Leander and taped on October 12 in Studio Three, with Ringo adding drums and Paul maracas.[187]

"Hello Goodbye"

McCartney wrote "Hello Goodbye" (known first as "Hello Hello"), the A-side of the Beatles' single for the Christmas 1967 market. The song was based on an apparently simplistic word-association game he'd played with Alistair Taylor.[188] Basic tracks included McCartney's piano (mixed very low), Lennon's organ (especially audible at **C**, **E**, and the final time through **B**), Starr's drums (with heavy double-sticking on the floor tom for every eighth in the coda), and Har-

Example 2.9 "Jessie's Dream."

rison's maracas (replacing the tambourine he'd played on Take 1, heard on Beatles 1990d), all heard left. These were recorded on October 2, and the tape was also given tambourine (right), bongos (center), and conga (left) that day for the coda.[189] A tape reduction on October 19 allowed the superimposition of two Leslied Casino parts by Harrison (right and, for the coda, center), two sped-up lead vocals by McCartney, and (at 1:15 and 1:30) handclaps (center except for **C**, mixed right, where heavy echo is added), and backing vocals from McCartney, Lennon, and Harrison (right except for the coda, when mixed center). Work done thus far is mixed for Beatles 1996a. The verse here contains a Casino part, example 2.10, omitted from the final master. Note that an F chord is suggested at **A+4**; following G[7], this is reminiscent of the V–IV "Strawberry Fields" ambivalence; is "Hello Goodbye" McCartney's pale copy of that passage? Two violas were added on October 20 (right), and McCartney's bass part was taped on October 25 and November 2.[190] The mono mix was made on November 2, the stereo on November 6.[191]

Joshua Rifkin sums up the primary value of "Hello Goodbye" as motivic. The once subordinate descending scale in the bass for the chorus (**B**, 0:21–0:38) is inverted, extended in diminution and emphasized by the lead guitar in the same passage and then by the backing vocals, which also have another inventive contrapuntal role, in relation to the lead vocal at **E** (1:53–2:04).[192]

Along with an intent about as innocuous as "Your Mother Should Know," if not "All Together Now," aspects of the more infectious "Hello Goodbye" recall other Beatles efforts. The vocal relations at **E** recall "Help!," the mixture-improved chorus (especially **B+4–7**, 0:28–0:38) comes from the keyboard part

Example 2.10 "Hello Goodbye" (Lennon-McCartney). © 1967 Northern Songs.

to "For No One," and the verse's descending vocal parallel thirds (d^2-f^2, c^2-e^2, b^1-d^2, a^1-c^2, **A**+1–4, 0:00–0:09) come from "Love of the Loved" and more recent efforts and will be reheard in Part II of "You Never Give Me Your Money" and in the bridge of "One of These Days" (McCartney 1980a).[193] Thus, much of the song's charm is derivative McCartney, freshened up by off-balance phrase lengths of eight and a half bars (verse) and seven bars (chorus) and by a bittersweet chromatic descent in the codetta (**F**–3–4, 2:36–2:40). The track is well crafted and fun, but putting "I Am the Walrus" on the A-side would probably have encouraged Lennon to lead the Beatles to new heights in the 1970s; as it is, "Hello Goodbye" was one more nail in the Beatles' coffin.

"Hello Goodbye"/"I Am the Walrus" sold more than 300,000 copies in the United Kingdom within one day of its November 24 release (Parlophone R 5655), achieving four weeks at #1. In the United States, the single (Capitol 2056, released November 27) had three weeks at #1. American Capitol also released a thirteen-song LP, *Magical Mystery Tour* (Capitol SMAL/SMAS 2835, November 27, eight weeks at #1), augmenting the film songs with all A- and B-sides released in 1967, three in fake stereo. The album sold 1.75 million copies within seven weeks and ultimately a total of 5 million. This format was popular enough to sell 50,000 copies as an American export to the United Kingdom, where EMI released it in its own right in November 1976 (Parlophone PCTC255). This is the only American compilation—a much more practical collection than the British EPs—to have been produced (although with variant mixes) as a compact disc as a member of the official EMI canon.

The Beatles in Late 1967

The Beatles concluded 1967 with another Christmas record for their fans, the opening of the Apple boutique, and a few other projects. The fan club record, taped November 28, mixed and heavily edited the next day, centers on a song, "Christmas Time (Is Here Again)." Authorship is credited to all Beatles, who chant—"Flying"-style—along with George Martin and actor friend Victor Spinetti over Ringo's drums, McCartney's piano, Harrison's Martin, and Lennon's timpani.[194] On the original fan club disc, choruses of this number punctuate a silly pre-Python skit of the boys at "BBC House," including "Michael" (McCartney) interviewing "Sir Gerald" (Lennon) on a bogus talk show, Harrison reading a radio dedication of "Plenty of Jam Jars" by the Ravellers (followed by a thus-titled Bonzo-like chorus, apparently Lennon's creation), Ringo introducing "Theatre Hour," and Lennon improvising a heartfelt holiday message in a broad Scottish burr over George Martin's "Auld Lang Syne" on organ.[195]

This recording follows the November production by John and Paul of Grapefruit's "Dear Delilah." This group, NEMS artists managed by Terry Doran and renamed by Lennon after Ono's book, represented Apple Publishing's first contracted writers, signed on December 11; their records appeared on RCA Victor. Lennon was also occupied on November 24 and 28 creating sound effects and spoken-word tapes for a stage production based on his writings, "Scene Three Act One."[196]

Two other extant recordings are supposed to date from late 1967: Ringo singing (quite off-key) "Daddy's Little Sunshine Boy" (Lennon 1988a) and Lennon and Starr together creating an inventively edited "Chi-Chi's Café" (Lennon c. 1989), a "You Know My Name (Look Up the Number)" sort of off-beat improvisation where Ringo makes up "Don't forget the apples when you go downtown" and Lennon vamps a "Hernando's Hideaway" in falsetto and a mangled bossa nova, all accompanied by the chord and rhythm section from Lennon's Mellotron, with lots of applause added for the "Edge Hill Country Club" atmosphere. (Edge Hill is a suburban Liverpool district.)

While McCartney was enjoying two and a half weeks in Scotland, Starr made his solo film debut, shooting for three weeks in Rome in a cameo part in *Candy* (based on a novel by Terry Southern, whose face adorns the *Sgt. Pepper* cover). Also at this time, Lennon and Harrison oversaw the December 7 opening of the Apple boutique on 94 Baker Street (at Paddington, in Marylebone, central London). This venture was a clothing shop modeled on the Edwardian "Granny Takes a Trip" shop (King's Road, Chelsea).[197] Both Lennon and Harrison saw Ravi Shankar once more in concert, in Paris on December 23.

The boutique and its clothes were designed by the Fool and represented the second project to be unveiled under the Apple moniker, following a mysterious mention of "Apple" on the back cover of *Sgt. Pepper's Lonely Hearts Club Band*.[198] "Magical Mystery Tour," produced by Apple Films, was the third. The "Apple" name was proposed by McCartney, inspired by one of three Magritte paintings he had acquired, *Le Jeu de mourre*, featuring an apple with the phrase "au revoir" across the middle.[199] Begun innocently enough, the post-Epstein Apple enterprise was to provide the impulse for both a 1968 vision and a 1969 migraine.

Summary of the Mid-Beatles Style

In the years 1965–67, many gradual changes can be traced in the Beatles' musical interests, and some will be summarized here. For starters, introductions become more subtle: while the chromatic intro of "Do You Want to Know a Secret" and "If I Fell" is rewritten in "Here, There and Everywhere," the starkly jarring opening chords of "All I've Got to Do" and "A Hard Day's Night" are replaced by more complex irregularities, such as the metrically tricky introduction to "Drive My Car." Gone too, for the most part, are the simple pandiatonic endings with added-sixth and -ninth sonorities; these chords are blended in "She's Leaving Love," which is also one of the rare midperiod rehearings of the Lydian II♯ after "Yesterday." But additive chords generally become more dissonant than sixths or ninths, as in "The Word," "Drive My Car," and "Taxman." Song endings themselves are more apt to fade out, often with quasi-mystical and stand-alone codas beginning with "Rain."

The frequency with which motives are reharmonized in early songs—"She Loves You," "Yes It Is"—drops significantly, but in the close of "With a Little

Help from My Friends," the technique does reappear, leading to a rare repeat of the ♭VI–♭VII–I "P.S. I Love You" cadence; this progression is expanded in "A Day in the Life." Another significant castoff is the wild retransition so crucial in the early singles; in 1965–67, only "The Night Before" and "Sgt. Pepper's Lonely Hearts Club Band" begin the bridge on the flat side, tonicizing IV, then moving to a tonicized dominant for the retransition, an effect so important earlier. Mixture from minor, touched upon in "In My Life," largely disappears, giving way to mixture from the pentatonic, truly creating the "sound" of rock music with the many uses of the ♭VII chord, particularly as nonfunctional neighbor to I ("A Hard Day's Night," "Tomorrow Never Knows," "For No One," "Hello Goodbye") or in the double-plagal cadence ("You've Got to Hide Your Love Away," "She Said She Said," "With a Little Help from My Friends") and with ♭III ("Sgt. Pepper's Lonely Hearts Club Band," "Lucy in the Sky with Diamonds," "I Am the Walrus").

Original "wrong mode" chords add to harmonic expressivity in "Think for Yourself," "Strawberry Fields Forever," "Only a Northern Song," and "I Am the Walrus," and modal scales are invoked in "Eleanor Rigby" (Dorian) and "Blue Jay Way" (Lydian). Daring tonicizations, nonfunctional modulations, and progressive tonality in "You're Going to Lose That Girl," "Day Tripper," "Doctor Robert," "Theme from *The Family Way*," "Penny Lane," "Lucy in the Sky with Diamonds," "Being for the Benefit of Mr. Kite," and "A Day in the Life" add to the creation of tonal ambiguity in ways different from those in the mysterious but simpler "And I Love Her" and "Girl."

The Beatles do not release a strict twelve-bar blues number in this period—the major-mode "Flying" comes closest, but the R&B language predominates, particularly in *Rubber Soul*. After "What Goes On," the rockabilly style goes into dormancy. Outside of "I'm Down," "Run for Your Life," and perhaps "Sgt. Pepper's Lonely Hearts Club Band," there is little pure rock and roll at all. There is a great new interest in counterpoint, largely stemming from the addition of the Rickenbacker bass ("If I Needed Someone," "Michelle," "With a Little Help from My Friends"), but also with the addition of chromatic descents ("In My Life," "The Word," "You Won't See Me," "Eleanor Rigby"), 4–3 suspensions (frequent in *Rubber Soul* and *Revolver* but then disappearing), î pedals ("The Word," "You Won't See Me," "Tomorrow Never Knows") and the common use of the tamboura, and woven-in quotations ("Paperback Writer," "It's All Too Much," "All You Need Is Love," and, for that matter, "I Am the Walrus"). With voices working more independently, there is little doubling of instruments other than in "Day Tripper" and "For No One," and there are fewer three-part vocals, and more solos, almost never in falsetto, after *Rubber Soul*. Structural aspects of voice leading often become quite expressive, as in "Nowhere Man," "Strawberry Fields Forever," "Penny Lane," "With a Little Help from My Friends," and "The Fool on the Hill."

The Beatles' music had always been driven by interesting rhythms—Ringo's fills, irregular phrase lengths—but as goal-directedness becomes less of an issue, the Beatles are more rhythmically inventive, with even more interesting drumwork, sections in contrasting meters ("She Said She Said," much of *Sgt.*

Pepper) and mixed meters ("Good Morning Good Morning," "All You Need Is Love").

McCartney and Lennon both begin composing on keyboards, which quickly include harmonium, harpsichord, clavichord, and Mellotron as well as an assortment of pianos and organs. George Martin adds barrelhouse ("You Like Me Too Much") and baroque ("In My Life") keyboard touches to several tracks. Beginning with *Beatles for Sale*, McCartney plays guitar—Texan, Casino, and Esquire—on many tracks, and the Beatles' guitars get hotter from "I Feel Fine" through "Ticket to Ride," "Think for Yourself," "Paperback Writer," and "And Your Bird Can Sing" to the heavily distorted power chords of "Sgt. Pepper's Lonely Hearts Club Band." Beginning with *Help!*, the Beatles call on outside musicians, including such masters as Alan Civil and David Mason, and even begin writing for orchestra. But the Beatles' most original colors come from their mid-period studio experimentations with various pedals and distortion effects, using an organ amplifier effect for the guitar and a guitar amplifier for the piano, speed-altered and reversed tape, heavy phasing and filtering, sound effects, and the musique concrète integration of "found" tapes. All of the Beatles' new musical and technical effects are artistically expressive of a rapidly widening array of poetic statements. Often these statements are intentionally obscure; as Lennon sings in two post-Beatles songs, "I don't expect you to understand." This obscurity enables the Beatles' millions of listeners to learn more about themselves as they explore and embrace a multitude of meanings, and it may indeed be a factor in what has made the Beatles represent, in a nearly one-to-one fashion, the musical thoughts and dreams of a generation.

THREE

SO LET IT OUT AND
LET IT IN (1968)

The year 1968 was a time of simultaneous rejuvenation and dissolution for the Beatles; McCartney's involvement in both solo and group projects continued to be prolific, Lennon found a new muse and a new voice, Harrison's confidence as a composer grew and he found success producing other artists, and Starr finally finished his first solo composition. But while a stay in India freed creative juices, there was also an increase of bile in the Beatles' system, even leading Ringo to quit the band for a brief period. Every member of the group—with the possible exception of McCartney—was to begin finding more pleasure in solo projects than in group endeavors. In fact, the year began with solo musical projects from McCartney and Harrison while the Lennons vacationed with actor-friend Victor Spinetti for a week in Casablanca, a far cry from the days when a year would begin with nightly concerts and preparations for an upcoming group film.

Musically, 1968 was a year of extremes for the Beatles. The acoustic guitars they strummed with delight in India—Lennon even worked diligently there at his fingerpicking technique—gave us some of the Beatles' lightest physical textures ever, as in "Julia," "Blackbird," and "Mother Nature's Son." But a new supply of Fender and Gibson electrics fit right in with the raucous rock and roll they returned to in "Lady Madonna" and continued with the likes of "Hey Bulldog," "Birthday," and "Back in the U.S.S.R." Lennon's own production ran the gamut from Dadaist musique concrète, of which "Revolution 9" was the year's most conservative example, to the airy, free-floating meters and soundscape of "Across the Universe," from the child's lullaby "Good Night" to the hellhound-

Table 3.1 Time Line of Major Events for the Beatles, 1968

Jan.–Feb.:	Lennon and McCartney producing recordings by McGough and McGear, by Grapefruit, and by Cilla Black, in London
Jan. 12–Feb. 8:	Recording of next single, EMI studios in Bombay and London
Early Feb.:	Beatles organize Apple Corps, Ltd.
Feb. 4–11:	Recording of "Across the Universe" and "Hey Bulldog," EMI, London
Feb. 15–Apr. 12:	Beatles retreat in Rishikesh, India
Mar. 15:	"Lady Madonna"/"The Inner Light" released in United Kingdom
Late May:	Lennon and Ono record *Two Virgins*, Weybridge
May 30–Oct. 17:	Recording and mixing of *The Beatles* (a.k.a. the "White album"), EMI and Trident studios, London
June–July:	McCartney records with Black Dyke Mills Band, Bradford, and Mary Hopkin, London
June 24–26:	Harrison records with Jackie Lomax, EMI and Trident Studios, London
July 17:	World premiere of film *Yellow Submarine*, London
July 31–Aug. 1:	Recording of "Hey Jude," Trident, London
Aug. 30:	"Hey Jude"/"Revolution" released in United Kingdom
Oct.–Nov.:	Harrison records with Jackie Lomax, Los Angeles
Nov. 22:	*The Beatles* released in United Kingdom
Nov. 29:	Lennon's *Unfinished Music, No. 1: Two Virgins* released in United Kingdom
Dec.:	McCartney produces recordings by Mary Hopkin, the Fourmost, Jackie Lomax, Steve Miller, Carlos Mendes, and Badfinger, through July 1969
Dec. 11:	Lennon performs in all-star band for "The Rock 'n' Roll Circus" television film

defying "Yer Blues." The work of the other Beatles was easily more predictable, but we should mention above all else the proliferation of compositions by George Harrison, who this year would be awarded his first song on a Beatles single and four cuts on the White album and would still begin writing a stockpile of songs for which there was no group outlet, songs that would eventually become cornerstones of his own solo albums. But we begin our account of 1968 with the always active Paul McCartney.

Early 1968: India, Return to R&R, Apple, and Yoko

"Step inside Love"

McCartney began 1968 by finishing a year-end 1967 project. He had written the verse and refrain of "Step inside Love," a brief bossa nova number recorded on November 21, 1967, as the theme song for Cilla Black's eight-week Tuesday night TV series beginning January 30.[1] The theme proved so popular that McCartney was required to write a bridge just before his departure for India so the song could be properly recorded, as arranged by Mike Vickers, on February 28 for release.[2] A reduction of the opening of Black's recording is given as example 3.1.

McCartney's 1967 demo recording, without bridge (heard on Beatles c. 1976a), was sung a fourth lower. The simple bridge added for Black was a four-bar turnaround through a mixture-enhanced deceptive cadence, following D[7] with the deceptive E♭, which went through A minor to regain D[7]. Note that the

Example 3.1 "Step inside Love" (Lennon-McCartney). © 1968 Northern Songs.

F-major chord of **A**+3 is not a modal ♭VII neighbor to the tonic G—as in "Got to Get You into My Life" and elsewhere—but an agent of modulation to C. The coda (not seen here), a repetition of G–F–G–F, is reminiscent of the conclusion to "A Hard Day's Night." In the promo film for the single, McCartney is seen, with Black and George Martin in Studio Three, playing the Martin D-28 on which he wrote the song.[3] McCartney also busied himself in January and February by producing an eponymous album for McGough and McGear (two-thirds of the Scaffold) and playing drums on Paul Jones's single "And the Sun Will Shine," a song written by the Bee Gees and produced by Peter Asher with contributions from Jeff Beck, Nicky Hopkins, and Mike Vickers for British EMI's Columbia label. In March he played ukelele on the Bonzo Dog Band's "I'm the Urban Spaceman," composed by Neil Innes, which McCartney also produced under the pseudonym "Apollo C. Vermouth." Lennon and McCartney are also said to have produced recordings for Grapefruit in the first months of 1968.

Wonderwall

Harrison composed and produced the soundtrack for the film *Wonderwall*, which had its premiere at the 1968 Cannes Festival. He began at Twickenham in November 1967 by "spotting" rough film edits with a stopwatch, then writing and recording accompaniments.[4] These were made with Indian musicians in London (November 22 and 23, 1967, and January 5, 1968) and in Bombay's HMV Studios (January 9–13, 1968) and with a Liverpool rock group, the Remo Four, in London (January 30). The eighteen tracks, ranging from 1'04" to 5'27" in length, include "Microbes," "Tabla and Pakavaj," "In the Park," "Guru Vandana," "Gat Kirwani," "Love Scene," "Fantasy Sequins," "On the Bed," and "Singing Om" by Indian musicians using tambouras, *shenhais*, harmonium, sitars, sarods, tabla, *tablatarangs*, svaramandal, and dilrubas.[5]

Rock instrumentations are heard in "Red Lady Too," a repeated binary form; the first half of its B section is given as example 3.2, with the Remo Four playing "Moonlight" Sonata–like suspensions on piano, honky-tonk piano, Mellotron, and drums. Other rock numbers for the soundtrack include "Drilling a Home"—sounding similar to the jazz section almost used in "Flying," with the tape speed gradually altered upward from G to B♭ major, "Greasy Legs" (for har-

Example 3.2 "Red Lady Too" (Harrison). © 1968 Northern Songs.

monium and Mellotron), "Ski-ing" (with Eric Clapton playing four distorted electric guitars, two of them backward, in C pentatonic minor, all dubbed over tambouras), "Dream Scene" (featuring the Fool on flutes and reeds, a Hendrix-style voice at three-quarters speed, and changing bells), "Party Seacombe" (a slow major-mode twenty-bar blues like "Flying," featuring Mellotron and two guitars with wah), "Crying" (using portamentos on two dilrubas for a crying effect, as in "Cry for a Shadow"), "Cowboy Museum" (a western number with slide guitar and boogie shuffle on skulls), "Glass Box" (including two trumpets and flügelhorn), and "Wonderwall to Be Here" (based on a minor-mode I–♭VII–♭VI–V progression, styled like Liberacian variations on "While My Guitar Gently Weeps"). The LP (Apple SAPCOR1) was first released in the United Kingdom on November 1, 1968, and in the United States (Apple ST3350, #49) a month later.

"The Inner Light"

When Harrison taped an appearance on "The Frost Programme" in September 1967, Cambridge Sanskrit scholar Juan Mascaró was an invited audience member. Six weeks afterward, Mascaró wrote the composer suggesting that—following the success of "Within You Without You"—Harrison try his hand at setting the professor's translation of a Lao-tse poem from the *Tao Te Ching* (sixth century B.C.), such as the following from a book he mailed to Harrison, *Lamps of Fire*:

> Without going out of my door
> I can know all things on earth.
> Without looking out of my window
> I can know the ways of heaven.
>
> For the farther one travels
> The less one knows.

> The sage therefore
> Arrives without travelling,
> Sees all without looking,
> Does all without doing.[6]

Harrison made very few changes to this text in creating "The Inner Light," his last Indian effort as a Beatle. Largely because of McCartney's support, "The Inner Light" was chosen as 1968's first B-side, Harrison's first song on a single. Lennon must also have respected the song; he was soon to create "Julia" in a very parallel process, troping a text taken from Lebanese poet Kahlil Gibran.

With *Wonderwall* taping nearing completion in Bombay, Harrison secured a backing track for "The Inner Light" on January 12 from the same musicians (on harmonium, *pakavaj*, tabla, and flute [left], sarod and *tablatarang* [right], and *shenai* [right-center]). He dubbed a lead vocal (center) in London on February 6, once the tape was copied from two- to four-track. On the 8th, Lennon and McCartney added backing vocals (**B**), and the recording was mixed for mono.[7] Of the finished product, McCartney says, "Forget the Indian music and listen to the melody. Don't you think it's a beautiful melody?"[8] Note that the Mixolydian tune begins with the same ascending arpeggiation of the diminished triad that was the featured motive (*ga–pa–ni*, the Indian equivalent of mi–sol–te) of "Within You Without You." David Reck says, "Most memorable is the sheer simplicity and straightforwardness of the haunting modal melody, somehow capturing perfectly the mood and truth and aphoristic essence of the lyrics."[9] The peace and joy of nirvana are made palpable in this most sincere effort.

"Lady Madonna"

McCartney is quoted as saying, "I was looking through this African magazine, and I saw this African lady with a baby. And underneath the picture it said 'Mountain Madonna.' But I said 'Oh no, "Lady Madonna,"' and I wrote the song."[10] The resulting lyrics, like those of "Fixing a Hole," are puzzling, and other writers' explanations of the central figure as destitute, prostitute, and even McCartney's mother, a nurse, are not wholly satisfying.[11] As Lennon complains, "The song never really went anywhere," and as with many McCartney lyrics, a neat interpretation does not seem possible or desirable.[12] We may need only accept that the litany of days of the week is McCartney's way of simultaneously marking time and drawing from his rock-and-roll heritage, as it is done in "Rock around the Clock" and "Reelin' & Rockin'," and also a vague indication that the Lady has day-to-day cares that invite sympathy.

When the Beatles heard McCartney's piano part and learned that he had based it on "Bad Penny Blues" by the Humphrey Lyttleton band, a traditional jazz (or "trad jazz") recording produced by George Martin in 1956, they wanted to build their arrangement around that model. Martin suggested that Ringo use brushes. The drummer: "So I used brushes and we did a track with just brushes and the piano and then we decided we needed an off-beat. So we put an off-beat on it and Paul decided to sing it in his sort-of Elvis voice."[13] The period sound was also invoked by the low-fidelity vocal brass imitation (McCartney, Lennon, and Harrison cupped their hands around their mouths for the backing scat vocals at **C** and **F**), the addition of two tenor and two baritone saxophones, playing McCartney's suggested lines, all in unison—but including a tenor solo at **F** by Ronnie Scott, and the use of a distortion-inducing inexpensive microphone along with "heavy compression and limiting" on the piano part.[14]

The basic track—McCartney's piano and Starr's brushing (left)—was followed on Tracks 2 and 3 with several overdubs, all made in Studio Three on February 3. McCartney played a distorted Rickenbacker, and Lennon and Harrison also used distortion on their unison guitars, probably the Casino and the SG, respectively. The guitars were played through the same overdriven amplifier, Ringo's drums marking the off-beat (all heard right). On Track 4, Paul recorded his Elvis-like lead vocals, and John and George provided their "pa-pa-pa" backing vocals, with tambourine at **F** (all center).[15] The tape was reduced on February 6 to allow for separate double-tracked vocal and piano from McCartney (now inaudible), the "See how they run!" refrain from all three singers, handclaps, and saxes (center, performed in the immense Studio One). The mono mix was done on February 15, the stereo not until December 2, 1969, for the *Hey Jude* compilation. The final piano chord is abruptly abbreviated, as it was spoiled by a sol-mi-do-te scatted by the composer; it survives only in a mix made before the February 6 additions including a Lennon Hammond part (as heard on Beatles 1991m).

The modal mixture in "Lady Madonna," most obvious in the "P.S. I Love You"/"With a Little Help from My Friends" ♭VI–♭VII–I cadence appearing at **A–1** and elsewhere, is no subtle innovation, but a raw rock-inspired doubling of a passing motion. No contrapuntal niceties in this passage: the Beatles barrel up the fingerboards and keyboard with primitive power. In fact, this song was at the forefront of a spring–summer 1968 rock-and-roll revival in the United Kingdom that saw British-only rereleases of Gene Vincent's "Be-Bop-a-Lula," Carl Perkins's "Blue Suede Shoes," Jerry Lee Lewis's "Great Balls of Fire," Buddy Holly's "That'll Be the Day," Little Richard's "Good Golly Miss Molly," and others.

The verse structure in "Lady Madonna" is unique among Beatles songs, but it is similar to "Old MacDonald" in that its opening phrase is truncated for an appearance after the bridge. A repeated four-bar phrase (**A-B**) is followed by an eight-bar bridge section (**C**) that neatly tonicizes ♭III (C major) before chorally intoning the retransitional V^7_{4-3} refrain, with the same chords, A–C–E, that form the harmonic guideposts of two other McCartney songs, "Another Girl" and "Birthday." The retransition leads to a four-bar rehearing of the opening phrase and an instrumental tag ending (**D**). The "bridge" extends the repeated-note stepwise descent in the bass from the "Hello Goodbye" chorus and the nearly-an-octave examples in the Who's "Pictures of Lily" (April 1967) and Procol Harum's "Whiter Shade of Pale" (May 1967), repeated in David Bowie's later "Changes" (April 1972); here, allowing one registral break, the descent extends a full twelfth. Backed with "The Inner Light," "Lady Madonna" was the first British Beatles single (Parlophone R5675, released March 15) since 1962 to not reach #1 (peaking with two weeks at #2) on the *Melody Maker* chart. The American release (Capitol 2138, released on March 18) reached only #4, but McCartney enjoyed reviving this hard-rocking piano number in his 1975–76 "Wings over America" tour.

"Hey Bulldog"

The Beatles were scheduled to film a promotional video for "Lady Madonna" in Studio Three on February 11. United Artists still wanted one number for *Yellow Submarine*, so Lennon brought to the session a half-written idea, "Hey Bullfrog," which the Beatles recorded while being filmed for the video.[16] An early home demo (heard on Beatles 1993a) known as "She Can Talk to Me," excerpted in example 3.3, shows that Lennon apparently had the chorus, with its brilliant imitative chromatic ascents (**B**+3–4, 0:57–1:01, following **B**+1–2 in the score, 0:52–0:56), before he wrote verses. Standing in for verses is an "Eleanor Rigby"–like chromatic and modal suggestion of the singer lonely in his room. McCartney's remembered contributions to "Hey Bulldog" include misreading the line "measured out in news" in Lennon's manuscript as "measured out in you" (preferred and adopted by the composer) and barking (to make Lennon laugh) at the end of the basic track take, leading the composer to change the title from "Hey Bullfrog" when it came time to cut the coda vocals.[17] Because the Beatles composed and recorded what was to become "Hey Bulldog" while the cameras were rolling, the resulting clip, first screened in the United Kingdom on March 13, was an openly clumsy marriage of these images to the "Lady Madonna" recording.

On the record, we hear the basic track of Lennon's piano, Harrison's Casino (as at **A**+6–7, 0:46), Starr's drums, Mal Evans's tambourine (all left), and McCartney's Rickenbacker bass (center), with just a few overdubs. These include Starr's off-beat drums, left, and Harrison's distorted SG, doubling the Casino's chromatic ostinato for the introduction (center), and Lennon's distorted lead guitar solo (entering at **C**), lead vocal from Lennon, and a final vocal take with Lennon doubling his lead and McCartney providing harmony (right).[18] McCartney's vocal part is actually below Lennon's at **A**, a texture that has rarely been heard before but was to recur a few times in 1968–69. Mono mixing (increasing the speed by 2 percent) was completed the same day, and stereo mixing was done for the soundtrack LP on October 29. Just as rock-oriented as "Lady Madonna," "Bulldog" takes on a heavy blues cast despite the superficial sharp-side chromaticism; this is largely because of the total absence of any seventh scale degree, the leading tone in particular.

Other than for any reasons already mentioned, this one-session recording is of historical interest, as it was the first of many appearances of Yoko Ono as Lennon's guest in the studio. Her reaction to the event was a rare criticism of the Beatles' music to their faces: "Why do you always use that [regular and repetitive] beat all the time, the same beat, why don't you do something more complex . . . ?"[19] As shall be noted regarding some of his 1968 compositions, Lennon was to take this and her many further judgments quite seriously.

Example 3.3 "Hey Bulldog" compositional draft (Lennon-McCartney). © 1968
Northern Songs.

"Across the Universe"

If "Hey Bulldog" was a throwaway recorded simply to fulfill a film contract, the
Beatles were at the same time recording a song that would always remain one
of Lennon's favorites, "one of the best lyrics I've written," "Across the Universe."[20] Lennon began composing while hearing the echoing words of his wife
as they lay in bed and—as McCartney claims of "Yesterday"—he was driven
to write as the words channeled through him: Cynthia "must have been going
on and on about something and she'd gone to sleep and I'd kept hearing these
words over and over, flowing like an endless stream. . . . But the words . . . were
given to me as *boom!* I don't own it, you know; it came through like that. . . .
Such an extraordinary meter and I can never repeat it! It's not a matter of
craftsmanship; it wrote itself. It *drove* me out of bed. I didn't want to write it, I
was just slightly irritable and I went downstairs and I couldn't get to sleep until

I put it on paper."[21] Several writers have cited "Across the Universe" in order to repeat George Martin's thought that Lennon's lyrics drive his music, indicating the verses' buoyantly irregular meter and their reflection in the flexible musical phrase rhythms.[22]

The evocative imagery of these verses, approaching the acid-dripping lyrics by Robert Hunter for the Grateful Dead, goes "The Inner Light" one better by using actual Sanskrit phrases. These are "Jai Guru Deva"—literally "Victory to the Guru-God," words of praise for God and for one's guru, a personal spiritual master—and "Om"—"the most sacred of the mantras, or holy sounds, in Hinduism, representing—connecting with, in its sonority the essence of the universe, all that is."[23] Note how the melody floats weightlessly, innocent and eternal, descending for three bars and then returning up to a nonresolving $\hat{7}$ at **A**+4, g^1 finally resolving down to $f\sharp^1$ at **B**+7 and the $c\sharp^1$ up to d^2 only in the coda.

Lennon has complained that "Across the Universe" has been issued in various forms, none to his liking. In fact, at least six versions have circulated, revealing the full history of the recording process. The first version is Take 2 from Studio Three, made on February 4 (heard on Beatles 1996a), with Lennon and McCartney on Martin D-28s (the composer strumming simple open-position chords in D major after the opening bar of parallel sixths), Harrison on tamboura, Starr on svaramandal, and Lennon singing. A practice mix of these tracks without McCartney's guitar is captured from a studio monitor on Beatles 1993d. The second version is a stereo acetate (heard on Beatles 1987a) of the released take, copied from the original four tracks before the first tape reduction. The live backing has Lennon's D-28 and Starr's tom-tom (entering at **B**) on one track and Harrison's tamboura on another, all with Leslie and ADT; the first overdubs have Lennon's sped-up first vocal on the third track, and the fourth track is given to two female fans who were recruited from the studio steps, doubling an octave higher, in falsetto, Lennon's vocal lines at **B**+4–11. The third version is a mono acetate, known as the "Hums Wild" mix (Beatles 1989), made for Lennon's own study at the completion of work on February 4, incorporating three new and reversed tracks of humming, guitar, and other effects, all rejected in later work.

Version Four is the earliest commercially released mix (Beatles 1988b) and thus is more complex. It begins with the previous tamboura (its entry delayed until **A**+5 [0:41]) and female fans left, and D-28, tom-toms, and first Lennon vocal center. Additions from February 8 include Lennon's double-tracked lead vocal and organ, at **B**, and Harrison's maracas and Martin's second organ, both entering at **B**+4 (all heard center).[24] Also from this date are Harrison's wah-heavy guitar, wordless ("ah") Lennon/McCartney backing vocals answering those of the fans at **B**+5–11 and, in the coda only, McCartney's bass line on the piano (right).[25] All of this was sped up from D major to E♭ and given wild (center/left) bird effects preceding the intro and in the coda on October 2, 1969. The fifth version is Glyn Johns's mix of January 1970, and the sixth is Phil Spector's D♭ remix with orchestration of March–April 1970; these last two will be discussed in chapter 4.

Lennon was unhappy with the work done on February 4 and 8; he felt no support from his mates and even felt that (as in other cases) McCartney was sabotaging his work, here by auditioning female fans on the steps of the studio rather than hiring professionals.[26] Lennon had initially offered "Across the Universe" as a potential A-side, but he did not feel that the end result was worthy. Comedian Spike Milligan, in the studio when the decision against release was made, asked if he could have the recording for a wildlife-benefit LP, and it was agreed—thus Martin's dubbing of bird effects in October 1969. If McCartney was party to this decision, it marks the beginning of his long career of public wildlife support. Lennon was finally able to participate in a re-recording of the song in January 1975 for David Bowie's LP *Young Americans*.

Rishikesh

The Beatles' long-postponed Himalayan stay with the Maharishi Mahesh Yogi at the Spiritual Regeneration Academy of Transcendental Meditation was finally realized in February 1968. The Lennons and Harrisons planned to leave London on February 15 for a three-month stay; the others were to leave on the 19th for a shorter visit.[27] McCartney stayed as long as planned, until March 26, but the others all cut their visits short, the Starkeys on February 29, the Lennons and Harrisons on April 12.[28] Along with the Beatles, their families, and friend Alex Mardas, the initiates included Mia Farrow and her sister Prudence; Donovan; Mike Love of the Beach Boys; jazz flutist Paul Horn; and about forty-five others. The Beatles' goal in this ashram, situated in a forest on a mountain ledge 150 feet above the Ganges as it enters the plains, directly across from Rishikesh (a town of 12,000, about 10,000 of whom were renunciants, about 140 miles north of New Delhi), was to renounce drugs, promiscuity, and all selfishness in order to attain bliss through meditation, which was to grow increasingly meaningful following twice-daily lectures.[29] While the experience no doubt changed the Beatles' lives, it was notably unsuccessful in the realms of drugs, promiscuity, and selfishness.

Most enduring are the products of the Beatles' Martin D-28s and Donovan's Gibson J-45, the instruments brought to India. The Beatles composed many songs for their next LP while at Rishikesh and enjoyed other musical expression as well. One Italian television feature shows the Beatles involved in many multiguitar choruses, singing such numbers as "(When) the Saints Go Marching In," "You Are My Sunshine," "Blowin' in the Wind," the Hare Krishna mantra, and Donovan's "Happiness Runs" (some of which are heard on Beatles 1993a). One recording made in Rishikesh on Mike Love's birthday (March 15) has McCartney, Love, and Donovan, two of them on acoustics, performing their dutiful yet droll "Thank You Guru Dev," excerpted in example 3.4.[30] Donovan wrote "Jennifer Juniper" (March 1968) for Pattie Harrison's sister and taught Lennon some fingerpicking techniques—compare the guitarwork in "Happiness Runs" with that in "Julia"—and Harrison wrote an unused verse for Don's tamboura-drenched "Hurdy Gurdy Man" (June 1968): "When truth gets buried deep / beneath a thousand years of sleep, time demands a turnaround / and once again the truth is found."[31]

Example 3.4 "Thank You Guru Dev" compositional draft.

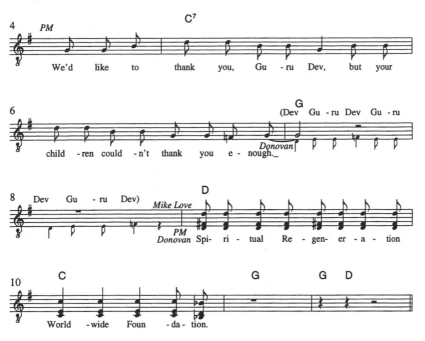

Alex Mardas, a friend with whom the Beatles visited Greece in the summer of 1967, whom they appointed to head their new electronics company, Fiftyshapes Ltd., in September 1967, and who had a nonspeaking role in "Magical Mystery Tour," spoiled the magic when he claimed that the Maharishi had made sexual advances on a woman in the party.[32] Lennon, already suspicious, confronted the guru with vague accusations and found the response disappointingly noncosmic, and the Beatles left India.

Apple

In 1967, Brian Epstein suggested that the Beatles invest their income in administrative, retail, and artistic ventures over which they could exercise control. The first openings came in publishing (Apple Music, registered in September 1967) and film (Apple Films, first producing "Magical Mystery Tour" and the "Lady Madonna" clip). Then, in February 1968, the Beatles invested $2 million in creating Apple Corps. Ltd. (directed for all of its thirty years, at this writing, by Neil Aspinall) to manage their interests in a mix of business and philanthropy.[33] The launch was announced by Lennon and McCartney in a series of New York appearances on May 11–15. On "The Tonight Show" on May 12, an idealistic McCartney said Apple would be "a controlled weirdness, a kind of Western communism. We want to help people, but without doing it like a charity. We always had to go to the big men on our knees and touch our forelocks and say, 'Please can we do so-and-so . . . ?' We're in the happy position of not needing any more money, so for the first time the bosses aren't in it for profit. If you come to me and say, 'I've had such and such a dream,' I'll say to you, 'Go away and do it.' "[34]

The Beatles were out of their depth. Apple soon turned out to be a half-baked pie in the sky. Rather than professional advisers, the Beatles supported a house astrologer to help them make decisions. The primary facilitator for philan-thropy was to be the Apple Foundation for the Arts, which hoped to subsidize writers, artists, and performers.[35] Their call for tapes went out in late April in the form of a full-page ad ("This man has talent"; see *Melody Maker*, April 27, 1968, p. 9) designed by McCartney, and Apple offices were deluged with appli-cations, but not a single grant was awarded—the staff could not be bothered to judge the applications. Apple Films' three projects—an adaptation of Lennon's two books, another of *Lord of the Rings*, and a vehicle for model Twiggy—never materialized for manager Denis O'Dell.[36] Apple Music, run by Terry Doran, never had a hit beyond the Beatles' direct involvement; their group Grapefruit even took to doing cover versions of music by others, such as of the Four Seasons' "C'mon Marianne." Apple Electronics, a realignment of Fiftyshapes, headed by "Magic" Alex Mardas, was a constant disappointment, and Apple Retail—Pete Shotton was replaced as manager by John Lydon—was such a disaster through shrinkage and mismanagement that the Baker Street boutique had to be closed in July 1968, at a total loss of over £100,000; all clothing stock was finally given away for the asking. Derek Taylor handled pub-licity in a professional manner; this and Ron Kass's Apple Records, to be dis-cussed later in this chapter, were the Apple success stories.[37]

The Theater

June 18, 1968, saw the National Theatre opening of John Lennon's *In His Own Write*, a one-act adaptation of *Scene Three Act One* (December 1967), coau-thored and directed by Victor Spinetti to weave some of Lennon's stories into a tale of a boy growing up with his fantasies. "The play had been heavily cen-sored by the Lord Chamberlain's office, for its blasphemous reference to 'Almighty Griff,' and disrespect to such world statesmen as 'Pregnant De Gaulle' and 'Sir Alice Doubtless-Whom.' "[38]

Yellow Submarine, the animated quest story with four new Beatles songs ("Only a Northern Song," "All Together Now," "It's All Too Much," and "Hey Bulldog"), several older ones ("Nowhere Man," "Yellow Submarine," "Eleanor Rigby," "When I'm Sixty-Four," "Sgt. Pepper's Lonely Hearts Club Band," "Lucy in the Sky with Diamonds," and "All You Need Is Love," and excerpts from "Think for Yourself," "Love You To," "A Day in the Life," and "Baby You're a Rich Man"), and incidental music composed and recorded by George Martin (in-cluding a bit of reversed music for the film's "vacuum monster"), was produced by TVC Studios in Soho for Subafilms.[39] The Beatles liked the early cuts, filled with imaginative pun-filled op-art, enough that they agreed to make a brief live appearance at the end of the feature-length cartoon; this scripted one-shot scene was filmed on January 25, 1968. The film opened on July 17 to a disappointing box-office reception.

With only four new songs, the format for the film's accompanying record release was in doubt. An EP was planned in September 1968 but was ruled out by the new year. The only release, then, was to be an LP with six of the Beatles' tracks on one side, the title track and "All You Need Is Love" flanking the four new film songs, and newly recorded versions of Martin's scores (done on October 22 and 23) on the other.[40] The album was delayed half a year after the film's opening, and the Martin-heavy format was not a fan pleaser; the American version (Apple SW153, released January 13, 1969) reached #2 for two weeks, the British disc (Parlophone PMC/PCS 7070, January 17), was #3 for only one.

JohnandYoko

Lennon's relationship with Yoko Ono had progressed to such a point in early 1968 that he considered bringing her to India; instead, she sent him instructionals ("I'm a cloud—watch for me in the sky") that he hid from his wife.[41] The affair was consummated in May and discovered by John's wife Cynthia, to Lennon's apparent indifference, when she returned unexpectedly from abroad.[42]

Lennon was excited about Ono's art; he was impressed by a tape of her performing a simple instructional with Ornette Coleman at the Albert Hall on February 29, released as "AOS" (Ono 1970); the opening phrase, featuring Ono's lyrical "voice modulation" over a Webernesque accompaniment, is shown in example 3.5. In his Weybridge music room in late May, John played his homemade electronic tapes for Yoko, and she decided that they should create one together.[43] The immediate result was an improvisation that would be released as the LP *Unfinished Music No. 1: Two Virgins* (Lennon 1968b; released first in the United States, November 11, 1968). In the spirit of Ono's *Grapefruit* pieces, this first of two "Unfinished" LPs was so named because Lennon and Ono believed that much of the album's music was not pressed into the grooves but was to be created in the mind of the listener. This LP, consisting of two intact excerpts, running fourteen and fifteen minutes, from several hours of tape, opens with two simultaneously rolling tapes of whistling: one slowed down and with heavy echo, the other a real-time loop. Over these (the loop continues beyond the live tape), Lennon demonstrates the piano setting of his Mellotron, and Ono's vocalizations blend neatly with the keyboard's many pitch bends. Yoko bangs a grand piano while Lennon invents a slow two-note ostinato at the Mellotron, both vocalizing above the whistling loop and a quarter-speed Irish tenor. On Side 2, with the use of tape echo, Lennon gets an effect like guitar feedback from the Mellotron, and then programs the instrument with random trad jazz snatches, replaying the sampled trumpet and rhythm fragments with the Mellotron's pitch bend.[44] The artists summed up their Dadaist aesthetics on August 24, 1968, in a live televised appearance: they "told David Frost that just about everything we see, hear, feel or smell about us should be classified as art. We are each works of art in ourselves—our bodies and our minds combining to make something which should be treated in the same way that an art examiner

Example 3.5 "AOS" (Ono). © 1970 Ono Music.

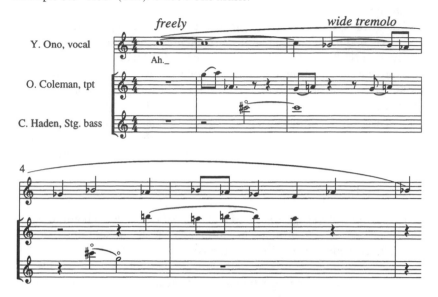

might treat a painting or a piece of sculpture. In gist, they said, the whole world is one vast gallery, one massive exhibition of art."[45]

Lennon and Ono were to collaborate in a wide range of media. In May 1968, they planted a pair of acorns "for peace," one facing east, the other west — symbolizing the merging of their cultural backgrounds — in a sculpture exhibition at Coventry Cathedral.[46] In July, John backed Yoko's art exhibition at London's Robert Fraser Gallery, "You Are Here," to which he contributed a sculpture entitled "Built Around" — to which viewers were to add objects — and 365 white balloons that he set free, each tagged with a request to return the fallen balloons. Ono's *Film No. 5* was simply the image of Lennon's smile slowed by a factor of thirty-six to imperceptible movement, à la Warhol, done by shooting several hundred frames a minute (expanding two and a half minutes to ninety), and her film *Two Virgins* superimposed the faces of the two artists, again symbolizing their oneness; both films had their premieres in Chicago in October 1968. Beginning when the two attended the June 18, 1968, opening of *In His Own Write* in very public hand-in-hand defiance of their marriages, they were lambasted in very hurtful ways by the press, often from an openly racist perspective. In reaction to this pain, the two began their experimentation with, and ultimate dependence on, heroin in July 1968.[47]

The Beatles (a.k.a. the White album) and
"Hey Jude"/"Revolution"

Lennon says that in Rishikesh, "we got our mantra, we sat in the mountains eating lousy vegetarian food and writing all those songs. We wrote *tons* of songs in India."[48] On June 29, McCartney said of the thirty songs to be included in the Beatles' massive 1968 LP, *The Beatles*, "Twenty were written while we were with the Maharishi in India; the other ten we have written in the time since we came back to London."[49] Lennon said in September that most of the songs for the White album were written on guitar, so "they have a different feel about them. I missed the piano a bit because you just write differently."[50] The songs that were furthest advanced were taped in composers' demos in the fourth week of May. All twenty-seven of these available recordings were made on one four-track Ampex machine at Harrison's home studio in Esher.[51] The source recording for these Ampex demos will henceforth be referred to as the "Kinfauns" tape, named for Harrison's house in Esher. Extant are fifteen demos offered by Lennon ("Revolution," "Everybody's Got Something to Hide Except Me and My Monkey," "Cry Baby Cry," "Sexy Sadie," "Yer Blues," "Dear Prudence," "I'm So Tired," "The Continuing Story of Bungalow Bill," "Julia," "What's the New Mary Jane," "I'm Just a Child of Nature," "Glass Onion," "Happiness Is a Warm Gun," "Mean Mr Mustard," and "Polythene Pam"), seven by McCartney ("Blackbird," "Ob-La-Di, Ob-La-Da," "Mother Nature's Son," "Rocky Raccoon," "Back in the U.S.S.R.," "Honey Pie," and "Jubilee" [later "Junk"]) and five by Harrison ("While My Guitar Gently Weeps," "Piggies," "Circles," "Sour Milk Sea," and "Not Guilty"). Most of the recordings have the composer at double-tracked acoustic guitar with double-tracked unison voices, but four Lennon songs have only a single guitar, two Harrison songs add harmonium and/or organ, and "Sour Milk Sea" adds electric guitar, bass, and percussion; harmony vocals are already sketched for three songs by McCartney and four by Lennon. Two McCartney offerings are without their eventual introductions, and not all the lyrics are yet there in three songs by McCartney, two by Harrison, and three by Lennon. Presumably, each Beatle received a copy of the tape to allow home practice on each others' compositions.

Given the abundance of new songs, packaging presented the opposite problem than that facing *Yellow Submarine*. The day before recording began, McCartney announced, "We might record all thirty songs and pick fourteen or so for an album, or it could turn out to be two albums or even a three album pack. We just don't know until we have finished."[52] A rock album released as an all-new three-record set would not be attempted before 1970, with Harrison's *All Things Must Pass*, but all-new two-record sets had come into vogue before the October 17 mastering of *The Beatles*. The Beatles knew intimately Bob Dylan's *Blonde on Blonde* (July 1966), Frank Zappa's *Freak Out!* (late 1966), Donovan's *Gift from a Flower to a Garden* (January 1968), and Cream's *Wheels of Fire* (August 1968), as well as pending two-disc sets by Jimi Hendrix and the Incredible String Band (both released before *The Beatles*). Before recording began, George Martin argued that the material should be distilled to a single LP, but he was overridden, so the result was a thirty-track double album with the following song order (dates of the first recordings for each song are given in parentheses):[53]

Side 1

"Back in the U.S.S.R." (Aug. 22)
"Dear Prudence" (Aug. 28)
"Glass Onion" (Sept. 11)
"Ob-La-Di, Ob-La-Da" (July 3)
"Wild Honey Pie" (Aug. 20)
"The Continuing Story of
    Bungalow Bill" (Oct. 8)
"While My Guitar Gently
    Weeps" (July 25)
"Happiness Is a Warm
    Gun" (Sept. 23)

Side 2

"Martha My Dear" (Oct. 4)
"I'm So Tired" (Oct. 8)
"Blackbird" (June 11)
"Piggies" (Sept. 19)
"Rocky Raccoon" (Aug. 15)
"Don't Pass Me By" (June 5)
"Why Don't We Do It
    in the Road" (Oct. 9)
"I Will" (Sept. 16)
"Julia" (Oct. 13)

Side 3

"Birthday" (Sept. 18)
"Yer Blues" (Aug. 13)
"Mother Nature's Son" (Aug. 9)
"Everybody's Got Something to Hide
    Except Me and My Monkey" (June 26)
"Sexy Sadie" (July 19)
"Helter Skelter" (July 18)
"Long Long Long" (Oct. 7)

Side 4

"Revolution 1" (May 30)
"Honey Pie" (Oct. 1)
"Savoy Truffle" (Oct. 3)
"Cry Baby Cry" (July 15)
[untitled PM outtake (Sept. 16)]
"Revolution 9" (May 30)
"Good Night" (June 28)

The album has been called a history of rock and roll, because of the wide variety of styles represented and parodied.[54] Tim Riley goes so far as to say, "The varied stereo mixes make them sound like a different band on each track. In moments like the relentless groove of 'Everybody's Got Something to Hide, Except Me and My Monkey,' the lazy upbeats of 'I'm So Tired,' and the tight grip of the bridge to 'Birthday,' their sense of ensemble is as strong as at any other point in their career. The disparity between songs is linked only by the musical currents that still flow between them."[55] The new emphasis on simplicity already seen in "Lady Madonna" and "Hey Bulldog" is part of Lennon's ripening preference for primitivism — for him, "realism" — in his art. Although several of his White album lyrics are intentionally obscure, he also begins here to react against the artifice of 1967. Lennon recalled in 1970 that the White album saw the beginnings of his rock-and-roll-inspired directness; he argues Platonically that rock and roll is "real, it's not perverted or thought about, it's not a concept, it is a chair, not a design for a chair, or a better chair, or a bigger chair, or a chair with leather or with design . . . it is the first chair. It is a chair for sitting on, not chairs for looking at or being appreciated. You sit on that music."[56]

Much is made of the small degree of collaboration on the White album, and it is true for each song that the composer has a great deal of control over the arrangement. In "Julia," Lennon produces his first track on a Beatles release not to involve other members, but this had already been done by both McCartney (first in 1965) and Harrison. The Beatles had long been sidemen for each others' tracks, but these sessions are different from those before because most of the group efforts here had been highly developed, in some cases finished, by a soloist before being brought to the studio.

McCartney said in May 1980 that the group chemistry was more tense for *The Beatles* than for any other album.[57] Part of this is due to the fact that Ono was now closer to Lennon than McCartney was. As a feminist and an artist, she always considered herself an equal of John's. She believed her opinion to be so valued that she once told Paul that the group could play better, in a July 19, 1968, control room hearing of "Sexy Sadie."[58] But McCartney, with his precisionistic control over every aspect of his songs' arrangements, was a major contributor to the bitter atmosphere. He even recorded his own drumming for "Back in the U.S.S.R.," the last straw that kept Ringo out of the studio until he was begged to return to film a promo after twelve days. McCartney's callous attitude lingers eighteen years later: "I'm sure it pissed Ringo off when he couldn't quite get the drums to 'Back in the U.S.S.R.,' and I sat in. It's very weird to know that you can do a thing someone else is having trouble with."[59] The ever impatient Lennon complained about having to work on "Ob-La-Di, Ob-La-Da" for five days running because McCartney started from scratch for a third set of basic tracks after other versions had already received many overdubs, but Lennon had his own sort of domination over studio time. His "Revolution" sequence — idiosyncratic, to say the least — monopolized the first week of recording, and a patient McCartney did not offer his first composition until Lennon was done and they had even recorded a song of Ringo's. McCartney offered the song, "Blackbird," to a silent reception; he recorded it — as he was later to do with "Why Don't We Do It in the Road" — in one studio while his mates were involved in another. Lennon was asked in May 1970 at what point he thought the Beatles had broken up, and he responded, "The Beatles' White Album. Listen — all you experts listen, none of you can hear. Every track is an individual track — there isn't any Beatle music on it. I just say, listen to the White Album. It was John and the Band, Paul and the Band, George and the Band."[60] For this universally recognized reason, our discussion below of the new compositions for the White album will proceed composer by composer.

Harrison continued to use his Fender Stratocaster and Gibson SG, McCartney his Rickenbacker, and Lennon his Casino and Jumbo, both newly stripped down to the bare wood.[61] Alongside these, however, a whole raft of new equipment was supplied by Fender and adopted. Making their first appearances on the White album are Fender Telecasters for both Harrison and Lennon, Fender Jazz Basses, the Bass VI, Bassman 100 amp, with two twelve-inch cones, and two Fender Twin-reverb amplifiers — each with a pair of twelve-inch speakers that were much better than the Vox units at maintaining a clear sound at high volumes. Several of the album's recordings run a piano through the new amp, "Penny Lane"–style. In addition, Harrison purchased a new C&W acoustic guitar, the Gibson J-200 (best-known as customized for Elvis in the 1950s), in New York, and was ultimately given a Gibson Les Paul that he had borrowed to use with the new Fender amp on July 18.[62] Ringo was still on his 1963-style Ludwig set, bass drum now without front head and heavily damped with towels, with a chamois damping the snare. The kit remained in the studio, as Ringo Starr never practiced at home.[63]

On May 14, the Beatles booked EMI's Studio Two for two sessions a day, for a total commitment running from 2:30 P.M. to midnight, five days a week, for two months.[64] Their attendance, as it turned out, would be much more relaxed, and they completed the work only after five months. By mid-1968, London's independent studios, to which the Beatles began to turn a year previously, were highly competitive, boasting the latest in technology, and at one of these the Beatles got their first taste of eight-track recording.[65] The recording staff was affected by the artists' heavy disagreements. Martin took an unprecedented three-week holiday during the sessions (ending October 1), handing the reins to new AIR assistant and one-time Who producer Chris Thomas, who is heard playing five different keyboards on four different tracks. Because of the tension, long-time engineer Geoff Emerick—so essential on *Sgt. Pepper*—quit on July 16, not to work with the group again until July 21, 1969.[66]

Each composer's contributions to the White album shall be addressed in a roughly chronological order of composition, determined as follows: (1) those pieces known to predate India, (2) those known to have been written in India, (3) others present on the Kinfauns rehearsal tape, and (4) all others recorded during this period, taken up in the order of their introduction in the studio.

New Songs by John Lennon

"Cry Baby Cry"   Five early working tapes of Lennon's "Cry Baby Cry" are ascribed to late 1967.[67] The two earliest drafts are played on piano with double-tracked voice. The piano, with its typical-for-1967 chromatic descent in the bass, is essentially finished here; the five-and-a-half-bar first verse (**B**) is repeated following the Mixolydian choruses (**C**), which at this point carry the text of an advertisement from which Lennon took the words "Cry baby cry, make your mother buy."[68] The third draft, for piano and voice, introduces as a bridge to the "Cry Baby Cry" chorus the germ of the "Across the Universe" chorus, "Jai Guru Deva, Om," here with an oom-pah piano basis. It is not known how this chorus was transplanted from "Cry Baby Cry" to "Across," but Lennon's method of raiding some of his compositions to provide sections of others seems to have been a regular practice, and it is particularly well documented in his thorough composing tapes of the late 1970s. The fourth "Cry Baby Cry" sketch tape is a fragment for piano and Mellotron (with strings setting) of the "Across the Universe" germ, and the fifth tape is a loud power-chord woodshedding of the chorus on the Casino.[69] The double-tracked Kinfauns demo has the lyrics and chords fully composed by late May, but the introduction (**A**) is lacking, and the coda, shown in example 3.6, has a metrically irregular overlapping of vocals—a technique reserved for "Julia"—that is smoothed out in the final version.

The "Cry Baby Cry" recording is fairly straightforward. Everything heard on the extreme left and right was taped as the basic tracks on July 16, following a

Example 3.6 "Cry Baby Cry" compositional draft (Lennon-McCartney). © 1968 Northern Songs.

day-long group rehearsal. Take 1 of these rehearsals, heard on Beatles 1996b, appears with Lennon's Jumbo and guide vocal, McCartney's bass, and Starr's drums. On the left channel from the basic tracks are Lennon's vocal for the introduction and choruses (onto which some bass bleeds in the first verse; choruses are given ADT in a reduction made on July 16) and McCartney's rhythmically flippant Rickenbacker (entering for the second verse, at 0:40). On the right are Lennon's Jumbo (with ADT) and Starr's drums. Some additions heard in the center were taped the same day; these include Lennon's piano (the score omits the lead-ins of C–1) and Martin's harmonium. All others were added two days later. These final dubs were Lennon's lead vocal, Lennon/McCartney falsetto backing vocals and tambourine for choruses, Martin's sea-chantey harmonium introduction, sound effects for tea (1:10–1:15) enjoyed in the third verse, and Harrison's bluesy guitar, also in the third verse. The guitar is a bright Gibson Les Paul borrowed from Eric Clapton and soon to be a permanent gift.[70] The guitar's sound, featuring the $b\flat2$-g^2 interval, is emphatically blue, particularly in following the $\natural3$ that sustains above the $\hat{6}$–$\sharp\hat{5}$–$\natural\hat{5}$–$\sharp\hat{4}$–$\natural\hat{4}$ bass descent.

In the chorus, Lennon's vocal adopts a spooky, breathy tremolo that may have inspired Tommy James's odd colors in "Crimson and Clover" (December 1968). Another creepy effect derives from the ending; as if to reverse the ending on VI♯ of "And I Love Her," Lennon ends "Cry Baby Cry" on the relative minor home of VI, itself negated by the chilling last note of the piano, a nonresolving but insistent low D♯. All in all, it's difficult to get too deeply drawn into this dark and rather unsympathetic taunting of a crying baby. "Cry Baby Cry" was mixed for both stereo and mono on October 15.

"Dear Prudence" and "The Continuing Story of Bungalow Bill"   Two Lennon songs on the White album tell Rishikesh stories and are known to have been composed there. Prudence Farrow's friends worried about her in Rishikesh; she was such a recluse, constantly meditating in her hut, that Harrison and Lennon were asked to try to reach her. "So we sang to her," speaks Lennon over his guitar at the end of the Kinfauns demo of the song that resulted, "Dear Prudence."[71] This song has been heard as a metaphor for a gentle encouragement

toward sexual awakening, but given Lennon's inclinations, a much more general sort of enlightenment involving a "brand new day" can be appreciated.[72]

The Kinfauns demo of "Dear Prudence," performed in C♯ rather than the eventual D, has the song intact except for a clumsy transition from a repeated bridge (**C**) directly to a new Who-like weight at **D**. The released version shows the possibilities of both the new eight-track recording equipment at Trident Studios, allowing a cleaner additive layering in the increasingly thick vocal and instrumental arrangement, and the new Fender gear—the Casino has new clarity through the Twin-Reverb amplifier, and a distorted Fender Telecaster introduces a dirtiness not heard before. Taped on August 28 and 29, we hear Lennon's Casino ("Guitar II," that part practiced in Kinfauns, and another based on the chromatic bass descent of "Lucy in the Sky with Diamonds") on the right. On the left are McCartney's Rickenbacker bass, Harrison's solo Telecaster (the pentatonic "Guitar I" at **C** [1:49–2:00] and then, after **D**, "Guitar IV"), with its 1963-style octaves (2:56–3:31) rising to Harrison's highest playing ever, to d⁴ (and note the final Hendrix-like effect at 3:33–3:39), and Lennon's second Casino ("Guitar III," a tamboura-like alternation of $\hat{1}$, $\hat{5}$, and $\hat{8}$. At center are Lennon's double-tracked lead vocal, McCartney's drums (the song was recorded during Ringo's "strike"), Harrison's Les Paul (a fourth, unnotated, guitar simply articulating the double-plagal cadence at **B**+4–5 [1:38–1:42], C–G–D chords in arpeggiating sixteenths, foreshadowing a technique featured on *Abbey Road*), and McCartney's piano (heard only in the coda—"rippling and glistening with brightness, irradiating everything around it").[73] Additionally, a chorus with tambourines and handclaps consisting of the Beatles, Mal Evans, cousin John McCartney, and Harrison protégé Jackie Lomax is heard both left and right.[74] Both mono and stereo mixes were done on October 13.

The ringing dronelike guitars give "Dear Prudence" a peaceful aura that, along with the tamboura-colored "Across the Universe," is about as "Indian" as a Lennon composition ever got. The openness of its invitation is a bright change from the impersonal world of "Cry Baby Cry."

Lennon found it ironically amusing when one of his fellow meditators took a break from the course to hunt tigers with his mother. Lennon combined the names Jungle Jim and Buffalo Bill to ridicule the safari with feigned Captain Marvel gravity in "The Continuing Story of Bungalow Bill," his second song to tell a Rishikesh story.[75] The well-rehearsed chorus heard on the Kinfauns demo has an identical voicing to that on the released version but is thrown off by the draft's meter, without a second beat in **A**+4 and **C**+4. Lennon hates "dead air" beats but relents and adds the rest for ensemble security. Recorded entirely on October 8 and mixed the next day on eight-track at EMI, "Bungalow Bill" has on its right channel Ringo's drums, Lennon's overdubbed organ, a few conclusory notes from an acoustic guitar, and Chris Thomas's Mellotron. In the song proper, the Mellotron features mandolin tapes until the bassoon stop—that used on "Flying"—appears beginning the second time through **C**, at 2:08. But it also has a solo role, spliced onto the song's opening, heard in the center: a Flamenco-style *tastar de corde*, reminiscent of the opening chord from "Do You Want to

Know a Secret." Also heard center are McCartney's Rickenbacker (with lots of glissandi in the choruses), and Lennon's lead vocal (aided by Ono as "mommy," her role in three White album songs, and concluding with whistling). On the left are Lennon's Jumbo, his second vocal (again with whistling), chorus (with Maureen Starkey as well as Ono and studio hands) and tambourine, McCartney's second Rickenbacker part (heard only at the end of the third verse), and Harrison's J-200 chime (at the second hearing of **B**+3, 1:00).

The chorus is harmonically interesting in that it literally transposes its one mixture-colored phrase, heard in the tonic of C (0:00–0:07) and then in A (0:07–0:15). The modulation is a new twist on a familiar relationship: the dominant of the first half cadence (0:06–0:07) pivots as ♮VII of the new key. The result pits against each other the two tonal centers of C and A, which Lennon will contrast in several other compositions before McCartney and Harrison take advantage of the same effect in their work. The corresponding modulation within the verse, from A-natural minor to IV♭ of C, is suitably melodramatic, with tremolo effects on a cliff-hanging fermata on ♭$\hat{6}$ (0:33–). As in "I Am the Walrus," Lennon's narrative voice is rich and playful, but this song is a comical portrait rather than a social satire.

"I'm So Tired" and "Yer Blues"   Apparently three weeks into a Rishikesh-enforced abstinence and sleepless at night, perhaps with recurring thoughts of Yoko, Lennon wrote "I'm So Tired."[76] The Kinfauns demo is as ultimately recorded through the third verse, after which point the first verse (**A**)-refrain (**B**) is repeated. This leads to a unique spoken verse with the text, "When I hold you in your [*sic*] arms / When you show each one of your charms / I wonder, should I get up and go to the funny farm," clearly flowing from this song's concern for sanity, but cut from "I'm So Tired" to form the basis of the finale of "Happiness Is a Warm Gun." The progression in the opening bars, I–VII^7–IV–V, is worthy of note. Seemingly a variation on the banal I–VI–IV–V that follows (**A**+3–4) — tarted up by the singer's emphatic unprepared ninth (vocal, **A**+1) — this also seems to substitute $\hat{7}$ for the $\hat{1}$ more commonly heard in a jazz use of ♭III°[7], a Beatles chord last heard in "If I Fell."[77] The comparison of tonic with a major triad a half-step below will also be explored in "Sexy Sadie."

The song was recorded on October 8 and mixed on the 15th; the eight tracks are filled as follows: (1) McCartney's Rickenbacker (mixed left); (2) Ringo's drums (left); (3) Lennon's Casino (right); (4) Lennon's lead vocal (with varying degrees of ADT) and organ (center); (5) a Lennon/McCartney backing vocal duet (with gain much higher in the mono than the stereo mix; center); (6) drums, Harrison's Stratocaster bleed-through, and electric piano (heard center, especially at **B**); (7) drums (center); and (8) snare, Lennon's second organ, and Harrison's Strat (deleted).[78] The recording ends with indecipherable nonsense muttered by Lennon (center) that would lead many fans to play the record backward, hearing something very much like "Paul is dead, man; miss him, miss him, miss him." "I'm So Tired" is relentless in its buildup from lazy fatigue through offbeat-accented "chick"-guitar frustration (0:16–0:20) to the anger and bitter imploring of the refrain (1:00–1:05) that can only be answered by silence until its last appearance is pounded away three times. Lennon thus has explored quite a range of moods in his first compositions for the White album, but the song discussed next, "Yer Blues," takes the frustrations of "I'm So Tired" to an even deeper level.

"Trying to reach God and feeling suicidal" in India, Lennon wanted to write a blues.[79] But he felt insecure in the face of Sleepy John Estes and the original blues artists to whom he listened in school, insecure "just like Dylan's 'Mr. Jones'" (a character in Dylan's "Ballad of a Thin Man," September 1965), and in the third verse's reminiscences of Robert Johnson's "Hellhound on My Trail" (June 1937), so Lennon wrote a parody of British blues imitators, "Yer Blues."[80] The pentatonic tune is based almost completely on the d (D–E–G) and a (E–G–A) [025] trichords, the latter sung in both opening and closing registers. Lennon begins with an extremely slow tempo ($\silent.$ = 56), but the band varies the texture with a stop-time passage (**B**), followed by a "rock-and-roll"-inspired swing blues (**C**) and tongue-in-cheek improvisational solos (**D–E**) before the original rhythm is regained with a splice at **E+**11 (at 3:17, the edit of reductions of Takes 6 and 14).[81] Given the highly irregular accents of regrouped beat divisions (**A+**5–6), as tried in the "Cry Baby Cry" demo, it seems like Lennon has reacted to Ono's criticism of the all-too-predictable rhythm in "Hey Bulldog," for these events are more complex than the changing meters of "She Said She Said" or the mixed meters of "Good Morning Good Morning" and "All You Need Is Love." Even the use of ♮III–V⁷ (**A+**5–6, 0:22–0:27) in the place of the twelve-bar model's V⁷–IV⁷ could be heard as a defensive complication.

Texturally, "Yer Blues" is the simplest group recording on the LP. Although vocals were dubbed separately, no instruments were added to the basic track of Ringo's drums (heard left), Paul's Fender Jazz Bass (center), George's Leslied Telecaster ("Guitar I," with its almost-large-enough string bends, right), and John's Casino ("Guitar II," right except for **D**, where heard left). The recording's immediate "presence" is due to Lennon's demand to record the track in an acoustically unprepared closet off Studio Two. Lennon's vocal and McCartney's cadential 1̂ descant were taped on August 13 and 14, and editing/mixing was done on August 14 (mono), August 20 (adding Ringo's count-in as if to verify the live procedure), and October 14 (stereo, fading out eleven seconds faster than the mono). Lennon's vocal is given a Jerry Lee Lewis–like echo at **B** and **C** and is heard from Take 14 only in the appropriately ghostly bleed-through onto the drum track (3:17 to the end). Even the unidirectional microphones were no match for the lack of separation between group members in the small closet. The song's ponderous earnestness — hear particularly the Jazz Bass from the start — belies the composer's satirical tone, which is really evident only in the deliberate switch to swing time (at 2:09) and the purposefully empty one- and two-note guitar solos.

"Julia"   In early 1968, Lennon must have read Kahlil Gibran's book of aphorisms, *Sand and Foam*, for he was apparently taken by two of its apothegms: "Half of what I say is meaningless; but I say it so that the other half may reach

Example 3.7 "Julia" compositional draft (Lennon-McCartney). © 1968 Northern Songs.

you," and "When Life does not find a singer to sing her heart she produces a philosopher to speak her mind." These sentences apparently provoked Lennon to daydream in India about communicating with his mother, as this experience is relived in the song "Julia," in which he paraphrases and tropes Gibran's text to illustrate the integration of dreamlike memories into waking consciousness.[82] Three demos are extant: instrumental and single-tracked vocal versions in C, and a double-tracked vocal in E♭ that includes a later-abandoned descant part, shown in example 3.7.[83]

Lennon says, "The song was actually a combination of an imagery of Yoko and my mother blended into one."[84] Some sort of mother-Yoko transference may have been operative; in "The Continuing Story of Bungalow Bill," Ono takes on the role of "mommy" and is elsewhere referred to as "Mother." Regardless of the reasons behind this blending, it is clear which of "Julia"'s metaphors refer to Julia and which to Yoko. In "Yer Blues," Lennon sang, "My mother is of the sky"; this song's lyrics refer to Julia through sky-related images: "windy smile," "floating sky," "the sun," "morning moon," and "silent cloud."[85] "Yoko" is Japanese for "ocean child" and is represented with references to "seashell eyes" and "sleeping sand." The dead Julia and the living Yoko represent a spiritual/physical polarity. Polarity is indeed a key concept in this song, which begins, "Half of what I say . . ." The second Gibran quote suggests a mind/heart polarity. Further, there is a distinction between the spectral "call"-ing and the physical "touch"-ing, as Julia communicated to John through verbal metaphors, while Yoko simply reaches out and touches him.

"Julia" was recorded, simply double-tracking Lennon's vocal and Jumbo, and mixed on October 13. The guitar part is fingerpicked in a C-major pattern with capo on the second fret in the manner John learned from Donovan.[86] This simplicity, in addition to Lennon's frequent repetition of a single pitch, is somewhat offset by mild complexities in phrase length proportions and surface harmonies. Textural and motivic aspects of the musical setting directly highlight the textual polarities summarized above. The "Any Time at All"–like elisions at the beginnings of three verses, allowed by the vocal double-tracking, illustrate Lennon's changing consciousness at Julia's sudden appearance in his mind. By following the two different vocal tracks, the listener can follow the two paths, one farther away from reality than the other, being traced in Lennon's mind. Other double-tracking, effecting a unison doubling of several lines —"just to reach you Julia," "so I sing a song of love, Julia"— usually (the bridge, **C**, being the exception) represents Lennon's whole self responding to the half of his self (single-tracked) that hears Julia calling him and feels Yoko touching him.

"Julia"'s motivic language helps define the polarities of the text. The static prolongation of $\hat{5}$ has two motivic shapes. The declamatory, telegraphlike monotone of $\hat{5}$ gives the Gibran readings at **A** and **D** a meditative trancelike quality, while the gentle floating around $\hat{5}$, especially through neighbor b, which causes the alpha-wave-like $\hat{5}$ to flicker, accompanies the imagery that is "call"-ed forth to John's mind by his reading. This stasis on $\hat{5}$, both through the repeated pitch and with the candle-flame neighbors, accompanies the spiritual and mental attitudes in the text. The emotional and physical aspects are heard in the tumbling and unsupported $\hat{3}$–$\hat{2}$–$\hat{1}$ down-to-earth "song of love for Julia," which takes place in an inner voice, and the a $(\hat{5})$ is regained each time through the wonderful reaching-over of the double-tracked elision.

The dreamy quality is also sustained by the colorful surface harmonies of the verse. In **B**+2–4, a V$\flat$ chord is followed by a VI$\sharp$ triad that is itself followed by a ninth chord built on IV$\flat$. This series floats, all in weak second inversions, without being function-bound, in a loose support of the upper voice's neighbor b^1 and chromatic passing tone b$\flat^1$ in the prolongation of tonic. There is not even a strong dominant in the retransition; the A–C–E chord at **C**+4–5 is undercut by an F$\sharp$ that pretends to be root.

And so Lennon's floating daydream, evoked by remembrance of his mother, wanders to a deeply inner place shared by Julia and Yoko and is undisturbed as the singer splits into two, one half expressing the trance of called-up mental images, and the other half responding with a song of love. "Julia" is not so much a lament as an illustration of the paths of imagination, relating the wonder of a daydream of successful spiritual communion.

"What's the New Mary Jane"   "What's the New Mary Jane," a song cowritten by Lennon and Alex Mardas, was a contender for the album but cut when the LP sequence was finally determined.[87] The Kinfauns demo, unusually tritone-heavy, is excerpted in example 3.8. The final chorus is repeated many times, for a total length of 2'34", while Lennon alternates between the chorus text and that of the incoherent title. The track was recorded on August 14, with Lennon on piano and Harrison on J-200; vocals and many percussion effects were supplied by these two, Ono and Evans, leading to an ersatz Zappa frenzy, with various percussion, harmonium, tin whistles, xylophone, handbells, and plucking and scraping of the piano strings.

Four different stereo mixes from the August 14 recording have circulated; they are identified here in increasing order of complexity. The first one runs 6'27" and was probably mixed on October 14, 1968, with very little separation and taking little advantage of Lennon's double-tracked vocal. This mix is distinguished by surface noise from the resulting acetate at about 1:00 (Beatles 1991n, vol. 2; Beatles 1989). The second mix runs 6'30" and was probably done on September 11, 1969, with double-tracked vocal but no ADT (Beatles c. 1980, A). A third mix runs 6'33" and was likely done on November 26, 1969, with constant vocals from Ono and heavy tape echo by the third verse (Beatles c. 1980, B). The fourth was mixed by Geoff Emerick in 1985 for the aborted *Sessions* LP; it runs 6'02", with ADT added from the second verse on-

Example 3.8 "What's the New Mary Jane" (Lennon-McCartney). © 1968 Northern Songs.

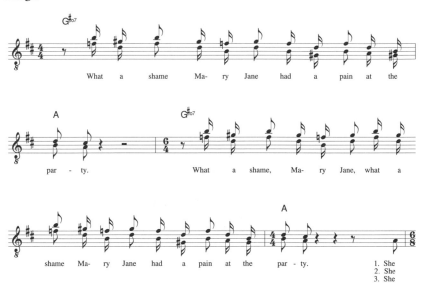

ward and heavy echo from the third onward (Beatles 1991l, 1993b, 1993e, and cleaned slightly for 1996b). Ultimately, the techniques are interesting, but too much reliance is made on weak material. "Revolution 9" is a similar free-for-all but much stronger, largely because little of it was recorded in real time.

The "Revolution" Series   In India, Lennon began writing a song that would take its fuel from uprisings by the revolutionary Maoists in China and by students in London (March 1968) and Paris (May 1968).[88] Despite Lennon's strong antiwar feelings, he was not against the establishment in 1968, as he would be a year later. Rather, he was a determined pacifist and wanted to see the plan before any government was to be toppled, so his "Revolution" counsels against that very approach.[89] The song, with two of its three verses intact, was very solid by the time the Kinfauns demos were made. At this time, the song was played in C at ♩ = 124. Apparently Lennon thought the tempo too fast to articulate the rapid-fire syllabic passages, because the first group takes at EMI on May 30 result in a recording, in B♭, that has a slower but gradually increasing tempo of ♩ = 92–104, with a gentleness appropriate for the espousal of peace. But with this recording—the group's first studio work since February 11—Lennon expresses ambivalence, quizzically telling the revolutionaries that they "can count me out—in," "because I wasn't sure."[90] Even though his mind was not quite made up about revolution, Lennon wanted this recording out as a single, "as a statement of the Beatles' position" on war and revolution. McCartney and Harrison demurred, citing the uncommercially slow tempo, but the composer sensed jealousy in that he was rivaling the dominance shown by McCartney over the previous year; "I was awake again and they weren't used to it."[91] After a long delay, Lennon decided to remake the recording at a faster, more "commercial" tempo, counting himself completely "out" of the revolutionary circle; this was done (at $\quarternote$ = 124, and in B♭) in July, but by then it was relegated to the B-side of McCartney's "Hey Jude," which even Lennon agreed was a stronger A-side for the single. Instead of discarding the May recording, Lennon retitled it "Revolution 1," and it went onto the White album.

"Revolution 1" originally endured for 10'17". As with "What's the New Mary Jane" and many other precedents over three years, the song proper led to a simple free-for-all jam, with Lennon continuing to promise "all right" in screaming, tremolo-heavy Ono-styled vocal modulations recorded as he lay flat on his back. Unlike "Strawberry Fields Forever," "All You Need Is Love," and so on, the LP version of "Revolution 1" lost its coda. The six-minute remainder formed the basis of a musique concrète work, largely a Lennon-Ono collaboration "painting in sound a picture of revolution," "Revolution 9," which was included on the album in spite of objection from others.[92] Guided by Ono's experience and enthusiasm, it was perhaps Lennon's most adventurous work ever.

In "Revolution 1," Lennon likely took pride in the funkiness of both his rhythm and his lead playing. And, as in "Bungalow Bill," he throws an odd bar of $\frac{2}{4}$ in among the $\frac{4}{4}$ meter; the verse phrases, **A–B**, are of $6\frac{1}{2} + 6\frac{1}{2} + 6$ bars. A revolting three eighths elbow their way into the third ending (3:24). Incredibly, these extra eighths were spliced in, as if in answer to the opening's inadvertently overlapping takes, as revealed in a reduction mix of vocal, Jumbo, and bass parts made on June 4 (heard on Beatles 1994b). The basic track was made on May 30; we hear Lennon's easy-to-transpose two-string boogie part on Jumbo ("Guitar II"), McCartney's piano (most noticeable in the retransitional backhand gliss at 2:25), and Starr's drums (all heard center). This was reduced the next day, making room for Lennon's lead and descant vocal parts, McCartney's Rickenbacker, and "shoo be doo wop" vocals from Harrison and McCartney (all center). On June 4, Lennon cut his vocal for the coda lying down (wild), joined by extraneous vocalizings by Harrison and McCartney. A second reduction allowed McCartney's sustained organ (unused), a second drum track from Ringo and echoing percussive noise heard in the introduction (all center), and Lennon's fine lead guitar ("Guitar I," probably a distorted Strat, using a tone pedal at **C**; generally heard left but wild in the third verse and coda).[93] Two trumpets (right) and four pedaling-then-boogieing trombones (right, with some ADT sent left) were added on June 21, on which date a third reduction permitted Harrison to add the syncopated chords at **A–1**, perhaps on his distorted SG. Mixes were done on June 25. This version may not have been very "commercial," but its slow tempo, laid-back brass, restful lead vocal, and smooth backing vocals have the calming effect counseled in the lyrics, an effective counterpoise to the revolution sizzling in the distance with metric stabs and distorted electric guitars.

"Revolution 9" was both more ambitious and more dire than the song proper. The coda of the May 30 basic track, alternating D and A triads while Lennon yelled "All right!" and Ono spoke such phrases as "if you become naked," was overdubbed on May 31 and again on June 4 before being separated from the song proper. This basic recording is heard at various points within "Revolution 9"

Example 3.9a Robert Schumann, *Symphonic Etudes.*

(2:07–2:09; 2:33–2:50, with some bass and guitars; 3:10–3:12; 3:26–3:29; 3:45–3:51; 4:05–4:06; 4:20–4:28; 4:59–5:02; 5:39–5:49; 5:55–5:57; 6:15; and 6:49–7:46, with very heavy echo and distortion from the STEED system), always on the right, panning center only at the end.[94] Above this basic track, Lennon and Ono assembled sound effects, many on loops and all taken from a wide variety of sources, on June 6, 10, and 11. On the 20th, Lennon and Harrison simultaneously improvised and/or read from a hodgepodge of stream-of-consciousness discourses (and, at 6:44–6:46, Ono sang a sustained a^1) and the stereo master was mixed—"Tomorrow Never Knows"–style—on May 20, with Lennon mixing inputs from the control rooms of EMI's three main studios.[95] On May 25, the tape was edited from 9'05" to 8'12", and the mono mix, a reduction of the stereo master, was made on August 20.

Altogether, 154 entries from at least 45 sources are heard in the final mix. They include the piano theme in B minor (as notated in the Wise score, heard at 0:00–0:15, 0:52–1:31, 2:02–2:17, 2:54–3:01, 3:28–3:44, 3:48–4:03, 5:18–5:37, 6:07–6:13, and 6:29–6:43, three times heard panning), the looped announcement of Lennon's lucky number, "number nine," taken from an EMI engineers' testing tape (0:02–0:22, 1:48–1:50, 2:02–2:11 with STEED, 2:25–2:31, 2:49–2:53, 3:28–3:30, 3:48–3:50, 4:18–4:34, and 6:22–6:29, twice panning), a snip of a violin section's b–c^1 trill from "A Day in the Life" (at **C+11**; 0:15–0:21), a reversed looped passage from the finale of Myra Hess's EMI recording of Schumann's *Symphonic Etudes*, op. 13 (the original form is given in ex. 3.9a; 0:21–0:37, 0:57–1:11, and 3:48–4:11), a looped eighteenth-century duet of oboe/horn arpeggiations (0:50–1:00, 1:27–1:47, 3:02–3:15, 4:18–4:49, and 6:15–6:25), a reversed looped passage from a $\frac{6}{8}$ movement from a nineteenth-century string quartet in E♭ (0:50–0:57 and 1:48–1:50), a loop from a passage in Vaughn-Williams's motet "O Clap Your Hands" (King's College Choir, Cambridge, with the English Chamber Orchestra conducted by David Will-

Example 3.9b–d "Revolution 9" loops (Lennon-McCartney). © 1968 Northern Songs.

cocks; 0:58–1:00, 1:33–1:39, 4:18–4:50, and 6:25–6:31; always heard right),
a reversed looped passage from electric guitar in E (see ex. 3.9b; 1:55–2:07, and
2:23–2:29), the looped final chord of Sibelius's Symphony No. 7 (2:09–2:32,
2:59–3:05, 3:20–3:23, 5:24–5:28, and 5:40–5:52, always heard right), a reversed looped choral passage for sopranos and altos (see ex. 3.9c; 2:16–2:43,
2:51–3:03, 3:48–3:54, 4:18, 5:15–5:34, 5:37–5:41, and 6:09–6:29, nearly
always on the left), a looped clarinet's "Swami" tune (ex. 3.9d; 2:20–2:28,
3:17–3:23, 3:29–3:31, 3:36–3:38, 5:13–5:30, 5:52–6:01 with heavy echo,
and 6:09–6:29), operatic soprano (1:09–1:14) and tenors (2:35–2:42,
6:09–6:29, and 7:04–7:43), gunfire (5:43–6:09), the chatter of the filled
STEED tape being rewound over a live playback head (3:24–3:29, right; this is
heard at 3:56–4:09 in the alternate mix), heavy crowd noise — often from a
football match (twice with an announcer calling "Number 30," and three times
with the chant "Hold that line, block that kick," including the track's conclusion),
and many others too numerous to list here.[96] A few of Lennon's and Harrison's
spoken additions from June 20, some inaudible in the released mixes but clarified
in the alternate mix, are given here:

LENNON:	HARRISON:
0:50: ". . . him is his Welsh Fred in a pair of brown underpants . . ."	
1:01–1:08: ". . . remember shows you his brain and nods at you; every one knew that as time went by they'd get a little bit older and a little bit slower, but they weren't . . ."	
	1:51–1:53: "Who was to know? who wants to know?"
2:14–2:17: ". . . I phoned him on the third night, but unfortunately he was . . ."	
	3:38–4:19: "unbeaten with the situation . . . the telegram from the late colonel . . . bit of falsies the headmaster reported."
"they are standing still, they are standing still, they couldn't . . ."	

"Who could tell what he was saying;
his voice was low and his mind
was high and his eyes were closed
and his legs were drawn and his
hands were tied and his feet were
bound and his nose was burning,
his head was on fire and glasses
were insane. This was the end of
his ordeal."

"... this thing on the radio
gets into it, which
enabled him to move
about all over the
classroom."

4:41– 5:15: "... told the nuns
they believe he's insane. He was
the same and there wasn't a thing
that they could do about him, when
the doctor had told him he had
better get somewhere like at the
booty because his lungs were gone for
a burden, so the wife told him he'd
better go to see a surgeon or what
the place would be safest to go for
to call a surgeon than he could a
pair of yellow underclothes, so any
at all he went to see the dentist,
instead he gave him a pair of teeth
which wasn't any good at all so, so
instead of that he joined the
fucking Navy and went to sea."

5:30– 5:37: "... my broken chair,
my wings are broken and so is my hair,
I am not in the mood for wearing blue
clothing ..."

5:49– 5:59: "the sheep were a' sheeping,
the cows were a' cowing, the dogs were
dogging, the cats were catting, the birds
were birding, the fish were fishing, the
men were menning, they went swimming."

6:08: "... only to find the
night-watchman unaware of his
presence in the building. ..."

6:25– 6:48: "personality complex,
onion soup ... industrial output,
financial imbalance, the watusi,
the twist. Take this brother, may
it serve you well."

"... thrusting in between
your shoulderblades ...
El Dorado ..."

"Thank you."

7:42: "I'd just like to say ..."

This essay in sampling and deconstruction was given an overture comprising a McCartney outtake from September 16, "Can You Take Me Back," and a control room conversation between Alistair Taylor and George Martin and was unleashed on millions of pairs of ears unwashed by Zappa's "Who Are the Brain Police" (1966), let alone Stockhausen's *Gesang der Jünglinge* (1955–56).[97] Few knew what to make of it then, and the imaginative track has since never caught on among Beatles fans not otherwise interested in electronic music. (The techniques did not appreciably influence other rock musicians either; the atonal synthesized music and the musique concrète heard on Jerry Garcia's first solo album *Garcia* [1972] were probably inspired more by ex-Dead keyboardist and Stockhausen student Tom Constanten, as demonstrated on *Anthem of the Sun* [1968]. In September 1998, theorist Jonathan Bernard and I shared mutual memories of the Buckinghams in 1967–68, and these conversations led to the uncovering of a number of electronic images in their works, created by their Varèse-inspired producer, ex-Mother Jim Guercio.) As Lennon was to later complain that one reason he left the Beatles was his discomfort in having to fit into some kind of "format," the 1968 arguments over the tempos of "Revolution" and whether or not to include "Revolution 9" on the White album may be seen as portents of the rejection a year later of a "Cold Turkey" single and of the McCartney-dominated arrangement of the *Abbey Road* LP. Lennon was soon to think that if Beatles fans didn't care for "Revolution 9," he could find his audience elsewhere.

The raucous quality of "Revolution 9" infects the single version, called simply "Revolution." This fast rendition is noted for its "dirty" electric piano solo by Nicky Hopkins and its highly distorted guitars—not from the usual pre-amp distortion but caused by overloading the pre-amp on the mixing board by mismatching impedances through direct injection.[98] After rehearsing the fast version in B♭ on July 9, basic tracks were made on the 10th. These comprise Ringo's heavily compressed and limited drums, left (and for introduction and the added backbeat at **D**, center), and John's Casino with George's Les Paul, both heavily distorted but George's very much the fouler, both right. In the same July 10 session, two reductions allowed for handclaps at **C** (left) and two unison Lennon lead vocals (center), and an acetate (heard on Beatles 1994b) was then cut for study. The next day, Nicky Hopkins added the electric piano solo and coda (center), and recording was completed on July 12 with McCartney's bass and Lennon's searing Casino solo (at **E**, ending on the raunchy two-bar retransitional half-step slow trill on $\hat{5}$; both center).[99] The mono mix was prepared on July 15, the stereo not until December 5, 1969 (for the *Hey Jude* LP). A promotional performance video (an edited version of which is seen in Beatles 1996c) was filmed on September 4 with the Beatles singing live but over prerecorded instrumental tracks. In the video, McCartney sings descant, he and Harrison sing the shoo-be-doo-wops, and Lennon compounds the confusion as to his so-important stance by singing, once again, "But when you talk about destruction, don't you know that you can count me out—in."

It is notable that such a monumental composition, the first White album track recorded, could have three so very different realizations and that Lennon's stance is so ambivalent about such an important subject. As if to make up for this ambivalence, for which he was criticized by political radicals, Lennon was to take much firmer radical stances in the music of the early 1970s.

"Sexy Sadie" and Other Rishikesh Work   One home tape made in spring 1968 called "The Maharishi Song" consists of Lennon in a major-mode talking blues—more a conversation with Ono in rhythm—in which he portrays the Maharishi as a sham with earthly interests, working with the help of a shill to boost his image. Lennon's sudden disenchantment with the Maharishi came out in "Maharishi," later "Sexy Sadie," written as the bags were packed to leave India.[100]

The Kinfauns demo, without introduction, is essentially complete but has no real ending, Lennon's problem since at least as far back as "Yes It Is." Instead, it cascades through a chromatic-line series of major-minor chords, IV$^{\flat 7}$–III$^{7}_{\sharp}$–$\flat$III$^{\flat 7}_{\flat 5}$–II$^{7}_{\sharp}$–$\flat$II$^{\flat 7}_{\flat 5}$–I$^{\flat 7}$—sort of a lickerish chromatic version of the "I Am the Walrus" coda—before settling on IV^{add6}. The first day's work at EMI, on July 19, produced twenty-one unusable takes of "Sexy Sadie," at a very slow tempo. Both known attempts, a control room monitor mix (heard on Beatles 1993d) and Take 6 (Beatles 1996b), are at $\quarternote = 68$ as opposed to the final $\quarternote = 80$.[101] Twenty-three more practice takes were done on July 24. An acceptable basic track came from the next session, on August 13. On this, Lennon's Jumbo, Mc-Cartney's echoing piano, and Harrison's Leslied Les Paul are heard right, Starr's drums right-center, and Lennon's lead vocal center. Lacking eight-track equipment at EMI until September, three reductions were required on August 21 for dubs. These include Paul's Rickenbacker, left; John's second vocal and organ and Ringo's tambourine, center; and two Leslied sets of Paul/John/George backing "wah-wah" vocals, right. The mono mix, somehow missing the first three beats of bass, was made on August 21, the stereo on October 14, both eliminating a minute from the basic tracks.[102]

Although IV–V^7–I cadences abound in "Sexy Sadie," the song never settles into its tonic of G major. Instead, it teases around Î, as did the "Day Tripper" ostinato. The first arrival of tonic, at **A** (0:04), slips immediately to a chord that acts as V^7 of III, making the tonic G sound retrospectively like $\flat$VI in B minor, an area also emphasized at **A**+2 (0:13–0:15) by the agogic accent in the harmonic rhythm.[103] G priority is regained at **A**+4, only to slip away again; this time, normal progress from F$\sharp^7$ is interrupted by C, regaining G as tonic. In **A**+6 (0:27–0:28), F$\sharp^7$ simply doubles chromatic passing tone G$\flat$ on its way to F, which chord prepares C for its use in the subsequent V^7 on D (0:30–0:31). The lascivious half-step G–F$\sharp$ is given an even stranger context after the return from the doggedly diatonic "Here, There and Everywhere"–based bridge. Here, the steady I–II–III–IV progression at **B** has too-safe parallel octaves that leave nothing to chance. This passage ends at **B**+5 with the unexpected half-step A–A$\flat$ (1:06–1:09), resulting in the bass descent, A–A$\flat$–G–F$\sharp$, certainly more lubricious than even the slick Maharishi could have been.[104]

While in India, Lennon composed at least four other songs for which Kinfauns demos were prepared. "Look at Me" and "I'm Just a Child of Nature" appear in later solo LPs (Lennon 1970 and 1971 [as "Jealous Guy"], respectively) and are thus beyond the scope of this book. "Mean Mr Mustard" and "Polythene Pam" remain forever incomplete but appear on *Abbey Road* and thus will be discussed in chapter 4.[105] "The Rishi Kesh Song," in which Lennon sings, "The magic's in the mantra. . . . Just swallow this, that's all you gotta do," is often mentioned in the context of Lennon's India work, but this draft is actually thought to date from 1980 (the date given in Lennon 1998).

"Everybody's Got Something to Hide Except Me and My Monkey"   Lennon dates "Everybody's Got Something to Hide Except Me and My Monkey" to a probable mid-May, when he says it is "about me and Yoko. Everybody seemed to be paranoid except for us two, who were in the glow of love. Everything is clear and open when you're in love. Everybody was sort of tense around us: You know, 'What is *she* doing here at the session? Why is she with him?' All this sort of madness is going on around us because we just happened to want to be together all the time."[106] Harrison says that "Come on is such a joy" was a saying of the Maharishi's.[107] The composer's carefree opening guitar chords — not yet present in the Kinfauns tape, otherwise essentially finished except for the absence of IV — hide the downbeat as effectively as he did in "I Want to Hold Your Hand" and "She's a Woman." Is Lennon again courting Ono with rhythmic inventiveness?[108] The verse's cadence (**B**+11–14, 0:32–0:39) impresses the listener with both its $\frac{7}{4}$ metric effect and its reordering of the bluesy [025]-based chord progression.

The song was rehearsed on June 26, and the basic track was cut the next day. This consisted of Starr's drums and McCartney's busy cowbell and *chocalho* (alternating verses), left, and Lennon's chords on the Casino ("Guitar II") and Harrison's lead on the distorted SG ("Guitar I"), right. Three reductions allowed overdubs on July 1, including Paul's loose Rickenbacker, left, and second bass at **D** (beginning at 2:03), right, and John's two compressed lead vocals, center. On July 23, the Beatles added Paul's shouts (as at 0:39), left, and handclaps and extra snare for cadence, center. The tape was sped up from D major to E as the tracks were mixed on October 23. The exuberance of Lennon's young love is heard in the Beatles' hardest and most infectiously rhythmic rocking since "Sgt. Pepper's Lonely Hearts Club Band."

"Glass Onion" and "Happiness Is a Warm Gun"   Although no other known Lennon tapes predate September, the *Anthology* project's liner notes maintain that its rudimentary demos of "Glass Onion" and "Happiness Is a Warm Gun" (Beatles 1996b) are from Kinfauns. "Glass Onion" grew out of Lennon's amusement in early 1968 over fans' fascination with finding hidden meanings in Beatles records — even playing *Sgt. Pepper* backward to do so — and out of his typical "Walrus"-like desire to confuse them even more.[109] The composer has obvious fun warping the tune of "Strawberry Fields Forever" (**A**+2, 0:03–0:04), reviving the swooping strings of "I Am the Walrus" (**A**+6–9, 0:11–0:18), and quoting the plastic recorder from "The Fool on the Hill" (**A**+4–9, 1:27–1:40). Paul says John "wrote it mainly, but I helped him on it; . . . we were thinking specifically of this whole idea of all these kind of people who write in and say, 'Who was the walrus, John? Were you the walrus?' or 'Is Paul the walrus?' So eventually he said, 'Let's do this joke tune "Glass Onion" [with] all

kinds of answers to the universe.' "[110] Of course the "answers" aren't plain but as mystifying as ever: in this song about peeling back transparent layers of riddles in "Strawberry Fields Forever," "I Am the Walrus, "Lady Madonna," "Fixing a Hole," and "The Fool on the Hill," the central riddle remains visible but not solved, no matter how many holes are fixed—a reference as much to the Sea of Holes in the *Yellow Submarine* film as to the *Sgt. Pepper* song, no matter how many dovetail joints are crafted. Lennon will not provide easy answers. In print interviews, though, at least one clue has led somewhere; John says that his fond words for Paul at **A** in the second verse are a thank-you for having led the group over the preceding year.[111] This reference, though, only seems to make the song more mysterious.

Only the first verse, heard three times, is present in the Kinfauns demo, and its lyrics are different from the ultimate version in declaring that the place seen through a glass onion is "just as real" as Strawberry Fields. What appears to be double-tracked gibberish following the refrains in the Kinfauns tape actually contains clues, with references to "me and my buddies," "me and my friends," and a "Gene Vincent Fan Club," that Lennon may again be recalling his boyhood, perhaps singing of another Woolton landmark such as the Allerton Park Golf Course or some other home of "the other half," where "everything glowed." The final statement of the verse has drastic, curious, and moving changes of tempo from $\JJ = 116$ to $\JJ = 80$ and back, which reverberate with the boyhood-reviving meter changes in "She Said She Said." These fascinating changes do not survive in the EMI version.

Basic tracks were recorded on September 11 and consist of McCartney's Jazz Bass, left; Harrison's Strat, center; and Lennon's Jumbo with Starr's drums, right. Lennon's two unison vocals (and a distant shout from McCartney at 1:15, a bit less tuneful and more immediate than the 1963 falsetto re-transitions) and tambourine (right) were added the next day, and Paul's piano (entering at **B** and recapturing the backhand glissando from "Revolution 1" at **C**+8, 1:16) and Ringo's double-tracked drums (both right) the day after that. McCartney double-tracked the recorder part (right) on September 16. A sound effects tape (with telephone, the smashing of glass, and a brief loop of rugby commentary, heard in Beatles 1996b) was compiled on September 26 but scrapped when Martin recorded in their place the parts for double string quartet (center) on October 10, the date on which both mixes were prepared.[112]

One wonders whether Lennon asked Martin for a coda that sounds like a taunting sneer at his audience, for that's the effect of the violins' and violas' sliding tritones over the cellos' pizzicato. And the song proper is tonal, but normal contexts for A minor are paid little heed. In the verse (**A**), the tonic triad is embellished by chords, F^7 and C^7, that each share with tonic a pair of common tones and a pair of contrapuntal neighbors. The cadence (**B**) takes a bluesy turn with the [025] relationship among roots of F, D, and G, and the bridge (**C**) prolongs I^7 with an inner-voice chromatic scale ($e^1-f^1-f\sharp^1-g^1$, 1:01–1:16) emphasizing the role of counterpoint over harmony. There is no easy V, only a tough neighboring $\flat$VII. Lennon dares you to make sense of it!

A popular platitude in 1966–68 was "Happiness is a warm puppy," created in Charles Schulz's "Peanuts" comic strip. The culture reacted with countless take-offs, including "Happiness is a warm gun," a phrase on the cover of an American gun magazine that George Martin showed Lennon. The latter was impressed enough with its audacity to write a song with that title.[113] Beginning with the rejected spoken verse from the "I'm So Tired" demo (transcribed from "Happiness Is a Warm Gun" as ex. 3.10a), Lennon was inspired by his relationship with Ono (referred to at **E** as "Mother Superior") to add a few gun-related sexual double-entendres.[114] This became the new song's finale (**F–I**), to which the three singers added some greasy "bang bang shoot shoot" doo-wop backing vocals over the idiomatic 1950s progression already written into "I'm So Tired," I–VI–IV–V. This finale is not present in the Kinfauns tapes, however; only sections **D** ("I need a fix," at that time still in a straight $\frac{4}{4}$) and **E** ("Mother Superior"), along with the later-discarded "Yoko Ono, oh no" passage on I–♭VII–IV (Beatles 1996b, 0:51+), seem to date back to May.

Lennon had trouble developing the song further, so while tripping with Derek Taylor, Neil Aspinall, and Pete Shotton, he sought interesting phrases from his friends, apparently hoping to compose another riddle song along the lines of "I Am the Walrus" and "Glass Onion." Taylor recalls, "First of all, he wanted to know how to describe a girl who was really smart and I remembered a phrase of my father's which was 'she's not a girl who misses much' " (thus the line at **A+1–2**). Then Taylor told of having met a man who enjoyed wearing moleskin gloves during sex, and of how the image of lizards "nipping up the window" (revised at **B+1–3**) was for him a Los Angelinian "symbol of very quick movement." Taylor takes credit for having read in a newspaper the stories of a voyeur caught at a soccer match with mirrors on his boots (**B+4–5**) and of "a man wearing a cloak [who] had fake plastic hands, which he would rest on the counter of a shop while underneath the cloak he was busy lifting things and stuffing them in a bag around his waist" (**B+6–7**, but highly suggestive of masturbation given Lennon's rewritten context). The line about donating something, once eaten, to the National Trust (**B+8–9**) came out of a conversation about having seen evidence of public defecation.[115] If the opening line is about Yoko, what follows is a rather perverse self-portrayal, and the poetic text as a whole is not only eccentric (nothing new for Lennon) but also less coherent than anything else (including "Walrus" and "Revolution 9") produced by the Beatles.

Like "I'm So Tired," the composition builds in intensity through a variety of textural and tonal changes. The music, though—despite the mishmash of styles in a highly sectionalized through-composed form—well compared by its composer in this regard to "God" (Lennon 1970)—is tightly unified by motivic relationships that recall on the large scale what "She Loves You" does on its surface. Of particular notice are the varied reharmonizings of the E–G motive with which Lennon opens the song, unadorned. Through **A**, this third is filled in for a descent, g^1–$f\sharp^1$–e^1, over two chords in E minor. This line, of course, had furnished the bass support in the verse of "All You Need Is Love."[116] At **C**, the same E–G third is supported by a major-minor seventh chord on A, in a new A-

Example 3.10a "Happiness Is a Warm Gun" (Lennon-McCartney). © 1968 Northern Songs.

Example 3.10b "Happiness Is a Warm Gun" compositional draft (Lennon-McCartney). © 1968 Northern Songs.

pentatonic-minor context that sets up the [025] (A–C–G) chord relations, as essential to "Everybody's Got Something to Hide Except Me and My Monkey" and "Glass Onion," in **C–E**. As in "She Loves You," the G–E motive is given a third harmonization. The finale (**F**) arrives with the same interval in a new, high register that opens up with great "happiness" at the arrival of C major (A major's ♭VII at **F–1** becomes C's V, reversing a "Bungalow Bill" modulation).[117] C major finally clarifies E as the primary tone prolonged through the entire piece, as this $\hat{3}$ descends to $\hat{2}$ at **I+4** and to $\hat{1}$ in the final bar, descending most clearly in Harrison's Telecaster. Once again, Lennon writes a White album song with stunning tonal relations, puzzling poetry, and a touch of satire.

But it is Lennon's rhythmic contrasts that make this song a standout, instead of just the tired old rock-and-roll number of which its clichés remind us. Seventy takes of the basic track were necessary, says Mark Lewisohn (1988, 157), because of the song's rhythmic complexity, unusual even for a Lennon piece.[118] In the version released, the basic track consisted of John's Casino, center; Paul's Rickenbacker (with glisses at **F**, 1:35–1:45, like those in "Bungalow Bill"), left;

and Ringo's drums and George's compressed Telecaster, right. There are six *different* meters in the first twenty-one bars, with cross accents in every first beat of **E** (1:13–1:34). At **G** (1:47–2:02), Ringo somehow maintains $\frac{4}{4}$ for four and a half bars while the rest of the band is agreed on three bars of $\frac{12}{8}$ (everyone's eighths being equal in this unique sesquialtera rhythm). A free tempo (2:15–2:21) presents a "She Loves You"–style cadenza on IV♭ just before **I** (where "yes it is" recalls the coda of that 1965 song). Tempo changes define the major sections: ♩ = 72 at **A**, ♩. = 54 at **C**, eighths moving at precisely half the tempo as before, and ♩ = 76 at **F**, and some wild changes of beat division occur in between (at **E** as well as **G**). No wonder "Mother Superior jump the gun"; Yoko's "Hey Bulldog" digs hit pay dirt here.

The backing track was complete with an edit (at 1:34) of Takes 53 and 65 made on September 25, after which all overdubs were added.[119] These include three lead vocals by Lennon—with descant in **B**+6–9, mixed out of **C**, and with odd octaves for the junkie's moan at **D**, 1:03–1:12 (center, moving to right at **F**), doo-wops (left), McCartney's second bass part at **C** (left), and tuba (deleted in both mixes). Additionally, a single track (heard on Beatles 1993d) has organ in **A–B** (the beginning of which part—derived from the Casino—is transcribed as ex. 3.10b), a punched-in fuzzed Telecaster solo by Lennon at **C**, silence at **D**, hi-hat and tambourine at **E**+1, and piano from **F** to the end; this track is heard center, but the organ and, at **F**, piano are deleted in both mixes, made on September 26 (mono) and October 15 (stereo). While none of the vocal or instrumental parts in "Happiness Is a Warm Gun" require any degree of technical wizardry, and none of the instrumental colors are wildly innovative, every note is just right, and the two-minute, forty-second song packs a wealth of imaginative variety and inevitable power.

"Good Night"   Discussion of Lennon's White album compositions closes on the subject of the only one not appearing among the Kinfauns demos. Lennon wrote "Good Night" on piano for son Julian.[120] He wrote the song in June, following the breakup of his marriage, and was inspired to have Ringo sing it with a lush orchestra: "So I just said to George Martin 'arrange it just like Hollywood.' Yeah, corny."[121] Preliminary work took place in the studio on June 28 and July 2. An early rehearsal from the former date, with Lennon on piano, Harrison on simple percussion, and Starr on vocal, is preserved in Beatles 1996b. On July 22, Martin taped his score for three flutes, clarinet, horn, vibraphone, harp, twelve violins, three violas, three celli, and double bass in Studio One, with a standard orchestral stereo image. To this, Ringo added his lead vocal, and eight members (four men, four women) of the Mike Sammes Singers, four of whom had chanted on "I Am the Walrus," added light-programme-styled backing vocals.[122] Mixes were done on October 11, the stereo receiving a fade-in.

The verse structure has Lennon's asymmetry, with two identical antecedents (**A**+1–8, 0:22–0:51) preceding a single consequent (**A**+9–12, 0:52–1:05), as in "It's Only Love." Also of interest is the verse's voice leading, descending from $\hat{8}$ to $\hat{5}$ once $\hat{1}$ becomes dissonant (**A**+2, downbeat), suggesting a gentle dropping-off, as with peaceful sleep. The major-major I^7 chords are very uncharacteristic of the composer, and the countermelodies and the sequential interlude at C might very well have been Martin's ideas, issuing from Ravel's style. Martin mimics his favorite composer well, particularly with his flute, horn, and harp figuration; Wilfrid Mellers finds Raveaux extended tertian sonorities.[123] This passage is also closely related to a song written by Martin, "The Game."[124] I have difficulty settling into "Good Night" after "Revolution 9" dies away, but most no doubt take it as a welcome bromide.

Succinctly summarizing John Lennon's compositions for the White album would be as difficult as doing so for his entire career. In no other single collection does he plumb his imagination in as many different directions as he does here. Among the most innovative powerful pieces are the dire electronic mayhem of "Revolution 9," the gentle daydream of "Julia," and the perverse puzzle of "Happiness Is a Warm Gun." Another puzzle, "Glass Onion," is more taunting, along the lines of "Bungalow Bill," and the satirical tone of "Happiness" becomes more subtle in "Yer Blues." The frustration of "I'm So Tired" cuts through the bliss of "Dear Prudence."

We have tied the composer's continuing exploration of rhythmic complexity, as exhibited in "Happiness," "Me and My Monkey," "Yer Blues," "Cry Baby Cry," and "Bungalow Bill," to an off-hand criticism of the Beatles from Yoko, but there is no neat corresponding explanation for Lennon's continued interest in complex tonal relations, as shown in "Sexy Sadie," "Bungalow Bill," "Happiness," and "Glass Onion." His strong interest in the blues, as in "Me and My Monkey" and "Yer Blues," could be tied to the fact that most of these 1968 songs were written on the guitar, but the piano-based "Cry Baby Cry" is as bluesy as it is modal and chromatic.

Whereas McCartney will be seen to have written in a host of different styles for this LP, nearly all of his offerings — save perhaps "Why Don't We Do It in the Road" and "Wild Honey Pie" — are more typical of the Beatles than of his solo work. The same cannot be said of "Revolution 9" (if only *Two Virgins* were this interesting), "Julia" (which would have fit perfectly into *John Lennon/Plastic Ono Band*), "Good Night" (*Imagine?*), or perhaps even "Happiness Is a Warm Gun" (which would have been a good counterpart to "(Just Like) Starting Over" on *Double Fantasy*). With his bass and voice, McCartney adds a great deal to Lennon's tracks, but we sense that Lennon is the master, McCartney the apt pupil.

New Songs by Paul McCartney

"Mother Nature's Son," "Rocky Raccoon," "Back in the U.S.S.R.," "Jubilee," and "Wild Honey Pie"   Although available documents confirm that five McCartney songs from the White album period — "Mother Nature's Son," "Rocky Raccoon," "Back in the U.S.S.R.," "Jubilee," and "Wild Honey Pie" — were written in India, many others undoubtedly were as well, and the composer's new comfort in 1968 with the acoustic guitar suggests a fair amount of exercise in Rishikesh.[125]

The bucolic "Mother Nature's Son" conveys an innocence deeper than that of the "Fool on the Hill." Lennon says "Mother Nature's Son" and his own "I'm Just a Child of Nature" were both inspired by a lecture on nature by the Maharishi.[126] Musically, McCartney's song also resounds with the simple folk style of "I've Just Seen a Face" and of the Incredible String Band and portrays McCartney as a natural busker, "singing songs for everyone." The Kinfauns demo (with the "Guitar I" part and vocal) is essentially complete, lacking the introduction, some of the vocal scatting, which proves Paul's facility with adding descant parts, and the final $Ib7$ chord, as it repeats for a projected fade-out. The slow first two bars were still not performed by the time Take 2 (Beatles 1996b) was recorded for vocal and guitar only. This run-through also lacks the two bars of the first ending and concludes with an unusual tempo change from ♩ = 86 to about ♩ = 54.

"Mother Nature's Son" was a simple recording. McCartney taped his lead vocal (center) and Martin D-28 part ("Guitar I," left) on August 9 and completed it on the 20th with his own parts for bass drum (introduction and **B**, from 1:10, center), bongos (entering at the second **A**+5, 0:59) and timpani (entering at the second **B**+5, at 2:04, both right-center), and second D-28 (fourth hearing of **A**, 2:16–2:37, including the McCartneian descending major scale) and vocal (coda, both right). Four horns were added (right, entering at the first ending, 0:42), and the song sat ready for mixing, which was done on October 12, cutting the introduction in half.[127] The song is laden with echo, particularly from the drums, which were positioned in a corridor for maximum effect, an effect well suited for setting the outdoor atmosphere ("beside a mountain stream") that has also been the milieu suggested by horns since the eighteenth century.[128]

The introductory $E9$ chord prepares a song in D, not the expected A; the denouement from this introduction has a surprising atmosphere of naïveté. Voice leading in the melody is limited to static but pretty contrapuntal neighbors: a^1–b^1–a^1 (**A**+1–2), d^2–$c\sharp^2$–d^2 (**A**+3–7), $f\sharp^2$–g^2–$f\sharp^2$ (**B**+1–6). This lack of a supported descending line expresses well a satisfaction with things as they are—not only a happiness in singing in a backcountry setting but also a contentment in the situation held since "born a poor young country boy." This song has been cited as a precursor to John Denver's "country boy" style, but it was a much more closely copied model for Justin Hayward in several songs for the Moody Blues, notably "Dawning Is the Day" (particularly with its chromatic descent over the tonic at "Miss Misty Meadow, you will find your way"; 1970).[129]

"Rocky Raccoon"—initially "Rocky Sassoon"—is supposed to have been jointly composed by McCartney, Lennon, and Donovan, but Lennon takes no credit.[130] This number is one of a genre of acoustic western ballads of the lawless West also represented by Dylan's "John Wesley Harding" (January 1968) and the Dead's "Dupree's Diamond Blues" (June 1969). The Kinfauns demo (Beatles 1991j) lacks the crucial verse at **G** (Lennon's lyrics?) and the free introduction (**A**) that both sets up the story and gives the drifting song some of its small amount of modest charm. The form is held together by a flimsy premise that is not rigidly followed: similar phrases are grouped in pairs set off by slight differences; cf. **B** (0:30–0:54) and **D** (1:19–1:42) as opposed to **C** (0:55–1:18) and **E** (1:43–1:55). Harmony is unified by the guitar's repeated descent, g^1–$f\sharp^1$–$f\natural^1$–e^1, which gets old quickly.

"Rocky Raccoon" was recorded and mixed for mono on August 15. The basic track consists of Paul's D-28 and John's harmonica at **B**−1 (0:28–0:30) only (right-center), Ringo's drums (entering at **B**+4, a bit later in mono; note the snare "gunshot" at **E**+1, 1:48), and John's Bass VI, preserved only at **F** (1:55–2:18, both left). This is augmented by McCartney's lead vocal (center) and Harrison's plodding Bass VI with Leslie (entering at **C**, 0:54, left), and Lennon's harmonica (entering at **D**+4, 1:28), Martin's saloon piano (at **F**, 1:55–2:18), Lennon's harmonium (entering at **G**+2, 2:21), and backing McCartney/Lennon/Harrison vocals (third time through **D**, 2:52) (all right). The loose atmosphere in recording the basic track, resulting in an improvisatory introduction (**A**), is most evident in comparing the final master with Take 8 (Beatles 1996b). The stereo mix was made on October 10. While I feel obligated to provide the above documentation for a fan favorite, I find nothing else particularly noteworthy in the song's musical or poetic content.

Stories as to the title of "Back in the U.S.S.R." present two origins: (1) Britain enacted the chauvinistic "I'm Backing Britain" campaign in January 1968 in hopes of raising funds to put toward the national debt; (2) in Rishikesh, Mike Love suggested that he and Paul do a U.S.S.R.-based rewrite of Chuck Berry's "Back in the U.S.A." (June 1959), and together they worked up a refrain as "I'm Backing the U.S.S.R.," later to revert to the final, more Berry-leaning title.[131] Lennon and McCartney help the song evolve into a tribute to the Beach Boys, completing the circle that began when the Beach Boys redid Berry's "Sweet Little Sixteen" (February 1958) as "Surfin' U.S.A." (March 1963). Berry's "Back in the U.S.A." provides the Beatles with material in both a litany of place-names and an opening about an international return flight.[132] Icing is added to the honorific cake at the end of the bridge, where McCartney shouts a reference to Ray Charles's "Georgia on My Mind," a wonderful turn on the name of the Soviet state.

The song's verse-refrain (**A**)/bridge (**B**) structure, most of its lyrics (excepting the third verse), all of its eventual chords, and even its offbeat accents measured 3+3+4 in the refrain's extension (second ending of **A**, 0:58–1:02) are present in the Kinfauns demo. The demo's feel, however, is very different from the more driving final track, because there McCartney must drop his original rhythm guitar part (a "Revolution 1"–like boogie) to take up drums in Ringo's absence. The basic track was recorded on August 22 and contained McCartney's drums, Harrison's Telecaster ("Guitar I"), and Lennon's Bass VI (heard only in the refrains and chorded [!] bridge), all heard right. All overdubs were completed the next day; these include McCartney's drum backbeat (left), compressed lead vocal with its Jerry Lee Lewis-like stuttering (double-tracked for the refrain, center), and piano (including the now frequent retransitional backhand glisses at 2:02 and 2:23), Rickenbacker bass fills at **A**+4 and Casino solo for the last verse (maintaining a $\hat{1}$ pedal as done by I° violin in "Yesterday") (all right); Harrison's Jazz bass (including the fifths of "Guitar II" in the refrain, left) and more Telecaster (including the octave doubling—"Guitar III"—in the refrain and the note-bending solo at **C**, right); and Wilson/Love/Wilson-style backing vocals by the three singers in the bridge and handclaps for the refrain, solo, and last verse (center). To polish the LP's solid opener, jet sounds were taken from the EMI archives and panned over much of the track, eventually crossfading over the arrival of "Dear Prudence." The mono mix—different from the stereo chiefly in its jet effects—was done on August 23, the stereo on October 13.

The "Sgt. Pepper" I–♭III–IV [025] progression, also a link to both "Glass Onion" and "Happiness Is a Warm Gun," dominates the verse-refrain. This passage contrasts major triads on A and C with a strength that hints at what will come in *Abbey Road*. The bridge features a novel chromatic bass descent, $\hat{4}$–$\hat{3}$–♭$\hat{3}$–$\hat{2}$ (**B**+5–6, 1:13–1:15), within an expansion of V⁷/V that is enriched by a chromatic change in contrary motion against the bass, $\hat{4}$ to ♯$\hat{4}$ (in moving from D to B⁷, 1:13–1:15). Even within a purposefully derivative song, McCartney writes an original number with loads of fresh energy.

The would-be whimsical Indian blues singalong "Wild Honey Pie" is one of McCartney's slightest efforts ever. Its title, which implies that this song is related to "Honey Pie," is misleading, for it has much closer tonal links to the more substantial "While My Guitar Gently Weeps," sharing its I–♭VII–♭VI–V structure, or to the coda of the later "Glass Onion," exploiting the same tritones within major-minor chords in the guitar voicings. On August 20, McCartney recorded three acoustic guitars (two center, one right), harpsichord (left), bass drum (center), tom-tom (right), and three vocals (left, center, and right); these were mixed for mono the same day and for stereo on October 13. Perhaps this throwaway can be explained as McCartney's answer to Lennon's "What's the New Mary Jane," which had been taped four days before this was.

"Ob-La-Di, Ob-La-Da," "Honey Pie," and "Blackbird"   Three other McCartney efforts, "Ob-La-Di, Ob-La-Da," "Honey Pie," and "Blackbird," appear among the Kinfauns demos. Conga player Jimmy Scott led the London-based Ob-La-Di Ob-La-Da Band, whose name was based on a Nigerian expression meaning "Life goes on."[133] The phrase caught McCartney's ear enough to lead him to write "Ob-La-Di, Ob-La-Da" in the clipped-backbeat Jamaican ska style popularized in the United Kingdom in August 1967 by Desmond Dekker and the Aces and later to govern Wings's "C Moon" (1972) and "Seaside Woman" (1973). McCartney fictionalizes the bandleader's family's story and in the second verse falls back on his weakness for expensive rings (cf. "Can't Buy Me Love," "I'm Down," and the early draft of "Drive My Car").

Three of four basic versions of "Ob-La-Di" have found distribution. The Kinfauns demo (Beatles 1991j), performed in A at ♩ = 128, is complete, but the coda's deceptive cadence, which derives from **B**+2 in the chorus, has only one bar of VI instead of the eventual two. The first studio version, still in A at ♩ = 126 with the one-bar deceptive resolution, was taped on July 3, 4, and 5.[134] This version has the same acoustic-guitar basis as the demo, along with drums, bass, two McCartney vocals—including a rejected third-verse descant part a third above the lead, maintaining $\natural\hat{7}$—and backing Harrison/Lennon vocals, three saxes, Jimmy Scott's conga, and marimba.[135]

Despite the heavy three-day production, McCartney rejected this tape and attempted two more sets of basic tracks, beginning on July 8 and 9, respectively, and opted to use the earlier of these, played in B♭ at a slower tempo, $\downarrow$ = 112. The much more percussive released version, centered on bass and piano, began with a basic track including Lennon's piano—borrowing McCartney's gliss at **C–**1 (2:08), Harrison's Jumbo overloading the tubes in the desk, Starr's drums, and McCartney's Rickenbacker—which does not enter until **A–**2, contrary to the score—all reduced to one track heard center.[136] On July 9, 11, and 15 this was overlaid with McCartney's lead vocals, vocal percussion, and handclaps, including Lennon's and Harrison's off-mike wisecracking "arm" and "leg" in answer to McCartney's "hand," **A+**4 (right, with ADT to left), and Lennon/Harrison falsetto backing vocals, three saxes in the bridges, and Latin percussion (all center). Mixes were made on July 15 (mono) and October 12 (stereo).[137] "Ob-La-Di, Ob-La-Da" became a #1 single, but not by the Beatles; it was recorded by five groups in Britain within a week of the release of the White album, the hit version done by the quintet Marmalade (released on December 4, 1968). It's a good pop tune in the "Hello Goodbye" or even the "Thank You Girl" vein and enormously popular, but the Beatles do not advance here.

"Honey Pie" is McCartney's compulsively obligatory vaudeville number for the White album, and it was covered in early 1969 by Alan Klein, once the lead singer of the New Vaudeville Band. Never has the composer so blatantly attempted to recapture the sound of the 1920s. The song incorporates a harmonic surprise (Ger$_5^6$–V7/II, **B+**3–4, 0:42–0:45) known elsewhere only in "Jelly Roll" Morton's "The Pearls."[138] The instrumentation and styling are straight from a preswing dance band. The nostalgic lyrics evoke the period's fascination with both Hollywood and the Atlantic, whose ocean winds inspire the clarinets in **F+**7–8 and again at the second time through **C+**3–4. McCartney can't resist a stagy reference to the reeds and the intense-but-restrained guitar, "Yeah! . . . I like that, aah, ooh . . . I like this kinda hot kinda music—hot kinda music!—play it to me, play it to me: 'Hollywood Blues!,' " at **E+**4–**F+**7.[139] And of course, the engineers re-create the sound of a scratchy 78-rpm shellac record from the era of the earliest electrical recordings at **A+**5–6 with very heavily compressed sped-up vocal run through a band-pass filter set with a very narrow midrange, along with surface-noise sound effects. All of this distances McCartney from his public, in an even more defensive way than with *Sgt. Pepper*, as if to say, "It's not *my* recording—I just found it in the attic; isn't it camp?"

The Kinfauns demo is lacking a few of the song's final lyrics—the opening line and the aptly pathetic line about feeling weak in the knee—but McCartney has the guitar chords, which he will teach to Lennon, already worked out. The verse has a very economical though sophisticated rhythm guitar part that uses the same finger pattern to produce all major triads on either strings 1–5 or, shifted one string over, 2–5. The basic tracks, cut at Trident on October 1, include McCartney on piano (heard left), Lennon on Casino (right), and Harrison's Bass VI and Starr's brushed drums (both center). The next day, McCartney added both lead vocal (center) and lead guitar on his own Casino, wiping Lennon's introduction with a light commentary featuring harmonics (right) and, on another track, adding the witty solo at **E** (center) that is usually attributed to Lennon, who only plays the chords on the basic track. On October 4, the vocal and effects for the "shellac" line were produced (left), along with Martin's score for two clarinets, two alto saxes, two tenor saxes, and baritone sax (right). Both mixes were made on October 5; the stereo wisely eliminates three bars of McCartney's solo that mar the mono mix at **E+5–7**. One of the song's unintentionally charming aspects is created by the difficulty McCartney has in matching the rhythm of his vocal overdub to the introduction's *senza tempo* backing track; it creates an appropriately tentative air, reminiscent of Lennon's introduction to "If I Fell." If the song remains light and fluffy, it is more than well crafted and authentic in all of its elements; the words have just the right tone and engender a warm nostalgia—despite the composer's staged distance—as surely as does "When I'm Sixty-Four."

McCartney, who was later to have a hit with his appeal for black/white harmony, "Ebony and Ivory" (April 1982), wrote "Blackbird" in Scotland as a reaction to the severe racial tension in America in the spring of 1968.[140] In the folk blues tradition, the song is scored simply for vocal, with very little double-tracking, and D-28 (with first string tuned down a whole step), accompanied by a pervasive metronome that sounds like an informal foottap for country-style percussion, along with added bird calls that function remarkably well in the G-major context. All was recorded on June 11 and mixed on October 13. Lennon says he contributed a line: perhaps the "And Your Bird Can Sing"–like reference to broken wings?[141] The song was one of McCartney's first Beatles numbers to be performed after the breakup, done on tour with Wings in 1975–76.

"Blackbird" is built on the guitar's parallel tenths; an open-g tonic pedal completes the guitar's texture. The motion in tenths is expressed in its most basic shape at the last three bars before the D.S. (1:41–1:46), as a rise in the bass from G to c and a descent interrupted by the cadential appearance of the dominant. This rise and fall is the model for the extended motion in tenths through the entire song; in **A+1–4** (0:04–0:12), the rise proceeds a third higher than in the basic shape. The bass line supporting the tenths rises here to e—the broken-wing chromatic nature of which may suggest the African American struggle through nonviolent resistance, which carefully descends in resignation through the same chromatics in **A+4–6** (0:12–0:18), a descent emphasized by the imitation of the chromatic line, $e^1–e\flat^1–d^1–c\sharp^1–c^1$, an octave higher. At **B** (at 0:47), the bass line reaches up a step higher still, when the "Blackbird" is encouraged to fly. Against the guitar's tenths, the verse's vocal melody carries the fundamental line, descending $\hat{5}$ (**A+2**)–$\hat{4}$ (**A+3**)–$\hat{3}$ (**A+4**)–$\hat{2}$ (**A+8**)–$\hat{1}$ (**A+8**).

The guitar's effortless register change (across the barlines at $A+1-2$, 0:06, etc.) represents the blacks' aspirations, the blackbird's rise, at this point only an unarticulated dream sensed in "the dead of night." This is made clear only at $B+4-6$ (0:54–1:00), where this g^1-g^2 octave is brought "into the light," expressed vocally in the song's only blues-related material. The bridge (B) had twice included modally inflected $f\sharp^1$ and $b\flat$, but these pitches might be interpreted as Mixolydian and minor touches until $B+4-6$ (0:54–1:00). The blues domain implied by the guitar soars brilliantly in the fully pentatonic vocal, stressing the blue notes already prepared by the guitar.[142] This is the height of black pride; the blues scale is the only material in "Blackbird" with an exclusively African American origin. The voice soars at the "moment" prescribed at $A+7-8$ (0:18–0:22): the V^7–I cadence. At the climax of the bridge, the voice arpeggiates downward, emphasizing the blue notes, in order to return to the obligatory register for the return of the neighbor f^1 to g^1 (0:58–0:59). That the coda's freely "arisen" birdsong cadenza (1:38–1:40 and continuing) prolongs an extended tonic harmony, rather than a cadential $^6_4$ or V^5_3, corroborates the notion that the blackbird can sing only once the struggle is finally over. So the blackbird, who had its early struggle for freedom, waits patiently for its proud pentatonic and cadential "moment to arise."

"Helter Skelter"   In early May 1980, McCartney said, " 'Helter Skelter' came about because I read in the *Melody Maker* that The Who . . . they were talking about a track they made. Now I don't know what the track was. . . . But the talk was 'the loudest, most raucous rock 'n' rolling dirtiest thing we've ever done, man.' . . . But that made me think, 'ooh, gotta do it. I really see that.' And I . . . said, 'We gotta do the most loudest, most raucous'—and it was 'Helter Skelter.' "[143]

The earliest McCartney song to postdate the Kinfauns demos, "Helter Skelter"—whose title refers to a helical English fairground slide as well as to haphazard confusion in general—was originally a twenty-four-minute, loud, grating, and out-of-tune free-for-all. The Beatles do it with the borrowed Les Paul cranked up all the way. After a rehearsal on July 18, all recording was done on September 9 and 10: we hear Lennon's Jazz bass, his squeaking sax mouthpiece, and Mal Evans's trumpet (the latter two heard especially after 3:14) (all left); McCartney's back-feeding Casino for rhythm ("Guitar I"), his lead vocal (with an Elvis-like STEED at 1:12–1:15), and backing vocals and chatter by Harrison and Lennon (the latter screaming with Ono-like vocal modulation at 2:48–2:55) (all center); Ringo's drums and "blisters" complaint (right); and Harrison's loud, distorted, sliding Les Paul ("Guitar II"; wild).[144] The mono mix (3'36") was done on September 17, the stereo (4'29") on October 12. Appropriately, the song features only the raunchy [025] related chords, E^7 (tonic), G, and A, the hard-rock "Sgt. Pepper" I–$\flat$III–IV progression also heard in "Back in the U.S.S.R.," "Glass Onion," and "Happiness Is a Warm Gun." This [025] relationship is made clearest, perhaps, in the "Day Tripper"–like sustained backing vocal chords at $B+3-7$ (0:23–0:37). There is no dominant and little tonal function; organized noise is the brief.

"Hey Jude"   Although by June McCartney was very happy with Linda Eastman (who did not move to England until October 1968), his breakup of a five-year relationship with Jane Asher brought him enough sadness that he was very much able to sympathize with young Julian Lennon, to whom he had always been a loving uncle and whose parents were now irrevocably split. One day while driving to visit Julian and Cyn at Weybridge, probably in the last days of June, Paul found himself singing what was to become a song of deep emotional support, beginning "Hey Jules, don't make it bad."[145] "And then I just thought a better name was Jude. A bit more country and western for me"; Jules "just seemed a bit of a mouthful, so I changed it to 'Jude.'"[146] One wonders whether McCartney was ever aware of the fact that Jude was the patron saint of desperate situations, and whether he would have known a certain liturgical work by John Ireland from his choirboy days. Ireland's "Te Deum laudamus" (1907) begins with, and returns to, the material given as example 3.11, which is untransposed in "Hey Jude" ($A+1-3$) but improved by McCartney with the unprepared "leap from the dominant seventh of the V^7 chord to a nonharmonic eleventh of that chord at the words 'a sad song.'"[147] The "Hey Jude" melody then (in $A+5-6$, 0:14–0:19) turns away from Ireland and toward the Drifters' "Save the Last Dance for Me" (August 1960; at "and don't forget who's taking you home and in whose arms you're gonna be," rising from $\hat{6}$ to upper-neighbor $\hat{2}$ before resolving the previous $\hat{6}$ to $\hat{5}$; note that Ireland also rises from $\hat{6}$ in his mm. 9–11) before the original cadence.[148] Regardless of its provenance, the "Hey Jude" melody is a marvel of construction, contrasting wide leaps with stepwise motions, sustained tones with rapid movement, syllabic with melismatic word-setting, and tension ("don't make it *bad*") with resolution ("make it *better*"), all graced, of course, by its composer's gift for a natural tune.

McCartney worked the song up in July and brought a tape of it to John and Yoko on the 26th. The composer thought "Hey Jude" still had dummy words, but Lennon, who at first took the song as McCartney's blessing of his and Ono's relationship even though that tie severely weakened the Lennon/McCartney partnership, insisted that such abstractly expressionistic phrases as "the movement you need is on your shoulder" stay the way they were.[149] Lennon recognized the song immediately as "one of his masterpieces," and both agreed that it would be the Beatles' next single.[150] "Hey Jude"'s most commented-on feature, however, is its great length of 7'11", making it the longest #1 single of all time, a result of the nineteen performances of the double-plagal cadence, a wordless four-minute mantra with a grandeur that seems to suggest that, given the proper understanding and encouragement, Jude has found his courage and moves on with grace and dignity.[151] Indeed, theorist Frank Samarotto has called "Hey Jude" the perfect example of a structural downbeat, a term of Edward Cone's, meaning that the song's first three minutes act as an expanded upbeat, culminating in the two-octave vocal ornamented arpeggiation at $C-1$ (3:01–3:08), all released at C.[152] Tim Riley points out how, especially after joined in the third verse by other singers, the lead singer's persona seems to gain confidence, so the coda brings enlightenment to the singer as well as to his friend.[153]

Example 3.11 John Ireland, *Te Deum.*

(*continued*)

Example 3.11 (*continued*)

When the Beatles gathered at Studio Two for rehearsal on July 30, cameras caught parts of several run-throughs of "Hey Jude," with McCartney's piano and vocal, Lennon's Jumbo and backing vocal, and Starr's drums—Harrison was in the control room with Martin—for *Music!*, a short documentary on popular music released in Britain in October 1969. The edited film and outtakes have yielded two partial attempts by McCartney of W. C. Handy's "St. Louis Blues" (1914), one performed while Evans was changing a string for Lennon, and a brief excerpt of McCartney busking something usually called "Las Vegas Tune," all in the F major of the hovering "Hey Jude."[154]

After rehearsing on July 29 and 30, the Beatles taped the basic track on Trident's eight-track machine on the 31st. This comprised McCartney's piano (heard right), Lennon's Jumbo (entering the second time through **A**, 0:26, left), Starr's drums (entering at the second ending, 0:50, center), and Harrison's Telecaster (only for the retransition, **B**+9–11, 1:23–1:28, and subsequent bridge fills, center). During the recording, McCartney told Harrison not to play "echoes" in each vocal rest, which, by the way, Lennon had done on the 30th to no apparent criticism. The composer has said, "I really didn't see it like that and it was a bit of a number for me to have to dare to tell George Harrison, one of the . . . greats, I think, to not play. It was like an insult almost. But . . . that was how we did a lot of our stuff you know."[155] When this incident was recalled during a similar disagreement in a January 6, 1969, rehearsal, Harrison said bitterly, "I'll play whatever you want me to play, or I won't play at all, if you don't want me to play; whatever it is that will please you, I'll do it."[156] Four days later that January, the tension would force him to leave the band for five days.

Overdubs completed on August 1 include McCartney's lead vocal, tambourine (entering the second time through **A**), backing vocals from the three singers (entering at the second performance of **A**+4, 1:42, including Lennon's harmony vocal, which begins below the melody but jumps above for the cadence, and a pretty three-part descending 5–6 sequence at **B**+1–3, 2:01–2:09), McCartney's bass (entering at **B** and ending at **C**, wiped there by string basses), and a bottom-heavy orchestra (two flutes, two contrabass clarinets, bassoon, contrabassoon, two horns, four trumpets, four trombones, percussion, ten violins, three violas, three celli, and two string basses) with handclaps (entering at **C**) (all center).[157]

Mixing proved difficult until new equalizations allowed for a good transfer of the Trident recordings to differently biased EMI machines, but the stereo was done on August 2, the mono on August 8. Additional difficulties were encountered in mastering because of the length of the single and because of a particularly loud drum fill at 5:56. John Bauch, who assisted Malcolm Davies in cutting the single on the usual Neumann VMS lathe, says, "The trick was to close the grooves up as much as the computer would allow but open them rapidly for Ringo's drum roll towards the end. If you look at the . . . pressing, you can see this 'opening' quite clearly."[158]

The Beatles performed "Hey Jude" on stage for promotional films on September 4. McCartney played an upright piano, Lennon his Casino, Harrison the Bass VI, and Starr his drums, with orchestra and scores of extras chanting the "na na na na" coda—as if a pre-"Give Peace a Chance" anthem—but they all played over the recording, in one instance getting significantly out of sync in the fade-out. These videos were televised on "Frost on Sunday," before which the Beatles busked the show's theme song (George Martin's composition), with Harrison carrying the melody on six-string bass.[159] Backed with "Revolution," "Hey Jude" was released on August 30 in the United Kingdom (Apple R5722; #1 for four weeks) and four days earlier in the United States (Apple 2276; #1 for nine weeks, the best American chart performance of any single in the period between 1959 and 1977), where it sold 3 million copies in two months. Worldwide, the single sold 6 million by year's end and a total of over 8 million. Perhaps its most lasting effect was the rash of rock songs that followed with mantralike repeated sections, as varied as Van Morrison's "Astral Weeks" (November 1968), "Donovan's "Atlantis" (March 1969), the Moody Blues' "Never Comes the Day" (May 1969), and the Allman Brothers' "Revival" (October 1970), but "Hey Jude" no doubt also had more benign and valuable effects on its imitators.

"I Will" and "Birthday"   McCartney introduced two songs to the studio in September. "I Will" is McCartney's sweetest love ballad since "Here, There and Everywhere," against which it pales in terms of its arrangement and relatively meek bridge (**B**) but which it resembles in its harmonic twists and well-crafted melody. Harmonic surprise registers in **A**+4 (0:08), where the first phrase dead-ends two beats early because of a motion from VI to the inactive III, especially odd as VI had normally led to II[7] in **A**+1–2 (0:02–0:03). Surprise strikes again in **C**+1 (1:23–1:25), where an unprepared V[7]–VI[7] cadence is jolted by the song's only mixture from the minor mode, leading to a soft plagal common-tone resolution of ♭VI$^6_5$–I—following repeated fragments as in the extended coda of "Yes It Is," rather than the potentially more disruptive function of the German $^4_3$—with which ♭VI$^6_5$ is enharmonically equivalent. McCartney's voice leading is expressive; the verse's sure $\hat{5}$ (**A**+1, 0:01)–$\hat{4}$ (**A**+5, 0:11)–$\hat{3}$ (**A**+6, 0:12)–$\hat{2}$ (**A**+7, 0:16)–$\hat{1}$ (**A**+8, 0:18) gives the singer's "I Will" promise a sin-

cerity not open to question. The "Here, There and Everywhere"–like $\hat{7}$ left hanging at the end of the bridge, not to be resolved in register until the coda ($\mathbf{C}+1$), strongly unifies all elements of greatest interest, giving the $\flat\text{VI}^6_5$ harmony the effect of direct pleading rather than its usual metaphor of deception, especially given the song's resolute air of triadically fixed determined purpose, integrity, and will.[160]

Both Paul and Donovan recall the music but not the lyrics of "I Will" taking shape in India (Miles 1997, 420), but the song does not appear among the Kinfauns tapes. The basic track was recorded on September 16 as one of sixty-seven takes, including several ad-libs such as "Can You Take Me Back" (Take 19, inserted on the album before "Revolution 9"), an off-the-cuff rehearing of "Step inside Love," the Santana-like Dorian alternation of Cm7 and F chords in "Los Paranoias," and another listed as "The Way You Look Tonight."[161] McCartney sang and played his D-28 ("Guitar II"; both vocal and guitar heard center), Ringo played maracas (beginning at **B**, 0:40, right) and drums (left), and Lennon was on temple blocks (beginning at **B**, 0:40, left). The next day, the composer added two vocals, one a descant in parallel thirds for the bridge, quoted in the coda (center), and the other a "doo doo" bass line (right), and also an acoustic twelve-string guitar last heard in "The Fool on the Hill" (at the first and second endings, bridge, the cadence for the third verse and coda, center). The mono mix, with the "bass" vocal silent in first verse, was made on September 26, the stereo on October 14.

Paul was the lead composer of "Birthday," in which all had a hand, as it was invented "on the spot" in the studio on September 18.[162] The basic track consists of Starr's drums, Harrison's Bass VI, Lennon's tambourine, and McCartney's Casino for "Guitar II" (all center; one can also hear McCartney's off-mike "A Day In the Life"–like counting through the bridge, **B**, as if other parts would eventually cover Starr's drum solo). Overdubs feature Lennon's Casino for "Guitar I," always roughly doubling McCartney's Casino at the higher octave, even in the pentatonic solo. Unlike "Day Tripper," the two guitars are always answered by the bass, which takes no rests. Also superimposed were McCartney's Leslied "Penny Lane"–like piano with STEED entering at **D** (1:10, at center with Lennon's Casino) and handclaps and chorus of all four Beatles (Paul and John having the lead duet), Yoko Ono, Pattie Harrison, and Mal Evans (all left, with ADT sent right).[163] The mono mix was done the same day, with the stereo prepared on October 14.

The simple song's tonal structure, an A-major verse based on a twelve-bar blues leading to a transitional half cadence at **C**, followed by a C-major party (**D**) that pushes to a shouted retransitional dominant (first ending) before returning to the tonic with the repeated verse, is just like that of the otherwise very different "Another Girl." This forward-moving structure carries material so hell-bent that Tim Riley has described the final Leslied piano tones as a siren, giving "the effect of a huge train blistering past, the listener left gaping at the force of its motion."[164] A definite party starter, "Birthday" endures as one of the most popular tracks of the White album.

"Martha My Dear" and "Why Don't We Do It in the Road"   "Martha My Dear"
takes its name but nothing else from McCartney's sheepdog (1966–81). The
rambling lyrics have the singer insist that he and Martha are "meant to be
with each other," even though he seems to prefer spending his days convers-
ing with others. The lyrics are not the point, but merely a flimsy cover on a
nice bit of modulating rhythmic counterpoint on the piano that barely as-
serts E♭ as tonic before the dominant is tonicized (mm. 2–5, at 0:09).[165] With
the music continuing to ramble as the lyrics do, F major is tonicized as well
in the first bridge (**B**, at 0:43). Was McCartney trying to emulate the slithery,
fast-moving tonal areas of "Sexy Sadie"? Metrically, the first-bar $\frac{5}{4}$ effect
slides into an easy $\frac{4}{4}$, a trick further developed in the second bridge, **C** (starting at 1:00), which begins with $\frac{6}{4}$ instead of $\frac{5}{4}$. The track's terraced dynamics—the instrumentation increasing markedly at **B**, 0:38, and again at **C**,
1:00—and its use of two bridges make this an unusually sectional song for
McCartney and thus related to a degree to the recently recorded "Happiness
Is a Warm Gun."

The vocal melody displays a similarly interesting variety, particularly in register. The verse remains mostly in McCartney's lower range (f¹–c²) but ends with
a flag ("Don't forget me," f²–e², 0:32–0:33) that signals the higher registers to
come. As Martha is asked to hold her head up, Paul sings up to a² and its upper
neighbor b♭² (0:44–0:46). As singer and subject stray farthest from the home
key of E♭, Martha is asked to look at "what is all around you." In one phrase, Mc-
Cartney glides effortlessly from a chalumeau d¹ (1:02) to a high a² (1:12). The
remote tonal areas and urgent registral contrasts attempt to broaden Martha's
horizons as far as possible. Despite the relatively short passages, the unusual
tonal, metric, instrumental, formal, and melodic divisions of "Martha My Dear"
point the way to McCartney's later large-scale "You Never Give Me Your Money,"
"Uncle Albert/Admiral Halsey," and "Band on the Run."

The basic track of "Martha My Dear," cut at Trident on October 4, reverts to
a *Revolver* procedure, with McCartney on piano (left) and Starr on drums (center, entering only at **C**, 1:00). A score for strings (4/2/2/0; left, primarily doubling the piano, entering at **A**) and brass (1/3/1/1; right, one trumpet doubling
on flügelhorn, which has the solo for the second **B**) was recorded the same day,
along with McCartney's double-tracked vocal and handclaps (entering at **D**)
with ADT (all center). Note the unchanging brass chord pedals at **C**
(1:00–1:13), like the pedal chords in "Got to Get You into My Life," thus another
Revolver reference. Dubs were finished the next day, with McCartney's Rickenbacker and Telecaster (both augmenting the texture at **C**, 1:00, center), as were
both mixes.

McCartney's blunt twelve-bar blues in D pentatonic minor, "Why Don't We Do
It in the Road," seems to be his response to both the Rolling Stones' "Let's Spend
the Night Together" (January 1967) and Bob Dylan's "Down along the Cove"
(January 1968). The basic track, recorded on October 9, has McCartney playing acoustic guitar—unheard except for the soundboard slapping that begins
the track—and singing, all compressed, with a James Brown falsetto beginning

the third chorus (at 1:08). He overdubbed a piano the same day, and Ringo's drums, Paul's second vocal (used in spots on the second chorus), and hand-claps, Rickenbacker, and bluesy high-register Casino (entering at **A**+7, 0:25), re-creating the "Wild Honey Pie" tritones for the cadential V^7, were taped on October 10.[166] Mono and (very narrow) stereo mixes were done on the 16th. Except for Ringo's dubbed drums, this is all McCartney, and Lennon perceptively wondered why his partner kept such a tight grip on the others even though he could at the same time busy himself alone in a separate studio with tracks like this.[167] Is it revealing that, despite his isolation, McCartney asked the same abiding loyalty of Martha?

Mark Lewisohn's research found that on August 20, McCartney recorded a ballad called "Et Cetera" during work on "Mother Nature's Son" and "Wild Honey Pie."[168] It is also known that studio visitors heard working versions of "The Long and Winding Road," "Let It Be," and "Maxwell's Silver Hammer" during the production of the White album, but no pre-1969 tapes of these songs are known to exist, so they will be addressed in chapter 4.

Even more prolific than the newly energized Lennon, McCartney could have filled three LP sides with his new 1968 compositions. How can this body of work be characterized? McCartney rocks his hardest and loudest on this LP, with his drumming on "Back in the U.S.S.R." and his Casino-energized "Helter Skelter" and "Birthday," with the hard-rock pentatonic-based ♭III chord an important function in all three and a key center of its own in "Birthday." Even though he hasn't lost his gift for counterpoint, as demonstrated in "I Will" and "Blackbird," or for wide-ranging tonal relations, as heard in "Honey Pie," these aspects of McCartney's craft are not as evident on the surface in most of his 1968 offerings, which tend to be simple and unpretentious.

Whereas Lennon turns most often to the blues when he picks up his acoustic, McCartney turns first to white, major/minor rural post-Appalachian styles, as he does in the folk-based "Mother Nature's Son" and "Rocky Raccoon" and in the ballad "I Will." "Blackbird" introduces a central blues lick within a diatonic (and even chromatic) context, and while "Why Don't We Do It in the Road" and "Wild Honey Pie" are as raucous as anything of Lennon's, they certainly lack the depth of "Yer Blues." Perhaps the greatest difference for McCartney between this album and earlier ones is that, thoroughly comfortable on piano, Martin acoustic, and Casino, he plays bass on only a single basic track among his own compositions, that for "Ob-La-Di, Ob-La-Da." He even leaves the bass to others altogether on several songs, including his most popular song of 1968, "Hey Jude."

As suggested by a number of criticisms in the pages above, McCartney is guilty of sloth more often than Lennon is on this LP. While his lyrics can be witty ("Honey Pie"), they are just as often incongruous ("Martha My Dear"), and his throwaway numbers add some relief to the album but represent only his idle moments. But in 1968, Lennon was wild and unpredictable, and McCartney was safe and secure. How fortunate were the Beatles that George Martin could give just as much of himself to "Glass Onion" as to "Honey Pie."

New Songs by George Harrison

The year 1968 marks a new beginning of Harrison's work as a composer the way 1963 does for Lennon and McCartney. Although he had had token success before, and on occasion—as with *Revolver* and *Sgt. Pepper*—important contributions, he becomes privately prolific during the making of the White album. During this time, he presents eight newly completed songs and works on several more in a rush seen publicly only two years later with the release of *All Things Must Pass*. Some of those later songs began life in 1968 as well, although documentation is sparse.[169]

"Piggies" and "Sour Milk Sea"   Harrison's "Piggies," with origins as far back as 1966—its topic reminds one of that year's "Taxman"—is the second-oldest number on the LP.[170] Running across the song's old manuscript in his parents' home in 1968, Harrison even got the line "What they need's a damn good whacking" from his mother before he left Liverpool.[171] Lennon supplied the assonant line, "Clutching forks and knives to eat their bacon"; in the Kinfauns demo, the line had ended, tentatively, "to cut their pork chops."[172] The basic track was recorded in Studio One on September 19.[173] Taped initially were Harrison's J-200 (right), Chris Thomas's harpsichord (center), and McCartney's Rickenbacker and Starr's tambourine (both left). Overdubs on September 20 included Harrison's three vocals (all center). Harrison changes his vocal color by pinching his nose in the bridge (**B**, 0:48–1:05) and by using a very narrow band-pass filter normally reserved for echo-chamber work.[174] He evidences a remarkable range in the third verse, singing a bass part that reaches down to a low $E\flat$ (1:28, a range he repeats only in intoning "Sir Frankie Crisp" in Harrison 1970) and a descant part that, in falsetto, climbs to $b\flat^2$ in its last bar (1:41).[175] Other dubs of that day consist of drums at the end of the retransition (center), and hog sounds collected by Lennon from EMI tapes, an old 78 record, and his own throat (right). The recording was completed on October 10 by four violins and two violas (center) with two celli (right)—the same octet, in the same session, as for "Glass Onion." Mono and stereo mixes were done on October 11.

"Piggies" is notable for its Baroque textures and harmony, including an implied but unfulfilled tonicization of VI in the bridge, **B**+1–2, and a change of mode on the tonic in the coda, in harpsichord and strings. But these are contrasted against guttural hog grunts and a rude final cadence inexplicably a diminished fourth away from tonic—although made superficially elegant by its ornamented anticipation—for an Orwellian comparison of pigs to socially horrid, though outwardly refined, tyrants.[176] (A musical setting of a similar comparison is found in "Village Ghetto Land," on Stevie Wonder's *Songs in the Key of Life* [1976] and *Natural Wonder* [1995].)

One of Harrison's Kinfauns songs, "Sour Milk Sea," must have been rejected by Lennon, because the composer gave the song away to another singer who recorded it with Harrison on rhythm guitar, McCartney on bass, and Starr on

Example 3.12a "Sour Milk Sea" compositional draft (Harrison). © 1969 Harrisongs Music.

drums before the Beatles began work on any Harrison songs for the White album. The other singer was Jackie Lomax, who'd sung for one of Liverpool's earliest groups, the Undertakers, and then, with the Lomax Alliance, signed with Brian Epstein in 1967. Harrison produced Lomax's first LP for Apple. "Sour Milk Sea," taped at Trident and EMI on June 24–26 with the above personnel plus Eric Clapton on lead guitar and Nicky Hopkins on piano, was the lead single. It was released on August 26, 1968, in the United States, and on September 6 in the United Kingdom, failing to chart in either country. Portions of the first verse and chorus are given as examples 3.12a and 3.12b, respectively, as played on the Kinfauns demo. The roots of the chord collection (A, C, D, E, G, B♭, some not shown here) would describe a pentatonic minor scale on A, allowing B♭ as a tritone-related ornament to E⁷, but the verse seems centered on E, while the chorus settles on D, the Mixolydian ♭VII area. All in all, this song's harmonic language represents an unstable version of chord relationships heard in the Beatles of 1964 and 1965. Like "Dear Prudence" and "Martha My Dear," "Sour Milk Sea" works to get its listener out of the doldrums. But in contrast with the Lennon and McCartney songs, no bright mood is offered here as a substitute.

"While My Guitar Gently Weeps"   Even with the Indian retreat, Harrison felt distant from his guitar.[177] But in Liverpool, when — in line with an *I Ching* sense of the aleatory — he opened a book "at random" to find an idea for a composi-

Example 3.12b "Sour Milk Sea" compositional draft (Harrison). © 1969 Harrisongs Music.

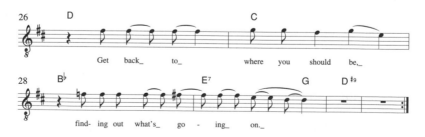

tion and read the words, "gently weeps," he began writing a song about the instrument that wept through "Cry for a Shadow" and *Wonderwall*'s "Crying" and
was to weep again in "This Guitar (Can't Keep from Crying)" (Harrison 1975).

The manuscript of the resulting song, "While My Guitar Gently Weeps,"
shows many rejected lines: for instance, "I look at the sky and I notice it's cloud-
ing," and "I'm wondering why your cigars keep on burning."[178] One entire verse
made it as far as an EMI session but was replaced by a repeat of the first verse
before the basic track was finished. The rejected verse reads:

> I look from the wings at the play you are staging,
>   while my guitar gently weeps;
> As I'm sitting here doing nothing but aging,
>   still my guitar gently weeps.[179]

Given such cuts, one wonders why Harrison kept such apparent filler as "I look
at the floor and I see it needs sweeping." Some of the rhymes are embarrassing,
particularly in the second bridge (**C**), which seems to be an attempt at rewriting Bob Dylan's "All I Really Want to Do" (September 1964). Still, the imagery
is evocative, and the musical setting is expert and riveting.

As they stand, the lyrics express regret at unrealized potential. The change
from the minor-mode verse (**A–B**) to the parallel major for the bridge might
hint that hope is to be fulfilled, but the continued minor triads (III, VI, and II, all
that are diatonically available) seem to express a strong dismay that love is not
to be unfolded, that the object of the song is not to be put right. In the bridge,
Paul's bass melody becomes expansive in support of George, presaging further
development to come in "Something," as Harrison recalls an early Lennon/
McCartney hallmark, $\hat{7}$ over III. The tragedy is well set with the verse's and
coda's inevitable bass line, $\hat{8}-\flat\hat{7}-\hat{6}-\flat\hat{6}-\hat{5}$—a slow retread of "Lucy in the Sky
with Diamonds"—and continues in the fade-out ending, which never resolves
the ever reappearing dominant.[180]

The Kinfauns demo of "While My Guitar Gently Weeps" (Beatles 1991j) still
retains many rejected lines of verse and is probably played in G minor (the final
version sounds in A minor), with the J-200 and, beginning with the bridge, a
sustained Hammond B-3 organ. This take is most notable for the later-discarded
retransitional V+ at each bridge cadence, at **C+**8 and the first ending. Work at
EMI did not begin until July 25, when Harrison recorded the song on his J-200
and an overdubbed harmonium, the latter audible in distributed mixes only in
bled-through spots. This "Take 1" includes the extra verse given above but re-
jects the V+ triad in guitar, though it continues on the harmonium.[181] The song
apparently did not catch fire with the dominant Beatles (who had first heard it
in May), because it was not approached again until it was remade on August
16, September 3, and September 5. These sessions produced another aborted
take, with Ringo's double-tracked drums, Paul's bass, John's organ, George's
J-200, two vocals, lead guitar, and backward electric guitar solo, plus maracas.

So an unsupported Harrison began a third version on September 5. The
basic tracks were remade with Ringo's drums (heard right), Paul's piano (left),
George's J-200 ("Guitar II," center), and John's Casino with tremolo (center, au-

dible only in the coda, especially at 3:43–3:46, 3:54–4:03, and 4:10–4:15), and they then received historic overdubs by Eric Clapton the next day. The composer recalled:

> I worked on that song with John, Paul, and Ringo one day, and they were not interested in it at all. And I knew inside of me that it was a nice song. The next day I was with Eric, and I was going into the session, and I said, "We're going to do this song. Come on and play on it." He said, "Oh, no. I can't do that. Nobody ever plays on the Beatles' records." I said, "Look, it's my song, and I want you to play on it." So Eric came in, and the other guys were as good as gold — because he was there. . . . So Eric played that, and I thought it was really good. Then we listened to it back, and he said, "Ah, there's a problem, though; it's not Beatley enough" — so we put it through the ADT to wobble it a bit.[182]

Clapton's Les Paul ("Guitar I," heard left), so hot it is constantly on the verge of feedback, was joined by dubs from Paul's Jazz bass, emphasizing his wide-ranging part in the bridge with glissandos (right), Harrison's organ for the bridge, and Ringo's castanets (entering at **B**; both left). Overdubs were complete with Ringo's tambourine, George's vocals (double-tracked at **C**), and Paul's descant vocal (all center). Both mixes were made on October 7; the Les Paul is given wider ADT and more volume in the mono mix.

Harrison's demos are pretty, but Clapton makes this a monumental track. His technique — a left hand supple enough for a wide range of vibrato and fluid position shifts, a sense of rhythmic placement, phrasing, and ornamentation unequaled among his peers — is remarkable. Notice the increasing lengths of the thrice-heard first scale degrees at 0:17–0:19, the restraint in the many bars of rests punctuated by brief unexpected appearances (as at 0:28–0:29), the command exhibited in his turnaround phrases (0:31–0:34), the expressive string bends unheard in any other Beatles track (0:47–0:53, especially marking the structural change of mode with c♮ rising to c♯), the sense of power in a retransition (1:21–1:24), the sobbingest vibrato possible (2:01–2:07). And the phrases of his solo (1:55–2:31) are, as usual, composed with the surest and most measured rise in intensity, rhythmic activity, tonal drive, and registral climb, so that its final culmination is nothing short of majestic. It is largely this majesty, revisited at times in the wobbling coda, that rescues the song from its otherwise pathetic air.[183]

"Not Guilty"   Two other Harrison compositions, "Not Guilty" and "Circles," appear among the Kinfauns demos.[184] The former was probably the last recording to be cut from the album's lineup. Harrison recalls it as a bitter song: "It was me getting pissed off at Lennon and McCartney for the grief I was catching during the making of the white album. I said I wasn't guilty of getting in the way of their careers. I said I wasn't guilty of leading them astray in our all going to Rishikesh to see the Maharishi."[185] The basic theme is presented with a pun in the third verse: "I won't upset the Apple cart, I only want what I can get." The song was rehearsed on August 1, and recording began a week later, when a basic track was laid with George's Les Paul (chiefly a rhythm part), Paul's Rick-

Example 3.13 "Not Guilty" compositional draft (Harrison). © 1979 Ganga Publishing.

enbacker, John's harpsichord, and Ringo's drums. The Beatles began overdubs on the 9th, with Ringo's second drum track, George's second Les Paul rhythm track, and a third track for solos recorded through the echo chamber, and Paul's new bass line. On the 12th, George finished the recording with his lead vocal.

No mixes were ever made for the album, but two have surfaced: Geoff Emerick's stereo mix (slick and heavily edited) made for the 1985 *Sessions* project and borrowed for Beatles 1996b, and another transferred directly from the eight-track working tape (heard best on Beatles 1991m). The track was remade—softer, featuring a Fender Rhodes—for Harrison 1979.

Just to provide a glimpse into McCartney's melodic bass writing and the composer's typically outlandish chord juxtapositions, an excerpt from the first verse and refrain is given with guitar chording as example 3.13. These lines show the usual Harrison interest in unusual chord colors ($I^7_\sharp$, $\natural VII^7_{\natural 3}$, and IIIb appear), at a new level of sophistication similar to jazz methodology. E minor is the key center, but A minor is tonicized to start the verse's phrases and is implied with the unusual progression $G-Dm^{8-7}-E^7$. The confident and loudly protesting G-minor chord appears through an unprecedented use of mixture from the Phrygian mode (thus the chord's Bb) into A pentatonic minor, an area heard more clearly in the [025] progression E^7-G-A. Wolf and Reger would probably have dug this track.

"Savoy Truffle" and "Long Long Long"   Seemingly a remake of the Byrds' less innocent "Artificial Energy" (January 1968), George Harrison's "Savoy Truffle"

teases Eric Clapton, who's just returned from a dentist instructing him to stop eating sweets.[186] The taunting attitude is heard clearly in the stretched meters beginning every verse.

The verses (**A+**1–10) list the contents of Mackintosh's "Good News" assortment (creme tangerine, montelimart, ginger sling, coffee dessert, and savoy truffle), with a few candies invented for good measure. The dentist's threat is repeated in the refrain (**A+**11–14), and the agony of a toothache is described in the first bridge (**B**). The second bridge is built around Derek Taylor's suggested line, "You know that what you eat you are," and the reference to "Ob-la-di" seems a sinister suggestion that, as David Crosby fears in "Artificial Energy," perhaps life will *not* go on.[187] As in "Yesterday," the harmonies of the bridge (E–A–G–B) recast those presented in the verse, with some condensation. One feature, the inner-voice line D–C♯–D–D♯ (**B+**3–4, 1:16–1:18), seems to borrow from a similar inner-voice line (D–C♯–E–D♯) with the identical rhythm in "Not Guilty."

The recording began on October 3 at Trident, with a basic track of Starr's compressed drums (left), McCartney's Rickenbacker (right, with characteristic repeated-note descending scales at **A+**5–7, **A+**12–14, and **B+**1–2), and Harrison's pentatonic electric piano with Lennon's Casino rhythm (both center). Harrison recorded his two vocals (right) on October 5. On the 11th, two baritone and four tenor saxes (all heavily distorted, heard right with ADT) were added. The saxes boogie with an ostinato that, like the guitars in "Day Tripper," successfully negotiates some unexpected harmonic changes. Work was completed on October 14, with the addition of Harrison's Telecaster parts (left and right), a sustained organ in the bridge (center), and a soft, whirling organ in the bridge and tambourine for the final refrain and coda (both right). The Telecaster doubles the taunting verse-opening vocal on the left, where it has downbeats at the end of the second verse (1:03–1:08), but its solo is moved to the right. Harrison gets in some good licks, but we can imagine that Clapton would have been more expansive. Time for the album's completion was running short; mono and stereo mixing of "Savoy Truffle" were completed on the 14th.

Harrison's final composition for the White album, "Long Long Long," captures the acoustic guitar/organ combination so familiar in his demos with a tune as close as the Beatles ever came to plagiarism.[188] Harrison says, "The 'you' in *Long Long Long* is God. I can't recall much about it except the chords which I think were coming from [Bob Dylan's] *Sad Eyed Lady of the Low Land*—D to E minor, A and D—those three chords and the way they moved."[189] Harrison plays "Long Long Long" on the guitar in a D-major pattern with a capo on the third fret, thus the difference in key between model (D major) and result (F major). In fact, only the metric change from Dylan's $\frac{12}{8}$ to Harrison's $\frac{6}{8}$, doubling the harmonic rhythm, and incidental rhythmic adjustments give the borrowing any subtlety. Comparison of examples 3.14 and 3.15 shows that Harrison takes Dylan's voice leading intact, beginning with the vocal in parallel fifths above the G–F♯m–Em–D progression, followed by a vocal e1–b above E minor repeated an octave lower, d1–a above D, moving to an implied $\hat{7}$ over the ca-

Example 3.14 Analysis of "Sad Eyed Lady of the Lowlands."

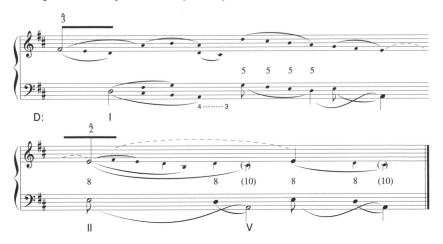

dential V.[190] As in the Dylan model, the progression never concludes. It is always left hanging unsatisfied on the repeated half cadence, unfulfilled for Dylan's Lady as "no man comes" and for Harrison as "how I want you." The song's subdued approach also reminds one of Dylan's backing group, known as the Band, which Harrison would come to admire so much by Thanksgiving 1968 that they were to have a full impact on his composition.

The recording of "Long Long Long" began with a basic track accomplished on October 7. Harrison strummed his J-200 (right) and recorded his vocal (center), Ringo drummed, and Paul played Hammond organ (both left). After a low C from the organ pedals rattled a wine bottle atop the Leslie speaker, Starr had to add to the resulting sound (heard wild, 2:31–2:54) some frenetic drumming for the coda. The next day, Harrison added a melodic J-200 part, its partials em-

Example 3.15 Analysis of "Long Long Long."

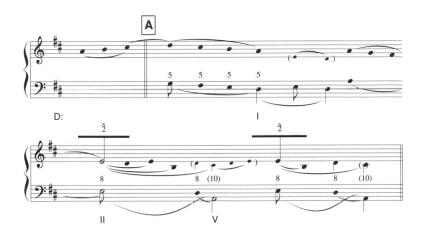

phasized by distortion so as to create a sitarlike sound, and a second vocal (both center), and McCartney added his Rickenbacker (left).[191] On October 9, McCartney added a descant vocal and Chris Thomas a gospel piano for the *All Things Must Pass*–like bridge (**B**) (both center). The stereo mix was done on October 10, the mono on the 14th.

Harrison brings some interesting text-painting to the White album through "Long Long Long." An extreme length of time is portrayed through verses divided unequally into three three-bar units, all in a slow $\frac{6}{8}$ meter but for a final, stretched-out bar in $\frac{9}{8}$. The extension in the final, stretched-out bar is thus an unambiguous representation of a "long, long, long time." The emphasis on three-bar phrases, although at a much more subtle tempo, recalls the verses of "Wait" (1965), which happens to begin with the same opening lyric and carry a related poetic theme.

Ringo Starr Composes

"Don't Pass Me By"   Ringo had received partial composers' credit in 1965 for "What Goes On," but his earliest composition, dating from at least as far back as 1963, was "Don't Pass Me By," which was finally allowed into the studio for the White album.[192] While well below normal Beatles standards, the insipid song is probably no worse than several minutes that McCartney brought to the LP. Not wishing to have his royalties siphoned off by Northern Songs (to which he was not contractually obligated), Starr created his own publishing company, Startling Music Ltd., in July. The C&W atmosphere reminds one of Ringo's days with Rory Storm and points to his subsequent song "Early 1970" (1970–71) and the *Beaucoups of Blues* LP (1970). The verse has an extra bar of $\frac{2}{4}$ (**A**+8) among an otherwise regular $\frac{4}{4}$ meter, a metric trick common with many songs on the White album.

The basic track was taped on June 5, in the midst of the "Revolution" recordings. These consist of McCartney's piano, miked and played through a guitar amplifier and Leslie speaker, and Ringo's drums, featuring the cowbell in the introduction (both left). The same day, McCartney taped an alternate piano track and sleighbells (left). Starr's double-tracked sped-up vocal (center, including in the coda a counting fill as heard in "A Day in the Life" and "Birthday") was added the next day, and McCartney's Rickenbacker (right) was taped on both June 6 and July 12. On the 12th, the tape also received a second amplified piano part from Ringo and country fiddling by one Jack Fallon (both right).[193] The amplified piano introduction was taped on July 22 and edited onto the completed mixes done on October 11, the procedure accounting for the false start in the third bar. The stereo mix sounds in C, the mono sped up to C$\sharp$.[194] The vocal sounds ridiculously high and totally without the expressive meaning of, say, the vari-speed vocals of "Lucy in the Sky with Diamonds."

Ringo was at work on two other compositions in 1968: "Octopus's Garden," begun in the second half of October and to be discussed in chapter 4, and "It Don't Come Easy," recorded in March 1970 with Harrison's guitar and production assistance but not released until 1971. This last-named is probably his best original song, and it was often a concert opener for his "All-Starr" tours of the 1990s.

With Ringo off to Sardinia on October 14 for a two-week break, and Harrison to Hollywood on October 16 for sessions with Jackie Lomax, several LP-finishing tasks were left to Lennon, McCartney, Martin, and staff. They had to decide what would be included and what left out, determine the final running order, mix "Why Don't We Do It in the Road," mix the crossfades and add some nonsense between a few tracks (cf. "Marrakesh Express" on *Crosby, Stills and Nash*, June 1969), and master the entire LP for mono and stereo. All of these tasks were done in a twenty-four-hour session in the three main control rooms and two other production rooms, beginning at 5 P.M. on October 16.

The idea of calling the LP *A Doll's House* had to be scrapped when Family's August 1968 release was titled *Music in a Doll's House*. The eventual minimalist title tied in perfectly with the idea of the pure white cover. The cover — perhaps a mute tribute to Brian Epstein, whose idea for a similar cover for *Sgt. Pepper* had been overruled—was the work of Richard Hamilton, a contact of Robert Fraser (the designer of the *Sgt. Pepper* sleeve). Hamilton also conceived of the collage poster for which Mal Evans and Neil Aspinall collected snapshots, and of the separate portraits shot by John Kelly. Exterior packaging was complete with a skewed embossed title on the front, light gray lettering along the spine, and consecutive serial numbers branded on the first 2 million copies, an emblem repeated for the 45 sleeve when "Ob-La-Di, Ob-La-Da"/"Julia" was released as a U.S. single in November 1976.[195]

The Beatles was a great commercial success: the British release (Apple PMC/PCS 7067/8, released November 22, 1968) sold over 300,000 copies (grossing £1 million) in advance of release, debuting on the album chart at #3 and spending ten weeks at the top. In the United States, the album (Apple SWBO101, released on November 25) drew advance orders of 1.9 million copies, topping the chart for nine weeks. Worldwide, the album sold 4 million within a month and 7 million altogether. This was the world's best-selling double album until the industry-stunning 1977 release of *Saturday Night Fever*, a multiartist extravaganza that defined the entire mainstream disco cult. If you were to ask any baby boomer about "the double album," *The Beatles* would undoubtedly be the first to come to mind.

Apple Records

On August 11, 1968, the Beatles launched Apple Records, the first such endeavor involving a major artist since Frank Sinatra and Phil Spector had introduced their own labels in 1961.[196] The division was headed by Ron Kass, who came from the European arm of Liberty Records, and the Granny Smith label was designed by Gene Mahon, who had done the back cover of *Sgt. Pepper*. Recording began within days upon a June 20 agreement allowing EMI to distribute Apple product. Among the first projects, Apple's A&R director Peter

Asher produced his new management client James Taylor, George Harrison produced Brian Epstein's client Jackie Lomax, and Paul McCartney produced the Black Dyke Mills Band and Mary Hopkin. The label released its first four records in the United Kingdom on August 30 and September 6: The Beatles' "Hey Jude"/"Revolution" (Apple R5722), Mary Hopkin's "Those Were the Days"/"Turn! Turn! Turn!" (Apple 2), Jackie Lomax's "Sour Milk Sea"/"The Eagle Laughs at You" (Apple 3), and John Foster and Sons Ltd. Black Dyke Mills Band's "Thingumybob"/"Yellow Submarine" (Apple 4).

Mary Hopkin

Mary Hopkin (b. 1950, Pontardawe, Wales) was seen by Twiggy performing folk songs on a Cardiff television program for amateurs, and following a few phone calls she auditioned for McCartney, who became her producer. Paul matched her instantly with a song, "Those Were the Days," adapted by Gene Raskin from an East European folk song that he'd heard in a London club in 1965.[197] Hopkin became very unhappy with her manager, Terry Doran, and also with McCartney's choices of material, but her first single — recorded at Trident in mid-July, orchestral parts imaginatively arranged by Richard Hewson — was Apple's second-biggest hit ever, behind "Hey Jude," selling 5 million copies worldwide through 1968.[198] McCartney had Hopkin record a song ("The Game") written by George Martin and brought Donovan to the studio to play on three of his own numbers for Hopkins's first LP, *Postcard*, completed in December 1968 (peaking at #6 in the United Kingdom the following April but stalling at a disappointing #28 in the United States).[199]

Other Original Apple Acts

Perhaps because his voice always sounded stuck at the back of his throat, Jackie Lomax never found commercial success. He made no showing on the British charts, and his American track record was little better: "Sour Milk Sea" peaked at #117, and his Harrison-produced LP, *Is This What You Want*, at #142.[200] Despite this disappointment, the recording project was a happy time for Harrison, and one of its side benefits was the Beatle's early introduction to the Moog synthesizer, played in the sessions by Paul Beaver and Bernie Krause. Harrison says,

> We finally got through the [White] album and everybody was pleased because the tracks were good. Then I worked on an album with Jackie Lomax . . . , and I spent a long time in the States and I had such a good time working with all these different musicians and different people. Then I hung out at Woodstock for Thanksgiving and, you know, I felt really good at that time. I got back to England for Christmas and then on January the first we were to start on the thing which turned into *Let It Be*. And straightaway again, it was just weird vibes.[201]

Apparently following the success of "Step inside Love," in the spring McCartney was commissioned by London Weekend Television to write a theme song for its comedy series to premiere in the fall, "Thingumybob." McCartney wrote a vaudevillian brass score ("Really, it's my dad's type of music") and tried to record it with a London group.[202] Not liking the results, he had Peter Asher book John Foster and Sons' thirty-nine-member Black Dyke Mills Band, the National Brass Band title winner seven times since 1945, and he went to Bradford, Yorkshire, on June 30 to re-record it. The instrumental, a ragtime march with oom-pah tubas, punchy trumpets, mellow F-horns, soaring trombones, and tinkling glockenspiel in B♭, works along the same lines as James McCartney's "Walking in the Park with Eloise," featuring similarly jaunty applied chords, but Paul's ditty pales in comparison with his dad's. "Thingumybob"/"Yellow Submarine" was the Black Dyke's only Apple disc; it did not chart.

The Iveys formed in Swansea, South Wales, in 1966 and were heard by Mal Evans and Peter Asher in London clubs by 1967. Evans heard some of their homemade demos and got them to Derek Taylor, who passed the tapes along to McCartney, and the Iveys were awarded contracts with Apple Publishing in April 1968 and Apple Records in July.[203] The Iveys' first single and Apple's fifth, "Maybe Tomorrow"/"And Her Daddy's a Millionaire" (released on November 15 in the United Kingdom), was a flop, despite McCartneian scalar bass lines, Mancunian harmonies, and Martinesque celli on the A-side, leading to a very limited release of the group's first LP. Only in 1969, after the quartet's name was changed to Badfinger—Neil Aspinall's suggestion—and there was much more direct involvement from McCartney and Harrison, would the group become successful.

Subsequent world-class artist James Taylor was discovered by Asher, who produced his first, eponymous LP for Apple in July–October 1968. McCartney plays bass on Taylor's first single, "Carolina in My Mind," released only in the United States, where it languished at #118 on the charts. The album failed but was reincarnated in 1969 when Harrison took the title line from "Something in the Way She Moves" for one of his own songs. The producer and artist blamed the album's failure on Derek Taylor's lack of publicity, and Derek blamed the artist's lack of promotion due to a nervous breakdown. Asher took Taylor to Warner Brothers, where he became a major attraction.

As if to add class to his roster, Peter Asher signed the Modern Jazz Quartet, who produced an Apple LP in 1968. Singles were planned for 1969 release for Trash and for Ashton, Gardner and Dyke (three of Liverpool's Remo Four, who'd played on the *Wonderwall* soundtrack). Among early plans, Keith Moon of the Who and Manfred Mann were to produce for Apple, and Harry Nilsson was to record, but these were some of the label's hopes that were never fulfilled.

The Beatles in Late 1968

JohnandYoko

Lennon and Ono began their film collaborations in August and September with *Smile*, a slowed-down ultra-high-speed shot of John's smile, and *Two Virgins*, superimposing a cloud with the intermeshing faces of the couple, and then had *Rape* professionally shot in December. This last film depicted the symbolic rape of a woman through an unrelenting invasion of privacy, a disturbance known by Lennon since 1963 and part of the message of *A Hard Day's Night*, by having a woman followed around London and into her home by a cameraman and sound technician.[204]

McCartney had Hopkin and Harrison had Lomax, so Lennon decided to release his and Yoko's May recordings as *Unfinished Music No. 1: Two Virgins*. With an increasing public openness, partly out of a sense of social responsibility, partly as artistic communication, they decided to use as cover photos two shots they had taken of themselves, nude (front and back), in early October, insisting that they were not so much being nude as forthrightly being themselves. John's rebirth was difficult. Considering the package obscene, EMI refused to distribute it, even when covered in a brown paper sleeve. Distribution was instead handled by Track in the United Kingdom (releasing the LP on November 29) and Tetragrammaton in the United States (November 11). Newark, New Jersey, police confiscated nearly 30,000 copies of the LP from a warehouse, but no charges were brought.[205]

The months of October and November 1968 were among Lennon's most difficult ever. In the space of forty-one days, he was arrested and convicted of possession of marijuana resin (an event that was to set the course for untold grief in the 1970s), he was divorced by Cynthia, and Yoko miscarried John's baby early in the third trimester. This last event was the basis for a ghoulish artistic statement. The fetal heartbeat was recorded just before the miscarriage, and it was released followed by two minutes' silence on a spring 1969 LP called *Life with the Lions*, which also depicted other Lennon trials in this period.[206] No wonder Lennon is heard in December 1968 singing his draft of "Everyone Had a Hard Year," which was a passage to be absorbed by McCartney's "I've Got a Feeling" the following month.[207]

Lennon and Ono ended the year with two more or less live performances, "The Rock 'n' Roll Circus" and "The Alchemical Wedding." A projected TV program that was never broadcast, "The Rock 'n' Roll Circus" constituted a filmed appearance in a band with Mick Jagger and Keith Richard of the Stones, Eric Clapton (ex-Cream), and Mitch Mitchell (ex–Jimi Hendrix Experience). Without prerecorded tapes, this December 11 performance for the cameras (with a rehearsal the day before) was the closest any Beatle had come to a live group performance in two years. Lennon led the band through an eight-and-a-half-minute version of "Yer Blues," which amounted to the Beatles' arrangement through **D**, followed by Clapton's solo twice through **E** and his instrumental version of **A**, concluding with many Richard-led choruses of a generic blues boogie graced by Ono's caterwauling.[208] Lennon also participated in the "Dirty Mac Jam."[209]

The other performance was for the "Alchemical Wedding" at the Albert Hall on December 18. Lennon and Ono remained on stage in a large white bag for a half hour, and their performance was over. "Bagism," a concept developed by Ono in 1965, was supposed to have been inspired by the phrase "The essential is invisible to the eye" from Antoine de Saint-Exupéry's *Le Petit Prince*.[210] This concept expresses the same idea Lennon and McCartney had stated for some time in speaking out against those with predetermined ideas about other people and their music—their "bag." The bag was supposed to prevent others from being prejudiced by appearances. Instead, it usually promoted ridicule. While doing his best to express himself clearly on important matters, John Lennon followed his music into a puzzling vortex.

The Group

The fan club's 1968 Christmas record was taped by four separate Beatles in the fall and edited by radio personality Kenny Everett for release on December 20. Ringo says hello over "Ob-La-Di, Ob-La-Da," McCartney busks Christmas/New Year wishes to his acoustic, John relates a thinly veiled tale of two balloons in love who "battled on against overwhelming oddities, includo some of there beast friends" against a lilting nineteenth-century parlor accompaniment on piano, and George and Mal Evans offer greetings from America. Then once more around, with Ringo having a Python-like telephone conversation with himself, John continuing with a punning stream of consciousness ("their loss was our gainsboroughnil") and George introducing Tiny Tim, who—with ukelele—sings "Nowhere Man" an octave higher than Lennon had.[211]

The year ended amid the usual press speculation that the Beatles would regroup for a live performance, but this time the sources were unusually reliable. McCartney and Derek Taylor jumped the gun as early as September by announcing several group performances at the Roundhouse, likely to be scheduled for December. But the other Beatles could never be convinced to make a go of it; Harrison and Starr were the most reluctant. While these musings led to no club dates, they prompted the climactic live performance of the "Get Back" sessions of January 1969.

While the Beatles took as much advantage of their compositional ingenuity and their engineers' creativity for the White album as for any previous effort, the plain cover was an emblem for the group's attempted return to their prepsychedelic simplicity. If they learned anything during their restful, contemplative stay in India, it may have been a disdain for modernism. One might not gather this from hearing "Revolution 9," but consider the album's emphasis on the acoustic guitar. Despite McCartney's stunning solo appearance for "Yesterday" and other notable examples from 1965, this was never an instrument strongly associated with the group. Rediscovered in Rishikesh, the acoustic guitar—after all, the first device on which John, Paul, or George played rock and roll—represents the group's musical roots as does no other. The electric guitar of course has a major role to play on the album, but it nearly always drives a securely grounded hard-rocking sound, rather than an ethereal fantasy like "I'm Only Sleeping" or "She Said She Said." The Beatles would try to give up studio gimmickry altogether in 1969, and only after a major effort to perform live resulted in failure would they find themselves through new sorts of experimentation in *Abbey Road*.

FOUR

LET IT BE
(1969–1970)

The Beatles disbanded in 1969, but not before recording their sloppiest and their slickest LPs. This chapter traces the on-again/off-again progress of their "Get Back"/*Let It Be* project, with close attention to the compositional process, and the remarkable achievement of *Abbey Road*, which—more than any other album—makes clear the differences between Lennon and McCartney, while Harrison twice takes center stage. Also to follow is a brief treatment of the personal and business differences that combined with incompatible musical interests to drive the group apart.

Both the "Get Back" and the *Abbey Road* projects contribute to an understanding of the basic musical differences between Lennon and McCartney. The Beatles had led a revival of rock and roll, as discussed in chapter 3 in relation to "Lady Madonna" and related compositions, culminating in a few White album tracks. The Beatles wished to go even further, with a return to live performances of simple rock arrangements, to "Get Back" all the way to their Quarry Men roots. For McCartney, this was to be a vehicle for reconnecting with his fans. For Lennon, it was a decision supporting an aesthetic statement that all of his art need not be complex, that the most profound ideas and feelings could best be expressed directly, without a lot of bullshit. For McCartney, psychedelia had been a Day-Glo breeze; for his partner, it was another perspective on the puzzle of himself. But both yearned for the simple innocence of youth. In *Abbey Road*, the rock-and-roll spirit comes through most strongly in Lennon's "Come Together" and "I Want You (She's So Heavy)," but also in McCartney's "Oh! Darling," "Carry That Weight," and "The End." The problem for

Table 4.1 Time Line of Major Events for the Beatles, 1969–1970

1969

Jan.–Dec.:	Harrison produces or records with Jackie Lomax, Billy Preston, Brute Force, the Radha Krishna Temple, Doris Troy, Jack Bruce, Joe Cocker, Ric Grech, Delaney & Bonnie
Jan. 2–31:	Recording and filming for "Get Back" project, Twickenham and Apple Studios, London
Jan. 17:	*Yellow Submarine* released in United Kingdom
Feb. 3:	John, George, and Ringo hire Allen Klein as manager
Feb. 5:	First mixing of *Get Back* material, continuing through Apr. 2, 1970
Feb. 22–Aug. 25:	Recordings and postproduction for *Abbey Road* LP, Trident, EMI, and Olympic Studios, London
Mar. 2:	John performs with Yoko, Cambridge
Apr. 11:	"Get Back"/"Don't Let Me Down" released in United Kingdom
Apr. 14–18:	Beatles record for next single, EMI, London
Apr. 30:	Beatles continue recording "You Know My Name (Look Up the Number)," EMI, London
May 9:	Lennon's *Unfinished Music, No. 2: Life with the Lions,* and Harrison's *Electronic Sounds,* released in United Kingdom
May 30:	"The Ballad of John and Yoko"/"Old Brown Shoe" released in United Kingdom
June 1:	John records "Give Peace a Chance," Queen Elizabeth Hotel, Montreal
July 4:	"Give Peace a Chance"/"Remember Love" released by Plastic Ono Band in United Kingdom
Sept. 13:	Plastic Ono Band performs, Varsity Stadium, Toronto
Sept. 25:	Plastic Ono Band records "Cold Turkey"
Sept. 26:	*Abbey Road* released in United Kingdom
Oct.:	"Paul is dead" rumors circulate
Oct. 24:	"Cold Turkey"/"Don't Worry Kyoko (Mummy's Only Looking for a Hand in the Snow)" released by Plastic Ono Band in United Kingdom
Oct. 27:	Ringo begins recording *Sentimental Journey* LP, EMI, Wessex, De Lane Lea, and Morgan Studios, London, continuing through Mar. 6, 1970
Nov. 7:	Lennon's *Wedding Album* released in United Kingdom
Dec.:	McCartney begins recording his first solo LP, continuing through Mar. 23, 1970, home studio (St. John's Wood) and EMI and Morgan Studios, London
Dec. 2–14:	George tours England and Scandinavia with Delaney & Bonnie
Dec. 12:	Lennon's *Plastic Ono Band Live Peace in Toronto—1969* released in United Kingdom
Dec. 15:	John and George perform in UNICEF benefit, Lyceum Ballroom, London

1970

Jan. 3–4:	Recording of "I Me Mine," EMI, London
Jan. 27:	Lennon records "Instant Karma," EMI, London
Feb. 6:	"Instant Karma"/"Who Has Seen the Wind" released by Plastic Ono Band in United Kingdom

Table 4.1 (*continued*)

Feb. 18–19, Mar. 8, 11, Oct.:	Ringo records "It Don't Come Easy" and "Early 1970," EMI and Trident Studios, London
Mar. 6:	"Let It Be"/"You Know My Name (Look Up the Number)" released in United Kingdom
Mar. 27:	Ringo's *Sentimental Journey* released in United Kingdom
Apr. 10:	McCartney announces the breakup of the Beatles
Apr. 17:	*McCartney* released in United Kingdom
May 8:	*Let It Be* released in United Kingdom

Lennon was that McCartney wished to elevate the rock songs by welding them into a grandiose "pop-opera" scheme, while he believed they should stand on their own merits. When invited on two days' notice to attend a September 1969 Rock and Roll Revival Festival in Toronto that was to feature Chuck Berry, Little Richard, Jerry Lee Lewis, and Bo Diddley, Lennon decided that he could only go as a performer. And did he ask the crowd-pleasing McCartney to join him on stage? No, he assembled his own band and decided on the return flight that he had replaced the Beatles with something more artistically true to himself. Meanwhile, Harrison found musical sustenance in 1969 in a continually growing group of collaborators that only sometimes included the Beatles.

McCartney wished to be close to his fans, but he could never be direct with them — recall the artifice of the "Sgt. Pepper" personification — so he had to turn down Lennon's offer to have the Beatles record "Cold Turkey" as a new single. The song's portrayal of heroin addiction probably precluded any consideration, but McCartney was likely suspicious of anything with tinges of Lennon's Dadaist tendencies, and the minimalist vocalizations of the harrowing coda were close to Yoko and far from Paul. Lennon had privately suffered over "Hello Goodbye" supplanting "I Am the Walrus" as an A-side, and in late 1969 he must have been seeing the Beatles as the vehicle for the fluffy and meaningless "Maxwell's Silver Hammer," not for the politically and socially important "Give Peace a Chance" or such verismo confessions as "Cold Turkey." So John asked for a divorce from Paul, "just like from Cynthia," and McCartney waited until the moment was right to make peace with himself.

"Get Back"

In September 1968 John Lennon described his new compositional interests as a step away from the psychedelic flowers of *Sgt. Pepper* and back toward his rock-and-roll roots: "We got a bit pretentious. Like everybody, we had our phase and now it's a little change over to trying to be more natural, less 'newspaper taxis,' say. . . . Really, I just like rock & roll. . . . I'm still trying to reproduce 'Some Other Guy' sometimes or 'Be-Bop-A-Lula.' "[1] This return to simplicity was closely tied to a desire to perform as a band again, live, without overdubs. By early 1968 Harrison expressed a desire to do so, but he did not wish to return to the madness of Beatlemania-afflicted crowds, so a small invited audience was envisioned.[2] Paul believed the group had to get over its stage fright and give the fans a show, but George was apprehensive; after his recent weeks of relaxed and inspiring musical collaborations in the States, he did not relish submitting once again to Paul's domination. Lennon was taking very little seriously — particularly the idea of disciplined rehearsal. McCartney says his partner was using heroin at the time, and several of the January outtakes provide circumstantial evidence of this.[3] When Paul suggested on January 2 that for a thrill, the group perform somewhere forbidden, John suggested Manila or Memphis, recalling the horror scenes of 1966; Ringo thought of the Liverpool Cathedral.[4] But McCartney was determined, and the show was to go on.

Initial hopes were to present White album highlights along with some older Beatles songs for a total of ten or twelve numbers, but as 1968 came to a close it seemed desirable to work up a group of all-new tunes, written with an ear toward live performance, along with some old rock-and-roll covers.[5] The group would rehearse for a few weeks in the new year with cameras so as to produce a documentary TV show directed by Michael Lindsay-Hogg (director of the "Rock 'n' Roll Circus" show), aiming toward concert performances to be filmed and recorded for a live LP in mid- to late January, the venue — perhaps an intimate gathering at the Roundhouse, or at the Twickenham studios — yet to be determined. Ringo had contracted in October 1968 to begin a heavy shooting schedule in early February for the Peter Sellers film *The Magic Christian*, so there was little time for delay.[6] As for the recording, Lennon was adamant that this was to be done completely without overdubs, without editing, "warts and all." But when it became clear that the show was to be performed not in concert but in the studio, the group eventually resorted to take after take, trying to get the perfect live run-through of each track, infuriating Martin, who thought that since the live concert appearance had been abandoned, normal studio procedure would streamline the process immeasurably.[7]

Filmed rehearsals were finally scheduled to begin at Twickenham film studios on January 2, and the TV concert shoot would be done there for two or three houses over a week's time beginning on January 17.[8] As rehearsals progressed, tensions mounted, Harrison quit the group, and the concert idea was dropped; filming ended at Twickenham on the 15th. A few days later, Harrison came back to the fold, having persuaded keyboardist Billy Preston to join the band so as to keep tempers under control, and filmed rehearsals resumed at Apple Studios on the 22nd, culminating in an impromptu noon-hour rooftop concert on the 30th and proper studio recording on the 31st.

Paul led with eight or nine new songs, featuring the project's theme song, "Get Back," a sort of boogified "Ob-La-Di, Ob-La-Da."[9] This song featured a double-plagal cadence, a device Lennon employed in his joyous "Dig a Pony." McCartney revisited the sudden twisting modulations of "Martha My Dear" for poetic effect in "The Long and Winding Road" and recalled the approach to the bridge in "Here, There and Everywhere" when "Two of Us" reminisced along a ♭III tangent. Aside from Harrison's twelve-bar number, "For You Blue," Lennon invoked the blues most strongly this go-round, as in the [025]-based cadence to "I've Got a Feeling" and in the revival of the 1963 blue-note reject, "The One after 909."

The Beatles' instrumentation is primarily that of the White album, with a few additions. Harrison plays his Les Paul, Telecaster, blue Stratocaster, and Gibson J-200, usually through a square Leslie cabinet given him by Clapton and for a few days with wah-wah. Lennon relies on the Epiphone Casino, Martin D-28, Gibson J-200, and Fender Bass VI, but we also hear him on the Hammond (with two three-and-a-half-octave manuals) and with an unidentifiable lap steel.[10] McCartney plays his Martin D-28, Höfner bass (presumably in anticipation of standing for live performances, where he preferred the lighter instrument), and the East German Blüthner grand piano, which is available at both Twickenham and Apple. Starr has a new set of Ludwigs, with yellow wooden shells, now with two upper toms in addition to the bass drum, snare, and floor tom, always with towels on the snare and floor tom, and a blanket inside the headless bass drum. Additionally, Ringo had a jangle box atop the hihat, perhaps so as to eliminate the need for an overdubbed tambourine. For Billy Preston, an electric piano would become available at the Apple Studios.

From a personal standpoint, the "Get Back" sessions of January 1969 represented a new low in collegiality. But from a professional view, very few previous months ever registered as much productive activity: some fifty-two new Beatles compositions were introduced, twenty-three of them receiving attention on four or more occasions. Because this was the most fully documented month of the Beatles' career—some seventy total hours of sound film are still extant today—it is difficult to know whether this apparent surge in creativity was something new or simply uniquely measurable. For our purposes, I will address primarily the five polished songs performed in the January 30 rooftop concert and the three others perfected in studio recordings and will then summarize the remaining work offered by each composer, all after a brief overview.

All January 1969 tapes enjoying distribution have been carefully catalogued in Doug Sulpy and Ray Schweighardt's *Drugs, Divorce and a Slipping Image* (henceforth abbreviated as S/S). These authors list 967 January recordings, of which I have studied 630. Their catalog and Lewisohn's datings (which, because they are based on non-EMI recordings, are made from film-company documents whose format is unfamiliar to him as an EMI archivist) are discrepant and undoubtedly have minor errors. The S/S-proposed chronology of extant film recordings seems to be based on the content of the Beatles' discussion and performance, the general progression of song arrangement, established continuities, and announcements of reel numbers every fifteen minutes or so done for synchronization purposes, all made from segments of tape rarely longer than six or seven minutes.[11] This said, S/S can only be seen as a first-rate document study of major import to Beatles scholars, and its provisional titles and catalog numbers will be adhered to here in nearly every case. What follows is a summary of "Get Back" recordings following the S/S chronology; in addition to the Beatles compositions listed here, 249 different identifiable covers and old Beatles songs are performed—some fully, most in brief excerpts—along with countless improvisations.

January 2: Rehearsals begin at Twickenham. "Don't Let Me Down," "All Things Must Pass," "Dig a Pony," "Let It Down," "I've Got a Feeling," "A Case of the Blues," "I'm Just a Child of Nature," "Sun King," and "Two of Us" are all introduced. Harrison displays his interest in the Band, likely intensified the previous Thanksgiving when he visited several members of the group at Woodstock.

January 3: New Beatles compositions include "She Came In through the Bathroom Window," "Paul Piano Intro," "Ramblin' Woman," "Picasso," "Taking a Trip to Carolina," "A Hole in the Heart Case," "Give Me Some Truth," and "Maxwell's Silver Hammer."

January 6: "Oh! Darling," "Hear Me Lord," and "Carry That Weight." An earnest and unusually sensitive McCartney tells Harrison, "I'm trying to help, but I always hear myself annoying you," leading to the latter's sulking capitulation.

January 7: "The Long and Winding Road," "Golden Slumbers," "Castle of the King of the Birds," "Get Back," and "For You Blue" are new.

January 8: "I Me Mine," "Mean Mr Mustard," and "Let It Be" are new.

January 9: "Another Day," "Her Majesty," "Suzy Parker," "La Penina," "Teddy Boy," "Junk," and "Commonwealth" are new.

January 10: Harrison, who has already contributed six new songs, has an un-recorded dispute with Lennon over lunch, disavows any interest in a television show, tells the others he's quitting the group, and leaves.[12] The others continue work, introducing "Through a London Window" and "John, John" and joking about finding a replacement guitarist; Lennon offers to get Clapton.

January 13: Harrison is absent, and Lennon doesn't arrive until 3 P.M. "With the status of the band in doubt, Paul eventually agrees to push the date of the live show back one week."[13] Those present work on seven previously re-hearsed numbers.

January 14: Harrison has gone to visit family in Liverpool. "The Day I Went Back to School," "The Back Seat of My Car," "It's Just for You," "Madman," and "Watching Rainbows" are the day's new compositions introduced by the re-maining Beatles.

January 15: Less than five minutes of tape from this day have appeared, work at Twickenham is over, and a private afternoon Beatles meeting is called, at which it is decided that all four will reconvene at Apple on the 22nd to per-form for cameras only — no audience.

Apple offices had moved in July to fashionable quarters at 3 Savile Row, just off Regent Street near Piccadilly Circus. Electronics "visionary" Alex Mardas had convinced the Beatles that with a reasonable budget, he could build a state-of-the-art seventy-two-track recording facility in the Apple basement, and they'd never again suffer EMI's many inconveniences. Why, he asked, did they continue to surround Ringo with frustrating sound screens, when it would be a cinch for "Magic" Alex to provide invisible acoustic dividers made of ultra-sonic waves?[14] When Martin's AIR staff inspected the basement in mid-January, they were appalled: the studio acoustics had untreated resonances that would color some pitches differently than others, the nearby heating plant was uninsulated and easily audible, no window or intercom linked the studio and control room, and—worst of all—the mixing board was a noisy handmade mess. Martin demanded that EMI's mobile recording unit be installed at once, and his ex-employer complied. A refurbished Apple Studio finally opened for business in September 1971.

The electronics resolved, Harrison took it upon himself to improve the group chemistry. Pleased by the others' 1968 behavior in Clapton's presence, Harrison decided to reemploy the tactic when he saw keyboardist and old friend Billy Preston on stage with Ray Charles. Preston was invited to the "Get Back" sessions and worked with the group from January 22 into May; as he says, "They just let me play whatever I wanted to play." [15]

> January 22: "Every Night" is the only nonimprovised number introduced on this first day at Apple, where the month's first eight-track sound recordings were made with EMI's remote equipment.
>
> January 23: Ringo introduced "Octopus's Garden" and "Hey, Hey Georgie," and a slow instrumental led by Preston is called "Billy's Blues." This date was Alan Parsons's first as Beatles tape operator. [16]
>
> January 24: "Polythene Pam," "There You Are, Eddie," "Pillow for Your Head," and "Dig It" are new.
>
> January 25: The Beatles continue work on previously heard numbers.
>
> January 26: "Isn't It a Pity," "I Look Out the Window," and "Suicide" are the day's new compositions.
>
> January 27: Previous songs are reworked.
>
> January 28: New compositions include "Old Brown Shoe," "Something," "How Do You Tell Someone," and "I Want You (She's So Heavy)."
>
> January 29: The Beatles continue work on previous numbers; oddly, S/S lists no songs that are to be performed in the following day's first live appearance in more than two years.
>
> January 30: The rooftop concert for nearby businessmen and passersby on the street consists of three hearings of "Get Back," two of "Don't Let Me Down," two of "I've Got a Feeling," and one each of "The One after 909" and "Dig a Pony," all previously rehearsed. Of these takes, the "I've Got a Feeling," "One after 909," and "Dig a Pony" performances were to make it to vinyl.
>
> January 31: "Two of Us," "The Long and Winding Road," and "Let It Be," all polished and considered worthy of an LP but as acoustic-based numbers not suitable for the rooftop concert, are recorded in numerous studio takes.

The "Get Back" film and sound tapes languished. Engineer Glyn Johns had been the film's sound man and, as Martin was rarely present—particularly at Twickenham—the Beatles often turned to him as de facto producer. Lennon says of the twenty-five miles of raw sound tape: "We didn't want to know about it anymore, so we just left it to Glyn Johns and said, 'Here, mix it.' That was the first time since the first album that we didn't want to have anything to do with it. None of us could be bothered going in. Nobody called anybody about it, and the tapes were left there."[17] Johns mixed the rooftop concert for stereo at Apple on February 5, but the rest was far more problematical. All along, he had been preparing acetates of selected takes for the Beatles, and these were the first takes to which he conveniently turned for mixing, even though many better versions existed elsewhere in the rubble.[18] Johns booked time at Olympic, where he mixed tracks on March 10–13. Along with bits of chatter added at Olympic by Martin and the Beatles on May 7 and 9, the LP *Get Back, Don't Let Me Down and 12 Other Songs* (reproduced in Beatles 1991d, and still rumored to be a potential forthcoming Apple release at this writing) was mastered on May 28. The lineup for the projected LP is given here. The parenthesized digits following the titles are the S/S catalog numbers, the first two digits representing the date in January on which the take was made, and the number following the divider point is the order number for that take in that day's work. For instance, "30.6" indicates that the recording in question was the sixth overall made on January 30.

Side 1	Side 2
"One after 909" (30.6)	"For You Blue" (25.24)
"Link Track" (a.k.a. "Rocker") (22.47)/	"Teddy Boy" (24.22)
"Save the Last Dance for Me" (22.48)/	"Two of Us" (24.39)/
"Don't Let Me Down" (22.49)	"Maggie Mae" (24.40)
"Dig a Pony" (23.35)/	"Dig It" (26.27)
"I've Got a Feeling" (23.36)	"Let It Be" (31.38, and April 30 dub)
"Get Back" (27.4)	"The Long and Winding Road" (31.20)
	"Get Back (reprise)" (28.1)

Also mixed in March but discarded by May were performances of "The Walk" (S/S 27.10; after Jimmy McCracklin, February 1958), "Lady Madonna" (31.16, the song that got the group back to rock and roll), and a ten-minute medley (26.29–26.32) comprising "Shake, Rattle and Roll" ("Big" Joe Turner, 1954), "Miss Ann" (Little Richard, 1955), "Kansas City" (Wilbert Harrison, April 1959), "Lawdy Miss Clawdy" (Elvis Presley, 1956), "Blue Suede Shoes" (Presley, April 1956), and "You Really Got a Hold on Me" (the Miracles, December 1962).[19]

The Beatles received acetates of all the live takes; McCartney says the LP was "great," and Lennon says, "I thought it would be good to go out, the shitty version, because it would break the Beatles, you know, it would break the myth. That's us, with no trousers on and no glossy paint over the cover and no sort of hope. . . . But that didn't happen. We ended up doing *Abbey Road* quickly, and putting out something slick to preserve the myth."[20] The "Get Back" album was slated for a June and then a late August or early September release, advance copies went out to disc jockeys (allowing for some of the earliest Beatles bootlegs in 1969, entitled "Hot as Sun" and "Kum Back"), and track-by-track reviews even appeared in *The Beatles Monthly Book* (July 1969) and *Rolling Stone* (September 20, 1969). At some point in the summer, likely in July, the more lucrative plan for a documentary feature film replaced the idea of the TV show;

the LP could wait a few more months to tie in with the film's release. In the meantime, work on the next LP was under way, and the Johns mix was never released at all, for the Beatles handed the tapes to Phil Spector in 1970 for the "slick" *Let It Be* LP production.

The Songs of the Rooftop Concert

The lunchtime rooftop concert of January 30, the climax of both the month's work and the eventual film (heard unedited in Beatles 1992d), consists of five songs played with Höfner, Casino, Telecaster, Ludwigs, and electric piano. Owing to the abundance of audio and video sources, much can be discerned about the genesis of the "head" arrangements for each composition, including the development of approaches to the lyrics, instrumentation, melody, harmony, and rhythm that will become the salient hallmarks of each song. The coverage below of each song, those performed on the roof and then those recorded in the studio, will sketch the development of these features, in presumed chronological order by tape source. Further discussion of most of these songs will be reserved for much later in the chapter, in connection with the mixes as finished for release in 1970.

"Get Back"   Of "Get Back," McCartney says, "We were sitting in the studio and we made it up out of thin air. . . . When we finished it, we recorded it at Apple Studios and made it into a song to roller-coast by."[21] The track seems to have been born in S/S 7.14 (that is, the fourteenth catalogued take from January 7), an improvisation in A major that sketches out a wordless melody for the verse. Work continues in 9.54–9.58, where the chorus (**B**, 0:43–0:59, the lyrics recalling "Sour Milk Sea") takes shape, featuring the pentatonic tumbling strain of "I Saw Her Standing There" at **B**+3–4 (0:47–0:51). Other than the double-plagal G–D–A cadence, the song never adds any chords to the tonic A and neighboring D.

McCartney's verse lyrics germinate in a post–"Back in the U.S.S.R." travelogue, mentioning both California and Tucson, Linda Eastman's haunts outside New York (and, in 1998, her place of death). They then lead to "Don't Dig No Pakistanis" (9.57, Beatles 1994j), an antidiscrimination ode in response to M.P. Enoch Powell's then recent speech and year-old racist tirade against the immigration of "coloureds" from the various Commonwealth colonies into London, squeezing into council flats (government-subsidized housing) and "taking other people's jobs."[22] In 9.57, the chorus is intact, as are the verse's tune and McCartney's ultrasimple bass line; Lennon makes wide use of the wah on his Casino, and Harrison plays tambourine, and still the double-plagal cadence has yet to appear. Main character Jo-Jo first appears in 9.58 and 10.4. While Harrison is away, 13.9–13.21 are devoted to inventing the lyrics to the second verse, first about Loretta Marsh then Loretta Marvin. Take 13.12 (Beatles 1975) is a run-through that begins with the second verse and continues with a few words of the first, leading to a wah solo from Lennon; a skeletal third verse still refers to the council flats.

The first two verses are in place in 23.4–23.14 (Beatles 1984), and McCartney accepts Harrison's suggested syncopated double-plagal cadence from the Telecaster (0:27–0:28) in 23.6. In 23.7, McCartney has a much more clearly formed idea of the lyrics, and he explains to his mates that Loretta is a drag queen in high-heeled shoes on a Tucson ranch waiting for Jo-Jo to return from California.[23] In 23.9, Starr's snare rhythm reminds Harrison of the Four Tops' "Reach Out I'll Be There" (August 1966), and this is kept. Lennon continues to work on his lead Casino part (largely a left-hand boogie), which the composer assigned him during Harrison's absence; Harrison's simple rhythm part takes shape very quickly on the 23rd, on Les Paul and then on Telecaster. Lennon works out his backing vocal part at **C** (1:14–1:28) in 23.12. Preston starts work on electric piano in 23.22 (adding the syncopated I^{7}_{43} chord at **B**); this take breaks down when Harrison catches Lennon making a typical "counting" error—"You're going on to D while we're still on A." But the solo, now without wah, has taken on its large rockabilly portamentos. The arrangement is essentially complete in 23.25.[24]

Rehearsals continue on the 24th: Lennon plays slide in 24.71, a warm-up; 24.76 evolves easily into a medley of Berry numbers inspired by Lennon's boogie.[25] Later work appears in 27.2 (Beatles 1991i), and 27.3 is in the sort of German the Beatles had used at the Star Club seven years earlier—"Gerraus nach deinem Haus!" (Beatles 1993b). Rehearsal 27.4, with Lennon's Casino switched to the neck pickup for a mellower tone, is the version released on both single— the coda of which comes from 28.1—and LP. The only other available tapes of "Get Back" are from the rooftop performance (Beatles 1992d). Here the theme song for the whole project is a warm-up, the program's opener (appearing in Beatles 1970c) and closer (during which Lennon's and Harrison's amps are turned off).[26] Following this, the end of the concert, Lennon is taken *way* back; he announces, "I'd like to say 'thank you' on behalf of the group and ourselves and I hope we've passed the audition."[27]

"Don't Let Me Down"   In a press conference in the last weeks of 1968, Lennon and Ono, with acoustic guitar, were asked to hum one of their latest tunes. Lennon sang and played the desperate chorus (**A**, 0:06–0:27) of "Don't Let Me Down," a passage based on the repeated $F\sharp m^{7}$–E change from Fleetwood Mac's instrumental "Albatross" (November 1968), a recording then being used as link music on the "Thames Television" program. Lennon said it was all he could remember of a song he would later say was about Yoko.[28] A late-1968 demo (part of which, from Beatles 1993b, is presented in ex. 4.1a) already has parts of the bridge (**C**, 1:19–1:47) and verse (**B**, with an "In My Life"–like $IV\sharp$-$\natural$–I, 0:28–0:57) and an unusual variation of the bridge (ex. 4.1a, mm. 13–16) that uses the German $^{6}_{5}$ (here, G^{7} applied to the dominant of E) of "Day Tripper," "Honey Pie," and "Sexy Sadie." In this early version, various sections are repeated, but the chorus (**A**, which perhaps postdates these other sections) is not yet heard.

"Don't Let Me Down" was the first song demonstrated in the New Year, in 2.1, 2.3, and 2.6 (all before McCartney arrives). In 2.18–2.24 (Beatles 1994g),

Example 4.1a "Don't Let Me Down" compositional draft (Lennon-McCartney). ©
1969 Northern Songs.

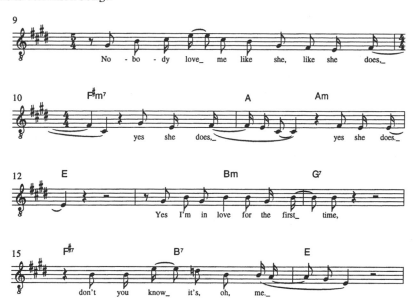

"Don't Let Me Down" grows out of the repeated F#m7–E opening of "Sun King,"
which is very closely modeled on "Albatross." In this preliminary run-through,
the "Don't Let Me Down" chorus is repeated so Harrison and Starr can work
out guitar, drum, and tentative harmony vocal parts, moving also to the two-
bar German $^6_5$ "variation" and bridge, but the structure is disorganized. In
2.39–2.43, McCartney considers playing piano, Harrison taking over bass, but
Lennon wants several guitarists. McCartney attempts an ordering of the
emerging song's various segments, beginning with the chorus, as Evans takes
dictation of the lyrics, in 2.43. By 3.28–3.30 (Beatles 1982b) and 3.90 (Beatles
1994d), McCartney has a valid, though not final, bass line and is working on a
vocal countermelody.

In 6.18–6.32, a highly productive forty-minute rehearsal (nearly all in Beatles 1991i and 1994d), McCartney has worked out his chorus vocal part and
wants to add a descant moving from repeated eighths on high $\hat{3}$ at **C**+2–3 to
more on $\hat{4}$ at **C**+4–7, returning to $\hat{3}$ at **C**+8–9. As if in charge, Paul gives
George the descending line, $\hat{8}–\hat{7}–\hat{6}–\hat{5}$, to be sung obliquely against his own re-

Example 4.1b "Don't Let Me Down" compositional draft.

peated high $\hat{3}$; both parts will eventually be dropped as too complicated. Lennon's Casino is well distorted, and Harrison uses the wah. In the spirit of simplification, the German $^6_5$ has disappeared. In 6.22, a fully structured performance except for an ending, McCartney has added the descant part to the verse, and the lyrics are intact except the beginning of the second verse. But many guitar features are yet to be worked out, and Lennon asks Harrison to invent some riffs. In 6.24, Paul asks for lighter drumming, with an "airy" ride cymbal in the bridge, and sings Harrison a suggested fluent guitar part (ex. 4.1b, from Beatles 1991i) for the verse that enhances the emerging cross-rhythm but is ultimately left unused. Although this is Lennon's song, it is McCartney who puts the sections in order and arranges specific instrumental and vocal parts for the others.

Lennon complains about overuse of the wah in 7.93 (Beatles 1991h). In 7.96, Harrison works on a descending two-part accompaniment to the verse, but it lacks the $3+3+2$ rhythm later set up by his articulation at **B**+2–3 ("Guitar I," 0:31–0:37); the bass line includes many frills, including chromatic passing tones, that are later to be dropped. Harrison's guitar introduction is born in 9.30, as is the $3+3+2$ rhythm at **B**+2–3. He finally exchanges the wah for a Leslie in 10.3 (Beatles 1975), on which take Lennon plays on electric piano a part virtually duplicated by Preston in 22.47–22.49 (Beatles 1991d). During these rehearsals, McCartney has created the bass line, Harrison has the guitar countermelody in the bridge, and all extraneous backing vocals are gone. Billy and George are in perfect concert with the touching tonic major-seventh chord at 0:38. Take 28.2 was released as the B-side of "Get Back," but not before Lennon's vocal was double-tracked in the bridge and third and fourth choruses. This finished arrangement is re-created in the two rooftop performances (30.3, where Lennon forgets the words of the second verse, and 30.12, where his similar error is in the first verse).

Mixes for the "Get Back"/"Don't Let Me Down" single were made on April 7 at Olympic Studios; for the first time, a Beatles single was issued in stereo, but in the United States only. The British release (Apple R 5777, released April 11, remaining at #1 for four weeks) sold more than half a million copies, and the American (Apple 2490, May 5, #1 for five weeks) sold more than 2 million. Never before had the Beatles gone eight months between singles, so the public was more than ready with its cash.

"I've Got a Feeling"   Lennon and McCartney each contribute sections that are superimposed quodlibet-style to create "I've Got a Feeling." Lennon ended 1968 with a demo of "Everyone Had a Hard Year," a number alternating B♭ and Gm⁷ chords with "Julia"-style fingerpicking. John took the melody of this draft a half-step higher and kept most of the same text—although there is not yet a reference to a "wet dream"—and came up with a section of "I've Got a Feeling" (**F**). By S/S 2.11, where we hear Casino, Höfner, and explorations on the Les Paul, the alternating chords have become A and D^6_4, and new words have been added, but the tune (example 4.2) carries only a clue in its voice leading of what it is to become.[29] Apparently this take is only Lennon's attempt to recall McCartney's previously written tune, because the latter sings **A** intact in 2.26,

Example 4.2 "I've Got a Feeling" compositional draft.

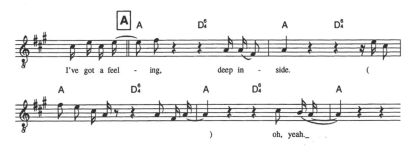

and backing vocals are there as well. Harrison plays the chords at **A+9** ("Guitar II," 0:29–0:32) in straight sixteenths and needs to be told the roots of the pentatonic [025] cadence, E–G–D (**A+10**–1, 0:32–0:35), Lennon's lower harmony vocal at **B** (0:41–1:01) is coming along, and McCartney calls out the chords of his shouted Little Richard–style bridge (**C**, 1:15–1:30). Note that, as in "Yesterday," the bridge chords, here forming the [025]-based progression E–G7–D7, are based on the resetting of a pattern from the verse. McCartney instructs Lennon on how to create imperceptible changes of pitch at **C+4**–5 (1:25–1:30): "It's got to be like pain; at the moment it's a riff." The third verse and quodlibet at **F** (2:45–3:08) are present in 2.35, complete but for an ending.[30] After this run-through, McCartney suggests triplets at **A+9** (0:29–0:32), but Harrison is working on **A+10**—he tries arpeggiating the cadential chords in triplets, not yet hitting on the chromatic scale. It seems that at some point in December, McCartney must have heard Lennon's sketch, built it into a real song, and taken it over as his own.

Work continues, Harrison adopting a wah briefly in 7.33 (Beatles 1994c) and, with the Les Paul, 9.32 (Beatles 1991e). McCartney still complains in 9.33 (seen in Beatles 1970c) about microtones not being close enough together in the guitar retransition; the chromatic triplets of **E** (2:34–2:39) appear first in 9.34 (Beatles 1975). By 22.54–22.58 (Beatles 1991g), Preston has added electric piano, and the arrangement—with Ringo's delayed entry and oddly syncopated bass drum, triplets at **A+9**, bass line finished, and ending composed—is nearly complete. But still the chromatic line at **A+10** is not yet heard; all are at work on triplet arpeggios at that point—"the waltz bits," as McCartney calls them. Although the next run-through, 23.36 (Beatles 1996b), breaks down, it was included in Glyn Johns's provisional LP. The arrangement has not changed in 27.5–27.8 (Beatles 1994f), 27.11 (mixed by Johns on March 13; Beatles 1991b), or 27.14–27.15 (Beatles 1991k) and was "finished" only on the rooftop, 30.4 (in Beatles 1970b and 1970c), and 30.9. Phil Spector must have enjoyed balancing the wall-of-sound backing, featuring three different but constant ostinato patterns from Lennon, Harrison, and Preston.

"The One after 909"   With the Beatles steeped in memories of their earliest compositions, many of which are demonstrated in these sessions, "The One

after 909" makes its first recorded appearance since March 1963.[31] Allowing for brief memory lapses, the vocals, guitars, and stop-time D-gesture are fairly set by 3.34–3.36 (Beatles 1982b); the song is treated to George's wah in 7.86–7.89 (Beatles 1991h), 8.17 (Beatles 1991e), and 9.36–9.39 (Beatles 1975 and 1970c); and Billy adds the gliss-ful keyboard in 28.4–28.5 (Beatles 1987e). The fine rooftop performance, 30.5–30.6 (far better without the wah), was mixed for the *Get Back* LP and appeared in both the *Let It Be* film and LP. Too bad this number hadn't been revived for *Beatles for Sale* in place of, perhaps, "Mr. Moonlight," but on *Let It Be*, it remains at least a major part of the only commercially available record of the Beatles' final live performance for the public, even if only in an unannounced rooftop session.

"Dig a Pony"   Little can be ascertained about the compositional process of "Dig a Pony." In 2.4, Lennon shows Harrison its chords, an unusually colorful expansion of V: II–♮VII⁷–V (**A**+7–13, 0:29–0:40) and a double-plagal (G–D–A) chorus (**B**, 1:00–1:09). But recordings are not again available until 7.85 (Beatles 1991h), by which point the group has the song pretty well down, even if the retransition to the D.S. hasn't been worked out and Lennon can't recall many of the words; he will still need the lyrics in front of him for the rooftop show.[32] The double-plagal introduction trebled in two guitars and bass and Harrison's joyous parallel sixths (0:31–0:41) have been perfected by 22.14–22.15 (Beatles 1984). Preston is not heard in the "Dig a Pony" sessions until 22.53 (Beatles 1991g), which captures only the finished coda.[33] The next available tape, 23.34–23.35, has two full performances, the second (Beatles 1996b) polished enough for Glyn Johns's LP, although the rooftop version (30.8) was chosen for *Let It Be*.[34]

The Studio Releases

"Two of Us"   The Beatles apparently felt that their rooftop performances achieved the desired effect, for the group did not bring those songs to the studio for remakes. Three acoustic McCartney numbers, on the other hand, too delicate for the rooftop, underwent multiple takes at Apple on January 31: "Two of Us," "The Long and Winding Road," and "Let It Be."

Both Paul and Linda Eastman have said that "Two of Us" was written about how they would drive aimlessly in London and the surrounding countryside and write postcards to each other (see Miles 1997, 470–1), but—perhaps in the "getting back" vein—the song evolved into a retrospective ode to the Lennon-McCartney partnership. The run-through presented on Beatles 1996b has Paul call "Take it, Phil!" (al 1:47), a vivid reminder that Paul and John began their vocal harmonizing in emulation of Phil and Don Everly. The paper-chasing reference in the third verse (**A**+6–8) predicts the similar Apple-bashing that would inspire "You Never Give Me Your Money."[35] Given this reading, the lyrics of the bridge (**B**, 1:31–1:44) predict a fast-approaching end to the relationship. The bridge is highlighted both by the shift to the parallel minor through ♭III, untransposed from "Here, There and Everywhere," and by the initial vocal skip up to d^2, which finally breaks the verse's barrier that always permits b^1 to rise only to c^2, which must always descend "back home" to $\hat{1}$.[36] Harmonically, the bridge is interesting for its gradual yet sure return from the remote $\flat$III area to the strong dominant at the early-Beatles-style retransition (1:42–1:44); only the falsetto "oohs" are missing in this more relaxed style.

In 2.45–2.47 (Beatles 1982b), McCartney plays the song on his Martin D-28 with Ringo drumming; as Lennon picks up his Casino and Harrison his Telecaster, McCartney calls out the bridge changes in rhythm: "B$\flat$–D minor–G minor–A minor, stay on A minor, A minor seventh to D." McCartney confuses the others because sometimes he counts three beats' rest in **A+11**, sometimes two, but the final metric arrangement is decided here. Otherwise, all his lyrics and parts are complete, and he already knows what his descant is to do— Lennon will be assigned the lower part—while Harrison already has his romping fourth-beat sixteenths figured out. By 3.45 (Beatles 1982b), the descant is learned. In 6.33–6.37 (Beatles 1994h), McCartney teaches Ringo the cymbal part for the bridge, and progress is slowed by a long argument between McCartney and Harrison as to incompatible working methods, leading to an inopportune recollection of the disagreement between the two over how to perform "Hey Jude." McCartney plays bass and impersonates Elvis in the bridge in 8.11 (Beatles 1992d, seen in Beatles 1970c), in which the vocal parts are solid. Takes 9.22–9.28 and 10.2 (Beatles 1994i, 1994j, and 1975) are all presto and electric, the composer playing roots on bass, and feature later-discarded wholenote backing harmonies in the bridge.

Harrison takes back the bass line on his Telecaster in 24.18, and acoustic guitars are tried in 24.20, McCartney arriving at the metrically bewitching broken-sixth introduction ("Guitar I") in 24.29. The carefree whistling coda appears in 24.33 (Beatles 1991k), but Harrison still doesn't have a bass part for the bridge. Lennon showcases his expert Scottish burr and McCartney his Jamaican head-tone in 24.35 (Beatles 1991e). Harrison's part for the bridge is developing in 24.39 (Beatles 1991d), a very slow take, and in another without an S/S entry (Beatles 1996b), and is finished in a thirteen-minute rehearsal of the bridge, 25.6 (Beatles 1994i), where McCartney sings and plays on the D-28 his suggestions for the desired bass part to his stand-in, followed by full-group repetitions of single bars until Harrison has invented the entire part on the Stratocaster. Things would have gone so much faster had the Beatles been able to read notation! As is true of nearly all of their arrangements, the parts themselves are not so technically demanding, but they do twist and turn with imagination and thus tax the performers' memory skills. Experimentation in 25.7–25.17 (seen in film outtakes) with a lower vocal part for Lennon at **B+3**–5 (1:35–1:42) is abandoned, but it is here that Lennon comes up with the guitar sixteenths on the J-200 ("Guitar II") in the other bridge measures. The arrangement is complete, and work is done except for the four finished takes done in 31.1–31.7 (Beatles 1991h); 31.5 (with D-28, J-200, Telecaster, and drums) is the released version.

"Two of Us" was originally called "On Our Way Home," under which title McCartney produced a recording by Mortimer, a New York trio discovered by

Example 4.3 Analysis of "The Long and Winding Road."

Peter Asher, planned for release as an Apple single in June but for some unknown reason never issued.

"The Long and Winding Road"   Apple officer Alistair Taylor claims that McCartney wrote "The Long and Winding Road" for his wife Lesley, and Steve Turner
surmises that the long and winding road itself is the B842, an artery that leads
to wind-swept Campbeltown, near the composer's Scottish farm on the Mull of
Kintyre.[37] One wonders additionally whether the song's highly poetic line "The
wild and windy night that the rain washed away has left a pool of tears" might
have origins in Lennon's inspiring reference to "pools of sorrow, waves of joy"
in "Across the Universe." McCartney has ascribed the song's musical origins to
Ray Charles (Miles 1997, 539). Regardless of its inspiration, the verse's tune begins to follow a long descent (see example 4.3) from $\hat{8}$ (e♭1, **A+**1, 0:00), leading
through ♭$\hat{7}$ (**A+**3, 0:09) to $\hat{6}$ (**A+**4, 1:10) and $\hat{5}$ (**A+**8, 0:24) before changing its
course and returning up to $\hat{8}$ (**B−**1, 0:39). The twists and turns of the melody—
which does not trace the descent and ascent quite directly, as can be followed
in the closed noteheads in the graph—echo in the harmony, which begins in C
minor and tonicizes A♭ major (**A+**4) before turning to E♭, a perfect musical description of a long and winding road. The melody of the bridge (**C**, 1:26–1:40)
seems to exist only so as to alternate twice between the two opposite nodes of
the melody, e♭1 and b♭, both symmetrically ornamented by upper neighbors
and under thirds, again underlining the road's winding nature.

Begun in 1968, "The Long and Winding Road" is introduced to the band in 7.1 and 7.3 (Beatles 1994g), where McCartney plays a solo piano and sings while waiting for others to arrive at Twickenham. He has lyrics for only the first verse (**A**) and a bit of the bridge (**C**), but the tune and piano part (including the striking V^{11} chord at **A**+2) for verse, bridge, and coda are virtually complete. The song reappears as a piano solo at 7.40 (Beatles 1991i) and 10.22 (Beatles 1994i), again played simply to pass the time. McCartney teaches the chords to Harrison in 8.82–8.85, but Lennon remains uninvolved for two more weeks. The next available recording, 26.38–26.39 (Beatles 1970c), with McCartney strong on piano, Lennon weak on Bass VI, Harrison on Leslied Telecaster, and Starr on drums, is an odd light cha-cha followed by a backing-vocal rehearsal. The lyrics for the second verse make their first appearance in 28.8 (Beatles 1987e), an A-major blues led by Preston, with McCartney on bass, Starr on drums, and Harrison on Telecaster. So, without any indication of how Lennon (Bass VI) and Harrison (Telecaster with Leslie) learn their parts, the next available tape includes fragments of the final recordings, 31.8–31.15 and 31.17–31.22 (Beatles 1991h except 31.20, which is on 1996b). One take (31.14) breaks down when Lennon plays an incomprehensible G in **A**+4. The Johns mix of the released take (31.20) adds nothing to the Beatles' sparse drums, expert piano, roughly articulated Bass VI, Telecaster with Leslie, and solo McCartney vocal, but this track will receive substantial later treatment, to be discussed in due course, before its 1970 release. A film of the recording of 31.22, in which the Beatles are joined by Preston on Hammond, appears in *Let It Be* and *The Beatles Anthology*.

"Let It Be"   In the summer of 1968, McCartney dreamed that he was comforted by his mother, Mary, who advised him to let his problems be.[38] Thus was born the song whose title would be lent to the entire project: "Let It Be." The chorus (**B**, 0:38–0:51) is based on the trademark McCartney stepwise-descending bass, but the gospel tone, which led many to interpret "Let It Be" as a Marian anthem, reminds one of the Band's similarly built chorus to "The Weight" (August 1968).

Paul runs through the first verse and chorus on piano in 8.50 (Beatles 1991c), working with Ringo on the hi-hat-based drum part while John maps out a few chords and lines on the Casino. George joins in 8.86, and John adds vocal harmony to the chorus in 9.5. McCartney leads a close rehearsal in 9.88–9.91 and 9.95–9.97 (Beatles 1975 and 1994i), directing Lennon's notes on the Bass VI, singing against the piano part the root names every two beats during the verse, **C**, and the A–G–F steps in the chorus, **D** (1:18–1:22)— "You'll get it, it's dead easy"—while Harrison struggles with guitar. McCartney sings the backing "ah"s in the chorus, then asks "who wants to take the one above" (c^1–b–a–g), which is elected by Harrison; then the composer says to Lennon, "Now you take the lower—the same notes as you're playing on the bass." McCartney and Lennon with Leslie continue alone through 9.89, the latter getting more proficient with bass lines. All four work at 9.95, but Harrison contributes little other than his vocal harmonies. Lennon wants to know when each is to come in, as the instrumental entries are to be staggered; this is worked out by McCartney and Johns, the break (**F**+1–2, 1:45–1:52)/ending is devised, and Harrison, working alone, devises his solo (**G**). Take 9.97 is a run-through, with McCartney's piano the only instrument before drums and jangle box enter at **C** (0:52), bass at **D** (1:18, a bit later than in the final arrangement), and guitar at **G** (1:59). All sing their parts, but lyrics exist for the first verse only.

Rehearsals continue with 25.27–25.42, with Lennon on Bass VI, McCartney on piano, Starr on drums, and Harrison now with the Strat through his Leslie, on which he plays his solo in nearly finished form. The second verse appears in a full run-through later that day (Beatles 1996b; there is no S/S entry) and in 26.33–26.37 (film outtakes and Beatles 1991b). Take 26.36 is a full performance, but the introduction is just a piano and bass version of **F** (at 1:45); Preston now plays Hammond, but his part is very rudimentary and largely covered by the backing vocals and the Strat's Leslie; the third verse is just a dummy combining lines of the first two. The released version comes from 31.23–31.29 (Beatles 1991h), before which the introduction has been readied, Ringo has restricted the hi-hat at **C** to the backbeat, Preston's part has become more prominent—including the solo at **F**+3–4—and the third verse has been written. Take 31.38 is the one released, with overdubs made even for the *Get Back* album, as well as for subsequent releases. McCartney judges the take "very fair; one more"; this last performance, 31.39, appears in the film. Agreeing with his fans, McCartney has remembered "Let It Be" as one of his own favorites, and he played it in 1979 benefit concerts for the victims of Kampuchea.[39]

Other New Compositions

McCartney's Aside from wordless improvisations, McCartney works on twenty-five compositions in the "Get Back" tapes. In addition to those discussed above, a piano solo copyrighted as "Paul Piano Intro" appears in the film, actually opening it. This piece, the beginning of which is transcribed as example 4.4, resembles more than anything else an early Baroque keyboard suite, a deft gigue with expert counterpoint along a descending chromatic line, followed by a stately pavane loaded with leaden parallel fifths. Likewise, a twelve-bar boogie played four-hands by Starr (*primo*) and McCartney (*secondo*) featuring the latter's busked lyrics, beginning "I bought a piano the other day, I didn't know the man could play . . . ," was kept in the film and copyrighted as "Jazz Piano Song." Six of McCartney's eight *Abbey Road* songs ("Maxwell's Silver Hammer," "She Came In through the Bathroom Window," "Oh! Darling," "Carry That Weight," "Golden Slumbers," and "Her Majesty," all to be discussed later in the chapter, in the context of that album) are worked through, as are seven songs ("Teddy Boy," "Every Night," "Hot as Sun," "Junk," "Suicide," "Another Day," and "Back Seat of My Car") that would be released only as solo McCartney works.

Four additional numbers and many improvisations were never heard again. In order of greatest development, these drafts are known as "It's Just for You," "There You Are, Eddie," "Castle of the King of the Birds," and "The Day I Went Back to School." The first of several verses of "It's Just for You" (14.22–14.23

Example 4.4 "Paul Piano Intro" (Lennon-McCartney). © 1969 Northern Songs.

[Beatles 1991i]) is excerpted in example 4.5; shown are the R- and D-gestures of the SRDC structure. This is a falsetto bel canto number with a Latin beat employing mode mixture like the use of IV♭ in Presley's "It's Now or Never" (July 1960), perhaps improvised on the spot, but played in A♭, A, then B♭. "There You Are, Eddie" (24.48 [Beatles 1981c] and 24.72 [1991g]) is an inconsequential ditty in D with Paul on D-28 and John keeping up on Casino. "Castle of the King of the Birds" is a piano fragment attempted over the course of a few days (7.4 [Beatles 1994d] and 9.4), shown in example 4.6, to which McCartney vocalizes as if he envisions future lyrics. "The Day I Went Back to School" (14.8 [Beatles 1994e]) is a simple number whose origin is captured on tape but which is not known to have been taken any further.

Lennon's   In addition to "Don't Let Me Down," "Everyone Had a Hard Year," and "Dig a Pony," eleven new Lennon songs appeared in January. Two were published in connection with the project. One was "Dig It," a jam copyrighted in the name of all four Beatles that appeared in both the film and the album. The highly repetitive I–IV–V–IV jam goes nowhere but its stream-of-consciousness litany of lyrics, including the initials "FBI, CIA, BBC, B. B. King"—not unlike the "LBJ," "IRT," "U.S.A.," "LSD," "FBI," "CIA" string in "Initials," from *Hair* (1968)—is a bit of a window into the composer's twisted mind. The other

Example 4.5 "It's Just for You" compositional draft.

Example 4.6 "The Castle of the King of the Birds" compositional draft.

number used in the film was "Suzy Parker," the published title of a blue number actually about Suzy's Parlour.

Four of Lennon's six *Abbey Road* songs, "Sun King," "Polythene Pam," "Mean Mr Mustard," and "I Want You (She's So Heavy)," are run through, as is a discarded number, "Watching Rainbows" (14.29 [Beatles 1994f]). This last provides the heroin-related "shoot me" that will later be grafted onto "Come Together." "I'm Just a Child of Nature," rewritten in 1971 as "Jealous Guy," and "Give Me Some Truth" are exposed here but saved for solo recording. Two other compositions are heard among various improvisations (such as "A Hole in the Heart Case"). "Madman" (14.27–14.28 [Beatles 1994f], 14.34, and 22.19 [Beatles 1984]) is an electric-piano cousin to the coexisting "Mean Mr Mustard." "A Case of the Blues" is a seeming remake of the Monkees cover "(I'm Not Your) Steppin' Stone" (December 1966) that in three January references (2.12 [Beatles 1994g], 7.72 [1991c], and 7.103 [1994c]) does not progress beyond a weak late-1968 demo (Lennon 1988f), other than to add some boogie figuration to a simple Casino part.

Lennon's other main contribution to the January product is in leading his mates through "Maggie Mae" (24.34, 24.36, 24.40 [Beatles 1991d]), the traditional skiffle tale of a Liverpool streetwalker that appears in both the Johns LP and *Let It Be*. The song is performed with Lennon's J-200 and lead vocal, McCartney's D-28 and descant vocal, Harrison's bass line on Telecaster, and Starr's drums.

Harrison's and Starr's   As central as Lennon's contributions are to the White album, Harrison's twelve new compositions in January 1969 (counting the untaped "Wah-Wah") are far more interesting than those of his elder, even if none are promoted to the final cut, the sessions of January 30 and 31. Two songs, "For You Blue" and "I Me Mine," are prominent in the film and thus also appear in the accompanying album. An off-screen performance of "For You Blue"— the title is likely a corruption of " 'For You' Blues," as it's a twelve-bar number— marks the film's transition from Twickenham to Apple. Harrison's elegant introductory hammer-ons promise more than they deliver, so the song's primary interest remains in preserving Lennon's only lap-steel performance with the Beatles, one that seems both clumsy and polished at the same time.

Harrison introduces the song in 7.25–7.26 (Beatles 1994h), at which point McCartney complains that no one other than himself wants to help organize the show; Harrison, ignoring the fact that his song is getting no attention, chimes in with an idea about continuity, but Lennon is distinctly uninterested. Band rehearsals on "For You Blue" begin in 9.17–9.20 and take better shape in 9.83–9.84 (Beatles 1975), with Harrison's guitar perfected, McCartney working on bass, Starr working on drums, and Lennon boogieing on his Casino. By 25.19–25.24 (Beatles 1996b, 1970c, 1992e, and 1991d), Harrison is on J-200, McCartney on piano (with a solo at **C** descending two octaves in rhythmically apt right-hand parallel sixths), Lennon on slide (solo at **B**), and Ringo brushing his drums with a heavy backbeat, and the sounding key has changed from E to D; the song was written in A and is played with a capo on the fifth fret. Take 25.24 (Beatles 1991b) was mixed by Johns for the *Get Back* LP and also appears on *Let It Be*.

Just as "Not Guilty" was Harrison's defense against the tyranny of his songwriting comrades, "I Me Mine" is a mocking complaint about their stifling egos.[40] The verse-refrain (**A–B**) is based on a tune Harrison heard played on television by an Austrian brass band. The melody has the European folk quality of Mary Hopkin's "Those Were the Days," well suited both to Harrison's favorite F-against-E^7 sound from "I Want to Tell You" and elsewhere and to the transition's descending chromaticism, A–G♯–G♮–F♯–F♮ (0:31–0:35), while the bridge (**C**, 0:39–0:57) is a simple twelve-bar blues.

January 1969 takes of "I Me Mine" were all done on the 8th. Takes 8.1–8.4 (Beatles 1991c) has Harrison play the song for Ringo on Lennon's Casino. Lyrics are finished, and the "Guitar II" part is finished except that the transition at **C**–1–2 (0:35–0:38) features a flamenco-style E–F$^{\mathrm{sus5}\,{}^{6}_{4}}$–E–F$^{\mathrm{sus5}\,{}^{6}_{2}}$–E–F$^{\mathrm{sus5}\,{}^{6}_{4}}$–E$^{8-7}$ that is later discarded. Lennon openly mocks the song in 8.39–8.40 (Beatles 1992e), seemingly jealous at Harrison's widening vocal range as well as his confidence in his compositional abilities. In 8.53, the song reminds McCartney of the 1951 French waltz "Domino" (Beatles 1975), which he plays expertly with enjoyable counterpoint in bass and vocal (with contrary motion in sequential applied chords); and in 8.75, it leads McCartney to recall King Oliver's "St. James Infirmary" blues of 1929 (Beatles 1992e). Serious group rehearsals, featuring Les Paul, Casino, Höfner, and Ludwigs, begin with 8.54–8.57 (Beatles 1975); despite Lennon's heavy insults as to the Spanish style, the composer wishes castanets. The one-and-a-half-minute arrangement is finished by 8.63–8.64 (Beatles 1994j) and 8.73–8.81 (Beatles 1994j and 1992e), with Harrison's comments to the others limited to an adjusted cymbal part. The song is not picked up again this month.

When filmmakers decided in late 1969 to use footage of both 8.1 and 8.81 (spliced together), particularly for the accompanying shots of John and Yoko's attempts at waltzing, the tie-in LP suddenly required a recording of the song despite its not having been taped properly. Thus, the Beatles were called back to EMI on January 3–4, 1970. John Lennon could not be bothered to return from Denmark to make what were to be the group's final recording sessions, but the others turned in a good performance, omitting the E–F$^{\mathrm{sus5}\,{}^{6}_{2}}$–E flamenco bit, with McCart-

Example 4.7 "I Look out the Window" compositional draft.

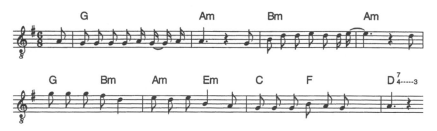

ney's organ, bass, and backing vocal; Harrison's J-200, two distorted lead guitars, and lead vocal; and Ringo's drums. The one-and-a-half-minute performance would be stretched, with one tape copy and an edit, to 2'25".

During the sessions, Harrison also works on "Old Brown Shoe" and "Something," both to appear in subsequent Beatles releases, and "All Things Must Pass," "Let It Down," "Hear Me Lord," and "Isn't It a Pity," all rejected by the group but polished for Harrison's *All Things Must Pass*.[41] Otherwise, Harrison also tries out three songs that seem to have gone no further. One was the acoustic number "Ramblin' Woman" (3.7 and 9.85 [Beatles 1975]), with Jesse Fuller–like applied V[7]s and VII°[7]. This may have been composed over the previous Thanksgiving, as Harrison is heard relating the song to two then unreleased Dylan songs that he would have heard at that time. The second was the folklike yet rich "I Look out the Window" (26.17, Beatles 1987e), transcribed here as example 4.7. The off-mike vocal renders the text indistinguishable, yet the lilting tune, poignant minor chords, and forward-driving cadential suspension make this one of Harrison's prettiest drafts. Regardless, McCartney ridicules it instantly. The third composition is "How Do You Tell Someone" (28.20, Beatles 1992e), an undistinguished Caribbean-flavored rewrite of "If I Needed Someone."

Ringo Starr brings three songs of his own to the sessions: "Octopus's Garden" will appear on *Abbey Road*; two half-minute fragments, "Picasso" (3.9) and "Taking a Trip to Carolina" (3.10), are unavailable to me.

Bad Business

The Beatles had withstood mounting personal and musical differences for years, but they would not be able to survive the myriad severe business troubles that would plague them in 1968–69. When the Apple boutique soured, it was simply closed and emptied; subsequent disasters could not be handled so summarily and with such unilateral control. By late 1968, employee thefts from Apple's offices added a crippling strain, and the Savile Row building was virtually held hostage through December by a handful of Hell's Angels living there at Harrison's invitation.[42] Failure met all corporate divisions but Apple Records, which had its problems as well, including botched signings of Buddy Guy and — after a full album was cut — Delaney and Bonnie. The BBC's February 1969 ban on an Apple record for the offensive name of its group, "White Trash," did not help either. Apple's accounting firm resigned in October 1968, "warning of dire consequences."[43] A powerful merchant banker — a stuffed-shirt type held in no high regard by the antiestablishment Beatles — offered to straighten the company out as a friendly gesture toward Beatles protector Joseph Lockwood, the chairman of EMI, but his magnanimous offer was met with silence.

The situation worsened. Nemperor Holdings, once Brian Epstein's NEMS but by 1969 under the control of his brother Clive, continued to draw 25 percent of the Beatles' artist's earnings despite having no role in the group's management, because of a clause Brian had put in the group's nine-year contract with EMI, binding until January 1976. To pay taxes, Clive Epstein resolved to sell Nemperor despite its income. Linda Eastman's father, John, a lawyer with extensive experience in the entertainment world, advised Paul to have the Beatles buy Nemperor, matching a competing £1 million offer from a bank, Triumph Investment Trust. EMI chair Lockwood pledged that his company would advance the cash to the Beatles — £1 million in royalties were presently due in any event — and Clive Epstein was sympathetic until proceedings were disrupted by one Allen Klein.

Klein (b. 1931) was a highly successful manager of entertainers, having built up an unassailable record by strong-arming record companies into coughing up back-earned royalties, which earned him Bobby Darin's gratitude, and by renegotiating astronomical royalties into artists' contracts, which brought Sam Cooke and the Rolling Stones enormous profits — much greater than anything ever sought by NEMS for the Beatles. So when he read Lennon's fear expressed in the *Disc and Music Echo* (January 1969) that if Apple "carries on like this all of us will be broke in the next six months," Klein wasted no time in gaining the confidence of Lennon, Harrison, and Starr in having him look into their accounts.[44] McCartney held out against Klein, even after the others signed a management contract with him in May 1969. Once given authority, Klein swept house; gone in a flurry were not only "Magic" Alex but also Denis O'Dell (manager of the Films division), Ron Kass (Records), Peter Asher (A&R), Brian Lewis (Legal), Alistair Taylor (general manager of Apple, with seven years of Beatles service), and personal assistant Peter Brown. Gone entirely were the offices of Publishing, Retail, and the Apple Foundation for the Arts. Several "internal" conflicts between the brutish Allen Klein and the circumspect John Eastman, McCartney's representative, led Epstein to sell a 70 percent share of Nemperor to Triumph, the Beatles' bidding competitor, on February 17.

Immediately following this sale, Klein had the Beatles inform EMI that all of their royalties were to be paid to Apple, with no portion to Nemperor. Lockwood, who had now been thrice offended by his one-time lovable moptops, declared that all recording royalties were to be held in escrow until the dispute was settled. Following intense negotiations, Triumph gave up its claim to future royalties and gave the Beatles shares in its own stock worth roughly £500,000, in exchange for 25 percent of current royalties, the group's 10 percent share of NEMS, and £800,000 in cash.

The Beatles' growing instability beginning early in 1968 and the unpredictability of Klein irritated Dick James, who decided upon the Nemperor transaction to sell the 23 percent that he controlled of Northern Songs, the Beatles' publishing company. His decision followed that of several other Northern investors who had sold to Associated Television Corporation (ATV), which bought James's share on March 28. ATV bid on all outstanding shares, and the Beatles counterbid on a controlling interest; together they owned 30.8 percent, or so all assumed before it was determined to Lennon's disillusionment that McCartney had secretly been buying up shares under Eastman's advice. A sizable consortium of shareholders, holding 14 percent, was wooed by the Beatles but was wildly insulted by an antiestablishment Lennon, so the Beatles lost them also to ATV on May 20 and, out of total frustration, ended up selling their own shares to ATV in late October.

Klein did some good for the Beatles; he convinced them that the January 1969 film would return a much greater profit if released to theaters than if mere broadcast rights were to be sold. But more important, he renegotiated their EMI and Capitol contracts for a fantastic increase in recording royalties. Klein increased their corporate income from £850,000 for the year ending March 31, 1969, to £1,708,000 for the nine months ending December 31, 1969, and the 1969 total was doubled to £4,350,000 in 1970.[45] This boon came at a fatal cost, however; the months of quarrelsome meetings in the spring of 1969 fairly destroyed what little fellowship the Beatles could still enjoy. This is doubly unfortunate in that, as bitter as the "Get Back" sessions frequently were, McCartney's plan to bring the band back to its earliest performing and recording methods was occasionally successful in rekindling the joyful spirit behind its most exuberant work.

The Beatles in Early 1969

John Lennon

Lennon was a paradox in 1969, simultaneously on a macrobiotic diet for his health and on hard drugs for his pain. His artistic endeavors continued to expand, even into lithography in February 1969, as he engraved a poem, "Bag One" ("A is for Parrot which we can plainly see . . .").[46] A primary intention was to confound expectations, to not be "put in a bag" by others. This determination led to his performance with Yoko Ono at a jazz concert at Lady Mitchell Hall, Cambridge, on March 2; she wailed and he accompanied with Casino feedback, along with John Tchicai on alto sax and Jon Stevens on drums. When the recording was released as Side 1 of *Unfinished Music No. 2: Life with the Lions*, one reviewer said of Ono's voice modulation: "Listening to Yoko's extraordinary voice one can detect the innocence of a yelling baby, the torture of a damned soul and the stamina of an Alpine yodeller. Miss Ono has unleashed the most terrifying sound since the development of the jet engine."[47] Lennon explained his emancipation from the mundane: "What she'd done for [my] guitar playing was to free it the way she'd freed her voice from all the restrictions. I was always thinking, 'Well, I can't quite play like Eric [Clapton] or George [Harrison] or B. B. King.' But then I gave up trying to play like that and just played whatever I could, whatever way I could, to match it to her voice."[48]

Lennon's major event of the spring, however, was his March 20 wedding to Ono, at some level a response to McCartney's March 12 marriage to Eastman. He turned the event into a true 1960s happening by staging events, producing a film, and recording a single and LP for worldwide celebration. Lennon and Ono headed to Southampton, hoping for a wedding at sea; this could not be done, so arrangements for Paris were attempted. This failing too, Peter Brown found that a ceremony could be arranged quickly in Gibraltar. The honeymoon involved a week spent in an Amsterdam hotel bed, with the world's press invited to the first "Bed-In for Peace." The bridegroom: "We knew that we could never get married and hide away on a honeymoon without being hounded by the press, so we decided to put the situation to good use and have a few laughs at the same time."[49] At the Amsterdam Hilton, Lennon declared, "Peace is our art. . . . We stand a chance of influencing other young people" by promoting the cause of peace to counter the way governments seemed to promote the cause of war. From Amsterdam, the couple traveled to Vienna for the world premiere of their film *Rape* and a press reception at the Hotel Sacher, where — on stage — they ate Sacher torte in a bag. They returned to London with a plan to send 100 acorns to the world's leaders, to be planted as a gesture of peace. The LP, comprising Amsterdam recordings on Side 2 and the sounds of their two heartbeats and their calling each others' first names filling Side 1, was of course called *Wedding Album*.[50] The events in Southampton, Paris, Gibraltar, Amsterdam, Vienna, and London are recounted in the narrative song recorded by the Beatles, "The Ballad of John and Yoko."

"The Ballad of John and Yoko"

Lennon sings current affairs directly from newspapers in "A Day in the Life" and reads clippings about himself in "No Bed for Beatle John" (Lennon 1969), but in "The Ballad of John and Yoko," he combines both approaches. The narrative style is spiced with Lennon's wit — he knows from dreadful experience the implications of comparing himself with Christ, but can't resist meeting the Bible Belt head-on anyway in the chorus ($A+8-16$, 0:16−0:31), and his pun about "only trying to get us some peace" in bed is a sly wink. But the bridge (**B**, 1:28−1:43) carries a direct and sincere sermon that reached millions of anti-materialistic sympathizers. The reference to crucifixion sounds impudent and resulted in radio bleeps and bans, but it is a sure measure of Lennon's pain at his and Yoko's poor personal treatment by his friends and by the world. Perhaps here is born, as well, the notion much better stated in "God" (Lennon 1970) that "God is a concept by which we measure our pain."[51]

Given its topical nature, Lennon wished to record the song immediately, an attitude shown by McCartney for other reasons in "She's Leaving Home" and elsewhere, even though Starr was busy filming and Harrison was out of the country. The two went right to EMI's Studio Three on April 14, laying down the following tracks, beginning with Lennon's Jumbo and vocal, and McCartney's drums:

1. McCartney's thundering bass (heard center)
2. Lennon's Jumbo (center)
3. McCartney's drums (right-center)
4. Lennon's widely echoing lead vocal, in an "I Saw Her Standing There"– or "Get Back"–like tumbling strain for the crucifixion (center)
5. Lennon's Casino (left, recalling the coda from "Lonesome Tears in My Eyes")
6. Lennon's second Casino part and McCartney's piano (right)
7. McCartney's descant vocal for the bridge and last two verses (center)
8. McCartney's maracas and Lennon's percussive tapping of the back of his Jumbo (left)

In the last choruses (A+9–16, as at 1:58–2:11), Lennon's first Casino part "mocks his self-pity," putting to illustrative use the alternating descending and ascending chromatic lines in sixths from "You Like Me Too Much."[52] The song became the A-side of the Beatles' first stereo single in Britain (Apple R5786, released May 30, 1969, sustaining three weeks at #1) and the second such in the United States (Apple 2531, June 4, stalling for three weeks at #8, where it peaked, perhaps due to radio bans in some major markets).

The month of May witnessed two significant events for the Lennon-Onos: they bought Tittenhurst Park, an eighteenth-century Georgian home on a seventy-four-acre estate (the setting for the 1971 film *Imagine*) in Ascot on May 5, and they released *Unfinished Music No. 2: Life with the Lions*, featuring events surrounding the November 1968 miscarriage and the February Cambridge concert. This LP was on the Apple subsidiary label, Zapple (United Kingdom: Zapple 01, May 9, 1969, no chart entry; United States: Zapple ST3357, May 26; #174), which was also supposed to carry low-budget spoken-word LPs by Ken Kesey, Richard Brautigan, Allen Ginsberg, and William Burroughs, overseen by Barry Miles of the *International Times*, until the project produced contractual obstacles and was eventually axed by Klein.[53] Lennon and Harrison each had one release on the label, and that was it for Zapple.

"Give Peace a Chance"

Lennon and Ono wanted to take their peace message to America with another bed-in, but Lennon's 1968 drug conviction led to visa problems. He scheduled a bed-in in the Bahamas (where Ringo and the *Magic Christian* cast and crew, finished ahead of schedule, were relaxing on a two-week holiday), but finding Freeport inhospitable, plans were taken to Montreal. Joined by friends (Allen Ginsberg, Tim and Rosemary Leary, Dick Gregory, Murray the "K," Tommy Smothers, and members of the local Hare Krishna group), met by skeptics (most notably cartoonist Al Capp), and given an eight-day (May 26–June 2) platform by the press, including many phone interviews with American radio stations, the Lennons took every opportunity to advance the cause of peace.

They knew that their method was ridiculous to many, saying, "We're quite willing to be the world's clowns if it will do any good. For reasons known only to themselves, people print what I say. And I say 'peace.' "[54]

Determined to get the message out, Lennon wrote an anthem, "Give Peace a Chance," that was recorded in Room 1742 of Montreal's Queen Elizabeth Hotel on June 1. In between the repetitive singalong chorus, Lennon offered topical talking verses over a strummed C chord on the J-160E, listing a confusing array of political and other factions (and finally documenting a number of the participants), each with their own approach to life. Each verse was then followed by a unifying V[7]–I singalong chorus for the fifty or so present, "All we are saying is 'Give Peace a Chance,' " which Lennon dreamed might someday supplant "We Shall Overcome."[55] Although this was purely a Lennon-Ono project, the song's composer was registered as "Lennon-McCartney"; Lennon said this was to thank his partner for the "Ballad of John and Yoko" recording, and it may also have been a conciliatory gesture, given the misunderstandings over Northern Songs over the previous weeks.

Lennon envisioned a string of non-Beatles projects, with different personnel involved in each, so he called this continuously flexible outfit the Plastic Ono Band, under whose name "Give Peace a Chance" was released (United Kingdom: Apple 13, July 4, three weeks at #2; United States: Apple 1809, July 7, #14). The flip side was Ono's "Remember Love," a folklike song in a diatonic D major leading to an "Albatross"-based coda, repeating the nonfunctional neighbor progression, II[7]–I. Yoko sang the song against John's simple "Dear Prudence"–like fingerpicking. The record's sleeve shows the band's only constant elements: recording and playback equipment, encased in Plexiglas: one tall cylinder enclosed a mike boom, and three rectangular columns held a Sony open-reel deck, an automatic turntable, and a loudspeaker. The playback equipment suggests the role that the consumer/listener has in the band, continuing Ono's and Lennon's "Unfinished Music" philosophy.[56] A bad car accident in Golspie, Scotland, on July 1 prevented the Lennons from attending the press party for the single two days later, but the sculpture itself stood in for them![57] The song was given a slow reggae treatment with completely new topical verse lyrics ("Childish, man!") by an Apple signee, the Hot Chocolate Band (United Kingdom: Apple 18, October 10, 1969; United States: Apple 1812, October 17), but it found no success there.[58]

Paul McCartney

Paul married Linda Eastman on March 12, and their daughter Mary was born on August 28, but these remained private matters. Linda would occasionally attend and photograph Beatles sessions, and her daughter Heather is seen in the Apple studio films on January 26. But compared to John's life, Paul's as a Beatle was clearly divided into the personal and the professional.

The first half of 1969 saw McCartney involved in at least six instances of working on an outsider's recording session. One was in producing a record in January, the jazz standard "Rosetta," for his old Merseyside friends, the Four-

Example 4.8 "Penina" (McCartney). © 1969 Northern Songs.

most. On this, McCartney revived a "Lady Madonna" practice by having band members imitate brass in a 1930s-style arrangement by cupping their hands around their mouths. The record was released only in the United Kingdom (CBS 4041; February 21, 1969) and did not chart.

McCartney had a hand in several other unsuccessful records in early 1969. On March 11, he produced the B-side ("Thumbin' a Ride") of Jackie Lomax's American single "New Day" (Apple 1807, June 2, 1969), playing drums alongside Harrison's guitar, Lomax's vocal, Preston's keyboards, Klaus Voorman's bass, and backing vocals by the Rascals. Also, the Steve Miller Band's "My Dark Hour" (United States: Capitol 2520, June 16; United Kingdom: Capitol CL15604, July 18), had McCartney—as "Paul Ramon"—playing drums and bass and singing backing vocal on May 9. Miller was one of the unfortunates under contract to Apple Publishing; this disc was produced by "Get Back" technician Glyn Johns. (McCartney and Miller were to collaborate on three tracks for McCartney 1997a.)

While vacationing on the Portuguese Gulf of Cádiz in late 1968, McCartney stepped into a hotel called "La Penina" and sat in on drums with Carlos Mendes. Asked for a song, he improvised a weak ditty he called "Penina." Mendes liked it so much that it was "given" to him, and the record was released in Portugal on July 18, 1969 (European Parlophone QMSP16459). This song, the only verse of which is excerpted as example 4.8 (from *The Songs* 1979), was perhaps the first McCartney "composition" too simple and repetitive to be a hit.

The fifth of these projects was much more successful, for McCartney wrote a catchy tune for Mary Hopkin, "Goodbye," the long-awaited follow-up to her

Example 4.9 "Goodbye" (McCartney). © 1969 Northern Songs.

1968 smash. The demo (Beatles 1991a) was probably taped in December 1968, the Hopkin recording—transposed with a capo from Paul's C major to Mary's E—made around February 1969. The song was unusually incomplete, lacking a bridge but substituting a vocalized verse above which McCartney played a descant line on his Casino, and with the most rudimentary of choruses. The verse (the first phrase of which is given as example 4.9), however, was perfect for Mary's sweet Welsh voice, particularly as it floated above the supporting chords with barely any reference to their roots, prior to the more affirmative cadences. McCartney played his D-28, notably for the introduction's parallel sixths, quite the Beatles hallmark of 1969. He also added bass to the track, and Ringo drummed along with Mary's guitar, female chorus, and strings. Mary promoted the single (United Kingdom: Apple 10, March 28, 1969, #2 for two weeks; United States: Apple 1806, April 7, #13) on a thirty-nine-show tour with Engelbert Humperdinck, selling a solid 200,000 copies in the United States.

Perhaps envious of White Trash's notoriety, the unsuccessful Iveys changed their name to the slightly risqué Badfinger and began Apple's best string of hits by an act other than the Beatles. They had strong support in that their records were variously produced by Paul McCartney, George Harrison, and Todd Rundgren. McCartney produced their version of his composition "Come and Get It" for the *Magic Christian* soundtrack.[59] Paul recorded a one-man demo (Beatles 1996b) on July 24 with piano, double-tracked vocal, maracas, drums, and bass, which the trio learned and reproduced on August 3 for a solid Top Ten hit (United Kingdom: Apple 20, December 5, 1969, #4; United States: Apple 1815, January 12, 1970, #7; the release dates tie in with the film's December 11 premiere). The song's harmony is inventive. It is mostly in E major, but the verse's D-gesture introduces mixture from the parallel minor and the Phrygian, even approaching V from ♭II with the chord progression, $C - Em - F - B^{8-7}_{6-5}{}_{4-3}$, which is further summarized in the coda's plagal ♭VI–I cadence.

George Harrison and Ringo Starr

Harrison followed the "Get Back" sessions with a rough month, as he was hospitalized February 7–15 with tonsillitis and then arrested for cannabis possession on March 12, but his spring continued with the completion of his second solo LP, production for other artists, and his second Beatles B-side. The solo LP was *Electronic Sound* (United Kingdom: Zapple 02, May 9, 1969, not charting; United States: Zapple ST3358, May 26, #191). Playing with studio test equipment once in March 1967, McCartney had told an EMI engineer that someone should connect a bank of oscillators with electronic controls: "It would be a new electronic instrument."[60] In fact, Robert Moog was developing just such an instrument, the modular synthesizer, at that time. Bernie Krause, a Moog pioneer, played one at Harrison's October 1968 Lomax sessions in Los Angeles and demonstrated its capabilities to the Beatle. Harrison bought one immediately, with model IIIp shipped in January 1969, and Sequencer Complement B following a month later.[61] Unbeknownst to Krause, his tutoring session was not only taped but also released as a full side of the *Electronic Sound* LP, entitled "No Time or Space."[62] The Beatle filled the other side, entitled "Under the Mersey Wall," with his own early experimentation.[63] Krause's side was taped completely live, and Harrison's was apparently made from the superimposition of two live sessions; the LP shows that George was impressed with the novelty of the instrument but unaware of its technical potential, let alone its artistic possibilities.

Harrison's early productions for Apple were for a singer called Brute Force, whose "The King of Fuh" (he's the "Fuh King") would not be released by EMI, although promo copies were pressed; the chanting British monks of the Radha Krishna Temple (beginning with "Hare Krishna Mantra," United States: Apple 1810, August 22, 1969; United Kingdom: Apple 15, August 29, #11); and Doris Troy (beginning with "Ain't That Cute," United Kingdom: Apple 24, February 13, 1970; United States: Apple 1820, March 16).[64] Harrison also did session work in the spring for Jack Bruce and Joe Cocker. Ringo contributed to the Apple stable as well: at his suggestion, classical composer John Taverner was signed, and his *The Whale* was produced in September 1970.

"Old Brown Shoe"   Harrison wrote "Old Brown Shoe" at the piano, basing his poetry (says he) on dualities — right/wrong, short/long, up/down — in a more interesting way than did "Hello Goodbye." The manuscript shows several discarded lines, such as "I'm going to hold you tight, I never want to let you loose," but all lyrics were intact when Harrison brought the song to the group on January 28.[65] In S/S 28.12 (Beatles 1992e), it is clear that the group has already worked on "Old Brown Shoe," as Harrison's piano part is essentially finished, McCartney has the roots down on bass, and Preston has decided on some Hammond licks. Starr plays along, but Lennon, on Casino, seems stymied or disinterested. This run-through is done in C, but despite the odd assortment and ordering of chords, they try A as well, recalling the early takes of "Strawberry Fields Forever." By 28.17 (Beatles 1993b), they are back in C, Harrison always at the piano. Preston plays pentatonic fills, rather than the composer's eventual sustained chords; McCartney has the chromatic passers in the introduction but not the fine triplets in the verse ($\mathbf{A}+1-8$, 0:07–0:20), bridge ($\mathbf{B}$, 1:04–1:24), or interlude ($\mathbf{C}$, 1:24–1:51). Starr's drum part is about finished, but Lennon is lost on guitar.

Example 4.10 Analysis of "Old Brown Shoe."

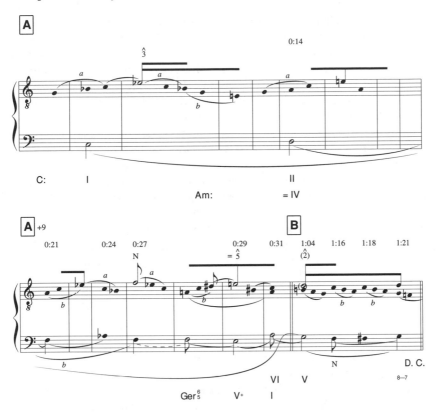

Despite this preliminary work, Harrison recorded a new piano demo with vocal and two overdubbed guitars (Beatles 1996b) on February 25. The band, needing a B-side for "The Ballad of John and Yoko," approached the song again on April 16, recording a basic track of Harrison's slide part on Telecaster (heard left), Ringo's drums (center), and McCartney's jangle piano (right); Lennon recorded a rhythm guitar part at the same time, but this was later wiped. That day's superimpositions include McCartney's Jazz Bass doubled in the bridge by Harrison's second Telecaster part, a line already present in Harrison's demo, featuring chromatically moving arpeggiations as in the bridge guitars in "And Your Bird Can Sing" (both left). Also added on the 16th were Harrison's compressed lead vocal and, in the bridge and coda only, backing Lennon-McCartney vocals (all center). On the 18th, Harrison added a Hammond part (left) and a stinging, highly Claptonesque solo (**C+9**–16, 1:38–1:51, center) on the Leslie-colored Telecaster given ADT treatment sent wild to both channels. In a rush for the single, the stereo mix was also produced on the 18th.

Example 4.10 presents a sketch of the voice leading and harmony in "Old Brown Shoe," which is far more subtle and interesting than those qualities of its A-side. Note the frequent alterations of C-major scale degrees, largely resulting from transpositions of the two motives in which the composer seems most interested. The first of these is the bluesy [025] trichord, labeled "a" and appearing in two pairs, as G-B♭-C ($\mathbf{A}$+1, 0:06–0:08) altered to G–A–C ($\mathbf{A}$+4–5, 0:13–0:15) and as E♭-C-B♭ ($\mathbf{A}$+2, 0:09–0:10) altered to F–E♭–C ($\mathbf{A}$+12, 0:25–0:26). The other is the diminished triad, labeled "b," with "roots" of E ($\mathbf{A}$+2–3, 0:10–0:11), A ($\mathbf{A}$+9–10, 0:20–0:23, and elsewhere, functioning enharmonically in the German $^6_5$ chord), F♯ for the bridge retransition (1:16–1:19), and in the verse's large bass motion D–F–A♭ (0:14–0:21–0:24). It is this harmony involving D, F, and A♭ that sets the song on its edge, for it begins as an innocuous II⁷ chord in C major but progresses to an unexpected German $^6_5$ in A minor, reminiscent of the modulation in the "Day Tripper" refrain. The bridge expands G major, making A sound like an upper neighbor to V while the structural upper voice descends along in antiparallel fifths to a dramatic interrupted $\hat{2}$. This leads nicely back to the C pentatonic material, and the song ends with a verse's final Am answered by a taunting fade on C^9_{b7}. The A/C duality not only fits well the composer's main concern in the poetic text but also revisits a harmonic scheme that had appeared several times in the White album and was soon to provide the tonal backdrop for *Abbey Road*, to which we turn next.

Abbey Road

The "Get Back" LP and TV show were still thought imminent when the single of that name was released in April, and there was still talk of a possible telecast in the first week of July.[66] But two weeks later it was announced that the "Get Back" LP, though thought ready, would be shelved until the film was to be distributed in December.[67] The Beatles ended a two-month absence from group appearances in the studio on July 1, marking the beginning of intensive work through August that would result in what would be their swan song.

The Beatles' corporate work in February through June was sporadic, partly due to Ringo's involvement with *Magic Christian*. These months saw eleven sessions at Apple, Olympic, and EMI, only three of which are known to have been attended by a Beatle, for postproduction work on the "Get Back" tapes. These sessions aside, all four Beatles met at Trident or EMI (usually in the small Studio Three) six times during these five months, and two or three met another four times, all for new recordings. Other than to help with the "Ballad of John and Yoko" single, Martin attended only two non–"Get Back" sessions. Martin says of his attitude at the end of the unhappy month of "Get Back," "I thought, gosh, this is the end, I don't want to be part of this anymore. And I really thought it was. And, I was really surprised when, after we finished that album, Paul came to me and said, let's get back and record like we used to. . . . Will you produce an album like you used to?"[68] Martin dictated that the LP would have to be a polished studio album "like the old days" (thinking of *Sgt. Pepper*), not like the January recordings or the miserable White album sessions. Given these circumstances, it is somewhat remarkable that *Abbey Road* is universally regarded as a coherent demonstration of inspired composition, impeccable vocal and instrumental ensemble, and clean and cleverly colorful engineering.

For the new album, McCartney and Martin wanted to have a series of interconnected songs, but Lennon dissented. It was decided that to satisfy both Beatles, Side 1 would consist of six separate songs, and much of Side 2 would be a medley.[69] Lennon could very well have considered this medley emblematic of his and McCartney's artistic differences when he said two years later, "By the time the Beatles were at their peak, we were cutting each other down to size, we were limiting our capacity to write and perform by having to fit it into some kind of format and that's why it caused trouble."[70]

Beginning with the White album, the three Beatles other than Ringo had become comfortable on acoustic or electric guitar, bass, or keyboards, and such flexibility is most apparent on *Abbey Road*. The album features a similar instrumentation to that used in January: Rickenbacker and Jazz Basses (one photo shows a Jazz Bass strung for a right-hander, probably George), Casino, Telecaster, Les Paul, Martin D-28, Gibson J-160E, Gibson J-200, and Ludwigs. Ringo's drums are now without jangle box and fitted with new heads; he remembers that *Abbey Road* "was tom-tom madness. I had gotten this new kit made of wood, and calfskins, and the toms had so much depth. I went nuts on the toms. Talk about changes in my drum style—the kit made me change because I changed my kit."[71] As part of his large contribution to the album, Harrison brought his Moog IIIp to the studio, where three Beatles recorded with it. Additionally, the guitars as well as the bass were now running directly to the board through DIT boxes, rather than being miked at the amp. Geoff Emerick, who rejoined the Beatles for this LP after a year-long absence, says, "I've always been against direct injection; it sounds wishy-washy to me and you don't get the power of the amp. Although it's rich in content it's also feeble, but I suppose it goes with the transistorized sound of today"; nevertheless, he acceded to the Beatles' desires.[72]

As biographer Philip Norman says, "Something had stopped the elements diverging, and restored them to their old unsurpassable balance. *Abbey Road* was John Lennon at his best, and Paul McCartney at his best, and George Harrison suddenly reaching a best that no one had ever imagined. It was John's anarchy, straight and honed. It was Paul's sentimentality with the brake applied."[73] For the Beatles' only real eight-track LP, all the elements come together. The adventurous yet systematic aspect of the chord relationships in Harrison's "Old Brown Shoe" find their most gorgeous expression yet in his "Something," which features new uses of a modal ♭III and a tonicized VI♯, its raised first scale degree reminiscent of that in "Strawberry Fields Forever." The sure double-plagal chords and the briskly confident rhythmic complexity of Harrison's "Here Comes the Sun" make the ambiguous harmonies and lugubrious tempo of Lennon's "Because" sound all the more mysterious. McCartney's contributions to the others' compositions, whether it was on the electric piano in "Come Together" or the bass in "Something," set new standards for collaboration, and Lennon plays perhaps his best lead guitar ever for McCartney's "You Never Give Me Your Money." Never before did a rock song end with an abrupt splice, but that's how both of this record's sides are finished. Having produced a double LP the year before, perhaps it did not seem too remarkable to present a double half-LP, and the format works not so much as a compromise between the opposing views of the two group leaders, but as further testament to the multifaceted nature of this highly imaginative group. Because of the integrity of the album's format, just as strong here as in *Sgt. Pepper*, our analysis will proceed in a similar manner. Each song will be addressed in its order of appearance, and then we'll turn to the nature of the medley as a whole. Because many of the *Abbey Road* songs figure in the "Get Back" rehearsals, we will again take advantage of the Sulpy/Schweighardt catalog in our discussions of the genesis of these songs.

Side 1

"Come Together"   The title of the LP's opening track, and one of its most recent compositions, "Come Together," was given to Lennon in late May by Timothy Leary, who wanted "Come Together—Join the Party" as a theme song for his 1970 California gubernatorial campaign.[74] Lennon is heard chanting the phrase in Montreal, but he had yet to mold the slogan to his own purposes, which before he could help it became mired in Walrus/Ono gobbledygook.[75] The gobbledygook may be heard as a disguise for Lennon's portrayal of the band members, one per verse: George as the long-haired holy roller, Paul as the good-looking player of Muddy Waters licks, and Lennon himself through images of the Walrus, Ono, and Bag Productions and a "spinal cracker" reference to his car accident, but Ringo is harder to make out so clearly.

Whereas Leary felt betrayed by Lennon's appropriation of his phrase, Lennon was sued for plagiarism from his song's obvious model, Chuck Berry's "You Can't Catch Me," a line of which appears directly in the song's germ, $\mathbf{A}+1-2$ (0:12–0:18).[76] The song's other source is far more subtle; the introductory "shoot me" was part of the abandoned January song "Watching Rainbows" (S/S 14.29, excerpted in example 4.11 from Beatles 1994f), which—given the context of various January discussions—expresses a wish not for martyrdom but for a heroin fix.

The basic track was recorded on July 21 in Studio Three; it consists of Paul's Rickenbacker, John's guide vocal and handclaps with heavy echo (all center), George's Les Paul boogie as in "Revolution" ("Guitar II," left), and Ringo's drums (right).[77] On July 22, Lennon recut his lead vocal (heard center); this was a simple part carrying the pentatonic d-trichord, $c\natural^2-d^2-f\natural^2$, above the blue $I^{\sharp 9}_{\natural 7}$, before the diatonic $\sharp\hat{3}-\hat{2}-\hat{1}$ cadence, colored by live echo recalling "The Ballad of John and Yoko." Also added that day were Lennon's heavily distorted guitar for refrains ($\mathbf{C}+9-10$, 1:10–1:15, "Guitar II") and interlude ($\mathbf{D}$, 2:02–2:24) (left); a maraca was shaken at $\mathbf{D}+5-8$ (2:14–2:25) and the coda (3:35 to end) (center), and McCartney added the electric piano for $\mathbf{D}$ (at 2:03, heard right but moving to the center at the guitar duet's close). Paul says John "wanted a piano lick to be very swampy and smoky, and I played it that way and he liked that a lot."[78] Other dubs made on July 23, 25, 29, and 30 include McCartney's backing

Example 4.11 "Watching Rainbows" compositional draft.

vocal (the *c*-trichord, sung below Lennon's part, as done occasionally over the past year) beginning in the second ("Ringo's") verse, a Les Paul duet double-tracked in hollow fourths and fifths by Harrison at **D**+5−9 (2:14−2:27), his Les Paul solo in the coda (3:12 to end), and a waterlogged tone-pedal guitar at **E** (3:02−3:11, all center). The Beatles' ensemble is at its rhythmic best in the re-transition (**D**+9−10, 2:25−2:31), where the group agrees on syncopations for one bar and then drifts in separate directions over the cresting hammered-on trill of the Rickenbacker. The mix was done on July 7; all of *Abbey Road* was mixed for stereo only.

"Something"   Harrison liked James Taylor's "Something in the Way She Moves," a song produced by Peter Asher in the summer of 1968, so much that he wrote his most popular Beatles song, "Something," from its first line, which is excerpted in example 4.12.[79] He began writing it on the piano, possibly on October 18, 1968, and on the 19th played it for Chris Thomas, who wished to produce it for the White album, but it was nowhere near ready.[80] We know more about the song's early history from the "Get Back" television film out-takes. Rehearsal S/S 28.18−28.19 (heard on Beatles 1992e) opens with Harrison asking McCartney what lyric could follow the line taken from Taylor: Something in the way she moves " 'attracts me' what?"; Lennon leaps in, "just say whatever comes into your head each time, 'attracts me like a cauliflower,' until you get the word"; what comes into the composer's head next is the use-less "pomegranate," but he does have the line "I don't want to leave her now" and the third verse. With a simple drum backing, Harrison's Leslied Telecaster

Example 4.12 "Something in the Way She Moves" (Taylor). © 1968 Blackwood Music.

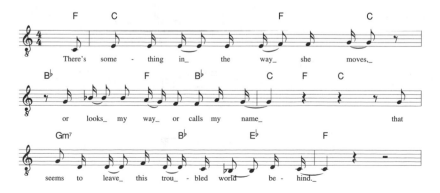

Example 4.13a "Something" compositional draft (Harrison). © 1969 Harrisongs Music.

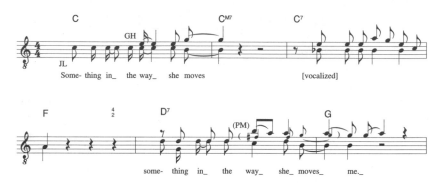

demonstrates all the chords and some moving lines, and he wishes to sing an early descant while Lennon sings the lead melody, both shown in example 4.13a, along with a few notes suggested by McCartney. The bridge (**B**, 1:14–1:41) at this time has for its lyrics "Do you know who missed the show? I don't know, I don't know," and the composer points out that the bass should descend stepwise from A at this point. McCartney complies with finesse while Preston comes up with some organ accompaniment. Lennon thinks he's singing, "What do you know, Mr. Show," and they pursue this direction for a few moments.

Harrison taped a demo on vocal, Telecaster, and overdubbed piano in A (moving to F♯) on February 25.[81] The piano carries mostly roots in the bass, but the melodic lines at **A**+4 and virtually all of **B** are set. All the lyrics are completed, along with a soulfully ornamented tune and verse at **C**, shown in example 4.13b, that will later disappear, and the guitar's tag intro is set as well. Perhaps out of a fear of rejection, the acetate was given not to the Beatles to re-

Example 4.13b "Something" compositional draft.

hearse but to Joe Cocker, who recorded the song in the key of A, probably in March (it was released in November 1969 on the LP *Joe Cocker!*, A&M 4224). Harrison played rhythm guitar along with Leon Russell and Cocker's Grease Band, ignoring the mixture-characterizing IV–♭III–V$^6_4$–I cadence and relying instead on a weak common tone for the modulation to F♯, and apparently improvising different words for the second verse. Oddly, both phrases of the bridge cadence on the local dominant, here C♯.

Perhaps Lennon and McCartney, both of whom later professed great admiration for the song, disagreed with Harrison's having given the song away, for the Beatles began their own recording on April 16. The basic track was remade on May 2, with McCartney's bass (later wiped), Ringo's drums, and Lennon's all-but-mixed-out piano (center; it remains at **B+4**, 1:24–1:28, and **B+8–C+6**, 1:38–2:02), and Harrison's Leslied rhythm part on Les Paul with Preston's echo-treated Hammond (both left). On May 5 at Olympic, McCartney replayed his Rickenbacker part (right), and Harrison added a second Leslied Les Paul, this time on lead (center, including some stray notes in the third time through **A+8** that would be mixed out). Harrison added a lead vocal (later wiped) on July 11, filling all eight tracks, necessitating a reduction that lopped off the last two minutes of a nearly five-minute coda, a simple repeated piano-led jam alternating A and C triads. This reduction mix, called Take 37, is heard on Beatles 1991k.

Harrison redid his vocal on July 16 (center, given ADT in the final mix). He has said that he was trying to sing like Ray Charles, who was among the many who were to cover the song; I don't hear much similarity, except perhaps in the neighbor ornamentation on "woos me" (0:22–0:24). On the same date, McCartney taped his descant vocal for the bridge, and Ringo overdubbed both a suspended cymbal and a hi-hat (both center). Strings were desired, requiring a second reduction, and Martin made a copy on August 4 from which to prepare his score. On August 15, strings (12/4/4/1, entering in the second verse with pizzicato in the bridge and echo applied to arco passages) were added from Studio One as Harrison simultaneously taped his Les Paul guitar solo (**C**) in Studio Two (both center). The August 19 mix deleted the coda's jam entirely.

The introductory plagal progression with passing chords, IV–♭III–V$^6_4$–I, borrows from the minor mode and may have evolved from the C, F, and E♭ triads appearing in the first phrase of Taylor's model (ex. 4.12), reordered to produce the ear-catching rising chromatic line, a^1–b♭^{1}–b♮^{1}–c^2.[82] Or perhaps Harrison had in his ear the last few chords of "Let It Be," where b♭ must change to b♮ before its resolution to c. This progression acts as the song's motto, as "Something" has no chorus or—excepting the introductory word of each verse—refrain.

The verse begins with a retrograde of the chromatic rise, in the vocal part (**A+1–4**, 0:05–0:16) that is sequenced a step higher in diminution (**A+5–6**, 0:19–0:24) to lead to the dominant, extending the phrase to six bars. This sequence is clarified by the "8–10, 8–10" marking in the voice-leading sketch, example 4.13c. What follows (**A+7–8**, 0:27–0:33) continues the chromatic descent in an inner voice in Preston's organ, with the same part he had recently played on "I Want You (She's So Heavy)," a^1–g♯^{1}–g♮^{1}–f♯^{1}. This leads not to V

Example 4.13c Analysis of "Something."

but rather, as did the Beatles' 1963–65-era Lydian II♯, to the plagal cadence motto, thus carrying the chromatic descent further in the bass to F♮. The intangible wonder conjured by surprisingly altered and redirected scale degrees is established as the song's musical focus, and it perfectly fits the poetic notion of a "something" that cannot easily be expressed in words.[83]

The motto allows the song's real surprise, its move to VI♯ with an alteration of Î for the bridge.[84] In terms of voice leading, the primary function of the bridge is to establish the song's primary tone, 3̂, which descends to Î in the guitar solo (**C**), as shown in example 4.13c. This intimates that the structural core of the song's melody, a fully supported $\hat{3}$–$\hat{2}$–$\hat{1}$ descent heard only in the guitar solo, is best expressed in a musical fantasy. A poetic text here would only get in the way. It might be extrapolated that the registrally rising wordless fantasy "shows" what was suggested in the bridge lyrics, that the singer's love will grow. Despite the song's profound surprises, almost everything—the hard-won lyrics, the vocal phrasing, the guitar work, the drums, Martin's strings—is understated. The exception to this texture is McCartney's overdubbed bass, which adds bold and fluent detail with passers, neighbors, and arpeggiations to Harrison's sure and pretty structural counterpoint, often dominating the other parts. Not at all out of place, the bass often adds just what seems needed; in the third time through **A**+2–4 (2:17–2:25), for example, McCartney's simple rhythm, repeated upper neighbors, an arpeggiation to $\hat{1}$, and a new resolution to $\hat{4}$ achieve the effect that a very vivid but elusive "something" is at the tip of the tongue.

Allen Klein's first musical direction for the Beatles was to choose "Something" as an A-side, following the standard U.S. practice of extracting at least one single from an album. Many writers see this as an attempt to curry favor with Harrison, who had waited for such recognition for some time. "Come Together" was selected as the B-side, and the two songs competed for radio attention, both placing high on the charts. The release of the record (United States: Apple 1813, October 20, 1969, #4; United Kingdom: Apple 24, October 24, #3/#2 then #1 combined) was accompanied by the only promotional film to have all Beatles shot separately.

"Maxwell's Silver Hammer"   "That's Paul's. I hate it. 'Cuz all I remember is the track—he made us do it a hundred million times. He did *everything* to make it into a single and it never was and it never could've been, but he put guitar licks on it and he had somebody hitting iron pieces and we spent more money on that song than any of them in the whole album." "Sometimes Paul would make us do these really fruity songs. I mean, my God. . . . After a while we did a good job on it, but when Paul got an idea or an arrangement in his head . . ." These are Lennon's and Harrison's recollections, respectively, of McCartney's single that wasn't, "Maxwell's Silver Hammer."[85] The giddy composer takes the vaudeville stage again with applied V[7]s of II, V, VI, and IV, pulling the audience with an interrupted verse-ending $\hat{7}$ (**C**–1, 0:35–0:36) like a bad riddle, and even announcing a sobriquet at the end (3:16–3:21) for a final bow; all in all, another audience-distancing performance of a performance.[86] But the glare of McCartney's spotlight keeps him from seeing that band members are marking their exits.

We have little idea of the song's origins, dating from October 1968, but the reference to the "pataphysical" is to a branch of metaphysics developed by turn-of-the-century Parisian playwright Alfred Jarry.[87] In S/S 3.86–3.87 (Beatles 1994d), McCartney sings the chord names as he plays bass, with Ringo and Harrison following. McCartney moves to the piano in 7.36, 7.41–7.50 (Beatles 1991i and 1994c), and 7.57–7.59 (Beatles 1992d and 1994c), where Harrison

Example 4.14 "Maxwell's Silver Hammer" compositional draft (Lennon-McCartney). © 1969 Northern Songs.

works on Bass VI, finding all the jaunty quarter-note passing tones, and Lennon plays Casino over Ringo's hi-hat, snare, and bass drum. The first two verses (**A**, supporting a structural $\hat{3}$–$\hat{2}$ motion) and chorus (**C**+1–8, 0:37–0:49, with the complete $\hat{3}$–$\hat{2}$–$\hat{1}$ line) are pretty well sketched out, but the third verse has only the words "court," "judge," and "guilty," and no interlude (**C**+9–12 [0:51–0:58], **E** [2:04–2:11], and coda) appears yet. By 7.58, McCartney, Harrison, and Lennon try a whistled intro/interlude, a repeated $\hat{8}$–$\hat{7}$–$\hat{6}$–$\hat{5}$ in half notes over a $I_3^{5}{}_{3}^{6}{}_{3}^{5}{}_{4}^{6}$ vamp, and Mal has found an anvil he clangs in **C**+1 (0:37) and **C**+5 (0:44). In 7.59, John offers a spoken intro, "Let me tell you the story about Maxwell's silver hammer; he got it from F. D. Cohen, the pawnbroker from Bayswater," and Paul suggests a corny ending: unison $\hat{8}$–$\hat{7}$–$\hat{6}$–$\flat\hat{6}$–$\hat{5}$– (clang!) half notes followed by $\hat{5}$–$\hat{6}$–$\hat{7}$–$\hat{8}$ in eighths. At one point, George and Paul invent a carnival harmonization for the chorus (see ex. 4.14), but this is not repeated in later takes. None of these early versions finds the slick I–V$_3^4$/VI–VI progression that is so characteristic of this song but that McCartney casts in an entirely different, tender glow for "Another Day" (February 1971).

The basic track of McCartney's piano, Harrison's clipped but authoritative Bass VI (both left), and Starr's drums (right), made on July 9, was augmented the same day with two guitars, probably Lennon's Jumbo (center, retained only at second and third choruses, and the third time through **B** and **D**) and the Telecaster that Harrison plays for fills at **A**+8–9 in the second (right-center) and third (left-center) verses.[88] The next day, the tracks were filled by George Martin's Hammond in the introduction and interludes (mixed out but bleeding through center at **E**+3–4, 2:08–2:10), Ringo's anvil (center), and more cymbals for downbeats in **B**+1 (0:30) and **B**+3 (left-center); Harrison's two Leslied Telecaster parts (harmonic intervals left-center and a single line right-center) for **D** (1:49–2:03) and the coda; McCartney's lead vocal (with Holly-like melismas at **A**+7–8 [0:11–0:13 and elsewhere], given ADT for the choruses in a July 10 reduction); and backing vocals from McCartney, Harrison, and Starr (center, but "Rose" and "Valerie" cry from the left). At this point, test mixes were made, resulting in a mono mix heard on Beatles 1991k. Harrison added another Telecaster part to the choruses on the 11th (center), and McCartney added the five different Moog parts on August 6 (two simultaneously at **C**+9–12, 0:51–0:59, the upper part right-center, and the lower left-center), expert pitch work on the fretless ribbon controller for the second verse (0:59–1:27, "Keyboard," stems up, center) and back to the keyboard for the ghostly third verse (beginning at 2:11, stems down, panning left-to-right) through the third time through **C**−1 (2:46 – 2:48, alternating c♯2 and b2), second **D** (3:03 – 3:15), and coda (3:20 – 3:23, center).[89] Mixing and editing (the drums/piano/organ/bass introduction, equivalent to the **C**+9 –12 passage, was lopped off) were done on August 12, 14, and 25. We're left with Rococo craftsmanship on a Gothic but hollow shell.

"Oh! Darling"   Paul McCartney might have based "Oh! Darling" on Fats Domino's slow $\frac{12}{8}$ piano rockers; Domino's "Can't Believe You Wanna Leave," with an identical verse/bridge structure and $\frac{4-3}{b2-1}$ ending, could have been a particular model. But the Beatle was probably also listening to Fleetwood Mac's B. B. King–like recording of Little Willie John's "Need Your Love So Bad," a nonhit single in July 1968, that has the identical meter and structure and even the same untransposed chords in the bridge, including the unexpected B (V/V) and F (neighboring ♭VI) triads, as heard in "Oh! Darling."

McCartney is heard playing and singing the first eleven seconds of the song in the *Let It Be* soundtrack (S/S 6.1). The next day, in 7.39 (Beatles 1991i) and 7.56 (Beatles 1992d), he plays it all the way through, with verses only partly written, teaching the chord progression in B♭— more a Domino key than the eventual A— to Harrison on Bass VI, Lennon on Casino, and Ringo on drums. At this point, **C**+2 (1:12 –1:16) has IV♭ rather than ♭VI. In 15.1 –15.2 (Beatles 1994f), McCartney performs alone, the falsetto octave of **B**+5 (0:55) is sung in each verse, and the bridge is spoken. Back in A, 27.1 (Beatles 1991i and 1996b, still with IV♭ at **C**+2) has McCartney move to bass with Preston on electric piano, Lennon attempting a lower vocal part along with his Casino, Harrison doing very little on Telecaster, and Starr on drums. For this take, McCartney's emerging bass line has little other than the arpeggiations of **B**+3 – 6 (0:48 –1:00) already in place, but Preston has devised the retransitional V' triad.

A proper recording was begun in Studio Three on April 20, with a basic track of Lennon's piano and Ringo's "tom-tom madness" drums (left), McCartney's Rickenbacker (center), and Harrison's Leslied Telecaster (right), this last with backbeats for the verse, dry staccato arpeggiations in the bridge, and curious Leslied harmonics for the song's last six notes. This tape sat for three months, and then McCartney attempted echoing lead vocals (center) on July 17, 18, 22, and 23 until he got the right effect; he later said, "I came into the studios early every day for a week to sing it by myself because . . . I wanted it to sound as though I'd been performing it on stage all week."[90] His very hot multiphonic-colored vocal hits with perfect intonation a falsetto e2 (first time through **B**+5) and even a gliss up to a2 (second performance of **C**+1, 2:16 – 2:17), actual pitch.[91] Following some aborted work on second lead guitar and tambourine, sustained three-part vocal harmonies were added on August 11, along the lines of similar vocal parts cut for "Because" a week previous. The song was mixed on the 12th. While McCartney's "Maxwell's Silver Hammer" and "Oh! Darling" have always been popular Beatles tracks, they are not the album's highlights.[92]

Example 4.15a–c "Octopus's Garden" compositional drafts.

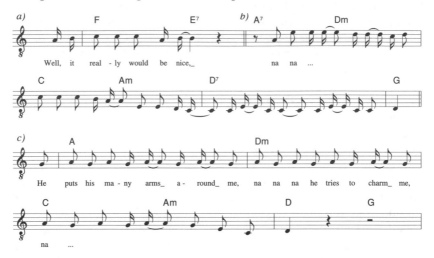

"Octopus's Garden"   When things had gone poorly for him on the White album, Ringo took off for Sardinia, where he heard a fisherman's story that captured his imagination. "He told me all about octopuses, how they go 'round the sea bed and pick up stones and shiny objects and build gardens. I thought, 'How fabulous!' 'cause at the time I just wanted to be under the sea, too. I wanted to get out of it for a while."[93] Ringo introduces the song that resulted from this conversation, "Octopus's Garden," on piano in S/S 23.1–23.2 and 26.5–26.15 (some of which is heard in Beatles 1991g, part of which is in the finished film). At this point, the song is in C, and he only has eight bars of one verse featuring the R-line "It would be nice, paradise," which would disappear. The silly lyrics raise a giggle from the crew, and Harrison—with J-200 and at times reaching over to demonstrate on the piano—coaches his drummer at composition the way Lennon had helped him a few years back. George continues the verse with a D-line, suggesting examples 4.15a–c (from Beatles 1991g), the last bringing back to life the 1965 image of "Eight Arms to Hold You," "just something to get back to where you started," while Lennon takes over the drums, and then Ringo indirectly asks George to come up with a bridge. "George was always great, because I'd write the song and give it to him because I could play only three chords. And he'd show me that it would take actually seven chords to play the song, because you have passing chords and things like that."[94]

The song appeared at Abbey Road on April 26, when a backing track was recorded, transposed to E major. From this day we hear Ringo's drums (right-center), John's broken chords on Casino (left), and Paul's Rickenbacker bass and George's countrified Strat with Leslie (both center).[95] The Strat was played through the entire song, but little of this track survives to the final mix. Overdubs waited three months, until July 17 and 18, and then consisted of Ringo's lead vocal with ADT and McCartney's jangle piano through a guitar amp (beginning at **B**, 0:31, both center); cloying backing vocals from Paul, George, and

Ringo (center for the first C-line refrain, at **C** [0:42–0:50], but thereafter right, with ADT sent left); undersea bass reinforcement from the piano for **B–C** (as at 0:31–0:50) and coda (right); more drums for the eighths at **B+4** (left); and two wild-panning tracks for the A-major interlude that strongly recalls "Yellow Submarine." Here, Ringo gurgled through a straw into a glass of water on one track, and Paul and George sang through a Leslie speaker, the result heavily limited for a gargling effect, on the other.[96] The mix was done on July 18, but the track was revisited in December to prepare for a mimed appearance by Ringo on a special put together by George Martin, "With a Little Help from My Friends," televised from London on Christmas Eve. Ringo entertains the kiddies, and the rest of us accept the colorful track as benign.

"I Want You (She's So Heavy)"   Side 1 closes with a nearly eight-minute track whose only lyrics are the often repeated "I want you so bad (babe), it's drivin' me mad (yeah); she's so heavy." Hearing that this fact was ridiculed on television, Lennon explained the simplicity as a new directness, and Ono said, "If you were drowning you wouldn't say: 'I'd like to be helped because I have just a moment to live.' You'd say, 'Help!' but if you were more desperate you'd say, '*Eiough-hhh*,' or something like that. And the desperation of life is really life itself, the core of life, what's really driving us forth."[97]

Lennon introduced the title and a fragment of the tune to his mates in S/S 28.25 – 28.26 (Beatles 1987e), doubling his vocal line on guitar in the manner of Eric Clapton or Jimmy Page. Group rehearsals apparently began only on February 22 at Trident, when the basic track was recorded with Ringo's drums (left), John's Casino ("Guitar II" through most of the track, but "Guitar I" at **A**, center), and Paul's Rickenbacker bass (right-center). In a marked departure from the goal of the "Get Back" sessions a month before, three different takes from this session were edited together the next day.[98] Lennon and Harrison added many guitars on April 18. These included two doubled Les Pauls, beginning as "Guitar I" in the introduction (0:02–0:13) but doubling the Casino arpeggiation at **B** (beginning at 1:56, left and center), and heavily distorted guitars doubling the bass through **D** (beginning at 4:36, left and right). Preston's Hammond and (entering at the second time through **C**, at 4:07) conga (both right) were added in Studio Three on April 20, Lennon added white noise from the Moog (right; "growing" out of the crash cymbal and most audible after 5:42) on August 8, and Lennon/McCartney/Harrison backing vocals were added to two tracks at **B** (center; only the f^2-e^2 descent at **B+4–5**, 2:04–2:07, and **B+7–8**, 2:10–2:14 — in parallel fifths above the bass — had existed previously) on August 11. That day and August 20 saw sessions for editing (inserting the first **B** section, 1:55–2:23, and the heavily repeated **D**, 4:37–end, into a previously mixed master with fewer dubs) and mixing. The texture is effective for both the formal structure and the length of the recording; such a dense, often repeated final section as we have here works only because of the sparse quality of the opening verse, where tape hiss is at times the dominant sound— and an unwitting foil to the white-noise vortex into which the track eventually spirals.

Despite the simplicity of its lyrics and the large amount of repeated material, "I Want You" is of some tonal interest. The listener would seem certain of the tonal center from the introduction: the opening D minor seems borne out as tonic by the rich but goal-oriented $V_7^{b9}/V-bVI^{b7}-V^+$ cadence, but the following verse tonicizes A minor instead (and the A-pentatonic-minor tune here is the song's only melody), so the Dm chord that arrives at **A+**12 (at 0:36) sounds more like the IV of a second phrase in blues than I.[99] As if to clarify matters, the verse ends with B♭ acting not as ♭VI of D minor but as ♭II of A, moving there to V_7^{b9} of A minor. But the matter is not settled, for the song ends after the fifteenth time through **D**, all in a D-minor wash. Once again, Lennon gives us a song where a single tonal center does not predominate; rather, the original tonal structure seems to be a game about the dual roles of tritone-related E_7^{b9} and B♭^{7} chords.

But of course, we don't really know *where* the song ends, as we don't feel we've heard an ending. Engineer Alan Parsons explains the abrupt splice: "We were putting the final touches to that side of the LP and we were listening to the mix. John said 'There! Cut the tape there.' Geoff [Emerick] cut the tape and that was it. End of side one!"[100] The harsh repetition of the E_7^{b9} chord and the minimalist post–"Hey Jude" redundancy are the main qualities that mark this as a 1969 recording; otherwise, "I Want You (She's So Heavy)" could almost have been a *Rubber Soul* outtake.

Side 2

Paul McCartney was inspired by twenty-minute-plus works by the Mothers, Keith West, the Who, and the Small Faces. And given the fact that both he and John Lennon had several unfinished bits that resisted development on their own, he also took notice of the way the Beach Boys could string together short snippets of material into larger wholes. McCartney wished to write something bigger than individual songs, and George Martin was highly encouraging.[101] The album's second side consists for the most part of a medley of complete songs and fragments that cohere by virtue of tonal organization and thematic recapitulation. It is introduced by one fully independent song and a second composition that, as a prelude, prepares the beginning of the medley proper, and the side ends with the brief "Her Majesty." Listed below are the songs and their composers for the whole of Side 2; those songs in the medley that were recorded as a piece are joined by a "plus" sign (+); those joined in postproduction by either a crossfade or a hard tape edit are marked by a slash (/).

7. "Here Comes the Sun" (Harrison)
8. "Because" (Lennon)

[MEDLEY:]
9. "You Never Give Me Your Money" (McCartney)/
10. "Sun King" (Lennon) + 11. "Mean Mr Mustard" (Lennon)/
12. "Polythene Pam" (Lennon) + 13. "She Came In through the Bathroom Window" (McCartney)/

14. "Golden Slumbers" (McCartney) + 15. "Carry That Weight" (McCartney)/

16. "The End" (McCartney)

17. "Her Majesty" (McCartney)

Lennon never liked the "pop opera," as he called it; he was rightly dissatisfied because "none of the songs had anything to do with each other, no thread at all, only the fact that we stuck them together."[102] But his partner, especially in *Band on the Run, Paul McCartney's Liverpool Oratorio,* and *Standing Stone,* would continue to experiment in this direction. Following discussion on the individual tracks on the album's second side, we will return to the question of the medley's unity.

"Here Comes the Sun"   "Here Comes the Sun" reflects both the brightness of the spring day on which it was written and the blossoming confidence of the composer. Harrison says that the song "was written on a very nice sunny day in Eric Clapton's garden. We'd been through real hell with business, and it was all very heavy. Being in Eric's garden felt like playing hooky from school. I found some sort of release and the song just came."[103]

Basic tracks of Rickenbacker, drums (both center), and Harrison's J-200 (left; played very simply in D with a capo on the seventh fret) were recorded on July 7, and a second J-200 part (left) was dubbed the same day.[104] Vocals were added on the following day; these are George's lead (center), plus sunny backing parts from Paul and George, on two tracks (right, panning to right-center at **B**+25–30, 1:36–2:03). After this, the seven tracks were reduced to two. Handclaps (right, entering the third time through **B**+25–30, at 1:48) and harmonium (left, entering the second time through **B**+10, at 1:16) were added on July 16, more acoustic guitar parts (center, entering with the handclaps) on August 6 and 11, Martin's orchestral score (two piccolos, two flutes, two alto flutes, and two clarinets all left-center, and 0/4/4/1 strings center) on August 15, and Harrison's Moog (left-center, panning to center for the descending glissando—"Strawberry Fields," anyone?—at **A**–1, 0:12–0:14, thereafter left or left-center) just prior to mixing on August 19. The addition of these details was nick-of-time work, done the day before the compilation of the master tape for the entire album.

The middle section, featuring the repeated text "Sun, sun, sun, here it comes" over lightly varied instrumentation, takes on the quality of a meditator's mantra. The voice leading here consists of a tri-plagal progression, C–G–D–A, quoting the dreamy retransition from "A Day in the Life," with a structural gentleness that enhances the suggestion of a meditative state. Harrison's meditation becomes truly transcendental when the V[7] of the fifth ending (2:04–2:11) reveals that the A chord of **A**+28, heard six times as a point of tonal arrival, truly functions as an upper neighbor to the structural dominant. The composer's enlightenment is seemingly celebrated in this fifth ending by the retransition's radiant unfolding of V[7], reminiscent of such retransitions in "Twist and Shout," "This Boy," "Day Tripper," and other early numbers, culminating on the exuberant seventh, the piccolos' d^3 (2:09–2:10).

"Here Comes the Sun" is a fine example of growth in rhythmic complexity. The song is introduced by increasing syncopation in the vocal parts, a characteristic noted in Harrison's earlier compositions. The stress of weak parts of beats is emphasized by cross-rhythms in the guitar break (**A**+6−7, 0:23−0:27), where two bars' length of common time is accented so as to produce a pattern in eighths of 12+4, free enough to suggest joyous abandon. Following the first verse/chorus, this break is extended by two $\frac{4}{4}$ measures (**B**+16−17, 0:55− 0:58), but the second verse/chorus is extended by only one $\frac{4}{4}$ bar (**B**+16, 1:27−1:28). These aspects of asymmetry prepare the middle section's constantly changing meter (beginning at 1:29), which is built on the irregular accent pattern of the eighths of the guitar break (**A**+6−7), but the cascading fourths create a new metrical grouping. A regular $\frac{4}{4}$ pattern in the retransition (the V[7] at 2:04−2:11) then aids the listener in predicting the timing of the verse's return. The coda (2:40 to the end) brings together the vocal syncopations from the chorus, the cross-rhythms of the guitar break, and a unique rehearing of the chorus's ending. Finally, the last four bars (2:54−3:04) juxtapose for one time only the guitar break with a rehearing of the bridge, but now A finally proves itself to be a steadfast harmony.

Dominated at first by layers of acoustic guitar and low strings, "Here Comes the Sun" represents the brightening sun in the bridge by the Moog motive that rises in register and culminates in a V[7]-prolonging retransition highlighted by brilliant frequencies in piccolos and well-placed cymbal crashes. The middle section features a patch probably based on a sawtooth wave, realized as the motive sounds in four different registers. With each higher octave, the edge of the sawtooth seems dulled a bit, approaching the purity of a sine wave but not so much that its last appearance, which concludes on a[2] in the opening of the fifth ending, doesn't lead perfectly to the bright attack of the piccolos on g♯[2] one bar later. A second patch, seemingly based on a triangle wave and featuring a light ribbon portamento, was used in two other passages that exemplify on a larger scale the rising octaves of the bridge: in the second verse (0:59−1:13) the Moog doubles the solo guitar line at the unison, and in the third verse (2:11 through the coda; these two verses straddle the "enlightening" middle section and retransition) the Moog adds an obbligato line an octave above. The high-register triangle wave (which heavily emphasizes the fundamental) joins the family of flutes and piccolos. The Moog performances completed the work on "Here Comes the Sun," following even the normally final orchestral overdubs. Martin's touch with the woodwinds was complemented perfectly by Harrison's final superimpositions, all working together to reflect the sun's increasing brilliance.

"Because"   In a recording made in Amsterdam on March 26 (Lennon and Ono 1969), Lennon can be heard picking arpeggiations on the Jumbo. The arpeggiations were later to become the accompaniment to "Because," a composition that in its final form is dominated by the hot Casino (right) doubled by Martin's Baldwin electric harpsichord (left).[105] In the film *John and Yoko: The Bed-In*, Lennon strums the same progression and adds the vocal part of the final arrangement into the third verse. Here he sings the middle part of the eventual

three-part arrangement, except for the g♯¹ on the first word and for the lowest part at "Love is old, love is new." In the Beatles recording, McCartney sings on top and Harrison nearly always on bottom, in parts arranged by George Martin. The three-part vocals, all mixed to the center, were recorded three times, so the end result is a nine-man choir, three on a part.[106] The full sound complements the exaggerated sustain of the keyboard and the long notes on the bass. Aside from singing backing vocals, McCartney plays Rickenbacker (center) and Harrison the Moog, apparently with three different patches. The first, a sawtooth wave modified in emulation of a horn, doubles the guitar part at the song's climax in **B** (1:30–1:43, center). The "horn" patch probably added some noise alongside the sawtooth, and both sources were led to voltage-controlled low-pass filters regulated by separate envelope generators. This would have allowed the noise to have a faster attack and decay than the slower-to-open, long-sustaining sawtooth would have. It may also have had a bit of regeneration to simulate the horn's natural resonance around 500 Hz and a touch of reverberation. The second and third patches sound simultaneously in the song's conclusion (2:12 to the end); on the left, an envelope generator with a slow attack regulates a low-pass filter, causing the upper partials to open up in sequence on each note, and a simple trianglelike wave is heard on the right channel. There is no percussion, although Starr kept a steady beat on his hi-hat during the recording of the basic tracks. The bass, harpsichord, and guitar were taped at once on August 1; the vocal tracks were laid on August 1 and 4, the Moog on August 5; and the tracks were mixed on the 12th.

"Because" is notable for its unresolved, circular harmonic structure. Vaguely reminiscent of the transitional nature of a slow movement from a Corelli or Handel sonata—a connection neatly enhanced by the presence of the harpsichord—this song ends on VII°$^4_3$ of what follows, which in this case is McCartney's "You Never Gave Me Your Money."[107] This VII°-type harmony had ended the first verse (**A**+10, 0:58–1:00), but with a highly ambiguous function. Because one could expect ♭II (**A**+9, 0:55–0:57) to lead to V, a hearing of V$^7_{♭5}$ with lowered $\hat{7}$ may be considered in **A**+10; f♮ would then be heard as a chromatic passing tone—all in all, an unlikely function. The nature of this chord is revealed at **B** (1:30) as VII°$^4_2$ of a structural IV. The chord's other appearance (**C**–1, 2:09–2:11) is wrapped in yet a new guise, due to a restructuring of hypermeasures as newly interpreted by the chorus, a technique reminiscent of the coda to "Sexy Sadie." In the first verse, phrases were initially arranged in groups of 4+4+2 measures; the final verse melts into a coda without a definite cadence and is grouped, by virtue of choral downbeats, as 4+4+4(!)+4+4, even though the instrumental tracks continue with the identical parts articulating the original groupings. So this time, the harmony heard once as a strangely altered V and twice as VII°⁷ (once applied to F♯ and once to A) is neither. It is finally understood as a contrapuntal entity that neighbors the tonic and has a common tone with it.

"Because" is typical for the Beatles only in that it is inspired by sources outside of rock music. The song is Lennon's recomposition of the first movement of Beethoven's "Moonlight" Sonata, and there are a few points of similarity between the song and its model. Both arpeggiate triads and seventh chords in C♯ minor in the baritone range of a keyboard instrument at a slow tempo, move through the submediant to ♭II, and approach VIIº7/IV via a common tone.[108] Lennon says, "Yoko was playing 'Moonlight Sonata' on the piano. . . . I said, 'Can you play those chords backwards?' and wrote 'Because' around them."[109] If one considers that in Beethoven, the opening arpeggiations appear in an ascending manner only, one might guess that Ono was instructed to reverse that direction; the resulting "circular" ascending and descending arpeggiations that characterize nearly every bar of "Because," then, can be related to a hearing of Beethoven with both forward and backward "chords."

Thus far, the adjective "circular" has been applied to both the harmonic structure and the surface figuration. The notion of circularity is at the heart of the poetic text, as in the play on words upon which the first verse is built: a second meaning of the word "turn" follows the word "round." The second verse reinterprets "blows" following "wind," and the third verse provides a double meaning for "blue" with "cry." Circularity is also inherent in the constant shifts back and forth in the poet's perspective: each verse alternates an external appearance with its effect on the composer's psyche. On the structural V in **B**+3–4 (1:36–1:42), Lennon makes his strongest point; he surprises the listener by extending the circle from the universal "all" not to the first-person "me" but to the second-person "you." This statement, about the universality of love, has a fully mystical quality only slightly less strongly suggested by the spiritual reactions to the world, the wind, and the sky in the three verses, and we must recall the role of the sky in the Lennon-Ono spiritual world, as expressed from *Grapefruit* onward. A final clue to the circularity of the relationships between Lennon and his outside world as expressed in "Because" can be heard in one of his last compositions, "Watching the Wheels" (Lennon and Ono 1980). Here the composer explains his years of daydreaming while watching cars roll by his Dakota apartment. Lennon says of "Watching the Wheels": "The whole universe is a wheel, right? Wheels go round and round. They're my own wheels, mainly. But you know, watching meself is like watching everybody else." The relationship in Lennon's mind between fantasy and circularity is expressed again in his 1980 memories of "I'm Only Sleeping": "It's got backwards guitars, too. That's me—dreaming my life away."[110] (The line "dreaming my life away" is a quote from "Watching the Wheels.") Perhaps "Because" could have borrowed the subtitle, "quasi una Fantasia," as well as the backward chords, from Beethoven's model.

"You Never Give Me Your Money"   Just as Harrison's "Here Comes the Sun" expresses a release from the woes of Beatles business, that same tension inspired McCartney's "You Never Give Me Your Money." The basic track was taped on May 6 and includes McCartney's piano (left), Lennon's distorted Casino (right-center, entering in measure 4, at 0:08), Starr's drums (right, entering the second time through **A**, at 0:47), and Harrison's Leslied Telecaster (center, entering only at **B**+4, 0:18, and faded up high after **C**, 1:31). In the climactic transition, **E**, 2:11–2:28, Lennon plays the lower part, Harrison the higher. The

original basic track ran for thirteen repetitions of **H** longer than did the final mix, and it was appended by an additional blues jam. McCartney cut his lead vocal (wild, between center and right) on July 1 (at **D–E+**1, 1:48–2:09; his part is the sustained f^2–e^2, sung three times).[111] McCartney conducted much further experimentation, but the only other overdubs to survive the final mix are McCartney's second vocal, taped with backing Lennon/Harrison vocals and tambourine at **H** (3:08 to the end, all wild, panning with the first vocal) on July 15, and McCartney's Rickenbacker (center, entering at the second **A**, 0:46) and heavily compressed and filtered piano (the same treatment is also given the vocal here) punched in at **B** (1:09–1:31) on July 31. Following the punch-in of the honky-tonk instrument, the first piano then continues from **C** (1:31, beginning with bass reinforcement like that noted in "Octopus's Garden"); at **E+4**–6 (2:17–2:25) it is faded up on each third beat, and it is mixed out entirely after **F** (2:28). To create continuity for the medley, a crossfade was devised to segue from the end of "You Never Give Me Your Money" into the following song, "Sun King." The tape used for the crossfade consisted of an overlay of tape loops, an e^4 bell (heard twice), birds, bubbles, crickets, and cicadas, all made at McCartney's home, mixed to four-track on August 5. The stereo mix was made on August 13, adding ADT to Paul's vocal to emphasize the phoniness of the "funny paper" at **A+4** (0:32–0:34), and adding tape echo at "break down," the second ending (0:40–0:43); the crossfade was applied on August 21.[112]

Expanding on the hint given in "Martha My Dear," "You Never Give Me Your Money" is McCartney's first multisection through-composed song. Part 1 (**A**, through 1:09) is a passage heard first on instruments only, then with a single vocal line and finally with three vocal parts, all bemoaning the Beatles' business hassles. The first system of example 4.16, a sketch of the tonal structure of the entire Side 2 medley, shows how the "Part 1" passage (**A**) is based on a 5–8 sequence with sevenths, prolonging primary tone e^2 in A minor. A dominant function in **B–1** (1:08–1:09) tonicizes C major for Part 2 (**B**, 1:09–1:31), a repeated phrase based on a descending sixth-progression with parallel thirds below, reversing the direction of the thirds in the "Hello Goodbye" verse. The evocation of nostalgia by the honky-tonk piano and the haze of the filtered colors may also have a "flashback" effect, as the singer remembers a time when he had "nowhere to go." A codetta to Part 2 (**C–D**, 1:31–2:09) prolongs C major with the repeated double-plagal cadence, B♭–F–C; the B♭ refers back to Part 2's brief tonicizations of IV. The lack of harmonic progression and the suddenly slow harmonic rhythm in new three-bar groupings, heard five times—a pattern akin to the gentle middle of "Here Comes the Sun"—characterize the singer's freedom from care, and the "magic feeling" expressed with the free-floating fourths recalls the "dream" in falling fourths in the "A Day in the Life" retransition. The special "magic feeling" is emphasized by Starr's ride and crash cymbals and by Harrison's Leslied guitar ringing with triad arpeggiations descending in fourths, which also may recall the bridge of "Here Comes the Sun."

E (2:09–2:28) constitutes a dramatic transition to Part 3. The transition contains three phases: the first (to **E+4**, 2:17) introduces both guitars in unison, supported with mixture from the C-pentatonic-minor scale (C–E♭–F–

G–B♭), all prolonging primary tone e². The E♭ of **E+3** prepares the second phase of the transition (through **E+6**, 2:24), wherein an octatonic system (C–C♯–E♭–E♮–F–G–A–B♭) develops B♭ a bit further in a move from C⁷ to A. Here, tonal centers of C and A battle for primacy in a three-part guitar flourish that alternates major triads and major-minor seventh chords, the roots of which articulate a diminished-seventh cycle, C–E♭–G♭–A, on the downbeats. The third phase (**F–1**, 2:25–2:28) supports a chromatic ascent to c♯³ on the Telecaster's very highest fret, at which point the tonal center of A declares victory over that of C.

The transcendence of the motion back to A highlights the text "one sweet dream, pick up the bags, get in the limousine," which has been heard as a suggestion of "the sweeping rush of early fame"—again, McCartney reliving his past.[113] Part 3 (**F**, 2:28–2:44) transposes the first phase of the transition, now heard in A, with pentatonic mixture and now with the same boogie guitar chords on roots of A and B with which Harrison had opened "Eight Days a Week"—a musical reference to the days of early fame. This section then transposes the falling fourths from the Part 2 codetta. A measure in slow triple meter (**G–1–2**, 2:44–2:47) heralds the structural close, 3̂–2̂–1̂ (**G**) in parallel octaves with the bass, confirmed by a soulful falsetto an octave above. The coda (**H**, beginning at 3:09) sounds like a youth's bedtime prayer—have Paul's memories reverted that far?—and, with its tenfold repetition, like another mantra. The multifaceted transition to the coda is of interest for formal reasons as well as tonal and metric; what begins as the C-gesture of Part 3, "One sweet dream came true . . . ," takes on a double role as the generative phrase of the conclusion. The coda's ringing guitar figure recalls that of the Part 2 codetta and therefore the contemplative middle section of "Here Comes the Sun."

Even for as gifted a contrapuntist as McCartney, the power of monophony has great value in rock music. John Covach has a theory that rock musicians may adopt a learned, contrapuntal style when performing on the keyboard (Billy Joel often exemplifies this), while music dominated by electric guitars thrives on the unified energy of parallel fifths and octaves (the Who, Led Zeppelin, and most grunge come to mind).[114] "You Never Give Me Your Money" begins with an elegant piano-oriented linear intervallic pattern (5–8, 5–8) and ends with hard-rocking guitar-based structural parallel fifths and octaves, and the transition from one instrumentation to the other is a gradual one that follows a shift in harmonic systems. The "regression" from a learned style to parallel octaves follows the increasing freedom from authority expressed in the poetic text. McCartney's piano, which carries the opening, begins to fade from center stage when it is overshadowed by the bass; the piano has a lesser role at **C** and then disappears. Harrison's guitar takes over gradually; it enters as a rhythm instrument and then dominates the song after its boost of volume at **C**. As example 4.16 shows, Parts 1 (**A**) and 2 (**B**) exemplify standard practice in the major-minor system, and the listener might even guess that Part 2 is to function as a divider in approaching the dominant of A minor, as had been done in "Another Girl," "Wait," and "Your Mother Should Know." The double-plagal neighbor harmonies of the codetta are functional, but here is planted the seed of ♭VII harmony. This is the chord that is to bring the composer away from the strong tension involving V and I and into the blues-derived pentatonic scale. Guitars adorn the transition with the new pentatonic materials. While the harmonic materials are altered in the transition, there is still a strong element of surface counterpoint in the outer parts of the transition as well as its transposition at the beginning of Part 3 (**F**). It is also revealed here that the C-major passage is to play no harmonic role; it is heard in retrospect as preparation for the C of the A-pentatonic-minor conclusion and so is labeled in example 4.16 as an inversion of tonic. But Part 3, with its play of A and C triads, is pentatonic-based; counterpoint is not implied, so parallel octaves, really a doubled single voice, become the norm.

The coda alternates C-major triads with A major-minor seventh chords, reminding the listener of the transition's octatonic passage involving C7 and A7 chords. The chord tones in the coda are, again, overtone doublings of nonfunctional roots a third apart, and Harrison's voice freezes G♮ as a pentatonic member of both chords; the G never really resolves, but remains above the A harmony. In fact, the C chord is heard as its consonant support. The song's opening chord is, of course, A–C–E–G, and as in "A Hard Day's Night," the piece ends with a dissonant sonority that relates to the work's opening. "All good children go to heaven," even those innocent transgressors who create a structural close by singing in octaves with the bass.

"Sun King" + *"Mean Mr Mustard"*   The instrumental parts of the **A** section of "Sun King" (through 0:51) started life in the "Albatross"-based chorus of "Don't Let Me Down," a repeated neighboring progression F♯m7–Eadd6. "Mean Mr Mustard" was "a bit of crap" that Lennon says he wrote in India; "I'd read somewhere in the newspaper about this mean [stingy] guy who hid five-pound notes, not up his nose but somewhere else."[115] Both songs are in E and were joined by the "Sun King" chorus (**B**, beginning at 0:58) when the Beatles performed them together on July 24 for the medley. By January 1969 (8.31, Beatles 1991e; and 14.28, Beatles 1994f), "Mean Mr Mustard" had its verses and an unadorned I–Ger$^6_5$–V7 structure and was played on electric piano with help from Ringo and stray leads from Harrison. But there as in the Kinfauns tape, the **B** section continued in $\frac{4}{4}$ and led to a later-dropped IV–I–IV–V7 bridge: "Mean Mr Mustard, he's such a dirty bastard," repeated.

The basic track for the two songs was recorded under the working title "Here Comes the Sun-King" on July 24. From this first performance we hear Ringo's drums (panning center to right at the opening), George's Leslied Telecaster ("Guitar I" in "Sun King," center but right-center for "Mean Mr Mustard"), Paul's grisly distorted Jazz Bass, probably overloading the board through direct injection, the effect more pronounced in "Mean Mr Mustard" (left), and John's Casino ("Guitar II" for "Sun King," silent in "Mean Mr Mustard," wild). Both Harrison's and Lennon's guitars have a good deal of "Albatross"-like reverberation.[116] The next day, July 25, Lennon led rich vocals by the three singers on two tracks (center and left-center, in quasi-Spanish/Italian), Martin played organ for "Sun King" (right-center, entering at **B**+7, 1:18), Lennon played

Example 4.16 Analysis of *Abbey Road* medley.

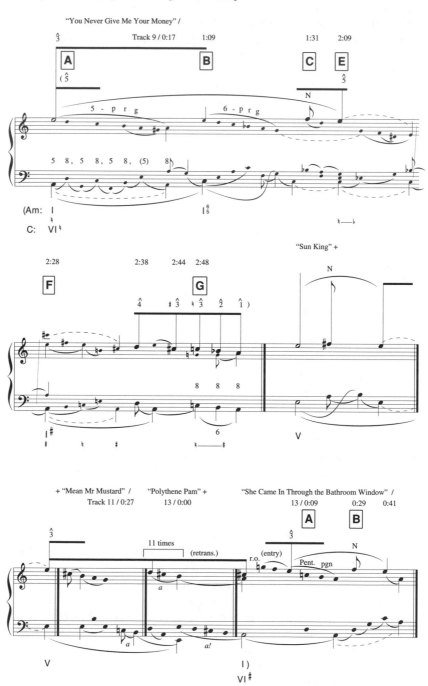

264

Example 4.16 (*continued*)

"Golden Slumbers" +
Track 14 / 0:21

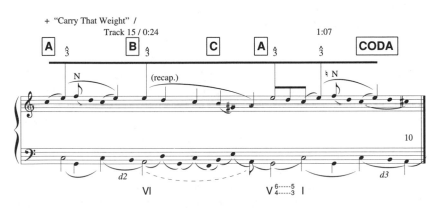

+ "Carry That Weight" /
Track 15 / 0:24

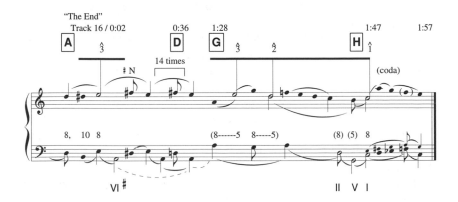

"The End"
Track 16 / 0:02

piano for "Mean Mr Mustard" (center), and percussion (bongos and maracas, left, added at the second **A** of "Sun King" [at 1:50], tambourine center for "Mean Mr Mustard") was added as well. Tests led to mixing, crossfading to "You Never Give Me Your Money" and joining to "Polythene Pam" with a hard edit on August 14; the "You Never Give Me Your Money"/"Sun King" crossfade was redone on August 21.

The two songs share a motive, a chromatic line of three semitones ("Sun King": organ and guitar, **B**+8 [1:21–1:22] and **C**+2 [1:22–1:23]; "Mean Mr Mustard": piano and guitar, **A**+6 [0:15–0:16] and **A**+8 [0:19–0:21]), but there are far more contrasts than similarities between the songs. The vulgarity of "Mean Mr Mustard" sounds all the more restless following the pompous repose of the "Sun King" chorus, an effect partly due to the use of primarily major chords—Gm7 being the exception—with roots forming the unperturbed [025] collections C–G–A and F–D–C–F, all from the C-pentatonic-major scale.

"Polythene Pam" + *"She Came In through the Bathroom Window"*   "Polythene Pam" was a half-written number from India in which Lennon conflated a Cavern fan, "Polythene Pat" (who would eat the substance), with a woman he met in Guernsey dressed in polythene.[117] The bag may also be a reference to Bag Productions (referred to directly in "Come Together"), John's and Yoko's production company, and the "drag" characterization keeps alive the Desmond Jones/Loretta Martin/John and Yoko as "gurus" imagery. Lennon dates his partner's "She Came In through the Bathroom Window" from mid-May 1968; it is supposed to have been inspired by fans' having climbed a ladder into McCartney's St. Johns Wood home.[118] McCartney recalls having completed the final "police department" verse in New York in October 1968 (Miles 1997, 521).

Both verses of "Polythene Pam" get a single acoustic guitar run-through with descant from McCartney in January 1969 (S/S 24.31, Beatles 1991c), but "She Came In through the Bathroom Window" is thoroughly rehearsed at that time (6.58, Beatles 1994d; 7.8, 7.20, 7.32, Beatles 1994h; 7.111, Beatles 1992d; 8.37, 9.41–9.49, Beatles 1975; 22.60, Beatles 1984; and a version lacking an S/S entry, that on Beatles 1996b). All three verses are intact by 6.58, performed on Paul's bass, John's Casino, and George's wah, with John and George both singing the same descant line to Paul's refrain, **B** (0:29–0:50). McCartney plays little other than roots on bass, but in 7.111 he has devised the passing tones in **B**+5 (0:41–0:43); the part becomes more active but still not recognizable by 9.46. Harrison quits the descant part by 9.41, at which point Lennon takes up the piano. In 22.60, McCartney asks for a tight three-part vocal arrangement at **B**, but he never gets it.

The basic track was taped on July 25, with Lennon's twelve-string acoustic ("Guitar II," left, except for the introduction to "Polythene Pam," center; parts of the guide vocal bleed through on this track, including the counting at **B** in "Polythene Pam"), McCartney's Rickenbacker (center), and Harrison's Les Paul ("Guitar I," right); Ringo redid his drums (right-center) the same day. Many more parts were taped on July 28 and 30, including vocals (John's Scouse lead for "Polythene Pam," backed by Paul and George, all center; Paul's lead and [at **B**] descant for "She Came In through the Bathroom Window," center, backed by Paul and John, left-center), percussion (tambourine from the second **A**+12 of "Polythene Pam" through the introduction and **B** section of "She Came In"; maracas and cowbell at **B** for "Polythene Pam"; all center), and more guitars (George's Les Paul E-pentatonic-minor solo at **B** in "Polythene Pam," continuing through "She Came In," right; and George's Telecaster's transitional descending scale, $\hat{5}$–$\hat{4}$–$\hat{3}$–$\hat{2}$, at **C** in "Polythene Pam").[119] The two songs were mixed and joined to "Mean Mr Mustard" with a hard edit on August 14.

"Polythene Pam," particularly Harrison's solo, is based on the double-plagal cadence (D–A–E) but is of further harmonic interest in **A**+7–8 (0:14–0:16), where the C–D–E progression anticipates an introduction to Pam with the "Billy Shears" fanfare. This appears right after the pentatonically divided I–♮III–V^7 progression that had provided the structure for "Birthday" (0:12–0:14). The A-major arrival at the start of "She Came In through the Bathroom Window," which halves the prevailing meter, makes the E heard since "Sun King" work as a large dominant, creating a nonrecapitulatory arrival as thunderous and affirming as the beginning of the "Hey Jude" coda.[120]

"Golden Slumbers" + "Carry That Weight"   During a (late?) 1968 visit with his father in Cheshire, McCartney happened upon a music book of his half-sister Ruth's containing a setting of "Golden Slumbers," a poem by Elizabethan dramatist Thomas Dekker (1572?–1632). Unable to read the musical notation, he composed his own setting, and the Beatles' "Golden Slumbers" resulted. The original poem reads as follows:

> Golden slumbers kiss your eyes;
> smiles awake you when you rise.
> Sleep pretty wantons do not cry,
> and I will sing a lullaby.
> Rock them, rock them, lullaby.[121]

Dekker probably intended a gentle rocking, but that is not McCartney's style, and he probably followed the poem with the hard-rocking "Carry That Weight" very early in the compositional process.

The two songs are already joined when we hear them in January 1969. In S/S 7.2 (Beatles 1994g), McCartney plays the songs solo on piano, having all of the eventual chords and suspensions in "Golden Slumbers," as in the E of **A**+8–9 (0:25–0:31) and the E and G of **B**+1–2 (0:34–0:39). Also present already is the right-hand rocking figuration, but the passing motions, as at **A**+3–4 (0:09–0:14), have not yet been developed. At this early stage, the song is metrically quirky, and McCartney can't reproduce the same irregular counts of vocal rests in each performance. The quirks are never fully ironed out; the "Golden Slumbers" chorus settles on phrases of 3+2½+4 bars. "Golden" moves directly to the **A** section of "Carry That Weight," which then returns to the lullaby.

The basic track (Paul's piano, right-center; Ringo's drums, entering at **B**

[0:32], left; and George's Bass VI) was taped on July 2, with a new inclusion: an unexpected recapitulation of the opening of "You Never Give Me Your Money," with new lyrics. The next day two takes were edited together, and McCartney recorded a wide-ranging lead vocal and (for "Carry That Weight") Harrison dubbed a Leslied Telecaster part (both center) before test mixes were made.[122] The same day, McCartney taped a second vocal, and all but the injured Lennon chanted on the "Carry That Weight" chorus (all center). Another drum track (right) was dubbed onto "Carry That Weight" on July 31, and Martin added a score of brass (four horns, three trumpets, trombone, and bass trombone; ADT to left and right) and strings (12/4/4/1; center) on August 15. The tracks were mixed on August 18 and crossfaded to "The End" on the 19th.

The pair of songs was covered by the Glaswegian quintet Trash (formerly White Trash) for a nonhit Apple single (United Kingdom: Apple 17, October 3, 1969; United States: Apple 1811, October 15). Their version is a very close copy, particularly in the bass line, of the Beatles' arrangement until **B** of "Carry That Weight" (0:24), when it goes very much its own way with a Baroque organ break and an English horn obbligato. The Beatles don't provide Trash with an ending, so following the "**Coda**," the cover group fades out on the chorus. Lennon enjoyed the imitation and insisted that it be released, which it was, against the composer's desires.[123]

"The End"   The Beatles' final LP was to conclude with McCartney's "The End," which Lennon describes as another "unfinished song."[124] Hardly unfinished— McCartney discusses his intention to write a rhyming couplet to indicate closure the way Shakespeare would end his scenes (Miles 1997, 558). One example of such a model would be the concluding lines from Act IV, scene iv of "All's Well That Ends Well":

> All's well that ends well: still the fine's the crown;
> Whate'er the course, the end is the renown.

"The End" was recorded in two parts, both begun on July 23, that were later extended by six added bars. Part 1 (through **E**+12, 1:17) has drums (recorded on two tracks with three sets of mikes so that the top tom is heard left; bass drum, floor tom, and cymbals center; and snare right), Rickenbacker bass, and Lennon's Casino ("Guitar") through **B** (0:19, both center), Ringo's eight-bar "solo" at **C**, and the A^7 (sometimes A^9)–D^7 alternation on Lennon's rhythm guitar through **D** and twelve bars of **E** (only to 1:17, marking the very subtle end of Part 1).[125] Part 2 was an overdub that began where Part 1 left off, allowing McCartney to move to piano. Along with the piano (center) were taped the Casino ("Guitar," right with the solo at **H**, center) and Harrison's Leslied Telecaster ("Others," left) at **G** and drums (entering at **H**–1, with the same stereo distribution as before). Although more work was to be done, these are the only tracks appearing in the medley test (audible on Beatles 1991k) compiled on July 30.

On August 5, 7, 8, and 18, additional instrumental and all vocal parts were added to "The End." Before **C**, we hear McCartney's lead vocal, a new guitar for the opening chords (**A**+1–2 and **B**+1–2), and McCartney's electric piano (the August 18 dub) for the low-register rising chromatic thirds at **A**+3–4 (0:04–0:06) and **B**+3–4 (0:15–0:17, all center). After **F**, we hear McCartney's lead vocal and descant (1:32 to the end), and Harrison's Leslied chords in the last four bars (1:47 to the end, all center). The **D**–**E** section (0:34–1:29) was substantially reworked, with new drums (right, here replacing the two-track recording), bass, and rhythm guitar (center) necessary to accommodate the vocals (chanting "The End," right then left). Most important, the Beatles added their traded solos at **E** on August 7, with McCartney's rocking Telecaster, Harrison's sublime Telecaster, and Lennon's grungy distorted Casino (all center) alternating two-bar passages, each improvising three times in A minor pentatonic. On August 15, the "Golden Slumbers" orchestra taped parts for "The End" (center, low in the mix). Mixing, editing, and the join to "Carry That Weight" were completed on August 19 and 21, and the master of "The End" itself was edited from 2'41" to 2'05", most likely cut between **D** and **E** (perhaps at 0:50), on August 25. The guitarists displayed fascinating pretensions in "The End," but they likely realized that the two-bar breaks were as far as they could go in that direction. Or, apparently, any direction.

"Her Majesty"   A brief tongue-in-cheek music hall ditty composed at the Scotland farm, "Her Majesty" appears first in January 1969, heard as S/S 9.8 and 24.47 (Beatles 1981c), with the composer first on piano and then on his D-28 with Lennon lost on the lap slide. McCartney taped the song live, vocal and D-28, on July 2, as if this were a demo to be considered for group performance as part of the medley. It never received further attention but was included in the July 30 medley test, originally situated between "Mean Mr Mustard" and "Polythene Pam." It was judged out of place, so McCartney asked that it be scrapped. Rather than dispose of a Beatles performance, engineer John Kurlander spliced it at the end of the medley, separated from the bulk of the test by some twenty-five feet of leader.[126] The composer liked the surprising effect at the end of the resulting acetate, so this trial tape of "Her Majesty," removed in an approximate form (the decay of the final chord of "Mean Mr Mustard" enters after fourteen seconds of leader, and the final D-major triad of "Her Majesty" is similarly chopped off the end), is the piece that closes the LP (panning right to left), a song whose title is not even listed on the original LP cover.

The LP ordering was established with the compilation of the master tape on August 20, with "Octopus's Garden" and "Oh! Darling" reversing position and a switch of the two sides, and McCartney had the master itself edited on the 21st, when the introduction to "Maxwell's Silver Hammer" was cut, and the 25th, when a few seconds of the "End" interlude material was cut. It remains now to examine, if only briefly, the nature of the large structure of the medley, from "You Never Give Me Your Money" through "The End."

The concept of the medley seems to have been a joint creation of Martin and McCartney, probably just before the recordings of July 1–4. Both claim credit for the notion: McCartney says, "I wanted to do something bigger, a kind of operatic moment. . . . We wanted to dabble and I had a bit of fun making some of the songs fit together, with the key changes. That was nice, it worked out well."[127] Martin says: "I wanted to try and make side two a continual work. That was Paul and I getting together. . . . I was trying to get Paul to write stuff that . . . referred back to something else. Bring some form into the thing."[128] Most of the medley songs had already been composed before Martin was asked to produce a new album. All of these songs had originally been performed in the same keys as the final versions, but several changes were made with an ear cocked toward overall unity: Lennon's decision to change the name of Mr. Mustard's sister from Shirley to Pam; the devising of the retransitional bars preceding "She Came In through the Bathroom Window"; and the inclusion of references to earlier material in "Carry That Weight."

Example 4.16 presents a deep-level analysis of the medley's tonal structure. Lennon's "Mean Mr Mustard" and "Polythene Pam" are chiefly concerned with inner voices in the dominant prolongation in A, but McCartney recaptures the upper voice with a G♮ in the context of A, to portray the sudden entry through the "Bathroom Window" (midway through the third system). The strong instrumental retransition to A that announces "Bathroom Window" is based on descents heard in "Mean Mr Mustard" and "Polythene Pam"; the two preparatory motions are marked in example 4.16 as "*a*" and the retransition as "*a!*," which refers to the completion of the bass line in its return to A. One might guess that McCartney was thinking primarily about this retransition when he spoke of "making some of the songs fit together, with the key changes." One aspect of "Polythene Pam" resurfaces in "The End": the former ends with an instrumental jam in which the double-plagal function is the basis of eleven guitar variations; in "The End," the choral section and the guitar solos are built on fourteen hearings of the plagal relationship, I–IV(–I).

Much more to the forefront, of course, is McCartney's recomposition of "You Never Give Me Your Money" in "Golden Slumbers" and "Carry That Weight." Like "You Never Give Me," "Golden Slumbers" (probably the older song) opens with an Am^7 chord on the piano and begins its structure with falling fifths in the bass (bracketed in ex. 4.16 and marked "*b*"). The bracket labeled "*c*" marks a quotation from the structure of Part 2 of "You Never Give Me," and those marked "*d*" indicate three different passages in "Golden Slumbers" and "Carry That Weight" that recompose the C–B–A bass line from the coda of "You Never Give Me." In the last version, "*d3*," Harrison's guitar quotes the "You Never Give Me" coda. Of course, the arrival point in "Carry That Weight" marked "recap.," introduced by the "*d*" motive, is a complete rehearing of the foreground diminution of Part 1 of "You Never Give Me Your Money."

McCartney's twist is that "You Never Give Me" is now heard in the context of C major. Robert Gauldin has discussed the relationships between the tonal areas of C and A in *Abbey Road* in terms of Wagnerian "double-tonic" juxtapositions, and many examples of C–A relationships can be seen throughout example 4.16, as well as in other *Abbey Road* compositions.[129] The medley's most telling juxtaposition of A and C comes in "The End," at the moment when the tonicized A major moves to II of C (**G**, at 1:43). The final structural cadence of the medley, followed only by a brief ornamental plagal coda that refers back to Part 3 of "You Never Give Me," sets the text, "and in the end the love you take is equal to the love you make," which Lennon praised as "a very cosmic, philosophical line."[130] Because of the coincidence of this return to C major and a graduated change of tempo, both tonal and metric modulations occur precisely on the word "equal," the word that separates the two halves of the equation.[131]

Despite the extremely varied circumstances of composition for the various medley songs, and also despite the fact that most of the basic composition was complete before the concept of the medley was voiced, one searches for an overarching theme in this group of songs that were chosen and joined in a very conscious manner. The juxtaposition of the tonal centers of A and C seems to be a central concern, and certainly a clue exists in "Golden Slumbers," wherein a desire to find a way home is sung in A minor, and the consequence of the return, a lullaby, is set in C major; thus, A contains tension, and C repose. Much of the poetic text of the medley deals with selfishness and self-gratification—the financial complaints in "You Never Give Me Your Money," the miserliness of Mr. Mustard, the holding back of the pillow in "Carry That Weight," the desire that some second person will visit the singer's dreams—perhaps the "one sweet dream" of "You Never Give Me Your Money"?—in "The End." These selfish moments are all set in the context of the tonal center of A. Generosity is expressed in the comfort offered in "Golden Slumbers"; in "Carry That Weight," the group can be heard to admonish the singer to stop being so selfish—recall McCartney's preoccupation with his personal financial difficulties. These are the points where C major is central. A great compromise in the "negotiations" is finally achieved in the equation of "The End." Apparently McCartney has understood the repeated C-major choruses, because he comes to the earth-shaking realization that there is only as much self-gratifying love ("the love you take"), that of A major, as there is of the generous kind ("the love you make"), that of C major. While not an unusual theme for the Beatles, and certainly one of central importance to John Lennon, as in "The Word" and "All You Need Is Love," it seems rewarding to hear this uplifting message as a very personal final gift from Paul McCartney to his mates, as well as from the Beatles to the world. 'Tis true that a good play needs no epilogue, but McCartney's ear for structural balance graces a fine medley with a better coda.

The LP title was changed from *Everest* to *Abbey Road* when the four could not be bothered to fly to the Himalayas for a cover shoot. *Abbey Road* (United Kingdom: Apple PCS7088, September 26, 1969, #1 for nineteen weeks; United States: Apple SO383, October 1, #1 for eleven weeks) remains the Beatles' biggest-selling album, with 4 million sold within two months and 9 million by 1992.

The End

The Beatles were essentially finished; only a regrouping of three members on January 3–4, 1970, interrupted the solo projects that would now become the regular outlet for artistic expression. Lennon and Ono showed many of their films, including the new *Apotheosis* and *Self-Portrait*, and prepared the previous year's "What's the New Mary Jane" for release as a Plastic Ono Band recording.[132] After hearing Dylan and the Who play a major festival on the Isle of Wight on August 2, Lennon offered to play at Toronto's Peace Festival on September 20, recruiting Eric Clapton to join the Plastic Ono Band for the occasion; this performance was filmed (*Sweet Toronto* 1988) and released on an LP (Plastic Ono Band 1969; December 12, 1969; United States, #10). Following Bo Diddley, Chuck Berry, Chicago, and the Doors, the Plastics played "Blue Suede Shoes" (with Yoko sitting in a bag), "Money (That's What I Want)," "Dizzy Miss Lizzie," "Yer Blues" (with Yoko wailing as she did for "Rock 'n' Roll Circus"), "Cold Turkey," "Give Peace a Chance," "Don't Worry Kyoko (Mummy's Only Looking for a Hand in the Snow)" (for Ono's six-year-old daughter, whose father had absconded with her), and twelve minutes of feedback with the high-wattage Marshall amps, later entitled "John, John, Let's Hope for Peace."

Lennon returned from Toronto beaming with confidence, and when McCartney, seeing the effect on his partner, proposed in a September meeting that the Beatles perform once again, Lennon could not contain himself and said that he wanted "a divorce" from the Beatles and from all of Paul's music, which he characterized that December as being "for the grannies to dig."[133] A shocked McCartney went home to Scotland for several months, recording his first solo LP, *McCartney*; he was to repeat the act a decade later, recording *McCartney II* as a response to the dissolution of Wings. A savvy Allen Klein kept the fact of the band's demise quiet through the negotiation of the EMI/Capitol/Beatles contracts. I have already suggested above that one of the sticking points between Lennon and McCartney was the latter's refusal to record the former's new song "Cold Turkey" (an answer to James Brown's 1967 record, "Cold Sweat"?), which portrays the agony of heroin withdrawal that Lennon and Ono undertook when they discovered that she was once again pregnant (she was to miscarry again in October). The Plastics—now John Lennon, Eric Clapton, Ringo Starr, Klaus Voorman, and Yoko Ono—recorded "Cold Turkey" and "Don't Worry Kyoko" on September 25 (United States: Apple 1813, October 20, 1969, #30; United Kingdom: Apple 1001, October 24, #12).

While in Scotland, McCartney found he had to disprove incredible October rumors that he had been killed in a 1966 car crash, his role filled by a double ever since. Such was the conclusion offered in a *Michigan Daily* review of *Abbey Road*, based on the interpretation of scores of clues found in record covers, lyrics, and backward messages.[134] Meanwhile (October 1969–March 1970), Ringo recorded his first solo LP, *Sentimental Journey*, a collection of standards by Cole Porter, Hoagy Carmichael, and others that he thought his mum might enjoy listening to. Harrison brought his Les Paul to early November sessions for a solo LP by Ric Grech (ex-Family) and toured briefly (December 2–12, in England and Copenhagen), playing his Les Paul and slide Strat with Delaney & Bonnie and Friends (including Clapton, who had hosted the two weeks of preliminary rehearsals in November), a crew that also joined Lennon and Ono on December 15 for a UNICEF charity concert in London.

Lennon stepped up his activism, seemingly believing that he had the answers to many of the world's problems. On November 25, he resigned his MBE award (the queen had decorated the Beatles as Members of the British Empire in October 1965), protesting Britain's support of both Nigeria's invasion of Biafra and America's war in Vietnam, and—for good measure—"Cold Turkey"'s slipping down the charts. In December, he vowed to film the story of James Hanratty, hanged in 1962 for murder but widely believed innocent. He and Ono declared the new year to be Year One A.P. (after peace), but few noted this on their calendars. The UNICEF concert inaugurated the "War Is Over (If You Want It)" billboard campaign, in which this message was plastered in a dozen large cities, and the Lennons met with Canada's prime minister, Pierre Trudeau, on December 23 to discuss world plans for peace. Lennon continued to challenge mores and laws by selling 300 signed sets of fourteen lithographs, entitled "Bag One," unveiled at the London Arts Gallery on January 15, 1970; the drawings depict his and Ono's life together, including their lovemaking.

Lennon also continued to produce music; his ominous Top Five single "Instant Karma," backed by Ono's plaintive "Who Has Seen the Wind," was written on January 26, 1970, recorded the next day, and released in the United Kingdom on February 6, and two weeks later, in the United States. Harrison contributed guitar to this heavy-echo warning that brings the Buddhist scriptures to life in a society of unrepentant instant gratifications. In the first months of 1970, Lennon and Ono assembled an art exhibition for the Fluxus group in New York that was unveiled in May. The two also got involved with heroin once again, cleaning up only by doing a stint in a detox center and undergoing the pain-unlocking Primal Scream therapy for three weeks in March in the United Kingdom and then in Los Angeles; they were admitted on a medical visa for four months beginning the last week in April 1970.[135]

McCartney and Lennon wanted to empty the Beatles vaults and release anything of value while they still had control over the material.[136] Lennon and Geoff Emerick prepared mixes of "You Know My Name (Look Up the Number)" and (once again) "What's the New Mary Jane" on November 26, 1969, for release on December 5 as a Plastic Ono Band single, but this was stopped. There was a final 1969 Beatles Fan Club Christmas record, but just as with the last, this was recorded individually; Ono is given more time on the record than Harrison, Starr, and McCartney combined. Klein was also busy; following his decision to release "Something" as a single, he authorized Capitol in the United States to compile a collection of ten A- and B-sides that had never appeared on LP, many to be mixed into stereo for the first time; these became the album *Hey Jude* (Apple 385, February 26, 1970, #2 for four weeks).

Let It Be

But these projects were small potatoes compared to the preparation of the January 1969 "Get Back" materials, left on the shelf until Allen Klein agreed on a film contract with United Artists in November. The finally edited film was to include shots of the Beatles working on "Across the Universe" and "I Me Mine," so recordings of these had to be prepared for the soundtrack album. Glyn Johns, who had overseen the original sound recording and had produced the first mixes, was called back in. He worked from the February 1968 take of "Across the Universe" that had just been released, sped up from D to E♭ and with George Martin's October 2, 1969, dubs of bird sounds, on Spike Milligan's World Wildlife LP, *No One's Gonna Change Our World*, on December 12, 1968. McCartney, Harrison, and Starr returned to EMI's Studio Two on January 3 and 4, 1970, to record "I Me Mine" and a few dubs for "Let It Be," and Johns recompiled the album on January 5 in accordance with the film, adding these recordings and deleting "Teddy Boy."

The Johns mixes excited no one. Upon Lennon's early-January return from Denmark, the "Get Back" tapes were handed instead to an eager Phil Spector, who produced the "Instant Karma" single on January 27. This was perhaps done at Klein's initial suggestion and certainly with Harrison's approval; McCartney was occupied elsewhere, writing material for his own LP.[137] Spector worked from March 23 through April 2, with EMI engineer Peter Bown and often with Harrison present as well.[138] He developed material from the Apple eight-track tapes, producing only tracks that had already been selected for mixing by Johns, so he did not have too much tape to wade through.[139] He certainly would not have been interested in the music rehearsals in the Twickenham recordings, although he did resurrect one brief snippet of dialogue from these sources. The following section presents a history of the Johns/Spector postproduction work on the "Get Back" tapes.

"Maggie Mae," "For You Blue," "One after 909," "Dig a Pony," and "Two of Us"
Five songs and extra bits of dialogue, the latter prepared on March 27, 1970, required very little work for the LP, and their original working tapes received only simple mixing and equalization from Spector. "Maggie Mae" (S/S 24.40) was mixed on March 26 with Lennon's vocal left, McCartney's right; Lennon's J-200 right, McCartney's D-28 left; Harrison's bass line on Telecaster and Starr's drums center. "For You Blue" (S/S 25.24; mixed March 25) is introduced by a typical Lennon non sequitur, "Queen says 'no' to pot-smoking FBI member" (from S/S 8.18, center), and places the lap slide left, McCartney's piano right, and Harrison's J-200 and vocal and brushed drums center. "The One after 909" (S/S 30.6 and 30.7; March 23) and "Dig a Pony" (S/S 30.8, March 23) both have Preston's electric piano and the Casino left; Maclen vocals, drums, and Höfner center; and Telecaster right. The rooftop performance of "The One after 909" ends with Lennon busking a line from "Danny Boy" (the 1918 adaptation of the Irish folk song, "Londonderry Air"), retained by Spector; "Dig a Pony" has the "All I Want Is You" vocals mixed out of the introduction and coda. "Two of Us" (S/S 22.42 and 31.5; March 25) has McCartney's D-28 left, Lennon's J-200 right, and Lennon/McCartney vocals, Telecaster bass line, and drums all center. This track is set up as the LP's opener by another Lennon ad-lib, his spoken intro to " 'I Dig a Pygmy,' by Charles Hawtrey and the Deaf-Aids," taken from rehearsals on January 22.

"Dig It," "Get Back," and "I've Got a Feeling"   Three other numbers required minor editing in addition to mixing and EQ. "Dig It" (S/S 26.27; March 27) was cut from 12'25" to 0'49", leaving primarily one of Lennon's many litanies of personages. We hear McCartney's piano left; Lennon's vocal and strummed Bass VI, drums, and Martin's shakers all center; and Preston's Hammond with Harrison's Telecaster right. "Get Back" (S/S 27.4; March 26), preceded by Lennon's word-twist, "Sweet Loretta Fart, she thought she was a cleaner, but she was a frying pan," consists of Casino boogie and solo left, Telecaster "chicks" right, and drums, Höfner, Preston's electric piano, and Lennon/McCartney vocals center. The track and LP conclude with a graft from the end of the rooftop performance (S/S 30.13; cut short in Beatles 1996b), where McCartney thanks Maureen for her applause and Lennon thanks everyone on behalf of the group. The master of "I've Got a Feeling" (S/S 30.4; March 23) did not edit a performance but spliced together several mixes, all with the same stereo distribution as the other rooftop numbers, "The One after 909" and "Dig It," except that the quodlibet vocals in the last verse are separated, Paul's left and John's right. Even though Johns had omitted McCartney's "Teddy Boy" (S/S 24.22) from LP contention, Spector produced a mix of this song on March 25, edited from 7'30" to 3'10".[140]

"Across the Universe" and "I Me Mine"   Because Lennon did not wish to join the 1970 sessions, Johns secured the February 4/8, 1968, take of "Across the Universe," kept it in D major, added Lennon dialogue ("all right, Richie") to the opening, and retained Lennon's D-28 and vocal, Harrison's tamboura (all with original Leslie and ADT effects), backward guitars, organ, and backing vocals in the refrain at **B**+4–11 by the female fans. Omitted are Ringo's tom-toms, Lennon/McCartney backing vocals, humming, Lennon's doubled vocal, Martin's organ, Harrison's maracas and wah, and McCartney's piano in the coda.[141] Spector slowed the tape to D♭; retained only Lennon's vocal and guitar, maracas for the refrains, wah at the second refrain, and the tamboura at **C** (all center); and added his massive wall of sound, scored by Richard Hewson, on April 1: a chorus of fourteen (right), more drums by Ringo (center), and brass (0/3/3/0) and strings (18/4/4/0, harp and two guitars, left, center, and right). Spector produced the LP mix on April 2.

A new recording of "I Me Mine" was begun and completed on January 3–4, 1970, without Lennon. The Johns mix (Beatles 1991a) of a performance lasting only 1'34" arranged the basic tracks with Harrison's J-200 left and McCartney's Rickenbacker and Starr's drums center; overdubs include McCartney's sustained organ (right), McCartney descant for **C**, two Harrison vocals, and staccato organ (all center); a lead acoustic part (left); and two distorted Les Paul parts (left for the introduction and the boogie at **C**, right for the lead at **C** and thereafter).[142] On March 23, Spector edited three mixes, deleting one of the double-tracked lead vocals but extending the length another fifty-two seconds by repeating the material from 0:31 to 1:21, taking the first ending twice. On April 1, Spector added the same brass and string forces used in "Across the Universe" and new drums from Ringo, the final dub on a Beatles recording. The April 2 remix placed first acoustic guitar, lead Les Paul, both organs, and brass (entering at the second time through **A**) left; lead acoustic guitar, boogie Les Paul, and strings right; and Harrison/McCartney vocals, bass, and new drums center.

"Let It Be"   Johns, Martin, and Spector all made adjustments to the original "Let It Be" recording (S/S 31.38). The April 30, 1969, Johns mix (Beatles 1991d) included a new Leslied Telecaster part from Harrison taped on April 30, wiping the original Strat. This new part, which entered at **F** (1:45), had a bluesy touch, with its ♭3̂–1̂ cadence at **H**–1 (2:23 – 2:26), but was otherwise diatonic and was undeveloped at the second hearing of **E** (3:22 – 3:36). We hear drums (entering at **C**, 0:52) and Telecaster (entering at **F**, not playing at all at the second **C** [2:40 – 3:08], and patterning the second **E** on the solo) all left; McCartney's piano, lead vocal with reverb, and Lennon/Harrison backing vocals center; and Preston's Hammond (on choruses, as at **B**, 0:38 – 0:51) with Lennon's Bass VI (entering at **C+**5, 1:05, playing only half-note roots) right.

The track changed drastically in Martin's hands on January 4, 1970; not only was his brass/strings score added on this day, but — contrary to the intentions of the original "live" recording, with which he did not agree — the song was given a new distorted Les Paul part, a new Rickenbacker bass part, a new electric piano, drums, and maracas. Harrison's Les Paul rises faster and higher at **G**, to a³, than did the April 1969 Telecaster solo, which rose to e³; both parts cadence with the wisdom-filled 3̂–2̂–1̂ descent that defines the chorus. The Rickenbacker replaces Lennon's plodding bass part with McCartney's much more graceful one. We hear organ left; Telecaster (from April 1969, including the Tele solo) and Les Paul (from January 1970 for the second time through **C+**4 – 5 only, *Past Masters, Volume Two,* 2:53 – 2:56) right (this channel is marred by a speaking voice at **C+**5, 1:07); Lennon/Harrison backing vocals beginning left and panning right, where they remain for the duration; and all else center: piano, lead vocal with echo, drums, new bass entering at **C+**4 (1:03, much lower in volume in this mix than in Spector's), brass (two trumpets, two trombones, and tenor sax) at **E** (1:32 – 1:45), electric piano at **F+**1 – 2 (1:45 – 1:52), maracas and new drums at the second **C** (2:42 – 3:09), and cellos at the second **E** (3:23 – 3:37). For the Beatles' last worldwide single, "Let It Be" was backed with Geoff Emerick's November 26, 1969, mono mix of "You Know My Name (Look Up the Number)" (United Kingdom: Apple R5833, March 6, 1970, #3 for two weeks; United States: Apple 2764, March 11, #1 for two weeks), sold 1.5 million in the United States, and inspired Billy Preston's Harrison-produced "That's the Way God Planned It" (recorded in April 1969, released United Kingdom: Apple 12, June 27, 1970, #7).

Martin's mix for the single had already peaked on the chart when Spector created the LP version. On March 26, he crossfaded from "Dig It" with a falsetto joke intro from Lennon ("that was 'Can You Dig It' by Georgie Wood; and now we'd like to do 'Hark the Angels Come,'" a line from S/S 24.70) and extended the length from 3'50" to 4'01", a length made grander by the repeat of **D** the last time, creating for this mix the second **E** (*Let It Be*), for a total of three choruses at the finish. Spector then mixed what he was given, omitting all guitars from the second **D** (3:08 – 3:22), bringing in the Les Paul for the second "E"

(3:22–3:35) for a terraced effect, all without the vocal echo that Johns had used but with heavy tape echo on Ringo's hi-hat for the second verse. The Telecaster is fully mixed out in favor of the stinging, arching Les Paul. We hear backing vocals with echo and (entering at the second **E**, 3:22) cellos, left; piano, lead vocal, drums with echo (entering at **C**, 0:52), new Rickenbacker part (entering at **C+4**, 1:02), and electric piano at **F+1–2** only (1:45–1:51; this may be McCartney's, as it is very similar to that instrument's overdub to "The End"), the latest guitar part by Harrison on the distorted Les Paul (entering first at **G**, 1:57), and maracas and the new drums (at the second **C**, 2:40), all center; and Preston's organ and brass at **E** (beginning at 1:31), right.

"The Long and Winding Road"   The final mix of "The Long and Winding Road" was taken a great distance from the original performance (S/S 31.20) on piano, Bass VI, Leslied Telecaster, drums, and single vocal. The orchestra, the choir, and Ringo's new drum track, the same forces added to "Across the Universe," were taped by Spector on April 1, and an edit was made the next day of two mixes: Beatles and chorus center, velvety strings and harp left, and brass right.

Klein had "The Long and Winding Road" released as an American-only single, backed by "For You Blue" (Apple 2832, May 11, 1970, #1 for two weeks), as a tie-in with both the film, which opened in New York on May 13, and the LP release. The album was still called *Get Back* in late December 1969 but became *Let It Be* by February 1970, when Lennon's full-circle cover idea—the Beatles matching their *Please Please Me* pose—was in preparation.[143] The *Let It Be* LP (United Kingdom: Apple PXS1, May 8, 1970, #1 for eight weeks; United States: Apple AR34001, May 18, #1 for four weeks) included a generous book of photos and dialogue from the film in the first British pressing (discontinued November 6) and featured the following track lineup:

Side 1	Side 2
"Two of Us"	"I've Got a Feeling"
"Dig a Pony"	"One after 909"
"Across the Universe"	"The Long and Winding Road"
"I Me Mine"	"For You Blue"
"Dig It"	"Get Back"
"Let It Be"	
"Maggie Mae"	

American outlets placed advance orders for 3.7 million, an industry record.[144] But at least two listeners were shocked by the results: George Martin professed ignorance that Phil Spector had even been given the tapes, and McCartney—given no opportunity, he says, to respond to an acetate of Spector's work—was crestfallen, particularly due to the treatment of "The Long and Winding Road."[145] Lennon, whose contribution to *Let It Be* was slight compared to his partner's, was Spector's champion: "He was given the shittiest load of badly recorded shit with a lousy feeling to it ever, and he made something out of it. . . . When I heard it I didn't puke."[146]

The Legacy

The other three had quit privately and temporarily, but the break was made public and permanent with a question-and-answer sheet prepared by Paul and the Apple publicity department as an insert to promo copies of *McCartney* (released April 10, 1970, nudged out of three weeks at #1 in the United States by *Let It Be*).[147] McCartney's insert was ostensibly in lieu of live press appearances in promotion of the album; it included such information as: "*Q:* Is your break with the Beatles temporary or permanent, due to personal differences or musical ones? *A:* Personal differences, business differences, musical differences but most of all because I have a better time with my family. Temporary or permanent? I don't know." On December 31, 1970, McCartney sued for the appointment of a receiver for the Beatles' interests. His suit was based on four arguments, including the group's threat to his creative control, citing Phil Spector's production of "The Long and Winding Road," and the unwelcome control over his work exercised by Allen Klein, with whom he'd refused to sign a contract.[148] The Beatles & Co. was formally dissolved in a January 9, 1975, ruling, and other ex-Beatles lawsuits against Klein, fellow ex-Beatles, and EMI/Capitol lingered until 1989.

The Beatles' musical influence on their times is often measured by the number of hit cover versions of their compositions and the variety of styles represented in these recordings. By mid-1965, Dick James reported over 1,900 recordings of Beatles compositions, but many of these were obvious coattail riders of the Beatles' hits; for instance, "A Hard Day's Night" had been recorded by 129 artists, and "Can't Buy Me Love" by 70, through 1986, hardly a testament to compositional integrity. "Yesterday" had been covered 425 times by that point, and by mid-1995, there had been more than 2,500 released recordings of "Yesterday."[149] Fifty-four Beatles covers charted on the Hot 100, and three reached the American Top Ten years after the Beatles broke up: Anne Murray's "You Won't See Me" (#8 in 1974), Elton John's "Lucy in the Sky with Diamonds" (#1 in 1975; Lennon played guitar and sang backing vocals), and Earth, Wind and Fire's "Got to Get You into My Life" (#9 in 1978). One notable tribute is Booker T. & the MGs' LP *McLemore Avenue* (April 1970), a cover of the entirety of *Abbey Road* and named after the address of their Memphis studio (Stax). The Beatles' music is heard in all imaginable styles and surroundings.

Another, more subtle measure of the Beatles' musical value is judged by their compositional traits surfacing in, or dominating, the compositions of others. Those instances cited within the text of this book are often directly contemporaneous with the Beatles' work, and many of these can be heard as stowaways on a gravy train. But such influences continued long into the following decades; the most heavily influenced artists include Spirit, Badfinger, Nilsson, Todd Rundgren, Chicago, NRBQ, Emitt Rhodes, Yes, Electric Light Orchestra, the Raspberries, Steely Dan, Slade, Billy Joel, the Flamin' Groovies, Klaatu, Cheap Trick, the Knack, Squeeze, XTC, Oasis, Nirvana, and Fastball.

But the Beatles' ultimate legacy lies in their own performances of their own compositions. It is natural that these recordings will always be of central importance to the largest demographic group of the century, the "baby boomers" who most often cite "A Day in the Life," "Hey Jude," "Yesterday," "Let It Be," "Help!," "All My Loving," "The Long and Winding Road," "She Loves You," "If I Fell," "And I Love Her," "Eleanor Rigby," "Back in the U.S.S.R.," "Lady Madonna," "A Hard Day's Night," and "I Am the Walrus" as their favorite Beatles tracks, and "Revolution 9," "You Know My Name (Look Up the Number)," "Helter Skelter," and "Do You Want to Know a Secret" as their least liked. Among the 19,851 records to appear on the *Billboard* singles charts from 1955 to 1992, "Hey Jude" ranks #8 in terms of chart performance; "I Want to Hold Your Hand," "Get Back," and "Can't Buy Me Love" also rank in the top 100, and the Beatles (group and solo) place forty-one titles among the top 5 percent. The group sold records in the hundreds of millions by the time they broke up, and it reached the billion mark in 1984, three years before the emergence of the first Beatles compact discs. The market for Beatles bootlegs has always been enormous, as has the market for reissues of old material. Largely because of bootleg pressures, Apple repackaged fifty-five of the most popular tracks into two two-record sets in 1973, the "Red" Beatles (Beatles 1973a) and the "Blue" Beatles (Beatles 1973b), which charted respectively at #2 and #1 in the United Kingdom and #3 and #1 in the United States. When EMI gained the authority in 1975 to reissue Beatles tracks as they saw fit, they placed "Strawberry Fields Forever," "Yesterday," and "Get Back" in the British Top Ten in April 1976, and "Got to Get You into My Life" in the American Top Ten that July. Parlophone reissued the Beatles' singles in color sleeves and picture disks on the twentieth anniversaries of their initial releases, and EMI has collected on a few discs through the years some "rarities" such as B-sides, alternate mixes, and finally, in 1994, a representation of BBC performances that was to sell 10 million copies worldwide in six months (Beatles 1994a, reaching #1 in the United Kingdom and #3 in the United States), culminating in the historical *Anthology* series of 1995–96. No one can predict the future, but while the surviving principals, particularly Harrison, obviously have their reasons for enjoying their time out of the limelight, it is difficult to imagine a world without a large audience for the Beatles.

POSTLUDE

WHATEVER HAPPENED TO . . . ?

The Beatles' solo careers will be summarized here very briefly only to set the stage for a treatment of the 1994–95 recordings for the *Anthology* series. Table 4.2 tallies the composition and recording activity of each of the Beatles as soloists through 1997.[1]

John Lennon

Lennon maintained an active pursuit of his music until 1976, when his EMI contract expired. Then, tasting a new freedom, he contented himself with New York family life as househusband and father to Sean (b. October 1975), not producing another record until late 1980.[2] He was murdered by a delusional fan on December 8, 1980. Lennon had eight singles and seven LPs reach the American Top Ten:

"(Just Like) Starting Over" (1980, #1 for five weeks)
"Whatever Gets You Through the Night" (1974, #1 for one week)
"Woman" (1981, #2 for three weeks)
"Instant Karma" (1970, #3)
"Imagine" (1971, #3)
"Nobody Told Me" (1984, #5)
"No. 9 Dream" (1975, #9)
"Watching the Wheels" (1981, #10)

Double Fantasy (1980, #1 for eight weeks)
Imagine (1971, #1 for one week)
Walls and Bridges (1974, #1 for one week)
John Lennon/Plastic Ono Band (1970. #6)
Rock 'n' Roll (1975, #6)
Mind Games (1973, #9)
Live Peace in Toronto/1969 (1970, #10)

Table 4.2 Musical Activity of the Solo Beatles, 1968–1998

Ex-Beatle	Solo albums	Additional A-Sides	New Compositions			Total new rel. titles
			Self-rel.	For others	Rec. but unrel.	
McCartney	28	19	273	48	76	366
Harrison	15	3	148	19	8	169
Lennon	17	6	96	7	38	144
Starr	15	3	46	2	4	142
Total	75	31	563	76	126	821

John Lennon continued to produce personal statements of deep introspection, perhaps most significantly in "God" (1970), and avoided indirect, second-hand narrations. His hopes for world peace, his support for political freedoms, his open feminism before it was an accepted stance, and his belief in a strong individual spirituality in everyone brought great social significance to his solo music, which could also celebrate love, his family, and personal joy. Lennon, who seldom reminded one of another composer except perhaps Dylan, reverted to his Beatles sound most clearly in "Love" (1970), "Jealous Guy" (1971), "Woman," and "Watching the Wheels" (both 1980).

Lennon was never an active performer after 1966, but he did make eight stage appearances before 1976, often in support of a social cause. His public outreach in the 1970s was through occasional exhibitions of art and films, the posthumous publication of his book *Skywriting by Word of Mouth* (largely a deconstructed pastiche of cultural history posing as comic novella, much more personal and mature than the early books), dozens of planned but unfinished recordings (some released in Lennon and Ono 1984, many others aired in the 1988–92 radio series "The Lost Lennon Tapes"), and philanthropy (made possible by wise investments managed by Ono, the daughter of a banking executive). Privately, the decade was divided into two halves, the first colored by a bitter three-year struggle against a U.S. deportation effort, in which Lennon was vindicated only after it was shown that he had been the victim of paranoid and illegal activities by the Nixon White House and the FBI, and the second a relaxed time for bread-baking in the Dakota apartments, directly across Central Park West from his memorial garden, Strawberry Fields.[3]

Paul McCartney

McCartney remained the most musically active of the Beatles, performing at least 349 concerts between 1972 and 1997, including a 1993 tour that was the second-highest-grossing American circuit that year, taking $32.3 million from twenty-four shows (behind the Dead's $44.5 million from seventy-eight dates).[4] His group Wings (1971–80) was highly successful, and although his records have not been major hits since 1986 (other than the two albums of 1997), his performances, recording contracts, and investments in music publishing and fine art have made him the thirtieth wealthiest Briton and one of the world's richest musicians, worth a reported £420 million. In the summer of 1995 he hosted an offbeat radio series called "Oobu Joobu," airing many solo-era outtakes. His Top Ten records in America:

"Ebony and Ivory" (1982, #1 for seven weeks)	"My Love" (1973, #1 for four weeks)
"Say, Say, Say" (1983, #1 for six weeks)	"Coming Up (Live at Glasgow)" (1980, #1 for three weeks)
"Silly Love Songs" (1976, #1 for five weeks)	"With a Little Luck" (1978, #1 for two weeks)

"Uncle Albert/Admiral Halsey" (1971, #1 for one week)
"Band on the Run" (1974, #1 for one week)
"Listen to What the Man Said" (1975, #1 for one week)
"Live and Let Die" (1973, #2 for three weeks)
"The Girl Is Mine" (1983, #2 for three weeks)
"Let 'Em In" (1976, #3 for one week)

"Junior's Farm" (1975, #3 for one week)
"Goodnight Tonight" (1979, #5)
"Another Day" (1971, #5)
"No More Lonely Nights" (1984, #6)
"Jet" (1974, #7)
"Spies Like Us" (1985, #7)
"Take It Away" (1982, #10)
"Hi Hi Hi" (1973, #10)
"Helen Wheels" (1974, #10)
"Maybe I'm Amazed" (1977, #10)

Wings at the Speed of Sound (1976, #1 for seven weeks)
Band on the Run (1973, #1 for four weeks)
McCartney (1970, #1 for three weeks)
Red Rose Speedway (1973, #1 for three weeks)
Tug of War (1982, #1 for three weeks)
Venus and Mars (1975, #1 for one week)

Wings over America (1976, #1 for one week)
London Town (1978, #2 for six weeks)
Ram (1971, #2 for two weeks)
Flaming Pie (1997, #2 for one week)
McCartney II (1980, #3 for one week)
Back to the Egg (1979, #8)
Wild Life (1971, #10)
Paul McCartney's Standing Stone (1997, #1 on classical chart for eleven weeks)

McCartney has continued to flaunt his expertise in counterpoint and his gift for expansive melodies in his solo work, both of which are constantly evident in his most beautiful songs, as in the poignant ode to Lennon, "Here Today" (1982). He continues to rock hard; ironically, he has composed far fewer vaudeville numbers than in the second half of the Beatles' career but has also written many more of his trademark sentimental vignettes, from "Another Day" (1971) to "Young Boy" (1997). His lyrics are often incoherent or, better, nonsensical; in the "Yellow Submarine" vein, McCartney is often silly, wasting himself on such comic-book creations as "Monkberry Moon Delight" (1971), "Bogey Music" (1980), and the more appropriate "Flaming Pie" (1997), let alone "Magneto and Titanium Man" (1975). McCartney is at home in every style from the simple folk tune to the epic classical form and arrangement and has constantly borrowed from his contemporaries, dipping into jazz, reggae, disco, funk, and techno-pop as he desires. Although perfectly happy recording all by himself, he has also collaborated with the luminaries of his time, including Stevie Wonder, Michael Jackson, Elvis Costello, and Steve Miller. His "My Brave Face" (1989) is the closest an ex-Beatle has ever come to "She Loves You."

McCartney realized a long-held dream of becoming a classical composer with his *Paul McCartney's Liverpool Oratorio* (cowritten with London commercial composer Carl Davis, 1991), "Appaloosa" (an orchestral work played by the Boston Pops in 1992), "The Leaf" (a solo piano work written with the assistance of John Fraser and recorded by Anya Alexeyev in 1995), and *Standing Stone* (a symphonic poem introduced at the Royal Albert Hall in 1997 in celebration of the centennial of EMI), all more successful ventures than his screen-play dabbling for *Give My Regards to Broad Street* (1984).

McCartney expanded his music-publishing holdings in the 1970s with the purchase of rights to Buddy Holly's music, then of Frank Loesser and many Broadway companies that gave him ownership of *Guys and Dolls*, *Annie*, *Mame*, *Grease*, *Hello Dolly*, *A Chorus Line*, *La Cage Aux Folles*, plus many standards such as "Stormy Weather," "Sentimental Journey," and "Autumn Leaves" as well as his own "Love Me Do" and "P.S. I Love You." He and Ono bungled their hopes of acquiring Northern Songs when it was put up for sale in 1981 and 1985, finally losing to Michael Jackson (whom McCartney had once advised to invest in music publishing), who paid $47.5 million for ATV, Northern's umbrella.[5] Mc-Cartney, knighted in 1997, has supported many causes with his cash — for example, underwriting animal rights and environmental protection groups; leading a $7.5 million fund-raising drive in 1995 for a hospital near his Sussex estate; sponsoring the $20 million renovation of the Liverpool Institute (once McCartney's school), which was reopened in 1996 as the Liverpool Institute of the Performing Arts; and leading a benefit concert for volcano victims in Montserrat in September 1997. Paul and Linda McCartney continued to perform together in addition to parenting their three daughters and son until her death from breast cancer on April 17, 1998.

George Harrison

Harrison has remained the most private Beatle, dividing much of his time between horticulture at his Henley-on-Thames home, driving for sport in the blue million-dollar McLaren F1 seen in the "Real Love" video, and tropical sun-bathing in Pacific Isle retreats. Following his Bangladesh benefit concert of August 1971 (which raised $13.5 million from concert, record, and film proceeds), he has toured twice, playing fifty-five shows in 1974 (the "Dark Horse" tour of the United States) and 1991–92 (leading a band with Eric Clapton in Japan and London), but his most consistent artistic activity since 1978 has been film production, beginning with a huge payoff from a $5.5 million investment in *Monty Python's Life of Brian* and the formation of HandMade Films, which produced twenty-three films before Harrison sold the company in 1994. McCartney's 1997 resurgence aside, Harrison has had the most recent ex-Beatle success with his occasional group the Traveling Wilburys (formed in 1988), featuring Bob Dylan, Roy Orbison (until his December 1988 death), Jeff Lynne, and Tom Petty. Harrison has battled throat cancer since the summer of 1997.

Harrison has probably not produced a solo LP quite up to the level of his breakthrough statement, *All Things Must Pass*, although *Cloud Nine* is consistently listenable. His style is much narrower, much more idiosyncratic, than those of Lennon and McCartney; he has even resorted to obvious restatements of his Beatles successes, "Here Comes the Sun" in "Here Comes the Moon" (1979) and "Only a Northern Song" in "This Song" (1976). But the Beatles sound shows through more successfully and less self-consciously in "Fish on the Sand" and "This Is Love" (both 1987). The prayerful devotion that marks many of his efforts often has a preachy quality not noticed in Lennon's tracts. Harrison's American Top Ten hits:

"My Sweet Lord" (1970, #1 for four weeks)
"Give Me Love (Give Me Peace on Earth)" (1973, #1 for one week)
"Got My Mind Set on You" (1988, #1 for one week, the last Beatles chart-
   topper)
"All Those Years Ago" (1981, #2 for three weeks)
"What Is Life" (1971, #10)

All Things Must Pass (1970, #1 for seven weeks)
Living in the Material World (1973, #1 for five weeks)
The Concert for Bangla Desh (1972, #2 for six weeks)
The Traveling Wilburys, Vol. 1 (1988, #3 for one week)
Dark Horse (1974, #4)
Extra Texture (Read All about It) (1975, #8)
Cloud Nine (1987, #8)

Ringo Starr

Ringo retired from a film career (with acting parts in *Candy*, *The Magic Christian*, *Blindman*, *200 Motels*, *That'll Be the Day*, *Sextette*, and *Caveman*, and producing roles in *Born to Boogie*, *Son of Dracula*, and *Princess Daisy*) in 1981 when he married Barbara Bach, with whom he lives in Monaco, Hollywood, and London.[6] Ringo played one concert in 1976 and two in 1984 and led full-fledged summer-long "All-Starr" tours of the United States in 1989, 1992, 1995, and 1997. He became the first ex-Beatle to be the subject of a radio series when he narrated "Ringo's Yellow Submarine" for twenty-six weeks in 1983, and he also narrated fifty-two episodes of the children's television show "Thomas the Tank Engine and Friends" in 1984–85. His best solo records were substantially assisted by ex-mates George Harrison, in "It Don't Come Easy" (1971) and "Wrack My Brain" (1981), and John Lennon, in "I'm the Greatest" (1973). Ringo had several Top Ten hits in the early 1970s:

"Photograph" (1973, #1 for one week)   "Oh My My" (1974, #5)
"You're Sixteen" (1974, #1 for one week)   "Only You" (1975, #6)
"No No Song" (1975, #3 for one week)   "Back Off Boogaloo" (1972, #9)
"It Don't Come Easy" (1971, #4)

Ringo (1973, #2 for two weeks)
Goodnight Vienna (1974, #8)

George Martin

In comparison with the Beatles, their producer has had a less distinguished but still quite successful career. For his recording concern since 1965, AIR, he has overseen the construction and management of three world-class sound studios, situated in London's Oxford Circus, the West Indies island of Montserrat (destroyed by hurricane in 1989), and Lyndhurst (in the North London suburb of Hampstead, replacing the Oxford Circus location). Martin has produced records by America, Cheap Trick, the Mahavishnu Orchestra, Sea Train, Jeff Beck, the Paul Winter Consort, and (for four solo projects) Paul McCartney. Beset by a steady deterioration of hearing since 1978, Martin retired from record production in 1998.

The Beatles Anthology

The 1995–97 *Beatles Anthology* releases mark four important additions to the Beatles corpus: (1) the group's own video version of their history (many clips taken from their personal archives), (2) EMI's release of eight compact discs of audio recordings, largely EMI outtakes—some never before distributed even on bootlegs—appearing on three two-CD sets and two CD "maxi-singles" with four tracks each, (3) the first post-1969 recordings involving all four group members, and (4) a group-authorized book history edited by Brian Roylance (which was due to be launched by Pavilion Books in the United Kingdom with a run of 500,000 copies in September 1997 but has been indefinitely postponed).

The project began in 1970 with Neil Aspinall's wish to produce a film history of the group called *The Long and Winding Road*, which, as mentioned in a 1980 document of John Lennon's, was to include a performance by the reunited four. Hopes for production remained alive through the 1980s, especially following upon the competing 1982 release of *The Compleat Beatles*, but the project was stalled by business differences that were not resolved until 1989, particularly Apple's lawsuit against EMI. Paul McCartney and George Harrison then talked about reviving the project and perhaps doing some composing together, as revealed by the former in a July 27, 1989, press conference. Apple announced Geoff Wonfor as film director in 1991; the three surviving Beatles taped interviews for the video separately in 1992, with Jools Holland asking questions, and as a group on May 18–19, 1995, with Bob Smeaton prompting discussion.

In December 1993, George Martin announced that the video release would be accompanied by a six-CD set of EMI outtakes. With occasional help from the Beatles, Martin combed through some 400 hours of outtakes and other rare audio documents at EMI's Abbey Road Studios in 1995, and Geoff Emerick mixed *Anthology* candidates on a 1970-vintage EMI TG analog eight-track desk with a restored acoustic echo chamber, Fairchild limiters, and vintage ADT and STEED processes, for the most authentic 1960s Beatles sound possible in the context of 1990s engineering.[7]

The three ex-Beatles met in London in October 1993 to plan new recordings for the *Anthology*. Apple asked Yoko Ono if Lennon had left any solo recordings that would be appropriate for Beatles overdubs, and in January 1994 she presented McCartney with rough homemade demos of four unfinished Lennon composition drafts, "Free as a Bird," "Real Love," "Grow Old with Me," and "Now and Then." Work began immediately in Los Angeles, where producer Jeff Lynne had engineer Marc Mann clean up the dubs of Lennon's informal stereo cassettes with digital filters, remove Lennon's rubato with digital time edits, reorder occasional sections, transfer the signals to twenty-four-track analog tape, and add a click track.[8] The three, led by Lynne, laid new parts onto the tape at Mill Studio, on McCartney's 150-acre farm in East Sussex, devoting four days each to "Free as a Bird" (in February–March 1994) and "Real Love" (in February 1995).[9] Says Paul on the completion of his partner's demos: "We just imagined that John had gone on holiday and had said to us, 'Finish them up, lads—I trust you.'"[10] The Beatles and Lynne shared credit for producing the tracks, while Geoff Emerick engineered with the assistance of Jon Jacobs. In June 1994, the three ex-Beatles—sometimes called "the Threetles"—were filmed at Harrison's Friar Park Studios, performing oldies, including what they could recall of the ancient Lennon-McCartney collaboration "Thinking of Linking," with two acoustic guitars and brushes.

"Free as a Bird"

Lennon composed "Free as a Bird" around 1977, reportedly as an exhilarated reaction to obtaining his hard-won U.S. "green card," but perhaps also in reflection of his unshackling from all artistic duties through the expiration of his EMI contract. Three varying takes of his vocal/piano demo are known to exist; Take 1 is the basis of the Beatles master.[11] This draft includes all of the melody, harmony, rhythm, and voice leading for the song proper, but only partial lyrics for the bridge, beginning "Whatever happened to the life that we once knew" before trailing off into wordless vocalizations. McCartney and Harrison completed the text jointly, apparently referring in their lyrics to the life the group once knew in the 1950s and 1960s and the estrangement of the 1970s and 1980s.[12]

In their first studio work together in twenty-four years, McCartney and Harrison added acoustic guitar parts (one is heard on each channel) and Ringo a Ludwig drum part (with multiple microphones) to Lennon's ghostly vocal on the forty-eight-track working tape. Next came McCartney's Höfner bass and Harrison's bright arpeggiating Telecaster—like Model 'T' Hamburguitar, reminiscent of *Rubber Soul* in its cadential 4–3 suspensions, and his distorted "grunge" slide guitar introduction and solo.[13] McCartney doubled Lennon's console piano, which had been engulfed in noise as well as a neglect of smooth voice leading, with a grand, and then all three Beatles added new vocals, descant, and backing parts for the verse and new lead vocals for the bridges. The backing vocals recall "Because" over the guitar solo beginning at 1:30; to keep things moving, Harrison's second bridge vocal abbreviates McCartney's first.[14] A pervasive sustained organ completes the texture.

The song's tonal attributes recall a number of the Beatles' efforts of the 1960s, as does its instrumentation. The song's voice-leading structure is described in example 4.17a; all is Lennon's except for the added coda, which bears the modal $\flat$VI–$\flat$VII–I cadence from "P.S. I Love You" and "With a Little Help from My

Example 4.17a Analysis of "Free as a Bird."

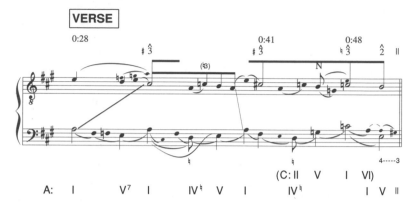

Friends" and is tacked on in the manner of "Hello Goodbye." The opening presents the chromatic descent in the bass from A to E introduced in "Lucy in the Sky with Diamonds" and carried through the White album, leading to minor-mode mixture on IV so important to the 1963–64 Beatles. Lennon's new twist is the rehearing of the D-minor chord, initially IV in A, as II of C, effectively like the turn from the A-major bridge to the C-major guitar solo in "Something." The surviving Beatles develop this potential by constructing a slide guitar solo in C (2:54–3:16), transposing the verse material for this *Abbey Road*–like A-versus-C fantasy. The solo returns to A via an altered deceptive cadence, ending V–VI♯ in C, a move borrowed from the "Something" coda, with "VI♯" (A) resuming its tonic status in the last verse and coda. While the upper voice as a whole is based on a 3̂–2̂–1̂ descent reflective of the song's interest in mode mixture, 5̂ characterizes the "bird" by floating freely above both the structural line and the battle between A and C, as an unobligated harmonic overtone of both areas.

Also new is Harrison's tacked-on ukelele performance, the final cadence of which is given in example 4.17b. Note the "Piggies"-like deflation caused by ending with a hackneyed cadence formula, Ger °3 [♭VI⁷]–V$^4_2$–I⁶, in a key unre-

Example 4.17b "Free as a Bird" (Lennon). © 1995 Lenono Music.

lated to the tonic. The ukelele puts the song's essential ♭VI chord, used to different ends in the verse, bridge, and coda, into a fourth, vaudevillian context emphasized by Lennon's verbal quotation of ukelele star George Formby's act-ending catch phrase, "Turned out nice again."[15] You didn't catch the phrase? Naturally, the Threetles reverse the recording so that it somehow resembles John Lennon speaking his own name.[16]

For the *Anthology* video series, Joe Pytka directed a video for "Free as a Bird" in October–November 1995 that makes use of a computer to integrate archival Beatles footage with new production, blending in a seamless flow some 80–100 visual references to the Beatles' works and lives, keeping the rec.music.beatles Internet newsgroup buzzing for weeks as the various "clues" were sifted out.[17] The video, shot continuously from a crane so as to simulate a bird's free per-spective, ends with a rear view of a ukelele vaudevillian playing to a packed the-ater. "Free as a Bird" was released as a single in the United Kingdom on De-cember 4, 1995 (reaching #2), and in the United States on December 12 (#6).

"Real Love"

Lennon distilled "Real Love" in 1979–80 from a brew of guitar and piano sketches that also produced sections of "Watching the Wheels" (Lennon and Ono 1980) and "I'm Stepping Out" (Lennon and Ono 1984). Some nine avail-able drafts of "Baby Make Love to You," "Real Life," "Real Love," and "Girls and Boys," as the evolving number was variously titled, were taped in the fall of 1980.[18] The "Real Love" chorus comes from perhaps the earliest of these demos (Lennon c. 1992a), a piano draft in C major that begins with the "I'm Stepping Out" verse ("Woke up this morning, blues around my head . . .") before moving into a gospel-flavored chorus ("Just got to let it go . . .") that was to be excised and included in "Watching the Wheels," and ending with the tune of the even-tual "Real Love" chorus but with the words "It's real life, it's real . . ." This in-carnation was a pessimistic song suggesting that in order to cope, one must shrug off the many unpleasant things that come with "real" life. This early ver-sion also contains an elaborate retransition based on a baroque sequence of ap-plied chords, progressing, two beats per chord, $V_\sharp^7/II–II–V_\sharp^7/III–III–V_\sharp^7/VI–VI–VI_2^4–IV$ to return to the verse's tonic, a passage that would not appear again. A second piano demo in C major (Lennon 1988c) completes the chorus, begin-ning once "Lonely to be afraid; it's just real life" and later "Why must we be alone; it's just real love." This version also introduces a section—"If it don't feel right, don't do it"—that would later form the bridge of "I'm Stepping Out."

The "Real Love" verse began life independently from the chorus, its melody

Example 4.18a "Real Love" compositional draft.

I   don't ex-pect you_   to_   un - der - stand

and chord progression in D having been discovered during piano/vocal work on "Baby Make Love to You" (Lennon 1996). There the tune supports the eventually unused text, "You told me you could do it too, have your cake and eat it too . . ." One D-major piano demo (Lennon c. 1992b) has no trace of the "Real Love" refrain but begins with the verse "All the little boys and girls livin' in this lonely world"; apparently the theme of loneliness led Lennon to eventually join the two separate sections. The verse ends with a rolling gospel-flavored codetta related to the "let it go" passage from previous demos that alternates I♭7 and IV7 chords, a motive that continues beneath a haranguing quote from "Isolation" (Lennon 1970), "I don't expect you to understand, now that the end is near at hand." This pessimistic gospel passage is excerpted in example 4.18a. All of these elements are joined with the "real life" chorus in Takes 4 and 6 (Lennon 1996 and *Imagine* 1988, respectively), a guitar piece that sounds in D♭ and ends in Take 6 with the curiously incomplete tag I–IIø7–V4–3.

The song underwent a wholesale transformation before Take 7 (Lennon 1996), the piano version that would be passed down to the Threetles. Now, a new parallel-minor introduction/interlude is foiled by a tone of optimism. All loneliness, referred to with the Fø7 chord, is put in the past; nothing that had occurred before matters, and Lennon's present love was preordained. This sentiment recalls "If I Fell," as does the text: "Oh I've been in love before, but in my heart I wanted more." There is no longer a place for the "I don't expect you" tirade, and "Real Love" looks to the future with definite plans in lyrics much further developed than those of "Free as a Bird." The group version takes advantage of the gospel-flavored verse piano codetta that is not present in the guitar takes. The Beatles' finished version speeds Lennon's demo up from D to E♭.[19]

McCartney says that the "Real Love" demo had a buzz that was cleansed and declicked in Los Angeles.[20] Returning to The Mill in February 1995, the Beatles composed a solo guitar passage and added Lennon's double-tracked vocal and piano to their own recording made on twenty-four-track tape. Harrison said, "We just dropped John's voice into the appropriate places," a procedure that led to an unfortunate alternation of clean and noisy sound textures.[21] The new recording consisted of Ringo's Ludwig drums, two acoustic six-string guitars (George's left and Paul's right), McCartney's grand piano, and both electric and double basses (the latter arco and most present in the third chorus, 2:50–2:58), the same Baldwin electric harpsichord once played by Martin on "Because," and the Abbey Road harmonium once played by Lennon on "We Can Work It Out" (both played here by their owner, Paul McCartney; the Baldwin is most audible during the introduction).[22] The arrangement also includes Ringo's

Example 4.18b Analysis of "Real Love."

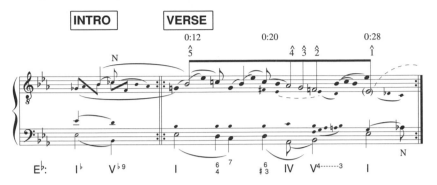

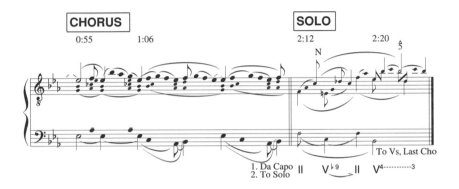

crotales and tambourine; Harrison's Hamburguitar, used for the distinctive fills (with two lines: lower, left, and upper, right) and the solo (2:12–2:25); Stratocaster slide for fills in the third chorus (at 2:47) and the coda; a "chick" rhythm guitar (heard right) and ukelele (center) for the coda; McCartney's descant vocal; and (at 2:02) Harrison's lower harmony vocal.

Example 4.18b exposes the structural voice leading of "Real Love." The keyboard introduction seems to symbolize Lennon's past "plans and schemes" with minor-mode mixture, making the major-mode forward-looking verse all the brighter. Referring to the $Bb^6_{\sharp 3}$ chord at 0:20, George recalls the music he and John heard on the radio in their youths: "He's got those augmented chords on there—which always featured in the old songs from the '20s, '30s, and '40s."[23] ("It's Only Love," from *Rubber Soul*, is a rare Lennon model with an augmented triad midway through the verse.) The verse structure traverses a $\hat{5}$-line, decorating the primary tone with its upper neighbor, now a whole step above as opposed to the half-step upper neighbor of the introduction. Because the repeated chorus ends the song, it must carry the final $\hat{1}$, decorated with its own upper neighbor, for the ending; but since it also leads back to other verses in previous hearings, Lennon elects to keep $\hat{5}$ in mind. The solo at 2:12 transposes the introduction's structure up from I♭ to a tonicized II, thus cleverly reassigning scale-degree functions to once-heard material. The solo combines the song's important neighbor motives by decorating the whole-step upper neighbor to $\hat{5}$ with its own half-step upper neighbor, emblematizing the change from past-related pessimism to future-based optimism, and then culminates in a high-register bent-note $\hat{6}$–$\hat{5}$ fantasy above a dramatic retransitional 4–3 suspension on V (at 2:20). The tonicization of II is particularly effective because it rectifies Lennon's material, which had contained F^{ø7} but not the Fm chord. "Real Love" (Beatles 1996d) was released on March 5, 1996, peaking in the United States at #11 and in the United Kingdom at #4.

Broadcast rights for the televised version of the video series, including first-run rights to "Free as a Bird," were bought by ABC-TV in the United States, by ITV in the United Kingdom, and by a hundred other networks worldwide by October 1995. In the United States, the program aired over six hours on November 19, 22, and 23, 1995, attracting an estimated 42 million viewers for the first installment; some 14.3 million saw the first hour in the United Kingdom. The ten-hour home video version (Beatles 1996c) was marketed by Turner Home Entertainment, released on September 5, 1996 (entering *Billboard*'s Top Music Videos chart at #1 despite its retail price of $159.95). The first pair of CDs, *The Beatles Anthology 1*, was released on November 21, 1995, the second, *Anthology 2*, on March 19, 1996, and the third on October 29, 1996.[24] Volume 1 shipped double platinum (200,000 additional copies pressed in a three-LP format) and, with 450,000 copies sold that day in the United States, outdid first-day sales of every other record in history; more than 1 million copies were sold in the United States in its first week, allowing the album to enter the chart at #1, where it remained for three weeks (in the United Kingdom, volume 1 debuted and peaked at #2 on the *BBC/Music Week* chart), and the album sold 10 million worldwide by the end of 1995. Volume 2 sold enough copies in its first week (442,000) to debut at #1 (in the United Kingdom, volume 2 debuted at #1, falling after one week in both markets) and selling 4.5 million through 1996. Volume 3 marked the first time in history that an artist achieved three consecutive debuts at #1 on the *Billboard* album chart. Following are the contents of the *Anthology* albums and maxi-singles; asterisks denote the respective first tracks of each side of the vinyl-format three-LP sets. The provenance of each track is in parentheses, and bracketed titles represent spoken-word recordings.

The Beatles Anthology 1

Disc One

*"Free as a Bird" (c. 1977; 2–3/94)
["We were four guys . . ."] (12/8/70)
"That'll Be the Day" (mid-1958)
"In Spite of All the Danger"
    (mid-1958)
["Sometimes I'd borrow . . ."] (11/3/94)
"Hallelujah, I Love Her So" (Spring '60)
"You'll Be Mine" (Spring '60)

Disc Two

*"She Loves You" (11/4/63)
"Till There Was You" (11/4/63)
"Twist and Shout" (11/4/63)
"This Boy" (12/2/63)
"I Want to Hold Your Hand"
    (12/2/63)
["Boys, what I was thinking . . ."]
    (12/2/63)

"Cayenne" (Spring '60)
["First of all . . ."] (10/27/62)
"My Bonnie" (6/22/61)
"Ain't She Sweet" (6/22/61)
"Cry for a Shadow" (6/22/61)
*["Brian was a beautiful guy"]
    (10/71)
["I secured them . . ."]
    (10/13/64)
"Searchin'" (1/1/62)
"Three Cool Cats" (1/1/62)
"The Sheik of Araby" (1/1/62)
"Like Dreamers Do" (1/1/62)
"Hello Little Girl" (1/1/62)
["Well, the recording test . . ."]
    (10/13/64)
"Besame Mucho" (6/6/62)
"Love Me Do" (6/6/62)
"How Do You Do It" (9/4/62)
"Please Please Me" (9/11/62)
*"The One after 909" (from Takes
    3–5; 3/5/63)
"Lend Me Your Comb" (7/2/63)
"I'll Get You" (10/13/63)
["We were performers . . ."]
    (12/8/70)
"I Saw Her Standing There"
    (10/24/63)
"From Me to You" (10/24/63)
"Money (That's What I Want)"
    (10/24/63)
"You Really Got a Hold On Me"
    (10/24/63)
"Roll Over Beethoven" (10/24/63)

"Moonlight Bay" (12/2/63)
"Can't Buy Me Love" (from Takes
    1–2; 1/29/64)
*"All My Loving" (2/9/64)
"You Can't Do That" (Take 6;
    2/25/64)
"And I Love Her" (Take 2; 2/25/64)
"A Hard Day's Night" (Take 1;
    4/16/64)
"I Wanna Be Your Man" (4/19/64)
"Long Tall Sally" (4/19/64)
"Boys" (4/19/64)
"Shout" (4/19/64)
"I'll Be Back" (Takes 2–3; 6/1/64)
*"You Know What to Do" (6/3/64)
"No Reply" (demo; 6/3/64)
"Mr Moonlight" (from Takes 1, 4;
    8/14/64)
"Leave My Kitten Alone" (Take 5;
    8/14/64)
"No Reply" (Take 2; 9/30/64)
"Eight Days a Week" (from Takes 1,
    2, 4, 5; 10/6/64)
"Kansas City"/"Hey, Hey, Hey, Hey!"
    Take 2; 10/18/64)

Free as a Bird

"Free as a Bird" (c. 1977; 2–3/94)
"I Saw Her Standing There" (Take 9; 2/11/63)
"This Boy" (from Takes 12–13; 10/17/63)
"Christmas Time (Is Here Again)" (edit of '66 and '67 fan club discs; 12/6/66,
    11/28/67)

The Beatles Anthology 2

Disc One

*"Real Love" (c. 1979; 2/95)
"Yes It Is" (from Takes 2, 14; 2/16/65)
"I'm Down" (Take 1; 6/14/65)
"You've Got to Hide Your Love Away"
    (from Takes 1, 2, 5; 2/18/65)
"If You've Got Trouble" (2/18/65)

Disc Two

*"Strawberry Fields Forever" ,(demos
    Takes 1, 7, edit piece; 11/66,
    12/9/66)
"Penny Lane" (remix of master;
    12/66–1/67)

"That Means a Lot" (Take 1; 2/20/65)
"Yesterday" (Take 1; 6/14/65)
"It's Only Love" (from Takes 2–3;
  6/15/65)
*"I Feel Fine" (8/1/65)
"Ticket to Ride" (8/1/65)
"Yesterday" (8/1/65)
"Help!" (8/1/65)
"Everybody's Trying to Be My Baby"
  (8/15/65)
"Norwegian Wood (This Bird Has
  Flown)" (Take 1; 10/12/65)
"I'm Looking Through You"
  (10/24/65)
"12-Bar Original" (from Take 2;
  11/4/65)
*"Tomorrow Never Knows"
  (Take 1; 4/6/66)
"Got to Get You into My Life" (Take 5;
  4/7/66)
"And Your Bird Can Sing" (Take 2;
  4/20/66)
"Taxman" (Take 11; 4/21/66)
"Eleanor Rigby" (Take 14; 4/28/66)
"I'm Only Sleeping" (from rehearsal
  and Take 1; 4/29/66)
"Rock and Roll Music" (6/30/66)
"She's a Woman" (6/30/66)

"A Day in the Life" (from Takes 1, 2,
  6; 1–2/67)
"Good Morning Good Morning"
  (Take 8; 2/8, 2/16/67)
"Only a Northern Song" (from Takes
  3, 12; 2/13–14, 4/20/67)
*"Being for the Benefit of Mr. Kite"
  (Takes 1, 2, 7; 2/17, 2/20/67)
"Lucy in the Sky with Diamonds"
  (from Takes 6–8; 3/1–2/67)
"Within You Without You" (remix
  of master; 3–4/67)
"Sgt. Pepper's Lonely Hearts Club
  Band (Reprise)" (Take 5; 4/1/67)
"You Know My Name (Look Up
  the Number)" (edit of various
  mixes; 5–6/67–4/69)
*"I Am the Walrus" (Take 16;
  9/5/67)
"The Fool on the Hill" (demo; 9/6/67)
"Your Mother Should Know"
  (Take 27; 9/16/67)
"The Fool on the Hill" (Take 4;
  9/25/67)
"Hello Goodbye" (Take 16; 10/2,
  10/19/67)
"Lady Madonna" (from Takes 3, 4;
  2/3, 2/6/68)
"Across the Universe" (Take 2;
  2/3/68)

Real Love

"Real Love" (c. 1979; 2/95)
"Baby's in Black" (8/29–30/65)
"Yellow Submarine" (new mix of master; 5/26/66, 6/1/66)
"Here, There and Everywhere" (from Takes 7, 13; 6/16/66)

The Beatles Anthology 3

Disc One

*"A Beginning" (7/22/68)
"Happiness Is a Warm Gun"
  (Kinfauns)
"Helter Skelter" (Take 2, 7/18/68)
"Mean Mr Mustard" (Kinfauns)
"Polythene Pam" (Kinfauns)
"Glass Onion" (Kinfauns)
"Junk" (Kinfauns)
"Piggies" (Kinfauns)

Disc Two

*"I've Got a Feeling" (S/S 23.36;
  1/23/69)
"She Came In through the Bathroom
  Window" (S/S 22.60; 1/22/69)
"Dig a Pony" (no S/S entry ; 1/22/69)
"Two of Us" (no S/S entry; 1/22/69)
"For You Blue" (no S/S entry ;
  1/25/69)
"Teddy Boy" (S/S 24.22; 1/69)

"Honey Pie" (Kinfauns)
"Don't Pass Me By" (from Takes 3, 5; 6/5–6/68)
"Ob-La-Di, Ob-La-Da" (7/3–5/68)
"Good Night" (from 6/28/68 rehearsal and 7/22/68 master)
*"Cry Baby Cry" (Take 1, 7/16/68)
"Blackbird" (Take 4, 6/11/68)
"Sexy Sadie" (Take 6, 7/19/68)
"While My Guitar Gently Weeps" (demo;7/25/68)
"Hey Jude" (rehearsal, 7/29/68)
"Not Guilty" (Take 102, 8/8–12/68)
"Mother Nature's Son" (Take 2, 8/9/68)
*"Glass Onion" (Take 33, 9/11–26/68)
"Rocky Raccoon" (Take 8, 8/15/68)
"What's the New Mary Jane" (Take 4; 8/14/68)
"Step inside Love"/"Los Paranoias" (from Take 35 of "I Will"; 9/16/68)
"I'm So Tired" (from Takes 3, 6, 9, 10/8/68)
"I Will" (Take 1; 9/16/68)
"Why Don't We Do It in the Road" (Take 4, 10/9/68)
"Julia" (Take 2, 10/13/68)

"Rip It Up"/"Shake, Rattle and Roll" /"Blue Suede Shoes" (S/S 26.28, 26.29, 26.31; 1/26/69)
*"The Long and Winding Road" (S/S 31.20; 1/26/69)
"Oh! Darling" (S/S 27.1; 1/27/69)
"All Things Must Pass" (demo; 2/25/69)
"Mailman, Bring Me No More Blues" (S/S 29.11; 1/29/69)
"Get Back" (S/S 30.13; 1/30/69)
"Old Brown Shoe" (demo; 2/25/69)
"Octopus's Garden" (from Takes 2, 8; 4/26/69)
"Maxwell's Silver Hammer" (Take 5, 7/9/69)
*"Something" (demo, 2/25/69)
"Come Together" (Take 1, 7/21/69)
"Come and Get It" (demo, 7/24/69)
"Ain't She Sweet" (7/24/69)
"Because" (SI to Take 16; 8/1, 8/4/69)
"Let It Be" (no S/S entry; 1/25/69)
"I Me Mine" (Take 16, 1/3/70)
"The End" (remix of Take 7; 7/23–8/18/69)
Final chord from "A Day in the Life" (Edit Piece Take 9, 2/22/67)

The musical and social impact of the Beatles has often been tied to their times; Lennon himself said, "Whatever wind was blowing at the time moved the Beatles, too. I'm not saying we weren't flags on the top of a ship; but the whole boat was moving. Maybe the Beatles were in the crow's-nest, shouting, 'Land ho,' or something like that, but we were all in the same damn boat."[25] In this age of marketing and profit, as opposed to peace and love, it remains to be seen what priorities motivate the Beatles' generation to make the resuscitated 1960s group part of their lives again in the 1990s; is it nostalgia for youth and rosier times? midlife crisis? the intrinsic value of the music? effective hype from EMI/Capitol? the long-reclusive nature of the members and their reluctance to regroup? crossover potential from Adult Contemporary radio to pop? While the *Anthology* realizes a twenty-five-year-old plan and closes a very long chapter in the Beatles' history, it also inspires a very strong sense that the Beatles are beginning anew. In fact, rumors circulate at this writing about upcoming television interviews, online Q&A sessions, and, as always, recording projects. As it has done since 1964, for whatever reason, the world waits for news of the next Beatles project.

APPENDIX A

Instruments Played by the Late-Period Beatles

Guitars and Electric Basses

Fender Bass VI   Fender marketed a six-string bass perfect for Lennon and Harrison, as it was tuned an octave lower than their usual guitars. Either would play a bass line with this instrument on the basic track for a McCartney number when the composer was occupied elsewhere, or might even overdub with it. Such is the case with four songs on the White album: "Rocky Raccoon," "Back in the U.S.S.R.," "Birthday," and "Honey Pie." John and George both used it during the January 1969 "Get Back" sessions while Paul played piano, and George played it on two July 1969 basic tracks for *Abbey Road*: "Maxwell's Silver Hammer" and "Carry That Weight."

The instrument has a single, gently sloping cutaway and a sunburst finish. Three Strat-like pickups were controlled by three on/off switches, a fourth "strangle" switch, and master volume and tone knobs, and the tone could be further altered with a Jaguar-style tremolo. The 30"-scale bound rosewood fingerboard is marked with block inlays.

Fender Esquire   The Fender Esquire heard on the title track of *Sgt. Pepper* is similar to the Telecaster but possesses only a single pickup with staggered poles. The ash body has a single cutaway—McCartney plays a right-handed model, restrung for a left-hander, so his cutaway is on the treble side—and the pickguard is laminated; the Custom model has bound top and back and a sunburst finish. All twenty-one frets are clear of the cutaway, and dot inlays are seen on the 1st,

3rd, 5th, 7th, 9th, 12th, 15th, 17th, 19th, and 21st frets, with a pair of dots at the octave. Two dome knobs control the simple electronics. Bruce Springsteen plays the Esquire.

Fender Jazz Bass   The Jazz Bass, with more snap to its articulation than the Beatles' other basses, is heard in five White album tracks. In August and September 1968, Paul plays a left-hander's Jazz Bass in "Yer Blues," "While My Guitar Gently Weeps," and "Glass Onion," and a right-hander's Jazz Bass is used by George in "Back in the U.S.S.R." and by John in "Helter Skelter." McCartney uses the instrument again in 1969 for "Old Brown Shoe" and "Sun King/Mean Mr Mustard." The body has a three-color sunburst finish, and the two pickups are controlled by a pair of volume knobs and a single tone knob. The bound, curved rosewood fingerboard, 34" scale, has block inlays.

Fender Stratocaster   The 1964 (pre-CBS) Strat had a solid body with an asymmetrical double-cutaway and rounded body edges; John's and George's model, first used in February 1965, was either Sonic blue or Daphne blue, with a nitrocellulose finish. The jack was angled into the top, which had a three-layer (white-black-white) celluloid pickguard with eleven screws, three pickups with white plastic covers, and three white plastic knobs. The thin peghead had a butterfly clip and topped an unbound fingerboard with dot inlays for the 3rd, 5th, 7th, 9th, 12th, 15th, 17th, 19th, and 21st frets. Harrison says, "I set up this Strat . . . for slide play before we did 'Nowhere Man.' In the late 60s I painted it psychedelic—it was the one I used for the '67 satellite thing for 'All You Need Is Love' and also on 'I Am the Walrus' on *Magical Mystery Tour*" (White 1990, 147; see also D. Forte 1987a, 86, and 1987b, 93–94). Harrison did extensive later slide work with this guitar, and he is seen playing it with Joe Cocker, Gary Wright, and others.

Fender Telecaster   In mid-1968, Fender gave Harrison and Lennon matching custom-made rosewood Telecasters, instruments perhaps associated most closely with countless C&W artists. The single-cutaway body is unbound, with a black laminated pickguard. Electronics are simple, with single-coil pickups at the bridge and neck controlled by two dome knobs and a three-way selector switch. The twenty-one frets are marked with dot inlays on the 3rd, 5th, 7th, 9th, 12th (double dots), 15th, 17th, 19th, and 21st frets.

Gibson Epiphone Casino   The 1964 Casino was a fully hollow sixteen-inch-wide thinbody with a 24 ¾" scale, rounded double cutaways, single-bound top and back, white three-ply pickguard, and sunburst finish. The single-bound fingerboard had twenty-two frets (sixteen clear of the body) and single parallelogram inlays on the 3rd, 5th, 7th, 9th, 12th, 15th, 17th, 19th, and 21st frets. The guitar was fitted with two Gibson P-90 single-coil pickups with poles across the center of chrome covers with triangular ears. The Tune-o-matic bridge and trapeze tailpiece were standard (lacking vibrato), as on Lennon's model; Harrison and McCartney both had right-handers' Bigsby units. In 1967, Lennon spray-painted the back and neck of his guitar, and all three Casinos lost their pickguards. Harrison and Lennon scraped the varnish from their instruments in mid-1968, leaving a breathing, bare, natural blond wood; according to Harrison, "they became much better guitars" (D. Forte 1987a, 88). McCartney's guitar was used in sessions from *Help!* through *Sgt. Pepper*, as well as in his solo career; Harrison and Lennon used theirs in the 1964–65 Christmas shows and on the 1966 tours; Lennon used hardly any other guitar in 1968–69.

Gibson Epiphone FT 79   The "Texan," a favorite C&W guitar, was McCartney's principal acoustic guitar until he acquired a Martin in 1967. The sixteen-inch-wide instrument had a round-shouldered dreadnought shape with mahogany back and sides and a spruce top with natural finish. The peghead had plastic tuner buttons and a vertical oval inlay; the rosewood fingerboard had single parallelogram inlays on only the 3rd, 5th, 7th, 9th, 12th, and 15th frets; fourteen cleared the body.

Gibson J-160E   The "Jumbo" (Model J-160E) is a sixteen-inch-wide, round-shouldered, dreadnought-shaped flattop guitar with a single-coil adjustable pole pickup at the fingerboard end of the soundhole and two knobs (for volume and tone) on the lower treble bout. The bridge has an upper belly, an adjustable saddle, and two inlaid dots. The laminated spruce top has a sunburst finish, the back and sides are of mahogany, and both top and back are bound in plastic. The bound rosewood fingerboard has fifteen frets clear of the body and trapezoid inlays on the 1st, 3rd, 5th, 7th, 9th, 12th, 15th, and 17th frets. The peghead has a "crown" inlay, and a small tortoise-shell pickguard follows the body-edge contour. The Jumbos, a pair of which were purchased for the fall 1962 EMI sessions, are heard in most early Beatles recordings; sometimes the only sound heard from them would be Lennon's strumming as it leaked onto his vocal microphone. Lennon would have to replace his original Jumbo, which was stolen during the Beatles' 1963–64 Christmas show. In 1965–67 photographs of both his and Harrison's Jumbos, the pickup has been moved to the bridge side of the soundhole; this is Lennon's guitar heard in "A Day in the Life." Regarding the use of both Jumbos during their first September 1962 recording session, see Shepherd 1964a, 9.

Gibson J-200   The seventeen-inch-wide, sunburst-finish jumbo-shape J-200 is Harrison's acoustic guitar for the White album and is featured most prominently in "While My Guitar Gently Weeps." It is distinguished by the engraved flower motif on its pickguard and its large moustache-shaped ebony bridge with pearl inlays. Top and maple back are multiply bound; single bindings protect the ebony fingerboard (with pointed end) and peghead (with crown inlay). The fingerboard has twenty frets, fourteen clear of the body, with crown inlays on the 1st, 3rd, 5th, 7th, 9th, 12th, 15th, and 17th frets.

Gibson Les Paul Deluxe   The Les Paul heard on four White album tracks has a small but heavy single-cutaway four-piece maple-and-mahogany body with bound carved top, cherry finish, and white pickguard. There is no vibrato bar, and two Mini-humbucking pickups—controlled by a switch on the upper bass bout and four clear bonnet knobs on the lower treble bout—are less responsive to treble than Harrison's other instruments are. Twenty-two frets, sixteen clear of the body, are all readily accessed. Pearloid trapezoid inlays mark the 3rd, 5th, 7th, 9th, 12th, 15th, 17th, 19th, and 21st frets on a bound rosewood fingerboard. Strings are anchored by a stud tailpiece behind a Tune-o-matic bridge.

Gibson SG   The SG Standard used by Harrison from 1966 is a solid-body instrument with beveled body edges, double cutaway with pointed horns pointing back into the neck, and cherry finish, made in 1963–66. The single-bound rosewood fingerboard (24¾ "scale) has pearloid trapezoid inlays on the 3rd, 5th, 7th, 9th, 12th, 15th, 17th, 19th, 21st, and 22nd frets, all clear of the body; the headstock carries a pearl logo. Electronics include two humbucking pickups with nickel-plated covers, controlled by four knobs and a switch. The Maestro vibrato arm, with lyre-and-logo cover, has been removed by the making of the "Paperback Writer" videos but is seen restored c. 1968.

Gretsch Nashville   The Gretsch Model 6120 double-bound hollowbody was sixteen inches wide and 2 ¼ inches deep, with double-rounded cutaway, painted f-holes, Chet Atkins's signature on the pickguard, and an "amber red" (orange) finish. The bound rosewood fingerboard (24¾ " scale) had a zero fret plus twenty-two frets, eighteen clear of the body, with thumbprint inlays on 1st, 3rd, 5th, 7th, 9th, 12th, 15th, and 17th. The bound peghead had a Gretsch nameplate and "Longhorn" inlay. Electronics featured two Filter 'Tron pickups, two knobs and switch on lower treble bout, knob on upper treble bout, two mute switches on upper bass bout, straight-bar bridge, and a Bigsby unit. Metal parts other than the nut and vibrato were gold-plated. The C&W instrument was played some by Brian Jones of the Rolling Stones before Lennon brought his copy to the studio in the spring of 1966.

Hamburguitar Model 'T'   As seen in the "Real Love" video, Harrison adopted a dark green burl-top Hamburguitar Model 'T' as a Telecaster copy in the 1990s. The single-cutaway instument, handmade by Detroiter Bernie Hamburger, has a mahogany body with white binding, maple neck, ebony fingerboard with twenty-two frets dotted in the Telecaster pattern, and two Seymour Duncan pickups.

Höfner 500/1 Bass   While this lightweight bass and its like replacements were relieved in most Beatles recordings by a Rickenbacker instrument beginning in late 1965, the "violin" bass (actually shaped like a bass viol) made and purchased in early 1961 is the instrument most closely associated with Beatle Paul. With a 30" scale and an unbound peghead with vertical logo, the rosewood fingerboard had twenty-two frets (featuring the usual Höfner "zero fret"), with dots inlaid on the 3rd, 5th, 7th, 9th, 12th, 15th, 17th, and 19th frets (with the octave marked by a pair). Sides and back were of maple, and the double-bound, warm-toned laminated spruce top featured a pearloid pickguard with strings attached to a trapeze tailpiece. Two double-pole, double-coil Nova Sonic pick-ups (with metal diamond-stamped covers concealing the poles) were fitted at neck and middle positions; electronics were controlled with two knobs and three flick switches (rhythm/solo, bass on, treble on). In October 1963, when electrician's tape could no longer hold its neck pickup in place, this instrument was replaced by a revised 1962-model 500/1 (with horizontal logo and new pickup configuration) for the London Palladium performance; this is the Höfner bass used to the present day. The original bass was redone with new pickup parts, potentiometers, and a three-color sunburst finish and retained as a backup instrument; Selmer presented McCartney with a third Höfner 500/1 (with gold-plated parts and bound neck) in the spring of 1964; this instrument now circulates on the collector's market.

Martin D-28   The guitars heard in "Flying" are likely the new Martin D-28s purchased by Harrison, McCartney, and Lennon for the Indian retreat, which was planned for the autumn of 1967 until both the death of Epstein and the continuation of the work on "Magical Mystery Tour" set the Beatles back. This instrument is an unadorned (save ivoroid binding and a checkered back stripe) and dreadnought-shaped acoustic, with spruce top (nitrocellulose finish, belly bridge, and plastic pickguard), its back and sides of Brazilian rosewood. It measures 15⅝" wide and 20" long. Fourteen of a total twenty frets are clear of the body, with single dot inlays on the 5th, 9th, 15th, and 17th frets and double inlays on the 7th and 12th.

Rickenbacker 360-12   Harrison's Ricky twelve-string was a full-scale thinbody instrument with a double pointed cutaway and Fireglo finish (red to yellow); all twenty-one frets were clear of the body. The flat-plate tailpiece was angled lower left to upper right and had no vibrato unit. Two chrome-bar pickups, at the neck and the bridge, were wired for stereo but not used in this manner; controls included five knobs (sectioned into eighths) and a pickup switch. The trim was deluxe, with triangular crushed pearl sparkle inlays on the 3rd, 5th, 7th, 9th, 12th, 15th, 17th, and 19th frets; white plastic split-level pickguard; double-bound top, back, and fingerboard; and bound slash holes. Harrison was given a second copy during an August 1965 press conference in Los Angeles; this instrument had a rounded top edge, no binding, and an opposite-oriented "R" tailpiece. Photographs also show Lennon with his own 360-12 in 1964, but he is not known to have performed with it.

Rickenbacker 4001S Bass   In 1965, McCartney took up the solid body Ricken-backer bass with cresting wave body and peghead shape, cut for a left-hander, with no binding, a Fireglo finish, and a one-piece pickguard. The rosewood fingerboard had dot inlays on the 3rd, 5th, 7th, 9th, 12th, 15th, and 17th frets (with two dots at the octave); nineteen frets were clear of the body, and all twenty were clear of the treble cutaway. There was a bar pickup at the neck and a heavy horseshoe pickup at the bridge; volume and tone were controlled with four knobs and a switch. Like Harrison's Strat and Lennon's Casino, this bass acquired a new coat of paint in 1967 (red, white, and gray), which was sanded away for a natural finish a few years later; the horseshoe magnet also disappeared during the Wings years.

Rickenbacker Capri   This was a three-quarter-size Capri Model 325 made in 1959, originally with a natural "Hi-Lustre Blond" finish, a hollow thinbody instrument with no soundholes, featuring a double-cutaway with pointed horns, both cut to the highest (21st) fret. The guitar had standard trim with no binding and the standard Rickenbacker recess at the tailpiece; dot inlays marked the 5th, 7th, 9th, 12th, and 15th frets. This instrument had a single-level gold Lucite pickguard, three chrome bar pickups, a Kauffman vibrato with roller bridges, and four diamond-shaped knobs. The guitar went through makeovers in the summer of 1961 and in September 1962 and is best known with the Bigsby tailpiece/vibrato unit it received in 1961 and with the black finish it was given in 1962. In honor of the Beatles' first appearance in America (February 1964), the Rickenbacker company presented Lennon with a replacement copy that finally retired this well-used original.

Keyboards

Hammond B-3   EMI's B-3 in Studio Two was mounted on wheels, its pedalboard detached. Its two keyboards were each of five octaves, and its tone was controlled by about twenty-five drawbars and four effect stops. It is heard in Beatles recordings as early as 1963, played by George Martin, Mal Evans, Billy Preston, and several Beatles. Its Leslie speaker was adapted by John Lennon for his voice in 1966, and by George Harrison for his guitar in 1966–69.

Mellotron   In 1963 and afterward, Lennon expressed interest in a guitar that could sound like an organ, so it was natural for him to be an early (November 1965) owner of the Bradley Brothers Mellotron (see Coleman 1992, 331, and Lewisohn 1988, 87). This instrument, with its two side-by-side keyboards — each of three octaves — that calls forth flutes, brass, or strings from 1,260 tracks on banks of magnetic tapes, also offering chord buttons, rhythm presets, and a pitch-bend knob, at a price of £975 (comparable contemporaneous keyboard prices: Selmer Pianotron, £71; Hohner Planet, £115; Philips Philicordia, £185; Farfisa Compact, £209; Lowrey models, £273-£1,049; see *Melody Maker*, February 27, 1965, p. 15).

This was the instrument, with flute stop, that McCartney wished to play on the "Strawberry Fields Forever" basic tracks on November 24, 1966. After "Strawberry Fields," the Mellotron is most closely identified with Mike Pinder of the Moody Blues (1966+) — probably the first rock group to record with it, for their fall 1966 single, "Love and Beauty"— but it was also adopted by the Rolling Stones (1967, especially as added by John Paul Jones), Jimi Hendrix,

Pink Floyd, the Bonzo Dog Doo Dah Band (all 1968), King Crimson (1969), Yes, and Led Zeppelin (both 1970).

Moog IIIP   Considering the Beatles' great interest in electronic keyboards, the Moog was a natural for them. Each Moog module, itself equipped with potentiometers and/or switches to regulate its effect, is capable of altering an incoming voltage. The resulting controlled voltage can then be applied by a patch cord to another module, controlling the effect of that oscillator, filter, or amplifier on a second incoming signal (along either linear or exponential scales). Thus, an oscillator might generate, from the incoming power supply, one of several basic periodic waveforms: a single frequency (ranging from 100 to 15,000 Hz) approaching a pure sine wave, or a preset combination of harmonic partials above a fundamental frequency producing various timbres, such as the flutelike triangle wave, the clarinetlike square wave, or the buzzlike sawtooth wave, or combinations of nonharmonic frequencies, as with random noise generators.

A "patch," a combination of cords, might determine that one of several filters, such as a low-pass filter (which produces a controllable reduction of partials above a dial-regulated or voltage-controlled frequency) or a band-pass filter (which allows the portion of a signal between two preset frequencies to pass unaltered while upper and lower frequencies are progressively filtered) might be applied to the output of an oscillator, the result of which is fed to an amplifier. The voltages of either the filter or the amplifier might be controlled in turn by an ADSR envelope generator, which would control the speed and intensity of a tone's attack, decay, sustain, and release. Other modules may have special effects, such as reverberation or regeneration; the latter is the resonant emphasis of a particular frequency. The IIIP model has two five-octave monophonic keyboards with portamento control, a ribbon controller, and various modules including ten voltage-controlled oscillators, a white noise generator, three ADSR envelope generators, voltage-controlled low-pass, high pass, and band-pass filters, three voltage-controlled amplifiers, a spring reverberation unit, and a four-channel mixer; these components are all visible in August 1969 photographs of Harrison's Moog.

Vox Continental   Through 1966, the Beatles toured with the Continental, a lightweight four-octave ($C-c^3$) single-manual keyboard with white-on-black keys, played through a 100-watt Vox amplifier. This was the model used by Manfred Mann; electric organs were also popularized in the United Kingdom by Alan Price of the Animals, Steve Winwood of the Spencer Davis Group, and Rod Argent of the Zombies.

Drums

Ludwig "Super Classic" Set   In June 1963, Ringo replaced his Premier kit with a black oyster Ludwig "Super Classic" kit with a 14" × 22" bass drum (a smaller one, at 20", was part of the two Ludwig Downbeat kits used for touring and so is visible in most photographs taken outside the studio), an all-metal 5" × 16" snare, and 16" × 16" and 9" × 13" tom-toms. He used a Clear Tone cowbell, a thin 18" crash cymbal, a medium 20" ride cymbal with rivets, and 15" hi-hats (originally Paiste Formula 602, but later Zildjian, cymbals) (Hayes 1968, 14; Clayson 1992, 81, 274 nn. 45, 46).

APPENDIX B

Musical Friends of the Late-Period Beatles

The Bonzo Dog Band   Led at the piano by future Monty Python composer Neil Innes and featuring singer Viv Stanshall and "Legs" Larry Smith on drums, the Bonzos were formed as a seven-piece 1920s-style dance band/comedy revue in 1965 and came to McCartney's attention via his brother Mike (Sharp 1988, 18). Mike McCartney's group, the Scaffold, and the Bonzos toured together in 1969, just before both bands split. In 1968, Paul was to produce "I'm the Urban Spaceman" for the Bonzos. Smith was featured on Harrison 1975, and Harrison produced Innes's "Lumberjack Song" for Python in 1975. Neil Innes was the brain behind the Rutles and their "All You Need Is Cash," a brilliant 1978 parody of the Beatles story made for NBC-TV (see Covach 1990).

Eric Clapton   Eric Clapton (b. 1945, Surrey) is one of the world's reigning guitarists. His technique and style are discussed briefly in chapter 2. Eric met the Beatles while a Yardbird in 1964; after that, they saw each other often in clubs and through mutual NEMS management. Collaborations began in 1968 when Clapton played on Harrison's *Wonderwall* (as "Eddie Clayton"), Lomax's "Sour Milk Sea," and "While My Guitar Gently Weeps." Clapton and Harrison together wrote "Badge," which was recorded by Cream with Harrison (as "L'Angelo Misterioso") in October 1968, and Clapton figures in the creation of Harrison's "Savoy Truffle" (1968) and "Here Comes the Sun" (1969).

   "Badge" would have worked well on the White album or on *Abbey Road*. With one line from Ringo, Harrison wrote most of the verse lyrics, and Clapton wrote most of the music—the verse moves simply Am–Dm–E^7—and the words for the bridge. On Cream's recording, Harrison plays rhythm guitar and Clapton the two solo parts, including the Leslied part that enters in the bridge, arpeggiating the chords of the many-times-repeated C–G–D double-plagal cadence in a prediction of Harrison's work on *Abbey Road* (Forte 1987b, 92).

Solo Beatle projects often involved Clapton. He worked with Lennon on the "Rock 'n' Roll Circus" project (1968), the "Cold Turkey" single, and the *Live Peace in Toronto* concert/LP (both 1969); with McCartney on *Back to the Egg* (1979); and with Starr in *The London Howlin' Wolf Sessions* (1971), *Ringo's Rotogravure* (1976), and *Stop and Smell the Roses* (1981). But his working relationship with Harrison has always been very close. They have played together on the Delaney & Bonnie and Friends tour/LP (1969); on Harrison's LPs *All Things Must Pass* (1970), *The Concert for Bangla Desh* (1971), *Cloud Nine* (1987), and *Live in Japan* (1991); on Harrison-produced LPs by Jackie Lomax (1968–69) and Doris Troy (1970); and as mutual sidemen on LPs by Leon Russell (1970), Ashton, Gardner and Dyke (1970), and Bobby Keys (1972). In 1979, Clapton married Harrison's ex-wife Pattie; the wedding celebration was the occasion for an impromptu jam with Harrison, Starr, McCartney, and Clapton.

Bob Dylan   With his roots in the blues of Jesse Fuller and Leadbelly and the folk songs of Woody Guthrie, Ramblin' Jack Elliott, and Pete Seeger, Dylan embodied folk protest of the early 1960s in his topical second and third LPs (*Freewheelin' Bob Dylan* [May 1963] and *The Times They Are A-Changin'* [January 1964]). Along with expressions of other social concerns, these records made poignant appeals for civil rights ("Oxford Town," "Only a Pawn in Their Game") and international peace ("Blowin' in the Wind," "Masters of War," "A Hard Rain's A-Gonna Fall," and "With God on Our Side"). Both of these topics were to appear in Beatles songs in subsequent years.

The Beatles became Dylan fans in January 1964—Lennon even took to wearing a Dylan-styled cap that month. "Guitar Blues," improvised in a New York hotel room in February, features Harrison with a guitar, singing a parody of Dylan's talking blues style (Beatles 1990a; compare with Dylan's "Talkin' World War III Blues" [1963], and hear also the Beatles discussing Dylan in 1964 on Beatles 1986c and 1992a). Lennon credits Dylan directly with raising the value of his song lyrics: "I think it was Dylan helped me realize that—not by any discussion or anything but just by hearing his work—I had a sort of professional songwriter's attitude to writing pop songs; [we] would turn out a certain style of song for a single and we would do a certain style of thing for this. . . . But to express myself I would write . . . *In His Own Write*, the personal stories which were expressive of my personal emotions. I'd have a separate songwriting John Lennon who wrote songs for the sort of meat market, and I didn't consider them—the lyrics or anything—to have any depth at all. They were just a joke. Then I started being me about the songs, not writing them objectively, but subjectively" (Wenner 1971, 124–26). With little precedent, "I'm a Loser" was Lennon's watershed.

The Beatles met Dylan in New York on August 28, at which time he introduced them to marijuana. Specific Beatles references to Dylan include the use of his photograph on the cover of *Sgt. Pepper*, Lennon's mentions of "Dylan's

Mr. Jones" in "Yer Blues," and "as they kill with God on their side" in "The Luck of the Irish." The Beatles used several Dylan songs for warm-ups in January 1969: "All along the Watchtower," "Blowin' in the Wind," "I Shall Be Released," "I Threw It All Away," and "Momma, You're Just on My Mind." At Dylan's New York home in 1970, Dylan and Harrison cowrote "I'd Have You Anytime" and "When Everybody Comes to Town"; Dylan's "If Not for You" was recorded by Harrison in 1970, and Dylan appeared in Harrison's August 1971 New York concerts to aid the refugees of Bangladesh. Lennon parodied Dylan in many home recordings of the 1970s. But the closest musical relationship between Dylan and any Beatle flourished when Harrison and Dylan formed the Traveling Wilburys in 1988.

The Fool   Simon and Marijke Koger and Josje Leeger were three pop-art designers from Amsterdam who called themselves "the Fool," hired by Epstein as stage designers for the Saville Theatre. The Beatles took to them immediately. Lennon had them paint the Bechstein upright on which he wrote "Lucy in the Sky with Diamonds" and "A Day in the Life"—this instrument was auctioned for $13,200 in August 1983—and a gypsy caravan he'd bought for Julian, which was exiled to an island, Dorinish, that Lennon bought in March 1967. Harrison had them paint much of his Esher home, and they designed the costumes for the "Our World" broadcast.

Perhaps their most famous work was the two-story exterior mural for the Apple boutique on Baker Street that opened in December 1967. Inspired by this work, Lennon commissioned a psychedelic paint job for his 1965 Rolls Royce Phantom (donated by Lennon to the Cooper-Hewitt Museum in 1977, which sold it for $2 million in 1985). Also under this influence, McCartney's Rickenbacker bass, Harrison's Strat, Starr's bass drum head, and all three Casinos were given wild paint jobs by their owners in June 1967; all of them but the Strat required scraping and some refinishing a year later.

Billy Preston   Billy Preston was gospel-rock keyboardist for Little Richard and Sam Cooke when the Beatles met him in Hamburg in 1962. Following that, he recorded for EMI, releasing his cover of "In the Midnight Hour" in July 1966. He was in London in January 1969 not only to play for Ray Charles's band but also to star in his own BBC-2 television show, recorded on the 19th, and to guest on Lulu's program on the 25th. His work with the Beatles on electric piano, piano, and organ was rewarded on January 31 with an Apple recording contract; Harrison produced his LPs *That's the Way God Planned It* (August 1969) and *Encouraging Words* (September 1970) and played guitar on others. Preston appears on Harrison 1970, 1971, 1974, 1976b, and 1982 and, in between other gigs as television talk-show band leader, toured with Ringo's All-Starr Band in 1989–95.

Phil Spector   In the period 1958–66, Phil Spector (b. New York, 1940) produced eighteen gold singles, including the Teddy Bears' "To Know Him Is to Love Him" (September 1958, a #1 hit covered by the Beatles), the Crystals'

"He's a Rebel" (August 1962, #1), the Ronettes' "Be My Baby" (August 1963, #2, featuring Spector's wife Ronnie), and the Righteous Brothers' "You've Lost That Lovin' Feelin'" (December 1964, #1). The Beatles met Spector in August 1966, when the Ronettes performed on the Beatles' final U.S. tour. His cloudy "wall of sound" style did not translate well to stereo—Todd Rundgren and Phil Ramone would achieve that effect in the 1970s—so the short-drama 45-rpm disc was much more his medium than the long-player (see Senoff 1969, 16). "Get Back" enticed Spector out of a two-year retirement.

Phil Spector went on to produce many projects for Lennon (a few singles, three LPs, and four more tracks for a fourth) and Harrison (two LPs and some singles) and collaborated with the latter in producing an Apple single for Ronnie Spector: "Try Some, Buy Some" (a song composed by Harrison)/"Tandoori Chicken" (Harrison/P. Spector) (United Kingdom: Apple 33, April 16, 1971; United States: Apple 1832, April 19, #77).

TABLE OF CHORD FUNCTIONS

The purpose of this table is to list the basic harmonies of tonal music, as identified by the roman numeral system adopted in this book, and to describe their most characteristic functions, both in common practice generally and as used by the Beatles. The chords in most of the Beatles' music conform to the major scale, even when melodic lines are drawn from the blues-related pentatonic minor; this is perhaps the strongest aspect of the tonal language of "Another Girl." True minor-mode pieces do occur as well, and of course the Beatles make ample use of mode mixture, borrowing scale-degree alterations from the minor into the major mode, for color contrast at a level that is often significant.

Chords other than those listed here, including the more exotic applied chords and such chromatic intensifiers as augmented-sixth chords, are referred to and discussed in the text, but their functions are based on a combination of the harmonic principles described below and more individualistic contrapuntal lines. Also, it should be borne in mind that all of these chords will occur most often in root position but that inversions are frequent and largely subject to the melodic development of McCartney's bass playing. Sevenths, ninths, suspended fourths, added sixths, and other passing or neighboring nonchord tones are added commonly and characteristically, and these events are discussed with ample attention in the main body of the text.

I Tonic harmony represents the home base, relaxation, consummation, and arrival. It is most effectively approached by V and can be embellished plagally by IV, but in blues-rock it can be ornamented by lower neighbor ♭VII as well.

I♭   This symbol refers to a minor tonic triad imported into the major mode. Such mode mixture is basic to "Norwegian Wood (This Bird Has Flown)" and "Penny Lane," both of which juxtapose the two colors for immediate contrasts of mood.

I♯   The symbol for a major tonic chord within a minor context, as in "Things We Said Today." Basically in the minor mode, "I'll Be Back" illustrates a powerful conflict of intentions by juxtaposing I against I♯; the song fades out indecisively.

♭II   An altered supertonic chord, a major triad built a half-step above tonic, with two typical functions. Most commonly a dominant preparation known as the "Neapolitan" chord, as in the introduction to "Do You Want to Know a Secret," but ♭II may also function as an altered V itself, by tritone substitution, even when the seventh of the chord does not sound as it would in most jazz applications. This is heard in the retransitions to "Things We Said Today" and "You're Going to Lose That Girl." The Beatles do not use ♭II in first inversion.

II   The supertonic harmony is typically a dominant preparation. In some rock music, particularly in acid rock, this chord works as a simple upper-neighbor embellishment of tonic, but before "Don't Let Me Down" and "Sun King," such a nondirected function is unknown in the Beatles' work. The Beatles often use a root-position II—considered too stable for such a usage in classical music—as a passing chord, as in moving from I to III within a tonic expansion. The verses of "If I Fell" and "Here, There and Everywhere," the chorus of "Getting Better," and the bridge of "Sexy Sadie" illustrate. II is tonicized for the bridges of "For No One" and "If I Needed Someone," in both cases leading then to a retransitional V^{4-3}.

II♯   The Beatles often use II♯—which is normally a dominant preparation (the applied chord, V of V) characterized by the rising raised fourth scale degree—for the melodic potential of its raised scale degree in a chromatically *descending* context. We refer to this usage as the Lydian II♯, and it is heard moving to IV in many Beatles songs, from "She Loves You" to "She's Leaving Home." II♯ is tonicized to illustrate transcendence in "Doctor Robert."

♭III   A major mediant triad appearing a minor third above tonic. This can be part of a blues-based I–♭III–I arpeggiation, as in the verse of "Helter Skelter," but much more often continues on to IV, as in the [025]-related, blues-inflected "Please Please Me," "The Night Before," "Sgt. Pepper's Lonely Hearts Club Band," "Lucy in the Sky with Diamonds" (where ♭III is tonicized), "I Am the Walrus," "Back in the U.S.S.R.," and the final cadence of "The End." In a minor key, ♭III will often be tonicized according to "normal" practice, as in "Another Girl" and "Your Mother Should

Know." In this minor context, ♭III may lead directly to V, as in "Girl" and most classical music, but the Beatles will also compose this in a pentatonically inflected major mode: witness the introduction of "You Like Me Too Much" and the whole of "Yer Blues." ♭III is tonicized in the minor-mode "Wait," "While My Guitar Gently Weeps," and "You Never Give Me Your Money" and, in a major context, "She Came In through the Bathroom Window."

III   The normally weak mediant triad is a source of strength for the Beatles, adding poignant color to songs from "She Loves You" to "Across the Universe." It normally provides initial consonant support for a melodic leading-tone that then is electrically charged by a succeeding V; one can practically smell the ozone as this occurs in "I Want to Hold Your Hand." Or it may act as a sensitive fifth above VI, as in the introspective verse of "Help!" Lennon's "I'm Happy Just to Dance with You" opens with a tonicized mediant, an emphasis that also appears in the verse of his "Sexy Sadie."

III♯ Aside from its applied role as V of VI, III♯ is known only as a surprising substitute for I⁶ on its way to IV in the reharmonizing codas of "I Want to Hold Your Hand" and "Yes It Is."

IV   IV has two important roles, as either a dominant preparation or a plagal ornament to the tonic. The Beatles will usually begin their bridge with IV, as in "The Ballad of John and Yoko," to set up the retransitional dominant. This IV will often be tonicized, as in "From Me to You" and "Because," to further intensify that form-defining V. In the minor-mode "I'm Only Sleeping," the bridge tonicizes IV but then withholds the dominant. In some similar cases, as in the chorus of "Ask Me Why" or the verse of "And Your Bird Can Sing," V does not appear at all, and IV thus takes on a greater role. In a blues context, IV may act as an upper-neighbor embellishment of I, even if directly following a cadential V, as in "Can't Buy Me Love."

IV♭ A minor subdominant chord in a major context. This usually drops to tonic as a plagal function weakened by mixture from minor, as in "All I've Got to Do," "I'll Follow the Sun," "Nowhere Man," and "The Continuing Story of Bungalow Bill." May be part of a larger use of the minor mode in a major context, as in the bridge of "Here, There and Everywhere."

V   The dominant, the tension-providing counterpoise of the tonic, strengthens the latter with the authentic V–I cadence or opposes the same by ending a phrase with the half cadence. Usually the structural goal of the bridge's retransition, and may be tonicized there, as in "I'll Get You."

V♭ The minor dominant is rare in the Beatles' music after "I'll Get You" but may embellish the modal ♭VII, as in "Good Morning Good Morning." "Strawberry Fields Forever" uses the minor dominant and other colorful "wrong-mode" chords to portray Lennon's sense of displacement.

♭VI   The major triad built a half-step above V is usually a modally inflected dominant preparation, often including a "seventh" that resolves as an augmented sixth. This occurs in the retransitions of "I Call Your Name" and "Mean Mr Mustard." In "Honey Pie," the resolution of ♭VI^7 to V^7 is delayed by two intervening applied chords. So as to further intensify their respective dominants in the minor mode, ♭VI is tonicized briefly within both the bridge of "Michelle" and the verse of "I'm Only Sleeping." ♭VI may provide a modally inflected plagal approach to the tonic, as in the simple ♭VI–I verse of "It Won't Be Long," the ♭VI–♭VII–I cadence of "P.S. I Love You," or the mixture-enhanced arpeggiation of the subdominant in the IV–♭VI–I succession heard in "Hello Goodbye" and "Oh! Darling." Rarely, ♭VI will work as IV of ♭III, as in the retransition of "A Day in the Life." More in line with traditional tonal practice, ♭VI as the goal of a modally inflected deceptive cadence precipitates the coda of "I Will."

VI   Lennon would frequently embellish the tonic by alternating it with its submediant, as in "All I've Got to Do," "Run for Your Life," and "All You Need Is Love." In the Dorian "Eleanor Rigby," VI is the only embellishment that McCartney allows the tonic. Lennon tonicizes VI in the opening of the bridge of "I'm Happy Just to Dance with You" and "You Can't Do That," in the middle of the bridge of "This Boy," in the end of the bridge of "There's a Place," and throughout the bridge of "We Can Work It Out." The descending arpeggiation, I–VI–IV, a rock cliché, is rare in McCartney's work but is one of Lennon's favorite ideas, as written into the verses of "I'll Get You" and "I'm So Tired," the chorus of "Happiness Is a Warm Gun," and many other songs. All three composing Beatles enjoy resolving VI plagally to III, as they do in "Please Please Me," "She Loves You," "No Reply," "I Need You," "I Will," and "Julia."

VI♯   In addition to its common applied role as V of II, the Beatles discover VI♯ as an area to be tonicized in its own right, a salient feature of *Abbey Road*. George Harrison anticipated his artful use of this relationship in the middle section of "Something" in the intentionally clumsy bridge of "Only a Northern Song."

♭VII   The major subtonic chord may prepare V^7 with a telling cross-relation on the altered seventh scale degree, as in cadences in "All My Loving," "I'm a Loser," "Yes It Is," and "Dig a Pony." This may be part of a larger dominant preparation, as in the II–♭VII–V^7 arpeggiation in the chorus of "Help!," or in the expanded tonicization of ♭VII in the chorus of "Penny Lane" that resolves in its retransitional V. In rock music but not in art music, ♭VII will be used as a lower-neighbor embellishment to tonic, beginning for the Beatles with "A Hard Day's Night" and "Every Little Thing." This I–♭VII–I progression will sometimes grind against a tonic pedal below, as in "Tomorrow Never Knows" and "Got to Get You into My Life." The Beatles progress from ♭VII through IV to I in the rock-defining "double plagal" cadence, used heavily from "You're Going to

Lose That Girl" and "The Night Before" to "Here Comes the Sun" and "Polythene Pam." ♭VII may also be a passing chord between the modal ♭VI and I, as in "P.S. I Love You," "With a Little Help from My Friends," and "Lady Madonna," and it appears as V of ♭III in a rare major-mode context in "The Word."

VII   Aside from an applied function to the mediant like that in "Martha My Dear," the Beatles rarely build any quality of triad on the leading tone, which in art music would typically appear as a passing diminished triad in first inversion. A major-minor VII⁷ chord appears in "I'm So Tired," and this is heard as a chromatic preparation of the dominant that follows after an intervening IV chord.

GLOSSARY OF TERMS

Acetate   an early test pressing made for production purposes, often for the home study of an experimental or otherwise preliminary mix; also called a "dub."

Aleatoric music   strictly, music in which many or most factors are controlled by chance; more loosely, music in which many or most factors are determined, often spontaneously, by the performer rather than by the composer.

Applied dominant   also called "secondary dominant"; a major triad or major-minor seventh chord whose root lies a perfect fifth above that of another major or minor triad which is thereby tonicized (q.v.), such as the chord on "green" in "You Can't Do That." The root of an applied diminished triad lies a chromatic half-step below the root of the major or minor triad being tonicized.

Banjolele   a type of ukelele given resonance by a banjolike body, popular in Britain in the 1930s and 1940s; played by John and Paul in the early 1950s.

Barre chord   a guitar chord formed with the left index finger stopping all strings, thus creating an artificial, movable nut, effectively reducing the length of all strings. This allows for several convenient methods of chord positioning and voicing with the three remaining fingers and thumb.

Basic track   the initial recording of a song, normally an instrumental performance only by "rhythm" instruments (drums, bass, rhythm guitar, keyboard), upon which vocals, solo instrumental lines, and parts played by outside musicians would be superimposed in subsequent recording.

Boogie   the repeated alternation of one or more chord tones, third or fifth, with their upper neighbors, usually idiomatic in guitar, keyboard, and vocal parts, such as in Lennon's guitar part in "Chains." Often but not always performed in a triplet "shuffle" pattern.

Bridge   a song's contrasting middle section, often beginning in an area other than tonic and usually leading to a dominant retransition.

315

Chorus   a song's section, nearly always affirming the tonic, usually appearing in the song's interior, with lyrics that remain constant with each hearing. If there is no refrain, the chorus is the container of the song's title.

Common-tone diminished-seventh chord   a fully diminished seventh chord, one of whose tones—usually that spelled as the chordal seventh—is also a member and most commonly the root of the principal chord being embellished. Usually, the common tone is maintained as a bass pedal; e.g., the embellishment of an F-major triad with a neighboring $g\sharp^{\circ4}_{2}$.

Compressors and limiters   electronic devices that would, respectively, either squeeze all constituent dynamic levels of a given recording in geometric ratios to add focus, or "clip" and thus eliminate extreme dynamic peaks so as to prevent distortion that would be caused by an overloaded signal. Used during recording, mixing, and mothering processes.

Cover   the recording of another artist's previously released song; when the rendition is in a different style from that of the original, the cover often brings an existing song to a new audience.

D-gesture or D-line   *see* SRDC.

Dominant preparation   a harmony, usually II⁶, II, IV, IV⁶, or VI but also including the more intense applied Vs, that sets the stage for the V.

Dorian mode   a pitch collection created by raising the sixth degree of the natural minor scale, as heard in "Eleanor Rigby."

Double-plagal cadence   the descent of two successive perfect fourths in roots moving to the tonic, ♭VII–IV–I, allowing both the interior anticipations of roots and stepwise descending resolutions in upper voices, as in "She Said She Said."

Double-tracking   The superimposition of one or more parts onto an already existing recording, made either by "sound-with-sound" onto a separate track of the existing tape or, through a reduction mix using "sound-on-sound," merging with the original material onto a new tape. The term is usually applied to the recording of two vocal parts, often at the unison, by the same singer, beginning with McCartney's vocal for "A Taste of Honey."

D.S.   Dal segno, or "[Repeat] from the sign."

Elision   here, a term used to designate the enjambment of two phrases, as in "Julia."

EP   An "extended-play" seven-inch single record, usually containing two songs per side. Aside from limited-release jukebox issues, EPs were far more common in the United Kingdom than in the United States after the 1950s.

Expansion (of harmony)   *see* Prolongation.

Fifth-progression   the melodic filling-in of a harmonic fifth with passing tones, as in the guitar retransition in "You've Got to Hide Your Love Away."

Gamak   melodic ornaments in North Indian instrumental or vocal music, adhering to the modal qualities of the Hindustani rags.

Guide vocal   vocalization, by a song's composer, of enough melody during the recording of a basic instrumental track to keep the ensemble together. If recorded, the guide vocal would be replaced by a subsequent more polished vocal overdub.

Hypermeasure, hypermeter   terms devised by Edward T. Cone to permit consideration of the metrical relations that exist among groupings of measures, thereby acknowledging strong and weak accentual relationships among consecutive downbeats.

Incomplete progression   a harmonic pattern that does not begin with tonic but "in medias res," e.g., the opening IV–V–I of "No Reply" or the structural II$\sharp$–V–I progression of "Lucy in the Sky with Diamonds."

Interruption   a voice-leading structure expressed in song as a period with an antecedent, leading to a half cadence, followed by its consequent, ending with an authentic cadence. The structural upper voice descends only to $\hat{2}$ over V at the first cadence and then returns to the beginning for the consequent, which descends fully to $\hat{1}$ for the second cadence. The entire descent is thus said to have been interrupted at the first half cadence. Exemplified in "All My Loving."

Limiters   *see* Compressors.

LP   the twelve-inch long-playing 33 1/3-rpm vinyl format for the album, a collection of songs either recorded for simultaneous release or repackaged in "best-of" compilations. The dominant form for the release of sound recordings from the late 1950s through the mid-1980s, the LP would contain 15–25 minutes of music per side and, in the United States, would retail for roughly $3 in 1964 and $7 in 1970.

Lydian II   A major triad built on $\hat{2}$, in a major key, but not functioning as V of V despite its inclusion of $\sharp\hat{4}$. This function is first heard in "She Loves You" and is perhaps best known in the cadence of "Yesterday."

Mixolydian ♭VII   A major subtonic triad built on $\flat\hat{7}$ in a major key. The modal alternation of I with ♭VII, common in the Beatles' music after 1964, descends from folk and blues but not from the classical world.

NEMS   The North End Music Stores, a Liverpool concern whose name was adopted for incorporation by Brian Epstein as the management company that would assist the Beatles in reaching beyond their bar-band status to become first-class touring and recording artists.

Nut position   Harrison's term for the most basic left-hand guitar position taking advantage of open strings; allows what are commonly called "cowboy chords."

Overdub   the superimposition of one recording over a preexisting one; *see* Basic track, Double-tracking.

Pentatonic minor scale   a five-tone collection of minor thirds and major seconds characteristic of the blues and blues-rock; its members correspond to scale degrees $\hat{1}$–$\flat\hat{3}$–$\hat{4}$–$\hat{5}$–$\flat\hat{7}$ of the chromatic scale.

Phrygian ♭II(7)   a major triad or seventh chord built on $\flat\hat{2}$, which does not necessarily act as a dominant-preparatory Neapolitan but instead may substitute for an altered V, as in "Things We Said Today."

Pitch class   the group of all pitches related by octave equivalence; e.g., the pitches . . . c$\sharp$1, c$\sharp$2, c$\sharp$3, . . . are all members of pitch class c$\sharp$.

Power chord   the open fifth on guitar, usually loud and distorted. Several often appear in parallel motion, usually adhering to the pentatonic minor scale (q.v.).

Predominant   *see* Dominant preparation.

Progressive tonality   a system characterized by the modulation from one key area to another without return or any other indication of an overriding single tonal center, as in "Being for the Benefit of Mr. Kite."

Prolongation (of harmony)   the expansion of a scale degree through its composing-out, which may involve (1) tonicization (q.v.) (as in the prolongation of C in "Birthday"), (2) the unfolding through time of intervals of its triad (as in the I♭7–I$^6_5$ progression in "I Saw Her Standing There"), or (3) contrapuntal elaboration, as with passing or neighboring chords (as with the F9 chord that helps prolong C in "Golden Slumbers").

Refrain   an optional final line of a song's verse, consisting of a lyric, usually containing the title, that does not vary from verse to verse.

Sesquialtera   a rhythmic ratio of 2:3, as exemplified by Ringo vs. the remainder of the ensemble at "When I hold you" in "Happiness Is a Warm Gun."

Single   the seven-inch 45-rpm nephew of the LP and the dominant carrier of music's most popular songs from the mid-1950s into the 1970s (and, arguably, further). The "single" contained one song per side, but only the "A" side was typically promoted on the radio and thus accounted for sales as well. Both airplay and sales would be tabulated to create the weekly singles charts, determining the national #1 records. The Beatles were quite unusual in that both sides of their singles usually received airplay, so it was typical for both sides to chart, making for the "double-sided" hit. During the 1960s, a single as long as three and a half minutes (such as the Beach Boys' "Good Vibrations") was unusual, but the outside practical limit was reached in 1968 with the seven-minute "Hey Jude." American singles sold for 69–89 cents through 1970 ("oldies" were a bit more).

Skiffle   an energetic folk style featuring simple acoustic and homemade instruments popular in Britain at the emergence of rock and roll in the mid-1950s. Exemplified by Lonnie Donegan with such hits as "Rock Island Line" and perpetrated by countless bands of teenagers who could find cheap guitars and washboards.

SRDC   an abbreviation for Statement-Restatement-Departure-Conclusion, the designation for the periodic functions, as well as motivic and tonal correspondences, among phrases of certain verses, as in "I'll Cry Instead." Individual phrases may be referred to as a D-gesture or a C-line.

Stop time   the abrupt cessation of sound from the background texture, thus no longer in support of a continuing solo voice or instrument that would often become at that point extra-emotive, creating a striking tension between musical forces. The Beatles found stop time effective on stage, so it is characteristic of many of their covers, but they would also compose it into their own songs, as in the brief domineering drum break of "You Can't Do That" or the anguished ornamental dominant retransitions of "Oh! Darling."

Tea-chest bass   a wooden crate (common around Liverpool's shipping docks) fitted with an upright broom handle; a string would be attached to both the chest (which functions as an amplifier) and the top of the broomstick; the open string is plucked by the free hand, and its tension (and therefore pitch) is governed by pulling and relaxing the stick with the other.

Tonicization   the temporary bestowal of "tonic" status on a scale degree other than $\hat{1}$, achieved by any of the techniques traditionally associated with modulation. The tonicized area will eventually resolve back to the original $\hat{1}$.

Track   may refer to a complete song on an album but, in this book, used much more often to refer to the portion of recording tape whose oxide particles would be aligned as they passed over the magnetically active area of a recording head during the taping process. The Beatles progressed from two-track, through four-track, to eight-track recording in their years at EMI, each track storing input from a different microphone or other source, as their tape machines and mixing boards gained in flexibility. Once recording was complete, these tracks of the working tape would then be reduced to a new tape in the mixing process, to a total of one track for a monophonic master, or two tracks for a stereophonic master.

Truck driver's modulation   the modulation to a tonal center one step higher, usually achieved very smoothly by stating or repeating the dominant at a half-cadence (analogous to depressing a clutch), transposing that V up a whole- or half-step (shifting to the next-higher gear) and then resolving to the new I (releasing the clutch). The technique can be an odious time killer in much commercial music but is made more subtle by the incomplete progression as the solo enters in "And I Love Her."

Trichord   any collection of three discrete pitch classes (q.v.); the [025] trichord is formed by any of the pitch classes (e.g., G–B♭–C or G–A–C) that contain among them the three intervals of a major second, a minor third, and a perfect fourth (and is named by a count of half-steps between constituents). The [025] trichord occurs in four places in the pentatonic minor scale.

Turnaround   the conclusion of one verse, usually on dominant harmony, that simultaneously prepares for the following verse, as in the last half-bar of the twelve-bar blues (q.v.).

Twelve-bar blues   the normal form of a blues chorus, comprising three lines, with four bars each. The first two lines share the same repeated lyric but differ in that the first maintains tonic while the second expands on this, with two bars of IV settling into two bars of I. The third line moves from a bar of V through another of IV to two of I; the twelfth bar will often be a turnaround to the succeeding verse, on V. Delta blues would follow this basic pattern very closely, whereas Chicago blues would typically introduce passing chords between I and IV, along with other embellishments, often chromatic. The chords are usually major, in support of pentatonic minor melody.

Verse   a song's section equivalent to the stanza, usually placed directly after any introduction, that nearly always appears with two or three (or, rarely, more) different sets of lyrics, but in rare early cases ("Love Me Do," "Not a Second Time") has one set only.

Wild track   one of the tracks of the working tape that, during the creation of the stereo master, is panned from channel to channel, thus seeming to migrate from one part of the stereo image to another.

NOTES

Preface

1. The songs referred to are, respectively, "Any Time at All," "When I Get Home," "Yes It Is," "It's Only Love," "Think for Yourself," "Rain," "Eleanor Rigby," "Penny Lane," "When I'm Sixty-Four," "Lucy in the Sky with Diamonds," "She's Leaving Home," "Being for the Benefit of Mr. Kite," "Within You Without You," "Lady Madonna," "Back in the U.S.S.R.," "Happiness Is a Warm Gun," "Julia," "Come Together," "You Never Give Me Your Money," and "Her Majesty."

2. I recommend Aldwell and Schachter 1989 for background on musical issues pertaining to harmony and voice leading that cannot be discussed in depth here.

3. The Beatles are often said to have enjoyed universal appeal. But despite their obviously enormous core pop following — and the band's popularity continues unabated, with sales of over 20 million CDs in 1996 — the group never once crossed over to *Billboard*'s "Country & Western" or "Rhythm & Blues"/"Soul" charts, whereas even the Beach Boys and the Four Seasons enjoyed R&B hits. As a solo artist, McCartney had one B-side enter the C&W chart in 1975 and three R&B hits in 1982–83, the latter all coperformed with Stevie Wonder or Michael Jackson.

4. Distinguished musicians have for many years compared the music of the Beatles to that of Monteverdi, Schubert, Schumann, and Poulenc; see the thoughts of Bernstein, Copland, Rorem, Rifkin, Perlman, and Foss in Kozinn 1995b, 31–34.

5. The Wise scores were apparently transcribed without recourse to either pre-overdub recordings or video archives, all of which permit a clear understanding of guitar voicings and other details masked by dense final-mix textures.

6. Unless otherwise stated, CD timings are intended for reference in commercially released EMI recordings, even if the passage being discussed is part of another recording, such as a compositional draft or a live performance, of that particular song.

Prelude

1. The teenage Lennon's "A Treasury of Art and Poetry" was sold by roommate Rod Murray in 1984 for £16,000 (Beatlenews roundup 1984, 4).

2. See BBC 1990 and Coleman 1992, 370–71.

3. McCartney discusses the delay in J. Goodman 1984, 110, and White 1990, 143.

4. Golson 1981a, 182.

5. The "boogie" technique ornaments a chord member, usually the fifth, with an upper neighbor or added seventh, using a finger pattern that alternates between the basic chord (such as G–B–D–G) and the ornamented version (G–B–E–G), usually with two strums on each.

6. Two of the five most popular major-mode songs in the 1955–90 era, Elvis Presley's "Don't Be Cruel" and Bobby Darin's "Mack the Knife," also feature [025] trichords in their verses. In the pentatonic minor, perhaps most familiar is "Hanky Panky" (Tommy James & the Shondells, 1966), which, like "Be-Bop-a-Lula" and "Dream Baby" (mentioned above), transposes the *c* trichord over I to *a* over IV in both the verse and the chorus.

7. The double-tonic complex is a construction noted in the operas of Wagner by Robert Bailey and applied to *Abbey Road* by Robert Gauldin. See Bailey 1985 and Gauldin 1990.

8. Martin labored as a salaried EMI employee through mid-1965, without any special monetary compensation, despite playing a defining role in the Beatles' remarkable achievements. Fed up with such a lack of recognition, Martin left Parlophone and created his own recording company, AIR, in August 1965. The Beatles elected to continue under his supervision, and he would still book their studio time at Abbey Road, but by declaring his freedom and setting his own fees, Martin made a major contribution to the growth of the independent record producer in the 1960s.

9. See A. Forte 1995, 42–51, for an excellent primer on reading such voice-leading sketches.

10. Lennon's crude draft tape is heard on Beatles 1992b. This document is also important for the light it sheds on Lennon's conception of the song's melody before it was arranged as a Lennon-McCartney vocal duet.

11. Perhaps because its tonal structure is so convoluted, the phrase rhythm of the introduction is a very square and easily grasped four-plus-four. Joshua Rifkin has commented on the odd phrase rhythm in the verse and the verse-bridge combination in Rifkin 1968, 119.

One

1. The performance was the group's August 15, 1965, New York concert at Shea Stadium for a then-world-record audience of 55,600. The tour-opening concert was filmed by NEMS for televising at Christmas, but after Epstein previewed a print in early November, it was decided that the soundtrack had numerous problems, so on January 5, 1966, the Beatles overdubbed parts for most of the songs (a restored "Everybody's Trying to Be My Baby" is heard on Beatles 1996a), and the EMI recording of "Act Naturally" was substituted for the live performance, necessitating several splices to fit the footage (Epstein halts 1965, 5). The color film, *The Beatles at Shea Stadium*, was finally aired on March 1, 1966.

2. George Harrison and Pattie Boyd, married on January 21, 1966, moved to Esher during the filming of *A Hard Day's Night*; John and Cynthia Lennon moved from a Kensington apartment to Weybridge later in 1964, and Ringo and Maureen followed shortly thereafter, though they kept a city apartment. In the summer of 1966, McCartney bought a dairy farm of 183 acres near Campbeltown, Scotland, as his retreat.

3. See *McCartney world tour* 1989, 50–51, Salewicz 1986, 179, and Miles 1997, 211–67.

4. Flippo 1988, 214.

5. Aspinall 1966a, 6; see also Miles 1997, 219–20.

6. Lennon had a similar studio in his own music room, also containing piano, organ, jukeboxes, and guitars, but admitted a lack of proficiency in recording himself. Harrison had actually been the first Beatle with home studio equipment, installed in 1964. See Wenner 1971, 128; James 1966b, 12; *Melody Maker*, February 27, 1965, pp. 12–13; Coleman 1992, 331; and Beatle news 1966a, 29.

7. Flippo 1988, 213–14.

8. See Tamla team 1966, 5, and Beatle news 1966a, 29. American Beatles recordings would have been preceded by the Rolling Stones' many sessions in Chicago and Hollywood in 1964–66. Brit Helen Shapiro recorded in Nashville with Presley's Jordanaires in 1963, and the Nashville sound was to shine in Bob Dylan's February 1966 recordings for *Blonde on Blonde*.

9. See Lewisohn 1988, 82.

10. McCartney in spring 1966: "Years ago, my Auntie Lil said to me: why do you always write songs about love? Can't you ever write about a horse or the summit conference or something interesting. So I thought, all right, Auntie Lil. And recently we've not been writing all our songs about love" (Beatlemania strikes 1966, 1, 18).

11. See Lewisohn 1988, 70–84, for details.

12. Clayson 1992, 113–14.

13. Lewisohn 1988, 72.

14. Lawrence 1978, 58; see also Lewisohn 1988, 70.

15. See O'Grady 1983, 96; Riley 1988, 182; and Lennon on the notion of the "head" of an album representing a "Starting Over" in Cott 1982a, 190.

16. Dowlding 1989, 145.

17. See Reck 1985, 91–92.

18. See Leary et al. [1964]. Harrison said in 1969 that his "The Art of Dying" (Harrison 1970) dates from 1966 (Schaffner 1982, 48) and likely relates to his reading of Leary. See also the Rascals' "Death's Reply" (December 1969) and Crosby, Stills, Nash and Young's "Deja Vu" (March 1970).

19. The "turn off your mind" quotation is found in Leary et al. [1964], 14; Lennon speaks in Miles and Marchbank 1978, 88.

20. Beatle news 1965a, 29. The phrase "Tomorrow never knows" is quoted in the Oasis song "Morning Glory" (1995).

21. Golson 1981b, 191.

22. Aspinall 1966c, 25.

23. The Leslie speaker features a revolving pair of horns, producing a whirring tremolo and Doppler-produced vibrato, and was normally enclosed within a Hammond organ case, as at EMI, but could also be purchased separately. The Beatles, particularly George Harrison, would use it throughout the remainder of their career.

24. Harrison owned a large number of Indian records, a tamboura, and two sitars by early April; he was to increase his collection of Indian instruments in July. See James 1966c, 11, and Aspinall 1966b, 24. The tamboura would be adopted in 1968 by both the Rolling Stones, in "Street Fighting Man," and Donovan, in "Hurdy Gurdy Man."

25. Coleman 1992, 370. Lennon's vocal is "punched out" for nearly three seconds at 2:46, where it deviates from a repeated pattern. The Leslied vocal was rerecorded on April 22.

26. See *McCartney world tour* 1989, 66, and the August 28, 1966, press conference on Beatles 1985e.

27. The laughter and guitars are noted in Friede et al. 1980, 214; Lewisohn 1988, 72; and Mulhern 1990, 33. Example 1.4d does seem to have some qualities of the guitar and sitar when played backward at slower speeds.

28. Quote from Lewisohn 1988, 72; see also Martin 1994, 80.

29. The pseudo-Indian ornamentation in example 1.4d is reminiscent of the Byrds' "Eight Miles High" (April 1966) and is heard again in many later works, such as the Hollies' "On a Carousel" (March 1967).

30. See Porter 1979, 285, and Reck 1985, 103–4. Wilfrid Mellers (1973, 81) compares the pentatonic cadence to that in "I Saw Her Standing There."

31. Leary et al. [1964], 54–55.

32. One early mono mix, heard on Lennon 1988e, applies no ADT.

33. Wade 1980, 83. At about this time, Harrison was reading Paramahansa Yogananda's (1893–1952) *Autobiography of a Yogi* (1946) (see Reck 1985, 92), a work to become so important to rock musicians that it was cited on the jackets of the Rascals' *See* (December 1969) and Yes's *Tales from Topographic Oceans* (December 1973). That book describes many blissful experiences of the yogic state of consciousness and warns against the cosmic delusion of maya that tempts human beings away from divinity and toward an individual ego and materialistic values. Harrison claimed Yogananda as an important influence on his life, and the guru's photo is seen on the cover of *Sgt. Pepper.*

34. Christgau and Piccarella 1982, 251; see also Mellers 1973, 82, and Robertson 1991, 53.

35. The track was also highly influential on an emerging psychedelic rock music. Halved and doubled tape speeds would be used by Jimi Hendrix and Frank Zappa; backward tapes by Hendrix, Pink Floyd, the Electric Prunes, the Byrds, Tomorrow, Spirit, the Who, Soft Machine, and the First Edition; and the Leslie effect by the Grateful Dead, Hendrix, the Moody Blues, Yes, Cream, Led Zeppelin, and Black Sabbath. The song's noises and I–♭VII–I basis are at the core of Pink Floyd's "Pow R. Toch" (1967). The LP-related aspect of the *Revolver* title would be revisited in Harrison's *Thirty-Three ⅓* (Harrison 1976b).

36. See Golson 1981b, 191, for Lennon's recollection. Lennon believes that both he and Harrison may have contributed to McCartney's lyrics (Dowlding 1989, 144).

37. The bass is mixed out of Beatles 1996a, but its [025] figure bleeds through at 1:14 and 2:02. The simplification of the vocal texture reminds me of the similar evolution of the simple solo vocal for "Can't Buy Me Love."

38. The I–♭VII–I progression over a Î pedal is emulated by Beatles imitators in the Rascals' "How Can I Be Sure" (September 1967) and "It's Wonderful" (November 1967), Chicago's "Beginnings" (May 1969), and Nazz's "A Beautiful Song" (May 1969).

39. Lewisohn 1988, 79; see also Beatles plus jazzmen 1966, 1.

40. A copyist's error mars the Wise score at **B–2**; McCartney concludes his line slurring $d^2-a^1-b^1$. The Leslie guitar becomes a Harrison trademark, but is occasionally heard in other recordings as well, such as the Beach Boys' title track from *Pet Sounds* (1966, as played by Carl Wilson), Cream's "Badge" (1968, as played by Eric Clapton), and Elton John's "Goodbye Yellow Brick Road" (1973, as played by Davey Johnstone).

41. Because McCartney ad-libs the vocal in the coda, his two takes are somewhat different and thus are not heard together at that point; the extended mono mix uses a different vocal take in the coda than the stereo does.

42. J. Goodman 1984, 107; Miles and Marchbank 1978, 88.

43. Beatles plus jazzmen 1966, 1. The session men are named in Lewisohn 1988, 79.

44. See O'Grady 1975, 344–45. This song's textural aspects were to mark hits as diverse as the Turtles' "Happy Together" (1967) and the Spiral Staircase's "More Today Than Yesterday" (1969). Micek (1994) finds that the saxophones' chromatic descent "reflects the intensity" of McCartney's desires at that point. Many, including Lennon, have ascribed a Motown influence to "Got to Get You into My Life" (see Miles and Marchbank 1978, 88); the single most likely Motown model is perhaps Stevie Won-

der's "Uptight (Everything's Alright)" (December 1965), whose brass arrangement emphasizes a I–♭VII–I neighbor function over a tonic pedal, as does McCartney's song. Perhaps Harrison had some Stevie Wonder mixed in among his Indian records!

45. Harrison's manuscript for "Love You To" is reproduced in Harrison 1980, 103.

46. See Batt 1966, 7; Beatle news 1966b, 29; Houston 1966, 6; Shankar 1968, 92–93; and Harrison 1980, 53–57, regarding Harrison's early relationship with Shankar. Harrison was still collaborating with the master thirty years hence, producing Shankar's album *Chants of India* in 1996–97.

47. See How about a tune 1966, 10, for the reference to Page.

48. See Raver 1966b, 2, for an early discussion of "raga-rock."

49. The London affiliation of the Indian musicians is given in Lewisohn 1992, 217. The Wise score is unaccountably missing b♭s.

50. Assertions by Harrison and by Bhagwat (see Harrison 1980, 102, and Lewisohn 1988, 72) as to the Beatle's playing sitar here have been questioned, but this recording would have required knowledge of no rags and only an elementary understanding of Hindustani formal patterns, easily attainable by a good guitarist within a few weeks.

51. Lewisohn (1988, 73, 84) notes that three different mixes were edited together for both mono and stereo versions; one splice is clearly audible in McCartney's vocal at 2:21.

52. This outline of Hindustani music draws from Shankar 1968, Jairazbhoy 1971, Wade 1980, and Vaughn 1994.

53. Wade 1980, 94.

54. Lewisohn 1988, 72.

55. *Melody Maker* announced on April 9 that the Beatles planned to record the two songs, "selected from fifteen songs that the Beatles have spent the past few weeks writing and rehearsing," "at a two-day session in London next week" (Beatles plan the new single 1966, 1). This report would imply that the Beatles had already discussed among themselves many songs for which recording had not yet begun, had perhaps even played sketchy versions of them for Martin, and had decided that of the lot, "Paperback Writer" would make the strongest A-side.

56. These suggestions as to the motivations for "Paperback Writer" are found in In the Beatles 1966, 10; Salewicz 1986, 179; and Cowan 1978?, 36.

57. See Friede et al. 1980, 98; see also Miles 1979, 238.

58. The manuscript is reproduced in *The Beatles Monthly Book* 36 (July 1966), 27. Lennon maintains that he assisted with the lyrics (Dowlding 1989, 128).

59. The comment from the interview is from Golson 1981b, 189.

60. The SG is identified in Mytkowicz 1987, 104. Take 2 is the released version. Take 1, which breaks down at the first change to IV, is heard on Beatles 1990d, which also presents Take 2 without echo, EQ, or balancing. Photos of the recording session (see *The Beatles Monthly Book* 35 [June 1966]) show the Beatles with many different instruments—Harrison holds a Burns bass, for instance—but no SG is visible.

61. See second engineer Phil McDonald's notes in Lewisohn 1988, 74.

62. Simply for experimentation's sake, says Emerick, the bass guitar is miked by a large bass-sensitive loudspeaker cone driven acoustically by the bass amp's woofer (Lewisohn 1988, 74).

63. The three singers are photographed at a piano, rehearsing their vocal parts at half speed, in *The Beatles Monthly Book* 81 (January 1983), cover, 2; see also *The Beatles Monthly Book* 35 (June 1966), 11. The quotation of the French folk song begins a long chain of Beatles songs that refer overtly to others; several, such as "All You Need Is Love" and "Glass Onion," refer to other Beatles compositions by name, in the spirit of Lennon's off-mike line to Ringo in "What Goes On" that apparently cites "Tell Me Why."

64. Compare Golson 1981b, 207; *The Beatles Monthly Book* 36 (July 1966), p. 19;

Lewisohn 1988, 74; and Buskin 1987, 40. The reversed vocal parts are transcribed in W. Everett 1986, 365, but the two staffs there should be interchanged.

65. The most popular early non-Beatles records would include the Buckinghams' "Susan" (December 1967) and Spanky & Our Gang's "Like to Get to Know You" (April 1968).

66. Emerick discusses how taping at slower or faster speeds than would be heard on the master, an outgrowth of the ADT process approximating voltage-controlled synthesis, alters the sound envelope in Lewisohn 1988, 74.

67. See Ringo's comments in Garbarini 1982, 50; Somach et al. 1989, 237; and Weinberg 1991, 181, 188.

68. An alternate mono mix heard on Beatles 1985b indicates that Lennon's descant part was originally recorded separately from the backing vocals, necessitating a tape reduction.

69. "Paperback Writer" was mixed for stereo on October 31, 1966, for inclusion on the Christmas compilation *A Collection of Beatles Oldies*.

70. Robertson 1991, 54.

71. Miles and Marchbank 1978, 88; Shotton and Schaffner 1983, 122; Dowlding 1989, 143; Turner 1994, 114.

72. The possibility of McCartney's input is mentioned in Dowlding 1989, 142.

73. The jam is noted in Lewisohn 1988, 75, but I have not heard it.

74. Lennon is quoted in Golson 1981b, 190; the manuscript appears in Campbell and Murphy 1980, xxxii.

75. Others have noted parallels between the tone of the lyrics in "And Your Bird Can Sing" and two Dylan songs from 1965: "Queen Jane Approximately" (Christgau and Piccarella 1982, 251) and "Positively 4th Street" (Riley 1988, 192).

76. Take 2 suggests that Lennon's chord sequence for the bridge (**B**), originally $F\sharp mM_2^4 - F\sharp mM_2^4 - F\sharp mm^7 - F\sharp^{o7} - D - Em^7 - Em^7 - A^7$, was likely improved by Harrison's obbligato lead parts.

77. McCartney is quoted in Flanagan 1990, 44; Harrison has also commented on the guitar thirds, in D. Forte 1987b, 92. The guitars in thirds are mimicked in many tracks by Cream, Led Zeppelin, the Allman Brothers, Spirit, Todd Rundgren, Steely Dan, and Boston.

78. Robertson 1991, 55.

79. Harrison's anger has lingered; a photo of his August 8, 1973, check to Inland Revenue for £1 million is given in Harrison 1980, plate 34. The $\sharp 9$ chord, a staple of the blues, would become the dissonant basis of Hendrix's "Purple Haze" (August 1967).

80. Lennon's claim is found in Golson 1981b, 161. The manuscript is reproduced in Harrison 1980, 95.

81. Lewisohn (1988, 76) discusses the original full close. The solo track copied onto the end repeats the structure of "Michelle" and the procedure used in "Rain."

82. Harrison's words are from D. Forte 1987b, 94; see McCartney's story in Mulhern 1990, 22, and Flanagan 1990, 44.

83. A half minute of rehearsal, featuring vibraphone—largely damped for the verse but fully open for the E-minor arpeggio—along with Lennon's Jumbo and drums, and Take 1 (Lennon and Harrison on acoustic guitars plucked at the bridge, Ringo on conga, and McCartney on tambourine, with double-tracked Lennon vocals, sounding in E♭ but at a tempo 15 percent faster than the final version) are heard on Beatles 1996a.

84. The tape speeds are given in Lewisohn 1988, 77.

85. George Martin discusses the procedure for recording the backward guitar lines in Buskin 1987, 40.

86. The nineteenth-century Lied, from Schubert's "Im Dorfe" through Brahms's Wiegenlieder to Wagner's "Träume," sought the effect of structural imperfect authentic cadences, floating between $\hat{3}$ and $\hat{5}$, without ever resolving to $\hat{1}$, as portray-

als of restful sleep and peaceful dreaming. The Beatles have stumbled upon the same device.

87. A grave marked "Eleanor Rigby," d. 1939, can be found in the south church-yard at St. Peter's, Woolton, a stone's throw from where McCartney first spoke with Lennon.

88. "Father Mackenzie," who was originally called Father McCartney in these lyrics, came from a telephone book. See Salewicz 1986, 180–81; J. Goodman 1984, 107; Miles and Marchbank 1978, 82; and Dowlding 1989, 134. Strangely, one McKenzie family has a plot adjacent to that of the Rigbys in Woolton.

89. A facsimile of McCartney's signed lyrics is in Campbell and Murphy 1980, 364. The bridge lyric, "Ah, look at *all the lonely people*," is added at top of the page. All of the conflicting claims as to lyric authorship come from Wenner 1971, 123; Golson 1981b, 151–52, 189; Dowlding 1989, 134–35; Coleman 1992, 23–24; and Shotton and Schaffner 1983, 122–23.

90. Lewisohn 1988, 77. See also Dowlding 1989, 135, and Golson 1981b, 152.

91. The miking technique, which preserved the gruff string articulations, is dis-cussed in Lewisohn 1988, 77. The original strings multitrack has been remixed for Beatles 1996a.

92. Riley 1988, 185.

93. J. Goodman 1984, 107.

94. The "monitor mixes" were live control room tapes made of the actual mix-ing process; they preserved various balance and filtering experiments, sometimes along with the engineers' discussions, and were never meant for potential release. The "For No One" monitor mixes are heard on Beatles 1993d.

95. The melody, just as in "Got to Get You into My Life," is based on an arpeg-giation of tonic leading to a neighboring ♭VII. In other popular music, the "offstage" quality of the horn often achieves the nostalgic effect suggested above. Note, e.g., how the horn answers "as I look back" in the Rascals' "I've Been Lonely Too Long" (January 1967).

96. I spoke with Civil, who was also to play in "A Day in the Life" and other Bea-tles recordings, on June 10, 1983. See Evans and Aspinall 1967 regarding the difficul-ties typically involved when session players were given no parts from which to read. "For No One" is performed in B♭ by McCartney with acoustic guitar, the Gabrieli String Quartet, and hornist Jeff Bryant in *Give My Regards to Broad Street*.

97. Hastings 1994. The keyboard part also recalls the Moody Blues' #1 hit "Go Now" (December 1964), which McCartney performed in his 1976 "Wings over America" tour.

98. The quote comes from Riley 1988, 194.

99. Miles and Marchbank 1978, 82–84; see also J. Goodman 1984, 107.

100. Golson 1981b, 189–90; Dowlding 1989, 138; Somach et al. 1989, 156. Mc-Cartney repaid the favor to Donovan a few months later by participating in the lat-ter's "Mellow Yellow" (November 1966). See Engelhardt 1998, 129.

101. Schaffner 1977, 62.

102. In the chorus, the four singers are on two parts as shown in the score, but at C+4 (0:43) and similar points, Harrison sings f[1] on the last sixteenth of beat two, illustrating that he has not lost his penchant for nonresolving nonchord tones.

103. Lennon's mocking of Ringo repeats the attitude captured in "What Goes On." Not heard is Ringo's thirty-one-second introductory declaration that his group will march from Land's End to John o' Groats, a reference to an actual 1960 feat (see the extreme southwest and northeast points on the British map), deleted in the mix-ing process but restored for the remixed multitrack for Beatles 1996c, which also in-cludes effects suppressed in the previous commercial mixes. Information on the ef-fects is drawn from Lewisohn 1988, 81; Buskin 1987, 42; Experiments 1966, 26; and Dowlding 1989, 139.

104. See Harrison 1980, 96–97, for the manuscript facsimile.

105. Harrison mentions McCartney's V♭9 of **A**+6 in connection with its reappearance in "Blue Jay Way," "I Want You (She's So Heavy)," and "When We Was Fab" (Harrison 1987a) in White 1987, 54.

106. The Spoonful's "Daydream" (February 1966) features the honky-tonk piano used in "Good Day Sunshine." It also has a Beatlesque staggering of the entrances of four differently textured guitars, the last with a volume-control pedal; "Good Day Sunshine" has no guitars at all. The drum triplets at the end of the intro of "Good Day Sunshine" are heard in the same place in the Spoonful's "You Didn't Have to Be So Nice" (November 1965). McCartney might also have been thinking of the Byrds' cover of "We'll Meet Again" (June 1965), which repeats "some sunny day-ay-ay-ay-ay" in three-part harmony, ending with reverb, as does "Good Day Sunshine." This song is one of Paul's several good-time-outdoors songs in the vein of other examples by the Beach Boys (McCartney's favorite Beach Boys LP, *Pet Sounds*, was released in late May 1966; honky-tonk piano is featured there as well) and the early Grateful Dead (1966).

Lennon may have contributed a few lines to "Good Day Sunshine." See J. Goodman 1984, 107, and Golson 1981b, 190.

107. The honky-tonk piano of "Good Day Sunshine" probably set the stage for its use in the Mamas and the Papas' "Words of Love" (December 1966) and "Dedicated to the One I Love" (February 1967).

108. The vocal arrangement of "Good Day Sunshine" in turn influences Cream's "I Feel Free" (April 1967), Yes's "Harold Land" (1969), and Chicago's "Wake Up Sunshine" (February 1970).

109. McCartney is quoted in *Melody Maker*, June 18, 1966 (actually published on the 16th), p. 18. Lennon and McCartney are heard together in Walsh 1966a, 3.

110. Gambaccini 1976, 66; J. Goodman 1984, 107; Elson 1986, 186–87. McCartney has also said (Miles 1997, 286) that his vocal was performed in imitation of Marianne Faithfull. "Here, There and Everywhere" was one of Lennon's favorite Beatles songs, and the harmonic structure of its verse is revisited in one of his last compositions, "Woman" (1980). After "Yesterday," it is McCartney's favorite of his Beatles songs (*McCartney world tour* 1989, 8), and it is the fourth *Revolver* track (after "Eleanor Rigby," "For No One," and "Good Day Sunshine") to be performed in *Give My Regards to Broad Street*. There it is abbreviated and played in F♯ with McCartney's guitar, flügelhorn, French horn, trombone, and cornet.

111. One can hear an early attempt with guide vocal and bass overdub, Take 7, on Beatles 1996c.

112. The shift to f♯2 in **B**+7 is of course an answer to the descent via register shift in **B**+2 (0:10–0:14), where b1 "descends" through a2 to g2. Aside from its registral glow, the f♯2 is highlighted by syncopation, further relating it to the similarly syncopated upper g2 of **B**+2.

113. Volume 1 shows that ever since his 1960 song "You'll Be Mine," McCartney has built polyphonic melodies of descending thirds, like those forming the basic structure of the highly ornamented bridge and into the recapitulation (from 0:56 to 1:08) of "Here, There and Everywhere": d2–b♭1, c2–a1, b♭1–g1; c2–a1, b♮1(!)–g1.

The motion from I to a bridge beginning on ♭III is not original here; the Beatles learned this in performing "To Know Her Is to Love Her." Closer to "Here, There and Everywhere" than that, though, are the two bars surrounding the move to the bridge in Herman's Hermits' "Mrs. Brown You've Got a Lovely Daughter" (April 1965).

114. This frustration is a topic in Hastings 1994.

115. See Golson 1981b, 190; Wenner 1971, 75–79; Miles and Marchbank 1978, 85; Somach et al. 1989, 213; An oral appreciation 1982, 217–18; and Turner 1994, 111.

116. Wiener 1992, 28. Sulpy (1995, 196) has heard a Lennon sketch that he calls "Hold On, I'm Comin'" and dates alongside these "She Said She Said" drafts.

117. See Walsh 1966a, 3.

118. The longing for past innocence recalls the opening verse of "Help!" Tim Riley (1988, 190) says, "At the core of Lennon's pain is a bottomless sense of abandonment, the same primal loss that gets recast in 'Strawberry Fields Forever' and again in 'Julia' and 'Mother.'" See also Rose 1985, 8.

119. Sections in contrasting meters like those in "She Said She Said" will be recreated by Jimi Hendrix ("Manic Depression," August 1967, and "One Rainy Wish," January 1968), Pink Floyd (1968), and Yes (1970).

120. The score has several a♮s in bass and lead guitar parts, all in error; in addition, Harrison's vocal part should read e♭2 for d2 in **A**+3 (third quarter) and **B**+2 (last eighth).

121. Lewisohn 1988, 84.

122. Shotton tells of the cover creation in Shotton and Schaffner 1983, 122. Voorman was a record jacket illustrator when the Beatles met him in Hamburg; he took up the bass with the popular Epstein-managed trio Paddy, Klaus & Gibson and with Manfred Mann before joining various post-Beatles Lennon and Harrison bands. Voorman "quoted" the *Revolver* cover in his sleeve for Harrison's "When We Was Fab" (January 1988). He was also called on for the multisection cover for *The Beatles Anthology* (1995–96).

123. Schaffner 1977, 214. Part of the "problem" with American reception of *Revolver* is likely related to the inferior track listing cobbled together for the original U.S. release, which pales in comparison with the original British release, not restored in the States until the 1988 compact disc release.

124. Both "Paperback Writer" and "Rain" are seen in re-edited versions in Beatles 1996c, vol. 5.

125. See *Melody Maker*, July 30, 1966, p. 1.

126. Coleman 1992, 310–11. "Rock and Roll Music" and "She's a Woman," opening the June 30 show, are heard on Beatles 1996a.

127. See Martin 1994, 7–8.

128. Beatles in interview row 1966, 4.

129. Schaffner 1977, 55. Of the Butcher photo, Lennon told a reporter at the time, "It's as valid as Vietnam!" (Walsh 1966a, 3), apparently referring to an American predilection for violence. Horribly similar to the "butcher cover" is the sleeve of Yoko Ono's "Now or Never" (November 1972), which features a famous color photograph of scores of My Lai villagers slain by American troops.

130. Beatles 1981b; see also Coleman 1992, 406–9. For more on the Christ controversy, see New York *Times*, August 6, 1966, p. 13; Beatles to face 1966, 1, 4; Grevatt 1966b, 15; Schaffner 1977, 57; Miles and Marchbank 1978, 28, 32; and Harry 1982, 142.

131. Grevatt 1966b, 15; Raver 1966c, 2.

132. See Wenner 1971, 131, and Miles and Marchbank 1978, 123.

133. McCabe and Schonfeld 1972, 59; compare Lennon's self-identity as a Beatle in Walsh 1966b, 3, and his tour memories in Wenner 1971, 14–20, 84–86.

134. Reck 1985, 106–7; Giuliano 1991b, 88.

135. See George's comments in *The Road* and Glazer 1977, 39–40, and Pattie's in Davies 1968b, 229.

136. Lennon had postproduction work on the film in London, February 11–March 3, 1967; the premiere took place on October 18, 1967.

137. Garbarini et al. 1980, 101.

138. Lennon et al. 1981, 17–18.

139. Countdown 1966, 3; Beatles to write 1966; Beatles take a rest 1966, 5; *Melody Maker*, November 19, 1966, p. 5. In January–February 1967, Shenson and Epstein commissioned a screenplay from award-winning London playwright Joe Orton; McCartney had liked his *Loot* and was also thinking of his friend Michael Antonioni to direct. Orton was told to give the Beatles parts that would allow them to

shine brighter than did the costars who had stolen scenes in *Help!* Orton wrote *Up Against It: Prick Up Your Ears*, submitted on March 6 but rejected by Epstein, perhaps because in the script the Beatles have been "caught in-flagrante, become involved in dubious political activity, dressed as women, committed murder, been put into prison and committed adultery" (Orton [1967], i). After the summer's woes, the Beatles' manager did not think this would promote a suitable image.

140. Beatles pic-script 1966, 1.

141. Lewisohn 1992, 214.

142. Martin 1979, 223; Elson 1986, 156; *The Beatles Monthly Book* 43 (February 1967), 11.

143. Beatle news 1966c, 13, 26, 29, 30.

144. Visiting George 1967, 12.

145. McCartney, a financial backer of the Indica (Hopkins 1987, 61), claims that Ono sought him out for Beatles manuscripts to auction for a New York John Cage benefit before she met Lennon (P. McCartney 1987). This strengthens biographer Hopkins's story that Ono originally approached Lennon with hopes of securing financial support. Her 1966 Indica catalogue is excerpted in Haskell and Hanhardt 1991, 14.

146. Wenner 1971, 173–74.

147. Haskell and Hanhardt 1991, 4.

148. Jones 1987, 142–43.

149. Hopkins 1987 is a thorough study of Ono's life; a generously illustrated survey of Ono's career through 1990 is given in Haskell and Hanhardt 1991. Her early art is summarized in Cott and Doudna 1982.

150. The Beatles also recorded Christmas messages for the "pirate" pop stations Radio London and Radio Caroline.

Interlude

1. Lennon recalls his inspiration for the song in Golson 1981b, 165–67, and Miles and Marchbank 1978, 9–10, 88.

2. Cott 1968; Miles and Marchbank 1978, 80.

3. Golson 1981b, 167–68. The "tree" may express another meaning as well; it was said of Lennon in 1964 that "childhood was happy enough for him, but he can remember being shot at by an irate owner of an apple-tree which John was busy 'scrumping'" (Shepherd 1964d, 174).

4. As testament to the Beatles' perfectionism in the recording process as compared to what normally would be expected, Lewisohn (1992, 244) presents an EMI document registering fiscal concern over the forty-seven acetate discs that would be cut during the making of "Strawberry Fields Forever" and "Penny Lane."

5. Martin 1979, 199–201; see also Martin in Beatles 1985c.

6. Takes 1–7 are heard on Beatles 1990d.

7. See Harrison on the Beatles' usually deleted codas in James 1967, 24. See McCartney on "cranberry sauce," and the furor to which this coda line contributed when taken for Lennon intoning "I buried Paul," in Miles and Marchbank 1978, 88.

8. This much of Take 7, crossfaded with selected tracks from Take 26, is heard on Beatles 1996a.

9. In the stereo mix released in 1967, the svaramandal track remains center. The 1971 stereo mix was for a German LP. Joshua Rifkin (1968, 120–21) finds that Harrison plays a rhythmically reduced version of the pitches of the chorus on the svaramandal at **B+9**; Martin (1994, 20) says that Harrison tuned the instrument very carefully, perhaps supporting Rifkin's observation. Harrison is seen with a fifteen-inch, twenty-one-string svaramandal in *Making of Sgt. Pepper* 1992.

10. Golson 1981b, 201–2.

11. In an exploitative way, the Buckinghams use backward cymbals in "Hey

Baby (They're Playing Our Song)" (August 1967) to express recollections; a more artistic use of tape effects is heard in the same group's "Foreign Policy" (June 1967).

12. "Strawberry Fields Forever" is placed in the context of the biography of Lennon's imagination in W. Everett 1986.

13. Lewisohn 1992, 235; see also James 1967, 24.

14. It seems likely that McCartney purchased back his own manuscript to "Penny Lane" when it was auctioned by Sotheby's in 1984 (*Sotheby's* 1984, 33); a facsimile appears in *McCartney world tour* 1989, 78. The lyrics are written on the reverse of a letter dated December 31, 1966; vocals were taped on December 30 and January 5. The only additions, marked by a different ink, to the otherwise complete draft are the retransitional words "very strange" and the smutty joke about "four of fish and finger pies" (see Miles and Marchbank 1978, 88).

15. Outtakes from the January 9 session, taped at the resulting pitch, are heard on Beatles 1992c and 1993a. Session musicians are named in Lewisohn 1988, 93.

16. The bus is an almost hidden premonition of McCartney's "Magical Mystery Tour."

17. Martin recalls the influence on McCartney of the Ashers' taste for Bach, Brahms, Handel, and Beethoven in BBC 1990; he discusses the Mason session in Martin 1979, 201–2. Mason's recollections, crediting the part to McCartney, are heard in Lewisohn 1988, 93, and *Making of Sgt. Pepper* 1992. One wonders if McCartney recognized the adaptation of the instrumental theme from Bach's "Jesu, Joy of Man's Desiring" in the twelve-string solo of the Byrds' "She Don't Care about Time" (October 1965), or the Toys' much more popular use of a Bach minuet in "A Lover's Concerto" (September 1965), and if these might have had any bearing on the Beatles' turn to the mid–eighteenth century for ideas.

18. The modulation up a whole step between verse and chorus is revisited in the Fifth Dimension's "Up, Up and Away" (May 1967), which traverses most of an equally divided octave, and in the Bee Gees' less artful "I've Gotta Get a Message to You" (August 1968).

19. In a 1994 conversation with me, Dan Kalbfus found the chorus more expressive than the verse, and Mollie Micek heard the brass fills during the chorus's vocal rests as wordless vehicles for reliving past events.

20. Mellers 1973, 83.

21. *Making of Sgt. Pepper* 1992.

22. Epstein, Beatles meet 1966, 20.

23. Martin 1979, 202.

24. Beatles single for Christmas 1966, 1. Many November–December press reports have the Beatles working on a single, not an LP. Flippo (1988, 201–2) elaborates that Epstein was relaying the pressure he felt from shareholders in Northern Songs, which had gone public in 1965.

25. The films were shot on January 30–31 and February 5 and 7 in London, Sevenoaks, and Liverpool locations; see the films in volume 6 of Beatles 1996c.

26. Martin 1979, 168.

Two

1. Whitburn 1993, 949.

2. Ibid., 958.

3. Mulhern 1990, 30.

4. Schaffner 1982, 126.

5. Hendrix was a transplanted native of Seattle.

6. Clapton's one LP with the Yardbirds, *Five Live Yardbirds*—recorded at the Marquee Club—parallels the Beatles' covers of Chuck Berry songs for their BBC performances.

7. Lewisohn 1988, 92, and 1992, 240–41. I have not heard the "Carnival" tape, but more details appear in Miles 1997, 308–9.

8. Radhakrishnan 1973, 95n.

9. The *Bhagavadgita* quote is from ibid., 204.

10. Martin 1992. One writer has it that McCartney was inspired to make a "concept" album upon hearing the Mothers' two-record set of 1966, *Freak Out* (Flippo 1988, 213).

11. Martin 1992.

12. *McCartney world tour* 1989, 53. This concern for stereotyping was to lead to Lennon's "bagism" campaign in 1969, and hiding behind a fictitious identity was to help Harrison find new freedom in 1988–90 as "Spike Wilbury" with the Traveling Wilburys. McCartney also hid behind pseudonyms such as "Percy Thrillington" in 1977 and "The Fireman" in 1993 and 1998, as did all Beatles when working in support of friends' recording projects.

13. Golson 1981b, 206–7; Martin 1994, 64.

14. The antiquarian turns of phrase are noted in Turner 1994, 118.

15. Miles and Marchbank 1978, 88.

16. Lennon speaks in Golson 1981b, 207; Starr in Clayson 1992, 114.

17. Ken Townsend, who oversaw the design of the transformer necessary for direct injection, believes that the technique was originated by the Beatles (Lewisohn 1988, 95).

18. Garbarini 1982, 47.

19. Martin 1992.

20. The Studer J37 tape machine on which *Sgt. Pepper* was recorded was auctioned, along with the studio's Mellotron, in October 1980 (Beatlenews roundup 1980, 22).

21. While in California in April, McCartney jammed with the Jefferson Airplane and the Beach Boys (munching crisply on "Vegetables," *Smiley Smile*, released September 1967) (D. Taylor 1987, 64). His and Mal Evans's home movies of this trip were auctioned in 1992 and released on videotape as *The Mystery Trip*.

22. Martin 1992.

23. The bass drum microphone placement is discussed in Buskin 1987, 44.

24. Lewisohn 1988, 101. Martin's horn score is shown in Kozinn 1995a, 157.

25. Sound effect origins are given in Lewisohn 1992, 248.

26. Examples of the hard-rock I–♭III–IV–I progression predating "Sgt. Pepper" are elusive — only the Temptations' "(I Know) I'm Losing You" (November 1966) comes to mind, and this postdates the turnaround in the Beatles' "The Night Before" (1965). But this quickly becomes a rock icon in many styles; it is basic to the verse of "I Can See for Miles" (the Who, October 1967), the bridge of "Think" (Aretha Franklin, May 1968), the title track of *Ogden's Nut Gone Flake* (the Small Faces, June 1968), and the chorus of "Magic Carpet Ride" (Steppenwolf, September 1968) and many to follow.

27. In Wenner 1971, 130–31, Lennon says the joint composition should be credited "fifty-fifty." Much of the song's composition process is given a contemporaneous account in Davies 1968a, 263–67.

28. Lennon speaks in Wenner 1971, 130. Reminiscent of the second verse of Dylan's "Ballad of a Thin Man" (September 1965), this mysterious line also seems to inspire a similar verse in Cream's "Take It Back" (*Disraeli Gears*).

29. Martin 1992.

30. Note the score's wrong note for backing vocals in the crucial last bar, which should read g$\sharp^1$.

31. Miles and Marchbank 1978, 89.

32. Martin 1992.

33. Ibid.

34. For earlier instances of the *Alice* books' influences on Lennon's poetry, see "Deaf Ted, Danoota (and me)" and "I Wandered" in Lennon 1964. From the latter:

"Past grisby trees and hulky builds / Past ratters and bradder sheep . . . Down hovey lanes and stoney claves / Down ricketts and stickly myth / In a fatty hebrew gurth / I wandered humply as a sock / To meet bad Bernie Smith." Carroll's likeness appears on the *Sgt. Pepper* cover. Lennon's inspiration from Carroll was predated by that of Grace Slick's "White Rabbit," first recorded by the Great Society in 1965.

35. Lennon has discussed the origin of the song's title in Wenner 1971, 136, and Golson 1981b, 191–92. McCartney, who insists that his total contribution to the song was on par with Lennon's, created at least the reference to "newspaper taxis." See Wenner 1971, 30, and Coleman 1995, 103. As to the psychedelic references, the boat, the taxis, and the train are highly suggestive of a "trip" (see Pichaske 1972, 59).

36. A manuscript with some transposed lyrics was auctioned by Sotheby's in August 1984 (*Sotheby's* 1984, 49). A second document indicates changes in instrumentation and chords along with key words from the text (Davies 1968a, 282).

37. The Lowrey is identified in Martin 1994, 101–2. An early take with Lennon's guide vocal is played and discussed by George Martin in Martin 1992 and distributed on Beatles 1993a. Beatles 1996a presents a new mix of components from the four-track tapes of both Takes 6 and 7 (the latter released on the 1967 LP).

38. What has been referred to as a "metric modulation," as in the work of Elliott Carter, is perhaps more properly understood as a modulation of tempos that pivots on submetrical relationships. Thus, triple groupings of quarters ("Lucy in the Sky with Diamonds," **B**), while retaining their individual durations, are regrouped as unarticulated triplets in a quadruple context (**C**–1, ♩. = ♩), and the new beat duration is in turn divided into two simple eighths (**C**), resulting in a tempo seeming one-third slower than the original. I thank Poundie Burstein for bringing "Lucy"'s use of this rhythmic technique to my attention in a November 1996 conversation; it is also discussed in Moore 1997, 32.

39. Davies 1968a, 268–69.

40. J. Goodman 1984, 110; see also Martin 1994, 112.

41. Lennon relates this violent past to his later cause for peace in Golson 1981b, 192; see also C. Lennon 1978, 25–26. McCartney's manuscript for "Getting Better" sold for a record $249,200 at Sotheby's, London, on September 14, 1995.

42. Martin 1994, 108.

43. The backing vocals session on March 21 was aborted when everyone realized that Lennon was incapacitated by LSD; see Davies 1968a, 271; Wenner 1971, 76; and Martin 1979, 206–7.

44. See Salewicz 1986, 190; Turner 1994, 125; Miles and Marchbank 1978, 89; and J. Goodman 1984, 110.

45. Mellers 1973, 90–91.

46. Martin 1994, 87.

47. Riley 1988, 217.

48. Most of the discussion on "She's Leaving Home" is taken from W. Everett 1987, which includes a full score transcription that clarifies all of the string assignments.

49. Miles and Marchbank 1978, 89.

50. The parents' moaning paraphrases the *Daily Mail* story's quotations of the actual parents (the original story is given in Turner 1994, 125) but also reverberates with antimaterialistic sentiments expressed in "Can't Buy Me Love" and "And Your Bird Can Sing."

51. The "Yesterday" connection is noted in Lewisohn 1988, 103. George Martin was hurt when McCartney went to Leander, which he did only because Martin did not satisfy his immediate wishes by canceling a session with Cilla Black to write and record the arrangement (Martin 1979, 207–8). Martin's adjustments are mentioned in Williams 1971b, 25. On August 27, 1992, at Sotheby's, London, McCartney paid £41,000 to recover his own manuscript to "She's Leaving Home" (Beatlenews roundup 1992, 10).

52. Davies 1968a, 275. A photo of the composer with poster in the Weybridge foyer is reproduced in D. Taylor 1987, 41; the text is transcribed in MacDonald 1994, 188n. Lennon did change the horse's name from the hard-to-scan Zanthus to an alliterative Henry, and other adjustments were made to create a rhyme scheme.

53. Martin 1994, 89. A carnival atmosphere pervades a number of early Dylan songs, such as "Ballad of a Thin Man" and "Desolation Row" (both September 1965). The metric contrasts of "Mr. Kite" help create a circus atmosphere in the later "Spinning Wheel" (Blood, Sweat and Tears, January 1969) and "The Night the Carousel Burnt Down" (Todd Rundgren, March 1972).

54. This identical arrangement is heard in Takes 1, 2, and 7—the last, the basis of the eventual master, crossfading into the February 20 effects tape—on Beatles 1996a.

55. Reverb was applied to different lines in the mono and stereo mixes; it was also useful in masking the drop-ins done on February 28 and 29.

56. The harmonicas were inspired by both the six-man Morton Fraser harmonica gang and the Beach Boys' use of bass harmonica on "I Know There's an Answer" (*Pet Sounds*, May 1966) (Martin 1992). In turn, the bass harmonica gives a carny sound to portions of Simon and Garfunkel's "The Boxer" (April 1969). Dietz 1995 suggests the hearing of a ringmaster's whistle blasts in the retransitional dominant.

57. Martin 1979, 204.

58. The production of the concrète collage of spliced-together steam organ tapes is discussed in Martin 1979, 204–5; Martin 1992; and Martin 1994, 90–91.

59. Martin 1994, 124.

60. Golson 1981b, 196.

61. Miles and Marchbank 1978, 89–92.

62. Reck 1985, 108–9.

63. Lewisohn 1992, 248.

64. Martin discusses the dilruba performances in Martin 1979, 203.

65. A new mix and edit of selected instrumental tracks (including dubbed strings only at **C**) was made for Beatles 1996a.

66. In *Khamaj thata*, the use of $\flat\hat{7}$ ascending is rare, but this is a favorite Harrison device.

67. Harrison 1980, 112.

68. See Jairazbhoy 1971, 103.

69. The tabla flurry is noted in Vaughn 1994.

70. See Wade 1980, 93.

71. Other rock songs influenced by "Within You Without You" include Spirit's "Mechanical World" (April 1968), the Incredible String Band's "Maya" (November 1968), and much of the Moodies' LP *To Our Children's Children's Children* (November 1969).

72. Dates are suggested in Miles and Marchbank 1978, 71; J. Goodman 1984, 110; and K. Everett 1967, 25.

73. McCartney's manuscript sold for $55,700 at Sotheby's, London, in September 1994 (Beatlenews roundup 1994).

74. Martin 1994, 35. An acetate of a December 21, 1966, mix in the original key of C was sold in August 1992 (Beatlenews roundup 1992, 10).

75. Riley 1988, 222; Golson 1981b, 193.

76. Golson 1981b, 206.

77. Miles and Marchbank 1978, 92. Bob Dylan's "Motorpsycho Nightmare" (September 1964) was inhabited by a frightening Rita protected by her father just as sisters protect McCartney's Rita. Dylan also makes a famous reference to parking meters in "Subterranean Homesick Blues" (April 1965).

78. Through the recording process, the speed of the tape was adjusted up 17.4 percent in one mixdown, down 7 percent in another, and mixed yet another 2.5 per-

cent slower (Martin 1994, 95–96), so the basic track had probably been recorded in D, though it sounds in E♭.

79. The comb and tissue paper are noted in Christgau and Piccarella 1982, 218–19.

80. The capstan effect is noted in Lewisohn 1988, 104.

81. Miles and Marchbank 1978, 92; Golson 1981b, 193. "Meet the Wife," mentioned at the end of the second bridge, **F**+4–5, is the name of a contemporaneous evening BBC-TV series, continuing the television references.

82. A new mix of the tracks made thus far is heard on Beatles 1996a.

83. An amusing anecdote has Lennon bewildered at the necessity of having the E♭ and B♭ saxes transpose parts differently: "Sounds bloody silly to me"; see Palmer 1968, 65; Martin 1979, 138–39; and Martin 1983, 82. Sounds Inc., a group from Kent that also included drums, bass, and two guitars, was signed by NEMS management in March 1964 and opened concerts for the Beatles in 1964–65.

84. The tape op is quoted in Lewisohn 1988, 102.

85. See Lewisohn 1988, 105, and the worksheet in Lewisohn 1992, 250. Riley 1988, 224, ties together Lennon's ennui, the coda's repeated phrase, and the animal chase: "As the sound recoils into its own whirlpool of repeated phrases, a fox hunt descends into the fore, satirizing the mad dash of life."

86. See Martin 1979, 203, and Lewisohn 1988, 109.

87. Tamm 1987, 214; Martin 1992.

88. O'Grady 1983, 135.

89. Such mixed meters, heretofore practically unknown in rock music, will be explored by the Airplane and the Dead (both in 1967), Cream (1968), the Allman Brothers (1969), and Led Zeppelin (1970).

90. Aspinall is mentioned in D. Taylor 1987, 26. The McCartney patter is from Beatles 1977a.

91. The master derives from Take 9; a nearly identical Take 5 basic track, with McCartney's guide vocal intact, is presented on Beatles 1996a.

92. Salewicz 1986, 184. News stories had served Bob Dylan in "Oxford Town" (May 1963) and "Lonesome Death of Hattie Carroll" (January 1964) and Frank Zappa in "Trouble Every Day" (March 1966), but these are all topical references, whereas Lennon's inspiration is more abstract and poetic. Lennon's manuscript was sold to Apple for £44,000 in August 1992 (Beatlenews roundup 1992, 10).

93. The story appears in Turner 1994, 132.

94. Miles and Marchbank 1978, 92. The Albert Hall, by the way, seats 8,000. Terry Doran, a car salesman, was a Beatles associate and the inspiration for the "motor trade" man in "She's Leaving Home."

95. Lennon provides the setting for this work in Wenner 1971, 138.

96. Riley draws an analogy to *Hamlet,* but one might also think of "Penny Lane": "We're never sure whether Lennon's section is the 'real' world or if it's merely the dream that Paul slips into atop the bus. The alarm clock blurs these boundaries: is Paul waking from Lennon's nightmare, or is Lennon imagining Paul's generic day in the life? The song inside a song works like the play within a play: the interdependence of reality and illusion is telescoped into one setting" (Riley 1988, 227).

97. See Gambaccini 1976, 23, and *McCartney world tour* 1989, 53.

98. Lennon is quoted in Golson 1981b, 193–94; McCartney in Miles and Marchbank 1978, 92. Lennon rewrote his partner's line as "My love will turn you on" in "Oh Yoko!" (Lennon 1971). Like Dylan's "Rainy Day Women #12 & 35" (July 1966) and the Byrds' "Eight Miles High" (April 1966), "A Day in the Life" was banned from many radio playlists, including that of the BBC, for apparent encouragement of illicit drug use.

99. Martin 1994, 156.

100. See Paul McCartney reviews 1967, 13. Only two other "quadri-plagal" examples come to mind—the Mothers' "Flower Punk" (March 1968), a send-up of

both Hendrix and Beatles models, and Deep Purple's "Hush" (August 1968), but "tri-plagal" progressions, ♭III–♭VII–IV–I, abound in 1968–69: see the verse of the Status Quo's "Pictures of Matchstick Men" (January 1968) and the choruses of the Stones' "Jumpin' Jack Flash" (May 1968) and the Bonzo Dog Band's "We Are Normal" (June 1969). The term "quadri-plagal" was suggested by Dan Kalbfus.

101. See Martin 1992 and Somach et al. 1989, 284.

102. Williams 1971b, 34; Martin 1979, 208–10.

103. McCartney instructed the orchestra members to perform without regard to their partners' rhythms but was amused to find that the string players followed their leader "like a herd of sheep," while the brass players remained quite loose (*McCartney world tour* 1989, 52; Lewisohn 1988, 14). The glissando was imitated on Mellotron by King Crimson in "The Epitaph" (October 1969).

104. "A Day in the Life" is the fifth song on the LP—following "Lucy in the Sky with Diamonds," "Being for the Benefit of Mr. Kite," "Within You Without You," and "Good Morning Good Morning"—to have metric contrast provided by the bridge, but this song has more rhythmic than harmonic coherence. Although the opening tempo (♩ = 80) quickens for the frantic bridge (♩ = 88, with heavy accents on the offbeat), the tempo of the final verse (returning to ♩ = 80) is heavily subdivided by Ringo in reference to the bridge (see Rifkin 1968, 119).

105. See Buskin 1987, 46, regarding the tape echo. The first fifteen bars of Take 1, along with a preliminary setup and Martin's added commentary, is heard on Beatles 1993a. Evans's counting is given progressively heavier echo, as McCartney says, "because we thought it was kinda freaky" (Lewisohn 1988, 14).

106. Martin 1979, 208.

107. This is the vocal marked by an "oh shit!" at **F**, preserved in the new mix of Take 6 edited between portions of the Take 2 basic track for Beatles 1996a, spliced there at 2:45 and 3:48.

108. This preliminary bass part contains all of the voice leading of the final version but is rhythmically simple (containing many half notes for the stepwise descents) and features a few harmonic intervals and three-part chords.

109. Martin 1979, 211.

110. A production schedule and £34,000 budget are given in Lewisohn 1992, 245. Only the film for "A Day in the Life" was produced; it is marked by multiple images and by rapid changes, each shot lasting less than three seconds.

111. The splice is identified in Martin 1979, 211. The orchestra parts reverberate not only because of the multiple layers of tape but also because of the "ambiophony" of Studio One, where they were recorded. This system involves a delayed live playback through a series of magnetic delay drums and 100 wall-mounted speakers, installed in 1958 for the ability to simulate various reverberation characteristics (Southall 1982, 57).

112. Pichaske 1972, 62. The sturdy chord is later relied on to carry the weight of the Beatles' entire recording career when appended to the end of "The End" in Beatles 1996b.

113. Three aborted stereo remixes can be heard on Beatles 1990d.

114. Riley 1988, 226.

115. Pichaske 1972, 59; see also Riley 1988, 225.

116. Buskin 1987, 68.

117. The high-frequency tone was there for dogs' enjoyment. Perhaps McCartney wished to answer the Beach Boys' *Pet Sounds*, which ends with dogs barking at a train.

118. Miles and Marchbank 1978, 93. The obscure gibberish, played backward, was interpreted as obscene by many British fans and became a major contributor to the craze of finding "hidden" meanings in the Beatles' recordings. The inner groove did not appear on American pressings, and because of its interference with

the disc-cutting process, it took on several different guises among worldwide releases. When Lennon produced Yoko Ono's LP *Plastic Ono Band* in October 1970, he repeated the inner-groove trick.

119. A preliminary order for Side 1 is given in Lewisohn 1988, 108.

120. See Martin 1994, 114–7.

121. The inner sleeve is replicated on p. 27 of the booklet in Beatles 1967b. The rejected gatefold is discussed in D. Taylor 1987, 32.

122. McCabe and Schonfeld 1972, 33. All personages on the cover are identified on p. 3 of the booklet in Beatles 1967b.

123. Beyond the rip-off cover shot by *Sgt. Pepper*'s photographer, the Stones use a Mellotron, harpsichord, oscillator, and backward guitars to try to re-create the tone of the Beatles' work; they even end one side with a ring-modulated version of "We Wish You a Merry Christmas" slowed down enough to contain "hidden" meaning. The Small Faces actually bring great originality to their Leslied guitar, honky-tonk piano, crowd noises, svaramandal, and harpsichord in creating a unified story of their second side. As homage to the Beatles, the Mothers include a reprise of a theme song, "What's the Ugliest Part of Your Body," and conclude on a long-held piano chord. One curious quotation from the LP appears in Marmalade's "Reflections of My Life" (March 1970), the intro, verse, and chorus of which are based on a half-time version of the first acoustic guitar bars from "A Day in the Life," vesting "Reflections" with an appropriate smoky pall.

124. Quoted are William Mann, in Martin 1994, 152, and Lees 1967, 94.

125. Leary speaks through Norman 1981, 287.

126. D. Taylor 1987, 41. Along with composer Philip Glass, McCartney collaborated with Ginsberg on an unusual recording (Ginsberg 1996) shortly before the poet's 1997 death.

127. Top 100 1987, 46. A much more comprehensive coverage of *Pepper* reception can be found in Moore 1997, 58–69.

128. The banjo, if audible at all, is indistinguishable from the harpsichord. The string bass and violin are quite audible in the broadcast mix (heard on Beatles 1990d) but nearly lost in the EMI version, where the violin can be heard scratching an open g on the first and second beats of **B**+3 (0:48–0:49), followed by its upper neighbor a two bars later, some amateurish noise at 1:32–1:36, and some undistinguished bowed tremolo at 3:13–3:20.

129. Bach was in the air: the C-major prelude from Book 1 of the *Well-Tempered Clavier* had just been woven into Gary Brooker's piano part in "Repent Walpurgis" (*Procol Harum*, May 1967).

130. Regarding the scatting of "She Loves You," compare the "All You Need Is Love" coda with the ending of "What's That You're Doing?" (McCartney 1982b), where Stevie Wonder recalls the 1963 hit once again. The orchestra was conducted by Mike Vickers, the ex–Manfred Mann guitarist who wrote film scores and arranged for Cilla Black and for Paul's brother's group, the Scaffold. See Martin 1979, 192–93, for more on the taping session. The film of the musical portion of the broadcast has been faithfully colorized for Beatles 1995b.

131. "Baby You're a Rich Man" emerged out of studio time otherwise wasted with "aimless" untitled jamming on May 9, June 1, and June 2, according to Lewisohn 1988, 111, 114, 116.

132. Lennon ascribes authorship to verse and chorus in Golson 1981b, 194. See McCabe and Schonfeld 1972, 38, regarding Epstein's desire to "entertain all the beautiful people."

133. See Harrison 1980, 100, for Harrison's notes on "Only a Northern Song."

134. See *McCartney world tour* 1989, 55.

135. The abridged basic track appears, with variant lyrics, in stereo on Beatles 1996a. So as to keep complete track of the known record of the Beatles' recording

history, it should be mentioned that on February 22, 1967, the group also recorded twenty-two minutes of drums with tambourine and congas labeled "Drum Track" in studio notes; this was never used (Lewisohn 1988, 99).

136. See Harrison 1980, 106, regarding the experiences that led to the composition of this song. The original mix, heard on Beatles 1993a, continues for eight and a half minutes, while the commercial version endures for 6'27".

137. The film version, while edited to 2'22" (see Beatles 1992f), still includes a verse that was cut from all record releases.

138. MacDonald 1994, 208, identifies the Merseys source.

139. The Beatles taped some effects for the film in the November 1967 sessions and produced more songs for the film in early 1968. See Lewisohn 1988, 130.

140. Turner 1994, 186.

141. See Lewisohn 1988, 15; Golson 1981b, 214; and McCoy and McGeary 1990, 225. A cassette, reputedly from Weybridge 1967, has surfaced (see Lennon 1988b), with Lennon struggling to find this song's chords on the piano, but this tape sounds more like an attempted but impaired recreation from the 1970s than a composing sketch.

142. Mixing and editing was overseen by Lennon. Because of complications arising from having edited a mono mix, this is the last Beatles record, and only the second since 1963, not to have been mixed for stereo. Beatles 1996a presents a new edit of stereo mixes from the multitrack and (from 4:29 on) what must be one of Lennon's alternate mono mixes, tape hiss and all. The passage in 0:46–2:16 there (a repeat of $A+1-7$ and a ska variation) had not appeared in the 1970 release, nor had that at 3:50–4:12 (eleven bars of D material), but this mix cuts thirteen bars from $D+5$ to $E+7$ at 4:21, at which point a different stereo mix is introduced—note the switch of vocal imaging.

143. Harrison says that this LSD controversy led to his song "See Yourself" (Harrison 1976a).

144. The drawing is shown in Beatlenews roundup 1993b, 4.

145. Regarding the Scaffold recording, see Paul in secret 1967, 1. "Catcall" was taped on July 20 at Chappell's London Studio and released that October 20, as Marmalade 598005, in the United Kingdom.

146. A. Taylor 1991, 89. See also Miles 1997, 378.

147. See Giuliano 1991b, 79–81, and Pules 1967, 11.

148. Norman 1981, 295–96; Reck 1985, 109–10.

149. Norman 1981, 277, 281, 300. Many have speculated that Epstein's decreasing role in the Beatles' affairs, combined with the looming date, October 1, 1967, of the end of his contract with them, led to a severe depression.

150. Wenner 1971, 52.

151. Regarding the *Daily Post* quote, the Alexandra Palace, and the Electric Garden, see, respectively, Haskell and Hanhardt 1991, 52; Lewisohn 1992, 254; and Raver 1967, 2.

152. See first-page stories on the Beatles' film plans in *Melody Maker* dated January 28, July 1, and September 9, 1967. Wolfe 1968, 122, says of the film edited from the Kesey trip: "It was the world's first acid film, taken under conditions of total spontaneity barreling through the heartlands of America, recording all *now*, in the moment." Kesey's bus, "Further," and its driver, Neal Cassady, are also the subject of the Grateful Dead's "The Other One" (August 1968): "Cowboy Neal at the wheel of the bus to Never-Ever Land."

153. The storyboard is reproduced in King 1987, 12; see also Gambaccini 1976, 47–48.

154. For Lennon's reaction to McCartney's plan, see Yorke 1970, 71; Miles 1981, 66–67; and Golson 1981b, 195. The job list is given in Giuliano 1991a, 121.

155. Walsh 1967, 12–13. Harrison had been perturbed by recent administrative hassles over the *Sgt. Pepper* sleeve and the "Our World" broadcast.

156. See Norman 1981, 310–11.

157. Regarding the *Strangelove* outtakes (erroneously attributed to *2001: A Space Odyssey*), see Turner 1994, 144, and Beatles 1996c, vol. 6. See "I Am the Walrus" outtakes inserted in Beatles 1996c. Regarding the cancellation of the American film broadcast, see *Melody Maker*, April 13, 1968, p. 1. "Magical Mystery Tour" enjoyed a limited theatrical release in the United States in 1974.

158. See Cowan 1978?, 31, regarding the poster search.

159. Dowlding 1989, 194.

160. Lewisohn 1988, 110.

161. The trumpeters again included David Mason, who had thus played on four Beatles sessions in 1967. Trumpet parts are ascribed both to McCartney and to the first trumpet, Elgar Howarth (Lewisohn 1988, 111).

162. Those authors would be Mellers 1973, 108; O'Grady 1983, 144; and Riley 1988, 236–37.

163. Turner 1994, 145–46. Lennon replied with a letter dated September 1.

164. Lennon reveals his motivation in Lennon et al. 1981, 154.

165. This is one of several variants of the chant and is cited in Shotton and Schaffner 1983, 124.

166. Some images are absolutely contemporaneous; "elementary penguin" is a jab at Allen Ginsberg, well-known for chanting "Hare Krishna" (Golson 1981b, 194), as he does on the Fugs' LP *Tenderness Junction* (October 1968); see also Wolfe 1968, 154, 194. The scholar-mocking citation of "Lucy in the Sky with Diamonds" is Lennon's most obvious self-reference to date, but "Glass Onion" will go further by referring to "I Am the Walrus," "Lucy in the Sky," and others. McCartney, in turn, would use a line from "Walrus," "See how they run," as the refrain of "Lady Madonna."

167. Golson 1981b, 194.

168. The cited Dylan songs are all from *Highway 61 Revisited* (September 1965). These songs tell of the mystery tramp, the one-eyed midget, Cinderella, Romeo, Cain and Abel, the Hunchback of Notre Dame, Ophelia, Noah, Dr. Filth, the Phantom of the Opera, Casanova, a tightrope walker, Ezra Pound, T. S. Eliot, Paul Revere's horse, Jack the Ripper, John the Baptist, Galileo, Cecil B. DeMille, Ma Rainey, and Beethoven. See also Murphy and Gross 1969, 42.

169. See Golson 1981b, 194, and Martin 1994, 139.

170. The *Lear* cast is given in Lewisohn 1988, 128. Lennon's "Radio Play," "Two Minutes Silence" (an elegy for Yoko's 1968 miscarriage), and "No Bed for Beatle John" (a recitation of news clippings), all from Lennon 1969, are other homages to Ono's interest in Cage. Lennon has said that "I Am the Walrus" was completed "after I met Yoko" (Golson 1981b, 194), so he connects her with this composition for some unstated reason. But we can guess that the coda is the basis of his remembrance.

171. Lewisohn 1988, 122.

172. See Golson 1981b, 101–2. The chorus, the Mike Sammes Singers, had recently been in the Top Ten with "I Was Kaiser Bill's Batman" (February 1967), released under the pseudonym "Whistling Jack Smith."

173. Lennon says the song derived from acid trips on successive (August–September?) weekends; see Golson 1981b, 194, and Cott 1968.

174. Cf. the cello trills here with the slow "turn you on" cello trills in "A Day in the Life." This hearing of anxiety seems incongruous alongside John Robertson's citation of Smokey Robinson's romantic "Ooo Baby Baby" (the Miracles, March 1965) as a model for Lennon's cry (Robertson 1991, 74), but such dis-ease is the fabric of "I Am the Walrus." For instance, Lennon's paranoia is ironically counterpoised by the restful English garden setting (see Wenner 1971, 185).

175. Monitor mixes of basic track rehearsal Takes 7–9 can be heard on Beatles 1993d: Take 7 fades in after the intro and breaks down two bars before **E**; Take 8 breaks down at **A+2**; Take 9 is a complete run-through. Take 16, heard without dubs on Beatles 1996a, was used for continued work.

176. Martin scored the work for session musicians.

177. The first four eighths are edited out of all mono mixes and from the first master of the American-released stereo mix. The drums at **B**–1 do not appear in mono; and the U.S. mono mix, pressed on both commercial and promotional discs, is the only version to include an extra bar (of D[7]) after **C**+5 (a measure present in the basic tracks, as heard on Beatles 1996a), perhaps removed elsewhere because Lennon has a vocal miscue. All stereo mixes are monophonic from **D**–1 (the point of both mono and stereo splices) onward, so as to incorporate the *Lear* material from the mono mixing session. This same sort of mess, resulting from the performance of overdubs after final mixing had already begun, was to complicate "You Know My Name (Look Up the Number)."

178. Lennon on playing second fiddle to McCartney's immeasurably less substantial but more pop-oriented A-side: "Can you believe it?" (Wenner 1971, 106).

179. The intention of McCartney's irony is revealed in a July 29, 1990, press conference: "When I wrote 'Fool on the Hill,' the idea for me was always just someone who's got the right answer but people tend to ridicule him" (McCartney 1991a). See also Miles 1997, 343, 365–6. An early vocal proclaims, in the coda, "He's no fool" (Take 4, Beatles 1996a). The released version is not so direct.

180. Lennon has praised his partner for the "complete" lyrics in "The Fool on the Hill" (Golson 1981b, 196).

181. The draft is heard on Beatles 1996a. Biographer Hunter Davies (1968a, 268) dates the song to even earlier origins in mid-March 1967.

182. See Davies 1968a, 321–23, and Harrison 1980, 114. The August 1 manuscript is given in Davies 1968a, 322, and Harrison 1980, 114; its lyrics are changed only slightly in the recorded version, but it also includes a fourth verse (in a different ink) sensibly omitted from the recording: "When I see you at the door / I know [you're] worth waiting for / for the moment when you speak— / I know I'd wait here all week."

183. The "Indian" sound, along with the fog, leads Wilfrid Mellers to hear the song as a "descent 'below' consciousness" in the "Tomorrow Never Knows" vein (Mellers 1973, 111). The rare Lydian scale is previously known only in the Left Banke's "Pretty Ballerina" (December 1966), among the popular-music repertoire.

184. See Evans and Aspinall 1968a, 11.

185. Note Lennon's backing vocal in the wordless introduction, which alternates $\flat\hat{6}-\hat{5}$ in the manner of a siren, the same effect he tried to achieve in the opening vocal of "Walrus." One August 22, 1967, acetate of Take 8 (on Beatles 1991a) contains only piano, drums, tambourine, and two McCartney vocals. Take 27, an attempted remake of the basic track of September 16 (see Beatles 1996a), features Ringo augmenting his snare rudiments with cymbal, supporting harmonium, and jangle piano, all underneath McCartney's guide vocal.

186. McCartney's guitar part is more ambitious than anything Harrison played in 1967 and is not unlike his own later "Hot as Sun."

187. Lewisohn 1988, 128.

188. MacDonald 1994, 218.

189. The extra-long coda (for Lennon, similar to that in "Ticket to Ride," Golson 1981b, 208) was referred to as the "Maori finale" from the start (Evans and Aspinall 1968a, 11). The Beatles saw Maori dancers in Dunedin, June 25, 1964 (Beatles 1981b). What sounds like an outtake from the October 2 session has McCartney abandoning the piano part of "Hello Goodbye" for an improvised I–IV–V–I number, "All Together on the Wireless Machine," sung for BBC personality Kenny Everett, who may have just entered the studio and who broadcast the ditty (Beatles c. 1976a) on November 25, 1967.

190. The viola parts were McCartney's own, notated by George Martin (Lewisohn 1988, 129).

191. A version without violas was mixed on November 15 for the mimed promo

video filmed in the Saville Theatre on November 10, but the fact of the miming was so obvious that the clip was banned in the United Kingdom as in defiance of the Musicians' Union (see Lewisohn 1992, 271–73).

192. Rifkin 1968, 122–23. Note also the bass descent in **A**+4. McCartney has said, "I've never practiced scales in my life" (Mulhern 1990, 23), but he writes many of them.

193. The structure of the first part of the chorus, **B**+1–4 (0:21–0:30), is transposed directly to A major by Graham Nash in the chorus of "Our House" (March 1970).

194. Lewisohn 1988, 131. The unedited (6'43") take of "Christmas Time," with ten choruses, is heard on Beatles 1992f. A brief (1'04") stereo mix was prepared for Beatles 1993e, and the first 2'18" are superimposed with messages from other Christmas tapings for commercial release on Beatles 1995d.

195. Evans and Aspinall 1968a, 8.

196. Lewisohn 1988, 131.

197. See D. Taylor 1987, 145.

198. Lennon has said that the boutique was intended as a tax dodge. It was managed by Liverpool friend Pete Shotton (Wenner 1971, 58).

199. Norman 1981, 315–16.

Three

1. The bossa nova is not a commonly represented style in 1960s pop music, but one example made the Top Five in Stan Getz's "The Girl from Ipanema" (May 1964), and the style is also heard in Simon and Garfunkel's "So Long, Frank Lloyd Wright" (February 1970). McCartney revisited the soft, chromatically modulating, syncopated dance style with its major sevenths in "Distractions" (McCartney 1989), which begins in G major and tonicizes B♭, just as "Step inside Love" does.

Ringo Starr made a guest appearance on friend Cilla's show, singing "Act Naturally" as a duet with his host on February 6.

2. The recording, produced by George Martin, was released as Parlophone R 5674 on March 8, reaching #8 in the charts. See How Cilla 1968, 11.

3. Black, whose history with the Beatles goes back to 1961, was to find success in Monte Carlo cabaret in July 1968. Her television show was picked up for another nine-week run in December 1968–February 1969. She produced eleven Top Ten British hits.

4. White 1987, 56.

5. Furthering his relationship with Indian music, Harrison was in California during June 7–18, 1968, to promote LPs and concerts by Ravi Shankar. During the visit they made appearances in the film *East Meets West*, wherein Shankar discusses his work with Harrison, who is seen practicing his sitar exercises known as *sargams*.

6. Mascaró's letter and translation follow Harrison's discussion in Harrison 1980, 118–19.

7. "The Inner Light" was not mixed for stereo before January 27, 1970, when it was apparently considered for Capitol's compilation LP *Hey Jude*. The stereo mix was not released until December 7, 1981, on the EP *The Beatles* (SGE1, United Kingdom).

8. Miles and Marchbank 1978, 97.

9. Reck 1985, 114–15.

10. Somach et al. 1989, 260–61.

11. These characterizations appear in Hertsgaard 1995, 232–33; Schaffner 1977, 95; and Flippo 1988, 265. Just to keep track of errors in the Wise scores' lyrics, the word at **C**+6 should read "bootlace."

12. Lennon is quoted in Golson 1981b, 211.

13. Walsh 1968a, 12–13.

14. Regarding the scat vocals, see Evans and Aspinall 1968b, 11. Ronnie Scott

had been a major jazz band leader since the early 1950s. Regarding the microphone, see Lewisohn 1988, 133.

15. For information on the guitars and amps, see Evans and Aspinall 1968b, 11. A monitor tape of one mixing session, where McCartney, Harrison, and Lennon can be heard singing along in the control room, features an early take of "Lady Madonna" with McCartney on harmonium and Lennon on Hammond (Beatles 1993d). The eventual backing track from Take 3, piano and brushed snare and McCartney's first vocal dub, are heard in isolation on Beatles 1996a, with occasional additions of saxophone and backing vocals from later tapes.

16. See Miles and Marchbank 1978, 102, and Golson 1981b, 213.

17. Cowan 1978?, 24. Just as McCartney borrowed the idea of the litany from old rock-and-roll numbers for "Lady Madonna," Lennon may have warmed to the idea of the "bulldog" based on its previous incarnations in Jerry Lee Lewis's "Big-Legged Woman," the Coasters' "Searchin'," and Little Willie John's "Leave My Kitten Alone."

18. ADT doubles Lennon's vocal to the left at **B** and thickens the texture of McCartney's barks on the right in the coda. The "Lady Madonna" film shows that the Casino, Rickenbacker, and Ludwigs all still carry the paint jobs done for the "All You Need Is Love" telecast.

19. Ono is cited in Wenner 1971, 101.

20. Lennon speaks in ibid., 116.

21. Golson 1981b, 201–2.

22. See Rose 1985, 8–9; Riley 1988, 296; and BBC 1990. Tempering Lennon's statement that the song "wrote itself," it should be noted that Take 2 does without the irregular last-beat rests heard in the finished version at **A+4** and **D−1**; they were probably added to provide for suitable breaths, but the effect creates appropriately gentle eddies in the flow.

23. I quote Reck 1985, 124, for the explanation of "Om." The correct lyrics at **A+3**, if one is consulting Wise for the lyrics, read "slither wildly as they pass away."

24. See Evans and Aspinall 1968b, 14, regarding these dubs.

25. The wah-wah guitar pedal, commercially introduced by Vox in April 1967, provided a foot-controlled sweep of partials and thus sounds just like its name. It was first popularized by Jimi Hendrix (in June 1967), Eric Clapton, Jimmy Page, and Pink Floyd's David Gilmour.

26. Golson 1981b, 201–2. I hear the girls' naïveté as an inspired touch.

27. Beatles single due 1968, 4.

28. The Beatles' visit coincided with the enterprising Maharishi's February release of an LP, one side of which is a sitar-accompanied discourse on "Love," the other a lecture titled "The Untapped Source of Power That Lies within You."

29. Short 1968, 12–13; Evans 1968a, 7.

30. Example 3.4 is taken from Beatles 1993b. The Beach Boys had planned to tour the United States with the Maharishi in May 1968, but the yogi pulled out after he was disgraced by the Beatles in April. Nevertheless, Rishikesh is reflected in "Anna Lee, the Healer," "Be Still," and "Transcendental Meditation," all on the Beach Boys' album *Friends* (June 1968). The Beatles' falling-out with the Maharishi probably doomed two April 1968 singles that were not to reach the Top Fifty: Scott McKenzie's "Holy Man" and the Strawberry Alarm Clock's "Sit with the Guru."

31. The information on Jennifer comes from Brown and Gaines 1983, 284. Harrison's unused verse, replaced by a hot Jimmy Page solo, appears in Somach et al. 1989, 157. The cover of Donovan's LP *A Gift from a Flower to a Garden* (April 1968) pictures the Maharishi; McCartney, who had participated in "Mellow Yellow" in 1966, may have sung a backing part on Don's "Atlantis" (March 1969). See Engelhardt, 1998, 129.

32. The unproductive Fiftyshapes is documented in Wiener 1992, 33.

33. McCabe and Schonfeld 1972, 83.

34. As quoted in Salewicz 1986, 198.

35. Walsh 1968b, 9.

36. Apple Films was to distribute the Lennon/Ono film collaborations to come. A much more successful support for offbeat films was Harrison's company, Hand-Made Films (active 1978–94).

37. The Apple fiasco has reaped profits in the retelling of the story. DiLello [1972] is a history told from inside the publicity office. A. Taylor 1991 tells of Apple's general manager. McCabe and Schonfeld 1972 is a full account of the company's wins and woes. Apple officers Peter Brown, Derek Taylor, and Pete Shotton have all told their stories in books.

38. Norman 1981, 331.

39. The "Hey Bulldog" sequence, beginning the film's final battle scene, did not make the American cut but is seen in British prints.

40. One suspects that the unpopular disc format might have been decided in favor of George Martin's potential for composer's royalties.

41. Rollin 1969, 37.

42. McCartney made for himself a very parallel personal experience. Jane Asher, his fiancée as of December 1967, found Paul with a fan *in flagrante delicto* when she returned home early from a theater tour; he had also by that time already begun a romantic relationship with his future wife, New Yorker Linda Eastman. Coleman 1992, 436–46, discusses well the early Lennon/Ono relationship, which is also the main topic of an interesting twenty-three-minute tape of Ono addressing Lennon, heard on Track 17 of Beatles 1994b.

43. Wenner 1971, 176.

44. Portions of Side 2 remind me of late 1967's "Chi-Chi's Café" and also of an early-1968 rumba played on the Mellotron's rhythm section (see Beatles 1994b).

45. James 1968b, 23.

46. See Robertson 1991, 93.

47. Hopkins 1987, 81.

48. Golson 1981b, 200.

49. Walsh 1968c, 5.

50. Cott 1968, 14.

51. See ibid. and Beatlenews roundup 1990, 5. The Ampex recordings are heard on Beatles 1991n and 1996b.

52. Walsh 1968c, 5.

53. Martin's argument is relayed in Norman 1981, 340. One speculates as to which titles would have made Martin's short list. Based on my knowledge of his preferences and constraints, I think he might have advocated an LP like this: Side 1: "Back in the U.S.S.R.," "The Continuing Story of Bungalow Bill," "I Will," "Ob-La-Di, Ob-La-Da," "Blackbird," "Not Guilty," "While My Guitar Gently Weeps," and "Happiness Is a Warm Gun"; Side 2: "Birthday," "Sexy Sadie," "Julia," "Martha My Dear," "Long Long Long," "Honey Pie," and "Good Night."

54. The history tag appeared as early as in Belz [1969], 65.

55. Riley 1988, 288.

56. Wenner 1971, 103; see also 100–101, 138.

57. McCartney 1980b.

58. The conversation is heard in Beatles 1993d. McCartney says, "It simply became very difficult for me to write with Yoko sitting there. If I had to think of a line, I started getting very nervous. I might want to say something like, 'I love you, girl,' but with Yoko watching I always felt that I had to come out with something clever and avant-garde" (Hopkins 1987, 124). See also Shotton and Schaffner 1983, 175; Robertson 1991, 91–92; and Lewisohn 1992, 277.

59. Dowlding 1989, 222–23; see Ringo's recollection in Weinberg 1991, 182.

60. Wenner [1970], 88.

61. Mytkowicz 1987, 106.

62. Regarding the J-200, see Evans 1968b, 31. Lennon is also supposed to have brought to the studio a new organ, perhaps the reed organ he bought in India and on which he wrote "Sexy Sadie," "The Continuing Story of Bungalow Bill," and "Julia" (Davis 1995c, 40). See also Evans 1968c, 11.

63. Hutton 1967, 15.

64. Lewisohn 1988, 135.

65. Southall 1982, 126. The first eight-track work was done at Trident Studios, which opened in March 1968 (Lewisohn 1992, 278). McCartney and Harrison had done production work there for other artists.

66. See Lewisohn 1988, 143.

67. This rough dating is based on a conversation related in Davies 1968a, 277.

68. It is clear that $\flat$VII is a Mixolydian substitute for V here because of the V^7/V that leads to it in **C+3–4**. The verse has a nursery rhyme basis—usually a folk trait, as in Simon and Garfunkel's "April Come She Will" (February 1966) — as does Lennon's "Cleanup Time" (Lennon and Ono 1980).

69. All of the "Cry Baby Cry" composing tapes are heard on Beatles 1993a.

70. During his June sessions with Ravi Shankar, Harrison realized that he would have to give up on trying to master the sitar, but he became discouraged about the fact that it had been so long since he had played the guitar seriously. Clapton thought the Les Paul Deluxe—not quite as good as the Les Paul Custom favored by British blues players Eric Clapton, Jimmy Page, Peter Green, and Mick Taylor, but still a beautiful instrument—would lead his friend out of the doldrums (Glazer 1977, 37; Harrison 1980, 57–58).

71. See also Golson 1981b, 208. Lennon's "Dear Prudence" manuscript sold for $19,500 at Sotheby's in June 1987 (Dowlding 1989, 224).

72. Those offering an interpretation with sexual overtones include Mellers 1973, 129, and Riley 1988, 265.

73. The piano is characterized in Riley 1988, 265.

74. Chorus members are identified in Evans 1968d, 12. McCartney is also supposed to have taped a flügelhorn, but I do not hear it.

75. Golson 1981b, 209; Turner 1994, 155. One is also reminded of Jumble Jim, a character in the short story "On Safairy with Whide Hunter" (Lennon 1964).

76. Golson 1981b, 209.

77. I thank Jim Dapogny for making clear the jazz derivation in a 1982 conversation.

78. Track 8, with many Stratocaster fills, is preserved on Beatles 1993d, and all eight tracks are reconstructed in Beatles 1992c. A seamless edit of Takes 3, 6, and 9 of the basic tracks appears on Beatles 1996b.

79. Lennon's words are from Golson 1981b, 209.

80. Lennon discusses his insecurity in Wenner 1971, 34. The acoustic rhythm guitar in the Kinfauns demo (Beatles 1991n) seems to use an open tuning and reverberates strongly of Estes.

81. Lewisohn 1988, 148, explains the edit. In Kinfauns, the original rhythm is maintained throughout.

82. Most of the discussion on "Julia" is taken from W. Everett 1986.

83. The C-major demos are heard on Beatles 1991j, and that in E$\flat$ is on Beatles 1991n.

84. Golson 1981b, 199–200.

85. Perhaps in regard to Yoko, John transposed the original lyrics of "Yer Blues," which read in Beatles 1991n, "My mother is of the earth, my father is of the sky . . ."

86. Donovan discusses the style used here and in "Dear Prudence" in Somach et al. 1989, 156–57; see also Mulhern 1990, 22. Perhaps the guitar lessons remind John of his instruction from Julia. The same half-measure ostinato with cross-rhythm reappears in Lennon's "Look at Me" (1968–70) and "Remember Love"

(1969). Take 2 of "Julia," in which the guide vocal gives way immediately as the composer concentrates on the fingerpicking, breaks down right after the complicated bridge (Beatles 1996b).

87. Composer credits are given in Harry 1982, 167.

88. James 1968a, 6; Turner 1994, 169.

89. See Wenner 1971, 131; Miles and Marchbank 1978, 97–98; and Golson 1981b, 196–97.

90. Miles and Marchbank 1978, 98.

91. Golson 1981b, 196–97.

92. The "painting" characterization is from Miles and Marchbank 1978, 98.

93. Several minutes of the June 4 overdub sessions are heard on Beatles 1994b.

94. About three minutes of the backing track for "Revolution 9" can be heard on Beatles 1994b, Track 17, 4:30–7:25 and 21:16–23:35.

95. Lennon discusses the recording procedure in Wenner 1971, 132, and Golson 1981b, 198.

96. EMI's tape librarians no doubt stored their holdings "tails out," thus the convenience of conclusory passages dubbed from the classical sources.

97. Alistair Taylor is identified in Evans 1969a, 7. The inclusion of "Can You Take Me Back" reverberates in later McCartney fragments, such as the portion of "Suicide" into which "Glasses" crossfades on McCartney 1970, and in the so-called link "Be What You See" on McCartney 1982b. McCartney's lounge-lizard performance of the entire "Suicide" is heard in McCartney 1992b.

98. Regarding the distortion procedure, see Schaffner 1977, 108–9, and Lewisohn 1988, 142.

99. The score conflates all three distorted guitar parts into one, but see the more accurate transcriptions in *Guitar World*, February 1994, p. 64.

100. See Golson 1981b, 201. "The Maharishi Song" is heard on Beatles 1991n. Regarding Lennon's break with the Maharishi, see C. Lennon 1978, 174; Reck 1985, 116; and Turner 1994, 167. Lennon: "I copped out and I wouldn't write 'Maharishi what have you done, you made a fool of everyone,' but now it can be told" (Wenner 1971, 55). A vulgar early verse of "Maharishi" is given in Lewisohn 1988, 144.

101. Take 6 features Lennon's vocal and Casino with heavy tremolo, McCartney's organ, and Starr's drums; the monitor mix has Lennon on Jumbo and vocal, Starr on drums, and McCartney on electric piano.

These slow takes surround both a six-minute version of Gershwin's "Summertime" and Lennon's "Brian Epstein Blues" (Beatles 1993d), the latter a busked G-major rewrite of "Sweet Little Sixteen," a boogie on Brian, brother Clive, and mother Queenie, and (triggered by "Sexy Sadie"?) the protagonist's sexual preference, "working in a coal mine."

102. The missing minute is heard in an early mix given by Ringo to friend Peter Sellers and comes to us through Beatles 1989.

103. The G–F#7–Bm progression works as a colorful substitute for the G–Em–Bm of "She Loves You," and in fact this use of a major triad on VII takes to a new level the consonant support for the seventh scale degree important in the early G-major songs: "She Loves You," "I Want to Hold Your Hand," etc.

104. As part of the continuing chromatic descent, the retransitional ♭II–I of "Sexy Sadie" does not have the same effect as the same formal/harmonic function in "Things We Said Today" or "You're Going to Lose That Girl."

105. See Wenner 1971, 21, regarding these other India compositions.

106. Golson 1981b, 200–201.

107. Harrison is heard in Beatles 1995b.

108. Lennon's count-in is preserved in the very rough mix heard on the "Peter Sellers tape" (Beatles 1989).

109. Lennon discusses his motivation for "Glass Onion" in Wenner 1971, 130.

110. Harry 1982, 145.

111. Wenner 1971, 106; Golson 1981b, 101, 208–9. It has also come out that the "cast iron shore" at **B** in the second verse is a Liverpudlian's term for the River Mersey's shipping docks.

112. The sound effects tape is discussed in Lewisohn 1992, 300–301.

113. Wenner 1971, 136.

114. Lennon explains the Ono connection in Golson 1981b, 199.

115. The words in the Wise score at **B**+8–9 should read "his wife." The Taylor story is recounted in Somach et al. 1989, 221, and Turner 1994, 157.

116. An accidental is missing in the vocal part at **A**+4. Additionally, Lennon's vocal half note in **I**+1 should be a^2.

117. **I**+1 has this ecstatic singer produce c^2 and d^2, some of his highest notes as a Beatle.

118. See Lewisohn 1988, 157.

119. The placement of the splice is suggested by MacDonald 1994, 255.

120. "Good Night" was written for Julian "the way 'Beautiful Boy' was written for Sean" (Golson 1981b, 209). Sean, born October 9, 1975, is Lennon's only child with Ono. "Beautiful Boy" appears on Lennon and Ono 1980.

121. Fallon 1969, 16–17.

122. Early outtakes, recalling the scrapped approaches to "Yellow Submarine," had Ringo intoning "Come on now, it's time you little toddlers were in bed" as a spoken introduction accompanied by Lennon's Casino vamping on D–E^7–A. One such approach is heard on Beatles 1995b.

123. Mellers 1973, 135.

124. The "Peter Sellers tape" (Beatles 1989) includes an only slightly different recording of "Good Night" from that released: in this recording, the bar before **C** is elided.

125. See a placement of McCartney's 1968 work in India in Cowan 1978?, Stannard 1984, and Elson 1986. "Jubilee," composed in India, was the working title for "Junk," a song essentially complete in the Kinfauns tapes and brought by McCartney to Beatles sessions in 1968 and 1969 but not released before McCartney 1970; hence, it lies beyond the limits of this book.

126. Golson 1981b, 210. McCartney has also cited the Nat King Cole Trio's 1947 recording of "Nature Boy" (Miles 1997, 490). The Cole hit (remade for a Top Forty hit in 1961 by Bobby Darin) is musically unrelated to "Mother Nature's Son," but Cole's piano break could have also inspired "Love in the Open Air."

127. Lewisohn 1988, 147.

128. The drums' hallway location is given in ibid., 150.

129. Denver is mentioned in Riley 1988, 279.

130. Compare Stannard 1984, 69, and Golson 1981b, 199.

131. See Turner 1994, 150; Cowan 1978?, 11; and J. Goodman 1984, 110.

132. "Back in the U.S.S.R." also has a less direct Berry connection; the repeated alternation of the vocal pitches in its verse reminds one of McCartney's similarly limited melody to the verse of "I Saw Her Standing There," another Beatles song with strong Berry roots. Paul's and Mike Love's recollections appear in Miles 1997, 422–23.

133. J. Goodman 1984, 110; Turner 1994, 153–54.

134. One take on Beatles 1991m is from an acetate mix done on July 5. This take was remixed with heavy editing, particularly for the bass line and a substitution of the second chorus for the first, for commercial release in Beatles 1996b.

135. Scott is identified as a performer in Turner 1994, 154.

136. The Jumbo overload, most noticeable in the lead guitar before the bass enters at 0:06, is mentioned in Lewisohn 1988, 11.

137. McCartney confuses Desmond's and Molly's names in the commercial version, but not in any earlier takes. Is the male protagonist named for Desmond Dekker?

138. I am indebted to Morton scholar Jim Dapogny for the reference to "The Pearls" (1923).

139. Cf. the off-mike approval, "That's nice," in the Bonzo Dog Band's "Hello Mabel" (June 1969).

140. This is what McCartney tells Donovan half a year after the recording of "Blackbird"; the conversation is preserved on Beatles 1978. Alternate versions of "Blackbird" in the Kinfauns demo, in Take 4 as heard on Beatles 1996b, and in a mono mix of June 11 heard on the "Peter Sellers tape" (Beatles 1989) are essentially as released except for the absence in each of any birdsong and for more vocal echo in the latter. The birdsong enters at different points in the mono and stereo mixes. In Miles (1997, 485), McCartney ascribes the song's origins to the treble/bass counterpoint of "a well-known piece by Bach," which may be a reference to the G-major outer-voice parallel tenths in the best known minuet from the Anna Magdalena collection. (The same counterpoint also appears in the same key in the Allemande of Bach's G-major French Suite.)

141. Lennon speaks in Golson 1981b, 209.

142. The Wise score misses the $b\flat$, as it does the g^1 at **A+3**.

143. McCartney 1980b. The Who were of course loud, but *Melody Maker*'s only mention of the Who in these weeks was in regard to the June 1968 single "Dogs." McCartney must have another source in mind, and "Helter Skelter" sounds more like an answer to Ono than to the Who.

144. In the July 18 rehearsal (part of Take 2 is heard in Beatles 1996b), McCartney apparently plays lead guitar over Lennon's bass and Harrison's distorted rhythm guitar; the lead sound resonates with McCartney 1970.

145. The June date is suggested in D. Taylor 1987, 103.

146. See Gambaccini 1976, 24, and Beatles 1995b. Julian purchased McCartney's recording notes for "Hey Jude" for a reported $39,030 in September 1996.

147. O'Grady 1983, 147. Ireland reset the same melody in his Magnificat and Nunc dimittis/Gloria Patri settings of an Evensong service of 1915. I am indebted to organist/choral director John Deaver for bringing the Ireland examples to my attention in a 1993 letter.

148. McCartney was well aware of the Drifters connection; see Dowlding 1989, 203.

149. Gambaccini 1974, 38.

150. Golson 1981b, 151, 196.

151. Richard Harris's previous "MacArthur Park" (May 1968) was a longer single at 7'20"; the Animals' "Sky Pilot" of four months earlier (7'20") was divided into two sides for the single. I recall that in the New York radio market (on WABC and WMCA), "Hey Jude" was played at its full length. But some stations apparently did not play the whole single, as Capitol Records provided a promo of 3'56", chopping off most of the mantra section (McCoy and McGeary 1990, 187). Capitol trimmed the hit to 5'05" for Beatles 1982c, and Martin cut one of the first six takes from July 29, 1968, to 4'00" (plus introduction) for Beatles 1996b.

152. Samarotto expressed this thought in a private conversation with me in November 1994.

153. Riley 1988, 251, 255.

154. The most complete July 30 take of "Hey Jude" appears on Beatles 1991l, and other segments are found on c. 1974 and 1991n.

155. McCartney 1980b.

156. Beatles 1994h, Track 2, 8:25.

157. George Martin tells about one orchestral player's refusal to sing and clap along: the player walked out, saying, "I'm not going to clap my hands and sing Paul McCartney's bloody song" (Martin 1979, 211).

158. Bauch's words come from a personal communication to me (March 1995).

159. See Beatles 1996c, vol. 8, and Beatles 1982a. The "Frost" program was a British-only broadcast; in the States, the videos were shown on "The Smothers Brothers Comedy Hour" (see Beatles 1994b).

160. The connection to "Here, There and Everywhere" is noted in Hastings 1994.

161. See Beatles 1996b regarding Takes 35 and "Los Paranoias." See Lewisohn 1988, 155, regarding "The Way You Look Tonight."

162. Golson 1981b, 200; Lewisohn 1988, 156. While "Birthday" was spontaneous, it spawned such imitations as the Nazz's "Hang On Paul" (May 1969), based on the "Birthday" riff, and Led Zeppelin's "Celebration Day" (October 1970), sharing McCartney's key scheme as well as the celebratory air.

163. The guitar ostinato comes from the school that produced Larry Williams's "Dizzy Miss Lizzie" (April 1958) and Bo Diddley's "Road Runner" (February 1960). Elton John makes a rare non-Beatles use of a Leslied piano in "Dirty Little Girl" (1973).

164. Riley 1988, 277.

165. Contrary to the score, the murky-bass left hand breaks an octave, not a fifth, in the opening, and plays octaves in mm. 3–4.

166. Take 5 received the overdubs. One can hear Paul's solo vocal and D-28 of Take 4 on Beatles 1996b. Oddly, much of this take has the softness of "Hot as Sun" (McCartney 1970), a quality buried in the White album version.

167. Golson 1981b, 199.

168. The 1968 recording of "Et Cetera" is recalled by an engineer but undocumented otherwise (Lewisohn 1988, 150). It may be the McCartney song of that name written c. 1964–65 for, but not accepted by, Marianne Faithfull (Miles 1997, 221–22).

169. In Beatles 1995b, Harrison recalls writing "Dehra Dun," the name of the closest town to Rishikesh, in India, and demonstrates it on a handy ukelele. This brief excerpt, all we have, sounds like Donovan's "Happiness Runs."

170. The origins are dated in Friede et al. 1980, 172.

171. This line appears in a different ink from surrounding material in the draft shown in Harrison 1980, 127. This manuscript also includes a verse not recorded: "Everywhere there's lots of piggies / Playing piggy pranks. / You can see them on their trotters / At the piggy banks. / Paying piggy thanks / To thee pig brother." The final words make it highly unlikely that George Orwell's work — especially his fable of autocracy masquerading as democracy, *Animal Farm*— is not the primary inspiration for "Piggies."

172. Lennon takes his credit in Golson 1981b, 210.

173. "Piggies" was probably recorded in G, as it was on the Kinfauns tape, and then sped up to A♭, where we hear it today.

174. The filter is discussed in Lewisohn 1988, 157.

175. Harrison's vocal pitches are given as they sound; at least the highest part was probably produced a half-step lower.

176. Kinfauns has no hint of the eventual ending, which relates to the joke ending of "Within You Without You" but seems quite appropriate and not defensive here. The Doors use a harpsichord to create a stark contrast of refined and coarse attitudes in "Touch Me" (December 1968).

177. This, of course, is due to his 1966 switch to sitar as his primary instrument. See Glazer 1977, 35.

178. The manuscript is given in Harrison 1980, 121–22. One of several "While My Guitar Gently Weeps" drafts sold for £8,500 in August 1992 (Beatlenews roundup 1992, 10).

179. This verse is heard on Beatles 1993e.

180. Following Cream's "Tales of Brave Ulysses" (November 1967), this repeatedly descending bass line becomes a staple of epic rock songs, such as "While My Guitar

Gently Weeps," Led Zeppelin's "Babe I'm Gonna Leave You" (January 1969), the Doors' "The Soft Parade" (August 1969), and King Crimson's "The Epitaph" (October 1969).

181. This take, when remixed for the abandoned *Sessions* project of 1985, includes the harmonium in the second bridge and last verse and creates an artificial fade-out ending by repeating two bars of the guitar's close. The same is heard on Beatles 1996b.

182. D. Forte 1987b, 91.

183. Harrison played guitar in Jeff Healey's 1990 remake of "While My Guitar Gently Weeps." I have not heard this version but would be curious to see how Harrison could fill in for Clapton.

184. The reincarnation-centered "Circles," showcasing a singularly expressive common-tone modulation down a half-step (Cm – G$^{4-3}$–f$\sharp$°– F$\sharp^{4-3}$–Bm), was not attempted by the Beatles but was resurrected for Harrison 1982, transposed up a fourth. The song will not be discussed further here.

185. White 1987, 55.

186. Harrison speaks of this in Glazer 1977, 38.

187. Taylor's contribution is documented in Somach et al. 1989, 221.

188. "Long Long Long" is Harrison's final song written for the LP, but by October, he is already at work on "Something" (Cowan 1978?, 43), which, however, is still in its early stages when available recordings appear from January 1969. This song will be discussed in chapter 4.

189. Harrison 1980, 132.

190. "Sad Eyed Lady of the Lowlands" is on *Blonde on Blonde* (July 1966), the only album a Beatle (Harrison) brought to India. "Long Long Long" is shown where it was composed, in D major, rather than where it sounds, to facilitate the comparison with Dylan's structure.

191. The Wise score presents a few errors; the fifth and sixth sixteenths in the J-200 part at **A**+3 should read f^1–g^1.

192. The title was mentioned in the press in 1963, and McCartney runs through its chorus when Ringo is asked about songwriting in press conferences of June and July 1964.

193. Perhaps it was Lennon who wished to retain the extra fiddling that outlasts the rest of the ensemble, as his harmonica repeats the practice on "Oh Yoko!" (Lennon 1971). While not known for any penchant for such styles, a wisecracking Lennon can also be heard calling a do-si-do and other square-dance steps in rhyming patter while bored with a McCartney run-through of "Teddy Boy" in January 1969 (Beatles 1996b).

194. The "Peter Sellers tape" (Beatles 1989) includes an early mono mix (in C$\sharp$) of "Don't Pass Me By" that includes, after **C**–1, a repeat of the first verse and another chorus, all of which was deleted from both released mixes. My ear finds it incongruous that George Martin's Raveaux forty-seven-second orchestral introduction taped on July 22 and given as "A Beginning" to "Don't Pass Me By" on Beatles 1996b could have ever been considered as an introduction to Ringo's recording. This edit piece does end on V$^4_2$ of C major but shares nothing else with the Beatles song. Beatles 1996b also includes a stereo mix in C of the June 5 – 6 pre-fiddle-and-bass recordings that indicates that editing was required to repair Paul's errant piano changes in the second chorus.

195. "Ob-La-Di, Ob-La-Da" and "Back in the U.S.S.R." were 1968 A-sides in some world markets, but no White album song was released on a single in the United States or United Kingdom before 1976.

196. In late 1967 the Rolling Stones were said to be in the process of forming their own label—they finally did so in 1971—and many 1968 reports had them in a merger with Apple.

197. Dawbarn 1968, 5; Schaffner 1982, 41; Miles 1997, 455.

198. For McCartney, against her wishes, she recorded "Those Were the Days" in

Italian, Spanish, French, and German. This was a successful maneuver, but could he have forgotten how he'd bristled over the "Sie Liebt Dich"/"Komm Gib Mir Deine Hand" episode in 1964? *Postcard*, her album produced by McCartney, contained numbers dating from 1927, 1933, 1956, and 1959 ("The Honeymoon Song"!) in which she had no interest, and he also insisted that she record "Que Sera, Sera" (instruments played by himself and Ringo alone) because it had been a childhood favorite of his; she refused to allow it to be released in the United Kingdom.

199. The sessions with Donovan also yielded very informal tapes of Paul busking a song for Linda Eastman's daughter, "Heather" (Beatles 1978), and another called "How Do You Do."

200. The LP was recorded October–November 1968, with orchestral dubs done the following January. Lomax's lead song, "Speak to Me," was a favorite of George's, who is heard playing this number, and Lomax's "Little Yellow Pills" as well, for his fellow Beatles several times during January 1969's "Get Back" project. During the same meetings, McCartney leads the group through Lomax's "You've Got Me Thinking."

201. Harrison speaks in Glazer 1977, 34. Woodstock, New York, was Bob Dylan's home. While there, Harrison wrote "All Things Must Pass" and, with Dylan, cowrote "I'd Have You Anytime," both on Harrison 1970.

202. McCartney is quoted in *Melody Maker*, July 6, 1968, p. 2. See also Pearson 1968, 10.

203. DiLello [1972], 39–40.

204. See Robertson 1991, 95–99.

205. Lennon's sleeve may have been a reaction to the Stones' having run into similar trouble in September over their *Beggars Banquet* cover, which showed no nudity but was found vulgar by Decca records and rejected. Hendrix's cover for *Electric Ladyland* (October 1968), with twenty-one nude figures, was not used in the United States, nor was Blind Faith's LP cover (July 1968), which featured a nude pubescent girl. Roxy Music and other groups ran into censorship for risqué covers in the 1970s, but there is no equal for the frankness of JohnandYoko's nudity for *Two Virgins*.

206. Ono's "Pulse Piece" (1963, in Ono [1964]) reads, "Listen to each other's pulse by putting your ear on the other's stomach."

207. At this time John and Yoko wrote a song for their miscarried child that would become "Oh My Love" on Lennon 1971. Also in the last weeks of the year, Lennon was composing "Don't Let Me Down" and "A Case of the Blues," both to be discussed in chapter 4.

208. "Yer Blues" is heard on Beatles 1991n, which also includes one and a half minutes of the December 10 rehearsal.

209. This track is heard on Lennon 1988d.

210. See Hopkins 1987, 51, and Harry 1982, 193, for the origins of "Bagism."

211. Lennon's contributions were taken from Lennon [1968a].

Four

1. Cott 1968.

2. See Davies 1968a, 283; Wilson 1968, 13; Norman 1981, 355; and Beatles to appear, 1968, 4.

3. McCartney 1987.

4. See Cott and Dalton 1969. Other locales considered: a Roman amphitheater in Tunisia (to escape Britain's winter weather) and the deck of an ocean liner (but Harrison pointed out the undoubtedly poor acoustics they'd find); Lennon: "I'm warming to the idea of doing it in an asylum" (Norman 1981, 355–56). On June 28, 1991, *Paul McCartney's Liverpool Oratorio* was first performed at the Anglican cathedral mentioned by Ringo.

5. See Beatle news 1968, 26; and Beatles plan for TV show 1968, 2.

6. The Sellers film, a spoof on those who achieve all they have with money, is a stepping-stone between the comedy of *A Hard Day's Night* and that of Monty Python; significantly, its humor is often supplied by actors from both casts. The film has a "cameo role" for the final chord of "A Day in the Life," used in the soundtrack.

7. Lennon is cited in Dowlding 1989, 253; Martin, in Schaffner 1977, 117.

8. Stannard 1984, 80–81; Evans 1969b, 9.

9. Beatles plan first live album 1969, 1.

10. The lap guitar is referred to as a Fender in James 1969, 9, but this is difficult to substantiate from films and photos. It has also been referred to as a Höfner 5140 Hawaiian Standard. It appears to be an unbound, brown guitar with a steel bridge, one pickup, and two knobs on the tailplate and played with a slide; the heavy neck supports a long fingerboard with twenty-five frets, with dot inlays—double dots on the twelfth and twenty-fourth frets. The Höfner Hawaiians, of a single slender trapezoidal wooden body, do have twenty-five frets, and a single pickup with volume and tone controls on the tailplate, so this is probably the make used.

11. Occasional discrepancies are unaccounted for; for instance, some film outtakes clearly show the date of January 25 on the clapper, but this material is catalogued—both in Lewisohn 1988 and Sulpy and Schweighardt 1994—for January 23.

12. Lewisohn 1992, 306; Sulpy and Schweighardt 1994. Harrison's ensuing headache leads to the composition of "Wah-Wah," a song not brought to the Beatles but appearing in Harrison 1970 (see Glazer 1977, 37).

13. Sulpy and Schweighardt 1994.

14. Martin 1979, 173.

15. *Compleat* 1982. Lennon argued in January that Preston should become a permanent member of the Beatles (Sulpy and Schweighardt 1994).

16. In 1973 Alan Parsons was to produce Pink Floyd's *Dark Side of the Moon*, an album that achieved a 741-week chart run, five years longer than the second-best. He also recorded three platinum LPs of his own.

17. Miles and Marchbank 1978, 103.

18. See Sulpy and Schweighardt 1994.

19. Little Richard's "Rip It Up"/"Shake, Rattle and Roll" (26.28–26.29) and "Blue Suede Shoes" (26.31), all with Harrison's Telecaster, McCartney's piano, Lennon's Bass VI, Starr's drums, and Billy Preston's Hammond B-3, are crossfaded for Beatles 1996b. This recording also includes a portion of Geoff Emerick's 1985 mix of a version of Buddy Holly's 1957 recording "Mailman, Bring Me No More Blues" (S/S 29.11).

20. McCartney 1987; Wenner 1971, 120–22.

21. Miles and Marchbank 1978, 105.

22. One full verse is quoted in Miles 1997, 535. The immigration theme is again taken up in the E-major boogie "Commonwealth" (9.77, in which the various colonies are described as "much too common for" Powell), "Aw, Enoch Powell" (9.78), and the E-major blues "Get Off!" (9.79–9.81) (all on Beatles 1975). A group called Liverpool Scene released an anti-Powell song in April 1969.

23. Loretta's Warhol-style drag-queen persona seems related to the accidental mix-up of Desmond and Molly in the released version of "Ob-La-Di, Ob-La-Da" and to the kinky dress of Lennon's "Polythene Pam."

24. "Get Back" Takes 23.22–23.29 are heard in Beatles 1991g, and a nearly polished 23.30 appears in Beatles 1991b, the latter from an acetate sweetened with echo.

25. Takes 24.71–24.79 are on Beatles 1991g; 24.82 (less Preston's solo) is on Beatles 1991c.

26. Apparently staged to satisfy McCartney's craving for the forbidden, the *Let It Be* film ends with police constables ascending to the roof, as if called by neighboring businessmen, and having the Beatles desist their public annoyance by turning off their amplifiers.

27. This "getting back" conceit governs the provisional jacket for the *Get Back* LP, which was posed similarly by Angus McBean at the same EMI House stairwell from a similar angle as used on the *Please Please Me* LP; title and graphics also matched. We have also noted this interest in going full circle at the beginning of *Revolver* and elsewhere; Lennon completes a cycle again with Lennon 1975b, the cover of which shows him in Hamburg in 1961, and the sound of which fades away with a farewell to the recording business (see Lennon et al. 1981, 63–64, 129–30).

28. Golson 1981b, 214. Allan Kozinn (1995a, 193) notes that the alternation of the optimistic E major and the cautious F#m emblematizes a new relationship, as if recalling "If I Fell."

29. Takes 2.11, 2.26, and 2.34–2.38 are heard on Beatles 1994g.

30. The quodlibet technique, first tried with "Frère Jacques" in "Paperback Writer," is used again by McCartney in "Silly Love Songs" (McCartney 1976a) and "Wanderlust" (McCartney 1984).

31. The structural aspects of "The One after 909" are discussed in volume 1.

32. John's vivid lyrics for "Dig a Pony," all suggestive of great confidence, were in a constant state of flux. Ringo: "It used to be 'I dig a skylight'"; John: "Yeah, but I changed it to groundhog — it had to be rougher." What was once "I con a Lowrey" became the title; John said, "It didn't sing well, so I changed it to Dug a Pony. It's got to be d's and p's, you know" (Cott and Dalton 1969). Probably for the same reason, John changed "wind glove" to "wind love" (**A**+4–5).

33. Note the similar texture in all guitars between "Dig a Pony"'s arpeggiations in **B**+1–2 (1:00–1:03) and the rejected arpeggiations of **A**+10 in "I've Got a Feeling" (0:32–0:34).

34. The released LP has spliced out a two-bar idea (like those at **B**+1–2) in two places: just before **A**, and just before the final chord, which is why the single word "you" can be heard following the instrumental coda.

35. Linda's memories are captured in Turner 1994, 175.

36. Beyond the "Here, There and Everywhere" reference, a second *Revolver* connection can be drawn: the change from $\frac{4}{4}$ to $\frac{3}{4}$ at **A**+11 (0:38) for the return home is reminiscent of the same change when Lennon returns to his childhood in "She Said She Said."

37. A. Taylor 1991, 152–53; Turner 1994, 182.

38. See Dowlding 1989, 262. The title had been highlighted in Hendrix's "If 6 Was 9" (January 1968).

39. McCartney speaks in *McCartney world tour* 1989, 8.

40. Harrison 1980, 158.

41. A solo demo of "All Things Must Pass," with vocal and two electric guitars (one Leslied), was taped by Harrison for the Beatles on February 25, 1969; it is heard on Beatles 1996b.

42. See DiLello 1983 [1972], 104.

43. Norman 1981, 348.

44. See Coleman 1992, 460. Twice before, beginning in 1966, unfounded publicity had linked Klein's name to attempts to buy the Beatles' contract from NEMS.

45. The royalty figures are given in Norman 1981, 181.

46. The engraving is reproduced in Lennon 1967, 42; see Robertson 1991, 105.

47. The review appears in *Melody Maker*, May 24, 1969, p. 19.

48. Hopkins 1987, 97.

49. Lennon 1967, 21.

50. Side 1 was recorded on April 22, 1969, the day John officially changed his name to John Ono Lennon, and mixed May 1. Compare the heartbeat idea with "Pulse Piece" from Ono's *Grapefruit*. The American LP (Apple SMAX3361) was released on October 20, 1969, and reached only #178; the British LP (Apple SAPCOR11) was released on November 7 and did not approach the Top 100 chart there.

51. See also Wenner 1971, 126.

52. The guitar's mocking is characterized in MacDonald 1994, 277.

53. For more information on Zapple plans, see DiLello 1983, 53, 85, 149–50, 163, 215.

54. Norman 1981, 374–75.

55. Wenner 1971, 110; see also Robertson 1991, 109–10, and *John and Yoko* 1990 [1970].

56. The record's full-page print advertisements follow Apple's typical publicity plan of running a teaser ad two weeks before the release announcement. The first ad (*Melody Maker*, June 28, p. 7) simply asks, "Who are the Plastic Ono Band?," and the follow-up (July 5, p. 12) superimposes the Plexiglas photo over a "Jones" page of the London phone directory, capped by the legend "YOU ARE THE PLASTIC ONO BAND," making clear the "Unfinished Music" conceit. For the ad for *Live Peace in Toronto 1969*, a television monitor appears among the "band" members.

57. Due to the accident, Lennon required seventeen stitches and a five-day hospitalization; Yoko and daughter Kyoko suffered similar injuries. The pain led to the use of more heroin.

58. Under a different label, the Hot Chocolate Band later revived itself with three Top Ten disco hits in 1975–79.

59. McCartney played piano on three other songs for the film as well.

60. Davies 1968a, 270.

61. Harrison was similarly impressed by Preston's playing of the Hammond B-3 organ and purchased one for himself in early 1969 (F. Kelly 1969, 5). Before the Moog was developed, oscillators and theremins had been used by the Beach Boys, the Rolling Stones, and the Mothers; the Grateful Dead incorporated a synthesizer in their 1968 concerts, and David Bowie used the synthesizer-like Stylogram on "Space Oddity," recorded at Trident in June 1969. According to Roger Luther of EJE Research, the Beatles received the ninety-fifth synthesizer produced by Moog, for about $8,000. Similar models had been shipped to the Stones in October, 1968, and to the Monkees in late 1967!

62. Harrison almost credited Krause with a note on the cover, but he decided to delete it (Schaffner 1977, 118–19).

63. See White 1987, 56.

64. Regarding Brute Force, see DiLello 1983, 125, 177, 216.

65. The manuscript facsimile is seen in Harrison 1980, 134–35.

66. Beatles—Plans 1969, 4.

67. Beatles' album 1969, 1.

68. *Compleat* 1982.

69. In a curiously related manner, many of Lennon's solo singles beginning with "Give Peace a Chance" would have his song on the A-side and one by Ono on the flip.

70. Interview of October 25, 1971, in Wigg 1976; Lennon may have been thinking of McCartney's say over the formats for *Sgt. Pepper*, "Magical Mystery Tour," and *Get Back* as well as for *Abbey Road*.

71. Weinberg 1991, 185. Elsewhere, Ringo remembers having switched to calfskin for *Sgt. Pepper's*, which also emphasizes the toms in different ways than heard previously.

72. Buskin 1987, 46.

73. Norman 1981, 381.

74. Leary dropped out of the race before the election, which gave the governorship to Ronald Reagan.

75. The Montreal chanting is heard in *John and Yoko* 1990 [1970]. "Come Together" regained its political import when John performed it in August 30, 1972, benefit concerts for a children's school in New York, ending the last verse, "Come together right now; STOP THE WAR!"

76. Leary's feelings are recalled in Golson 1981b, 210–11. The publisher who complained about the Berry plagiarism settled in October 1973, stipulating that Lennon record "You Can't Catch Me" and two other of the Big Seven Music's numbers; he chose "Sweet Little Sixteen" (Berry) and "Ya Ya" (Lee Dorsey), all three heard on Lennon's *Rock 'N' Roll* LP (1975).

77. Take 1 of the basic tracks, including John's tambourine with guide vocal and the otherwise final arrangement of Take 8—that used for the master—is heard on Beatles 1996b.

78. J. Goodman 1984, 87–88. The electric piano sound is reminiscent of that on Marvin Gaye's version of "I Heard It through the Grapevine" (November 1968).

79. By 1980, "Something" had been recorded by more than 150 artists (Harrison 1980, 152); at that time, the only Beatles compositions to attract more cover versions were McCartney's "Yesterday," with 425, and "Michelle," with 201 (Okun 1981).

80. Lewisohn 1988, 156.

81. The demo is heard in Beatles 1991a, dubbed directly from an acetate; Beatles 1996b omits the piano from this take.

82. Even in a minor key, the progression is unusual; one precedent is found in Beethoven's Sonata op. 10, no. 3, I°, mm. 141–49. The passing motion opening "Something" also resembles in a small way that of the chromatic opening, III–♭III♮⁵–II, of "Here, There and Everywhere."

83. Harrison reworks these chromatic descents in his solo ballads "Learning How to Love You" (Harrison 1976b) and "Your Love Is Forever" (Harrison 1979).

84. The I–VI♯ cadence is not strictly new; the relationship had been tested in the surprise ending of "And I Love Her."

85. Hear Lennon in Golson 1981b, 212, and Harrison in Glazer 1977, 35.

86. This characterization of $\hat{7}$ was inspired by an April 1995 conversation with musicians Susan Belleperche and Devon Dietz.

87. The 1968 date is supplied in Evans 1968d, 14; the Jarry connection is discussed in White 1988, 50.

88. Take 5 (Beatles 1996b) suggests that the retransitional piano arpeggiations at **E** were not played in the basic track (the master originates in Take 21). Paul's inspired scatting in Take 5 suggests that—taking a page from "When I'm Sixty-Four"—a solo wind such as a clarinet might have been considered for overdub solos.

89. Harrison's Moog was set up in Room 43, with the signal sent to the control room of Studio Two; all Moog patches were created by Mike Vickers (Lewisohn 1988, 185). Many excellent photos of the August 5–8 Moog sessions are seen throughout *The Beatles Monthly Book* 74 (September 1969).

90. Miles and Marchbank 1978, 102.

91. Various vocal outtakes can be heard on Beatles 1978 and 1987a; another (1991k) has unused backing, as well as lead, vocals, including two different McCartney parts for the last verse.

92. When EMI compiled the "Red" and "Blue" collections of the Beatles' most memorable recordings in two two-record sets in 1973 (Beatles 1973a and 1973b), Harrison's two *Abbey Road* compositions were chosen, as was Starr's, but none of McCartney's last Beatles songs made the cut.

93. Dowlding 1989, 283; see also Starr 1983, no. 14 (September 3).

94. Weinberg 1991, 183.

95. The basic track required thirty-two takes. The last led to the master; Take 2 (capped with Ringo's comment from the end of Take 8), with essentially the finished arrangement, is heard on Beatles 1996b.

96. One early mix (July 17?) on Beatles 1991k contains the full Stratocaster part and an unused Starr harmony vocal but has no backing vocals or interlude effects, likely identifying these as the final superimpositions.

97. Cott 1982b, 124; see also Wenner 1971, 124.

98. One take of the unedited basic track with one vocal, purportedly Paul's but it could all be John's, is audible on Beatles 1984. Another tape of Lennon singing the song with Jumbo for an Israeli radio station—probably at one of the 1969 bed-ins—is heard on Beatles 1987a. For the Casino introduction, the score's tablature is correct, but two pitches are not; the reader should substitute g♯ for f♯ in measure 3 and a♭ for a♮ one bar later.

99. The rich introduction, with its inner-voice chromatic descents A–G♯–G♮ and B–B♭–A over common tone F, reminds me of two bars of the vocal arrangement of "The Word" (**D**+7–8), where one inner voice descends D–C♯–C♮–B over common tones F and A. Harrison recalls "I Want You (She's So Heavy)," along with "I Want to Tell You" and "Blue Jay Way," when discussing the E chord with added F♮ (White 1987, 54).

100. Lewisohn 1988, 191.

101. See Miles and Marchbank 1978, 102.

102. Ibid.; Golson 1981b, 212.

103. George Harrison on *Abbey Road* 1969, 8. He says more on the song's having been inspired by his escape from meetings with bankers and lawyers in Wigg 1976 and Harrison 1980, 144. Harrison also mentions in Wigg that "I finished [the song] later when I was on holiday in Sardinia"; that holiday was taken in June 1969.

104. The capo divides the normal string length in thirds, creating a tone almost as bright and brittle as that of a twelve-string.

105. The Amsterdam guitar playing amounts to the following progression in C (not the eventual C♯) minor, played with the same figuration as heard in the final version: I–V⁶–VII°$^4_3$/V–V$^6_4$–I; against this, Yoko sings, "Stay in bed for peace . . . grow your hair." The part is equally playable in C or C♯ minor, and the arpeggiation on the Casino is very much like that heard in Feb. on "I Want You (She's So Heavy)."

106. Lawrence 1978, 56. The three vocal tracks are isolated on Beatles 1996b, where it sounds like John and George sing on two of the tracks, John and Paul on the third, providing the greatest total weight on John's lead line and the least on Paul's airy descant. George discussed his fondness for these vocal harmonies in November 1969 (Wigg 1976).

107. "For No One," featuring both a clavichord and a piano, had ended on V$^{4-3}$ but did not resolve into "Doctor Robert," the next song on *Revolver.*

108. "Because" is the Beatles' only song performed or mastered in C♯ minor.

109. Golson 1981b, 201.

110. See Cott 1981, 39, regarding "Watching the Wheels," and Golson 1981b, 208, regarding "I'm Only Sleeping."

111. The tracks recorded thus far are heard on Beatles 1991k.

112. The crossfade (replacing a sustained E harmonium chord attempted in one draft; Beatles 1991k) sounds like that from "Lordly Nightshade" to "The Mountain of God" (which uses *crotales*) on the Incredible String Band's *The Big Huge* (November 1968). For a full score of "You Never Give Me Your Money," see W. Everett 1995, 201–16.

113. Riley 1988, 328.

114. Covach discussed this notion with me in a November 1989 conversation.

115. Miles and Marchbank 1978, 75; Golson 1981b, 212. "Sun King" retains more of the "Albatross" sound than "Don't Let Me Down" does, especially by virtue of the soft cymbal crashes. The "Mean Mr Mustard" and "Polythene Pam" Kinfauns demos of May 1968 (both on Beatles 1996b) develop no further from that point through their final recordings, save for the name change within the former from "Shirley" to "Pam."

116. The reverb in John's Casino provides an odd coloring for one outtake from this session, "Ain't She Sweet" (Beatles 1996b), done in E, just as in 1961.

117. Miles and Marchbank 1978, 75, 102; Golson 1981b, 212–3; Turner 1994, 196.

118. Golson 1981b, 212; Friede et al. 1980, 192; Norman 1981, 377.

119. The $\hat{5}$–$\hat{4}$–$\hat{3}$–$\hat{2}$–$\hat{1}$ approach is reminiscent of the transition in "You've Got to Hide Your Love Away."

120. The metric relationship is mentioned in Riley 1988, 330.

121. As in Schaffner 1977, 126.

122. A mono mix of work mentioned thus far is heard on Beatles 1991k; the guide vocal is audible the second time through "Golden Slumbers" and in "Carry That Weight." The mix used for the medley test (also heard on Beatles 1991k) was made on July 30 and thus lacks the extra drums, brass, and strings.

123. DiLello 1972, 203–6.

124. Golson 1981b, 213.

125. The drum solo is accompanied by guitars and tambourine in Martin's remix for Beatles 1996b, which also has two sustained notes from McCartney's guitar before his solo proper begins. The gratuitous final E-major chord from this latter-day revisionist mix comes, of course, from the final pianos/harmonium chord of "A Day in the Life," taped on February 22, 1967.

126. Lewisohn 1992, 327–28.

127. Lewisohn 1988, 14.

128. Hodenfield 1976, 87.

129. See Gauldin 1990.

130. Golson 1981b, 213.

131. The text is certainly in sympathy with Lennon's essential line in the middle of "Because." Due to an altered tape speed, the intonation in this portion of "The End" is unnervingly more than a quarter-tone sharp; McCartney belatedly corrected this error by performing a medley of "Golden Slumbers"/"Carry That Weight"/"The End," all well in tune, during his 1989–90 world tour (see McCartney 1990). For the metric modulation, simple groupings of eighths ("The End," **F**), while retaining their individual durations, are regrouped as compound triplets (**G**+5–8, a move encouraged by the vocal syncopations in **G**+1–3), and the new beat duration is in turn divided once again into two simple eighths (**H**–1), resulting in a tempo one-third slower than the original. With the Beatles, this technique is heard previously only in "Lucy in the Sky with Diamonds."

132. A Lennon composition from August 1969 called "Rock Peace" has not surfaced.

133. Williams 1969, 21. The Beatles' December 1969 refusal to accept a $1 million offer for a one-night concert in Holland (Million 1969, 1) was followed by many multi-million-dollar offers, as high as $50 million in February 1976 and $225 million in March 1996, for the group to reunite for live appearances.

134. See Schaffner 1982, 48–49. Both Mick Jagger and Roger Daltrey had been widely reported dead in 1966, as was Engelbert Humperdinck in 1967.

135. The heroin detoxification is mentioned in Hopkins 1987, 124–25.

136. See McCartney c. 1985.

137. See Wenner 1971, 120–22.

138. Lewisohn 1988, 348.

139. Sulpy and Schweighardt 1994.

140. The version of "Teddy Boy" included on Beatles 1996b conflates one take unknown to Sulpy and Schweighardt with S/S 24.22 (they are joined at 1:15).

141. The Johns mix is heard (in mono) on Beatles 1994b.

142. George Martin's mix for Beatles 1996b is essentially the stereo reverse of Johns's.

143. See Paul McCartney solo 1970, 4, and Coleman 1992, 486. While the "full circle" cover was scrapped for *Let It Be*, the two photo sessions of 1963 and 1969 furnished the covers for the 1973 Apple reissues, known as the "Red" and "Blue" albums.

144. Stannard 1984, 252.

145. See Williams 1971b, 35; Gambaccini 1976, 23; and Norman 1981, 389–90. When "The Long and Winding Road" was remade by McCartney and Martin for McCartney 1984, they arranged orchestral and choral forces much larger than those used by Spector, but the voice leading was much leaner.

146. Wenner 1971, 120–22.

147. As late as November 1969 and February 1970, Lennon spoke about possible Beatles projects; see You never 1969, 30, and Wigg 1976. See also DiLello 1983, 244, 251–55. McCartney has cited an argument of May 9, 1969 (postdating the basic tracks of "You Never Give Me Your Money" by three days) as the point of no return in the Beatles' irrevocable split. See Englehardt 1998, 287–88.

148. See McCabe and Schonfeld 1972, 172–73. Klein received no further Beatles monies after March 13, 1971.

149. Beatles 1995b, 33.

Postlude

1. Note that each "album" may include one, two, or three LPs and that compilations of previously released products are not included. "Unreleased" compositions, many fragmentary, are those circulating on unauthorized releases.

2. John's first son, Julian, wrote and recorded two Top Ten hits in 1984–85. Sean recorded his first album in 1997.

3. See J. Wiener 1991 [1984] regarding the deportation effort.

4. In April 1990, McCartney played a house in Rio of 184,000, triple the Beatles' largest-ever crowd. This contrasts with many unannounced shows for handfuls of people in 1972 and 1990–91.

5. See Coleman 1995, 127–42. In November 1995, Sony paid a reported $100 million to merge with Jackson's ATV.

6. A 1979 fire in Hollywood Hills destroyed most of Ringo's Beatles mementos.

7. See G. Smith 1995, 84, 86, and Stapley 1995, 61, 62, 64.

8. See Rule 1996, 46, 48.

9. Jeff Lynne, a Wilbury and producer of Harrison 1987a, probably passed his "audition" for this project by having added tracks to a posthumously procured Roy Orbison recording (Rense 1995, 21; see also Stapley 1995, 68).

10. ITV announces 1995, 33. "Grow Old with Me," a piano/rhythm-box ballad demo taken from the Elizabeth Barrett Browning poem that had appeared on *Milk and Honey* in 1984, was rejected for group overdubs. The group began work on "Now and Then," which Lynne called "a bluesy sort of ballad in A minor" (heard on Lennon 1996), but left this piece unfinished (Rense 1995, 21). The new group composition, "All for Love," was apparently never completed, and it remains unclear as to how well McCartney and Harrison have resolved their personal differences, which have stood in the way of many potential collaborations since 1970.

11. Takes 1 and 3, without the later additions, are heard on Lennon 1996.

12. "Free as a Bird" seems unrelated to a faster Lennon demo of the 1970s, "Whatever Happened To . . . ," which has the refrain, "Whatever happened to the woman we once knew" (Lennon 1988b). A minor controversy greeted the release of "Free as a Bird" when rhythmic and textual similarities were discovered between its bridge and the Shangri-Las' "Remember (Walkin' in the Sand)" (1964), which has the lines "Whatever happened to the boy that I once knew" and "Whatever happened to the life I gave to you."

13. Harrison had used a yellow/red sunburst Telecaster, one of his favorite guitars, onstage in 1991.

14. The sequence of events is suggested by Lynne in Rense 1995, 20.

15. The Formby connection is explained in "Anthology" debuts 1995.

16. Harrison had played his uke at a March 3, 1991, convention of George Formby fans in Blackpool (A. Wiener 1992, 96). The ukelele was Lennon's mother's

instrument, on which she taught John his first chords. McCartney plays the uke in "Ram On" (McCartney 1971).

17. Here's another 1995.

18. Demos have been released as both "Real Love" (*Imagine* 1988) and "Girls and Boys" (Lennon 1990). See A. Wiener 1992, 66, 244, 247.

19. The bootleg sounds in D♭.

20. Kozinn 1995c, 17.

21. White 1996, 87.

22. McCartney's purchase of the Baldwin is discussed in Davis 1996b, 30. The acoustic bass is also of great historic value; it was the instrument played by Bill Black on Elvis's "Heartbreak Hotel," and Linda McCartney bought it at auction as a gift for Paul (see Rense 1995, 21). McCartney first recorded with the bass on Yoko Ono's recording "Hiroshima Sky Is Always Blue," on January 28, 1995 (Beatlenews roundup 1995, 6).

23. White 1996, 87.

24. EMI abandoned plans to issue a substantial book including recent Beatles interviews in its first 1.5 million copies of *Anthology 3*. Genesis, publisher of finely crafted books, used previously by George Harrison and Derek Taylor, has apparently postponed or shelved plans for a 300,000-word book originally to have appeared in late 1997.

25. Sheff 1981, 105.

REFERENCES

Aldwell, Edward, and Carl Schachter. 1989. *Harmony and voice leading*, 2d ed. New York: Harcourt, Brace, Jovanovich.
"Anthology" debuts at No. 1! 1995. *Beatlefan/EXTRA!* 54 (Dec. 4).
Arnold, Sue. 1998. Roll over, Beethoven! *Smithsonian*, Jan.
Aspinall, Neil. 1966a. Neil's column. *The Beatles Monthly Book*. no. 33 (Apr.).
———. 1966b. Neil's column. *The Beatles Monthly Book*, no. 37 (Aug.).
———. 1966c. Neil's column. *The Beatles Monthly Book*, no. 38 (Sept.).
Bagley, J. J. 1969. *The story of Merseyside*. Liverpool: Parry.
Bailey, Robert. 1985. An analytical study of the sketches and drafts. In *Wagner: Prelude and Transfiguration from* Tristan and Isolde, ed. Robert Bailey. New York: W. W. Norton.
Baird, Julia, with Geoffrey Giuliano. 1988. *John Lennon, my brother*. New York: Henry Holt.
Barrett, John. 1983. *The Beatles at Abbey Road*. EMI film.
Barrow, Tony. 1963. Their manager Brian Epstein. *The Beatles Monthly Book*, no. 1 (Aug.).
———. 1983. Facts and shocks. *The Beatles Monthly Book*, no. 81 (Jan.).
Batt, Shodan. 1966. By George, a Beatle is in India. *The Beatles Monthly Book*, no. 40 (Nov.).
BBC [British Broadcasting Corporation]. 1990. Lennon and McCartney as songwriters. Part 6 of series, *Lennon remembered* (Nov. 10).
Beatlemania strikes again. 1966. *Melody Maker*, June 18.
Beatle news. 1963. *The Beatles Monthly Book*, no. 5 (Dec.).
Beatle news. 1964. *The Beatles Monthly Book*, no. 6 (Jan.).
Beatle news. 1965a. *The Beatles Monthly Book*, no. 19 (Feb.).
Beatle news. 1965b. *The Beatles Monthly Book*, no. 27 (Oct.).
Beatle news. 1966a. *The Beatles Monthly Book*, no. 33 (Apr.).

Beatle news. 1966b. *The Beatles Monthly Book*, no. 39 (Oct.).

Beatle news. 1966c. *The Beatles Monthly Book*, no. 41 (Dec.).

Beatle news. 1968. *The Beatles Monthly Book*, no. 65 (Dec.).

Beatlenews roundup. 1980. *Beatlefan* 2, no. 6.

Beatlenews roundup. 1984. *Beatlefan* 6, no. 6.

Beatlenews roundup. 1987. *Beatlefan* 9, no. 3.

Beatlenews roundup. 1990. *Beatlefan* 12, no. 2.

Beatlenews roundup. 1992. *Beatlefan* 14, no. 1.

Beatlenews roundup. 1993a. *Beatlefan* 14, no. 6.

Beatlenews roundup. 1993b. *Beatlefan* 15, no. 2.

Beatlenews roundup. 1994. *Beatlefan* 16, no. 1.

Beatlenews roundup. 1995. *Beatlefan* 16, no. 4.

The Beatles. 1963a. *Please please me*. Parlophone CDP7464352.

———. 1963b. *With the Beatles*. Parlophone CDP7464362.

———. 1964a. *Beatles for sale*. Parlophone CDP7464382 (U.K.).

———. 1964b. *The Beatles story*. Capitol (S)TBO2222 (2 LPs).

———. 1964c. *A hard day's night*. Parlophone CDP7464372.

———. 1964d. *A hard day's night*. MPI Home Video MP1064.

———. 1964e. *A hard day's night*. Voyager CD-ROM.

———. 1964f. *Hear the Beatles tell all*. VJ PRO202.

———. 1964g. *Something new*. Odeon 1C06204600 (Ger.).

———. 1965a. *Help!* Parlophone CDP7464392.

———. 1965b. *Help!* MPI Home Video MP1342.

———. 1965c. *Rubber soul*. Parlophone CDP7464402.

———. 1966a. *A collection of Beatles oldies*. Parlophone PCS7016 (U.K.).

———. 1966b. *Revolver*. Parlophone CDP7464412.

———. 1967a. *Magical mystery tour*. Parlophone CDP7480622.

———. 1967b. *Sgt. Pepper's lonely hearts club band*. Parlophone CDP7464422.

———. 1968. *The Beatles*. Parlophone CDP7464438/42 (2 CDs).

———. 1969a. *Abbey road*. Parlophone CDP7464462.

———. 1969b. *Yellow submarine*. Parlophone CDP7464452.

———. 1970a. *The Beatles featuring Tony Sheridan: In the beginning (circa 1960)*. Polydor 244504.

———. 1970b. *Let it be*. Parlophone CDP7464472.

———. 1970c. *Let it be*. United Artists (film).

———. 1973a. *1962–1966*. Apple CDP077779703623.

———. 1973b. *1967–1970*. Apple CDP077779703920.

———. c. 1974. *L. S. Bumblebee*. Cumbat CBM 3626.

———. 1975. *Sweet Apple trax*. Wizardo 343 (2 LPs).

———. c. 1976a. *Abbey Road revisited*. Wizardo 353.

———. 1976b. *The Beatles featuring Tony Sheridan*. Contour CN2007 (U.K.).

———. 1977a. *The Beatles at the Hollywood Bowl*. Capitol SMAS11638 (U.S.); Parlophone EMTV4 (U.K.).

———. 1977b. *Live! at the Star-Club in Hamburg, Germany; 1962*. Bellaphon BLS5560 (Ger., 2 LPs).

———. 1977c. *Love songs*. Capitol SKBL11711 (U.S., 2 LPs).

———. 1978. *20 × 4*. Remime JPGR.

———. 1979. *Youngblood*. Audifon BVP005.

———. 197?. *The Beatle interviews*. Everest CBR1008 (U.K.).

———. c. 1980. *What a shame Mary Jane had a pain at the party*. R8028 (12-inch 45 rpm).

———. 1981a. *Air time*. Warwick M16051.

———. 1981b. *The Beatles talk downunder*. Raven PVC8911.

———. 1981c. *Wonderful picture of you*. Circle SKI5430 (2 LPs).

———. 1982a. *Strawberry fields forever*. Clue 9.

————. 1982b. *Sweet Apple trax III*. Sweet Sound W909.

————. 1982c. *20 greatest hits*. Capitol SV12245.

————. 1983. *Live at Abbey Road studios*. ARS29083 (2 LPs).

————. 1984. *I had a dream*. King MLK001.

————. 1985a. *East coast invasion*. Cicadelic 1964.

————. 1985b. *Not guilty*. Poverty NG.

————. 1985c. *Nothing is real*. NEMS BUD280.

————. 1985d. *Ready steady go! Special edition: The Beatles live!* Video 45 R0043.

————. 1985e. *West coast invasion*. Cicadelic 1966.

————. 1986a. *All our loving*. Cicadelic 1963.

————. 1986b. *Fun with the Fab Four*. Movietime.

————. 1986c. *Not a second time*. Cicadelic 1961.

————. 1986d. *'Round the world!* Cicadelic 1965.

————. 1986e. *Things we said today*. Cicadelic 1962.

————. 1987a. *Dig it*. NEMS FAB1234.

————. 1987b. *Here, there and everywhere*. Cicadelic 1968.

————. 1987c. *Liverpool May 1960: John Paul George and Stu*. Indra M56001 (2 LPs).

————. 1987d. *Quarrymen rehearse with Stu Sutcliff [sic]: Spring 1960*. Pre Beatle VD15/16.

————. 1987e. *Soundcheck*. Rock Solid RSR256.

————. 1988a. *Past masters, Vol. 1*. Parlophone CDP7900432.

————. 1988b. *Past masters, Vol. 2*. Parlophone CDP7900442.

————. 1988c. *Radio-Active, Vol. 2*. Pyramid RFTCD006.

————. 1988d. *Ultra rare trax vols. 3–4*. Swinging Pig TR2190S.

————. 1989. *Unsurpassed masters Vol. 4*. Yellow Dog 004 (Italy).

————. 1990a. *The first U.S. visit*. Apple Video MP6218.

————. 1990b. *Unsurpassed masters, vol. 1 (1962–1963)*. Unique Tracks 001 (Italy).

————. 1990c. *Unsurpassed masters, vol. 2 (1964–65)*. Unique Tracks 002 (Italy).

————. 1990d. *Unsurpassed masters, vol. 3 (1966–67)*. Unique Tracks 003 (Italy).

————. 1991a. *Acetates*. Yellow Dog 009 (Lux.).

————. 1991b. *Celluloid rock*. Yellow Dog 006 (Lux.).

————. 1991c. *Complete Apple trax vol. 6*. Ada, VIII (Ger.).

————. 1991d. *Get back and 22 other songs*. Yellow Dog 014 (Lux.).

————. 1991e. *Let it be sessions*. Chapter One CO25144.

————. 1991f. *The Silver Beatles: The original Decca tapes (1 January 1962) and Cavern Club rehearsals (early 1962)*. Yellow Dog 011 (Lux.).

————. 1991g. *'69 rehearsals, vol. 1*. Blue Kangaroo 01.

————. 1991h. *'69 rehearsals, vol. 2*. Blue Kangaroo 02.

————. 1991i. *'69 rehearsals, vol. 3*. Blue Kangaroo 03.

————. 1991j. *Unsurpassed demos*. Yellow Dog 008 (Lux.).

————. 1991k. *Unsurpassed masters, vol. 5 (1969)*. Yellow Dog 005 (Lux.).

————. 1991l. *Unsurpassed masters, vol. 6*. Yellow Dog 012 (Lux.).

————. 1991m. *Unsurpassed masters, vol. 7. (1962–69)*. Yellow Dog 013 (Lux.).

————. 1991n. *White album sessions*. Chapter One 25151/52 (2 CDs).

————. 1992a. *From Britain with beat*. Cicadelic OW10842.

————. 1992b. *The garage tapes*. Sel 18.

————. 1992c. *Hodge-Podge*. Black Dog 001 (Lux.).

————. 1992d. *The "Let it be" rehearsals, vol. 1*. Yellow Dog 015 (Lux.).

————. 1992e. *The "Let it be" rehearsals, vol. 2*. Yellow Dog 016 (Lux.).

————. 1992f. *Magical mystery demos*. Chapter One 25197.

————. 1993a. *Arrive without aging*. Vigotone 6869.

————. 1993b. *Artifacts*. Big Music (5 CDs).

————. 1993c. *The complete BBC sessions*. Great Dane 9326/9 (Italy, 9 CDs).

————. 1993d. *Control room monitor mixes: Unsurpassed outtakes.* Yellow Dog 032 (Lux.)

————. 1993e. *Sessions.* Spank SP103.

————. 1994a. *Live at the BBC.* Apple CDP724383179626 (2 CDs).

————. 1994b. *Revolution.* Vigotone 117.

————. 1994c. *Rockin' movie stars, vol. 1.* Orange 3.

————. 1994d. *Rockin' movie stars, vol. 2.* Orange 4.

————. 1994e. *Rockin' movie stars, vol. 3.* Orange 7.

————. 1994f. *Rockin' movie stars, vol. 4.* Orange 8.

————. 1994g. *Rockin' movie stars, vol. 5.* Orange 9.

————. 1994h. *Rockin' movie stars, vol. 6.* Orange 10.

————. 1994i. *Rockin' movie stars, vol. 7.* Orange 11.

————. 1994j. *Rockin' movie stars, vol. 8.* Orange 12.

————. 1995a. *Baby it's you.* Apple 724388207324.

————. 1995b. "The Beatles anthology," video produced by Apple for ABC-TV.

————. 1995c. *The Beatles anthology,* vol. 1. Apple CDP724383444526 (2 CDs).

————. 1995d. *Free as a bird.* Apple C2724385849725.

————. 1996a. *The Beatles anthology,* vol. 2. Apple CDP724383444823 (2 CDs).

————. 1996b. *The Beatles anthology,* vol. 3. Apple CDP724383445127 (2 CDs).

————. 1996c. "The Beatles anthology," video. Apple 5523V (8 VHS tapes).

————. 1996d. *Real love.* Apple C2724385854422.

————. 1997. *It's not too bad.* Pegboy 1008 (Ger.).

Beatles—Plans for yet another album. 1969. *Melody Maker,* July 5.

Beatles after new script for third film. 1965. *Melody Maker,* Dec. 18.

Beatles' album switch. 1969. *Melody Maker,* July 19.

Beatles blast own hit disc! 1963. *Melody Maker,* June 22.

Beatles in interview row. 1966. *Melody Maker,* June 4.

Beatles pic-script meeting. 1966. *Melody Maker,* Dec. 31.

Beatles plan first live album from next TV show. 1969. *Melody Maker,* Jan. 4.

Beatles plan for TV show. 1968. *Melody Maker,* Sept. 21.

Beatles plan the new single. 1966. *Melody Maker,* Apr. 9.

Beatles plus jazzmen on new album. 1966. *Melody Maker,* June 11.

Beatles single due March 15. 1968. *Melody Maker,* Feb. 24.

Beatles single for Christmas. 1966. *Melody Maker,* Nov. 12.

Beatles take a rest. 1966. *Melody Maker,* Sept. 10.

Beatles to appear live and John in the nude. 1968. *Rolling Stone* 21 (Nov. 9).

Beatles to face knockers. 1966. *Melody Maker,* Aug. 13.

Beatles to write entire film score. 1966. *Melody Maker,* Aug. 6.

Belz, Carl. [1969]. Rock and fine art. In *The Beatles reader,* ed. Charles Neises. Ann Arbor: Popular Culture Ink, 1984.

Best, Pete, and Patrick Doncaster. 1985. *Beatle!: The Pete Best story.* New York: Dell.

Braun, Michael. 1995. *"Love me do!": The Beatles' progress.* London: Penguin.

Brown, Peter, and Steven Gaines. 1983. *The love you make: An insider's story of the Beatles.* New York: McGraw-Hill.

Buk, Askold. 1994. Magical mystery tour. *Guitar World* 15 (Feb.).

Buskin, Richard. 1987. Jogging George Martin's memory. *Musician,* no. 105 (July).

Byrds go for Bach, ragas, Coltrane. 1966. *Melody Maker,* May 28.

Campbell, Colin, and Allan Murphy. 1980. *Things we said today.* Ann Arbor: Pierian.

Casey, Howie. 1963. The silver Beatles. *Mersey Beat* 2 (June 20–July 4, 1963). Reprinted in *Mersey beat: The beginnings of the Beatles,* ed. Bill Harry. New York: Quick Fox, 1977.

Christgau, Robert, and John Piccarella. 1982. Portrait of the artist as a rock and roll star. In *The ballad of John and Yoko,* ed. Jonathan Cott and Christine Doudna. Garden City, N.Y.: Rolling Stone.

Clayson, Alan. 1992. *Ringo Starr: Straight man or joker?* New York: Paragon.

Coleman, Ray. 1964a. Pop probe. *Melody Maker*, Oct. 24.

———. 1964b. When we stop selling records . . . *Melody Maker*, Oct. 31.

———. 1965a. Beatles say . . . *Melody Maker*, Jan. 9.

———. 1965b. Wish Elvis all the best in *Aladdin*. *Melody Maker*, Jan. 16.

———. 1965c. Here we go again. *Melody Maker*, Feb. 27.

———. 1989. *The man who made the Beatles: An intimate biography of Brian Epstein*. New York: McGraw-Hill.

———. 1992. *Lennon: The definitive biography*, 2d ed. New York: Harper Collins.

———. 1995. *McCartney: Yesterday & today*. London: Boxtree.

Compleat Beatles, The. 1982. Delilah Films MV700166 (video).

Cooke, Deryck. 1959. *The language of music*. Oxford: Oxford University.

———. 1968. The Lennon-McCartney songs. [Feb. 1, *The Listener*] In *The Lennon companion: Twenty-five years of comment*, ed. Elizabeth Thomson and David Gutman. New York: Schirmer, 1987.

Cott, Jonathan. 1968. Interview [Sept. 17–18, 1968] with John Lennon. *Rolling Stone* 22 (Nov. 23).

———. 1981. A conversation [Dec. 5, 1980]. *Rolling Stone* 335 (Jan. 22).

———. 1982a. John Lennon: How he became who he was. In *The ballad of John and Yoko*, ed. Jonathan Cott and Christine Doudna. Garden City, N.Y.: Rolling Stone.

———. 1982b. Yoko Ono and her sixteen-track voice. In *The ballad of John and Yoko*, ed. Jonathan Cott and Christine Doudna. Garden City, N.Y.: Rolling Stone.

Cott, Jonathan, and David Dalton. 1969. *The Beatles get back*. London: Apple. [Substantial but non-paginated book, printed in 1969, issued in record box with first British pressing of *Let it be* (Apple PXS1, available May 8–Nov. 6, 1970).]

Cott, Jonathan, and Christine Doudna, eds. 1982. *The ballad of John and Yoko*. Garden City, N.Y.: Rolling Stone.

Countdown for the third Beatles film. 1966. *Melody Maker*, May 7.

Covach, John. 1990. The Rutles and the use of specific models in musical satire. *Indiana Theory Review* 11.

Cowan, Philip. 1978? *Behind the Beatles songs*. London: Polytantric.

Davies, Hunter. 1968a. *The Beatles: The authorized biography*. New York: McGraw-Hill.

[Davies], Hunter. 1968b. Encyclo(Beatle)pedia. *The Beatles Monthly Book*, no. 59 (June).

Davis, Andy, ed. 1995a. Beatles '95. *The Beatles Monthly Book*, no. 231 (July).

———. 1995b. Beatles '95. *The Beatles Monthly Book*, no. 232 (Aug.).

———. 1995c. Beatles '95. *The Beatles Monthly Book*, no. 233 (Sept.).

———. 1995d. Beatles '95. *The Beatles Monthly Book*, no. 236 (Dec.).

———. 1996a. Beatles '96. *The Beatles Monthly Book*, no. 238 (Feb.).

———. 1996b. Beatles '96. *The Beatles Monthly Book*, no. 239 (Mar.).

Davison, Peter, ed. 1971. *Songs of the British music hall*. London: Oak.

Dawbarn, Bob. 1968. You know what I'd love to do? *Melody Maker*, Sept. 14.

Dawson, Jerry. 1965. Lennon's eye view. *Melody Maker*, Nov. 13.

Day, Aidan. 1989. *Jokerman: Reading the lyrics of Bob Dylan*. Oxford: Basil Blackwell.

Dean, Johnny. 1978. How "Love Me Do" became a hit. *The Beatles Monthly Book*, no. 28 (Aug.).

DeWitt, Howard. 1985. *The Beatles: Untold tales*. Fremont, CA: Horizon.

Dietz, Devon. 1995. Unpublished paper on "Mr. Kite."

DiLello, Richard. 1983 [1972]. *The longest cocktail party*. Ann Arbor: Pierian Press.

Dowlding, William J. 1989. *Beatlesongs*. New York: Fireside.

Elson, Howard. 1986. *McCartney: Songwriter*. London: W. H. Allen.

Engelhardt, Kristofer. 1998. *Beatles Undercover*. Burlington, Ontario: Collector's Guide Publishing.

Epstein, Beatles meet to discuss future. 1966. *Melody Maker*, Nov. 12.

Epstein, Brian [ghost. Derek Taylor]. 1964. *A cellarful of noise*. Garden City, N.Y.: Doubleday.

Epstein halts "Boys"/"Kansas" U.S. release. 1965. *Melody Maker*, Nov. 13.

Evans, Mal. 1968a. Beatles in India. *The Beatles Monthly Book*, no. 58 (May).

———. 1968b. Ringo and George in California. *The Beatles Monthly Book*, no. 61 (Aug.).

———. 1968c. Mal's [diary]. *The Beatles Monthly Book*, no. 63 (Oct.).

———. 1968d. Thirty new Beatle grooves. *The Beatles Monthly Book*, no. 64 (Nov.).

———. 1969a. Your album queries. *The Beatles Monthly Book*, no. 67 (Feb.).

———. 1969b. Mal's diary. *The Beatles Monthly Book*, no. 68 (Mar.).

Evans, Mal, and Neil Aspinall. 1967. Recording: Why it takes so long now. *The Beatles Monthly Book*, no. 45 (Apr.).

———. 1968a. How the magical EPs were made. *The Beatles Monthly Book*, no. 54 (Jan.).

———. 1968b. New single sessions. *The Beatles Monthly Book*, no. 57 (Apr.).

Everett, Kenny. 1967. Beatles' dinner party. *The Beatles Monthly Book*, no. 48 (July).

Everett, Walter. 1986. Fantastic remembrance in John Lennon's "Strawberry fields forever" and "Julia." *Musical Quarterly* 72, no. 3.

———. 1987. Text-painting in the foreground and middleground of Paul McCartney's Beatle song, "She's leaving home." *In Theory Only* 9, no. 7.

———. 1990. Grief in *Winterreise*: A Schenkerian perspective. *Music Analysis* 9 (July).

———. 1991. Voice leading, register, and self-discipline in *Die Zauberflöte*. *Theory and Practice* 16.

———. 1992. Voice leading and harmony as expressive devices in the early music of the Beatles: "She Loves You." *College Music Symposium* 32.

———. 1995. The Beatles as composers: The genesis of *Abbey Road*, side two. In *Concert music, rock, and jazz since 1945*, ed. Elizabeth West Marvin and Richard Hermann. Rochester, N.Y.: Univ. of Rochester.

Experiments with sounds. 1966. *Melody Maker*, Sept. 17.

Fallon, B. P. 1969. Is the real John Lennon now standing up? *Melody Maker*, Apr. 19.

Flanagan, Bill. 1990. Boy, you're gonna carry that weight. *Musician*, no. 139 (May).

Flippo, Chet. 1988. *Yesterday: The unauthorized biography of Paul McCartney*. New York: Doubleday.

Forte, Allen. 1995. *The American Popular Ballad of the Golden Era, 1924–1950*. Princeton: Princeton University Press.

Forte, Dan. 1987a. George's guitar gallery. *Guitar Player* 21 (Nov.).

———. 1987b. The jungle music and posh skiffle of George Harrison. *Guitar Player* 21 (Nov.).

Freeman, Robert. 1983. *Yesterday: The Beatles 1963–1965*. New York: Holt Rinehart & Winston.

Friede, Goldie, Robin Titone, and Sue Wiener. 1980. *The Beatles A to Z*. New York: Methuen.

Frith, Simon. 1988. *Music for pleasure: Essays in the sociology of pop*. New York: Routledge.

Fulpen, H. V. 1982. *The Beatles: An illustrated diary*. Quoted in William J. Dowlding, *Beatlesongs* (New York: Fireside, 1989).

Fulper-Smith, Shawn. 1984. Chicago: Who's on first? *Beatlefan* 6, no. 3.

Fury, Billy. 1963. *We want Billy!* Decca TAB62 (U.K.).

Gambaccini, Paul. 1974. Interview with Paul McCartney. *Rolling Stone* 153 (Jan. 31).

———, ed. 1976. *Paul McCartney in his own words*. New York: Quick Fox.

Garbarini, Vic. 1980. Paul McCartney: Lifting the veil on the Beatles. *Musician*, no. 26 (Aug.).

———. 1982. Ringo. *Musician*, no. 40 (Feb.).

Garbarini, Vic, Brian Cullman, and Barbara Graustark. 1980. *Strawberry fields forever: John Lennon remembered*. New York: Delilah.

Garry, Len. 1997. *John, Paul, & me: Before the Beatles*. London: CG Publishing.

Gauldin, Robert. 1990. Beethoven, *Tristan*, and the Beatles. *College Music Symposium* 30.

George Harrison, Ringo Starr—1980s Press Conferences. 1984? YOURE16.

George Harrison on *Abbey Road.* 1969. *Rolling Stone* 44 (Oct. 18).

Gerry and the Pacemakers. 1991. *The best of . . .* UA CDP7960932.

Ginsberg, Allen. 1996. *The ballad of the skeletons.* Mercury 6971201012.

Giuliano, Geoffrey. 1991a. *Blackbird: The life and times of Paul McCartney.* New York: Dutton.

———. 1991b. *Dark horse: The private life of George Harrison.* New York: Plume.

Glazer, Mitchell. 1977. Growing up at 33 1/3: The George Harrison interview. *Crawdaddy* (Feb.).

Golson, G. Barry, ed., 1981a. John Lennon: His final words on the Beatles' music. *Playboy* 28 (Apr.).

———. 1981b. *The Playboy interviews with John Lennon and Yoko Ono: The final testament.* New York: Berkley.

Goodman, Joan. 1984. Interview: Paul and Linda McCartney. *Playboy* 31 (Dec.).

Goodman, Pete. 1965. Norman Smith continues talking about balancing the Beatles. *The Beatles Monthly Book,* no. 23 (June).

Gottfridsson, Hans Olof. 1997. *The Beatles from Cavern to Star-Club.* Stockholm-Premium.

Grevatt, Ren. 1966a. Beach Boys' blast. *Melody Maker,* Mar. 19.

———. 1966b. Radio stations ignore ban on Beatle records. *Melody Maker,* Aug. 20.

Griffiths, David. 1987. Three tributaries of *The River. Popular Music* 7, no. 1.

Hand, Charles R. 1910. *The story of the Calderstones.* Liverpool: Hand & Co.

———. 1912. *Calderstones.* Liverpool: Hand & Co.

Harrison, George. 1970. *All things must pass.* Apple STCH639 (3 LPs).

———. 1971. *The concert for Bangla Desh.* Apple STCX3385 (3 LPs).

———. 1974. *Dark horse.* Apple SMAS3418.

———. 1975. *Extra texture—Read all about it.* Apple SW 3420.

———. 1976a. *A personal dialogue with George Harrison.* Dark Horse PRO649.

———. 1976b. *Thirty-three & ⅓.* Dark Horse DH3005.

———. 1979. *George Harrison.* Dark Horse DHK3255.

——— [with Derek Taylor]. 1980. *I me mine.* New York: Simon & Schuster.

———. 1982. *Gone troppo.* Dark Horse 237341.

———. 1984. Interview on "Eyewitness news," Auckland, New Zealand (Nov. 28).

———. 1987a. *Cloud nine.* Dark Horse 225643.

———. 1987b. Interview of Aug. 25. In Timothy White, *Rock lives: Profiles and interviews.* New York: Henry Holt, 1990.

———. 1992. *Live in Japan.* Dark Horse 9269642 (2 CDs).

Harry, Bill. 1982. *The Beatles who's who.* New York: Delilah.

———. 1983. The Beatles at the Star Club. *The Beatles Monthly Book,* no. 81 (Jan.).

———. 1984. *The Book of Lennon.* New York: Delilah.

———, ed. 1977. *Mersey beat: The beginnings of the Beatles.* New York: Quick Fox.

[Harry], Virginia. 1962. Merseybeat roundabout. *Mersey Beat* 1 (Mar. 22–Apr. 5). Reprinted in *Mersey beat: The beginnings of the Beatles,* ed. Bill Harry. New York: Quick Fox, 1977.

Haskell, Barbara, and John G. Hanhardt. 1991. *Yoko Ono: Arias and objects.* Salt Lake City: Peregrine Smith.

Hastings, Joel. 1994. The ballads of Paul McCartney. Unpublished paper.

Hayes, Chris. 1968. Expert advice. *Melody Maker,* Jan. 27.

Here's another clue for you all. 1995. *Beatlefan/EXTRA!* 54 (Dec. 4).

Hertsgaard, Mark. 1995. *A Day in the life: The music and artistry of the Beatles.* New York-Delacorte.

The Hits of 1963. 1988. EMI CD-MFP6033 (U.K.).

Hit-trick for Cilla?. 1964. *Melody Maker,* Aug. 8.

Hodenfield, Chris. 1976. Interview with George Martin. *Rolling Stone* 217 (15 July).

Holly, Buddy. 1985. *Legend*. MCA 24184 (U.K., 2 LPs).

———. 1990. *The Legendary* . . . Pickwick PWKS523/560/595 (U.K., 3 CDs).

Hopkins, Jerry. 1987. *Yoko Ono*. London: Sidgwick & Jackson.

Houston, Bob. 1966. Ravi Shankar: Doubts about East ever meeting West. *Melody Maker*, June 11.

How about a tune on the old sitar? 1966. *Melody Maker*, May 7.

How Cilla got fed up singing that hit. 1968. *Melody Maker*, Apr. 13.

Howlett, Kevin. 1983. *The Beatles at the BEEB: The story of their radio career, 1962–1965*. Ann Arbor: Pierian.

Hutton, Jack. 1967. Ringo on drums, drugs, and the Maharishi. *Melody Maker*, Dec. 2.

Imagine: John Lennon. 1988. Capitol C190803 (2 LPs).

Ingham, Peter, and Mtoru Mitsui. 1987. The search for "Sweet Georgia Brown": A case of discographical detection. *Popular Music* 6, no. 3.

Inside Abbey Road Studios. 1983. *Beatlefan* 5, no. 6 (Oct.–Nov.).

In the Beatles song writing factory. 1966. *Melody Maker*, July 16.

Isler, Scott. 1988. John Lennon: Lost in sound. *Musician* 114 (Apr.).

ITV announces anthology. 1995. *The Beatles Monthly Book*, no. 231 (July).

J. and P. stay faithful. 1964. *The Beatles Monthly Book*, no. 7 (Feb.).

Jairazbhoy, N[azir] A. 1971. *The rags of North Indian music*. London: Faber.

James, Frederick. 1966a. Beatles talk. *The Beatles Monthly Book*, no. 30 (Jan.).

———. 1966b. Beatles talk. *The Beatles Monthly Book*, no. 33 (Apr.).

———. 1966c. Beatles talk. *The Beatles Monthly Book*, no. 34 (May).

———. 1967. Beatles talk. *The Beatles Monthly Book*, no. 44 (Mar.).

———. 1968a. Revolution report. *The Beatles Monthly Book*, no. 60 (July).

———. 1968b. John and Yoko talk. *The Beatles Monthly Book*, no. 63 (Oct.).

———. 1968c. Tracks you've never heard. *The Beatles Monthly Book*, no. 64 (Nov.).

———. 1969. World's first in-depth preview. *The Beatles Monthly Book*, no. 73 (Aug.).

John and Yoko: The bed-in. 1990 [1970]. Original film, Bag Productions. Video rerelease, Picture Music International.

Jones, John. 1987. Meeting Yoko Ono. In *The Lennon companion: Twenty-five years of comment*, ed. Elizabeth Thomson and David Gutman. New York: Schirmer.

Kaye, Peter. 1987. *Beatles in Liverpool*. Parbold, England: Starlit.

Kelly, Freda. 1969. July newsletter. *The Beatles Monthly Book*, no. 72 (July).

Kelly, Michael B. 1991. *The Beatle myth*. Jefferson, N.C.: McFarland.

King, William. 1987. The making of a *Magical mystery tour*. *Beatlefan* 10, no. 1 (Dec.).

Klimecky, Chris. 1994. Unpublished paper on George Harrison.

Kozinn, Allan. 1987. The Beatles on compact disc: A conversation with George Martin. *Beatlefan* 9 (Feb.–Mar.).

———. 1994. John Lennon's first known recording is for sale. *New York Times*, July 21.

———. 1995a. *The Beatles*. London: Phaidon.

———. 1995b. The Beatles: Great classics. *BBC Music*, Oct.

———. 1995c. McCartney on the "Anthology." *Beatlefan* 17, no. 1 (Nov.–Dec.).

Kramer, Billy J., and the Dakotas. 1991. *The Best of* . . . Imperial/EMI CDP7960552.

Lawrence, Paul. 1978. I was a very nervous character: An interview with George Martin. *Audio* 62 (May).

Leach, Sam. 1992. *Follow the Merseybeat road*. Liverpool: Eden.

Leary, Timothy, Ralph Metzner, and Richard Alpert. [1964.] *The psychedelic experience*. New York: Citadel Press, 1995.

Lees, Gene. 1967. Beatles, op. 15. *High Fidelity* 17 (Aug.).

Leigh, Spencer. 1984. *Let's go down the Cavern*. London: Vermilion.

Lennon, Cynthia. 1978. *A twist of Lennon*. New York: Avon Books.

Lennon, John. 1964. *In his own write*. London: Jonathan Cape.

———. 1965. Blind date. *Melody Maker*, Dec. 11.

———. 1967+. *Skywriting by word of mouth*. New York: Harper & Row, 1986.

———. [1968a.] Two virgins. In *Skywriting by word of mouth*. New York: Harper & Row, 1986.

———. 1968b. *Unfinished music no. 1: Two virgins*. Apple T5001.

———. 1969. *Unfinished music no. 2: Life with the lions*. Zapple ST3358.

———. 1970. *John Lennon/Plastic Ono Band*. Capitol CDP7467702.

———. 1971. *Imagine*. Apple SW3339.

———. 1972a. Interview in *Hit Parader* (Apr.). Cited in William J. Dowlding, *Beatlesongs* (New York: Simon and Schuster, 1989).

———. 1972b. *Some time in New York City*. Capitol CDP746782/3 (2 CDs).

———. 1973. *Mind games*. Apple SW3414.

———. 1974. *Walls and bridges*. Apple SW3416.

———. 1975a. Live appearance on Scott Muni's WNEW-FM, New York, radio program (Feb. 13).

———. 1975b. *Rock 'n' roll*. Capitol/EMI CDP7467072.

———. 1980. *The last word*. Baktabak BAK2096.

———. 1986. *Menlove Avenue*. Capitol CDP7465762.

———. 1988a. *The lost Lennon tapes, vol. 2*. Bag 5074.

———. 1988b. *The lost Lennon tapes, vol. 3*. Bag 5075.

———. 1988c. *The lost Lennon tapes, vol. 5*. Bag 5077.

———. 1988d. *The lost Lennon tapes, vol. 8*. Bag 5080.

———. 1988e. *The lost Lennon tapes, vol. 9*. Bag 5081.

———. 1988f. *The lost Lennon tapes, vol. 10*. Bag 5082.

———. c. 1989. *The lost Lennon tapes, vol. 11*. Bag 5083.

———. 1990. *Lennon*. Capitol CDS7952202 (4 CDs).

———. c. 1992a. *The lost Lennon tapes, vol. 25*. Bag 5097.

———. c. 1992b. *The lost Lennon tapes, vol. 26*. Bag 5098.

———. 1993. *The lost Lennon tapes, vol. 28*. Bag 5100.

———. 1996. *Free as a bird: The Dakota Beatle demos*. Pegboy 1001 (Australia).

———. 1998. *John Lennon Anthology*. Capitol C2724383061426 (4 CDs).

Lennon, John, and Yoko Ono. 1969. *Wedding album*. Apple SMAX3361.

———. 1980. *Double Fantasy*. Geffen 2001.

———. 1984. *Milk and Honey*. Polydor 8171601Y1.

Lennon, John, Yoko Ono, and Andy Peebles. 1981. *The last Lennon tapes*. New York: Dell.

Lennon, Pauline. 1990. *Daddy come home*. London: Angus & Robertson.

Lewisohn, Mark. 1988. *The Beatles: Recording sessions*. New York: Harmony.

———. 1992. *The complete Beatles chronicle*. New York: Harmony.

Macca on his album. 1996. *Beatlefan/EXTRA!* 65 (Aug. 10).

MacDonald, Ian. 1994. *Revolution in the head*. New York: Henry Holt.

Madow, Stuart, and Jeff Sobul. 1992. *The colour of your dreams: The Beatles' psychedelic music*. Pittsburgh: Dorrance.

The making of Sgt. Pepper. 1992. George Martin's made-for-television documentary.

Mann, William. 1963. What songs the Beatles sang . . . [The London *Times*, Dec. 27] Reprinted in *The Lennon companion: Twenty-five years of comment*, ed. Elizabeth Thomson and David Gutman. New York: Schirmer, 1987.

Marchbank, Pearce, ed. 1982. *With the Beatles: The historic photographs of Dezo Hoffmann*. New York: Omnibus.

Marsden, Gerry, with Ray Coleman. 1993. *I'll never walk alone: An autobiography*. London: Bloomsbury.

Martin, George. 1983. *Making music: The guide to writing, performing and recording*. New York: Quill.

———, exec. prod. 1992. "The making of Sgt. Pepper." Television program aired on

ITV in the United Kingdom (June 14) and on the Disney Channel (Sept. 27) in the United States.

Martin, George, with Jeremy Hornsby. 1979. *All you need is ears*. New York: St. Martin's.

Martin, George, with William Pearson. 1994. *With a little help from my friends*. Boston: Little, Brown.

McCabe, Peter, and Robert D. Schonfeld. 1972. *Apple to the core*. New York: Pocket.

McCartney, Michael. 1987. *Mike Mac's white and blacks plus one color*. New York: Penguin.

——. 1992. *Remember: Recollections and photographs of the Beatles by Michael McCartney*. New York: Henry Holt & Co.

McCartney, Paul. 1970. *McCartney*. Capitol CDP7466112.

——. 1971. *Ram*. Apple SMAS3375.

——. 1973. *Band on the run*. Apple SOP3415.

——. 1976a. *Wings at the speed of sound*. Capitol CDP7481992.

——. 1976b. *Wings over America*. Capitol CDP7467152 (2 CDs).

—— [as "Percy Thrillington"]. 1977. *Thrillington*. Capitol ST11642.

——. 1980a. *McCartney II*. Capitol CDM7520242.

——. 1980b. *The McCartney interview*. Columbia PC36987.

——. 1982a. Interview in *Jamming!* (June). Reported in William J. Dowlding, *Beatlesongs*. New York: Fireside, 1989.

——. 1982b. *Tug of war*. Capitol CDP7460572.

——. 1984. *Give my regards to Broad Street*. Capitol CDP7460432.

——. c. 1985. *Paul McCartney press conferences*. BROADS 3.

——. 1987. *Interview picture disc*. Baktabak BAK2003.

——. 1988. *CHOBA B CCCP*. Capitol CDP7976152.

——. 1989. *Flowers in the dirt*. Capitol CDP7916532.

——. 1990. *Tripping the live fantastic*. Capitol CDP7947782 (2CDs).

——. 1991a. *Press conferences Tokyo/Chicago 1990*. LMW 28IF (U. K.).

——. 1991b. *Unplugged (the official bootleg)*. Capitol CDP7964132. (Notes by Mark Lewisohn.)

——. 1992a. *Paul McCartney's Liverpool oratorio*. Capitol CDS7543712 (2 CDs).

——. 1992b. *The piano tape [1974?]*. Mistral Melody Maker 9231.

——. 1993a. *Paul is live*. Capitol CDP724382770428.

—— [as "The Fireman"]. 1993b. *Strawberries oceans ships forest*. Capitol CDP724382716723.

——. 1994. Introduction to *The man who "framed" the Beatles: A biography of Richard Lester*, by Andrew Yule. New York: Donald I. Fine.

——. 1995. "A Leaf." Anya Alexeyev, piano. EMI Classics 724388217620.

——. 1997a. *Flaming pie*. Capitol CDP724385650024.

——. 1997b. *Paul McCartney's standing stone*. EMI Classics 724355648426.

—— [as "The Fireman"]. 1998. *Rushes*. Hydra 724349705524 (U.K.).

McCartney: The Beatlefan interview. 1984. *Beatlefan 7*, no. 1 (Dec.).

McCartney world tour, The. 1989. [Substantial program booklet for the U.S. leg of his 1989–90 concert tour.]

McCoy, William, and Mitchell McGeary. 1990. *Every little thing: The definitive guide to Beatles recording variations, rare mixes and other musical oddities, 1958–1986*. Ann Arbor: Popular Culture.

Mellers, Wilfrid. 1973. *The music of the Beatles: Twilight of the gods*. New York: Schirmer.

Micek, Mollie. 1994. Unpublished paper on Beatle horn arrangements.

Miles, Barry. 1997. *Paul McCartney: Many years from now*. New York: Holt.

Miles, [Barry], comp. 1981. *John Lennon in his own words*. New York: Quick Fox.

Miles, [Barry], and Pearce Marchbank, eds. 1978. *Beatles in their own words*. New York: Omnibus.

Million dollar offer for Beatles. 1969. *Melody Maker*, December 13.

Moore, Allan F. 1993. *Rock: The primary text—Developing a musicology of rock*. Buckingham, England: Open University.

———. 1997. *The Beatles: Sgt. Pepper's Lonely Hearts Club Band*. Cambridge: Cambridge University Press.

"Morecambe and Wise show." 1963. Recorded Dec. 2, aired ATV Apr. 18, 1964.

Mulhern, Tom. 1990. Interview with Paul McCartney. *Guitar Player* 24 (July).

Murphy, Karen, and Ronald Gross. 1969. All you need is love. *New York Times Magazine* (Apr. 13).

Mytkowicz, Bob. 1987. Fab gear!: Guitars of the Beatles. *Guitar Player* 21 (Nov.).

Norman, Philip. 1981. *Shout!: The true story of the Beatles*. London: Elm Tree.

O'Donnell, Jim. 1996. *The day John met Paul*. New York: Penguin.

O'Grady, Terence. 1975. The music of the Beatles from 1962 to *Sergeant Pepper's Lonely Hearts Club Band*, vol. 1. Ph.D. diss., University of Wisconsin, Madison.

———. 1979. *Rubber Soul* and the social dance tradition. *Journal of the Society for Ethnomusicology* 23 (Jan.).

———. 1983. *The Beatles: A musical evolution*. Boston: Twayne.

Okun, Milton, ed., 1981. *The compleat Beatles*. New York: Delilah.

On drums: Ringo Starr. 1963. *The Beatles Monthly Book*, no. 1 (Aug.).

On lead guitar: George Harrison. 1963. *The Beatles Monthly Book*, no. 1 (Aug.).

Ono, Yoko. [1964.] *Grapefruit*. New York: Simon and Schuster, 1970.

———. 1970. *Plastic Ono Band*. Apple SW 3373.

An oral appreciation. 1982. In *The ballad of John and Yoko*, ed. Jonathan Cott and Christine Doudna. Garden City, N.Y.: Rolling Stone.

Orton, Joe. [1967.] *Up against it: A screenplay for the Beatles*. London: Eyre Methuen, 1979.

Palmer, Raymond. 1968. Danger—Beatles at work. *Saturday Review* 51 (Oct. 12).

Paul in secret session. 1967. *Melody Maker*, July 22.

Paul McCartney reviews the new pop singles. 1967. *Melody Maker*, Feb. 25.

Paul McCartney solo album? 1970. *Melody Maker*, Feb. 21.

Pawlowski, Gareth L. 1989. *How they became the Beatles*. New York: E. P. Dutton.

Pearson, Stan. 1968. Paul's shout up at Shipley. *Melody Maker*, July 13.

Peer, Elizabeth, and Ralph Peer II. 1972. *Buddy Holly*. New York: Peer International.

Perkins, Carl. 1977. *The Sun story, vol. 3*. Sunnyvale 9330903.

Pichaske, David. 1972. Sustained performances. In *The Beatles reader*, ed. Charles P. Neises. Ann Arbor: Popular Culture, 1984.

Plastic Ono Band. 1969. *Live peace in Toronto 1969*. Apple SW 3362.

Porter, Steven C. 1979. Rhythm and harmony in the music of the Beatles. Ph.D. diss., City University of New York.

Pules, Harry. 1967. George in hippyland. *Melody Maker*, Aug. 19.

Radhakrishnan, S., trans. and ed. 1973. *The Bhagavadgita*. New York: Harper Torchbooks.

Radio series and tour for Beatles. 1963. *Melody Maker*, Mar. 2.

Raver, The [pseud.]. 1965a. Inside showbiz. *Melody Maker*, Jan. 2.

———. 1965b. Inside showbiz. *Melody Maker*, Jan. 30.

———. 1965c. *Melody Maker*, Dec. 4.

———. 1966a. *Melody Maker*, Feb. 26.

———. 1966b. *Melody Maker*, Apr. 23.

———. 1966c. *Melody Maker*, Sept. 10.

———. 1967. Weekly tonic. *Melody Maker*, May 20.

Reck, David R. 1985. Beatles orientalis: Influences from Asia in a popular song tradition. *Asian Music* 16, no. 1.

Rense, Rip. 1995. Recording with the fab three. *Beatlefan* 17/1 (Nov.–Dec.).

Repka, Charles. 1977. Resurrecting the Beatles. *High Fidelity and Musical America* 27, no. 8.

Rifkin, Joshua. 1968. On the music of the Beatles. In *The Lennon companion: Twenty-*

five years of comment, ed. Elizabeth Thomson and David Gutman. New York: Schirmer, 1987.

Riley, Tim. 1988. *Tell me why: A Beatles commentary*. New York: Knopf.

Roberts, Chris. 1963. The night a mouse took the mickey out of the Beatles. *Melody Maker*, Sept. 28.

———. 1964a. Lennon and McCartney tell you how to write a hit. *Melody Maker*, Feb. 1.

———. 1964b. John Lennon. *Melody Maker*, Apr. 4.

———. 1964c. Beat's secret weapon. *Melody Maker*, Apr. 18.

Robertson, John [Peter Doggett]. 1991. *The art and music of John Lennon*. New York: Birch Lane.

Rollin, Betty. 1969. Top pop merger. *Look* 33, no. 6 (Mar. 18).

The Rolling Stones. 1965. *Out of our heads*. Decca (U.K.).

———. 1966. *Aftermath*. Decca (U.K.).

Rose, Lloyd. 1985. Long gone John: Lennon and the revelations. [Boston *Phoenix*, 10 Dec. 10] In *The Lennon companion: Twenty-five years of comment*, ed. Elizabeth Thomson and David Gutman. New York: Schirmer, 1987.

Rowland, Mark. 1990. The quiet Wilbury. *Musician*, no. 137 (Mar.).

Rule, Greg. 1996. You say you want a revolution. *Keyboard*, no. 4 (Apr.).

St. Barnabas Church Mossley Hill, Seventy-fifth anniversary 1914–1989 souvenir brochure.

Salewicz, Chris. 1986. *McCartney*. New York: St. Martin's.

Sauceda, James. 1983. *The literary Lennon: A comedy of letters*. Ann Arbor: Pierian.

Schaffner, Nicholas. 1977. *The Beatles forever*. Harrisburg, Pa.: Cameron.

———. 1982. *The British invasion*. New York: McGraw-Hill.

Schwartz, David. 1990. *Listening to the Beatles*. Ann Arbor: Popular Culture Ink.

Senoff, Pete. 1969. Spector on pop today. *Melody Maker*, Oct. 11.

Shankar, Ravi. 1968. *My music, my life*. Los Angeles: Vikas.

———. 1997. *Chants of India*. Angel CDQ724385594823.

Sharp, Ken. 1988. A Rutle remembers: Talking with Neil Innes. *Beatlefan* 10, no. 1 (Dec. 1987–Jan. 1988).

Sheff, David. 1981. Interview: John Lennon and Yoko Ono. *Playboy* 28 (Jan.).

Shelton, Robert. 1986. *No direction home: The life and music of Bob Dylan*. New York: Ballantine.

Shenson, Walter, exec. prod. 1995. *You can't do that* (video).

Shepherd, Billy [Peter Jones]. 1963. A tale of four Beatles. Parts 2–3. *The Beatles Monthly Book*, nos. 3 (Oct.); 4 (Nov.).

———. 1964a. A tale of four Beatles. Part 6. *The Beatles Monthly Book*, no. 7 (Feb.).

———. 1964b. Filming with the boys in *A hard day's night*. *The Beatles Monthly Book*, no. 11 (June).

———. 1964c. Beatles on holiday. *The Beatles Monthly Book*, no. 12 (July).

———. 1964d. *The true story of the Beatles*. London: Beat.

——— [as Peter Jones]. 1979. Love Me Do. *The Beatles Monthly Book*, no. 34 (Feb.).

Shepherd, Billy, and Johnny Dean. 1966. Behind the spotlight. *The Beatles Monthly Book*, nos. 31 (Feb.) and 32 (Mar.).

———. 1967. Behind the spotlight. *The Beatles Monthly Book*, no. 43 (Feb.).

Short, Don. 1968. With the Beatles in India. *Melody Maker*, Mar. 9.

Shotton, Pete, and Nicholas Schaffner. 1983. *John Lennon: In my life*. New York: Stein and Day.

Slawson, Wayne. 1985. *Sound color*. Berkeley: University of California.

Smith, Giles. 1995. The Beatles' straight man. *New Yorker* (Nov. 20).

Smith, Joe. 1988. *Off the record: An oral history of popular music*. New York: Warner.

Smith, Richard. 1987. British Rickenbackers. *Guitar Player* 21, no. 7 (July).

Solt, Andrew, and Sam Egan. 1988. *Imagine: John Lennon*. New York: Macmillan.

Somach, Denny, Kathleen Somach, and Kevin Gunn. 1989. *Ticket to ride: A celebration of the Beatles based on the hit radio show*. New York: William Morrow & Co.

The songs Lennon and McCartney gave away. 1979. EMI NUT18 (U. K.).

Sotheby's London rock and roll memorabilia: 1955–1984. 1984. [Auction catalogue (Aug. 30).]

Southall, Brian. 1982. *Abbey Road*. Cambridge: Patrick Stephens.

Standby for Beatle single. 1966. *Melody Maker*, May 7.

Stannard, Neville. 1984. *The long and winding road*. New York: Avon.

Stapley, Patrick. 1995. The Beatles: Yesterday and today (and tomorrow). *EQ* 6, no. 11 (Nov.).

Starr, Ringo. 1983. *Ringo's yellow submarine*. Syndicated series for ABC Radio Network.

Steinem, Gloria. 1964. Beatle with a future. *Cosmopolitan* (Dec.). Reprinted in *The Lennon companion: Twenty-five years of comment*, ed. Elizabeth Thomson and David Gutman. New York: Schirmer, 1987.

Stewart-Brown, Ronald. 1911. *A history of the manor and township of Allerton*. Liverpool: E. Howell.

Sulpy, Doug. 1995. *The 910's Guide to the Beatles' Outtakes*. Princeton Junction, N.J.: The 910.

Sulpy, Doug, and Ray Schweighardt. 1994. *Drugs, divorce and a slipping image*. Princeton Junction, N.J.: The 910.

Sussman, Al. 1992. Interview with Mark Lewisohn. *Beatlefan* 14, no. 3.

Sweet Toronto. 1988. Pennebaker Assoc.

The Swinging Blue Jeans. 1992. *The Best of . . .* EMI CDP7992352 (U.K.).

Tamla team pen for Beatles. 1966. *Melody Maker*, Jan. 1.

Tamm, Eric. 1987. Beyond Strawberry fields. In *The Lennon companion*, ed. Elizabeth Thomson and David Gutman. New York: Schirmer.

Taylor, Alistair, with Hal Schuster and Hal Roberts. 1991. *Yesterday: My life with the Beatles*, rev. ed. Las Vegas: Pioneer.

Taylor, Derek. 1987. *It was twenty years ago today*. New York: Fireside.

Thomson, Elizabeth, and David Gutman, eds. 1987. *The Lennon companion: Twenty-five years of comment*. New York: Schirmer.

Top 100: The best albums of the last twenty years. 1987. *Rolling Stone* 507 (Aug. 27).

Tropman, Matt. 1994. Unpublished paper on "For no one."

Turner, Steve. 1994. *A hard day's write*. New York: Harper Perennial.

Vaughn, Ben. 1994. Unpublished paper on Hindustani influences on the Beatles.

Visiting George. 1967. *The Beatles Monthly Book*, no. 42 (Jan.).

Wade, Bonnie C. 1980. Some principles of Indian classical music. In *Musics of many cultures*, ed. Elizabeth May. Berkeley: University of California.

Walsh, Alan. 1966a. George: More to life than being a Beatle. *Melody Maker*, June 25.

———. 1966b. Beatle doubletalk. *Melody Maker*, July 9.

———. 1967. The George Harrison interview. *Melody Maker*, Sept. 9.

———. 1968a. Will the real Richard Starkey please stand up? *Melody Maker*, Mar. 16.

———. 1968b. Revolution! *Melody Maker*, June 1.

———. 1968c. We have a handful of songs. *Melody Maker*, June 8.

Weinberg, Max. 1991. *The big beat*. New York: Billboard.

Welch, Chris. 1965. *Melody Maker*, Nov. 27.

"Well now—dig this!" 1961. *Mersey Beat* 1 (Aug. 31–Sept. 14). Reprinted in *Mersey beat: The beginnings of the Beatles*, ed. Bill Harry. New York: Quick Fox, 1977.

Wenner, Jann. [1970]. One guy standing there shouting "I'm leaving." In *The ballad of John and Yoko*, ed. Jonathan Cott and Christine Doudna. Garden City, N.Y.: Rolling Stone, 1982.

———. 1971. *Lennon remembers: The Rolling Stone interviews*. San Francisco: Straight Arrow.

Whale, Derek. 1984. *Lost villages of Liverpool*. Part 2. Prescot, Merseyside: T. Stephenson & Sons.

When did you switch on? 1969. *The Beatles Monthly Book*, no. 69 (Apr.).

Whitburn, Joel. 1993. *Top pop albums, 1955–1992*. Menomonee Falls, Wis.: Record Research.

White, Timothy. 1987. George Harrison reconsidered. *Musician*, no. 109 (Nov.).

———. 1988. Farewell to the first solo era. *Musician*, no. 112 (Feb.).

———. 1990. *Rock lives: Profiles and interviews*. New York: Henry Holt & Co.

———. 1996. Magical history tour. *Billboard* 108, no. 10 (Mar. 9).

Whittaker, Lyndon. 1962. I'll remember Frank Ifield. Reproduced in Mark Lewisohn, *The complete Beatles chronicle*. New York: Harmony, 1992.

Widders-Ellis, Andy, and Jesse Gress. 1994. Take a rad song and make it better: Exploded views of three Beatles classics. *Guitar Player* 28 (Sept.).

Wiener, Allen J. 1992. *The Beatles ultimate recording guide*. New York: Facts on File.

Wiener, Jon. [1984]. *Come together: John Lennon in his time*. Urbana: University of Illinois Press, 1991.

Wigg, David. 1976. *The Beatles tapes from the David Wigg interviews*. Polydor 2683068 (U.K., 2 LPs).

Williams, Allan, and William Marshall. 1975. *The man who gave the Beatles away*. London: Elm Tree.

Williams, Richard. 1969. John and Yoko. *Melody Maker*, Dec. 6.

———. 1971a. Produced by George Martin, part two. *Melody Maker*, Aug. 28.

———. 1971b. Produced by George Martin, part three. *Melody Maker*, Sept. 4.

Wilson, Tony. 1968. George, the A&R man. *Melody Maker*, Sept. 28.

Winn, James. 1985. The Beatles as artists. In *The Essayist*, ed. Sheridan Baker and C. Jeriel Howard. New York: Harper and Row.

Wolfe, Tom. 1968. *The Electric Kool-Aid Acid Test*. New York: Bantam.

Wooler, Bob. 1961. The roving I. *Mersey Beat* 1 (Oct. 5–19). Reprinted in *Mersey beat: The beginnings of the Beatles*, ed. Bill Harry. New York: Quick Fox, 1977.

Yogananda, Paramahansa. [1946.] *Autobiography of a yogi*. Los Angeles: Self-Realization Fellowship, 1977.

Yorke, Ritchie. 1970. A private talk with John. In *The ballad of John and Yoko*, ed. Jonathan Cott and Christine Doudna. Garden City, N.Y.: Rolling Stone, 1982.

You never give me your money. 1969. *Rolling Stone* 46 (Nov. 15).

Yule, Andrew. 1994. *The man who "framed" the Beatles: A biography of Richard Lester*. New York: Donald I. Fine.

Zimmer, Dave. 1984. *Crosby, Stills and Nash: The authorized biography*. New York: St. Martin's.

INDEX OF NAMES, SONGS, ALBUMS, VIDEOS, AND ARTWORKS